Georgia State Capitol.

THE STORY OF GEORGIA

AND

THE GEORGIA PEOPLE

1732 to 1860

COMPLETE IN ONE VOLUME

BY

GEORGE GILLMAN SMITH, D.D.

SECOND EDITION

Baltimore

GENEALOGICAL PUBLISHING COMPANY

1968

Reprint of the Second Edition
Originally Published Circa 1901

Reprinted
Genealogical Publishing Company
Baltimore, 1968

Library of Congress Catalog Card Number 68-9359

PREFACE.

I have tried to write the Story of Georgia and the Georgia People from 1732 to 1860. I have rather aimed to give a series of pictures than a mere detail of events. I have freely used the labors of those who have gone before me, and have endeavored to put a fair estimate on their work.

Hewitt, the dignified and careful old Loyalist, who wrote a History of South Carolina, which was afterward republished by Mr. Carroll in his Historical Collections, gives an account of the Georgia Colony up to the Revolution. His story of the early Colony is very accurate. Major McCall, who wrote the first History of the State of Georgia, drew page after page from Hewitt, making no acknowledgment of his source of information, and all that is valuable in his account of the colony is found in Hewitt's History. McCall participated actively in the revolutionary struggle, and had a Scotchman's hate for all opposed to him, and his account of revolutionary matters is to be taken somewhat cautiously.

Bishop Stevens,* who wrote the second History of Georgia, is very painstaking and reliable. His style is classic and his pages are stately, his stateliness becoming sometimes almost ludicrous. Colonel Charles C. Jones,† whose two portly octavos reach to the close of the Revolution, has left no stone unturned in his effort to discover everything which could interest the student of Georgia history. Geor-

* Stevens's History of Georgia, Vol. I. D. Appleton & Co., New York 1847. Vol. II., 1859. E. H. Butler, Philadelphia.

† History of Georgia. By Charles C. Jones, Jr., LL.D. Boston. Houghton, Mifflin & Co. 1868. 2 vols.

gia was in her swaddling clothes when his story reached its conclusion. His somewhat untimely death was a great loss to Georgia, and the completion of the work he had laid out for himself was left to other hands.

Colonel Avery begins his history fifty years after Stevens ends his, and has given in a large octavo a full and graphic story of a stirring time.*

Professor Lawton B. Evans has written a school history of Georgia, which is very full and reliable. I have used the first edition of it very freely, and find it to be very trustworthy. A second and improved edition is now used in the Georgia schools. Professor Evans has added to my obligations by putting the collection of illustrations used in his first edition at my disposal,† and his obliging publishers, the University Publishing Co., have done the same.

Colonel Charles H. Smith has written an excellent sketch of Georgia, which has been published by a Northern firm. It is a mere sketch, but, like everything from the pen of the gifted writer, sprightly and valuable.

I have been much indebted to Adiel Sherwood, who published the first Gazetteer of Georgia in 1829, and who followed it by a new and improved edition in 1837.‡ His little book published in 1829 was the first effort to show the progress of the young State along industrial lines. It is thoroughly truthful. Mr. George White,§ who has done so much for Georgia history, has drawn largely from Mr. Sherwood, not always giving him proper credit.

Mr. White's two books are invaluable, and I am very

*The History of the State of Georgia from 1859 to 1881. Brown & Derby, New York.

† A Student's History of Georgia. By Lawton B. Evans. J. W. Burke & Co., Macon, Ga.

‡ Sherwood's Gazetteer, Washington, D. C., 1837.

§ White's Statistics. W. T. Williams, Savannah. 1849. White's Historical Collections, New York. 1856. Pudney & Russell.

largely indebted to him. He devoted much attention to Biography, and his personal sketches are excellent.

I am under special obligations to the Georgia Historical Society of Savannah for the use of its rare and valuable collection of books and newspapers, as well as of MSS. bearing on Georgia history. And I must render publicly my thanks to the courteous and well-informed Colonel Harden, the librarian, who has given me very valuable assistance.

My friends of the Macon bar have given me free access to their collections of Georgia law books, and Colonel J. R. Saussy and Colonel S. B. Adams of Savannah have given me access to some very rare and important works not to be found elsewhere.

I have tried to be strictly non-partisan in my statements, for I can but think the bitter animosities of the Revolution and the fiery heat of early politics have in some degree prevented a fair treatment of those who were under the public ban.

I have aimed to make a book of moderate size and to give prominence to facts to a large degree overlooked by other histories of Georgia, and I have been much less minute in my account of the first years of the Georgia Colony than I would have been had not those who preceded me given it such attention.

The aim I set forth at the beginning of this preface I have kept constantly before me, and have used a homeliness of treatment and a particularity of statement that would not have been warranted if I had designed to write a complete history for general circulation and reference.

The interesting story of De Soto in Georgia, which has so fascinated the early historians, has been so well told by Pickett, Jones and Stevens, that it was not necessary that I should tell it again, even if I regarded it, as I do not, as a part of the story of the Georgia people. It is an incident in the history of the Spaniards which is of very great interest, and the account given by the Spanish chronicler is an amusing illustration of the temptation, never resisted in those days, to draw largely on the fancy for facts. To find bushels of precious pearls, wonderful princesses and great cities in the Georgia forests was possible only to those Spanish romancers.

A glance over the Bibliography appended will show my sources of information. I have in almost every instance referred to the original copies of the books referred to, and have been compelled in only one instance, that of DeBrahm's account of the province of Georgia, to take my facts at second-hand. I am indebted to Colonel C. C. Jones for the facts recited by this German engineer.

I have found the work of preparing this volume a difficult one, not because I had no sufficient supply of material, but because of the difficulty of bringing into a moderate compass so much of interest to the Georgia people.

Through the kindness of Mrs. W. L. Peel of Atlanta, who devised the plan of publishing a list of the Revolutionary soldiers and who secured the cooperation of the ladies of the Atlanta Chapter, I have had access to this compilation. The well-informed and untiring Captain B. F. Johnson did the work, with the cooperation of the Secretary of State, Colonel Cook. In the Appendix is found the result of this labor.

GEORGE G. SMITH.

Vineville, Macon, Ga.

PREFACE TO SECOND EDITION.

The first edition of this book was disposed of in three months after it appeared.

There were some errors in my statements of fact, to which my attention has been called and which I have corrected. There were some accidental omissions which, in my anxiety to reduce the compass of the book, I made, which I have tried as far as possible to remedy: in one instance I find I have failed to give the true place to that chief of the tribunes, my own personal friend and my commander in the Army of Northern Virginia, General Robert Toombs, than whom Georgia never had a truer or more gifted son. I have largely increased the number of illustrations, have added an index, and a number of names of grantees of land and revolutionary soldiers which have been lately discovered. I have had no occasion up to this time to correct any statement of an important matter. My attention has, however, been called to the fact that I have not in so many words denounced the Yazoo sale as an infamous fraud. I have simply given the facts as they appear on the record; if they show that the Yazoo sale was a Credit Mobilier transaction the past verdict stands. My own opinion I have not thought it proper to obtrude.

GEO. G. SMITH.

Vineville, Macon, Ga., 1901.

BIBLIOGRAPHY.

1. Journal of Wm. Stephens, Esq., 3 vols., London, 1744.

This very rare and very valuable book is to be found in the library of the Georgia Historical Society in Savannah. It has been freely drawn upon by Hewitt, McCall, Bishop Stevens and Colonel Jones. It is very full and very reli able. It covers the period between 1738 and 1741.

2. Bartram's Journal of a Botanist.

3. Journal of John Wesley, Wesley's works, vol. I., Eaton & Maines, New York. Journal of Charles Wesley, in Jackson's Life. Whitefield's Letters and Journal as found in his life by Gillies, and in his works. London, 1770.

These books are of great service, especially the Journal of John Wesley, in which he gives much valuable information about the first days of Georgia and the Letters of Whitefield, which extend over thirty years.

4. Hewitt's History, as found in Carroll's Collections.

Dr. Hewitt was a Presbyterian minister of Charleston, and an intense Loyalist.

5. Bancroft's History, 2 vols.

6. Memorials of Oglethorpe, by Dr. Harris of Boston.

This biography, the only one we have of Oglethorpe, is, as far as the facts go, a valuable work. As is not unusual with biographers, he aims to magnify the subject of his story unduly.

7. TRANSACTIONS OF GEORGIA HISTORICAL SOCIETY, Vols. 1, 2, 3, 4, 5. Savannah.

These are very valuable, and cast much light on the early days of the colony. They contain:

A New and Accurate Account of the Province of South Carolina and Georgia. London, 1733.

A Voyage to Georgia, by Francis Moore, 1744.

An Impartial Inquiry, 1741.

Reasons for Establishing the Colony of Georgia, 1733.

The State of the Province of Georgia, 1740.

A Brief Account, a Tract against the Trustees, 1741.

Tailfer's Narrative, antagonistic to Oglethorpe. Published in Charleston, S. C., 1741.

The Trustee's Statement. London, 1742.

Governor Wright's Letters.

Oglethorpe's Letters.

8. McCALL'S HISTORY OF GEORGIA, 1811.

9. STEVENS'S HISTORY OF GEORGIA, vol. 1. D. Appleton & Co., 1847. Stevens's History of Georgia, vol. 2. E. H. Butler & Co., 1858.

10. HISTORY OF GEORGIA, by Colonel Chas. C. Jones, 2 vols., 1883.

As far as Colonel Jones goes he has left nothing behind him. Fair, non-partisan, graceful in style, his two large volumes are invaluable.

11. LIFE OF JAMES JACKSON, by Judge T. U. P. Charlton, 1809. Reprint of Thomas Meghan, 1896. A full account of General Jackson's army life.

12. PAMPHLETS OF GEORGIA HISTORY, by A. H. Chappell, Esq.

This series of pamphlets, which were published in Columbus in 1873, and republished by Thos. Meghan in

Atlanta in 1896, are very valuable and I have drawn freely on them.

13. HISTORY OF SAVANNAH, by Lee & Agnew.

14. HISTORY OF SAVANNAH, by C. C. Jones.

15. HISTORY OF AUGUSTA, by C. C. Jones.

16. HISTORY OF ATLANTA, by E. Y. Clarke.

17. HISTORY OF MACON, by J. C. Butler, have all aided me in making up my history of the cities. Mr. Butler's book is especially valuable in recovering everything which concerns Macon's infant history.

18. MEMOIRS OF GEORGIA, published by the Georgia Historical Association.

Two large volumes, to which contributions were made by Colonel Avery, Mr. J. Chandler Harris, Mr. W. P. Reed, Chas. N. West, Esq., General C. A. Evans, Dr. Foster and others, and in which there are a great many biographical sketches. There is much in this book which is very valuable.

19. KING ALCOHOL IN THE LAND OF KING COTTON, by Professor Scomp.

It is a very voluminous, accurate and carefully written story of the temperance reform. It is a work of great research, but is unreadably minute in its statements.

20. HISTORY OF GEORGIA, 1850 to 1881. Avery. This is a full and sprightly account of a stormy time.

COLONIAL LAWS OF GEORGIA. Lewis Johnson, 1771.

There are only three volumes of this collection of which I have knowledge, one in the Historical Society in Savannah, and two owned by J. R. Saussy, Esq., that city.

The Egmont Papers, published by Mr. DeRenne, which shed much light on colonial history.

Watkins's Digest of Georgia Laws to 1800. R. Aiken, 1st Ed., Philadelphia.

Marbury's Georgia Laws. R. Aiken, Philadelphia.

Compilation of Georgia Laws, by Augustine S. Clayton, to 1810.

Compilation of Georgia Laws, by L. Q. C. Lamar, Sr., to 1820.

Compilation of Georgia Laws, by W. C. Dawson, to 1825.

Digest of Georgia Laws, by O. H. Prince, 1837.

Sherwood's Gazetteer of Georgia, 1st Ed., 1829. Second edition, Washington, D. C., 1837.

It is difficult to speak too highly of this unpretending work. It casts a flood of light over the second period of Georgia history.

White's Statistics. Mr. White was largely indebted to Sherwood, but was a laborious and patient investigator himself, and his Book of Statistics, somewhat inaccurately called such, is invaluable. His larger work, Historical Collections, gives a very great amount of valuable matter out of which a history can be made, and has been of great service to me.

Georgians, by Governor Gilmer, is a rare book, full of reminiscences, very interesting and generally reliable.

Bench and Bar of Georgia, a series of biographical sketches of distinguished lawyers, by Stephen F. Miller, is a very carefully prepared, trustworthy and somewhat diffuse account of some of the leading lawyers of the State. It was published by J. B. Lippincott & Co., Philadelphia.

Reminiscences of a Georgia Lawyer, by Judge Garnett Andrews, is a pamphlet which aims at showing some of the ludicrous things in early Georgia, but casts some light on the early history of the period.

Georgia Scenes, Wm. Mitten; by Judge A. B. Longstreet. These books are invaluable for the information they give of the social life of the second generation of Georgians.

Asbury's Journal, giving an account of early Methodism.

Bishop Stevens's Centennial Address, presenting a sketch of the Episcopal Church in Georgia.

Campbell's History of the Baptists. J. W. Burke & Co., Macon. History of Baptists, Christian Index Pub. Co.

Wilson's Necrology of the Presbyterian Church, Atlanta, 1887.

Smith's History of Methodism in Georgia. J. W. Burke & Co., Macon.

Life of Edmond Bottsford. Mallary.

Life of Jesse Mercer. Mallary.

Life of James O. Andrew. Smith.

Life of Geo. F. Pierce. Smith.

Life of Robert Toombs. Stovall.

Life of B. H. Hill. Hill.

Life of Alex. H. Stephens. Brown & Johnson.

Life of Linton Stephens. Waddell.

Memorial of Howell Cobb. Boykin.

Georgia Gazette, from 1765 till its suspension.

The *Augusta Chronicle*, from 1796.

The *Georgia Messenger and Telegraph*, in Macon

The *Milledgeville Federal Union*, from 1825.

CONTENTS.

CHAPTER I.

CHAPTER II.

CHAPTER III.

CHAPTER X.

CHAPTER XI.

The Story of Georgia and the Georgia People.

CHAPTER I.

GEORGIA UNDER THE TRUSTEES—1732 TO 1754.

Preliminary—Carolina Settled—Mr. Oglethorpe Plans a Benevolent Colony—A Board of Trustees Organized—The King Makes a Grant of Territory West of the Savannah River—Proposal Made to Immigrants—Immigration of Thirty-five Families—Dr. Herbert First Clergyman—Immigrants Arrive at Charleston and Beaufort—Colonel Bull and Mr. Oglethorpe Select a Place for the Settlement of the Colony—Tomichichi and his People—Savannah Laid Out—Coming of the Salzburghers—Coming of the Highlanders—Second Immigration of English People, Salzburghers and Moravians—Troubles with the Spaniards—Mr. Oglethorpe Commissioned a Colonel, Raises a Regiment and Commands the British Forces—The Spanish War—The War Over—Mr. Oglethorpe at Frederica—Trouble with Malcontents—Mr. Oglethorpe's Return to England—Number of Immigrants up to his Date of Departure—The English Settlement—Allowance to Immigrants—Beneficiaries of the Trustees—Rum Forbidden—Slavery Prohibited—Reason for the Prohibition of Slavery—Difficulties Encountered by First Settlers—Failure of the Attempt to Make Wine and Silk—Discontent of the Colonists—Controversy—The Side of the Trustees—The Side of the Malcontents—List of the Malcontents—The First Office-holders and their Occupation—Mr. Oglethorpe's Treaty with the Creeks—The Scotch Settlement—Origin of the Immigration—John More McIntosh—Pastor McLeod, the First Presbyterian Minister in Georgia—New Inverness Founded—Partial List of the Colonists in New Inverness in 1740—Change of Name to Darien—Breaking up of the Scotch Settlement—The German Settlement—The Coming of the Salzburghers and their First Settlement at Ebenezer—Failure of the Settlement—Second Settlement—Partial List of the First Immigrants—Coming of a Second Colony of Germans—Frederica—Description of St. Simons Island—Settlement of Frederica—Rapid Growth of the City—Its Rapid Decline—Mr. James Spalding—Augusta Settled in 1735—A Sketch of its First Years—George Galphin—Indian Slave Trade—Results of the Efforts of the Trustees—Change of Laws—Slavery Permitted—Practical Failure of the Colony—The First Assembly Called—Surrender of the Charter—Amount of Land Granted—Religious History of the Colony for the First Twenty Years.

Authorities: Hewitt, McCall, Stevens, Jones, Historical Collections I., II., III., IV., Wm. Stephens's Journal, Wesley's Journal, Whitfield's Journal, Harris's Memorials of Oglethorpe.

Georgia History, so far as it concerns itself with much the larger part of its first settlers, begins in Virginia. Those European immigrants who settled near Savannah, and who came directly to Georgia from England, Germany, Scotland and Ireland, were not many.

There was little progress in Georgia until after 1752, when the tide of immigration came in from South Carolina, Virginia and North Carolina, and the American origin of the first Georgians is largely to be found in the old Virginia records.

The researches of Mr. Alexander Brown, the Rev. Dr. Niele, Dr. R. A. Brock, Mr. W. G. Stannard, Mr. A. C. Bruce, the collections of the Virginia Historical Society and the various histories of Virginia, all cast light on the origin of the Georgia people.

To begin the study of the larger part of the Georgians we must begin with the London company.

England claimed the whole North American continent by virtue of John Cabot's discovery of Newfoundland, but one hundred years had gone before she made any effort to settle the wilds. After Sir Walter Raleigh's failure to make a permanent settlement in the latter part of the sixteenth century, in the early part of the seventeenth a company of English adventurers, known as the London company, was organized. This was a great stock company, whose avowed aim was to Christianize the Indians, and whose real aim was to get large dividends from the mines and the fields and forests of the new world. The list of the members of this company and the amount of money each man contributed has been preserved. For near twenty years this company made constant efforts and spent much money in order to settle the colony, and by the year 1624 the inhabitants of the colony were about twelve hundred. In 1624 the London company passed out of sight, the charter being revoked by the king. This company took in all classes of Englishmen of means. Noblemen, gentlemen, tradesmen, clergymen and corporations all invested, allured by the returns secured by the Spanish in South America, the

Portuguese in Africa, and the Dutch in India. The immense profits which these people gained inspired the hope of those who invested their money in Virginia stock that they would be equally fortunate.

The stockholders of this company, when it went into liquidation, received lands for their investment at one half shilling per acre, and the foundations of the immense landed estates of Virginia were laid by the shareholders of the London company, and it was in this way that so many of the descendants of these people were found in Virginia in its early history, and afterwards in Georgia. The first settlements in Virginia were made on the rivers, and a large body of Virginians were found in eastern North Carolina early in the eighteenth century, and from thence came into Georgia. Many Georgia families count their origin as North Carolinian when it was really Virginian, and many South Carolina people who came to Georgia had an ancestry which one hundred years before was in Virginia. There were very few people of any considerable estate who came to Virginia in its first settlement. The days of Virginia's splendor, when the old Virginian begins his story, were not for fifty years after the first settlement of the colony, and though many of the early settlers were sons of noblemen and of gentlemen, they were very poor, and many a man entitled by his birth to a coat of arms had some difficulty in getting a coat of frieze to cover his arms. In those early days men who came from lordly halls in England lived in log cabins and toiled with their own hands. Not a few people of distinction in after time were redemptioners who worked for five years after they came to America to pay back their passage money to the planter who bought them for that time from the ship captain.

While this last stated fact is true, it is only exceptionally true, and it will be seen that the men of small means, who came from the upper and middle classes of England, Scotland and Wales, men who had some education and some small means, were largely the ancestors of the present race of Georgians.

That part of the colony of South Carolina, now Georgia and Alabama and Mississippi, was only settled by a few scattered Indians, and in it the Indian trader had now and then a warehouse and a ranch.

GEN. JAMES OGLETHORPE.

Florida was held by the restless and grasping Spaniard, who also laid claims to the lands on the Tombigbee and the Mississippi. The Spaniards menaced the South Carolina colony, and the English authorities realized the importance of settling a strong colony nearer Florida; so when Mr. Oglethorpe and his associates asked George II. for a grant of land for their projected refuge for the unfortunate, they met with a ready response, and all of the country originally granted to the proprietors which lay west of the Savannah was granted to them for the benevolent purpose they had in view. George II. made the grant, and in his honor the colony was called Georgia. There were associated with Mr. Oglethorpe in the trusteeship of the new colony twenty others. They were noblemen and gentlemen, and had a charter carefully drawn, which was to run for twenty years. Mr. Oglethorpe was selected by them for the work of planting the colony.

He was a member of Parliament, an English gentleman in easy circumstances and of excellent family. He had been educated at Oxford and had in his youth entered the army and served on the continent under Prince Eugene. He served on the prince's staff until the peace, then returned to England and was elected to Parliament, of which he was an active member in 1730. He was a man of gentle nature and of philanthropic spirit, and was led to enterprise an over-the-sea colony by finding that a friend of his, a baronet who had become involved in debt and who was confined in a debtors' prison, was in irons for some infraction of prison laws. The severe punishment inflicted on his friend led him to look into the matter of imprisonment for debt, and to ask if a plan could not be devised by which those who were poor and embarrassed might be kept out of debtors' prisons. An over-the-sea colony suggested itself. He would give the poor a chance in the new world to make a living, and, if in debt, to pay their creditors. His plan was not, as many have supposed, to pay poor debtors out of prison, but rather to give poor men a chance to keep out. To accomplish this extensive grants of land were to be made by the crown, and then by public aid and private contribution means were to be provided to settle needy families. They were to be those who could not make a comfortable living in England, men of good morals, who were not in debt, or, if in debt, whose creditors were willing for them to leave England. The grant was secured, the charter was written, and the trustees were given large powers by the crown.

Mr. Oglethorpe, who had charge of the colony, was perhaps a little visionary, but he was nobly unselfish and heroic, and devoted himself to the interest committed to his charge with great zeal.

The English Parliament granted £10,000 to the new colony in order to put it on its feet, and the English philanthropists subscribed liberally to the funds the trustees were securing for their project. They were now prepared to offer inducements to those who were willing to emigrate to the new colony. The colonists were to have a free passage across the sea, a town lot and a section of land, and were to be clothed and fed at the expense of the trustees for a twelvemonth.

The land to which they were going was contiguous to prosperous Carolina, and was pictured to them as an Eden. The silkworm and the vineyard they were assured would enrich them in a few years.

There should be no negro slaves to compete with them, and no large landed proprietors to monopolize their territory. They should have vines and fig-trees, and none should make them afraid.

So thirty-five families — carpenters, brick-layers, and farmers—with Dr. Herbert, a clergyman of the Church of England, as their chaplain, took passage at Deptford on the 16th November, 1732, and on the 12th of January, 1733, the Ann reached Charleston, S. C., on its way to Georgia.

The Carolinians received these new adventurers very kindly and convoyed their ship to Beaufort, where a smaller craft was provided to take them to some point on the west side of the Savannah river. Mr. Oglethorpe and the benevolent Colonel Bull made a prospecting tour up the Savannah river while the immigrants remained at Beaufort, and they decided to fix the settlement near Yamacraw town, some eighteen miles from the mouth of the Savannah, on a high bluff on the west side of the stream. This city stands to-day near where it was located by Oglethorpe in 1733, and Yamacraw still holds its old name on the map and in common parlance. The settlers were provided with abundant

TOMICHICHI AND NEPHEW.

supplies of necessary things. The generous Mr. Whittaker from South Carolina furnished one hundred head of cattle to give them a start, and Colonel Bull, Mr. Barlow, Mr. St. Julian, Mr. Woodward and Mr. Joseph Bryan, all wealthy planters, brought over a number of their slaves from South Carolina to assist them in building their houses.

There was no trouble to be expected from the poverty-stricken band of runaway Indians at Yamacraw, and Mr. Oglethorpe soon made a good friend of Tomichichi, who was head chief of the tribe. The colonists were sheltered in cloth tents on their first landing, and as it was in a Savannah February they were abundantly comfortable.

The bluff on which they had pitched their tents was covered with wide-spreading live-oaks, and a short distance away from the river was a wide stretch of pine forest. Colonel Bull and Mr. Bryan brought over some sawyers from their plantations, saw pits were dug and the pines were cut into boards, and the carpenters went to work to provide houses for these homeless Englishmen.

The little houses, 16 x 24, made of pine boards, were soon erected, a board tabernacle for a church was built, and then Mr. Oglethorpe proceeded to select a place for a fort for the protection of the colony from the Spaniards. He went across the country some twenty miles to the Ogeechee and built a fort called Fort Argyle, and settled a few families around it, and north of Savannah he located the village of Abercorn, where there were placed ten families.

The next immigrants to the colony were a body of Salzburghers. They were originally Austrians who had been driven from the Tyrol and who had been living for a time in Germany. They were Lutherans of the Pietist wing, people famous for their solid worth, and they had been invited to settle in this new colony, and the society for the propagation of the gospel in foreign parts had consented to pay the cost of transporting them. They were cordially welcomed by Mr. Oglethorpe and were permitted to select a home for themselves. Their agents selected a place in what is now Effingham, and they settled a village called Ebenezer. This spot was not happily chosen, and the next year they removed to another spot nearer the river, to which they gave the same name. There were a few Jews, originally from Portugal but directly from England, and a few French Huguenots who came from South Carolina. These were the first immigrants.

In July, the city having been tastefully laid out, there was allotted to each immigrant a town lot, a garden of five acres and a farm of forty-five acres, in all fifty acres. This property, however, was not granted in fee simple but was to descend to heirs, male, and in case there were none, then it was to revert to the trust. The English settlers received their grants in and around Savannah, and the Salzburghers had lands granted them some twenty miles away.

A body of Scotch Highlanders was the next considerable body of immigrants. They came from the north of Scotland and were settled by Oglethorpe at a place near the mouth of the Altamaha, which they called New Inverness, near what is now Darien.

Early in 1735 Mr. Oglethorpe, having settled these first colonists, returned to England, and in the fall of that year came again to Georgia with a large body of immigrants composed of Germans and Englishmen, and located a new town on the island of St. Simons, which he called Frederica. With these German Salzburghers there came another body of German religionists, the Moravians, who came to Georgia to Christianize the Indians, but after making a settlement called Irene, they removed to Pennsylvania to their larger settlement at Bethlehem.

The troubles with Spain were increasing, and it was evident that there would be a collision between the English and the Spaniards, and Mr. Oglethorpe went back to England to get a commission as colonel and to recruit a regiment for service in the colony. He endeavored to secure married men for his recruits, that they might bring their wives with them, so that when discharged they would remain in the colony.

The war came, as was expected, and Mr. Oglethorpe, now

commander-in-chief, with the aid of troops from the South Carolina colony, made an abortive effort to capture St. Augustine, and the Spaniards in return made a failure in their effort to capture Frederica, and the war ended ingloriously. Mr. Oglethorpe, henceforth known as General, became involved in some unpleasant affairs with some of his subalterns and demanded a court of inquiry. He returned to England and was fully vindicated.

He did not again visit the colony for whose interests he had labored so hard and sacrificed so much. He was very bitterly assailed by some malcontents, and vigorous pamphlets making all kinds of charges were written against him. The reader of these attacks will decide that they are unsupported by facts and do great injustice to one whose motives were of the noblest kind, although his judgment on the practical affairs of the colony was none of the best.

During his administration there were sent over, at the expense of the trustees, 1,521 immigrants, of whom 687 were foreigners. These immigrants were settled at and around Savannah, Ebenezer, Darien and Frederica.

General Oglethorpe has received so large a share of attention on the part of all who have written of Georgia that it is hardly necessary that I should say much of him here. Save to bring over the first two bodies of colonists and to conduct the Spanish war, he had but little to do with the Georgia colony or the Georgia people. He only spent seven years in Georgia. He went back to England and retired to his estate. Here he remained until the troubles with the Pretender began, and he was selected as brigadier to command some of the militia, but did little military service. He had a nominal connection with the British army, and living to a great age, was at one time the oldest general in the service. He has been very highly eulogized, and perhaps he has been overpraised and his services to the Georgia colony have been rated too highly, but he is worthy of very high commendation.

We will now take a more careful view of the social condition of the people and glance first at the English settlers.

The colonies in Virginia and New England were over one hundred years old. They were thickly peopled, and their inhabitants were in many respects in as comfortable circumstances as people of the same class were in Europe. Large fortunes had been made in many cases, especially in Virginia and Maryland and in the New England cities, and all the comforts and many of the luxuries of London and Bristol and Rotterdam were brought into Virginia, Massachusetts, Pennsylvania, South Carolina and New York.

The valley of Virginia was now being opened to settlement, and bodies of fine settlers were finding homes in the fertile valley of the Yadkin in North Carolina. South Carolina, in which slavery was allowed, was very prosperous, and there was a great area in that colony yet unsettled where free homes were awaiting all comers.

There was but little inducement for men of capital to emigrate to Georgia, and she was dependent upon the poorer class for her settlers.

In 1735, when the second body of English emigrants was to be sent out, in order to induce emigration it was agreed to give to every man who would go to the new colony a watch-coat, a musket and a bayonet, a hatchet, hand-saw, shovel, spade, three hoes, a gimlet, a drawing-knife, and a frying-pan. There should be given to each one during the year, 312 pounds of beef or pork, 104 pounds of rice, 104 pounds of cornmeal and peas, 104 pounds of flour, 1 pint of beer for each working-day, 52 quarts of molasses, 16 pounds of cheese, 12 pounds of butter, 12 pounds of sugar, 4 gallons of vinegar, 24 pounds of salt, 12 quarts of lamp oil, 20 pounds of soap, and 1 pound spun cotton. The same allowance of food was to be made to women and half that to each child.

In consideration of this they were to work for the colony for twelve months, and then settle in the town or country near by, on lots granted to them. These lots were not to be united and could not be sold without a special license. If the land was not improved in ten years it should be forfeited to the colony. A rent charge of two shillings for each fifty acres was to be a fixed charge.

None could take advantage of these offers but persons in decayed circumstances and those who had large families and whose habits were good. Emigrants might take a male servant or an apprentice whose expenses in three years should be repaid to the trustees. To us of this day it would seem as if stupidity could have gone no further than in the adoption of some of the regulations of the trustees, and that if they had aimed to prevent the settlement of the colony they could not have worked more effectively. The trustees made a provision that no rum should be sold in the colony, and that if any one brought in any of the fiery spirit the casks should be staved and the same poured out. When the drinking habits of the people at that time are remembered, when there was as yet no temperance societies, when at the raising of church buildings in New England the keg of rum was always opened, when pious deacons distilled the spirit with a good conscience, when the good pastor had his rum toddy to recruit his exhausted strength after his long Sabbath labors, when ministers and physicians defended the use of rum as a necessity in the malarious sections, it was a remarkable evidence of advanced views that the trustees endeavored to prevent the introduction of rum into the Georgia colony. Their well-devised scheme came to naught, and it is probable that rum was openly sold in Savannah almost from the beginning.

If the views of the trustees on rum and on African slavery could have been carried out as perfectly in all the colony as they were for twenty years in the Ebenezer settlement, the prosperity that from the beginning marked that community might have attended all Georgia from the first, but the unhappy regulation concerning land tenures, added to the prohibition of negro slavery, turned the tide of immigration into South Carolina and North Carolina, and the Georgia colony was neglected. The law forbidding the introduction of slaves was not made because slavery was thought to be a moral evil, but for purely economic reasons; and the practical workings of the law soon demonstrated the fact that its enforcement would prevent all development, for the country on the coast could not be developed by white labor. So most of the few people of means who came into the colony at its first settlement, and who tried to use white men as laborers, were compelled to remove to South Carolina, where they could get negroes.

There was no commerce. Rice and indigo, which made South Carolina rich, could not be cultivated without negro labor. There was no manufacturing of any kind. The few men of means, for none could be called wealthy, soon had stock ranches and depended on the wild grasses and nuts for food for their cows and ponies and hogs. The poorer classes, many of whom were day-laborers and artisans or small farmers, were dependent largely on the company stores to keep them from want. The country on the coast was far from fertile, and life was very hard at best.

The main part of the poorer Englishmen were not farmers but came from the cities and were dependent upon handiwork for a living, and those who attempted to farm on their small tracts near Savannah made a poor out of it. Mr. Wesley,* who came in 1737, says "the land was of four sorts, pine-barren, oak, marshes and hummocks. The pine

* Wesley's Journal.

land was cleared with difficulty, and produced the first year from two to four bushels of corn and from four to eight bushels of peas. The second year it produced half as much and the third year nothing. The oak lands were better, producing as much as ten bushels of corn per acre.

"The savannas and marshes furnished some pasturage. There were two kinds of grapes, the fox-grape and the cluster. The chinkapin and huckleberry and persimmon were wild fruits." As Mr. Wesley had never been twenty miles from the coast, his knowledge of the real value of the lands of the interior was exceedingly limited, but his account of the farming lands near Savannah and down the coast to Frederica is very correct, and these were the lands upon which the first comers were located. When one thinks of an Englishman who had been brought up in the fertile island going with his axe into a Georgia pine wood or a Georgia swamp to clear his field and make it ready for the hoe, for he had neither team nor plow, and that in an almost torrid clime; and when he adds to that the wide sweep of deadly malaria in the fall, he can well understand the supreme disgust with which the immigrants looked upon farm life in Georgia. The trustees had hoped to found in Georgia a silk-raising colony; the same scheme which had fascinated the Virginians over a hundred years before, and which had resulted in failure there, was to be found practicable in a softer clime.

So they had planted the mulberry and had brought over Mr. Camuse and his too bibulous wife and a supply of cocoons and began to raise silkworms and make silk, and when raw silk was made sufficient to weave a robe for the queen they were quite sure failure was impossible. Silk-raising was the "will-o'-the-wisp" to the Georgia colony for several disappointing years.

The raising of grapes from which to make wine began well and promised well, but it was soon found to be impracticable to make good wine in a climate so hot, and this enterprise was also given over.

The colonists were not prosperous and laid the blame of their straitened condition on Mr. Oglethorpe, who spent all his time at Frederica, and there was formed an anti-Oglethorpe party. The Oglethorpe party was under the control of the secretary of the colony, afterwards Governor William Stephens, who was the son of an English baronet, and had been a member of Parliament, and the anti-Oglethorpe party was led by his son, Thomas Stephens.* This last named gentleman was selected by sundry citizens to go to England and present their grievances to the trustees, which he did very vigorously, if not very skilfully. The result of it was that he was compelled to apologize for his reflections upon the good governor, and the friends of Mr. Oglethorpe published in 1740 a statement of the Province of Georgia, attested upon oath, which was designed to show how successfully all things had been managed. This account stated that the ground produced corn, rice, peas, potatoes, pumpkins, melons, wheat, oats, barley, mulberry trees, vines and cotton. That hogs and cattle increased beyond imagination. That there was considerable trade in the river.

That there was a court-house, a gaol, a storehouse, a wharf, a guard-house, and some other public buildings. A garden of ten acres in the city. Oranges had not yet been grown successfully, but would be. Silk was increasing. Vines grew luxuriantly, and some good white wine had been made. The trustees had a number of cattle. There were villages at Abercorn, Highgate and Hampstead. The houses in Darien were mostly huts, but tight and warm, and there was a little fort there. Frederica was very prosperous.† The people sent on charity from England were

* Mr. Stephens's Journal.

† Georgia Historical Collections, Vol. 1.

of the unfortunate. Some of them had thriven. Some were worthless and ran away to South Carolina to live by cunning. The servants picked up in London had proven worthless. The Germans had done well. This cheering report was signed by Patrick Graham, John Burton, William Stephens, Joe Fitzwalter, Joe Pavey, Henry Parker, James Carswell, Robert Hanks, Thomas Jones, Thomas Upton, Samuel Mercer, John Milledge, Giles Bean, Thomas Bailey, Aaron Campbell, Thomas Egerton, George Johnson, John Rae, Thomas Cindlell, Samuel Parker, Noble Jones, Anthony Camuse, Thomas Palmer, Thomas Young, Thomas Ellis.*

The anti-Oglethorpe people were not to be suppressed, and so Mr. Thomas Stephens, still sore over his experience at court, and Sir Richard Everhard prepared a spicy rebuttal, supported also by oaths. They said: "The agricultural condition was very bad. There was no magistrate in Darien or Ebenezer. The magistrates in Savannah and Frederica had so disregarded law as to be worse than none. The militia was untrained. The land was held on unsatisfactory tenures. Rum was not allowed and negroes were forbidden. Thomas Jones, the storekeeper, was a felon." These charges they tried to support by affidavits of the malcontents from all parts of the colony. But the affidavits do not support any charges of a serious nature against General Oglethorpe or his chief officers. They only show the great discontent of the colonists and the low state which the colony had reached. The fact was the poor people had many of them been grievously misled by the glowing pictures presented by the first visitors to the colony, and were not prepared to adjust themselves to the condition of things ; and it is evident that, while the trustees were perfectly sincere and unselfish, they knew nothing of the real difficulties which were to be overcome.†

* Georgia Historical Collections, Vol. 2.

† Georgia Historical Collections, Vol. 2.

The malcontents who signed the declaration were:

John Amory, Ben Adams, Thos. Andrews, Thos. Atwill, Thomas Antrobus, James Anderson, Hugh Anderson, John Brownfield, John Burton, Chas. Brittain, Jas. Burnside, F. Brooks, M. Bright, R. Bradley, M. Burkhalter, J. Blands, W. Barbo, P. Balliol, E. Bush, G. Bean, G. Bunch, P. Butler, T. Baillie, A. Bell, H. Buckley, L. Brown, W. Blecheman, A. Ban, T. Becher, W. Calvert, W. Carter, T. Cross, W. Cothred, J. Clark, J. Cundale, Wm. Cooksey, Jno. Jacob Curl, A. Camuse, T. Clyatt, John Carneck, J. Cuthbert, J. Coln, John Clark, J. Dormer, J. Desborough, R. Davis, T. Delegal, Andrew Duchie, Thomas Dawson, J. Dodds, D. Douglas, J. Duddery, D. Douglas, S. Davidson, W. Davy, J. Dean, P. Delegal, E. Davidson, C. Dasher, W. Elbert, Thomas Edgerton, John Evans, W. Ewen, T. Ellis, P. Emery, W. Evans, H. Frazer, J. Fitzwalter, H. Fletcher, W. Francis, John Fallowfield, W. Fox, E. Foster, T. Frazer, J. Foulds, R. Gilbert, P. Gordon, Pat. Grahame, John Grahame, D. Grendee, W. Greenfield, C. Greenfield, W. Grechson, J. Hetreman, Jas. Galloway, Jas. Gould, G. Herbougl, A. Glenn, Thos. Gaulet, Jas. Houston, M. German, Geo. Gorland, T. Hetherington, Jno. Gould, H. Green, J. Harboughs, C. Grunaldi, A. Grant, Jas. Jeansack, John Goldwire, R. Howes, Peter Jouberts, S. Holmes, J. Haselfoot, Ed. Jenkins, John Kelly, Wm. Kennedy, L. Lacy, R. Lobb, J. Cannon, P. Cantey, M. Lowley, H. Lloyd, L. Lyon, J. Loudry, Thomas Lee, S. Mercer, S. Marrauld, S. Montford, F. Mellichamp, J. McDonald, P. McKay, B. McIntosh, J. McIntosh, B. McKay, J. Muse, A. McBride, J. Miller, T. Neale, T. Ormston, C. Arlman, K. O. Brien, H. Parker, Wm. Parker, T. Morris, Sam'l Parker, J. Prestwood, Jno. Pye, R. Parker, J. Penrose, W. Pendicke, J. Papot, J. Pemberton, J. Perkins, G. Phillip, S. Rienwell, R. Rogers, Jno. Robe, Geo. Rush, J. Rae, A. Rose, J. Roberson, A. Rantowle, J. Watson, W. Rigdon, Hugh Ross, A. Reynolds, J. M. Rizer, L. Stamon, W. Starflichts, J. Stanley, D. Stewart, J. Smith, A. Simes, L. Sumners, J. Smith, J. Sellie, L. Salter, J. Scott, J. Smalley, D. Snook, G. Stephens, D. Snook, J. Spielberger, Jno. Spencer, G. Stephens, J. Smithers, John Scott, Jas. Springer, W. Stenhouse, J. Smalley, Jno. Scott, J.

Mackfield, L. Sparnell, W. Speeling, R. Williams, Peter Ector, E. Townsend, Geo. Tyrrell, S. Tarrian, J. Truan, T. Tripp, T. Tibbetts, P. Tailfer, A. Taylor, T. Upton, J. Williams, J. Watts, S. Ward, Geo. Waterman, J. Wilson, W. Williamson, W. Wood, J. White, T. Wattle, A. Walker, W. Woodruff, T. Webb, W. Wardrop, J. Warwick, Isaac Young, John Young, Thos. Young.

These composed a very large part of the freeholders of the colony and were from all the settled parts of it. This list of names is specially valuable, as it gives us a knowl. edge of some of the first settlers. In the declaration there is also information as to the avocations of those who signed the other paper. It will be seen that there are a number of names found on both papers. The malcontents endeavored to show that those who did not sign their paper were interested in some way with the Government. It gives the avocations of some of the first people.

Patrick Graham was apothecary to the trustees; J. Fitzwalter, gardener; J. Carwells, jailer; T. Upton, commands a garrison of five men; Giles Beca, a baker; Thomas Egerton, grandson of wheelright; A. Camuse, silk man; John Burton, town officer; James Pavey, in pay at Augusta; R. Hankes, town officer; Thomas Bayley, smith; George Johnson, sawyer; S. Parker, son-in-law of Mercer; William Stephens, secretary of colony; H. Parker, magistrate; T. Jones, magistrate, overseer, storekeeper; Samuel Mercer, constable; James Campbell, jailer; James Rae, scout, boatman; Noble Jones, commands a garrison; Thomas Young, wheelright; Thomas Ellis, surveyor. The storekeeper of the trustees had been Thomas Causton. He was the prosecutor of John Wesley. He became involved in his accounts with the trustees and was called home to England to settle them and died on his returning voyage.

The silk industry had failed. The people were not prospering, and when Mr. Oglethorpe returned to England he gave up his place and never came back to Georgia. He lived long and honorably after his return to England, and his honest intentions to do good have never been questioned. Few men were less capacitated to do the work he had in hand than he was, but no man ever tried more earnestly to do what duty demanded.

While Mr. Oglethorpe was here he made a treaty with the Creeks, going to the nation to do so, which was of great value to the colony. He was evidently more anxious to build up Frederica than Savannah, and was by no means popular with the colonists who had located themselves near the city which had been the first founded by him in Georgia.

BETHESDA.

The people who came to the colony were in the main Church of England people and brought with them a pastor from England, Dr. Henry Herbert. His health failed and he returned to England and Mr. Josiah Quincy was his successor, and after he left the colony Mr. John Wesley was the rector of the church, and after two years Mr. Whitfield came out. Bishop Stevens and Colonel Jones have given a full account, in whose histories the story of the early days of the church in Savannah is given at length. This is, however, the proper place to recognize the fact of Mr. Whitfield's establishment of the Bethesda Home for orphans, of which a full account will be found in the chapter on the Story of the Cities (chapter 14).

This English settlement, as I designate the one near Savannah, was by no means purely English. Some of the leading settlers in it were Scotchmen, and as we have seen elsewhere, some of them were Jews and Italians. The planters, at the time that Oglethorpe left the colony, were few and perhaps none of them in easy circumstances, and the larger part of the people were poor and disheartened. Secretary Stephens has left a copious journal, beginning with 1737 and going to 1742, and from it we gather that Patrick Houston, afterward Sir Patrick, Mr. Cuthbert, Mr. Noble Jones, Mr. Fallowfield, Mr. DeLacy, Mr. Thomas Jones, Mr. Mathews (who married Mary, the Creek princess), Dr. Patrick Grahame and a few others were the only people near Savannah who had any considerable quantity of land. Savannah was a straggling village of small log huts or houses built of sheathing plank. In the account of the cities the reader will find a more satisfactory statement of the first years of this principal village of the colony. The larger part of the inhabitants of the English colony lived near the village of Savannah and made a scanty livelihood by cultivating the land contiguous to it, and by doing such work as was to be found to do in so small a hamlet. When Mr. Whitfield began to build his orphans' home at Bethesda he gave employment to many of the people, much to their relief. They had their forty-acre fields on the outskirts and their little houses in the village, and soon gathered about them some cattle and hogs, and managed with their fishing-nets and fowling-pieces and the produce of their herds and fields to live in a plain and simple way. There were very few of them who were prosperous. There was some small trade, and, as we see from the account of the city, there was some gaiety to be found in the city even then. There was, however, for the first twenty years in this English settlement nothing like prosperity.

THE SCOTCH SETTLEMENT.

The sturdy Scotch Highlanders had little sympathy with the House of Hanover, and finding life hard among the wild hills of their native land were easily persuaded by Captain Mackay to come to the new colony of Georgia, which was pictured to them in the glowing language of the times as a land where all that man wanted could be had for the asking. Mr. John More McIntosh, a Scotch laird, the head of his clan, consented to lead the colony, and one hundred and thirty of them, with fifty women, took shipping from Inverness for Georgia. They reached Savannah in due time and then went in flat-bottomed boats to find their new home sixteen miles from Frederica, on the Altamaha.

Calling their town New Inverness, they established their settlement, built their huts and were just getting settled when the war with Spain began.

Mr. McLeod was their minister, and he had established the first Presbyterian kirk in Georgia, and he tells of how the sad failure of their hopes led the poorer Highlanders all to enlist in General Oglethorpe's army. By a night attack at St. Augustine over half of these brave Scotchmen were massacred by the Spaniards. They had not had an easy life in the Highlands, but their life in Georgia had been far harder, and so after this massacre many of the poorer members of the colony went elsewhere. Mr. John More McIntosh and his immediate family remained, and as he was a man of substance and kept the storehouse of the colony and traded with the Indians, he was well-to-do.

The settlers were in the main very poor peasants, only seventeen, according to General Oglethorpe's Letters, being able to pay their way across the sea. Some of the immigrants were, however, men of property and lairds of the clans from which most of the immigrants were recruited by Captain Mackay, and while many of the poorer members of the colony became dissatisfied with New Inverness and joined the malcontents, these leading families sided with Mr. Oglethorpe's adherents and signed a document in which they indorsed him and his measures. This list is the only one of these first settlers I have been able to secure. These were John Mackintosh Moore, John Mackintosh, Roland McDonald, John McDonald, John MacLean, John McIntosh, John McIntosh Bain, James Mackay, Daniel Clark, Alex Clark, I. Burgess, D. Clark, Jr., A. McBain, Wm. Munroe, John Cuthbert. These are all the names of the first immigrants I have been able to recover. These were Scotch without an admixture and most of them traders. At a later period there are found some English names among them.

The remnant of the Highland company, who were discharged after the Spanish war ended, did not return to Darien but distributed themselves over the lower part of the colony. Some of them settled in St. John's parish and some of them in what are now Camden, Glynn and McIntosh counties.

The removal of the restriction to the use of negroes led to the opening by the wealthier part of the settlers of rice plantations, and when the first assembly was called in 1750 John More McIntosh was a member from this section. In 1775 among those who sympathized with the revolutionists there were Lachlan McIntosh, Richard Cooper, George Threadcraft, Seth McCullough, Charles McDonald, Isaac Hall, John McIntosh, Thos. King, Raymond Demere, John Roland, Giles More, P. Shuttleworth, Joseph Slade, Samuel McClellan, Isaac Newsome, A. D. Cuthbert, John Witherspoon, John Hall, John Fulton, John McCullough, Samuel Fulton, Peter Sallen, Isaac Cuthbert, James Clark, M. McCullough, Wm. McCullough, B. Shuttleworth, John McClelland.

Some of these first comers engaged in Indian trade and had their warehouses and trading-post in Florida, and their rice plantations on the river and their summer homes on the islands. Some of the descendants of these immigrants fixed their homes in Savannah and engaged in mercantile pursuits.

After the breaking up of the kirk in Darien and the departure of their minister, there does not seem for some years to have been any religious teacher among those who remained, but after the Church of England was established under Governor Ellis, there was likely occasional service held by an Episcopal missionary. The wealthy planters sent their children to Savannah and Charleston and Sunbury for education, and the poor grew up in ignorance.

As we shall see in a future chapter, there was another body of Scotch Highlanders who came to Georgia at a later time, who came through North Carolina.

THE GERMAN SETTLEMENT.

The Germans who came with Mr. Oglethorpe on his first coming to the colony chose in their location a section of land in what is now Effingham county, and established a village which was called Ebenezer. The glowing description of Mr. Van Reck, who was deputed to select the spot for their home, is so extravagant that one acquainted with the country finds it hard to understand how the good man could have seen so much and have been so deluded, and it was as disappointing to the honest Germans who settled it as it has been to the modern observer.

The Salzburghers were a body of Austrian Protestants who had been exiled from the native hills and found a temporary refuge in Germany, and from thence a body of seventy-eight came to Dover, in England, from which place, at the expense of the society for the propagation of the gospel in foreign parts, they were transported free of charge to Georgia. They had with them their two pastors, Bolzius and Gronau. Their commissary, Van Reck, went with

Oglethorpe into the wilderness to find a home for them. It was in early March when the pine woods were in their fairest garb.

Finding a spot in the wilderness of what he thought was matchless loveliness, he decided that was the place in which the weary exiles could find rest. "It was," he said, "between two rivers which fell into the Savannah, a little rivulet with crystal water glided by the town, the woods are open, the air balmy, there are wide meadows, there is the cedar, the walnut, the pine, the cypress, the oak, the myrtle and the sassafras, the ground is fertile, and the woods full of game." This was the land the German dreamer found, but when the settlement was made it was found to be a barren waste, and after two years of effort to make it productive they found it would be necessary to remove to another spot. They found that nearer the river and settled the New Ebenezer. They were a very thrifty people and secured help not only from the trustees, but from their kinspeople and sympathizers across the seas, and in a few years they were in very comfortable circumstances. Their history was written some years ago by Mr. Strobel, the pastor of Ebenezer, and is a very full and satisfactory account of them. These German immigrants were connected with the great Lutheran body, and they brought into Georgia and planted in its forests a German village.

They soon had a school and a home for widows or orphans, and away from the temptations of city life they developed a model community. Mr. Strobel has given the following list of persons who belonged to the community in 1741:

Messrs. Bolzius, Gronau, Rieser, Laub, Grewandel, Mamer, Kaigler, Zittreur, Runter, Rottenberger, Zubli, Ortman, Kulcher, Ramer, Reidelsparger, Moller, Hertzog, Hessler, Pletter, Sigismund, Hernberger, Bruckner, Ott, Zettler, Tribner, Eischberger, Arnsdorf, Ruter, Brandner, Lumberger, Lackner, Steiner, Schwarzer, Schmidt, Crause, Gruber,

Schutner, Lietner, Corberger, Grimmuger, Bergshammer, Landseller, Ernst (Ernest), Rieser, Pickler, Spurlbergen, Niedlinger, Helfenstein, Rabenhorst, Lembke, Muhlenberg, Wertch, Muller, Treutlen, Floerl, Wiesenbaker, Schubtrien, Kramer, Goldwire, Kraus, Beddenbach, Waldhauer, Pauler, Rahn, Helme, Remshart, Grau, Heil, Buchler, Hanleiter, Bollinger, McCay, Zimmerbuer, Oechele (Exley), Kimberger, Winkler, Witman, Dasher, Schrampa, Schwenger, Mohr, Liemberger, Buntz, Micheal, Beckley, Hausler, Gugel, Schremph, De Rosche, Moeler, Deppe, Metzger, Seckinger, Mack, Schneider, Schuele, Helfenstein, Freyermouth, Keifer, Tarringer, Pfluger, Meyer, Ditters, Rentz, Bergman.

Those who examine this list will find names which have since been Anglicized and slightly changed, but they will find many unchanged which are still borne by Georgians. No people have been more noted for industry, probity and intelligence. The little hamlet they founded, and which for so many years was the center of so much of interest to the Salzburghers, has long since ceased to be anything like even a village, but the church still stands and many of the descendants of these German refugees are still living. While the Pilgrim Fathers, who were a smaller number than these Salzburghers, have a high place in American history, this noble band of Austrian refugees has been almost lost to sight by the historian. They came to Georgia from their native Tyrol because of their devotion to Christian principle, and wherever their descendants are found the spirit which belonged to their fathers is manifested in them.

This people resided in what was afterward the upper part of St. Matthew's parish. They had been accustomed to farmers' work in their native land and to live in a simple, frugal way, and receiving help both from the trustees and from their German coreligionists across the seas, they had prospered from the first, and in 1754 their part of the colony received an accession by the coming of a body of German

Lutherans, not Salzburghers, who were brought into the colony by Captain De Brahm and settled at a place five miles north of Ebenezer. This colony increased very rapidly, and, according to Jones, the one hundred and fifty were multiplied tenfold in a little over a twelvemonth. This must, however, be a mistake, as it is not all probable that fifteen hundred Germans came at that time. They settled a village called Bethany in what is now Screven county, and De Brahm says there were three hundred and twenty Germans who came.*

There were, before the negroes were allowed, a small number of Germans who were brought over by the trustees, indentured for five years as servants, and in 1739 General Oglethorpe, in one of his letters to the trustees, mentions the coming of sixty-nine, who were distributed among the planters; but there was so little demand for them that there were several for whom homes could not be secured. There were in the number twelve marriageable females, who were taken by Mr. Bolzius to Ebenezer to furnish wives for the unmarried men.† Mr. Stephens mentions some German laborers who came with Captain Hewitt. It was a regular thing for the shipmasters coming to the American colonies to bring over a ship-load of young laborers, who were sold to the planters, and Virginia is not the only colony in which the wives of some of the planters were procured by paying the passage money across the seas. These last coming Germans evidently were absorbed by the already considerable bodies of their countrymen who were in the colony.

FREDERICA.

One of the objects of establishing the Georgia colony was to protect the more northern colonies from the aggressive Spaniards, who were in strong force in St. Augustine,

* See De Brahm's account, Wormsloe ed.

† Mr. Oglethorpe's Letters in Historical Collections.

and General Oglethorpe on his first visit determined to establish a fort and build a city on St. Simons Island at the mouth of the Altamaha. On his second coming to Georgia he brought with him quite a number of emigrants whom he intended to locate on this beautiful island, where he had a military post. Colonel Jones, to whom Georgia is so greatly indebted for having recovered so much of lost history, gives an account of Frederica in his "Dead Towns of Georgia." It was located on St. Simons Island, opposite to where the city of Brunswick now is, and was called Frederica in honor of Frederick, the son of George II. The town was located near the beach, where there had been once an Indian town. It was settled by the emigrants which Mr. Oglethorpe brought with him in his second coming to Georgia. The emigrants intended for it were landed at Savannah and reshipped in broad flat boats, which reached the bluff at St. Simons after six days of voyaging. The people found shelter from the March weather in booths made of the palmetto boughs. The city was laid out on forty acres of cleared land covered with grass sod. Around it was a beautiful forest of live-oaks, water-oaks, laurel, bay, cedar, sweet-gum, sassafras and pines. The muscadine and fox-grape and the fragrant yellow jessamine festooned the forest trees. The island abounded in deer, rabbits, raccoons, squirrels, wild turkeys, doves, red-birds, mocking-birds and great flocks of rice-birds. The marshes were crowded with wild geese, ducks, herons, cranes, plovers and marsh-hens, and the waters were filled with fishes of all kinds, crabs, shrimps and oysters.

This is not an exaggerated statement of what was to be found on St. Simons and the islands contiguous at that time. The island was said to be fertile and healthy, It was hard land to be cleared, and when the land was cultivated it soon was apparent that those crops which were indispensable to an Englishman's or a German's comfort were not suitable to the climate and the soil. The settlers reached the island too late the year of their first coming to do any farm work for that year, and before they could get fully settled the Spanish war was upon them. The money which came to the troops and for furnishing the supplies necessary for the subsistence of the small army helped to build up the little city and make it prosperous for a time. It is evident that this new city was a favorite of General Oglethorpe. The only land he located in Georgia was on St. Simons, and here he spent the larger part of the time he was in America. Up to the period when Oglethorpe returned to England Frederica prospered, but when peace came the town began to decline and soon ceased to be a place of any note at all. It afterward became the home of Mr. James Spalding, who carried on quite a trade with the Creek and Seminole Indians. There was nothing in the location or its surroundings to give anything like permanent prosperity to it, and after its bright and vigorous infancy it declined constantly until there was nothing left of the second city of Georgia—not even the name. Mr. Bartram, the French botanist, who visited this country just before the Revolution, found only the ruins of what had once been the city, and when it was decided some years ago to take a picture of the live-oak under which John Wesley and his brother Charles had preached, they found the oak still standing in magnificence, but no vestige of a living being near-by. Frederica was truly a dead town.

AUGUSTA.

Before Mr. Oglethorpe came to Georgia there was a trading-post near what is now Hamburg, S. C., on the South Carolina side of the river called Fort Moore, and Mr. Oglethorpe decided to build a fort on the Georgia side and garrison it. This he did, and in honor of the Princess

Augusta it was called by her name. In the pamphlet to which we have referred, by Wm. Stephens, there is the following list of Indian traders who had headquarters at Augusta. The names given are: Wood, Brown, Clark, Knott, Spencer, Barnett, Ladson, Mackey, Elsey, Facy, McQueen, Wright, Gardner, Andrews, Duvall, Cammell Randel, Chauncey, Newberry.

There were beside these traders, living near the fort, Kennedy O'Brien, Frazer, Miller, Brown, a saddler, a tailor, William Clark, H. Overstreet, L. Bean, William Grey, William Calahan, McGilveray, Casson, Gilmore, Goodale, Ross, Galphin.

On the east side of the Savannah, in South Carolina, where negroes were allowed, there were numbers of plantations opened, and the corn consumed by the large number of horses needed in the trade with the Indians was produced there.

These Indian traders sent out their men to the towns of the Chickasaws, Uchees, Creeks and Cherokees, and in the spring season great crowds of Indians came with their ponies loaded with peltry to trade at the post for powder and lead, and especially for rum. There was a mean rum known as tafia which was the main article of traffic. It was brought by Indian traders from the coast and traded for all kinds of products and for Indian slaves.* These slaves, taken by their enemies in war, were brought to Augusta and sold and carried to Charleston and shipped to the West Indies. The traders were oftentimes wretchedly dissolute. They lived shameless lives with the squaws, and when they grew weary of them went from them without hesitation.

There was a large trading-post owned by Galphin in Ogeechee Town. This old Galphinton is ten miles south

* See Logan's History of South Carolina, p. 180 and beyond, for a full account of this traffic.

of Louisville, on the Ogeechee river. George Galphin was a famous Indian trader, who had an elegant home at Silver Bluff and was recognized as a king by the various tribes. They brought all questions to him for settlement. It was told of him that once a chief, attracted by the red coat Galphin wore, said to him one day:

"Me had dream."

"Oh!" said Galphin, "what was it?"

"Me dream you give me dat coat."

"Then you shall have it," said the trader.

A long time passed, when one day, when the chief was at the post, Galphin said:

"Chief, I had a dream."

"Ugh! What you dream?"

"I dreamt you give me all the land in the fork of this creek."

"Well, you shall have it, but we dream no more."

Augusta was not a place for a quiet residence in those wild days. Two thousand ponies owned by the traders were loaded with goods in Charleston and with peltry at the fort, and kept the now almost deserted old road to Charleston alive. As one now rides over the deep sands through which the old highway runs, he can bring before him the great train of Indian slaves doomed to a life worse than death, who had been bought and branded by the traders with a red-hot iron, and who were now to go in weary procession from Augusta to Charleston. There were great fortunes made in this Indian slave-trade and in furnishing the Indians with rum and gunpowder; and it was to pay the debts due George Galphin and other traders that Sir James Wright secured from the Indians their cession of Wilkes, Oglethorpe, Elbert and Lincoln counties. Augusta was not affected by the laws concerning negroes, and as far as rum was concerned it was the main article of traffic, but that rum was sold to the Indians, and the slaves she sold were captives secured in war.

There may have been, and I think it likely there were, sundry settlers who were scattered among the Indians and who had squatted on lands belonging to them ; and it is probable that Mr. Galphin had around his settlement at Galphinton some of his countrymen before Oglethorpe came, and I find some proof of it. Colonel Jones puts the emigration of the Scotch-Irish to St. George's parish as late as 1768. I find that certainly as early as Governor Reynolds's grants in 1752 there were grants of land made to men whom I know were in Jefferson.

General Oglethorpe had done his best to make a model colony, and though he left it in a sadly depressed condition, it was not from any failure on his part to endure hardships or face danger. When he returned to England the trustees selected Mr. William Stephens, who had for some years been his secretary as the *de facto* governor. He was at one time a member of Parliament in England, and was a man of excellent family and good cultivation. He had been a servant of the trustees from his first coming to the colony, and was devoted to their interests. He had been virtually the governor of the Savannah part of the colony during Mr. Oglethorpe's stay, and after Mr. Oglethorpe's return to England he was in entire control of affairs.

In 1749 there occurred the famous Bosomworth trouble, to which a ludicrous prominence has been given in the Georgia histories and in Hewitt's History of South Carolina, and a trifling affair has been magnified into an event of immense importance. Mary Bosomworth was a half-breed Creek woman, the daughter of a Scotch father. She had some education and spoke both the Creek and English languages. She had been employed by Mr. Oglethorpe as an interpreter. Having lost her first husband, Musgrove, she had married a worthless fellow by the name of Mathews, who gave Governor Stephens much annoyance. When he died she married a scapegrace clergyman whose name was Bosomworth. She made some claims to back-pay due her as interpreter, and laid claims to some landed property and threatened the infant colony with her vengeance if her claims were not allowed, and finally, with a small body of vagabond Indians, she came toward Savannah to enforce her demands. The few militia in the province, one hundred and seventy in all, under command of Captain Noble Jones, met the Indians, who were two hundred in number, and disarmed them without any trouble; and eventually, after Mary, in her drunken rage, for she was a sad reprobate, forced Governor Stephens to lock her up, the Indians were all invited to the governor's house and took a glass together with the whites, and smoked the pipe of peace and went back to their wigwams.* Mary's claim was at last settled by Governor Ellis, and she secured some money and a grant to St. Catherine's Island, which was sold to Button Gwinnett.†

Governor Stephens was old and feeble and the burdens of his office were borne by his associates, Parker and Habersham. He voluntarily, after a short incumbency, retired to his plantation near Savannah, where very suddenly he died. He wrote a copious Journal, often referred to by the

* In Hewitt, McCall, Stevens and Jones there is substantially the same account. There were only two hundred Indians in all. They had no ammunition and had not, in all likelihood, the slightest idea of doing any violence. The great army who saved the people from massacre were one hundred and seventy militia, under Captain Noble Jones. There was not a single drop of blood shed, and no threat or danger of a massacre. I am a little regretful that the brilliant rhetoric of Bishop Stevens, in giving account of this occurrence, has so little to support it; but he merely followed Hewitt, who was copied by McCall. The Journal of Mr. Wm. Stephens gives the best account of the whole affair. Colonel Jones has given all the facts with his accustomed accuracy.

† See Stephens's account in his Journal.

historians of Georgia, which was published in three volumes. This Journal was the first book written in Georgia, with the exception of the small collection of hymns published by John and Charles Wesley.

The colony, as we have seen, was in a depressed condition, and it was apparent to all on the ground that the chief cause of the state of things was the inability of the

JAMES HABERSHAM.

planters to secure cheap labor and the nature of the tenures of the granted land. Even Mr. Bolzius recognized that something was the matter, and James Habersham was requested by him to draw up a statement setting forth the condition of the colony and the cause of it, and Mr. Habersham wrote an article in which he attributed the depression to the prohibition of negro labor.

This paper came into the hands of the trustees, and they, becoming convinced by it that the restriction was not a wise one, decided that under certain conditions the colonists might import negroes. They had not been led to prohibit slavery at the first from any moral considerations, but had been led to it by their opinion that it was best for the temporal interests of the colony. They were now convinced that they had been mistaken, and so they prescribed the conditions under which the planters would be permitted to purchase and hold slaves.

These conditions were: The slaves should not be in large numbers on any plantation. They should be enjoined and encouraged to marry; they should be forbidden to use profane language; they should not be sold without registry, and should not learn any mechanical arts; they should not be worked on the Sabbath day, but should be compelled to go to church and be instructed by the Protestant ministry. Under these conditions the restriction against slave labor was removed.

The law against the admission of rum had probably been disregarded for some time, and it was repealed, and the restriction concerning land tenure was removed and the property was to be held in fee. There was nothing now, save that Georgia was still governed by trustees, to distinguish the youngest of the colonies from her older sisters; and this government by trustees was nearly at an end, for in 1751 the trustees surrendered their charter to the crown and the colonial office took the government of Georgia in hand. For two years and nine months the old appointees held over, and Mr. Henry Parker and Sir John Graham were successively in charge of the government.

In 1754, however, Sir John Reynolds was duly appointed to the position of governor.

In 1751 the first Assembly met in Savannah. The members were Francis Harris, John Milledge, William Francis, Wm. Russell, Savannah; Geo. Codagan, David

Douglas, Augusta; Christian Riedelsperger, Theobald Kiefer, Ebenezer; Wm. Ewen, Abercorn; Patrick Houston, Vernonsburg; Peter Morel, Acton; Jos. Summers, Little Ogeechee; Jno. Barnard, Skidaway; Audley Maxwell, Midway; Jno. More Mackintosh, Darien.*

The names of the places from which the delegates came give us some idea of how the population had moved and of the advance of the settlements into the interior.

In taking a survey of the colony for these twenty years one cannot but be impressed with the elevated aims of its founders. The trustees doubtless made grave mistakes, and in endeavoring to do too much had failed to do what might have been done for the good of the colony; but their motives were of the highest kind, and, with the single exception of Mr. Causton, there seems to have been among the officers of the colony only men of probity and intelligence. Men like Wm. Stephens, Noble Jones, James Habersham, and ministers like Jno. and Charles Wesley, Geo. Whitfield, and Pastors Gronau and Bolzius would have ornamented any State.

Up to the time the trustees surrendered their trust there had been granted in trust forty-one thousand acres, and sold outright twenty-seven thousand acres. The colony had been settled twenty years, and while it had had but little prosperity, it had had no disasters. There was no Indian massacre as in Virginia, no Indian war as in New England, no servile insurrection as in South Carolina, but it had by no means met the hopes of those who planted it. Perhaps no colony ever had a better class of first settlers. They were most of them quite poor, but so were the first settlers of Virginia and New England, the Huguenots and German emigrants to Pennsylvania. They were hampered at first by impracticable regulations, and many of them left the colony for South Carolina, but many remained

*Jones.

in Georgia, and many of those who left the colony returned in an after time. These first settlers had none of the calamities which befell the early settlers in the older colonies, but there were all the discomforts of frontier life. There were no mills driven by wind or water, and the settlers were dependent for bread upon Indian corn which was beaten in a mortar or ground on a hand-mill. The houses out of the villages were of round logs, and sometimes of clapboards. The floors were of dirt, and the chimneys were made of clay and stakes. The settlers had no comforts, but there was generally a sufficiency of food. Turkeys were caught in pens and quails and rabbits in traps, and near the towns where ammunition could be easily secured the pot-hunter provided ducks and wild geese and venison for the table. In a few years cattle were abundant and hogs in large numbers were raised on the acorns in the swamps.

There was no wheat flour save what came from New England, but soon after the settlements were made there were patches of rice. Even those planters who at this early date were considered well-to-do had few comforts, and even near the coast, where there was some shipping, living was plain, but away from it it was exceedingly hard.

There was comparatively little difference in the style of living among the rural people, and there were but three small villages—Savannah, Augusta and Ebenezer. Frederica had been almost abandoned and Augusta was merely a trading-post. There were only a few settlers above Savannah or below Brunswick, and these were far from prosperous.

In the sketch of Savannah in a later chapter an account is given of the religious history of the colony—the founding of Bethesda and the growth of Ebenezer. There was but little attention paid to churches and schools during the time of the trustees, although there was a school in Savannah and a tabernacle and a church and school in Ebenezer; but there were, so far as I can find, neither churches nor schools at the time when the trustees gave up their charge out of these villages. The Presbyterians had abandoned the colony, the Moravians had gone to Pennsylvania, and save at Bethesda and at Ebenezer there was little attention given to religious matters.

CHAPTER II.

UNDER THE ROYAL GOVERNORS.

Governor Reynolds—Some of his Difficulties with the Colonists—Dr. Little—Clement Martin Removed from the Council—Governor Reynolds Asks to be Recalled—Georgia as it Appeared in his Time—The Dorchester Settlement—The English Emigration to Dorchester, Mass.—The Settlement of Dorchester, S. C.—Removal to Georgia—List of the First Patentees—Midway Church Built—Lyman Hall and Button Gwinnett—The Land Grants Made by Governor Reynolds—Slavery in the Colony—Native Africans—The Condition of the New Negroes—Laws for Regulation of the Slaves—Governor Ellis—His Administration—Church of England Established—Episcopal Churches in Georgia—The First Presbyterian Church—The Congregational—The Lutheran—The List of Parishes—Governer James Wright—The Capital Settled in Savannah—Governor Wright's First Assembly—Condition of Affairs in the Colony—Troubles Impending in Consequence of the Stamp Act—Collision between Governor Wright and the Assembly—The Newly Ceded Lands and the Middle Georgia People—General View of the Colony to 1774—Mr. Whitfield's College Plan—The Moral Tone of the Colony—Sabbath Laws—Governor James Wright's Administration—Education in the Colony—Advance of the Colony among the English, the Scotch, the Germans, in St. George's Parish, Augusta, and St. Paul's Parish—Social Changes—Religious Movements—Baptists Enter the State.

Authorities: McCall, Stevens, Jones, Georgia Historical Collections, White's Statistics, White's Historical Collections, Whitfield's Journal, Colonial Laws, Hewitt, Records in Secretary of State's Office, Bartram, De Brahm.

Governor Reynolds, who came into his office in 1754, had been a captain in the British navy, and as a reward for his naval services he was made the first royal governor of the Georgia colony. He was officially designated as captain-general and governor-in-chief of his majesty's province in Georgia and vice-admiral of the same.

He was received by the people of the colony with great enthusiasm and began his administration very promisingly. He selected an able council consisting of the leading men in the colony. They were Sir Patrick Houston, Patrick Grahame, James Habersham, Noble Jones, Pickering Robinson, Francis Harris, Alex Kellett, Jonathan Bryan, Wm. Russell, Wm. Clifton and Clement Martin, Sr.

The bluff old sailor found things in a rather cheerless condition and was evidently greatly disappointed in the outlook. Savannah was not a well-built city, as he expected to find it, but a dilapidated village; and the governorship of a province in which there was not five thousand people, and whose most important public building was a board tabernacle, was not a place to be coveted. He began, however, to do some very needful things. He organized the courts and ordered all previous grants of land recalled, and proposed to issue new patents. He called the Assembly together, but soon found he had some troublesome men in it. One of these was Edmond Gray, a Quaker from St. Paul's parish. Gray, in connection with Farmer, McIntosh and Carr, issued a call for the people of the colony who valued their liberty to appear as soon as possible at Savannah. This Governor Reynolds thought was open rebellion, and as such denounced it. What led to the call of Gray we do not know, but we can conjecture it was to protest against the proposed measure of Governor Reynolds to recall the grants of land hitherto made and issue new warrants upon new conditions. These conditions were so hard that the entire Assembly united in a successful petition to the king for a negation of them, and the governor reluctantly withdrew them.

Edmond Gray, of whom we know too little, went afterward to the neutral ground south of Darien, and was visited by Governor Ellis at his home. Governor Ellis speaks of him kindly, and says he was a man of remarkable ability but had no common sense.

There was perhaps not a man in Governor Reynolds's council who did not know better than he did how to govern the Georgia colony, for every one of them, and they were superior men, knew the condition of things in the colony as Governor Reynolds could not have possibly known it; but the blustering old sea captain, who knew nothing of the conditions about him, and who, in addition to his own incompetency, was under the control of his private secretary, Dr. Little, another newcomer who was thoroughly detested by all of the council, treated their suggestions with contempt, and was not even satisfied when they expelled Mr. Carr and Mr. Gray and Mr. Farmer from the Assembly, but dismissed Mr. Clement Martin from the council and was generally offensive.

There was no easy time for the captain-general and commander-in-chief in the new colony. His salary was small, his expenses were heavy, and the home government was not disposed to make further grants to a colony which made so poor a return.

The Assembly was impertinent, if not rebellious, the council was as bad, and so, as matters did not improve when he had spent two years of a troublous kind in the province, and had done some hard work, he asked relief, and went back to England to his congenial place on the quarter-deck once more.*

The colonists had not been pleased with Governor Reynolds, and he fretted at the idea of being an exile to a small American town, so there was mutual pleasure at the separation. He said there were only one hundred and fifty houses in Savannah; the biggest of them was used for the meeting of the president and council; "but one end fell down whilst we were there, and obliged us to move to a kind of shed behind the court-house which was quite unfit. I have given orders, with the advice of the council, to fit up a shell of a house which was lately built as far as the laying of the sills, but never made use of. The prison

* Stephens and Jones.

was an insecure structure, which I ordered to be strengthened with bolts and bars."

Captain De Brahm, who came during Governor Stephens's last incumbency, confirms the governor's story. He says he could have bought the best improved lot in Savannah for a few pounds, and somewhat complacently intimates that if he had not come when he did the colony would have been deserted.

Governor Reynolds, however, did much good work. He organized the courts and put the government machinery into operation. He was governor in a very important day for Georgia, for the opening wide the gates to new settlers brought in the first American immigrants to the colony, except the few settlers who had come from lower South Carolina into the country below Savannah. There were the Virginians and North Carolinians, who came near this time to St. George's parish, then including all of Burke, Jefferson, and a large part of Screven county. In my sketches of these counties I have given a fuller account of these settlers than I can give here. They were numerous enough to send a representative from Halifax to the first Assembly called by Governor Reynolds, and when the parishes were laid off by Governor Ellis, to call for a special parish known as St. George's. A body of Quakers, before 1754, had settled some lands on Little river at a place which was called Blendon. It was in St. Paul's parish, on Little river, and was near the spot where Wrightsboro was afterward located. These Quakers were led by the Edmond Gray who became so obnoxious to Governor Reynolds. The Indians, however, menaced the peace-loving Quakers and they decided to abandon the settlement. The project was however revived during the time of Governor Wright, under the care of Joseph Mattock and Jona Sells, and a road joining the Savannah road, in St. George's parish, known still as the Quaker road, was cut at that time. There is near Wrightsboro a Quaker graveyard, but the Quaker settlement was abandoned during the Revolution.

While Jones, who is remarkably accurate, puts the settlement of the Scotch-Irish on the Ogeechee as late as 1768, I am sure there were many of these people in St. George's parish as early as the days of Governor Reynolds. Some who were associated with Galphin in the Indian trade were doubtless in the Nation before Oglethorpe came; but after the country was fairly opened and all restrictions on landholders had been removed, the tide of settlement from the north of Ireland set in very rapidly. The same class of Scotch-Irishmen who came to Pennsylvania, to Virginia and to the Carolinas came to Georgia and made quite a settlement. Captain De Brahm says that there were two hundred families in this section of the colony when his account was written, and, as will be seen by examining the list of land-patents, there were a large number who are registered as having received grants of land before 1768, whom one recognizes as being the progenitors of families who were afterward prominent in Jefferson, Screven and Burke counties, and a Mr. Edward Brown, Andrew and James Lambert, Arthur Thomas, Jacob Depford and Solomon Kempe had a settlement on the Ogeechee as early as 1756, in what is now Jefferson and Screven counties.

The little hamlet about Fort Augusta continued to grow, and there was now at the fort a considerable village of log huts, and hundreds of Indians came to it on trading expeditions every season, bringing peltry and slaves and ponies, and buying rum and ammunition and Indian guns.

These traders, of whom we spoke in the last chapter, were now quite numerous and had posts in various parts of the nations, and, whether among Creeks or Cherokees or Choctaws, they took to themselves Indian wives, generally the daughters of the chiefs, and in after time their children by these Indian squaws were chiefs of the tribes, and the Adairs, Rosses, McIntoshes, McGilverays, and many others had their descendants among the Indians, much to the grief of the white man. Nor were they alone, but Englishmen of high birth left the homes of the white people and married, lived and died among the Indians, and their children led in many a foray against the white invaders in after

MAJOR RIDGE (INDIAN).

time. To these must be added not a few Virginians who were traders.

The settled portion of the colony, if any could be called settled at that early day, was confined to a narrow strip stretching along the Savannah, the Ogeechee and the Altamaha rivers, and on the lands near the coast. The recognized western boundary of the white settlement was the Ogeechee. The section east of this river was slowly filling up with white people, but beyond the Ogeechee river, save a few small and scattered Creek and Chickasaw towns, all was an Indian hunting-ground. The Cherokees occupied, without any one disturbing them, the northern and northwestern part of the State, but they had their principal towns in East Tennessee. The Spanish gold-digger, under De Soto, had traversed their country in search of gold, and had left a record of his stay in the pits he had dug, but other than these no whites had as yet disturbed the dusky denizens of these valleys.

Hitherto our attention has been directed to those settlers who came from over the sea, but now we are to speak of a colony of native Americans, who were to do much for Georgia and to have a great influence on her future history. During the time when Governor Stephens held over, and before Governor Reynolds reached Savannah, the Dorchester settlement, in what was afterwards St. John's parish, was made.

Captain De Brahm, a German engineer who made the first map of the colony and brought over the German emigrants, came to the colony at that time, and says he induced these settlers to come.

In Plymouth, England, in the heat of the persecution of the Puritans by Archbishop Laud about 1630, a colony of Church of England people, weary of bishops and of liturgies, resolved to emigrate to then just settled New England. This they did and fixed their home at Dorchester, Mass. They accepted the Congregational form of government they found there, and became a Congregational church, with a Calvinistic confession. Fifty years after this they found themselves cramped for land, and as South Carolina had been settled largely by those who sympathized with their religious and political views, they secured a large grant of land on the Ashley river and planted a colony there, which they called Dorchester also. Here they planted rice and became large slaveholders.

They received an addition to their number from Virginia. The rice country about them was not sufficient for their needs, and as soon as Georgia allowed the planters to bring slaves into the colony they sent over some of their congregation to survey the land. There were some extensive swamps between Savannah and Darien, in what is now known as the swamp land of Liberty county. They were admirably adapted to the growth of rice, but, save to a rice-planter accustomed to malarial swamps, certainly uninviting. The Dorchester people succeeded in getting grants from the colonial government which covered over thirty thousand acres of this fertile country. They did not at once remove, but, remaining a part of the year in South Carolina, they came to Georgia after their crop was made and opened land and built shelters until they were ready to change their habitations.

These immigrants fixed their homes on the edge of the swamps, building their humble cabins in the very center of the malarious district. The heavy timber was cleared away, the swamps were ditched and the dams made, and they moved their families and the cultivation of rice began. The only tool used in culture after the land was cleared, says Colonel Jones, was the hoe, and the rice was brought from the field on the head of the negroes and cleaned from the husks with pestle and mortar. Corn was ground in hand-mills. The market was Savannah, to which the rough rice was shipped by coasting schooners. The colony prospered and was soon quite populous. We give here a list of persons who received grants of five hundred acres: John Davis, John Maxwell, James Maxwell, William Maxwell, John Stevens, Benjamin Baker, John Lupton, Rev. Mr. Osgood, Samuel Stephens, Sarah Norman, Daniel Slade, Edward Sumner, Andrew Way, Richard Spencer, William Brumley, Sarah Osgood, Rich Giraudeau, Joseph Bacon, Jonathan Bacon, John Norman, Sarah Mitchell, John Edwards, John Ellrod, John Way, William Graves, James Norman, John Stewart, Samuel James, Robert Glass, Robert

Eccles, John Quarterman, David Ross, William Lupton, Richard Baker, John Stevens, Joseph Oswald, Jacob Weston, Joshua Clarke, A. Gleve, William Mackay, David Fox, Willoughby West, Palmer Gaulding, William Russell, Parmenus Way, Jacob Riden, Benjamin Andrew, and James Andrew.

It was decided by them to establish a market town nearer to the colony than Savannah, and in 1758 the town of Sunbury, on the western bank of Medway river, was laid out. Colonel Jones, who gives a history of the dead towns of Georgia, gives not only a plot of the young city but a list of the lot-holders, which is interesting as showing who resided in this county at that time. They were: Mark Carr, Grey Elliott, Francis Arthur, William Graves, John Cubbege, James Maxwell, Mary Spivey, Samuel Bennerworth, Stephen Dickerson, James Fisher, Schmidt & Molich, Swinton & Co., Darling & Munro, Thomas Peacock, A. Darling, Thomas Young, Roger Kelsal, John James, John Bacon, John Stewart, John Lupton, Dunbar, Young & Co., James Dunham, Lyman Hall, Samuel Miller, Kenneth Bailey, Samuel Benniworth, William Stevenson, Tabitha Bacon, John Winn, David Jerray, Francis Arthur, John Steward, John Lawson, Thomas Ralph, John Quarterman, Thomas Goldsmith, James Houston, Ivan Stevens, William Baker, Elijah Simmons, Robert Bolton, John Humphrey, Francis Guilland, Henry Saltus, Donald McKay, Stephen Dickenson, James Hurley, Francis Lee, John Quarterman, James Dowell, John Irvine, Jemima Irvine, Math Smallwood, William Peacock, John Osgood, Rebecca Way, Hugh Clark, Paris Way, Nath Yates, William Dunham, Charles West, Samuel West, Thomas Carter, Audley Maxwell, John Graves, John Baker, James Fisher, Jno. Elliot, Jno. Lyman, John Sutherland, Sam Jeanes, Joseph Tichenor, William Mullen, William Davis, James Sergeant, John Jones, Strong Ashmore, F. Arthur, George Morris, Joshua Snowden,

James Andrew, Samuel Morcock, George Bodington, Mary Bateman, Patrick McKay, Benjamin Andrew, Marmaduke Gerry, John Winn, Richard Mills, James Hatcher, John Perkins, William Low, Barnard Romans, Ed Mahone, R. Spencer, John Mitchell, Morgan Tabb, Joseph Watcher, Jno. Gasper Stirkey, John Jones, Joseph Richardson, Robert Smallwood, John Futes, Arthur Carney, Isaac Linder, Frederick Holsendorf.

The first thing these good people did after fixing their homes was to build them a log church in the midst of their plantations. This church was succeeded by a better one, which was burned during the Revolution, and that by a still better one. For many years the Midway church with its chapels, first at Sunbury, then at Walthourville, commanded the best talent of the Presbyterian Church, and the congregation was large, wealthy, and intelligent, but after the last war reluctantly the church was given up by the whites and is now occupied by the negroes.

The Rev. Mr. Osgood, for whom Bishop James Osgood Andrew was named, was the pastor they brought with them from South Carolina. Like his parishioners, he was a planter and a man evidently of some estate. He was virtually a Presbyterian, and after Mr. McLeod, who only remained a little while in Georgia, was the first Presbyterian minister who had a charge in Georgia; for while Midway was a Congregational church during almost its entire history, the pastoral office was filled by Presbyterian ministers, with whom the Congregationalists of an early day in America were always in accord.

It was to be expected that the Puritans of Dorchester would sympathize with their New England kinsmen in their resistance to the course of the English government, and they were in advance of all others in Georgia in their spirit of rebellion. They were represented in every public movement in Savannah, and sent hundreds of barrels of rice to the poor in Boston, and when the convention failed to send delegates to the Constitutional Congress the parish of St. John sent Dr. Lyman Hall as its representative. Two signers of the Declaration—Lyman Hall and Button Gwinnett—were both from this parish, though Mr. Gwinnett was not a member of the Dorchester colony.

The list of grantees as I have given it is necessarily very imperfect, and is confined to those who received grants of five hundred acres. The list of those receiving grants

BUTTON GWINNETT.

from the State published in the appendix will give many more than those mentioned above, while the memorandum of those who had lots in Sunbury will give a still clearer idea of the people who composed this colony when it was in its infancy.

As slavery was now legalized in the colony the Assembly passed sundry laws with reference to the treatment of slaves. It must be remembered that the larger part of the slaves were savages direct from Africa. They had been captured by their own countrymen in the cruel wars the tribes waged with each other, and driven like cattle to the west African ports, where they had been sold to the Portuguese and English traders. They had no idea of honesty, no feeling of pity to a foe, no conception of sexual purity or marital fidelity. They could not speak the language of the people who owned them and understood nothing of what was said to them except a few plain commands. Accustomed to nakedness and hunger in their own land, they found the regular supply of rice and potatoes and the scanty apparel furnished by the rice-planters a great advance beyond all they had in negro-land. Slavery was permitted everywhere at that time and was condemned by none, not even the Quakers. The slavery, however, which was to be allowed in the colonies was by no means Roman or Grecian or African slavery, for the control of the slave was restricted by law, and the slave was carefully protected from all bodily harm. The acts passed provided: 1. That the slave should not leave his place without a written permit. 2. Unusual assemblages of slaves were to be dispersed. 3. If he was guilty of a capital crime he should be tried by two justices and punished with death. 4. A justice and two freeholders were a sufficient court for ordinary offenses. 5. Arson should be punished with death. 6. Stealing a slave or effacing his *brand* should be a felony. 7. If a slave was condemned to death the colony should pay his value to his owner, but not more than fifty pounds. 8. No slave should carry firearms. 9. If a slave struck a white man he should be punished. If he struck him the third time he should be put to death. Cruelty to slaves was forbidden. If any one should wilfully murder his slave he should be adjudged guilty of a felony, with the benefit of the clergy, for the first offense; but if he did it the second time he should be deemed guilty of a *murther*. 10. If he should kill a slave in heat he should forfeit fifty pounds. 11. If he should maim him or cruelly maltreat him, he should forfeit ten pounds. 12. If he did not give him sufficient food and clothing he should be fined. 13. If an owner was charged with inhuman conduct, he should be presumed to be guilty, unless he showed his innocence. No one could have a plantation occupied entirely by slaves.

Governor Reynolds was succeeded by the scholarly and considerate Governor Ellis. Governor Ellis made an honest and successful effort to conciliate the offended colonists and to secure peace to all the colony. The Assembly, which had been called by Governor Reynolds, was by no means a representative body, and those who were eligible to seats in it were by the restrictions laid down reduced to a very few.

The Assembly called by Governor Ellis met and established the Church of England and divided the colony into parishes. The administration of Governor Ellis was uneventful and unimportant. He left the colony after a short stay in it and went back to England, carrying with him good wishes to all the colonists and a holy horror of the hot summers in Savannah. The most important and really the only notable act of his administration was the establishment of the Church of England and the division of the State into parishes. There was in Georgia at that time Christ Church, in Savannah; St. Paul's Church, in Augusta; St. George's, a log church, in Burke county; a Lutheran Church, in Ebenezer; a Congregational in Liberty county; and these were all the churches from above Augusta to Amelia Island. There was the rector of Christ Church in Savannah, and a missionary sent out by the Society for the Propagation of the Gospel in Foreign parts, Mr. Jonathan Copp, whose home was in Augusta. These were the only Episcopal ministers in the colony. Mr. Osgood was the only Congregationalist and Mr. Bedgewood the only Baptist, and he had no organized church to serve. The Lutherans had two pastors, Mr. Bolzius and Mr. Gronau, but they preached only in German. The Lutherans built them a small church in Savannah, which was supplied by these Ebenezer pastors.

There seems to have been little opposition to the establishment of the Church, and it was after all a mere form of church establishment. It was abandoned in twenty years, and did not exist long enough to accomplish any noticeable results.

The parishes were: Christ Church, which included all of Chatham and the islands adjacent.

St. Matthew's, which included all of Effingham and much of Screven.

St. George's, all of Burke, Jefferson, and a part of Screven.

St. Paul's, all of Richmond, Columbia, McDuffie, and a part of Warren.

St. John's, all of Liberty.

St. Andrew's, all the section south of the Altamaha, near Darien.

St. Philip's, the section on the south side of the Ogeechee, west of Liberty.

St. James's, Frederica and the county south of it to the disputed line.

In 1765 four new parishes, St. Patrick's, St. David's, St. Thomas's and St. Mary's, were laid out in the section south of the Altamaha, and now contained in Camden, Charlton, and the adjoining counties. These parishes were not really organized, and were such in name only.

There was a feeble effort to build a church in each of these parishes, but save the log church in Augusta and in St. George's parish I can find no evidence that any others were built.

Governor James Wright, who succeeded Governor Ellis, was by far the ablest man who had ever been governor of

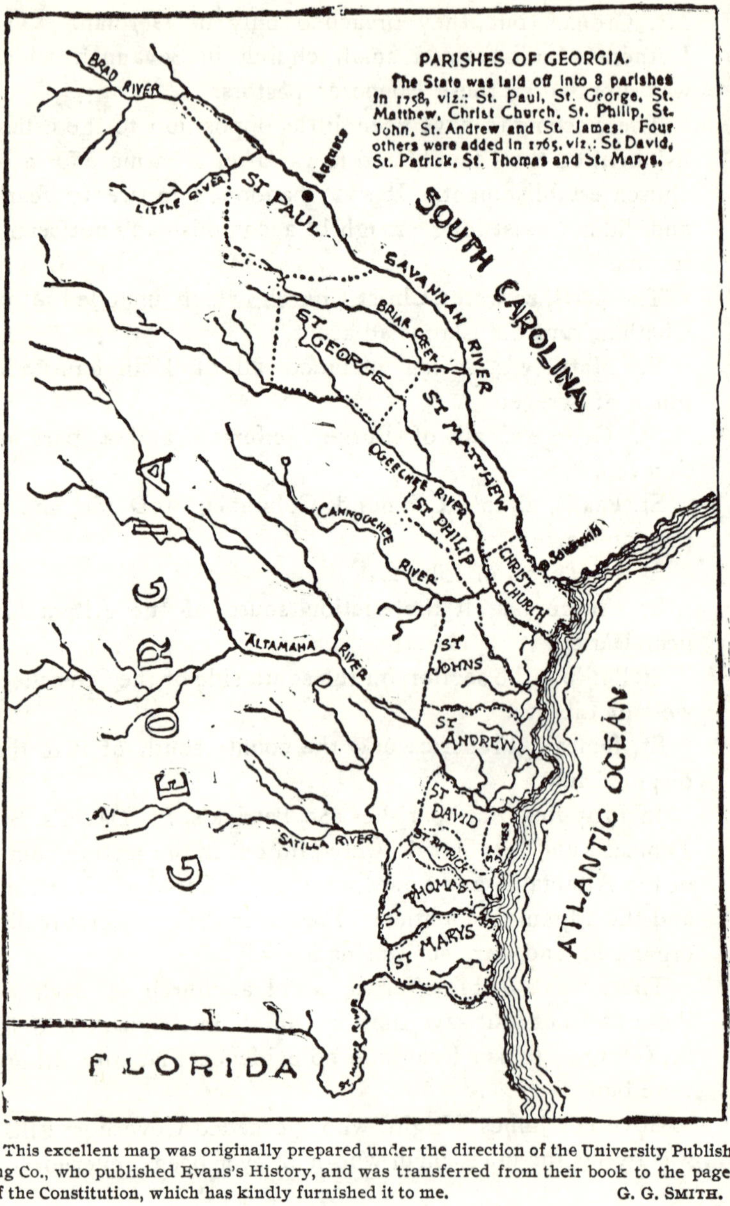

This excellent map was originally prepared under the direction of the University Publishing Co., who published Evans's History, and was transferred from their book to the pages of the Constitution, which has kindly furnished it to me. G. G. SMITH.

Georgia, and he has had no superior in that office since his day.

He was a South Carolinian by birth, and was a gentleman of fine culture. He was a lawyer, as his father, Chief Justice Wright of South Carolina, had been before him. At the time he received his appointment as governor he was colonial agent ot Georgia in London. He was a man of large estate and great purity of character. He had a strong will and great common sense. The question of removing the capital from Savannah to the new city of Hardwick, which had been settled by Governor Reynolds and Governor Ellis against Savannah, he reopened and decided that the capital should remain where it was and where it had been in Savannah, and the scheme of the new city was abandoned.

Governor Wright found the civil government well organized. The difficulties arising from the impracticable measures of the trustees had now been removed, and there was a prospect of a prosperous and peaceful rule. He surrounded himself with a wise council and made himself fully acquainted with all the needs of the growing colony. The Indians had given some little trouble to the frontier people, but in the main were peaceful. He called the Assembly together in Savannah. It consisted of: Jos. Ottalenghe, Grey Elliot, Lewis Johnson, Jos. Gibbons, Christ Church; Wm. Francis, N. W. Jones, Abercorn; Wm. Ewen, James De Vaux, Ebenezer; Alex Wylly, Halifax, James Whitefield, St. George's; Edward Barnard, John Graham, —— Williams, Lachlin McGilveray, St. Paul's; Elisha Butler, John Maxwell, Great Ogeechee; Thomas Carter, Parmenus Way, John Winn, St. John's; Robert Baillie, Jno. Holmes, St. Andrew's ; Lachlin McIntosh, St. James's.

As will appear, the members of the Assembly did not always reside in the parishes which they represented. Halifax, in St. George's, a comparatively new section in what is now Burke and Screven, was represented by Alex Wylly, of Christ Church, and Wm. Ewen and James De Vaux represented Ebenezer; while John Holmes, the Episcopal minister, represented St. Andrew's.

The Assembly seems to have been a harmonious body of able and intelligent men. The colony was now prospering. The wild schemes of raising silk and wine had been surrendered. The restrictions on land holdings and on slavery were given up and everything promised well for the future.

Shortly after Governor Wright began his career as governor, the governors of Georgia, South Carolina, North Carolina and Virginia met in Augusta and secured a cession of lands, and ten years after he purchased another body. As these two cessions were only ten years apart, and the sections purchased were contiguous, it is hardly necessary to consider them separately. The country first secured lay in the oak and hickory lands north of Augusta, in what is now Columbia county, and extended westward to what is now the west boundary of McDuffie county; in the second purchase in 1773 a body of land very much like this was also secured in what was afterward Wilkes county. This country was wonderfully beautiful and attractive. The land was mainly of two kinds, the oak and hickory lands and what was then known as the pine-barrens. There were no Indian settlements of importance in the section, and it was reserved by them as a hunting-ground. The first comers regarded the pine woods as uninhabitable, and settled along the creeks and rivers of the red lands. The Indians came annually in large hunting parties to kill the game which was in such abundance, and every winter they burned the woods to provide for the growth of the wild pasturage.

There had doubtless been some intruders on these lands, and no doubt horses and cattle were being raised on the range by South Carolina ranchmen and Indian traders.

There had been an effort to settle a colony on Little river in this section ten years before, but as we have seen it was broken up by the Indians. Now that this land was secured, and the Indians pacified, it was opened to settlement on

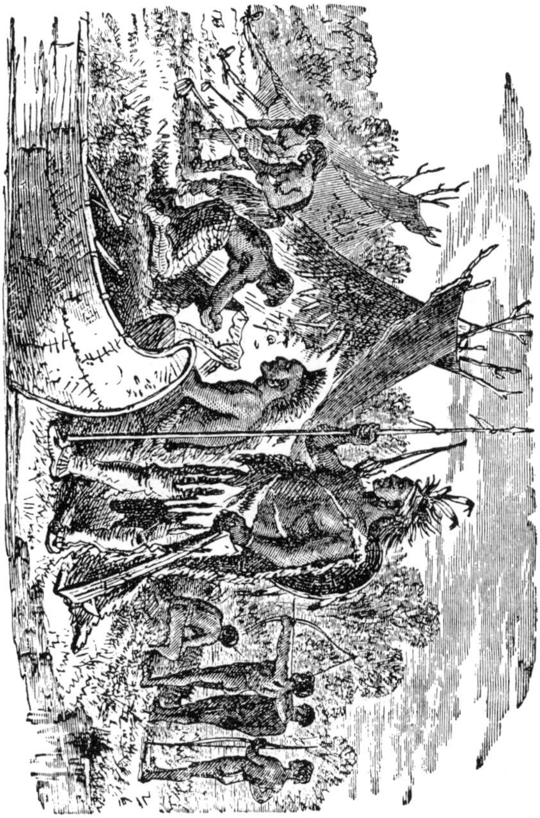

INDIAN LIFE.

most liberal terms. Any one who would file before a magistrate his purpose to settle in the land could get one hundred acres if he was single, two hundred if he was married, and an additional fifty acres for each child and each slave until five hundred acres were secured, at a nominal rental of two shillings a hundred acres. The offers of free farms were so generous that the tide of settlers poured in with great volume and covered the country. These people came from Virginia, North Carolina and Maryland, and settled on the banks of the Savannah river, the Kiokee creeks and Little river. In a study of the counties I have given a fuller account of the country and of the people. The tide of prosperity was rapidly rising.

When the Stamp Act troubles began there was but little excitement in Georgia outside of Savannah and Sunbury. In Savannah the young men paraded and burned in effigy obnoxious persons. The governor was furiously indignant, and in loud yet vain proclamation denounced the acts of the seditious.

The Liberty Boys were organized and the governor ordered out his little army of fifty-four men to take the stamps to the guard-house. The stamp-distributer came, and the intrepid governor protected him as well as he could, but he found himself unable to do so perfectly, and the English officer left the town. Governor Wright was menaced and the good and loyal James Habersham threatened also. Mobs gathered, a collision seemed imminent, but no further harm came than the burning of the governor in effigy. The stamps were in Savannah, but the people would not use them; though much to the indignation of the sister colony, South Carolina, the governor did use them on the clearance papers of the seventy sail in port at that time. The governor had barely held his own when the Stamp Act was repealed, much to his relief. But it was only a temporary lull. The Assembly refused to grant supplies to the soldiers quartered among the people. The Assembly appointed a new London agent, which the governor denied their right to do, and thus the contest between him and his Legislature grew more violent. Then the Assembly wished to issue twenty thousand pounds paper money. The governor thought twelve thousand pounds sufficient, and the king agreed with the governor. The Assembly passed an act for the government of the negroes; the governor approved it, but the king vetoed it. The colony was in a bad humor with the whole British government, and when Benjamin Franklin went to England to attend to the affairs of other colonies, Georgia appointed him to attend to her interests too, much to the disgust of the governor, who had but little use for the Pennsylvania printer. Then the Massachusetts colony sent out a circular

BENJAMIN FRANKLIN.

letter, and Mr. Alexander Wylly, the speaker, replied to it, approving its contents. When the Assembly met, although the governor expressed his disapproval of the circular, the Assembly passed resolutions of approval. The governor was very much angered at this procedure and, coming in, dissolved the Assembly.

The Assembly, now at open war with the governor, had sent an address to Dr. Franklin to be delivered to the king, which address the king refused to receive.

Then the merchants and planters began to hold meetings, and even Mr. Jonathan Bryan, one of the council, presided over their meetings; and Mr. Alexander Creighton introduced a resolution forbidding any importation of taxed products. The king promptly displaced Mr. Bryan, and twice the governor dissolved the rebellious Assembly. When this body met again in 1770 Dr. Noble Wimberly Jones was elected speaker. This was a gross affront to the governor, who had little use for the rebellious doctor, and

DR. NOBLE WIMBERLY JONES.

he ordered a new election. The Assembly held it and re-elected Dr. Jones, and as they would elect no one else the governor sent them home.

Then Sir James gladly took a respite from this incessant fight with his Assembly and went on a visit to England, and James Habersham took his place for the time being. Mr. Habersham was a man of remarkable probity, and while he sympathized with the colony to a great extent, he was loyal to the crown. The Assembly was composed of men with whom he had been associated from their first coming into the colony. He had been in the colony for nearly forty years, he had stood by it in all its struggles, he deplored this conflict of opinion and sympathized with the colonists, but his duty was plain, and when the members persisted in electing Dr. Jones he promptly dissolved the Assembly. Then there was for a time quiet, and colonists continued to flock into the new lands on Little river and the Ogeechee.

There was no fairer land in Georgia than the lands in St. George's and St. Paul's parishes, which were now open to settlers. Along the clear streams, for as yet they were as crystal, there stretched great bodies of cane in which the bear found his home, and on the rich wild grasses the myriad of deer fed. The hills were covered with a magnificent forest. The undergrowth had been kept down by the Indians, who burned the woods annually that the grasses might flourish. The forests were like a king's park. Herds of deer, droves of turkeys, and great flocks of rich-hued birds were found in every part of the land. The cattle needed no pasturage that the woods did not furnish. There were thousands of streamlets and springs, and when the land was opened there was a rich reward to the tiller's toil. It was no wonder then that, as soon as the land was offered to the settlers, they came in such numbers. Life with them was at first hard. There were no roads, and they came with their small supply of needful things on pack-horses. They built their cabins of round logs and covered them with split boards. At the first the floor was of packed clay, and the great chimney, with its wide hearth, was made of clay and stakes. There were no glazed windows and the door was made of split boards. Oftentimes there had not been a single nail used in building the cabin. The saw and axe and auger and frow had been the only tools. There was a scant supply of furniture, and it had been made mainly by hand; a three-legged stool, a puncheon bench, and, after the chair-maker came, a stout chair of hickory, with a raw-hide seat, were the conveniences. The bedsteads were made by hand, and the cattail and the long moss, and sometimes the leaves and pine straw, provided a couch for the sleepers.

The frontiersman had no easy time in providing food supplies. A few cattle he brought with him. Deer were abundant, and he killed an occasional bear, while wild turkeys were so plentiful that they were caught in pens and their flesh was dried and used as bread.

EARLY SETTLER'S CABIN.

There were some goods to be bought in Augusta at the stores of the traders, but there was little money on the frontier. By carrying peltry to the markets he secured powder and lead and salt. This was the condition of things on the frontier, but on the coast there was access to markets, and even at this early period comforts were common, and in the cities there was much elegance and many luxuries.

The new immigration was very large. The first comers had reported so favorably of the land that great crowds of immigrants came from the older counties of Virginia and from middle and eastern North Carolina into St. Paul's, St. George's and St. Matthew's parishes. Many Scotch-Irishmen came directly from Ireland and settled in what is now Jefferson county, which was then St. George's parish. Many Marylanders came into the lands on Little river, and another body of Quakers came from North Carolina, led by Mr. Jos. Mattocks, and settled near what was known as the

PIONEERS.

village of Wrightsboro. When the newly ceded lands in 1773 were opened for settlement there was at once a large immigration into that section, which was afterward known as Wilkes.

The tide of settlers was not checked by the beginning of the Revolution, for it was several years after the war had begun that these frontier people were at all disturbed.

The wondrous fertility and healthfulness of these lands drew at once a rush of settlers from the older colonies.

The lands were given away, and, without waiting to secure headrights or patents, the new immigrant came into these woods to choose his home. He found the tract upon which he wished to settle, put down his stakes and began to build his cabin. It was only necessary for him to file with the governor's council an affidavit that he intended to settle in the colony, and an order was given to the surveyor to lay out for him two hundred acres of land as his headright, and fifty acres additional for each negro he might bring with him. These newcomers, while of the same transatlantic stock with the settlers in lower Georgia, were not their close kinsmen; they were, as their grandfathers had been, native Americans. Mr. Anthony Stokes, who was judge of one of the king's courts, and wrote a book concerning Georgia, speaks of them as convicts and renegades driven out of the older States, but Mr. Stokes was a cockney who knew nothing of these people.

The early settlers of upper Georgia were not all of the same class, but they were much more homogeneous than the white people of the lower part of the State. The low-country people were English, Scotch, and Germans, but the up-country people were all native Americans. The low-country English and Scotch people were much more under the influence of English traditions, and there was a wider division between classes than in the up-country. Among these up-countrymen there were not a few ignorant unaspiring people. They were not peasants; they lived in their own cabins, and worked their own fields. They had never known anything of luxury and had a sovereign contempt for it. Their origin was probably an humble one. Their ancestors of three generations before had been brought over to Virginia by an enterprising ship-owner and sold to a tobacco planter for five years, and received a peck of corn a week and two suits of plain clothing during the year for wages, and after five years of servitude were freed.

When they were no longer in bondage they went out to the newer parts of Virginia and into North Carolina, and now their descendants came to Georgia. Some of them were thriftless and ignorant and degraded. That there were such among the early Georgians it would be folly to deny. The ubiquitous cracker we will never lose sight of, but it would be as untrue to history to put the mass of the upper Georgians among them, as to put men like James Habersham, or Noble Jones, or John More McIntosh, or the Salzburghers among the English paupers, the German servants and the Scotch peasants who composed a part of the first immigration to Savannah. These up-country people were not many of them men of means at the first. They had but little education and were plain people in manner and plain in dress and surroundings, but they had never been in bondage to any man. Many of them sprang from the best yeomanry of Scotland, Ireland, Wales, and England, and many of them were direct descendants of the landed gentry of England. These were the first comers into upper Georgia. An examination of the minutes of the council gives us an insight into their circumstances. There was an Irish colony, as it was called, near what is now Louisville, a large settlement of Quakers near Wrightsboro and on Little river, and a constant influx of Marylanders, Virginians and North Carolinians into the newly ceded lands. There were quite a number of slaves brought into this section, but few of the settlers had more than three or four. There was no farming, all were stock-raisers. Horses and cattle were turned on the range and rapidly increased in number. The low-country was receiving settlers from South Carolina, who came with many slaves, and who lived in great elegance, but the up-country was still a land of pioneers.

Their fathers had continued the old English custom of bequeathing their landed property to the eldest son, and the younger children were compelled to seek homes in the lands of new Virginia and North Carolina. They had no opportunities to secure an education, and grew up with oftentimes no more than was necessary to enable them to read. Their children were given homes in Georgia if they would occupy them, and they came in large numbers. The headright of two hundred acres was free, and the settler had but to choose his land to have it granted to him. There was little in outside appearances to distinguish a man whose ancestry went back to the Conquest from the man whose ancestors had been serfs for generations. They dressed in the same garb and used the same dialect, common dangers united all classes, and common interests caused them to blend. They married and intermarried, and soon they were by men like Sir Anthony Stokes grouped together as composing one class.

These various classes in after-times became to some extent distinct, but up to the Revolution there was little to mark them. After the Revolution the lines were more distinctly drawn. Every interest was advancing in the colony, and the enterprising Mr. Whitefield projected another grand scheme. The orphanage which he had founded, and which was fairly opened in 1741, had been carefully watched over by him for over thirty years, and had been fostered by his constant care. As the prosperity of the colony during Governor Wright's time had greatly increased the means of the people, the necessity for a home for orphans diminished. Mr. Whitefield then conceived the plan of establishing a college for the young men of the Southern colonies and of the English West Indies. He had now about sixty orphans, one thousand eight hundred acres of land and thirty negroes, and the Legislature granted him two thousand acres of land additional on Turtle river, not far from Brunswick, for the endowment of the college. He proposed to go to England to collect funds, and invest five thousand dollars in negroes to cultivate his newly granted rice land, near the Altamaha, but on his way to England, in Newberryport, Mass., he suddenly died. Not long after the college buildings were consumed by fire. He had left the property to his friend and patron, Lady Huntington. She rebuilt the house, but it never was properly established as a college; and, as Colonel Jones, who has given so full a sketch of Bethesda, says, was in moribund condition when it came into her hands.* It never rallied. The troubles with the mother country came. Its great friend, James Habersham, died in New Jersey in 1775. The property was confiscated and passed into the possession of the State, and after sundry unhappy experiences it was finally sold in 1808, and the proceeds distributed among certain benevolent institutions in Savannah. In 1854 a society of benevolent men of all classes, known as the Union Society, bought the site again and established a home for orphans which abides to this day.

The moral sentiment of the colony, so high in the first years, was not lowered during Governor Wright's time. The influence of men like Mr. Habersham and Mr. Bryan, and especially Mr. Whitefield, of the pious Lutherans, and now of the Puritans at Dorchester, all united to give to the colony a decidedly religious complexion.

Although the Church of England was established, an act was passed by which dissenters were not required to even take an oath before the courts in a way objectionable to them, and there was no interference at all with their religious privileges. The most rigid Puritan could not have asked for laws which were more sweeping on the subject of gaming, lotteries, Sabbath observance, profane swearing, or horse-racing. The law against Sabbath-breaking made in 1765, and revived, with the exception of two features, after

* See Stevens and Jones for fuller account.

the Revolution, required the most scrupulous observance of that holy day. The law required every one to go to church, under a penalty, every Sunday, and forbade any work, trading, traveling, reveling, hunting, fishing, or gaming on that day. It required justices and town wardens to carry out the law, and that the act should be read yearly in every church. The act was modified, but not repealed, when the independence of the State was secured. The administration of Sir James Wright was a clean one, and the morals of his council were of the highest kind. The laxity of conduct found in the young State was not in the colony. There were schools in Savannah, Sunbury, and at Ebenezer, Bethesda and Augusta, and doubtless there were private tutors in the homes of the rice-planters on the Altamaha, and some schools in St. George's parish; but the settlers in the newer sections were as yet struggling with the question as to how they were to be fed, and their educational privileges were very few.

In material things the older part of the colony had very rapidly advanced, but nowhere had the advancement been so great as in the Dorchester settlement. The marshes had been ditched and banked, rice-fields had been opened, and large plantations were made. Sunbury had become quite a populous little village of eight hundred to one thousand inhabitants, with a considerable trade from all the country about, and was exporting to England direct. The sea furnished rich supplies of fish and oysters, the woods were full of deer and turkeys; the bear and the panthers, or tigers, as the people called them, were in the swamps, and great droves of wild fowl came annually to lakes and lagoons. There was the church at Midway where the planters assembled for their weekly service, and the social life in so homogeneous a community was of the most delightful kind. The people of this community brought culture, refinement and religion with them, and in this section of Georgia, where for countless miles to the westward there was a forest of pine woods unbroken save by a few Indian villages, there was a community rarely equalled for intelligence and piety, and in which was found solid comfort, and even elegance of living. The change in the condition of things on the Altamaha during the years since slavery had been allowed had been very decided. The people living near Darien were nearly all of them kinspeople. John More McIntosh, who had founded the colony, had become a man of large fortune, and on the main on the rice plantations were a large number of his kinsmen. The Scotchmen who came to New Inverness were now scattered all over the tide-water country and were prosperous stock-raisers. There were many Scotchmen engaged in mercantile business in Savannah and Sunbury, and who were in the Indian trade in Augusta.

The large incoming of new settlers brought a lively trade to the three main markets, and as the visionary schemes of raising silk and wine were given up the colonists gave their attention to corn, indigo, rice and cattle.

Negro slaves were very cheap, and they were becoming very numerous on the sea islands and the rice plantations. The sea island planters were large producers of indigo, while the rice plantations were above the salt water on the coast. The people in the interior gave their attention almost entirely to corn and live stock. There was some lumber cut by whip saws; some crude turpentine and pitch and a large quantity of peltry of all kinds, myrtle-wax, hogs and cattle, which found a market in Savannah.

The counties below the Altamaha were very thinly peopled. Where St. Marys now is was a frontier post, and in the interior there were a few people on cattle ranches, but up to the Revolution the population was very small and the people very poor and very lawless.

The Germans were increasing. The new coming Germans brought in by Captain De Brahm and the Salzburghers had become one. They were of the same tongue and of the same faith, and naturally coalesced. These people were small farmers but very thrifty, and were constantly extending their lines and improving their estates. They had good pastors and intelligent schoolmasters, and when the Revolution began no people could have been more thrifty.

Up the Savannah river above the pine forests of St. Matthews there was a large section of valuable land unsuited for rice planting, but very fertile. It was on the Savannah and Ogeechee rivers and the creeks flowing into them, and was included in St. George's and St. Matthew's parishes. It was known as the borough of Halifax. In that part of this country now known as Burke, Screven and Jefferson, as we have seen elsewhere, there had come a great many worthy settlers from Virginia and North Carolina, and in the western part of it, as we have already seen, there was a large settlement of Scotch-Irish people. The Savannah river for much of its course through these counties was bordered by a thick swamp of cypress and water-oaks, and great cane-brakes, but along Briar and Bark Camp, McIntosh and McBeans, and Rocky creeks and the Ogeechee river there were fine lands adapted to the cultivation of corn and the raising of stock. People of moderate means had come in numbers into this country where land was easily secured and preempted small farms, which in course of time became large cotton plantations. But for the civil strife which the Revolution brought in, there would have been little disturbance to them during the war, but the Tories made sad ravages of these frontier homes.

Of the history of Savannah and Augusta I speak more particularly elsewhere, and it is not needful to do more here than mention the fact of their rapid growth and great prosperity. They were the chief commercial marts and were largely peopled by cannie Scotch traders who drove a thrifty business.

The twenty years which had elapsed since the trustees had surrendered their charter had brought about great changes in the social life of older parts of the colony, in which now everything had taken shape. The removal of the restriction concerning slavery, the admirable adaptation of the lands on the Ogeechee and Savannah and the Altamaha for rice culture, and the low price of negroes and the fact that the land was given away, led to the opening of large plantations and the establishment of homes of elegance in Savannah. The inventory of the property shows that before 1774 in Savannah and in Liberty county some of the planters had every elegance, even to phaetons and horses. There was a life of luxurious indulgence among the gentlemen, whether they lived on their estates or in their city residences. The importers brought into Savannah silks and satins from France, Madeira wine, cognac brandy, cases of Geneva gin, Jamaica rum, as well as the cheaper New England rum for the common people. In all the homes the decanter had a place on the sideboard, and was always brought out at every gathering. Society had taken a shape on the seaboard in 1774 from which there was little departure for over forty years, except during the Revolutionary war. The plain people of St. Matthew's, conservative and thrifty, had now after forty years of careful industry surrounded themselves with many substantial comforts, and were independent and prosperous. The rice-planters of St. John's parish had but transferred the long-established homes in South Carolina to Georgia, and society in the Midway and Newport section had not had any infancy. There was a frontier in upper Georgia and in the country south of the Altamaha, and all the hardships which had been encountered by the first comers to Georgia forty years before were encountered by the newcomers to St. George's, St. Paul's, and St. Andrew's.

An Independent Presbyterian Church, of which I speak more fully elsewhere, had been built in Savannah, and Mr. John Joachim Zubli, a Swiss, was the minister, and while the church people went to hear Mr. Haddon Smith read the service, and Governor Wright and Captain Tattnall, Judge Stokes, Messrs. Habersham and Bolton, and other old Englishmen had their pews in Christ's church, Sir John Grahame, Mr. Gibbons, and Mr. McGilveray went to the kirk to hear the sermon and sing the Psalms. The steady-going Lutherans had their churches at Ebenezer and Goshen. The Congregationalists went to hear Mr. Osgood, and now the Baptists came. Mr. Daniel Marshall moved into the Kiokee settlement, and did some wonderful work, and Mr. Bottsford organized some Baptist meetings on Briar creek, in Burke county, and a young Presbyterian licentiate was working in the neighborhood of the old church in St. George's and gathering the scattered Presbyterians together; but as a general thing these colonists had no one to preach to them, and no one to teach their children, save now and then a wandering Irishman, who taught a subscription school for a few months in the year. There was everything, however, to be hoped for in the future, when the events of which we shall speak in the next chapter occurred, and then for near a decade of years there was desolation.

The list of public officers in 1774 gives us a good insight into the colony as it then was. There were:

Sir James Wright, governor; James Habersham, Lewis Johnson, John Graham, Jas. Read, Clement Martin, Gray Elliot, Jas. Mackey, Jona Bryan, Jas. Edward Powell, counsellors; Noble Jones, Alex. Wylly, Jno. Adam Truetlen, John Mullryne, Patrick Houston, John Smith, David C. Braddock, Jno. Simpson, Geo. McIntosh, Thos. Vincent, Thos. Moody, Wm. Ewen, Edward Barnard, N. Jones, Jona Cochran, Andrew Johnson, John

Milledge, Josiah Tattnall, Assemblymen; Button Gwinnett, J. P. St. John's; H. Preston, notary; C. Prest, attorney-general; C. Watson; M. Roche, provost marshal; Chas. Pryce, notary; David Emanuel, David Lewis, Thomas Burton, J. P. St. George's; Sam Bullock, J. P. Christ Church; James Brown, dep. surveyor; Wm. Graems, attorney; Sam'l Farley, solicitor; John Glen, lawyer and attorney-general; L. Claiborn, lawyer; Henry Yonge, lawyer; Thos. Schender, lawyer; John Smith, lawyer; Anthony Stokes, lawyer and chief justice; James Hume, lawyer, Savannah; Wm. Belcher, lawyer; Arthur Carney, jnstice of the peace for the four southern parishes and captain of militia; Reymond Demere, ditto; John Holmes, J. P. St. George's; Thos. Stone, J. P. St. Phillip's; Stephen Smith, J. P. St. George's; Thomas Ross, solicitor; Wm. Stephens, clerk Assembly, Savannah; John Hume, secretary and registror, Savannah; Lewis Johnson, treasurer, Savannah; Wm. Stewart, N. P.; Isaac Perry, dept. surveyor; Frank Bigbee, surgeon; John Stephens, 3d lieutenant; James Whitefield, quartermaster; Benj. Lewis, dept. surveyor; Richard Scruggs, J. P. St. Matthew's; J. T. Russell, J. P. St. Andrew's; Jno. MacLean, J. P. Christ Church; John Dunbar, J. P. St. John's; Sam'l Creswill, D. S.; Jos. Houghton, James Cosby, D. S.; James Pannel, D. S.; Basil Lamar, D. S.; John Dooly, D. S.; Jona Sells, D. S.; George Walton, solicitor; David Tait; Andrew Elton Wells, clerk of market and marshal; Geo. Barry, justice; Francis Arthur, D. S.; James Robertson, solicitor; J. Pickens, D. S.; Thomas Waters, J. P.; Edward Keating, J. P.; J. Wood, J. P. St. John's; James Lucina, J. P. Christ Church; D. Frazer, Sunbury; James Seymour, J. P. St. George's and St. Matthew's; Stephen Matthews; J. Walthaur, J. P. St. Matthew's; Jno. Stirk, captain; Jas. Seymour; Quinton Pooler, captain 4th; Philip Howell, J. P. St. Matthew's; Samuel Strong, D. S.; James Kitching, collector; Robert Hamilton, solicitor; James Peart, D. S.; Elijah Lewis, D. S.; James Cantey, deputy surveyor; John Graves; Thomas Chisholm, deputy surveyor; Alex Wyly; Isaac Antrobus, deputy surveyor; J. Lewis, deputy surveyor; Jos. Marshall, J. P. St. Georges; Jno. Douglass, deputy; Josiah Cantey, D. S.; Isaac Antrobus, collector Sunbury; Elijah Brazeal, J. P. St. George's parish; Rich Cunningham; Patrick Houston, J. P.; William

Evans, lieutenant; Wm. McKenzie; Jos. Johnson, J. P.; Wm. Candler, D. S. St. Paul's; Alex. Thompson, J. P. Christ Church; James McFarlane, J. P. St. Paul's; Robert Baillie, D. S.; Andrew Way, D. S.; James Kitchings, collector; Francis Paris, J. P. St. George's; Wm. Harding, D. S.; Philip Young, solicitor; Wm. Haven, naval officer; Henry Yonge, solicitor; John Houston, solicitor; Wm. Sims, deputy surveyor; Alex Thompson; Jed Smith, deputy surveyor; Sanders Walker, deputy surveyor; Thos. Pittman, deputy surveyor; J. P. Romans, J. P.; Thomas Carr, collector Sunbury; Francis Lee, naval officer; Chas. Pryce, dep't reg. and examiner in chancery; Jno. Simpson, clerk in the house; Wm. Brown, searcher for the port of Savannah; John Thomas, John Mann, militia officers Burke; Wm. Graeme, attorney-general; Mat. Roche, provost marshal; Isaac Ford, J. P. St. George's; Moses Nunez, searcher port Savannah; Alex. Findley, Jas. Seymour, schoolmasters; Jared Nelson, Benj. Stirk; D. M. Neal, Wm. Barnard, deputy surveyors; Jno. Oliver, J. P. St. Paul's; James McFarlane, deputy surveyor; R. Wylley, N. P.; Wm. Harding, J. P. St. George's; Wm. McKenzie, comp. searcher and solicitor in chancery, Sunbury; James Kitchings, collector Sunbury; James Maxwell, J. P. St. Phillip's; Elijah Lewis, D. S.; Wm. Downs, D. S.; Jno. Stuart, councilor; Leon Marbury, D S.; Ben Lanier, J. P. St. Matthew's; John Chisholm, D. S.; Wm. Ewen, J. P. Chatham; Sam'l Elbert, captain, Chatham; Thomas Skinner, captain, Chatham; T. Netherclift, St. John's; Alex Hogg, captain. The following were captains, of Chatham: Jos. Habersham, Henry Yonge, Geo. Houston, Philip Morn, Alex. Martin, James Roberson, Alex. McGorm, Jno. B. Randell, Peter Bard, John Lucina, Wm. Stephens and Thos. Ross.

CHAPTER III.

REVOLUTION.

The Call for a Meeting of the Disaffected—Appointments of the Revolutionary Committee—Passage of Resolutions—Governor Wright's Counter Movement—Call of a Congress—Failure—Dissatisfaction of St. John's Parish—Lyman Hall—Increase of Excitement—Stealing Gunpowder—War Begun at Lexington—Call for a Congress—Members of the Congress—Archibald Bulloch the President—Dr. Noble Wimberly Jones, John Glen, John Houston, Edward Telfair, Dr. Zubly, Wm. Gibbons, John Adam Truetlen, Geo. Walton—Organization of the Council of Safety—Governor Wright Virtually Deposed—The Formation of the Battalion of Georgia Troops—Lachlan McIntosh, Samuel Elbert, John Habersham, James Jackson—Mr. Bulloch Elected Temporary President—Convention Called—Expedition to St. Augustine a Failure—Peaceful Condition of Affairs in the Colony 1776–1778—Constitutional Convention—List of Members not to be Found—Constitutional Provisions—Formation of Counties—Act of Confiscation and Amercement—Truetlen Elected Governor—Gwinnett's Duel with McIntosh—Both Wounded—The War in Earnest 1779—Triumphant March of the British—Capture of Savannah—Flight of Legislature—Trouble with Tories—Capture of Augusta—Colonel Twiggs, the Fews, Wm. Candler, Elijah Clarke—Sir James Wright, at Home Again—Act of Proscription—The Battle of Kettle Creek—Defeat of General Ash—Exode to North Carolina—The Itinerating Capital—The Loyalists and the Tories—Bloody Days—The War Drawing to a Close—Return of the Government to Augusta—Governor Brownson—Assembly in Session—Act of Confiscation and Amercement—Condition of Things in 1783—Religious Affairs—The Quakers—The Baptists—Marshall, Mercer, Bottsford—Characteristics of the People—General View of the Churches—Social Conditions just after the War.

Authorities: McCall, Stevens, Jones, White's Collections, Life of Wm. Candler, Life of James Jackson, Gilmer's Georgians, Lee Memoirs Ramsay, History of South Carolina, files of Georgia Gazette in Georgia Historical Society.

As McCall, Stevens and Jones have each given such a careful account of the difficulties between Governor Wright and his Assembly and of the events of the Revolutionary war, I shall throw what it is necessary for my purpose into one chapter of moderate length, and refer those who are anxious to make a careful study of those times to these valuable works where, with painstaking care, and, as far as Jones and Stevens are concerned, with praiseworthy impartiality everything of importance is detailed. Major McCall was perhaps not free from the influence of personal resentment, and was, perhaps, not prepared to do strict justice to a people he so thoroughly detested as the loyalists.

Governor Wright had been very efficient as a governor, and was highly esteemed by all the people until the troubles resulting from the Stamp Act began. He was, while American born, an Englishman in every fiber of his being, and was in full sympathy with the Tory ministry and with its measures, but he found his Assembly sadly poisoned by what he thought was the virus of rebellion, and as we saw in the last chapter, he had at one time an open rupture with his Assembly, and went to England for a twenty months' stay. The storm, however, blew over; he returned to America and had good reason to hope there would be peace, but after a short respite from contention the Boston port bill was passed, and things began to look warlike in the northern provinces.

There was only one paper in Georgia at that time, the *Georgia Gazette*, and in that paper, on the 29th of July, 1774 only one year after Governor Wright had made the great purchase from the Indians and opened a new world to Georgia, Dr. Noble Wimberly Jones, Mr. Archibald Bulloch, Mr. John Houston, and Mr. John Walton called a meeting of the citizens of Savannah to meet in Tondee's Long Room and consider the situation.

The governor and several of these gentlemen had been at outs for some time, and Dr. Jones had been especially offensive, and the governor's indignation against these rebellious subjects, of whom Dr. Jones was one, rose high. The convention met in August and considered the condition of things, and a large committee was appointed, consisting of John Glen, John Smith, Joseph Clay, John Houston, Dr. Noble Wimberly Jones, Lyman Hall, of St. John's parish; Wm. Young Esquire, Edward Telfair, Samuel Farley, George Walton, Joseph Habersham, Jonathan Bryan, Jonathan Cochran, Geo. McIntosh, Sutton Banks, Wm. Gibbons, Benj. Andrew, of St. John's; John Winn, of St. John's; John Stirk, of St. Matthew's; Archibald Bulloch, James Screven, David Zubly, H. Bourquine, Elisha Butler, Wm. Baker, John Mann, John Bennefield, John Stacy, and John Morel, to prepare resolutions. The committee prepared resolutions which were all the Boston people could have asked, and another committee was appointed to secure contributions for the relief of the Boston poor, and it collected and forwarded five hundred and twenty-nine barrels of rice to Boston for their relief. The action of this convention did not meet the approval of the old and staunch friends of a king who had always been a kind friend to the Georgia colony, and when Governor Wright wrote a protest against these utterances, and sent his messengers through the parishes to secure signers to it, he had no difficulty in securing a large number who expressed most decidedly their dissent from the course of these Savannah agitators. Men who fought afterward long and bravely for the American cause were found in large numbers among these signers.

The convention in Savannah could not see its way clear to the appointment of delegates to the Continental Congress, and much to the displeasure of the more ardent Sons of Liberty, and especially of those of St. John's parish, it adjourned and sent no delegates.

So another Congress was called to appoint delegates, but when the time came for its assemblage there were only five parishes represented. This meeting, insignificant as it was, still hoped to get the Assembly to appoint delegates to the

Continental Congress, and it might have succeeded but that the shrewd old governor dissolved the Assembly and checkmated it. The convention went through the form of an election, however, and Mr. Noble W. Jones, Mr. Archibald Bulloch and Mr. John Houston were selected as delegates to Philadelphia, but as they had no proper authority, and as the Georgia colony had not complied with the conditions of membership in the association, the delegates did not go, but sent a letter. This conduct was displeasing to the people of St. John's parish, who accepted all the conditions prescribed, and they sent Lyman Hall, a Connecticut man who practiced medicine in Sunbury, as their delegate, and he went to Philadelphia and took his seat in the Continental Congress, but did not vote.

Things were in a turmoil. The governor thought he had stamped out the fires of rebellion as they were kindled at Tondee's tavern, but to his dismay and disgust those irrepressible rebels broke out again. Some of them were men of years, for there was Mr. Jonathan Bryan, a staid, pious, wealthy old man; Dr. Noble Wimberly Jones, who came to the colony forty years before a child, who was now a wealthy and well educated physician; Mr. Edward Telfair, a native Scotchman and a successful merchant, and among the young men were James Habersham and John and Joseph his brothers, whose father was one of the staunchest friends of the king; these, as well as that young madcap, James Jackson; the hot-headed youth, John Milledge, and that Virginia adventurer, George Walton, were all in the conclave of rebels and were defying him. To crown all they broke open the powder magazine in Savannah and stole the gunpowder, and soon after this Major Habersham, in connection with the rebellious South Carolinians, captured a ship-load of gunpowder and turned it over to the rebels.

The brave old loyalist was powerless. Nominally he was captain-general and commander-in-chief, but really he was a prisonor in his own home. The up-country parishes were, however, not disaffected, and he had good reason to hope this storm would blow over as the one raised by the Stamp Act had, and that he would be in power again, but matters, instead of getting better, grew worse. Men whom he thought he could rely on in the up-country were becoming disaffected.

After Lexington and Concord the whole colony was aroused, and a convention was called to meet in Savannah July 4, 1775, and there assembled delegates from all the parishes. The delegates were:

From Savannah: A. Bulloch, Noble Wimberly Jones, Jos. Habersham, Jonathan Bryan, Ambrose Wright, William Young, John Glenn, Samuel Elbert, John Houston, Oliver Bowen, John McCluer, Edward Telfair, Thomas Lee, George Houston, Joseph Reynolds, John Smith, Wm. Ewen, John Martin, Dr. Zubli, Wm. Bryan, Philip Box, Philip Allman, Wm. O'Bryan, Joseph Clay, Seth John Cuthbert.

District of Vernonsburg: Joseph Butler, Andrew Elton Wells, Matthew Roche, Jr.

Acton: David Zubli. Basil Cowper, Wm. Gibbons.

Sea Island district: Colonel De Vaux, Colonel Delegal, James Bulloch, James Morel, John M. Giradeau, John Barnard, Robert Gibson.

St. Matthew's: Jno. Stirk, Jno. A. Treutlen, Geo. Walton, Edward Jones, Jacob Waldhauer, Philip Howell, Isaac Young, Jenkin Davis, John Morel, John Flerl, Charles McCay, C. Cramer.

St. George's: Henry Jones, John Green, Thos. Burton, Wm. Lord, David Lewis, Benjamin Lewis, James Pugh, John Fulton.

St. Andrew's: J. Cochran, W. Jones, P. Tarlin, L. McIntosh, W. McIntosh, George Threadcraft, John Wereat, Roderick McIntosh, John Witherspoon, Geo. McIntosh, Allen Stuart, John McIntosh, Raymond Demere.

St. Philip's: Colonel Butler, Wm. Lecompte, Wm. Maxwell, James Maxwell, S. Drayton, A. F. Brisbane, L. Mains, Hugh Bryan.

St. David's: Daniel Ryan.

St. Thomas's: J. Roberts.

St. Paul's: John Walton, Jos. Mattocks, Andrew Burns, Robert Rae, James Rae, Andrew Moore, Andrew Burney, Leonard Marbury.

St. John's: James Screven, Nicolas Brownson, D. Roberts, Jno. Baker, Jno. Bacon, J. Maxwell, E. Ball, William Baker, Wm. Bacon, Jno. Stevens, John Winn.

There had been very decided changes in the colony, and this Georgia congress had in it a number of able men of Georgia birth. Savannah was no longer a village. It had for the sixteen years of Governor Wright's governorship been continually advancing, and the South Carolina colony had given to Georgia some very valuable citizens, among them Archibald Bulloch, who was made president of this provincial congress. He was an ardent patriot, a man of great purity of character, and was so highly esteemed for his virtue and ability that he was chosen president of the Provincial Congress, and elected a delegate to the Continental Congress, and when Governor Wright was deposed and fled the State, and a council of safety was appointed to take charge of things in the interim before the adoption of a constitution, he was selected as the president and commander-in-chief. He was in this position when the Declaration of Independence was made, and it was his office to read the document to the assembly of citizens, who with due honors celebrated the event in Savannah. He called the convention to form a constitution, and would doubtless have been elected the first governor of the State under it, but was taken ill and died before its adoption, and John A. Treutlen was chosen. It was while Mr. Bulloch was president of the council that an abortive movement was made by General Lee on St. Augustine.

Mr. Jonathan Bryan, the son of Joseph Bryan, who had assisted Mr. Oglethorpe forty years before with his sawyers and carpenters, was himself a venerable man, a man of large means and a member of the council. His sympathies were with the Whigs and he became obnoxious to the governor, and when the governor threatened him with his displeasure indignantly threw up his office and left the council. He was an ardent patriot to the last, and was captured by the British and imprisoned in a prison-ship until he was released.

Dr. Noble Wimberly Jones was the son of Noble Jones, one of Mr. Oglethorpe's emigrants and a trusted man in the colony. Dr. Jones was himself an Englishman and could not have been less than fifty years old at this time, as he is mentioned as one who received the grant of a lot in 1733. He was a man of means, intelligence and character, and was a physician by profession. He was an ardent Whig, much to the sorrow of his excellent father, who was loyal to the last. He was obnoxious to Governor Wright because of his liberal views, and when he was elected speaker, as we have seen, Governor Wright dissolved the Assembly, and when he was again elected on its reassembling, James Habersham, acting governor, did the same thing.

Dr. Jones was elected twice a delegate to the Continental Congress, but did not go on account of his great respect for his aged father, who was, like his friend James Habersham, near the end of his life, and who died during these troubles.*

John Glen was a prominent lawyer in Savannah. He was son-in-law of Noble Jones and brother-in-law of Noble Wimberly Jones. He was so obnoxious to Governor Wright that he was ostracized by his proclamation, and so moderate

* Stevens and Colonel Jones both pay a lofty tribute to this excellent man, and to his descendant, Mr. De Renne, to whom Georgia is much indebted for the recovery and reproduction of much bearing on her early history.

in his Whigism that he was denounced by the Legislature of 1782 as a Tory. This censure was afterward, however, removed. Samuel Elbert, who rose to be a brigadier and governor, was the son of a Baptist preacher; born in South Carolina, he came to Georgia when quite young, married in Georgia, was captain of a volunteer company of grenadiers, and was selected as a field-officer in the first battalion of Georgia troops. He was captured at Briar creek, was exchanged, re-entered the army and was at the surrender of Yorktown.

In 1785 he was elected governor of the State by an almost unanimous vote* and made a treaty with the Indians at Shoulderbone creek. Three years after he left the governor's chair he died.

John Houston was the son of Sir Patrick Houston, who was one of the first settlers in the colony. He was one of the leading patriots and was appointed as one of the first representatives to the Continental Congress, and in 1778 he was chosen as governor of the new state, and in 1784 was governor a second time. He was a commissioner for the settlement of the boundary line between Georgia and South Carolina. After a life of distinguished service he died in Savannah in 1796.

Edward Telfair was a Scotchman who came with his brother to Savannah when he was thirty-one years old. William, the brother, was a Loyalist, but Edward was a Whig. He threw himself fully into the ranks of the patriots, and was with Jones, Habersham, Milledge and Walton at the breaking into the magazine. He was governor for two terms and elected twice to Congress. He died in 1807. He was a man of fine business judgment, of large wealth, and of great intelligence and public spirit.

Wm. Ewen was an Englishman by birth and came to the colony a poor boy. He was a potter and became a man of

* White.

substance and a lawyer. He took the side of the Americans, and was one of the council of safety and afterward president of the council.*

The Rev. Dr. Zubly was the first pastor of the Independent Presbyterian church in Savannah. He sympathized, no doubt, sincerely with the first movements of the Whigs and was sent as a delegate to Philadelphia. While there he became satisfied that the independence of the colonies would be declared. He was bitterly opposed to going so far, and when he was assured that the Congress would be satisfied with nothing less than independence, he divulged that fact to Sir James Wright in a letter. When it was discovered that he had done this he left Philadelphia hurriedly and fled to Savannah. The story of his treachery, as his course was called, followed him, and he was driven into exile and a large part of his property confiscated. He died before the war was over in South Carolina.

Wm. Gibbons was a prominent lawyer, whose family were leading and wealthy people in Savannah. He was very famous in after time as a lawyer and a man of large wealth and great enterprise.

John Adam Treutlen, the second of the name, descended from one of the Salzburghers, and the name is found among the deacons of the church.† He was possibly a son of the first Treutlen. He was elected governor at the first election by the legislature after the adoption of the constitution of 1777. When Col. Wm. Henry Drayton was trying to arouse a sentiment in favor of a union of the Georgia and Carolina colonies, he said some things which irritated the fiery German, and he published a loud protest and offered $100 reward for the arrest of the "said Wm. Henry Drayton." He was killed by the British in South Carolina.‡

* White, 2.

† See Strobel's History of the Salzburghers.

‡ White.

John Wereat was an Englishman of fine mind and extensive attainments. He was a leading man in the colony and the patron of James Jackson, whose father had been his friend in England.

George Walton was a Virginian. He was a member of an old and highly respected family in that State, but having lost his father and his estate being small, his guardian put him as apprentice to a carpenter. When his time was out he came to Georgia, where he had relatives, and resolved to study law, which he did with Colonel Yonge in Savannah, and began to practice there. He was heart and hand with the Whigs from the first, and was with the Savannah coterie in their daring measures. He was sent a delegate to the Continental Congress, signed the Declaration of Independence, was in the army as colonel and was wounded and taken prisoner. Was president of the council, governor, chief justice, and six times elected to Congress. He died in Augusta while judge of the superior court, in the early part of the century.*

These were some of those who were in this memorable convention of 1775. Few bodies of men have ever assembled in Georgia of more ability. The convention represented all parts of the young colony. At this time Georgia had in it only 17,000 white people in all.† .

The Assembly took charge of the government of the colony as the Long Parliament had taken charge of English affairs in the days of Charles I., and Governor Wright found himself powerless. He needed some troops to bring these recusants to order, and he wrote the British general and the British admiral to supply his needs, but the unconscionable rebels of South Carolina secured his letters and substituted others for them, telling the general and the admiral that all was well in the Georgia colony. The Assem-

* White.

†Jones.

bly finally ordered his arrest, and Major Habersham did the work as gently as possible. The old governor was subjected to no indignity, but simply confined to his home. He was allowed to escape, and he left the colony, much to its relief and doubtless to his own, and went to England, where he was received with due honors. The Assembly appointed delegates to the Continental Congress, who were: Dr. Zubly, Dr. Jones, Arch Bulloch, John Houston and Dr. Lyman Hall; provided for the issuing of paper money, which soon became worthless, and proceeded to organize a battalion of State troops. The officers of the battalion were: Colonel, Lachlan McIntosh; Lieutenant-Colonel, Samuel Elbert; Major, Joseph Habersham.

First Company: Captain, Francis H. Harris; First Lieutenant, John Habersham; Second Lieutenant, John Jenkins; Third Lieutenant, Ensign Rae, Savannah.

Second Company: Captain, Oliver Bowen, commodore; First Lieutenant, George Hanley; Second Lieutenant, John Berrien (afterward treasurer of the State, and father of John MacPherson Berrien), Savannah.

Third Company: Captain, John McIntosh; First Lieutenant, Lachlan McIntosh; Second Lieutenant, Francis Archer; Ensign, J. Morrison, Darien.

Fourth Company: Captain, Arthur Carney; First Lieutenant, Benj. Odinsell; Second Lieutenant, John Eman; Ensign, DeLaplaine, Liberty.

Fifth Company: Captain, Thomas Chisholm; First Lieutenant, Caleb Howell; Second Lieutenant, Daniel Cuthbert; Ensign, Wm. McIntosh, St. Philip's.

Sixth Company; Captain, John Green, Burke; Lieutenant, Ignatius Few, Columbia.

Seventh Company: Captain, Chesley Bostwick, Richmond; First Lieutenant, John Martin, Jefferson.

Eighth or Rifle Company: Captain, Colson; First Lieutenant, Shadrach Wright; Second Lieutenant, George Walton;* Chaplain, John Holmes, Episcopal minister, Wilkes county.

Lachlan McIntosh, who was to command the battalion, was one of that famous clan who settled at Darien, the son of John More McIntosh, the chief of the clan. He was himself born in Scotland, but had spent his early years in Georgia on the southern frontier at Darien, where his father kept the store of the trustees, and after that had a trading-post for the Indians and a rice plantation. In his youth he was in Charleston in a commercial house. He was a Whig from the beginning of the struggle, and when the First battalion was organized he was appointed to command it. He was a hasty, fearless Highlander, and became involved in a difficulty with Button Gwinnett in the early part of the war. There was a duel; both men were wounded, Gwinnett fatally. Colonel McIntosh then went to Virginia and had a command under Washington. He returned to Georgia and was in command of a brigade at the siege of Savannah, and was captured at the surrender of General Lincoln in Charleston. He died in Savannah in 1806.

Joseph Habersham, the major of the battalion, was the son of James Habersham, the staunch Loyalist. He was a native of Savannah, and was not twenty-five years old when the troubles began. He was educated at Princeton, and when only twenty-three years old was one of the committee appointed by the Liberty Boys. He was connected with the group who broke open the magazine and who captured the ship-load of powder. He was often in the General Assembly, and at one time was Speaker of the House; afterward he was postmaster-general of the United States. He died in Savannah in 1815.† The First company was composed of Savannah people and was commanded by Captain

* This George Walton was George Walton of Wilkes county, a relative of George Walton the signer.

† White.

Francis Henry Harris, the son of Francis Harris, who had long been in the colony, and was one of its trusted officers. Young Harris was at school in England when the war began. He came home at once and entered the army. His career was a brief one. In 1782, when the victory was nearly won, while he was in the army in South Carolina, a Georgia refugee fighting against the common foe, he died.*

The officers of the battalion came from all parts of the State, and as there was no immediate call for active service the little army was not put into the field, and only a few of the officers selected won any laurels during the war.

Among the most ardent of the young Liberty Boys was James Jackson, a fiery young Englishman, whose name does not appear among them, for he was a comparative stranger and not yet of age. Young Jackson had been invited to Georgia by Mr. Wereat, his father's friend, and had been in the province only a few years. He was a law student when the war broke out, and sympathizing with the Americans he threw himself with his whole soul into the contest. He so distinguished himself in the first military movements in Georgia that he was given a command as captain. He was in Savannah when it fell, and fled with John Milledge to South Carolina to join the army there. He was put in command of some refugee troops and was at the surrender of Augusta and commandant there. Then he raised and commanded a battalion of cavalry, and when Savannah fell he was the officer to whom was delegated by General Wayne the honor of leading the first troops into the evacuated city.

He threw himself after the war into politics, and at one time opposed his old commander, General Wayne, for a seat in Congress, and up to his death in 1806 he was perhaps the most prominent figure in Georgia. He was a man

* White.

of perfect fearlessness and exceedingly hasty temper, and in those days a word was followed by a blow and a blow by a duel. He fought a duel to the death during the Revolution with Lieutenant-Governor George Wells, who had affronted him, and fought several duels after that. He was intensely devoted to his adopted State, and there was no honor which she had it in her power to confer that she withheld from him. We shall see him often in the course of this history.

The council to whom all the matters connected with the government were referred consisted of George Walton, Wm. Ewen, Step Drayton, Noble W. Jones, Basil Cowper, Edward Telfair, J. L. Girardeau, Jonathan Bryan, John Smith, Wm. Gibbons, John Martin, Oliver Bowen, Ambrose Wright,* Samuel Elbert, Jos. Habersham, Francis Henry Harris.

Of a number of these we have already spoken. Of some few of them we know little, and one of them was denounced in an after time as a Loyalist. John Martin, known by Governor Wright as black John from the northward, was afterward governor, and was in that position when the Legislature returned to Savannah. Ambrose Wright had been Mr. Whitefield's traveling companion and his trusted friend, who was in charge of his interests at Bethesda and received a generous bequest from him when he died. Oliver Bowen was the leading naval officer in Georgia.

The council elected Geo. Walton temporary president and commissioned the officers of the battalion, and elected Mr. Archibald Bulloch the first president of the council. Mr. Bulloch called a convention to form a constitution. It was duly chosen and a constitution was adopted, but all record of its members and of its doings have been lost. We have the constitution it formed, but no other trace of it. The constitution was adopted by the

* He was the ancestor of General Ambrose R. Wright of the C. S. A.

convention which met in Savannah in 1777; but President Bulloch, who called the convention and presided over its sessions, died soon after its adjournment, and Button Gwinnett was chosen by the council to succeed him.

There was but little attention paid to the weak province of Georgia by the British during the years 1775, '76, '77 and '78, and there were no military operations of any importance. There was a little skirmish near Savannah, dignified by Bishop Stephens as the first battle in Georgia. An abortive movement was made on St. Augustine in 1776, and a second of the same character in 1777. A successful campaign, conducted by John Jones, Captain Twiggs and Captain Marbury, from the new settlements, against the Cherokees, and loss of an insignificant fort on the Altamaha, were about all the military movements of the first two years. The fact was, many denizens of Georgia did not know there was a war save from rumor.

There was so little trouble in Georgia that the convention had an uninterrupted session, and in 1777, in the city of Savannah, adopted the first Constitution of the State of Georgia. It provided that (1) all persons who were elected representatives should be Protestants, and should have two hundred and fifty acres of land or two hundred and fifty pounds of other property. 2. That all voters must have ten pounds of property. 3. That delegates to the Continental Congress should be annually chosen. 4. The governor was to be chosen annually by the Assembly. 5. There should be a superior court in every county. 6. There should be a supreme court, consisting of a chief justice and three or more justices of the peace, in every county. 7. Estates should not be entailed. 8. Schools should be established in every county, supported by the State. 9. No clergyman should be a member of the House of Delegates.

It proceeded at once to disestablish the Church of England and to form the parishes into counties. These counties were all, save one, named in honor of those Englishmen who had stood by the colonies in Parliament. Christ

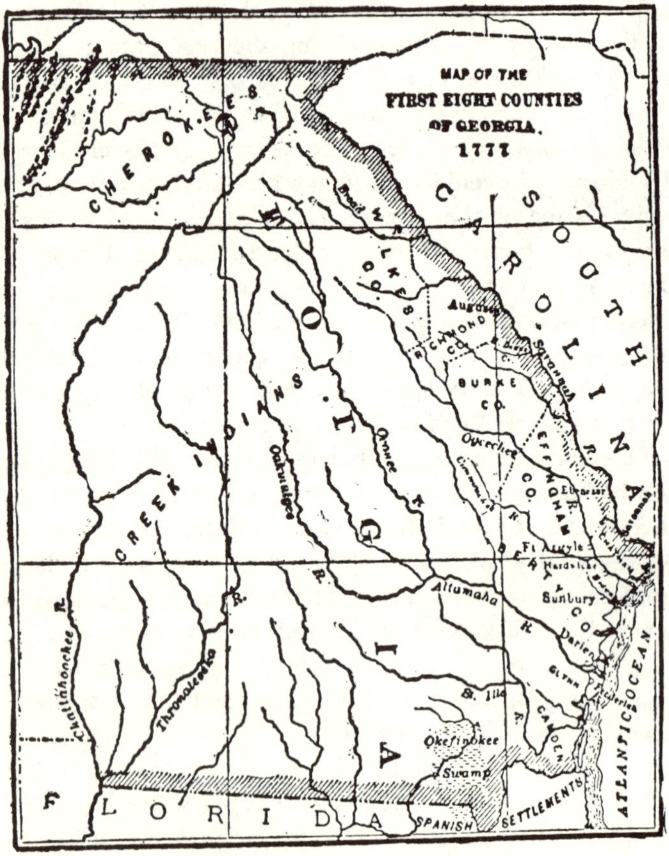

Church was called Chatham; St. Matthew's, Effingham; St. Philip's, Glynn; St. Andrew's, Camden; St. George's, Burke; St. Paul's, Richmond; the new county west of north and west of St. Paul's, Wilkes; St. John's, Liberty.

Acting in accordance with this Constitution the Assembly proceeded to elect a governor, and, as we have seen, elected Jno. Adam Treutlen.

The Constitution being adopted, the Legislature proceeded to take severe measures against the Loyalists. Many of the worthiest men in the State were not in sympathy with these rebellious movements, and those who had ventured all had no disposition to show the laggards, or, worse, the enemies to the cause, any mercy.

It could not have been expected that all the people, or even a majority of them, would fall in with the measures of the Whigs. There were many of the people sincerely attached to the British government. They were among the most intelligent and the wealthiest, and were not to be classed at all with those brigands who were afterward known as Tories. They were, however, very obnoxious to the patriots, and the Assembly adopted severe measures against them. They were pronounced guilty of high treason and banished from the State and their property confiscated. The list of these attainted ones is found in Watkins's Digest and in that of Marbury and Crawford. Those included in the act were among the very best people of the State; they were men who had done faithful work in and for the colony. They had occupied leading places and were often people of large means and some of them of great intelligence. While one is not disposed to detract from the noble group who espoused the cause of the colonies, it is too late now to throw odium on these who were denounced by this first act of ostracism as Loyalists.

The names as given in the official list are: Sir James Wright, R. Reed, Andrew Hewitt, Wm. Moore, Thos. Reed, Geo. Baillie, James Hume, Esq., John Bond Randall, Geo. Webb, Wm. John Yonge, Esq., H. Yonge, Sr., John Love, Charles W. McKennon, P. Yonge, Jos. Johnson, George Barry, Jas. Robertson, John Johnson, Alex Wylly, Jas. Brown, Wm. Love, Wm. Johnstone, D. Johnson, Chas. Hall,

John Lightenstone, A. McGowan, James Moore, John Mullryne, Wm. Sims, Wm. Colville, Josiah Tattnall, Sr., John Inglis, John Murray, Wm. McGilveray, P. Dean, Sir Anthony Stokes, J. J. Zubly, D.D., T. Johnson, John Wood, Geo. Kincaid, Henry Yonge, Jr., Chas. Wright, Geo. Borland, Jas. Downey, Thos. Eaton, John Graham, Wm. Frinkfield, Jas. Ed. Powell, John Hume, Esq., Geo. McCauley, Gerymyn Wright, Jos. Farley, Esq., Jno. Jameson, Chas. Wright, Thomas Eaton, James Taylor, Geo. Finch, Philip Moore, Wm. Panton, John Simpson, Charles McCulloch.

This act of confiscation and amercement was passed very promptly by the first Legislature, but before it could be carried into effect the tables were turned, for Governor Wright was restored to his place, and a retaliatory act of attainder was promptly passed, and we may well judge with great heartiness, against the prominent Whigs.*

The campaign against St. Augustine was a pitiable failure. There were great discord and contention in the American ranks between the leading officers. A few small skirmishes, in one of which Colonel Elijah Clarke was wounded, and the British had the advantage; and then the Americans retired toward Savannah and abandoned the effort to invade Florida for the time. This was the first campaign of the Georgia forces, and its results were by no means encouraging. Then the British began to move northward, and the attempt to resist the advance of their forces in the latter part of 1778 was a gallant but fruitless one. At Midway church there was a sharp skirmish in which the brave General Screven was killed, and in which young James Jackson, then a lieutenant, distinguished himself; but the British troops reached Savannah, and after a sharp engagement, in which the Americans, badly handled, were routed, the city fell again into the hands of the British.

The only relieving feature of the dark time was that

* The list of the proscribed Whigs is given on pp. 93–95.

Colonel John White, for whom White county was afterward named, with a small body of militia succeeded in capturing, on the Ogeechee, five armed vessels and one hundred and five troops.

The account of the capture of Savannah has been fully given by McCall, Bishop Stevens and Colonel Jones, and we have little more to do with it than to recognize the fact.

As soon as Governor Wright was reinstated he called a Legislature together. The members of it were:

Savannah—Samuel Farley, James Mossman, John Simpson, and James Robertson.

Little Ogeechee—Wm. Jones.

Midway—Jno. Irvine, Jos. Fox.

Ebenezer—Alex. Wright, Basil Cowper, Nathaniel Hall.

Acton—David Zubly.

Wilmington—Philip Yonge.

St. Andrew's—Robert Baillie James Spalding.

Frederica—Wm. Panton.

St. David's—Sam'l Douglas.

St. Patrick's—Robert Porteus.

St. Thomas's—Simon Paterson.

St. Mary's—Wm. Ross.

Halifax and St. George's—Alex. Wylly, John Henderson.

Of these, however, only fifteen qualified.*

Although the war had continued for nearly four years from its first beginning at Concord and Lexington, there had been but little disturbance in upper Georgia up to this time. The Indians were somewhat menacing, but they were a considerable distance from the remotest settler. People from North Carolina and Virginia came without fear into the new country above Augusta in the early years of the war. The people from Liberty and the counties below had some of them been forced to take refuge in parts of the State more remote from the coast, and there was little

* Jones, Vol. 2, 419.

change in the condition of affairs in any other part of the State; but in the latter part of 1778 and during the whole of 1779 war with all its horrors swept over Georgia. No part of it escaped, and no State save South Carolina was so devastated.

After Savannah was captured and General Howe had retreated to South Carolina, the British column almost without resistance marched northward, and there was a battle or skirmish with a body of Tories near where Waynesboro now is. In this fight Twiggs, Few and Inman, Whig captains, won the field. McCall says that Captain Inman, who was doubtless a kinsman of the captain of the same name who fell at Kings Mountain, killed three Tories with his own sword. This skirmish did not interfere with the progress of Colonel Campbell to Augusta. He captured that then little village without any difficulty, and then marched on through the upper part of Richmond county to the extreme limit of the white settlement at Fort Charlotte, where Petersburg stood and where the Broad river joins the Savannah.

The few partizan troops in Georgia had gradually fallen back before the advancing British column until they formed a junction with a column of troops under Colonel Pickens, who had crossed the river from South Carolina. These troops pursued a body of Tories under command of Colonel Boyd, a gallant British officer, who had gone into the new county of Wilkes and taken position on Kettle creek, near Washington. There were eight hundred of them, and the troops under Pickens, with Dooly and Elijah Clarke, attacked Boyd and won a decided victory.*

* In the battle Boyd was mortally wounded. General Pickens treated him with great kindness, and when the Briton was in his last hours he gave his watch and other valuables to General Pickens to be sent to his wife. This the chivalric Irishman did. Years after, when Mrs. Boyd died, she bequeathed that watch to the family of General Pickens, and they have it now.

The Tories in the up-country were now so disheartened by this defeat that they fled the country. The British troops then returned from the up-country and Augusta came once more into the hands of the Americans. General Ashe now crossed the Savannah river into Georgia and with quite a considerable force took position on Briar creek, in what is now Screven county. He was attacked by the British under General Prevost and signally defeated* and his army was broken to pieces. Many very severe things have been said of this brave and patriotic North Carolinian. It is not my office to exonerate, or condemn him. His case was brought at his instance before a court of inquiry, and he was fully vindicated from all other charges than the one of handling an army so large without proper caution. His forces were mere militia from different States. They were poorly equipped and badly disciplined. It is certain that the defeat was an entire and a crushing one, and destroyed the last vestige of hope that Georgia was likely to be recovered from the clutches of the British.

When Governor Wright was placed in his seat again he called a meeting of a loyal assembly, and they at once retaliated on the Whigs by passing an act of attainder and confiscation. This roll of honor has been preserved and is herewith given. It aimed to take in all those who were obnoxious to the crown, and contained the names of sundry persons who were afterwards denounced by the *Georgia Legislature of 1782 as Tories*. These men were :

John Houston, governor; Noble W. Jones, speaker; John Adam Treutlen, counselor; M. Sheftall; Lachlan McIntosh, general; Wm. O'Bryan, treasurer; George Walton, member of Congress; John Wereat, counselor; Wm. Stephens, attorney; Ed Telfair, member of Congress; John McClure, major; Ed Davies, assemblyman; John Clay, paymaster; Samuel Elbert, rebel general, Savannah; Seth John Cuthbert, major, Darien; W. Holsendorf, coun-

* For a very full account of this engagement see Jones, Vol. 2, 348–352.

selor, Darien; R. Howley, governor; George Galphin, superintendent Indian affairs, Silver Bluff; Andrew Williamson, rebel general; John White, colonel; N. Wade, treasurer; John Twiggs, colonel, Richmond; Wm. Few, rebel counselor, Columbia; E. Langworthy, rebel delegate; Wm. Glascock, counselor, Richmond; Robert Walton, commissioner, Richmond; Jos. Wood, clerk; Piggin, colonel; Wm. Hornbay, distiller; Pierce Butler, rebel officer, Darien; Jos. Wood, member of Congress; Rev. Wm. Piercy; Thos. Savage, planter; Thos. Stone, councilor; Benj. Andrew, councilor, Liberty; John Baker, colonel, Liberty; Wm. Baker, rebel officer, Liberty; Francis Brown, planter, Liberty; Nathan Brownson, member rebel Congress; John Hardy, captain; Thos. Morris, officer; Thos. Maxwell, planter, Liberty; Jos. Woodruff; W. Le Conte, counselor, Liberty; P. Chambers, shopkeeper; T. Washington, rebel officer, died in Charleston; C. F. Chevalier, counselor, French refugee; E. Maxwell, planter, Liberty; Thos. Maxwell, mayor of Sunbury, Liberty; Wm. Gibbons, Jr., planter, Savannah; Wm. Davies, officer, Burke; Jno. Graves, yeoman, Liberty; Charles Kent, counselor; Jno. Bacon, mariner, Liberty; N. Saxton, tavern-keeper; P. Lowe, officer; S. Spencer, mariner; Jno. Winn, Sr., planter, Liberty; Dev Jarrett, assemblyman, Richmond; S. West, gent., Liberty; J. Dupont, planter; Frederick Pugh, planter; James Rae, planter, Richmond; James Martin, planter; John Martin, sheriff, Jefferson; Thos. Pace, officer, Richmond; Benj. Few, officer, Richmond; D. Wright, planter, Richmond; C. Bostick, shopkeeper, Richmond; L. Bostick, planter, Richmond; L. Marbury, officer, Richmond; Jno. Sharp, planter, Richmond; Jno. McIntosh, colonel, Liberty; James Houston, surgeon, Chatham; James Habersham, Jr., merchant, Savannah; Jno. Habersham, major, Savannah; John Milledge, assemblyman, Savannah; Levi Sheftall, butcher, Savannah; P. J. Cohen, shopkeeper, Savannah; Jno. Sutcliff, shopkeeper, Savannah; Jonathan Bryan, counselor, Savannah; John Spencer, officer, Savannah; Rev. Jno. Holmes, chaplain, Burke; Wm. Gibbons, Sr., counselor, Savannah; Sheftall Sheftall, officer, Savannah; P. Minis, shopkeeper, Savannah; C. Pollock, shopkeeper, Savannah; R. Hamilton, attorney, Savannah; Benj. Loyd, officer, Savannah; J. Alexander, officer, Savannah; John Jenkins, assemblyman; S. Stirk, secretary, Effingham; P. Densler, yeoman; H. Cuyler, officer, Savannah;

Jos. Gibbons, assemblyman, Savannah; Ebenezer Platt, shop-keeper, Savannah; M. Griffin, planter; P. De Vaux, gentn., Savannah; John Gibbons, vessel master, Savannah; John Smith, planter; Jos. Oswald, planter; Josiah Powell, planter; Samuel Saltus, planter, Liberty; John Sandeford, planter; Peter Tarling, officer, Savannah; Oliver Bowen, commodore, Savannah; Lyman Hall, member of Congress, Liberty; Andrew Moore, planter; Joshua Inman, planter, Burke; John Dooly, colonel, Wilkes; Jno. Glen, chief justice, Savannah; Rich Wyley, member council, Savannah; A. F. Brisbane, counselor, Savannah; Shem Butler, assemblyman, Savannah; Jos. Habersham, colonel, Savannah; Jno. Stirk, colonel, Effingham; R. Demere, general, Darien; C. Odingsel, captain, Effingham; Wm. Peacock, counselor, Liberty; John Bradley, sea captain; Jos. Reynolds, bricklayer; Rudolph Strohaker, Chas. Cope, Lewis Cope, butchers, Savannah; Hepworth Carter, captain, Jefferson; S. Johnson, butcher; Jas. Harris, planter; Henry Jones, colonel, Burke; Hugh McGee, captain; John Wilson, gent., Richmond; George Wyche, officer, Richmond; Wm. Candler, officer, Richmond; Z. Fenn, planter, Richmond; Wm. McIntosh, colonel, Darien; Dr. Brydie, surgeon, Savannah; A. MacLean, merchant, Augusta; Pat Houston, baronet, Savannah; McCarty Campbell, merchant, Augusta; James Gordon, planter; Jno. Kell, gent., Darien; John McLean, planter; John Snider, planter, Effingham; Jno. Elliott, officer; R. Swinney, yeoman; Hugh Middleton, officer; Joe Pray, mariner; J. McLean, planter.

The French allies, assisted by the Americans, made an effort to recapture Savannah in September, 1779. Count D'Estaing, the French commander, directed the movements. He was wounded, and Count Pulaski, a Pole, who was an American ally, was fatally wounded. The battle was a fierce one and the loss of the French and Americans considerable. The victory of the British was complete, and they were the masters of the whole of Georgia.

Early in 1780 the British forces reoccupied Augusta and strengthened their works. They were attacked by Elijah Clarke and Major James Jackson, but they resisted the assault successfully and the Americans suffered greatly; and McCall says, what Brown indignantly denied,* that Brown was guilty of great cruelty to the helpless captives, hanging a large number. Brown admits there were some fifteen persons hung, but says they were atrocious criminals, who were hung for their murders and thefts. He denied the charge of Ramsay that he had allowed any cruelty from the Indians, and denied that there was any committed. The fearful story of the massacre of the prisoners rest on McCall alone, who gives as his authority certain letters from some unnamed British officers, who he says gloated over it. General Lee makes no mention of it, and it is probably not true. Governor Wright says "thirteen of the prisoners who broke their paroles and came against Augusta have been hanged, which I hope will have a very good effect."† Governor Wright had reached Savannah in July, 1779, and finally left there in the spring of 1782. He had the title of governor-general, but his rule was after a short time almost entirely confined to the limits of the garisoned city of Savannah. Here his Rump Parliament assembled and passed sundry laws that they could not execute. He was the most detested of the British officers, and the partizan troops took great pleasure in swooping down on his large estates and burning his barns. He says he had nine burned. He did his best to carry out the decree to confiscate rebel property, but he was handicapped and thwarted on every hand. The tide of disaster to the Americans reached its flood when Count D'Estaing failed in his attack on Savannah. When Lincoln fled Cornwallis swept victoriously over South Carolina, and Campbell subjugated all upper Georgia. In 1781 the tide began to turn and the staunch old governor began to see the end of his sway, and called lustily for help, which never came.

* See White's Historical Collections, Richmond county.

†See Governor Wright's Letters, Georgia Historical Collections, Vol. 4.

SEAL CONTINENTAL GOVERNMENT.

GEO. WALTON.

LAFAYETTE.

JOS. HABERSHAM.

He was game to the last, and had regular sessions of the courts and the Assembly, and the lawmaking body gravely passed its sweeping acts and observed all the forms of a peaceful government, even though the governor could see from his upper windows the smoke of his burning barns, fired by that pestiferous young Englishman, James Jackson, whose legion was making havoc in the loyal province. But this was in 1782. Nothing could have been blacker than the sky in Georgia from 1779 to 1781 was for the Whigs.

The State authorities had been driven from Savannah and Ebenezer to Augusta, and there was in the times of confusion no possibility for observing the forms of law. Trivial disputes divided the disorganized Whigs, and Wereat, Walton, Wells, Howley and Heard acted as governors during one year. While Heard was acting as governor at Heard's fort, Howley, with his council, was in South Carolina. Everything was in confusion. John Milton had fled with the archives of the State to Charleston; thence he conveyed them to Newbern, N. C., and finally lodged them in Baltimore, from whence they were returned to Georgia several years after the war ended. Farming was impossible, cattle were driven off, and starvation was threatened to the upcountry people. The great-hearted Clarke and Wm. Candler gathered the women and children and led them over the mountains to the Holston country, where they were fed till the war ended.

But despite all these adversities the Whigs were unsubdued, and again Augusta was attacked, and successfully. General Lee had come, and Clarke, Jackson and Dooly were there, and at last Brown surrendered to the Americans. There had been little quiet in Georgia from early in 1779 to the spring of 1781, and the saddest feature of it all was the bitter strife between the Whigs and Tories. As we have seen, many of the best people in Georgia were Loyalists. They had every reason to love the king for whose father the colony was named. Georgia had been the petted child of the crown. There was nothing England could do for her that she had not done. No young colony had ever been more prosperous than she had been since the crown had taken charge of the government, and the substantial old Englishmen who had always loved the king refused to follow the lead of these hotheads, as they called those who brought on the war; and now, after these disasters had come in such succession to the Whigs, others doubted the wisdom of any further resistance and were disposed to accept the terms proposed by the British, and thus increased the number of the disaffected. Taking advantage of this turmoil, the lawless and rapacious on both sides began a war of unrelenting severity and of unbridled robbery. The Loyalist from principle and devotion to his parental government and the Tory brigand were very different people, but they were soon classed together. The loyal Highlander, who was true to his king and was anxious to fight for him, and the quiet German who only wanted peace, were put in the same category with the robber Tory. It was a war to the knife. There was no pity on either side. John Dooly, the father of Judge Dooly, had been murdered in his own home by the Tories, and when nine Tories had been captured by a band of Wilkes county Whigs the furious sons of the murdered man slaughtered them all.* Grierson was shot to death after his surrender in Augusta, and Patrick Carr in cool blood shot an officer to death as he was handing his sword to Colonel Jackson. There had been developed a number of brave partizan leaders. John Twiggs, a Marylander, was always in the field and never defeated in the fray. He came with his kinsmen, John and David Emanuel, and was a young mechanic. He was first

* Gilmer's Georgians.

a captain and rose to the post of major-general. He chastised the Cherokee Indians, and protected the frontier on the Ogeechee from the Creeks. He was nearly always in partizan service and proved himself a soldier of the highest merit. He became the founder of a distinguished family, who have been an honor to the State of his adoption.

Jno. Jones, who is generally found in connection with Twiggs, was the son of a wealthy and prominent man in Virginia, and one of a number of brothers who came to Georgia just as the Revolution began. He and his brother James were members of the second Constitutional Convention, and his brothers Abram and Seaborn were both famous for their mental ability and warm patriotism.

Wm. Few, Benj. Few and Ignatius Few were three brothers who had settled in Columbia county just before the Revolution. They were of Welsh origin and were people of intelligence and wealth, and Wm. Few was, as we shall see, one of the leading men in civil life in Georgia. His brothers Ignatius and Benjamin were with Twiggs in his forays and stood by the struggling State till the hour of victory. From this family sprang the distinguished lawyer and preacher, Dr. Ignatius A. Few, who was the first president of Emory College, and connected with them was Wm. Candler, who was among the most distinguished men of this period, and one of the best educated men then in St. Paul's parish. He was a native Irishman, who came from Belfast, Ireland, to North Carolina. He came to St. Paul's parish as soon as it was opened for settlement, and was an officer of the militia under Sir James Wright. In common with all the citizens in the Wrightsboro neighborhood he was opposed to the first movements of the Liberty Boys, but when the war was fairly on he took his place with the Whigs. He was forced to flee to South Carolina, and there formed the refugees into a regiment of which he was the commander.

He was one of the escorts for the fleeing Georgians who went with Colonel Clarke to the Holston country. He did good service in the upper Carolina army after that, and as soon as the Georgians could again reach their homes, he came to his Georgia home and was selected as probate judge and was a member of the first Assembly after the war. He died in 1784. He was the progenitor of a very distinguished family of Candlers and Fews, for his daughter was the mother of Ignatius A. Few, the distinguished founder of Emory College, and his descendants of the Candlers have been noted for their ability in almost every walk of life—distinguished as teachers, jurists, soldiers, congressmen and divines, and one of them is now governor of the State of Georgia at this writing (1900).

ELIJAH CLARKE.

But perhaps the most active and intrepid and untiring man of the partizan leaders, who was long the idol of the common people of Georgia, was the rugged Elijah Clarke. He was, if not a native born Scotch-Irishman, but once removed from it. He came to Georgia on the first opening of the upper country. It was a wild country then and demanded strong men to subdue it. He had no wealth and no education, and no concern for the refinements of life. Born a freeman, he revolted at the idea of any restraint, and, devoid of fear, he went into the struggle for liberty with all ardor. He soon evinced the fact that he was a born soldier, and at the battle of Kettle creek he showed his qualities as a commander. When the war was over he settled on a large estate granted him by the Legislature and

Wilkes county. He was an impetuous, intrepid patriot. The Indians were troublesome and he was always ready for a foray. They invaded Georgia, instigated by McGilveray. Clarke pursued and defeated them. They were the last formidable body of Creeks who raided eastern Georgia.

In 1792 the French Republic commissioned him a brigadier, whose work was to invade Florida. He became involved in trouble with the State government in 1794 by making a settlement on the Indian lands, of which I speak more fully elsewhere. He died in 1799.

Colonel Wm. Glascock, whose name appears so often in the history of Georgia, was a gentleman of culture and wealth, who settled an estate near Augusta before De Brahm made his first map, probably before 1760. He was an old man when the Revolution began, and his son Thomas was a lieutenant in the army in Virginia and afterward in Georgia. Judge Glascock, for he was one of the first lay judges in Richmond county, was a vestryman of St. Paul's church, a trustee of Richmond Academy and of the State University. He died in Richmond in 1795.

His son Thomas, who was afterward general of the militia, was not the General Glascock who was in active service in the Indian war of 1818, and was a member of Congress. General Glascock the first was as intense a Federalist as his son Thomas was a pronounced Democrat. He was a bold operator in finances and left a large estate.

Colonel Stephen Heard was one of a large family of seven, who came to Georgia and fixed their homes in the ceded lands. Here on the frontier a fort was built, known as Heard Fort. He was a gallant soldier, and being a man of more than usual education for those days, when the disasters of 1779 had driven the seat of government from Augusta, he was elected by those who fled to the West nominal governor. He was afterward prominent in public life in Georgia, being often in the legislative councils.

The whole American cause in Georgia was in an almost hopeless condition, and the older colonies were seriously discussing some plan of settlement that would leave poor Georgia overrun and occupied by the British forces in the hands of the English Government. But brave George Walton and the members of the Continental Congress from Georgia united in an earnest remonstrance. It might have been of little avail, however, if France had not consented to interfere and if the tide of victory had not turned. This remonstrance of the Georgia delegation has been preserved by Mr. Geo. W. Jones-De Renne, and is found in a pamphlet published by him and reproduced in White.

After Augusta was evacuated the wandering State government returned to its old quarters there, and Dr. Nathan Brownson, a Liberty county man who had been a member of the Continental Congress, was elected in August, 1781, as governor for the unexpired term. He held the office less than six months, and was succeeded by John Martin, whom Governor Wright called "Black Jack from the Northward."

The legal capital was Savannah and the Legislature met at Ebenezer, the nearest point to it, and in July, 1782, after the city of Savannah was again in the hands of the Americans, the Assembly adjourned to meet there. It was in so hilarious a mood when it reached its old quarters that it instructed Governor Martin to buy, for the use of the executive, the council and Assembly, twenty-three pounds of coffee, three hundred and seventy pounds of sugar, sixteen bushels of salt and forty-two gallons of rum. (White.)

While the Assembly was in Augusta, before the evacuation of Savannah, a sweeping act of attainder and amercement was passed. It would seem from the published record that this act, which was enacted in May, 1782, was passed in *Savannah*. As Savannah was not evacuated till July, it must have been passed in Augusta. It was the act of five years before with the number of the denounced largely increased. Without giving the accused a hearing, merely on a suspicion of their disloyalty, or because of a rumor that they had not been true to the American cause, they were sentenced to the penalty of confiscation and banishment.

All debts due British subjects were sequestered. All bequests made to British subjects were taken by the State. The act was to go at once into effect. Many innocent persons were included in it, and for several years following there were numerous acts passed for the relief of those involved. There were, however, many cases of great hardship and injustice.

Poor Sir Patrick Houston was attainted by Sir James Wright because he was a rebel, and then by this act because he was a Loyalist. The same was true of sundry others, and many who were found in this list aspersed as Tories are found afterward to be leading men in the councils of the State.

Special acts were passed for the relief of some of those mentioned, and as will be seen elsewhere, Josiah Tattnall, whose large estate was confiscated and who was banished from the State, twenty-five years after this act was passed, when his son was governor, was relieved of the penalties it inflicted.

This act was passed in May, 1782. Those denounced in it were:

Sir James Wright, Geo. Houston, Sir John Grahame, P. Delegal, Alex Wright, P. Delegal, Jr., Lachlan McGilveray, Jno. Glen, Jno. Mullryne, John Boyd Randal, Josiah Tattnall, Sr., Jas. Mossman, Basil Cowper, J. C. Lucina, Wm. Telfair, N Hall, Alex McGown, T. Gibbons, Thos. Talmash, Jno. Fox, Samuel Douglas, John

Simpson, L. Johnson, Sr., M. Stewart, L. Johnson, Jr., Jno. Sutcliff, Wm. Johnson, B. Farley, Thos. Johnson, Thomas Rosse, Samuel Farley, J. J. Zubly, James Alexander, David Zubly, Joseph Spencer, Geo. Baillie, James Butler, Wm. Wylly, John Wood, Campbell Wylly, Robert Reid, John Starr, Levi Sheftall, Thomas Reid, James Harriot, Samuel Moore, R. Porteus, John Hubbard, Alex Creighton, Matthew Marshall, R. Moody, Joseph Marshall, Wm. Clark, Thomas Brown, James Chapman, Thomas Scott, Charles Watts, Wm. Frazer, Wm. Bosomworth, Timothy Hollingsworth, Sampson Williams, Val. Hollingsworth, G. Vansant, Wm. McDonald, George Vansant, John McDonald, Daniel McGirth, John McDonald, James McGirth, Wm. Ross, George Proctor, Daniel McLeod, James Shivers, Alex Baillie, John Spear, Alex McDonald, John Marten, David Ross, John Frost, Daniel McDonald, Wm. Frost, Roderick McIntosh, Cornelius Dunn, Angus Bacon, John Dunn, Thomas Young, John Pettinger, Simon Munroe, Robert Abrams, Simon Patterson, Joseph Raines, Wm. Lyford, Basil Cowper, Robert Baillie, Thomas Stringer, James Kitching, John Hopkins, Robert Kelsall, William Oldes, James Spalding, James Hume, Alex Inglis, Charles McDaniel, John Hume, James Brisbane, John McDonald, Thomas Goldsmith, William Miller, William McIntosh, Major James Wright, William Moss, Donald McDonald, James Robertson, Philip Moore, Dan'l McLeod, Henry Young, William Panton, Daniel McIntosh, Jos Farley, Thomas Skinner, John Fowles, I. M. Tattnall, John Polson, Thomas Fleming, C. McKenney, Wm. Ross, Alex Thompson, Alex Ross, John Wesley, R. McCormick, Charles Wright, John Shave, Thomas Forbes, Robert Porteus, Richard Shave, Colonel Thomas Brown, Jermyn Wright, A. Carney, Jas. Thompson, Charles Wright, Wm. Davidson, William Irvine, John McGilveray, Charles Watts, George Kincaid, Tim Barnard, James Carson, William Knox, Isaac DeLeon, William Clark, John Murray, Peter Edwards, Sir Pat Houston, Geo. Cuthbert, Samuel Langley, John Martin, William McGilveray, Samuel Early, John Williams, Wm. Stephens, Roger Kelsal, R. Demere, Benjamin Wilson, Thomas Young, John Proctor, Peter Dean, Simon Munroe, George Fox, Henry Muirel, D. McGerth, Moses Kirkland, James Spalding, George Aarons, John Lightenstone, R. Baillie, Wm. Willis, Wm. Lyford, A. Creighton, Andrew Menery, Andrew Hewitt, Rory McIntosh, Henry Cooper, John Johnson, Thomas Waters, William Calker, Henry Williams, Ed Corker, John Douglas, William Mangum, William White, James Douglas, Samuel Williams, Wm. Durgin, John O'Neal, James Hunt, Avington Perkins, John Young, Daniel Philips, Robert Tilman, James Gordon, Wm. Young, Abram Wilkins, Math Moon, Samuel Wilkins, Henry Sharp, Jonathan Wilkins, Jacob Sharp, Luke Binow, Cordy Sharp, Wm. Tidwell, Wm. McNott, Reuben Sherral, Saul Montgomery, James Gordon, Ed Pitcher, Benjamin Brantley, Colonel James Grierson, Henry Overstreet, Andrew Moore, Elias Bonnell, John Howard, Wm. Brown, Benj. Howard, Aug. Audentood, Thomas Howard, Absalom Wells, And. Robertson, John Ferguson, David Cameron, Wm. Reid, John Jameson, Thomas Beaty, Wm. Oates, Benj. Lanier, Robert Walsington, John Boykin, W. Tucker, Joshua Pearce, John McCormick, William Pierce, Paul McCormick, Philip Dill, R. Henderson, James Dill, Lew Mobley, John Goldwire, James Herbert, James Pace, James Moore, Rev. C. F. Triebner, Samuel Moore, S. Dampier, Joseph Cornells, P. Blythe, R. French, John Blythe, William Balfour, Samuel Cooper, Isaac Daronny, George Weekly, Isaac Eaton, W. Gruber, Andrew McNiely, Joseph Johnston, Jas. Robertson, John Johnson, James Lyle, Wm. Powell, Jos. Marshall, William Love, John Peg, John Love, John Brown, John Thomas, Thomas Rutherford, Daniel Russell, Cader Price, Matthew Lyle, John Hammett, Robert Miller, David Grimes, John Robertson, Philip Helverton, Daniel Howell, Wm. Hammond, Alex Carter, George Johnson, Thomas Scott, Richard Baillie, John Coppinger, Thos. Manson, Jacob Watson, Andrew Johnson, Charles Weatherford, John Furlow, James Jackson of Augusta, Wm. Johnson, Francis Folliot, Dr. Taylor, Simon Paterson, Thos. Polhill, Nath'l Polhill, John Maxwell, Samuel Kemp.

It will be seen that this act was but the act of five years before repeated, with the addition of many other names. Many of those attainted were not Tories or Loyalists and escaped the penalties of the act, and many were pardoned by special statute, and in many cases while the father was a Loyalist the son was a Whig, and so the property involved did not really pass from the family.

So much attention has been given to the Revolution by McCall, Stevens, and especially Jones, that there is nothing more to be said, and as their narratives are too extended to be repeated here I have contented myself with merely giving a short history. It will be seen the number engaged was not large. In all there were but about three thousand five hundred, and the battles fought, except that of Savannah and Briar creek, of but little importance. There was much courage displayed and much self-sacrifice made, and no men could have been truer than the Georgians were to the cause of the Continental Congress. There were comparatively few arms-bearing men in Georgia when the Revolutionary war began, but of those few much the largest number were in the war.

Up to 1779 everything in upper Georgia had been so peaceful that there was a steady flow of newcomers from North Carolina and Virginia. These years of war had however, desolated all the new settlements, and when the war was over there was much to do to repair its ravages There were cabins to rebuild and deserted fields to be once more brought into cultivation. The stock had been driven off, and the negroes had many of them escaped, but by 1782 things began to settle down.

The social condition of the Georgia people just after the Revolution was just such as might have been expected when everything had been overturned. The people had all suffered; none had escaped. From the Florida line to the limits of the Cherokee nation, and back to the last line of western settlements, the country had been ravaged. The hardships of the first frontier were reproduced in all the rural districts, and the villages, for there were no cities, were devastated. The first section to rally was the southern, and that too little known but remarkale man, John Wereat, who had a plantation on the neck in what is now Bryan county, loaded his flat-boats with rice and other supplies and had them poled up the Savannah river as far as he could go to relieve the destitution of the people of Wilkes and Richmond. The country, however, was so fertile that the pinching poverty of the people was soon at an end, but it was several years before there was comfort, much less luxury. The coast country had been devastated, and for several years there was almost the same condition which was found on the frontier. Our chapter of the cities will show the two villages, Savannah and Augusta, came out of the war almost in ruins.

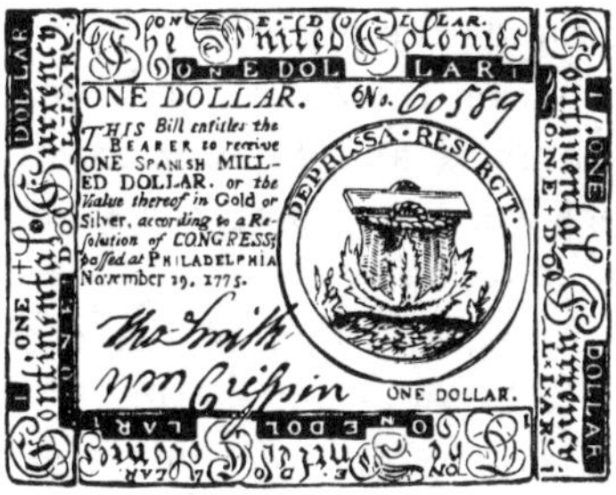

CONTINENTAL SCRIP.

There was no money. Georgia scrip was worthless, and Continental money was about as bad. There was nothing for market when the ports were again open, except some peltry, and for some years there was but little commerce.

Society was in a fearful state. When human life was held at so cheap a rate and when brutal courage was at such a premium; when men had no compunction about getting drunk, if rum could be had; when it was no robbery to take all a Tory had, and no murder to hang him; when children grew to manhood who had never spent a month in the schoolroom, and who had never heard a sermon, it was not to be expected that the morals of the people would be high, or their manners refined, or their intelligence considerable.

There was much lawlessness; there were neither judges nor courts; but there was no lapse into real savagery. There was still much among the rudest of the people which was praiseworthy. There was a scorn for lying, duplicity, and above all, for cowardice. There was a boundless hospitality, a kindness to all comers except Tories, a chivalric treatment of women, a genuine sympathy for the weak, and an unquestioning faith in the truths of religion.

The up-country people, mainly newcomers from Virginia and North Carolina, soon after the Revolution ended, took into their hands the government of the State. Many of the best people on the coast had been true to the crown and were now in exile, and those who stood for the cause of Independence were not numerous enough to overbalance the vote of the up-country.

In the first census, in 1790, of the eighty-two thousand people, black and white in Georgia, thirty-two thousand were in Wilkes county alone, and perhaps not an adult among them had been born in Georgia. There was an elegance and high culture in the few gentlemen planters, lawyers, and counselors of the coast who had been members in the old Assembly, that was not to be found in the sturdy men who had come into the wilds of upper Georgia—men who could barely write their names, who had always lived in log cabins, and worked with their own hands, but who had fought the Tories at Kettle creek and rode with Clarke and Twiggs, and Candler and Dooly on many a foray, as well as men like Few and Candler, and Walton and Glascock, father and son, who were equals in all respects to any in Georgia. These were prominent in the up-country at the end of the war, but the ruling element was still on the tide-water.

There had been no possibility of carrying on any schools, and those children who grew up during the war never entered a schoolroom. The larger number of persons from the better classes who could not write, who were found in Georgia in the early years of the nineteenth century, both men and women, grew up at this time, when there were neither primary schools nor academies.

SEAL OF THE STATE OF GEORGIA.

The war was virtually at an end in the early part of 1782, and with a devastated territory, an empty treasury, and a heavy debt, with an imperfect constitution and a discordant people, Georgia began her career as a free and independent State. There had been seventeen thousand white people when the war began,* and probably, despite the ravages of the war, there were as many at its close.

There was from 1777 to 1783 almost a complete suspension of all the religious work in the new State. The Rector of the Episcopal church in Savannah was a Loyalist. Mr. Triebner, the Lutheran, was a Loyalist and a fugitive, and the church in Ebenezer had been used as a stable. The Reformed Presbyterian minister in Burke, now Jeffer-

* Jones.

son county, was a Loyalist, and had fled the country. St. Paul's church in Augusta and the church at Midway had been burned. The Baptist preachers, Mr. Marshall, Mr. Bottsford, and Mr. Mercer, had been driven from the State, and there was no resumption of regular religious work until after the war had nearly ended.

The Quakers had been so persecuted in Georgia by the Whigs that they left the State and never returned to it.

CHAPTER IV.

1782 TO 1789.

Georgia a Free and Independent State—Governors Houston, Elbert, Handley, Telfair, and Mathews—Gloomy State of Affairs—College Projected—The Decision to Remove Capitol to Louisville—The State Government Temporarily in Augusta—Military Land Grants Issued—Rapid Settlement of the State—Indian Troubles—Oconee War—Paper Money Issued—Call for a Convention to Form a more Perfect Union—Delegates Appointed—Ratification of the Constitution of the United States—State Conventions—History of the Counties of Chatham, Effingham, Burke, Richmond, Liberty, Camden, Wilkes, Franklin, Washington, and Greene.

Authorities: Stevens, Jones, Sherwood, White's Statistics and Historical Collections, Chappell's Pamphlets, Watkins's Digest Georgia Laws, Marbury & Crawford's Digest, Madison Papers, Gilmer's Georgians, Files of the Georgia Gazette, and Personal Researches into County Records.

The war was virtually at an end when Cornwallis surrendered at Yorktown, and the last British soldier had been removed from Georgia and the State government fully reestablished for a year before the news reached Savannah that Georgia was recognized as a free and independent State. When this news reached Savannah, John Houston, who had been one of the four who called the first Revolutionary meeting, was governor, and the city in which that meeting was held was the recognized capital of the new State.

After Governor Houston's term expired, General Samuel Elbert, whom we have seen was the lieutenant-colonel of the first battalion of Georgia troops, and who was so true a soldier to the end of the war, was elected by an almost unanimous vote of the Legislature as governor. In 1786 Edward Telfair, the wise and wealthy Scotchman who had been so faithful to the cause of independence, succeeded him. Governor Telfair was followed by General George

Mathews. General George Mathews, while not born in Ireland, was a full-blooded Scotch-Irishman. He was born in Augusta county, Va., in the days when Indian forays were fearfully common. He became an Indian fighter in his boyhood, and distinguished himself at the battle of Point Pleasant. When the Revolutionary war began he threw himself ardently into it. He was made colonel of a regiment, and was at Germantown and Brandywine. He was wounded, captured, and then exchanged. He came to Georgia with some Virginia troops toward the close of the war. He was a shrewd speculator, and he bought at a bargain a claim to a large body of land known as the Goose Pond tract on Broad river and decided to move to it.* He brought in the famous Broad river settlers, of whom we shall hear more. He was a rough, quick-tempered, uneducated Irishman, thoroughly fearless and impetuous, and sundry stories are told of his want of culture, of his impetuous temper, which are not sufficiently authentic for these pages. He was a man of strong common sense and sterling honesty of purpose.

General Jackson was elected to succeed Governor Mathews, but declined the office, and Governor Handley, an Englishman likewise, was chosen and served the term. The condition of things was far from cheerful. The supplies of food were insufficient, there was no money in the State treasury, and there were heavy debts to be provided for. Many of the best citizens of the State were proscribed and were in exile, and their property ordered to the block. There was discord in the public councils. The Legislature was unwilling to comply with Governor Houston's urgent request that it should levy a tax for what he said were imperative demands, but gloomy as matters were a body of intelligent men secured from the Legislature a grant of ten

* Gilmer.

thousand acres of land for a college, to be located at some place to be afterward selected.

The Legislature had its sessions in Savannah from July, 1783, to the spring of 1786, when an act was passed providing for the selection of a place for the capital, which should be in twenty miles of Galphin's old town, which place should be called Louisville, but in the meantime the Legislature would meet in Augusta. The times even then were so disturbed that a guard was called for from each county along the route to see the body to its destination.

The State had much land and but a few people, and many of those who had been faithful to the cause of independence were now to receive a generous grant as a reward for their military services. In addition to these grants, in order to secure immigration, the State proposed to all newcomers to give them from two hundred to five hundred acres of land as headrights. Of these military grants there were five different classes of warrants issued.

First. Those citizens who bravely remained in Georgia during the struggle and served in the militia when called for were to have two hundred and fifty acres. There were 2,923 persons who received grants under this head.

Second. Refugees who fled the State, but fought in the American army; there were six hundred and ninety-four of these.

Third. Those who were not in active service, but were enrolled as minute-men; there were five hundred and fifty-five of these.

Fourth. Citizens of other States who came to the help of Georgia as continental soldiers; there were two hundred of these.

Fifth. To those who had served in the navy; to these only nine land-warrants were issued.*

* See Appendix for full list of grantees.

These military warrants were mainly to be located in the newly opened territory which was included in the two immense counties of Washington and Franklin. In addition to these grants, which were to classes, there were special grants made to certain individuals, one to General Greene of the Mulberry Grove property, near Savannah; one to General Wayne, and twenty thousand acres ganted to Count D'Estaing.*

The headrights were many of them granted before the Revolution by the colonial government, but many more were granted to the newcomers as soon as the war ended, A land-office was opened in Augusta and Bishop Stevens, who had access to the private papers of Mr. Jos. Habersham, who was one of the commissioners for issuing these warrants, gives a somewhat lively picture of the disorder in the land-office when the warrants were called for. The larger number of claimants were from the newly settled lands of now Columbia and Wilkes, who, becoming impatient at the necessarily slow progress of the commissioners, and perhaps a little too much under the influence of the tafia so abundant in Augusta, broke into the office and snatched the warrants from the table and made off with them. Many of these abstracted warrants were returned, and many were not recognized.

When the war ended, as we have seen, the counties in Georgia were Camden, Glynn, Liberty, Chatham, Effingham, Burke and Richmond, and to these were now added Franklin and Washington, which included the new ceded lands.

Up to the war of the Revolution there had been no serious disturbance with any of the Indians in Georgia. The ruling tribes were Creeks and Cherokees and in that contest

* This large estate was given by the count to a relative who married Colonel De Lapraier of the French army. His descendants still own a part of the land.

both sided with the English, and against the Cherokees an expedition under Colonel Twiggs had been sent out early in the war. As soon as peace came the Georgians took advantage of the victory won and coerced the Creeks into a cession of all the land which lay between the Ogeechee and Oconee rivers, and the Cherokees into the ceding of a considerable strip of their territory, and this new country was now divided into two great counties, Franklin and Washington. The Creeks were by no means reconciled to this seizure of their land and went upon the war-path, and there were frequent raids into the country taken possession of by the whites.

For several years the war known as the Oconee war raged between the Creeks and the Georgians. Forts and blockhouses were built in all the border counties, and the Creeks made a formidable invasion into the country east of the Oconee, and Elijah Clarke, with his forces, had a sharp fight with them as they retreated in what is now Walton county, at a place known now as Jack's creek, said to have been so called in honor of the courage of young Jack Clarke, who distinguished himself in the battle (Chappel). The Creeks gave the early settlers a great deal of trouble and the new village of Greensborough was burned by them. These troubles continued for nearly ten years, and after the formation of the Federal Union the United States troops garrisoned the frontier until the final settlement made by the general government, after which there was peace for near twenty years.

Georgia was now an independent State and as the land was given away, immigration came in a rapid tide into all parts now opened for settlement. The immigrants were of the same class we have already seen as coming into Burke and Richmond. They were mainly from Virginia, North Carolina and Maryland. Some of them were men of property, but the larger number were in very humble circumstances. They began life in a very primitive way. The houses were almost universally at this time of logs, and nearly all consisted of but a single room. There were as yet few stores in which merchandise could be bought; there were but few sawmills and even grist-mills were few. In the low-country rice and corn were the staple articles, and they were prepared for the table by being beat in a mortar, and in the up-country, where ashes were abundant, the corn was made into lye hominy. There was along the whole frontier, from Camden to Franklin, a constant menace from the Indians, and men, as in the early days of New England, were required to take their arms with them to church services. Troops of horsemen were organized in every county to be ready at any moment to pursue the marauding bands of savages who were likely to dash into the remote settlement to rob and murder.

We have seen in other chapters of the coming of the different churches into the province, and now we have the coming of the first Arminian Methodists into the State. In the year 1786 John Major and Thomas Humphries, two itinerant preachers from Virginia, at the instance of Bishop Francis Asbury, came into Georgia. The Methodists differed from any other denomination in some of their doctrines and most of their usages. These first preachers were from Virginia, and the good Virginians who had been brought up in the church of England found in these itinerants, preachers who were nearer akin to them than any other, and they gave them a cordial welcome to their homes, and many of them adhered to the societies the preachers established. The itinerants had no churches, but went from cabin to cabin and held services every day in the week except on Monday. The preachers were peculiar men in every way. They dressed like Quakers, in straight-breasted cutaway coats of brown homespun, wore white cravats and broad-brimmed hats. They sang lustily, preached boisterously, wept and stormed and exhorted, and were intensely in earnest. They preached a full and free gospel and a salvation possible to all men; they went everywhere and success attended their efforts. They began their work in Wilkes and extended it into Burke, and gathered quite a membership during their first year.

In 1788 there came to Georgia a Methodist preacher who was to have much to do with the future of the State, and whose descendants have been among its most honored children. This was Hope Hull, born in Worcester, Md.; he was a soldier in the Revolution before he was of age, and a Methodist preacher when he was twenty-one years old. He was a man of handsome presence, of fine intellect, of fluent and eloquent speech, and of broad views. After he located in Wilkes county he established the first high school in the county and employed a Presbyterian minister to teach it. He was a trustee of the State University and an ardent friend of that institution from its foundation.*

There was now in Georgia one organized Episcopal church, the one in Savannah, and several organized Presbyterian churches in Burke and Wilkes and one in Savannah, a Lutheran church in Effingham, and a Congregational church in Liberty. There were few church buildings, and in the rural districts religious services were held in private houses.

During Governor Telfair's term business began to revive and there was a crying need for a circulating medium. He addressed himself to the work of providing a currency for the State which would be trustworthy and hoped he had accomplished it by adopting, with certain careful restrictions, the usual resource of States, issuing promises to pay and making them a legal tender. The result was, as it has always been, the paper currency was first at par and then

* In my chapter on Religion in the Colony and the State I have given a fuller account of Methodism in Georgia.

declined more and more rapidly until it was worth only four to one.

During his governorship Nathan Brownson, Wm. Few and Hugh Lawson were commissioned to select a place for a State capitol and to provide for the erection of a building for the various departments and for establishing a State university. The capitol and university were to be in twenty miles of Galphin's old town, and the town was to be called Louisville, and £2,000 from the sale of confiscated property was to be appropriated for the building of the new State house. The place was selected, the town was laid out and in 1795 it was made the seat of government and continued such for nearly ten years, when the capitol was removed to Milledgeville.

The confederated government had secured large loans, based upon its confidence that the States would cede to the government their wild lands. This had been done by all of them except Georgia and North Carolina. The leading people in the new State were newcomers, mainly from Virginia. The State was young and feeble and penniless. A large debt which it could not pay was due to the Confederacy, and it had only this land to pay it with. It made some rather hard stipulations, which the confederated States thought were too rigorous, and it refused to accept the State's tender on such grounds, and the cession was not made.

The question of title, which was raised between Georgia and South Carolina as to the title of Georgia to the almost unknown land beyond the Chattahoochee, and as to where the eastern boundary of the new State really was, had been settled at Beaufort by commissioners in 1785, and so the free and independent State had a clear title, save as it was menaced by the Spanish claims, to all the territory included now in Georgia, Alabama and Mississippi.

The very unsatisfactory condition of things for the five years after the Revolution, when the old confederation was going to pieces and the Continental Congress had lost all hold on the various States, led the leaders of Georgia to fall readily into the scheme for a convention of all the States to form a new constitution and a closer union, and during Governor Mathews's time delegates were appointed to go to Philadelphia and take seats in the convention.

Wm. Few, Abraham Baldwin, Wm. Pierce, Wm. Houston, George Walton and Nathaniel Pendleton were selected as the delegates. Of these Few, Baldwin and Houston took part in the convention, but Mr. Few was the only one of the delegation who signed the original Constitution.* When the Assembly in Philadelphia adjourned † the Georgia Legislature called for a convention to meet in Augusta and ratify the new instrument, and on the second day of January, 1788, this convention did "fully and cordially assent to ratify and adopt the proposed Constitution."

The convention which ratified the Constitution of the United States and made the first draft of a new Constitution for the State, which was adopted in May of the next year, consisted of:

John Wereat, Wm. Few, Jas. McNeal, Wm. Stephens, Jos. Habersham, Edward Telfair, H. Todd, Geo. Mathews, Florence Sullivan, John King, James Powell, Jno. Elliot, James Maxwell, George Handley, Christopher Hilary, J. Milton, Jared Irwin, Jno. Rutherford, Joshua Williams, Jas. Seagrove, Henry Osborne, Robert Christmas, Thos. Daniel, R. Middleton, Jenkins Davis, N. Brownson, Wm. Gibbons, President.

No debate concerning the propriety of ratification was engaged in. Georgia was the fourth State to ratify the Constitution, and when it was ratified by five

* See Madison Papers.

† Appendix.

other States, as it was in October, she became a member of the Federal Union. There was no submission of this ratification to a popular vote, but the free and sovereign State, *acting as a State* in convention, without any dream that she was surrendering anything more than was delegated to the general government, became one of a Federal Union of thirteen sovereign States.

It is now my purpose to give a bird's-eye view of each county as it was established, giving a larger amount of attention to the parent counties, and not confining myself to the limits of time I have fixed to the general history, but bringing the history of the counties as such to the present time (1900), avoiding, however, all allusion to the part borne by the county during the great war between the States.

CHATHAM.

This county was named for the Earl of Chatham, and was the earliest settled of any portion of Georgia. It has the Savannah river on the east and the Ogeechee on the south and west and includes the islands adjacent. On these two rivers are some fine rice lands, but away from the rivers the land is mainly marsh or sterile pine woods. The agricultural resources of the county apart from its rice lands are not considerable. The river bottoms upon which rice was grown were magnificent estates before the war; and even since it ended, although the slaves have been freed, there have been some very extensive plantations, and though some of them have been worked for over a century they are still planted profitably. Many of these rice plantations have, however, been abandoned, and where there were in the beginning of the century well-kept fields there are now only marshes. Some of these old rice plantations are now market gardens, where great quantities of early vegetables are grown for the northern markets; but many of these fine old places are simply abandoned. Raising vegetables for the northern markets is carried on in the county very extensively. Some of the swamps around the city have been drained by canals and ditches and there is much land now arable which was waste, and many of the freedmen have gone into these low places and bought small tracts and now make a scanty living by planting small crops.

There are some famous plantations near the city. Mulberry Grove, where General Greene died, is a market garden. Bonaventure, where the Tattnall family had their home, is now a famous cemetery. The Hermitage, the seat of the McCallisters, with its magnificent avenue of live-oaks; and Beaulieu, the seat of Governor Stephens; Whitefield's Bethesda Orphanage; Jasper Springs, where Jasper captured the British guards and released the prisoners, are places of interest in the county. The history of Chatham is so interwoven with the early history of Georgia, and especially that of Savannah, which is given at length elsewhere, that it is not necessary to say much of the county in this place.

There is a comparatively small white population outside of the city and the various suburban villages. Thunderbolt, Tybee, Isle of Hope and White Bluff are on the seashore, and Pooler and Monteith and a few other small villages on the lines of railway. There are few schools and churches save for the negroes in the country districts around Savannah, but the villages are well supplied. In 1790 there were only twenty-five hundred white people in the county, Savannah included, but there were eight thousand two hundred slaves on the plantations and the sea islands. The sea islands were famous for the homes of planters who resided in the city during the winter and on their estates during the summer. They were not adapted to the production of rice and were devoted at their first settlement to indigo culture and stock-raising. They were congenial homes for the Africans who were imported in large numbers and who, when they were placed on the islands, rapidly increased. Before the Revolution there was much wealth and much luxurious living on these islands. The planters, after they gave up indigo culture, began to raise sea-island cotton, and as this staple was very high in price, they had large returns from their crops and increased in wealth very rapidly. The sea island planter in Chatham and along the Georgia coast presented much the same features as is pictured elsewhere in people of the wealthy class of planters. Their situation was an exposed one, and they suffered during the Revolution and the war of 1812. They rallied from these losses at those times, but from the disasters of the war between the States there was no recovery, and the islands are now largely peopled by negro tenants who make their living by fishing and oystering.

EFFINGHAM.

As we have seen elsewhere this county, which took the place of St. Matthew's parish, was settled mainly by Germans, and in the account of the German settlement we have already had a picture of the natural features of the county and of the people. In common with all the parts of the tide-water country this county suffered greatly during the Revolution. The bulk of the people, speaking only the German tongue and concerned only about their small farms and domestic interests, knew little and cared less about the issue between the colonists and England. Most of them desired to hold a neutral place. Some of them, however, were loyal to the king, and some of them were sympathizers with the colonies, and one of them, John Adam Treutlen, was a Georgia governor, and pronounced a rebel by Governor Wright. They were thus sadly divided and suffered on all sides. Their villages were occupied at different times by both armies, and their church was desecrated and defaced, for though their pastor took the side of the British and invited the English troops to Ebenezer, the rude soldiers turned their revered church into a stable. The whole country was desolated by the repeated raids of the soldiers on both sides, but the people were industrious and thrifty, and after peace came the herds of cattle on which they largely relied were soon replenished. The church was at once repaired, their schools were reopened, and the fields of the farmer put once more into cultivation, and though for the two years after the close of the war they had no pastor, they then secured a pious man from Germany to take the place. In 1790 there were 2,420 people in the county, of which only seven hundred and fifty were slaves, and in 1830, forty years afterward, there were only five hundred more inhabitants. The proximity of the county to Savannah, and its want of any commercial advantages, prevented its having towns of any considerable size, and yet gave it a fine position as a place for gardens and dairies. Its climate was excellent, and when the Central railroad traversed it some residence villages sprang up, and Guyton and Marlow have become favorite places for the country homes of Savannah merchants.

Springfield is the county site, and while it is a small village, it has been famous in days gone by for its excellent schools and the high character of its people.

Ebenezer, of which we have so often spoken, which was at one time a thrifty village, has long since ceased to be a place of any importance, and is now unpeopled. The old Lutheran church, famous as the first church in Georgia, still stands and has a congregation and a pastor.

The county, being originally peopled by Germans, has many of their descendants still in it. They are good people, honest, thrifty and religious. There are Lutherans and Baptists and Methodists in the county, and good churches and good schools are found in all parts of it.

There are few sections in Georgia where there is a better type of plain, good, contented, pious people than in Effingham, and their descendants are found in all sections of the low-country of Georgia, and wherever found are recognized as among the worthiest of the people.*

RICHMOND.

Richmond was named in honor of the Duke of Richmond. It was originally St. Paul's parish, and when it was made in 1777 it included all of Columbia and parts of McDuffie, Warren and Jefferson counties. As these counties will come under our survey in the proper time, it will only be necessary now to give attention to Richmond as it stands.

ST. PAUL'S CHURCH.

In the early parts of this history and in the chapter on Augusta nearly everything of interest connected with this county, up to the Revolution, has been narrated, and in the history of Augusta much of the after revolutionary history is given. Richmond is in the main a county of rather sterile pine woods, save on some of the creeks and on the river, where the land is a rich alluvial which at one time was very productive. Before

* In the first chapter of this History, in the account of the German settlement, the early history of these people is to be found.

Cotton Exchange, Augusta.

the lands on the river above Augusta were cleared of their forests the river-bed was deeper and the stream more rapid than it is at this day, and the freshets which come now almost annually were infrequent a hundred and twenty years ago. Then these lands were considered very valuable, and wealthy planters had large plantations in the swamps which brought a rich return. They are now turned largely into hay farms and are still valuable. The pine lands were for a long time esteemed only for their timber and as a range for cattle. There was some of this land, however, which had a good subsoil of clay which was, when manured, quite productive, and while it was not esteemed as first-class land, it repaid the tiller's toil, and even much of the land which was very sterile when well fertilized produced fine crops of melons and vegetables.

The rural population of Richmond, save on the river and on Rae's creek, were plain, poor people who ran small farms. There was quite a settlement of well-to-do Virginians some distance north of Augusta which was called Bedford, probably after the Virginia county from which they emigrated, and quite a settlement of Burke county planters in the healthy pine woods near what is now Hephzibah. A college was projected in the early part of the century, called Mt. Enon, which was to be located in the southern part of this county and opened as a Baptist college; but a charter was refused and it became the first Baptist high school in Georgia.

There was a fine water-power on the creeks, which, rising in the pine hills, ran into the river; and one of the most successful country factories was built on Spirit creek long before the war, and another known as Schley's, at Bellevue, where the shrewd old governor had his country home.

The building of the railway from Augusta to Sandersville opened up the lower part of the county, and there is a considerable village known as Hephzibah, where the Baptists have a school.

The county had been well supplied with Methodist and Baptist churches, and the school facilities had been moderately good; but the establishment of the public school system after the war provided all classes with excellent educational advantages.

Among the oldest Methodist and Baptist churches in upper Georgia are the Baptist church at Hephzibah, formerly Mt. Enon, and the Methodist church at Liberty, which antedate the beginning of this century.

Among the industries which have made the county famous the celebrated nurseries of the Berckmans are very notable.

Dr. Berckmans, an intelligent German, was struck with the great advantages of the climate and soil near Augusta for the raising of fruit trees and flowers, and he began his nurseries on a very extensive scale over forty years ago, and from them the most beautiful flowers and the finest fruits have been distributed throughout the land.

The fine climate of the Sand Hills, which stretch through the northwest part of the county, has invited summer residents, who have beautiful homes, chiefly at Grovetown, sixteen miles from the city.

The county is so linked with the city that it is not possible to separate them, and I shall in a future chapter devote a considerable space to Augusta, and as Columbia county includes much of what was historic Richmond, it is not needful to say more of the county as it is at present.

BURKE.

Burke county was formed from St. George's parish, and was named Burke in honor of Edmund Burke, the great statesman who stood so firmly for the colonies.

There were doubtless a few whites in this section before

Oglethorpe came, for the Indians who lived in this county complained to Governor Glen of South Carolina, that the whites, among whom were John Jones and John Whitehead, were making inroads on their hunting-grounds. It is certain that George Galphin had a trading-station at Galphinton, on the Ogeechee, when Fort Augusta took the place of Fort Moore in 1733. The settlements in South Carolina reached to the Savannah river, and it is hardly probable they stopped there. Before the parish of St. George was laid out the borough of Halifax sent two representatives to the Assembly of Governor Reynolds, and in the grants made by Governor Reynolds are sundry grants to persons who were found in Burke, Jefferson and Screven counties. After St. George's parish was made Burke county, it gave off Jefferson and Screven, leaving it still a large county. It was at its first settlement a county of wonderful fertility and sufficiently undulating to secure good drainage, except where there were deep depressions and ponds. It had in it no very lofty hills, and being possessed of a tenacious limestone soil, the rains and floods left it uninjured.

The Savannah was on the east, the Ogeechee on the west, and the great Briar creek traversed the whole county. Bark, Camp, Buckhead, Rocky, McIntosh, Beaverdam, and Walnut creeks were all considerable streams. Along the banks of each was a large strip of oak and hickory land. The great pine forests, valued only for pasturage, filled up the area unoccupied by the oak and hickory forests. There was beneath the surface an inexhaustible deposit of rotten limestone which now and then cropped out on the surface. The land was very productive, and there came into it as soon as it was opened for settlement great crowds of immigrants.

On the Ogeechee river, and on the various creeks flowing into it, as well as on the Savannah and its tributaries, there were many settlers before the Revolution. There was in 1774 six justices of the peace in the parish, and where Waynesboro now is there was a prison known as Burke jail.

In 1774, when the Liberty Boys began their rebellion, as it was regarded by Governor Wright, he received a very decided protest against their course from this parish, among others, and we find the names of:

George Wells, afterward lieutenant-governor; Peter Shand, James Doyle, S. Barrow, Dan'l Thomas, Gideon Thomas, John Thomas, Robert Henderson, F. L. Frier, John Red, James Warren, Jas. Williams, Sam'l Red, Alex. Berryhill, Ed. Hill, Charles Williams, Thos. Pennington, John Rogers, John Anderson, John Catlett, David Green, Jno. Pettigrew, Wm. Catlett, Jno. Rotten, Jno. Frier, James Davis, Wm. Milner, Elijah Dix, Sam'l Berryhill, Thos. Red, John Bledsoe, James Rae, Jos. Gresham, Wm. Doyle, Jos. Tilley, Job Thomas, Drury Roberts, Joel Walker, Jas. Red, W. McNorrell, Jno. Kennedy, F. Stringer, P. McCormick, H. Williams, J. Greenway, R. Blaishard, H. Irwin, T. Carter, J. Brantley, W. Weathers, W. Moore, W. Godbe, R Cureton, W. Cureton, P. Helvestien, Elias Daniel, E. Odom, B. Brantley, T. Gray, J. Brantley, John Greene, John Burnside, S. Jordan, P. Dickey, Zach Wimberly, S. Lamb. B. Warren, Sol. Davis, Jno. Gray, Frank Hancock, Pleast Goodall, Wade Kitts, Dan'l Logan, Myrick Davies, John Roberts, R. Douglas, Jesse Scruggs, Henry Mills, Jos. Moore, Amos Whitehead, John Robinson, John Thomas, Sr., Wm. Younge, E. Benniefield, Jacob Sharp, C. Yarborough, J. Hunt, B. Lamb. S. Slockcumb, L. Hobbs, Jno. Forth, N. Williams, Ed. Walters, Jno. Stephens, F. Francis, M. Davis, Arthur Walker, A. Davis, Allen Brown, Joseph Allday, Jas. Douglas, L. Ashberry, C. Golightly, John Howell, Bud Cade, J. Moore, John Whitehead, John Sharpe, T. Odom, W. Hobbs, R. Cade, John Tillman, C. Whitehead.

Many of these names belong to Virginia and North Carolina, and some are evidently Scotch-Irish in their origin. These constituted a small part of the heads of families in the at present three counties, but serve to give us a little insight as to whence the Burke people came and who they were. White gives another list at a later day (1792) of the officers of the first battalion of Georgia militia.

During the Revolution the patriots of Burke had considerable trouble with the Tories, who made repeated raids into the county. While many of the people were not in the army, they were patriots, and were in danger all the time.

The first settlers of Burke were not large slaveholders, nor was there a large influx of slaves until after the invention of the cotton-gin. It is likely that among the first cotton-gins ever put into operation in the world was the one set up in Burke county. Before Whitney secured his patent he put up one of his machines, as they were called, in Burke county, and ginned what cotton was brought him from all quarters. The wonderful value of the cotton lands in this county, low price of negroes, and the depression of the tobacco and indigo culture caused cotton plantations to spring up as soon as the gin was invented.

The oak and hickory section of the county when opened soon became quite unhealthy, and the white people were forced to the pine woods in the malarious seasons, and many of the smaller landholders sold their holdings in Burke and went farther west, and large plantations became the rule.

Waynesboro was laid off in 1783 and was named in honor of Mad Anthony Wayne, who was a great favorite in Georgia. The Legislature incorporated an academy and granted two thousand acres of land as an endowment, and incorporated the village with Thomas Lewis, Sr., Thomas Lewis, Jr., Jas. Duhart, Edward Telfair, and John Jones as commissioners. Two hundred lots were to be sold and the proceeds were to be devoted to paying for the public building. The academy was among the first houses built and the court-house was soon erected. The town grew and there was a race-course near by, and the famous comedy, "The Wax Works" of "Georgia Scenes," was acted in this village. There was no church, however, for many years, and the only preaching was an occasional sermon in the court-house; but in the early part of the century two Presbyterian churches, one of which had been organized at Walnut Branch and the other at Old Church, united and built a small Presbyterian church in Waynesboro, which was served by a pastor who in winter preached in Burke, and in summer to the same people who went to the village of Bath, in the pine woods of Richmond.

A Methodist church was built near where the cemetery is now soon after the Presbyterian church was built. The building was very inferior and the congregation very small. It has long since given way to what is now an elegant building with a large congregation. Six miles from Waynesboro was an old church which was built before the Revolution, and long used as a Methodist church, and in the east of the county is Bottsford Baptist church, one of the first Baptist churches in Georgia. The Baptist churches at Rocky Creek and Bark Camp and Buckhead were famous churches in the beginning of the century and for fifty years afterward.

The county of Burke became early in the century a county of large plantations and wealthy planters. Some of these lived in beautiful homes on their places during the winter and in summer went to the pine woods. Habersham, Alexander, Summerville, Bath and Brothersville were each piny wood villages, to which the planters repaired before the sickly season set in. There was much comfort and fine taste in these ante-bellum winter homes, and the hospitality of the planters was boundless. The villages to which they repaired during the summer time afforded a delightful social circle, and the commodious winter homes were filled with guests from the cities and the neighboring plantations. Nowhere was old Virginia life of a century gone by so reproduced as in Burke sixty years since. The large plantation was under the management of the overseer. The factor in Augusta or Savannah cashed the drafts of the planter and supplied his larder with such luxuries as he might desire from the city. His carriages and his horses were of the best order, and he supplied his library with the best books and periodicals. The wealth he enjoyed he had inherited, and he was often dependent upon the sagacity of others to keep it from leaving him. This was one kind, and the number was not large, of Burke county planters, and there were a few in all the neighboring counties of the same class. Then there were others much more numerous who had made their fortunes by hard work, and who, while they gave their children all that wealth could secure in the way of luxury, were themselves hard-working, close-trading men, who read no books and put on no style, but who knew how to manage negroes and make cotton. Then there was a class of poor plain people who lived in the pine woods, few of whom had any slaves. They lived in log cabins on small bodies of land, and lived by their own labor. They rafted ranging timber down the Savannah river, made shingles in the cypress swamps, and raised some cattle and sheep. They had little to do with the wealthy people of the oak woods, and knew but little of them. There was no county in the State before the war began in which there was a worthier, more contented or more prosperous people than the people of Burke county.

The wonderful cotton-producing quality of the land turned the county into one great plantation, except in the pine woods. Negroes increased in numbers, and men who began life with a few found themselves the owners of scores. They put a high estimate on negro property and did all they could to increase the number of their slaves. They neglected their lands, incurred large debts, and when the slaves were freed many were bankrupt.

Burke sent forth a large emigration, and the descendants of the people who came from Virginia and North Carolina, and from the north of Ireland, and settled in St. George's parish, have been scattered over all western and southern and southwestern Georgia. The smaller landholders from the oak and hickory country gave way at an early time to large landholders, and great bodies of negroes under the charge of an overseer were the sole inhabitants of some parts of the county during the summer and fall. When the rich cotton lands of the newer part of Georgia were opened the Burke planter removed a part of his force to them and opened a new plantation there. Much of the land was turned out and grew up in old field pines. A planter owned sometimes what had once been the separate homes of twenty sturdy frontiersmen. When the war ended and the negro was a freeman, the negroes were found in far greater numbers than the white people, and the few whites who lived on their estates came to the county town, and Waynesboro, from being a deserted village, became a flourishing little city. The plantations were left in the hands of negro tenants. The old field pines were cut down, and while the white people in Burke are no longer distributed over the county, but are concentrated in the villages, they are in larger number than in the older day. Where there was for many years a mere railroad station, the junction of the Augusta & Savannah railroad with the Central, Millen is now a prosperous little city. Midville, Herndon, Munnerlyn, and Perkins are all villages of some importance, and there are sundry hamlets in other parts of the county.

In the pine woods, where for many years the chief resource was ranging timber and cattle, there are now many small well-cultivated farms, where there are good substantial prosperous farmers. There are good schools and churches and a contented, well-to-do people.

I have devoted some care to this account of Burke, since it was one of the oldest counties, and its history is found largely reproduced in the other large cotton-producing counties of Middle Georgia. The people of Burke have always been noted for their hospitality and generosity. They have been, as a rule, plain, unpretentious, religious people. The population of this county in 1790 was 9,467, of whom only 2,392 were slaves. It then included Screven and Jefferson counties. In 1810, 6,166 whites and 4,691 slaves; in 1850, 5,268 free and 10,832 slaves. The population of whites is greater now than it has ever been, and the negro population is not diminished.*

This county has had its share of distinguished men. Lyman Hall, David Emanuel, Edward Telfair, Herschel V. Johnson. John Martin, all governors, lived in Burke. The Hon. J. J. Jones, S. A. Corker, R. E. Lester, congressmen, were from this county. The Shewmakes, legislators and jurists, and Judge Lawson, a prominent democratic politician, were from this county. Colonel T. M. Berrien long lived here. Edward Byne and the Kilpatricks, famous as Baptist preachers; Professor James Elmore Palmer, noted as an educator and long a professor in Emory College, and many others have cast luster on this good old county; but the county has been chiefly famed for its great planters, who have been noted for their intelligence and enterprise.

WILKES.

Governor Wright in 1773 made a purchase from the Indians of a large tract of land north of Little river and stretching westward to the Ogeechee. It was while he

* The court-house in Burke has been burned and all the records which antedated the war are destroyed, but in the Appendix may be found a list of the first comers to the county.

was in office known as the ceded lands. By the Constitution of 1777 all this section was included in one county, called Wilkes in honor of the reckless John Wilkes, who had distinguished himself as the friend of the colonies. It was a section of great fertility and beauty, possessing the features which we have found in Burke and Columbia counties.

The people from the older colonies speedily found homes in this newly-opened territory and, as we have seen before, in 1790, when Georgia had in it only eighty-two thousand people, Wilkes had thirty-six thousand in its boundary. These people were nearly all native Americans. They came mainly from Virginia, though there were a number of North Carolinians. Governor Gilmer gives in his "Georgians" a racy description of some of the first comers who settled in the county at that time. He says:

"On Long creek and extending southwardly from Savannah river a settlement was made before and during the Revolutionary war by the Clarkes, Doolys, Murrays, Waltons, and others. They were from Bertie and adjoining counties of North Carolina and were all connected by blood or intermarriage. These North Carolina settlers lived upon game and the milk of the cattle they carried with them in their emigration. Hogs, sheep, and poultry were not to be had except in the fewest numbers. A sufficient supply of these indispensables for a new country could only be obtained from South Carolina, whither the people went for that purpose when they had sufficient money to purchase. Many years passed before they owned hogs and sheep enough for bacon and clothing. It was a hard time when the breakfast of a family depended upon catching an opossum over night or a rabbit in the morning. The range was so unrestricted that the cows often wandered away beyond returning or finding, so that the children had no milk to wash down their otherwise dry bread. The horses that did the plowing had to be turned on the wild grass to get their food. They strayed away beyond finding if their legs were not fastened together, so that the art of hobbling was as important as the blacksmith's. Bells were put upon them for the purpose of indicating their whereabouts, and then the Indians, if on the frontiers, carried them off. It was difficult to clear of its timber enough land for corn and tobacco. The term patch was for a long time used for land sown in wheat, because only a small quantity was allotted to that grain. Even these patches were not seen for years after the settlement began, so that flour could not be had for love or money. It was a long time before the children had more than one biscuit apiece on Sunday mornings. Traps, snares and other contrivances were resorted to for catching rabbits, birds and turkeys.

There were no tanneries or well instructed shoemakers. Skins were hung in running streams till the hair could be slipped off, and then they were tanned in a trough. Most went without shoes the greater part of the year.

The first houses were log cabins with dirt floors and clapboard coverings. Toads and serpents were often found crawling over the floors. The rattle of the rattlesnake and the cry of the panther often sent the children home in a hurry when hunting the cows. After working all day they sat around the hearth at night picking the lint from the cottonseed. Their only fruits were wild haws and grapes.

In speaking of their social pleasures he said: "The great pleasure indulged in was dancing. The men went to musters, shooting matches and horse-races. The whisky bottle was always drawn out by the hospitable settler. The clothing of the girls was provided by their own weaving. Hollow trees provided cradles for their babies." The old governor gives an inventory of some estates, in which we get an insight into the prices of things and the general condition of the people just after the Revolution:

One negro boy, £50; 1 bed, 7s.; 1 pail and 1 piggin, 4s.; 1 wash-tub, 2 keelers, 4s.; 1 horse, £24; 1 saddle, 00; 1 razor and 2,000 acres of land in Richmond county, £50; 1 old gray horse, 5s.

Another appraisement shows:

One sorrel mare, £6; 1 mare, £1; 1 horse, £3; 1 horse colt, £4; 6 head cattle, £20; 1 negro boy, £20; 1 negro girl, £30; 1 axe, frying-pan and pothook, 5s.; 1 linen wheel, 5s.; old pewter, 15s.; butter-tub, 2s.; 5 old feather beds, £5; 1 pot, 10s.

Another estate was:

Four negroes, 3 ould basins, 7 plates, 1 frying-pan, 1 piggin, 1 earthen plate, 2 chairs, 1 table, 2 sides leather.

Another was:

Thirteen negroes, 6 horses, 7 sheep, 60 hogs, 23 cattle.

And another:

Sixty hogs, 8 sheep, 10 cattle, loom, knives and forks, flax wheel, turkey feather bed, 9 plates.

In 1795 an inventory calls for:

Eleven negroes, 29 hogs, 1 still, 30 pounds pewter.

Up to this time the only well-furnished house is that of a physician in Washington, and the only library is that of Mr. Wm. Rogers, a teacher. The condition of the roads and the difficulty of transportation forbade anything like the complete furnishing of any home, but, as is seen, a few years after the Revolution there was a great abundance of the necessaries of life.

These inventories give a better insight into the domestic affairs of the first settlers than any general description. They show that the first comers were men of some property, who had but few comforts and fewer of the luxuries of life. The description of Governor Gilmer of life among the first North Carolinians who came to Georgia and settled in Wilkes is borne out by the inventories of the first estates, but belonged to all the first comers. There was, however, immediately after the Revolution a large influx of Virginians who were in better circumstances, and who brought with them in their large wagons from Virginia a supply of better furniture, and furnished their tables more bountifully. As illustrative of this we have the inventory of John Wingfield, or as he is written, John Winkfield, who died in 1798, and whose inventory is elaborate and extensive. He had, besides a sufficient supply of plain household and kitchen furniture, some articles mentioned in no other inventory up to that time. They were bacon, sugar, turkeys, a riding-chair, some books, some lard, and some table-cloths. He had twenty-seven negroes, the largest number reported up to that time.

The land was generally secured by headright, or if purchased cost about two shillings per acre for the best quality. These Virginians, who knew the value of good land, bought large bodies and laid the foundations for the great estates their children had in after time.

There was no court-house till 1785 and court was held in private houses. The jury sat on a log and consulted on their verdict. Governor Gilmer says the jury saw a fleeing Tory and left their log and gave chase. "Prisoners," he says, "in the absence of a jail, were bound with hickory withes, and confined occasionally by putting their heads between the rails of a fence, and sometimes putting them in pens." The Tories had little chance for fair trials. In 1779 seven were condemned at one court. One man was indicted for treason, hog-stealing, horse-stealing, and other misdemeanors. While those tried for treason were convicted, I doubt their being hung, as I find men of the same name afterward in the county. If one was acquitted and the mob thought he was guilty his chance of escape was slim. Even after the war, when a man who was accused of stealing a horse from General Clarke was acquitted by the jury, the old soldier arrested him and marched him to a convenient tree and was about to hang him anyhow, when Nathaniel Pendleton, a distinguished lawyer, succeeded in begging the poor fellow off. The old governor gives some extracts from the presentments of the grand jury, as follows: "We present Hezekiah Wheat for profane swearing, and Thomas Brooks for profane swearing, also Wm. Vardeman for profane swearing, also Andrew Frazier, also John Parham, also Thomas Osborn, also Wm. Osborn, also Moses Harris, also Peter Carnes, also Wm. Moor, also Jeffry Early, also Wm. Thornton, also Grant Taylor, also Richard Powell, also Samuel Creswell, also Daniel Young, also Peter Stubblefield, also Jos. Cook, also James Stewart, also B. Smith, also Jos. Spradling, also Jno. Bragg for fighting and gambling, Jos. Parham for gambling, Grant Taylor and Wm. Osborn for fighting, Jos. Ryan for profane swearing, Daniel Young for gambling and suffering it to be done in his house, Peter Stubblefield for gambling, Dan'l Terondit for gambling, Owen Shannon for swearing, Thos. Shannon for gambling, Frederick Lipham for suffering gambling to be done in his house. The magistrates knowingly allow the Sabbath to be broke by merchants dealing with negroes and others, playing fives and other vices, in particular the magistrates about town who see it frequently, Micajah Williamson, Wm. Moor, and Henry Mounger, Esqs.; also that the militia officers in different districts do not keep up a patrol, from which the inhabitants suffer great damage by negroes riding horses at night, and many other mischievous acts; also that people are suffered to gallop and run horses through the streets of Washington."

These copious extracts drawn from Governor Gilmer's invaluable book give us a little insight into the beginning of the great county of Wilkes. The most of the earliest comers to every new country are poor. People in easy circumstances are not willing to endure the privation of a frontier life, but these first settlers are soon followed by those of larger means who enter into their labors. And so those who came first, bringing no property and settling on land granted to them by the State, who came without slaves or furniture, were soon followed by those who had both.

This immigration of people of means from Virginia and North Carolina came very rapidly after the Revolution. While, as the census will show, a very large number had no negroes, there were quite a number of slaves in this section soon after the war.

These slaves and those of the low-country planters were a very different class. They were Virginians by birth, though Africans by lineage. The negroes were not many in any family. In looking over the tax-lists in Wilkes there is not a slaveholder who has over thirty negroes up to the beginning of the century, while on the coast there were not a few slaveholders who had largely over one hundred.

The country in Virginia was much impoverished, and the prospect of finding good tobacco land in Georgia drew large colonies from all the central and tide-water counties of that State. The larger part of the immigration to Georgia had been from Dinwiddie, Prince George, Henrico, Hanover, Goochland and Halifax, and now there came a large colony from Albemarle led by Colonel George Mathews, afterward governor. He had served in Georgia during the Revolution, and had visited the new county of Wilkes on a prospecting tour. He was delighted with the land, so like the Piedmont country in which he lived, and finding that he could buy a large tract of preempted land at a small price, he bought what was known as the Goose Pond tract in then Wilkes, now Oglethorpe, county. He persuaded some of his neighbors to return with him to

Georgia and spy out the land. They, too, were delighted, and they formed a colony known afterward as the Broad river colony, and settled near together on that river. These Broad river people were well-to-do, who brought with them from their homes a few negroes and such furniture as could be brought in wagons, and their live stock. They found excellent land and a fine range and were soon independent, and many of them became quite wealthy. They were a people of great worth, and their descendants have been distinguished for their public services. Governor Gilmer, in his "Georgians," enters with interesting particularity into the family history of this remarkable colony. While these people preempted the rich valley of the Broad river, there were a number of other families of the same class who settled on the Little river. They were originally from Virginia, but some of them came directly from North Carolina. Among these comers were David Merriwether and Daniel Grant, and his son Thomas Grant. The Grants had one of the first mercantile establishments in middle Georgia, and built the first Methodist church in the State, and the second Methodist conference was held at their home. Daniel Grant was the first man in the State from conscientious motives to emancipate his slaves.

The country was very rapidly settled, and in 1790 there was in its then boundaries 24,000 free and 7,268 slaves. In 1810, when the county was divided, 7,603 free and 7,248 slaves; in 1830, 5,227 free and 8,960 slaves, while in 1850 there were only 3,826 free and 8,261 slaves. The entire population had declined 3,000 in twenty years.

Washington was selected as the county site. It was Heard's fort during the war, and was not laid out till 1783. The lots were to be sold, an academy and a court-house were to be built. It was the first county site called Washington in the new republic. At Judge Walton's instance the name was changed to Georgetown, but it held the name only for a little while, and the only evidence that it ever bore it is found in the Georgetown road from Louisville, and a record in Warrenton. It was soon settled by intelligent and well-to-do people, and was for years the leading county town west of Augusta. It had large commercial establishments, branch banks, an academy and handsome residences, but up to 1822 it had no church, and many of its leading citizens were noted for their skepticism and immorality. There were some leading people among them who were Baptists, and some Presbyterians and Methodists, but they had their membership in the country churches. In 1822 the Methodists built a church in the village, and soon after the Baptists and Presbyterians had each a place of worship.

Jesse Mercer, the most progressive and influential Baptist in Georgia, married a lady in Washington and settled in the village in a comfortable and handsome old-time residence. He here published one of the first hymn books ever printed in Georgia, "Mercer's Cluster of Sacred Songs," and established one of the first newspapers among the Baptists in the South, *The Christian Index*.

In the beginning of the century a hymn-book was published in Washington for the Methodists by Hope Hull, which was the first ever printed in Georgia.

When the tide of settlement moved westward Washington began to lose its prominence, and after the railroads were built it became a quiet, dignified, elegant old town with but little commercial importance, not even commanding the trade of its own county; but after the war a new era came and a new prosperity, and it has more than trebled its population and has become one of the most attractive of central Georgia towns. One of the first, if not the first, female academies in Georgia was established in Washington by Madame Dugas, and it had for a long time an important male school. In has now a graded school which has a very handsome house well equipped. The attractive homes and beautiful oaks and elms make Washington one of the most charming cities in the State.

It was here that the Cabinet of the Confederate States held its last session, and from this historic town the President of the Confederacy, with a few of his Cabinet, rode out to what he hoped would be exile, but which was to be captivity and a dungeon.

Wilkes had at the beginning of the century a newspaper published by David Hillhouse. He not only published a newspaper, but had the first job printing-office in the then interior of Georgia. He was an enterprising and successful northerner. He died in 1804 and his wife took charge of his newspaper and job office and successfully conducted them. Once she published the laws of Georgia, being the first and only woman who was ever State printer.

The county of Wilkes is most of it very hilly, with many streams and narrow valleys. It was a fine stock-raising country, and was admirably adapted to tobacco and cotton. Up to 1800 no cotton was grown for market. After that the planting of cotton became a prominent industry, and as new lands opened for the stockmen the farms were sold and great plantations absorbed them. It was not in Wilkes as in Burke that the planter was nearly always forced to employ some one to see after his interests while he fled from the malaria to a piny woods village. The Wilkes planters lived on their plantations and the country homes were commodious and elegant, but as in Burke the plantations absorbed the farms, and the war found Wilkes with but few white people in the country sections. The land was wretchedly worn, the homes in many cases dilapidated, and the yard full of little negroes. The result was as in Burke, but perhaps in no other middle Georgia county was the recovery from the evil effects of the war more rapid. The negroes were freed, but the planter found it cheaper to pay them wages than to hold them as slaves and support their dependents. The negroes clung to their old homes, and often to their old masters. The old fields which had grown up in second-growth timber and Bermuda grass were brought into cultivation. Pastures were made where the Bermuda grass had grown at will, and while there were sad reverses, perhaps the general prosperity of the county is beyond that of any period in the last fifty years.

The people of Wilkes have always been noted for their high religious character. While it could not be claimed for the early comer that as a rule he was very moral, it is certain he had great respect for religion and his house was open to the preachers. He was ready at any time to fight for the church, and there were prosperous churches in the county from the earliest settlement. The Baptists were in the adjoining county before Wilkes was settled, and as soon as it was laid out they had an organization in it. Many of the early comers were Presbyterians from North Carolina, and some of the earliest teachers were Presbyterian ministers. The first presbytery in Georgia was organized under an oak in the town of Washington. The Methodists, as we have seen, came in 1786, and the Roman Catholics came in 1794. The first Catholic church organized in a rural part of Georgia was in Wilkes, the first Methodist song-book in Georgia was published in Wilkes, and the first Baptist song-book and Baptist newspaper were published in Wilkes.*

The county of Wilkes during the Revolution and for some years afterward was on the frontier, and while what is now Wilkes was protected to some degree by the cordon of settlers who were nearer the Oconee, it was always in danger of Indian raids until the Creeks were at last subdued.

To merely mention the men of distinction who have

---

*See Chapter XIV., Religion in Georgia.

come from this famous old county would take much more space than we can give to any one county.

Here Elijah Clarke, who shared with Twiggs the place of highest honor as a partizan chief, had his home, and here John Clarke, his famous son, who was afterward twice governor, was brought up.

Matthew Talbott, for so many terms a member of the Georgia Legislature, and governor during one term, lived here.

Peter Early, the distinguished judge, and afterward governor, who died in Greene, began the practice of law in this county when he came from Virginia.

The celebrated Nathaniel Pendleton once lived in Washington, and Peter Van Allen, who was killed by W. H. Crawford in a duel, lived in this county.*

David Meriwether, the sterling Virginia soldier and Georgia statesman, lived here.

Duncan G. Campbell, one of the most gifted and astute of early Georgia politicians, and his gifted son, John A. Campbell, long judge of the Supreme Court of the United States, lived here.

Robert Toombs was born in this county and lived in it all his life, and died in the home of his youth in Washington.

Jesse Mercer, the wise philanthropist, was born in this county and died in it.

Hope Hull, one of the most valuable men of early Georgia, as we have seen, had his home near Washington.

The famous Bishop James O. Andrew was born in this county.

Daniel Grant and his son Thomas, noted for their advanced views, large wealth, and philanthropy, lived in this county.

[NOTE.—I have given much more attention to Wilkes

*Van Allen married a sister of Lorenzo Dow. See Dow's Journal.

General Robert Toombs.

than I can give to any other county of middle Georgia, but it was a parent county, and in giving its story I have told the story of others in this part of the State. I am very much indebted to that enthusiastic antiquarian, Miss Eliza Bowen, whose careful researches into the early history of the county ought to be carefully preserved and published. I have had furnished me by her the newspaper clippings from which I have gathered much information.]

LIBERTY.

St. John's, St. Andrew's and St. James's parishes were thrown into a county which was called Liberty. This county adjoined Chatham on the north and Glynn on the south, and its western boundary reached to the Altamaha. I have already given an account of part of it and a glimpse of the people in writing of the Dorchester settlement.

There was little of internal strife in this section during the Revolution. The Dorchester Puritans, who were the main body of the people, were almost universally Whigs, and the Tories gave little trouble; but the county was the most exposed part of the colony to the British ships, and being on the direct line of march from Savannah to St. Augustine, and from St. Augustine to Savannah, suffered much from the ravages of war.

Whether the army is a hostile or a friendly one, the people among whom it moves are always sufferers. Three times the American troops had marched into Liberty, and then came the British. There was a sharp conflict at Midway, the church was burned, the country devastated. The invaders carried off the negroes, burned the houses, broke the rice dams, drove off the cattle, and left the country desolate. As soon as peace came the planters who had fled to the back country returned and began life over again. They had scarce begun to recover from the ravages of the war when the Creek Indians went on the war-path and made frequent and disastrous forays into the settlements, murdering the whites, stealing the slaves and cattle, and rendering it dangerous for the people to go to church unarmed. Despite all these difficulties and drawbacks the thrifty people in the Dorchester settlement continued to improve their condition, and one of the most delightful chapters in Colonel Jones's history of Georgia is the account he gives of this part of Liberty after society had settled down again in the last year of the old century and the first in the new. He says: "Ordinary journeys to church and of a social character were performed on horseback. When he would a wooing go the gallant appeared mounted upon his finest steed and in his best attire, followed by a servant on another horse, conveying his master's valise behind him.

"Shortly after the Revolutionary war stick-back gigs were introduced. If a woman was in the vehicle and unattended the waiting-man rode another horse, keeping alongside and holding the check-rein in his left hand. When his master held the lines the servant rode behind. Men went often armed to church for fear of the Indians.

"The country was full of game, ducks and wild geese in innumerable quantities filled the rice-fields, wild turkeys and deer abounded, bears and beavers were found in the swamps, and buffalo herds wandered northward and southward. There was no lack of squirrels, opossums, raccoons, rabbits, snipe, woodcock; wild-cats were the pests; the rivers teemed with fish."

The planters had their homes in summer at Sunbury, where they had schools and where they had all the privileges of cultured society. Sunbury, after Dr. McWhir took charge of the academy, became the educational center of lower Georgia. While there was much culture and elegance in one part of the county, there was another in which it was not to be found. In the pine woods rice could not be planted, and rice culture demanded such an outlay that when a man had nothing, or had very limited means, he went from the swamps to the pine-barrens and began to gather his flocks and herds about him. These two classes of citizens, the rice-planter and the inland stock-raiser, were widely separated and hardly knew each other. The Liberty county rice-planters were in the main the Midway Congregationalists. They had removed from South Carolina together. They were many of them kinsmen, and they were generally in independent circumstances. They lived near each other, sent their children to the same school, and worshiped at the same church. Their slaves were generally recently imported Africans, and were at first exceedingly ignorant and degraded, but the planters did much to improve them. The owner of the plantation grouped his negro cabins together on some high spot on his plantation, generally in a thick wood. The overseer was a white man and the driver was a trusty negro slave. The overseer gave the laborer his task and the driver saw to it that the slave did his work. The discipline of the plantation was very rigid. The negro was fed on rice and potatoes, and his work, except for a few times in the year, was very light, then it was excessively heavy. He had little to do with his master, and was responsible only to the driver and the overseer. The rice-plantation negro was content with no other place, and while he was perhaps the lowest specimen of his race in America, he was the most contented. The house slaves of the rice-planters were generally of a different class from the field hands and superior to them. These house servants were better fed, better clad, and had more civilizing influences around them.

The white man who lived in the pine woods has already been pictured in the account of Burke. There was but little difference in the life of the piny woods denizen as he was found in all this coast country. He had few or no negroes, and while an independent man lived a very plain life. As yet his timber was of but little value to him, and he depended on the cattle on his range, his sheep, his goats, and sometimes on some tar and pitch he carried to the market at Sunbury. He had no taxes to pay, no school bills, or store bills. He built his cabin with his own hands, and raised on his farm all that was necessary to supply his simple needs. In describing him I describe the men of his class as they appeared until the middle of this century, for no people ever presented fewer variations than the piny woods people of lower Georgia, until the railroads reached them over forty years ago. Then a great change passed over them, and a greater passed over the rice-planters.

Up to the beginning of the last war there were two different types of southern life side by side in this county, but when it ended there was but one. The elegance and culture and wealth, not at all overstated by Colonel Jones, disappeared as if it had been a dream. The negroes came back to their old homes, but the master did not. The rice-fields were marshes again, the homes were deserted or burned, the old Midway church was given up to the negroes, and the people who had worshiped there found homes in other sections of the State. The pine woods were brought into market by the building of the railways. Turpentine farms were opened, mills were set up, and lands which had been considered worthless were found to be of real value. The culture of long cotton, of sugar-cane and of upland rice gave profitable employment to these small farmers, and there are few sections of the State where there is more solid comfort than is now to be found in what was considered at one time the barren lands of Liberty.

Along the line of the Savannah and Florida railway flourishing villages have sprung up, and the white population is considerably increased. The population of the county in 1790 was 5,355, of whom 4,025 were slaves; in 1810 there were 5,828 free and 4,408 slaves; in 1850, 8,000, of whom nearly 6,000 were slaves.

The account given of the Dorchester settlement has rendered any further account of Liberty needless, and the history of Midway church told elsewhere is a part of early Georgia history. While the Congregationalists were nominally in charge of the pulpit, the Presbyterians were really the preachers. There was virtually the same congregation, but there were really two organized churches of this denomination, one at Midway and one at Walthourville. The Methodists have been in Liberty since the latter part of the last century. The Baptists have a considerable following in the county.

No county has sent forth more distinguished sons than Liberty. Especially has it been famous for distinguished preachers who have gone from the Midway neighborhood.

CAMDEN AND GLYNN.

The county of Camden was on the extreme southern border of the State, and was at the time it was made a county very sparsely settled and by very poor people. In 1790 there were in the large area which was then embraced in it two hundred and thirty-five white people and seventy negroes. Many of those who were scattered over these pine hills were that class who were impatient of the restraints of civilized life and had gone into the wilds for greater freedom. There was not a church south of the Altamaha, and not a single public school in the beginning of the century in all the section. There were doubtless in the homes of the Spaldings, the McIntoshes and the few families of wealth around Darien, St. Marys and on the islands, private tutors; but the people who were scattered through the pine forests were without any religious and educational privileges, and when in 1799 the Methodists decided to establish a mission at St. Marys, and Jesse Lee rode from Charleston to that village on horseback to see after the mission, he said:

"The country is very level and very poor except near the watercourses, being mostly a low pine-barren, and almost covered with what is called saw-pimento; but on the river Satilla and a few other places the land is good. The county is no doubt very sickly, except on the Satilla and at St. Marys, which is open to the sea and situated on a dry, sandy bluff. The country is very good for cattle, but it is at present a poor place for piety or morality, few people making any profession of religion and many who are addicted to bad habits find a dwelling in these parts. Drunkenness is very common amongst the people. Persons who violate the laws of their country find it convenient to flee from justice, either to the Indians on the west or the Spaniards on the south, and thus get out of the laws of the United States. I heard of some people in those two counties, *Glenn* (Glynn) and Camden, that were grown up, and some had families who had never heard a sermon or a prayer in all their lives till last summer, when George Clark first came among them."*

This picture of an expanse of country which stretched back from the coast as far as the Georgia line extended was a true picture of much of all this section for years after this. The inhabitants were cattle-raisers, who drove their cattle to the little city of St. Marys, whence they were shipped to the West Indies.

When Dr. Lovick Pierce was quite a young man he was presiding elder in this section, and such was the state of society that he found a local preacher of mature years who had never been married legally to the mother of his children. There were neither magistrates nor parsons in these

* Thrift's Life of Lee. 257. 258.

wild woods, and young people, ignorant of the laws requiring a license to marry or the need of an officiating priest, paired like wild doves.

The rich lands on the rivers were opened early in the century, and the sea islands were planted in cotton and there were rice plantations on the main, and nowhere was there to be found a society more elegant than was to be found in this section near the seashore.

St. Marys, in Camden, has a commanding position, as it was the extreme southward town on the Atlantic coast, only separated from Florida by a river. It has had varied fortunes. Sometimes it was a place of importance, and then declined and then revived. For years it was an important shipping point for lumber, and at one time it commanded a large trade in hides, tallow and wax, which came to it from the pine woods lying west.

General John Floyd, the famous Indian fighter, lived in Camden, and General Duncan L. Church, a candidate for governor, had a rice plantation in this county. The county has never been thickly settled, but in St. Marys there have been good schools and churches for over a hundred years.

Glynn, apart from the sea islands and Brunswick its chief city, has never had any marked features. The land is low and very poor and the inhabitants few. The sea islands, which before the war between the States were the homes of men of means, were abandoned during the war, and after the overthrow of slavery were not reoccupied, and were no longer cultivated on any considerable scale; and one entire island, Jekyl, has been purchased by a body of wealthy men of the North as a seat for a club-house and as a great game preserve. Brunswick has, however, become a city of very considerable importance. The country tributary to it has been very rich in its pine forests, and great quantities of lumber and ship stores have been shipped from this port to North American and European cities.

There have been in Glynn and Camden from the first settlement two very different classes of people—the poor and the wealthy; but the wealthy have been very few, and the entire population at no time has been considerable.

FRANKLIN.

Franklin county, which was laid off in 1784, named in honor of Benjamin Franklin, embraced a very large part of upper Georgia, extending from the borders of what is now Rabun and Towns counties to Clarke, from the Savannah river to the Oconee in Hall and Jackson.

It is still quite a large county of high hills and narrow valleys, lying along the base of the Blue Ridge, with some large and fertile valleys along the Tugalo and the Savannah. The county site, Carnesville, was laid out in 1805, and was named in honor of Thomas Peter Carnes.

Franklin has sent forth into other parts of Georgia many most excellent people. It was for a long time by its location shut out from the world, but since the building of the Southern railway and the branch to Elberton it has been brought into close contact with other parts of the State.

The people generally have been people of moderate means, but famous for thrift, plainness and independence. It adjoined Anderson district in South Carolina, and as Scotch-Irish people came from Pennsylvania into western North and South Carolina their children came to Franklin in Georgia, but with them came many of pure English origin. The Cleveland, Humphreys, Gorham, Payne, Harden, Echols, Watson, Little, Chandler, and Blair families are all Scotch-Irish; while Wilkins, Sewell, Epperson, Rucker, Terrell, Hooper, Shannon, and Stovall are names of English people who came to this country from Virginia or North Carolina.

Lands were given away to actual settlers. They were productive, the health of the people good, and the population rapidly increased.

The Presbyterians, who came into Franklin at a very early day, organized several churches over a hundred years ago, which are still in existence. The Rev. Mr. Cartledge, who resided in Franklin, was pastor of one church for fifty years, having the longest pastorate ever held by a preacher of any name in Georgia.

The Methodists and Baptists came into the county at an early day and are very strong in the county. There are two famous camp-grounds belonging to the Methodists in the county where meetings have been held annually for many years. There has always been a good high school in Franklin, and good common schools are found in every neighborhood.

Franklin was very thinly settled for a considerable time after it was laid out, and in 1790 there were only in all the vast area which it covered 1,041 people, of whom 156 were slaves. When it was much reduced in size in 1810 there were 9,156 free and 1,056 slaves; in 1830 there were 10,107, of whom 2,370 were slaves.

There was up to 1792 great danger from Indian forays, and the scattered inhabitants lived much of the time in blockhouses. Near this period the Indians massacred a family of nine persons at one time, but after the formation of the Union in 1789 the troubles with the Cherokees were largely settled, and there was but little disturbance after that time.

The county is now much worn, and the people are generally in moderate circumstances, many of them quite poor, but the population is still considerable, being in 1890 over fifteen thousand of all classes. The people are entirely dependent on agriculture but are very industrious and moral, and are a happy, independent people; and while there is little attention paid to the higher education, there is a general attention to the fundamental branches of English.

WASHINGTON.

Washington in 1784, when it was first laid out, was a county of immense area, including what is now Greene, Hancock, Washington, Johnson, Montgomery and a part of Laurens and Oglethorpe, but the account we give now refers merely to that part of the original county which bears the name. It is very near the center of the State and is a still a county of large size, of which the flourishing little city of Sandersville is the county site. It includes in its boundary a section of what is known as the rotten limestone country, and is famous for the fossiliferous deposits belonging to the tertiary period. This limestone exists in such quantities that good lime has been made from it for market.

On the Ogeechee, the Buffalo and Kegg's creeks and Williamson swamp, and on the oak and hickory hills north of Sandersville the land at its first opening was very fertile, but the pine woods, which included much the larger part of the country, were in the early days of the century looked upon as of no value. The early comers took the oak and hickory lands, and the pine woods were thinly settled. The county was much exposed in its early settlement to Indian forays and was settled slowly.

The State had devoted a large part of Washington and Franklin for bounty land to its soldiers, and it was granted in lots of two hundred and fifty acres free from taxation for some years, and if one preferred to pay taxes he was to have two hundred and eighty-seven and one-half acres. Much of this land was of the best quality and many people came to the land granted them and made homes, though not a few sold their warrants. The long list of grants found in the Appendix does not show the settlers of Washington alone, but belongs to many who never came at all.

There was but little to attract to this dangerous frontier before the end of the Indian war, but although the danger was great the lands on the creeks and rivers and the oak and hickory lands north of Sandersville were so fertile that they drew many daring settlers, who had received their warrants from the State, and the population grew steadily, if not rapidly, for some years. In 1790 there were in all the country originally Washington 4,500, of whom only 649 were slaves; in 1810, 6,427 free and 3,313 slaves; in 1830, 6,000 free and 3,909 slaves; in 1890, 25,237 of all classes.

The first settlers as given by White were: Alexander Irwin, John Rutherford, Wm. Johnston, Jared Irwin, Wm. Irwin, Elisha Williams, Jacob Dennard, J. Beddingfield, P. Franklin, A. Sinquefield, Jos. Avant, John Sheppard, John Thomas, John Daniel, John Martin, B. Tennille, J. Burney, Hugh Lawson, John Shellman, Wm. Sapp, M. Murphy, John Jones, John Montgomery, John Stokes, M. Saunders, Geo. Galphin, Jacob Dennis, J. Nutt, D. Wood, W. Warthen, Jacob Kelly, Wm. May.

Many of these names are of Scotch origin, and many of these first settlers came from North Carolina, where a large colony of Scotch-Irishmen had settled. There were some of the settlers from Burke, Effingham and Wilkes and a few Virginians among the first comers. There were some slaveholders who had a small number of slaves, but the bulk of the people were poor and the fortunes possessed by them in after years were of their own making.

There was for twenty years after the settlement of Washington little to induce wealthy people to emigrate to it, but the land was so cheap and so fertile that those who came into the woods poor soon became independent and were rich in herds and flocks. There was no market nearer than Augusta, and there was but little to be sold and but little was bought. The houses were log cabins and the people were generally dependent entirely on their own labor, but the cotton machine was invented and one was brought to the county, and cotton planting began on a considerable scale after the century opened.

The tide of settlers came rushing in. They came with slaves to open new plantations. The poorer stock-raisers gave way and large plantations in the better lands became the rule, and by 1830 in the richer sections negro laborers had entirely supplanted the white yeomanry. This was, however, true only of the richer lands; there was much of the country occupied by the pine woods people, and there was among them the same condition of things that we have alluded to as belonging to the settlers in Liberty. There were a few very wealthy people in the county and a great many in moderate circumstances, and only a few who were very poor. The people as a rule lived plainly, and, while not famous for culture, were highly valued for their thrift and honesty.

The county site was not fixed until 1796, and the courts were held near what is now Warthen's. Saundersville, as it was first written, was named in honor of a Mr. Saunders who had a plantation on the place selected as the county site. It was in the center of the county near the pine belt, though in the oak woods. It was for many years an insignificant town, deriving its importance from its being the county site. It was incorporated and had an academy.

The academy at Sandersville was endowed by the State with the usual benefaction of one thousand acres of land, and afterward of an annual appropriation, and in addition to this it was allowed the privilege of running a lottery which was to be for the benefit of the academy. The lottery was in existence for a long time, as by the provisions of its charter it could continue until a certain sum was realized. The lottery and the endowment disappeared with the end of the war, and now the Washington county academy is merged into the graded school at Sandersville.

The Central railway passed directly through the poorer part of Washington, within three miles of Sandersville, and before the war much of the best retail trade of the county went to that city, but after the war the trade was given to the near-by villages of Tennille and Davisboro.

Sandersville began to improve rapidly and has continued to grow up to this time. It was surrounded by a wealthy country, and was for many years noted for its disregard of religion and morality. Some of the citizens were avowed infidels, and the lives of many of them openly profligate. There was but one apology for a church in the village, a dilapidated, unpainted shell of a house on the outskirts of the town. There was occasional preaching in the village, and no Sunday-school, but a change for the better set in about 1858.

The epicureans, who gave tone to society, either left the county or died, and a new and better class of men took their places. A neat church was built by the Methodists, then one by the Christians, and then one each by Baptists and Roman Catholics. Now in all these churches there are regular services.

The old uncomely academy has long since been abandoned, and one of the handsomest school buildings in the State has been erected.

The Federal army burned the court-house with its valuable records, and its place was taken by another, which is now being replaced by a very handsome and convenient edifice.

While there was little attention paid to religion in the first settlement of Washington, there were a few log churches both among Baptists and Methodists before the beginning of the century. Bishop Asbury mentions in his Journal preaching at Harris meeting-house and on Williamson's swamp. The Baptist church Bethlehem, near Warthen's, has a history going back to the early settlement of the county.

For many years after the county was settled all the wild revelry of frontier life was freely indulged in by the people. They drank almost universally, and often to excess, raced, gambled, and there was fair play given to all who chose to settle their quarrels in the ring. On court days and musters as late as 1850 there was fighting and drinking and gaming without any vigorous restraints, but now the county has the prohibition of the whisky traffic, and Sandersville and Tennille city governments, a law-abiding people, good schools and good churches.

Tennille, from being a mere station known as No. 13 on the road, has become quite a little city. The Central railroad, the Wrightsville and Tennille road, the road to Augusta and the short line to Sandersville give to the county all needful railroad facilities. Governor Jared Irwin, so famous in the early history of this county, lived and died in it, and his monument erected by the State stands on the public square in Sandersville.

GREENE.

Greene was formed from Washington in 1785. It was named Greene in honor of General Nathaniel Greene, and was composed of what is now Greene and Hancock and a part of Taliaferro, Oglethorpe and of Oconee. It was a magnificent county. The Oconee and Apalachee rivers and several large creeks ran through it, and the bottoms were wide and fertile. The larger part of the county was forest-covered hills of rich red land. The lower part, toward Hancock, was a fine gray land which was covered with a growth of small oaks, and at the first settling of the county was regarded as the least desirable part of the county, but is now the most thickly settled and prosperous part of it.

The first settlers, as Mr. White gives them, were: Thos. Haines, D. Gresham, W. Fitzpatrick, H. Graybill, Oliver Porter, John Bailey, Chas. Cessna, T. Baldwin, M. Rabun, Jno. George, Alex. Reed, M. Rogers, D. Dickson, W. Harris, Peyton Smith, E. E. Parks, Peter Cartright, G. W. Foster, Jno. Armour, Dr. Poullain, Jesse Perkins, Joel Newsome, James Armstrong, Major Beasly. To these might be added the Abercrombies, the Dales, Fouches, and Brewers.

These names are nearly all Virginia and North Carolina names. Greene was largely settled by people from these States and had in it a very few people from any other section. The list which is given by White includes many who were afterward in Oglethorpe and Hancock.

The first settlers lived on the creeks and near the river, and for their own protection in close proximity to each other. A blockhouse was generally built at a convenient distance, and the families upon the approach of the Indians fled to it for protection. The men left their families in the blockhouse and went into the fields to cultivate the corn patches from which they hoped to make their bread. Until the cessation of the Oconee war there was constant peril and the immigration of people of means was small; but by 1790 there were five thousand four hundred and five people in the several counties then known as Greene, of whom one thousand three hundred and seventy-seven were negroes. There was constant apprehension of Indian forays and troops of soldiers were kept under arms.

In 1794 there was a troop of dragoons commanded by Captain Jonas Fouche, of which we have a roster in White's collections. These dragoons were:

Captain Fouche, Peyton Smith, Geo. Phillips, William Browning, Chas. Harris, John Young, S. B. Harris, Wm. Heard, S. M. Devereaux, John Harrison, Abner Farmer, Isaac Stocks, Samuel Dale, Josiah McDonald, Douglas

Watson, Jesse Standifer, Wm. Scott, Arthur Foster, Wm. George, John Capps, R. Patrick, J. Jenkins, Chas. Watts, T. Byron, Jos. White, R. Finks, Geo. Owing, Wm. Coursey, Jos. Shaw, Jno. Pinkard, L. B. Jenkins, P. Watts, T. Scott, R. Walron, H. Potts, D. Lynch, S. Standifer, Jos. Heard, Jas. Moor, H. Gibson, R. Grimatt, George Reed, M. Wall, Jas. McGuire.

The militia districts mentioned were: Armour's, Browning's, Taylor's, Beard's, Melton's.

Although the county was organized in 1786, the first court does not seem to have met until 1790. The first estate is appraised in 1786. It consisted of:

Fifty bushels corn, 1 bay mare, 1 cow and calf, 1 heifer, some hogs, an ax, a hoe, a linen wheel, a brass kettle, a tea-kettle, a wash-tub, churn, candlesticks, bottles, slaye, tea-pots, bole, mugg; 200 acres land, £75.

The first will is that of Jos. Smith, a surveyor, made in 1786. His estate was, 17 cows, surveying instruments, 4 horses, 3 Bibles, 3 Testaments, 3 sermon books, 4½ yards gray cloth.

The first grand jury was: Thos. Harris, David Love, Walton Harris, David Gresham, Jno. A. Miller, Wm. Fitzpatrick, Wm. Heard, Moses Shelby, James Jenkins, Joseph White, Robert Baldwin, Wm. Shelby, Jesse Connell, Joseph Spradling, Wm. Daniel.

The grand jury presents as a "greate greavance" that these were more land-warrants than there was land.

The judge prescribes as a rule for lawyers that: "For the sake of a decent conformity with an ancient custom, and of a necessary distinction in the profession, that attorneys shall be heard in a black robe, but this rule was not to be enforced till the next session."

The cases in the early courts were largely for assault and battery, and when parties were convicted the fines were generally from three to ten dollars. One who had been convicted of manslaughter was sentenced to be branded on the left thumb with the letter M, and four convicted of forgery were to be hung.

The court-house in 1798 was a very inferior building, and the jail was a mere hut. As late as 1798 the United States soldiers were still quartered in the country to protect the settlers from Indian raids, for, though the Indians were nominally peaceable, they were likely at any time to give trouble. Despite the dangers from Indians and the hardships of the frontier immigrants poured in from North Carolina and from Virginia. Many of the North Carolinians came from Rowan and Mecklenburg and settled on Shoulderbone creek in Hancock. The Virginians came from Franklin, Brunswick, Prince George, Dinwiddie and Prince Edward and settled on the Apalachee and Oconee. The first comers to Greene were, as they were in Wilkes, generally men of small means. They were industrious and thrifty and prosperous. The tide of settlers was very constant and very full. At first nothing was produced but food crops, principally corn and cattle and hogs, but there was a large quantity of these. The range was wide and cattle and hogs fattened in the woods. A little tobacco was raised for market, but there was but little to sell and few purchasers for anything. The people lived within themselves. They made everything needful for comfort, and up to the war of 1812 Greene and Wilkes and Hancock were filled with plenty. The county produced everything needed for man or beast. There was corn, barley, rye, wheat, hogs, cattle, horses. There were few people of large wealth in the county up to 1812, and none who were squalidly poor. There were a few people like old Joel Early, who kept up the style of an old English baron, but the larger part of the people lived in solid comfort and made no pretenses. Living was exceedingly cheap, and board was two to four dollars per month. Unfortunately the drinking habits of the people were universal, and brandy and whisky were freely used, and they were distilled in quantities. Life in all this middle Georgia belt was so much the same that the story of one of these counties is the story of all.

The people of all these counties came from the same section and had the same features. They were, as far as education was concerned, beyond their children, who grew to manhood on the frontier, and who twenty years afterward settled in Jasper, Morgan or Jones. Most of those who signed deeds in Greene could write their names, but it was not so twenty years afterward. Those who grew to manhood during and just after the Revolution had scant opportunities for learning even elementary branches.

After the bringing in of the cotton-gin in the first years of the century, and as the country on the west of the Oconee was opened, the men who had small farms and raised provision crops entirely began to seek other homes and the farms were absorbed by the plantations.

After the war of 1812 wealth very rapidly increased in Greene and cotton planting was vigorously pressed. As was the case in Wilkes and Columbia negroes began to take the place of white people, the plantations of farms, and cotton of grain.

The effort of the planter from 1815 to 1850 was to raise all the cotton possible. Grass is the deadly foe of this textile plant, and now the Bermuda grass was brought into Greene. Mr. John Cunningham, a merchant of Greensboro in the early twenties, told the author that he brought the first small tuft of this grass to Greensboro and planted it in his garden. The garden was soon covered, the farm was next to follow, and the pestiferous grass, as it was regarded, spread so rapidly that in some cases the fields were simply surrendered to it and the planter counted his plantation as ruined. With the new lands opening, the Bermuda grass spreading, the fields once so fertile becoming washed and worn, the planters of Greene began to seek fresher lands in the west, and as in Wilkes the farms were absorbed by the plantations. The after history told of Wilkes and Burke is true of Greene.

It is now no longer a county of planters, but is a county of villages. The owners of the land reside in the small towns and the negro tenants work the fields. But while this is the fact now, it has been a fact to some extent for over forty years. Save that the freedman has taken the place of the slave, it is as it was when the overseer controlled the plantation before the war. This is true of the red lands, but not true of poorer lands in other parts of the county. Here there is improvement in every line.

The Presbyterians and the Baptists came into Greene with the first settlements and organized churches before they had meeting-houses. The Baptists had churches at Scull Shoals and Bairdstown shortly after the county was settled, and occupied jointly with the Presbyterians the building called Siloam meeting-house, then on the hill overlooking Greensboro. Here Mr. Ray had an academy, and for its support an appropriation was made by the Legislature.

The Methodists entered the county as soon as they came into Georgia, and soon had a number of preaching places. Bishop Asbury preached at Little Brittain, and at Bush's, now known as Liberty, and the South Carolina Conference was held at this church in 1808. Asbury and McKendree were both present. Lovick Pierce was ordained an elder and Bishop Wm. Capers was admitted into the connection as a preacher on trial. There was a famous camp-ground at Hastings, where the people of Greene used to assemble annually for religious meetings. One of the most remarkable revivals of religion ever known in Georgia reached

Greensboro in 1827, when Judge Longstreet and many of the most prominent men in the county were converted. Greene is now well supplied with churches and school-houses, and while the country neighborhoods have declined, the villages of Greensboro, Union Point, White Plains, Penfield, Woodville and Veazy have grown up, and the people of the county have religious and educational advantages beyond those at any previous time; and while much of what was once the most fertile land in Greene is not now productive, the average of production per acre is perhaps greater now than at any time since 1820.

Greensboro was selected as the county site as soon as the county was laid off, and an academy was provided for. The trustees were granted one thousand acres of land for its endowment. Commissioners were appointed to lay off the town and build the academy and repair Siloam meeting-house. The Rev. Jas. Ray was appointed rector.

Greensboro drew to it from its first settlement a fine class of citizens and soon became famous for its culture and refinement. It was the county site of a wealthy county, and while in the early days the planters mainly lived on their plantations, the lawyers and doctors, preachers and teachers, as well as the court officers, nearly all lived in the town. Here Dr. Lovick Pierce practised medicine during the time he was a local preacher, and here Dr. Adiel Sherwood, the great Baptist preacher, lived, and while living here in 1829 he published the first book, "Gazetteer of Georgia," which attempted to tell of the resources of the State. Here Judge Longstreet began the practise of law and became famous as a wit and jurist. Here he married and as has been seen became a Christian and Methodist preacher. Here Wm. C. Dawson, long time senator and one of the most popular of Georgians, had his home and practiced his profession. Thomas Foster, the genial and gifted young Congressman, practised law in this village.

John Bethune and Vincent Sandford, each clerks of the court and men of position and influence, lived here. Near here the great Georgia bishop, Geo. Foster Pierce, was born, and here he spent his childhood, and from Greensboro he went to college at Athens. Here he decided to enter the Methodist itinerancy, and laid down his law books and entered the ministry.

The eccentric but sterling Governor Peter Early lived in this county, and is buried on what was his manor. His father, Joel Early, came from Virginia, and purchased a very large body of land on the Oconee river, where he located what he called Early's Manor. His will is on record and is a striking document. It gives direction not only as to the distribution of his property, but as to the methods of pruning his apple orchards and resting his fields. He bequeathed his land to trustees to be given to his favored sons when they were thirty-six years old. Two of his sons he disinherited, one for extravagance, the other for disrespect. The descendants of the Greene county people are found in all sections of the Southern country, and they have been among the most useful and distinguished of the people.

CHAPTER V.

1789 TO 1800.

George Walton Governor—Convention 1789—Some of its Provisions—First General Thanksgiving Day Observed—Governor Telfair—General Washington's Visit to Georgia—Governor Mathews—New Counties—Educational Advancement—The Old Field School—Shooting Matches—Gander-pulling —Dancing—Fighting in the Ring—Horse-swapping—Drinking Habits—General Character of the People—The Yazoo Troubles—General Jackson's Course—Rescinding of the Act—Convention of 1795—Convention of 1798 General Jackson Governor — Pine-barren Frauds — History of Elbert, Columbia, Screven, Oglethorpe, Hancock, Bulloch, Bryan, McIntosh, Jackson, Montgomery, Lincoln—Georgia in the Federal Union.

Authorities: Stevens, Vol. II., White's Statistics, White's Historical Collections, Sherwood, Chappel's Pamphlet on the Yazoo and Pine-barren Frauds, Jackson's Letters of Sicillius, State Papers Quoted by Chappel, Watkins's Digest, Marbury & Crawford's Digest, Clayton's Compilation, Campbell's Georgia Baptists, Smith's History of Methodism, Wilson's Presbyterian Necrology, Georgia Scenes, Georgia Gazette, Georgia Chronicle, Cranch's Reports U. S. Supreme Court, Vol. VI.

Georgia ratified the Constitution early in 1788, but it was late in the year before the needful nine States had acted and the Union formed. George Walton, of whom we have spoken elsewhere, was governor when the Constitution was ratified. He had been of the four who called the first meeting of the Whigs in Savannah. He had signed the Declaration of Independence, had been a member of the Continental Congress, a member of the Council of Safety, and officer in the army, and one of the first of the Georgia judges. His published charges are not the best specimens of clear expression and of faultless English, but they are vigorous and sensible. Walton has not received his just meed from Georgia historians. He did not get on well with General McIntosh or Edward Telfair, who were Scotch lairds both, and rich men, and clashed with the Virginian. A convention had been called in the latter part of the year 1788, which met early in November. This convention was composed of George Handley, Jos. Clay, Jr., Mathew McAllister, Nathan Brownson, Thomas Lane, Edward Telfair, George Walton, James McNeil, Chas. Crawford, Wm. Few, Arthur Fort, Florence Sullivan, John King, Christopher Hillary, John Milton, Henry Osborne, James Armstrong, Nathaniel Pendleton, John Rutherford, Jared Irwin, John Watts, N. Cleveland, M. Woods, Sam'l Gardner, Chas. Abercrombie, Wm. Grier, Thomas Houghton.

This convention formed a Constitution which was submitted to one which met in May. The members of this convention were : Wm. Gibbons, Asa Emanuel, Justus H. Scheuber, Jos. Carmichael, Henry Carr, Benj. Lanier, Jno. Green. Nathan Brownson, David Emanuel, Hugh Lawson, Wm. Little, Abraham Marshall, W. F. Booker, Leonard Marbury, John Talbot, Jeremiah Walker, Lachlan McIntosh, Alex. Brisset, Jared Irwin, John Watts, Joshua Williams, M. Woods.

The convention revised and accepted the Constitution proposed. The instrument adopted required two Houses. Senators were to be twenty-eight years old, and have £250 in property; members of the House £150; no clergyman was eligible to a seat in either House; representation was to be equalized; the Senate should elect a governor on nomination from the House. This Constitution was in force about ten years. It was in full force in November, and Seaborn Jones was Speaker of the House, and ex-Governor Brownson President of the Senate. The House sent to the Senate the names of two nominees for governor. Ex-Governor Houston and ex-

Governor Telfair were the parties nominated. When the vote was counted it was found that each had the same vote. On the next ballot Governor Telfair was unanimously chosen.

The first Thanksgiving Day ordered by the United States authorities came while the Assembly was in session, and one of the first acts of the new Legislature was to provide for the observance of this day.

The church in Augusta had now been made habitable, and was being supplied for the time by Dr. Palmer of the Richmond academy. He was requested by the Legislature to provide a form of prayer and to preach a Thanksgiving sermon, which he did to the great satisfaction of the body, who very decorously attended service, and who the next day returned thanks to Mr. Palmer for his well-adapted sermon.

GEORGE WASHINGTON.

Georgia had already elected her two senators, and now made provisions for electing the three members of the House.

General Washington, who was making a tour through the United States, came to Augusta from Savannah and was received by the governor with due formality. The president always fixed his quarters at a public house, and positively refused to be entertained privately, but accepted the civilities which were always extended, so he had his dinings and the inevitable ball, attended the commencement of the Richmond academy, and gave the young students sundry

copies of the classics, which had been offered as prizes, with his autograph in them.

There had been up to this time no great deal of political strife in Georgia. The bitter antagonisms of the past had been personal rather than political, and the sectional feeling had not been as yet manifest. Savannah and the low-country had ruled the State from its first settlement without resistance or protest, but it now became evident that the people of the up-country were not to be ignored or overshadowed by the wealthy and cultured men of the low-country. These educated low-country men were all Democrats in public life and aristocrats in their social affinities. They were bitterly opposed to Federalism and sympathized with the French, and so when Mr. Telfair of Burke, formerly of Chatham, offered for governor the second time he was defeated by the rugged and uneducated Federalist, Colonel Geo. Mathews, who had only been in the State ten years, and who had been governor for one term already.

While Governor Mathews was in office that irrepressible old soldier, Elijah Clarke, decided the time had come to take possession of the Indian lands on the west of the Oconee, and so gathering a body of daring spirits about him they went together into the wilderness. Governor Mathews ordered him to withdraw, but he refused, and only after the militia was ordered out would he return.

It was during this period that Georgia became greatly excited by what many Georgians have always called the Yazoo fraud. Such was the extent of the angry feelings aroused by the act thus characterized that anything like a calm consideration of the matter was impossible then, and for fifty years afterward there was but one side of the case looked at; and such is the verdict of history even now, that I may find it difficult to make a fair, calm and judicial statement of the facts concerning the sale of the western lands.

The English colonial office before the Revolution, against the protest of South Carolina, recognized the colony of Georgia as having the title to all the lands lying west of Savannah river, containing what is now Georgia, Alabama, and Mississippi, and when England recognized the State of Georgia as free and independent, she gave to this State, composed then of less than thirty thousand people, a clear title to all that land. That part of this territory beyond the Chattahoochee was claimed by two separate parties. The Spanish claimed it by right of conquest, and the State of South Carolina claimed that it was a part of the original grant to the proprietors to which she had fallen heir.

The United States Government now came in with the plea that as large expenses had been incurred by the Continental Congress in conducting the war to a successful conclusion, and as the public lands had been pledged for payment of the national debt, that Georgia was bound in honor to do as Virginia and the other States had done, to relinquish her title to this unoccupied section. The general government also claimed that by the Constitution which Georgia had adopted the United States was the only party who had a right to treat with the Indians, and that Georgia by accepting the Constitution virtually gave her consent to the cession of this territory.

Georgia consented to make the cession, but the conditions she laid down were such that the general government refused to accept her proposition. Mr. Chappel, who examined closely into the matter, is of the opinion that these conditions were made purposely offensive by those who expected and intended to buy the land for a mere pittance. (Chappel's Pamphlet on Yazoo Fraud.)

The treasury of the State was empty, the State troops were unpaid, the people were not able to pay heavy taxes and were unwilling to pay any. The State currency was greatly depreciated, and the only hope of relief was the sale of the Indian lands.

In 1789 three companies—the Virginia Yazoo Company, the South Carolina Land Company, and the Tennessee Land Company—each composed of prominent men, proposed to purchase the land. The members of the South Carolina Land Company mentioned in Watkins were Alexander Moultrie, Isaac Huger, Wm. Clay Snipes, and Thos. Washington; and the Virginia Yazoo Company were Patrick Henry, David Ross, Wm. Cowan, Abraham B. Venable, Jno. B. Scott, Wm. Cock Ellis, Francis Watkins, and John Watts; and of the Tennessee Land Company, Zach Cox, Thos. Gilbert, John Strother, and, as appears from a record in the Wilkes county court, Steven Heard, Wm. Downs, Henry Candler, Jno. Gardner, Middleton Woods, Wm. Cox, and Thos. Carr were admitted into the company after the purchase was made.* This last company, which purchased the valley of the Tennessee, was exclusively a Georgia company.

These companies bought fifteen million five hundred thousand acres for about two hundred thousand dollars, payable in two years. The sale was made in good faith, and as far as we can see no complaint was made about it. Ed Telfair was governor and he signed the act; and it would have been a fact accomplished if the purchasers had been able to pay the amount agreed on, but they were not able to pay in coin, and tendered State currency and certificates, which the Legislature refused to receive, and the sale was declared a nullity because of this failure of the purchasers to pay the price. There was no charge of corruption made against any of the parties engaged in this first purchase, although they were fairly warned by the authorities of the general government that they could not

* See original record in Washington.

lawfully sell the land to which the Indian title had not been extinguished and which they proposed to buy.†

In 1794 the land was still unsold. The soldiers were clamorous for money, the treasury was still empty, and there was little hope of replenishing it unless Georgia could realize something from her rather uncertain interest in these western lands. It was known they were for sale and five companies came forward to buy them. Four of these companies united and agreed to give Georgia five hundred thousand dollars in cash for her interest, the purchasers to take the titles as they were and to get rid of all difficulties and arrange matters with the general government and with Spain and the Indians. These companies were the Georgia, the Upper Mississippi Company, the Georgia-Mississippi Company, and the Tennessee Land Company. These companies were not all Georgians, but a company of Georgians offered seven hundred thousand dollars for the property on somewhat different conditions.

The combined companies bought the land, but Governor Mathews vetoed the bill. They then had another introduced which was not so objectionable to him, and it finally passed.

There was a sharp contest between the rival companies and much lobbying. There was a small party who was unwilling to sell at all, a larger one who preferred the Augusta company, and a majority who favored a sale to the consolidated companies.

At last, after a long discussion, on February 7, 1795, the sale was made by a vote of 10 to 8 in the Senate, and 19 to 9 in the House.

The senators who voted for the bill were: Mr. King, Mr. Wright, Mr. Oneal, Mr. Wylie, Mr. Walton, Mr. Hampton, Mr. Cauthorn, Mr. Gresham, Mr. Thomas, and Mr. Mann.

† They were severely censured afterward, but not at that time.

Those who voted against it were: Mr. Milledge, Mr. Lanier, Mr. Morrison, Mr. Irwin, Mr. Blackburn, Mr. Pope, Mr. Mitchell, Mr. Wood.

The members of the House who voted for the sale of the lands were: Mr. T. P. Carnes, Mr. Longstreet, Mr. Gindrat, Mr. Lachlan McIntosh (not General McIntosh), Mr. Gresham of Greene, Mr. Mowbray, Mr. Gilbert, Mr. Moore, Mr. Howell, Mr. Musgrove, Mr. Harden, Mr. Watkins, Mr. Stephen Heard, Mr. Worsham, Mr. Thomas Heard, Mr. Wilkinson, Mr. King, Mr. Rabun, Mr. Geo. Walker.

The members who voted against it were: Mr. George Jones, Mr. D. B. Mitchell, Mr. John Jones, Mr. McNeal, Mr. Clement Lanier, Mr. Shepherd, Mr. J. B. Maxwell. (U. S. State papers.)

The governor reluctantly signed the bill and it was a law. The members of the combined companies are not all given in Watkins's Digest, where alone the act is found, but as there given they were Senator Gunn, Judge McAlister, Judge Nathaniel Pendleton, George Walker, Nicolas Long, Thomas Glascock, Ambrose Gordon, Thos. Cumming, Jno. B. Scott, Jno. C. Nightingale, Wade Hampton, Zack Coxe, Mr. Maher. There were associated with them many whose names are not given, among them the celebrated Judge James Wilson of Pennsylvania.

Among those whose bid was not accepted, but who tried to buy the lands for a little over a cent an acre, were General John Twiggs, Jno. Wereat, Wm. Gibbons, Wm. Few.

No men stood higher in Georgia than the men who composed these several companies and the members of the Legislature who made the sale, and no men were in higher repute than some of these in an after time. The charge has been made, and is by many believed, that this sale was effected by corrupt means, and it has been known in history as the Yazoo fraud.

It was charged that the companies who made the purchase bribed the men who sold the land by giving them shares in the land companies, and there was a color of truth to the charge brought out when it was found that all who voted for the sale did have shares of stock in the land company except one man, Robert Watkins. The governor who signed the bill was never accused of being a participant in any of the profits. The members of the Legislature did have stock in the companies, but it was never proved that any one of them had not paid for his stock a fair price and was guilty of selling his vote.

The excitement on this subject did not, however, immediately follow the passage of the act. It was quietly acquiesced in, and but for the efforts of one man would probably have received no further attention than had been given to the act of 1789. The first of the purchase money was paid, the title passed, when James Jackson, the senator from Georgia, in a series of articles signed Sicillius, violently assailed the act. These articles appeared in the two papers in Georgia, the *Gazette* in Savannah and the *Chronicle* in Augusta. They attracted wide attention and secured general indorsement. General Jackson resigned his seat in the Senate and came home and ran for State senator from Chatham, with the avowed purpose of having the act repudiated by the Legislature. The act was rescinded, and it was ordered that it be consumed by fire, and in front of the newly occupied State-house in Louisville the engrossed act was burned.

The money paid was to be refunded to those who called for it, and the Legislature ordered that all record of the act should be expunged from official documents.

The first digest of Georgia laws made by Watkins, for which the State had subscribed largely, was rejected because it contained the odious act, and for a hundred years with the masses in Georgia the one thing needed to render a public man odious was to say he was connected with the Yazoo fraud.

It is not my province to express any opinion on the issues involved, nor to take any part in the angry discussion of those days, but I think it due to the truth of history to make a full statement of the whole matter. That the sale was made legally there was no question, and though a free and sovereign State might repudiate the act of her officials and refuse to carry out an obnoxious measure, it was evident to all that if the matter could come before any court, State or Federal, the act would be recognized as regular; and it was quietly decided to end the discussion by rescinding the act and selling the land to the United States government, and leave it to settle with the claimants. This was done during the next decade, though in doing it the fiery Jackson, one of the commissioners, became involved in a difficulty which resulted in a duel with Mr. James Seagrove, a representative of the United States. A treaty was made between "the two sovereignties," * and Georgia thus surrendered her western lands. The price agreed on was $1,500,000 in cash, and the extinction of the title of the Indians to all lands east of the Chattahoochee.

At the time the sale was made, and for many years afterward, the conviction was general that the sale was fraudulent and all connected with it were criminal, and Judge Chappel, in his pamphlet, is exceedingly severe on all who had part in it. I have confined myself to a simple statement of facts, and leave my readers to draw their own conclusions. If these facts, which are easily verified, remove the odium which for this hundred years has rested on men whose character was otherwise untarnished, and show that there was no proof of criminal intent, and that this Legislature was not exceptional in being the only bribed body

* Language of the treaty.

in Georgia history, it ought to be a gratifying fact to all Georgians.

The Supreme Court of the United States in a celebrated decision on this subject did not admit any fraud, and sustained the legality of the sale.*

The Legislature elected in 1795 was elected on the one issue of repudiating and annulling the acts of the one which preceded it, and Jared Irwin, a Scotch-Irishman by descent but a native of North Carolina, who had been a brave soldier and a famous Indian fighter, was chosen as governor.

There was little difficulty encountered in carrying any measure which looked to the undoing of that which had been done the year before, and as soon as the acts could be passed the act of 1794 was declared null and void, and the order was made to return the money paid to those who applied for it.

The excitement in the State rose very high. It was openly charged that every man in the Legislature who voted for it but one had shares in the company and was corruptly influenced, and one man at least lost his life because of his course.

The list I have given of the members of the House contain the names of men whose reputation was never assailed before. It is I think clearly shown that the members of the Legislature and many others had shares in the venture, but it has never been shown that they did not come honestly by them or designed to defraud the State.

While there may be some question as to whether those connected with the Yazoo act were guilty of fraudulent

---

* I have referred to all the sources of information on this subject accessible to me, and while each separate statement has been carefully established, I have not attempted to support each by designating the place where it is to be found. The books referred to are Stevens's History, White's Statistics, Chappel's Tract, Watkins's Digest, U. S. State papers, the Georgia *Gazette*, Journal of the Legislature, Gilmer's Georgians, Cranch Reports, Vol. 6.

intent, there can be none that the Pine-barren frauds, were many of them frauds pure and simple. These frauds were the securing of fictitious grants to immense areas of pine lands in the unsettled parts of Georgia, chiefly Montgomery county. It is needless to enter now into a detailed statement of how these frauds were brought about; how, as will appear from a study of the list of headrights appended to this history, grants for not only thousands of acres were made, but hundreds of thousands, where not a single condition had been met. Men had granted under the great seal five hundred thousand acres of land, not one foot of which had been legally secured and not an acre of which they had in possession. How many grants of large bodies of barren land were legal we have no means of knowing, but all the large grants of 1794 and 1795 are suspicious, and nearly all of them were repudiated. It was never designed by the men who secured the grants to take possession of them, but it is possible that those in whose names they stand were innocent purchasers.

Judge Chappel in his "Reminiscences" recovers this almost lost chapter in Georgia history, and as late as the year 1899 men have appeared in Georgia with old grants to land which never existed. These grants were all professedly located in Washington, or what was afterward Emanuel, Johnson and Laurens counties, and a much larger amount was granted in the new county of Montgomery, which was cut off from Washington. There were granted altogether over seven million acres—more land than was to be found in all the territory of the county.

The State repudiated nearly all these grants and cancelled the patents, and no lands were actually taken under them; but the speculators who had secured possession of the fraudulent patents sold them to parties ignorant of the true state of things, and an earnest effort has been made for many years by the defrauded purchasers of worthless scrip to secure from the State some compensation for their losses.

Judge Chappel, who was in the Legislature and on a committee to look into this question, in 1839, has given a full account of these Pine-barren frauds in his interesting "Reminiscences."

A convention had been called by the Legislature of 1794 to revise the Constitution, and it met in the spring of 1795. It was composed of the following members:

Chatham—Josiah Tattnall, Jr., Thos. Gibbons, Noble W. Jones.

McIntosh—Jos. Clay, John Wereat. These gentlemen did not live in McIntosh but were permitted to represent it and were elected by the electors in that county.

Burke—B. Davis, D. Emanuel, Thos. King.

Elbert—L. Higginbottom, S. Heard, W. Barnett.

Glynn—Jno. Girradeau.

Greene—David Gresham, Phil Hunter, W. Fitzpatrick.

Richmond—John Milton, Geo. Walker, Phil Clayton.

Screven—B. Lanier, Wm. Skinner, P. R. Smith.

Warren—Levi Pruitt, Jno. Cobbs, P. Goodwin.

Washington—John Rutherford, Geo. Franklin, R. Wilkinson.

Wilkes—B. Catchings, Silas Mercer, D. Creswell.

It made no changes in the Constitution and only a few additions to it, and referred the question of repudiating the sale of the Yazoo land to the succeeding Legislature.

This convention made provision for another convention which should meet in 1798 and which met accordingly. It was the largest which had ever assembled in Georgia, and the ablest. All the previous Constitutions had prohibited ministers of the gospel from being members of the General Assembly.

Jesse Mercer, a sterling young Baptist preacher, was a member of the convention, and when it was proposed to introduce the same provision into the new Constitution, he proposed to amend by excluding also lawyers and doctors. The amendment resulted in having the whole provision rejected, and since that time it has been no disqualification for a member of the Legislature to be a minister of the gospel.

The convention was composed of the following delegates:

Bryan—Jos. Clay, J. B. Maxwell, Jno Pray.

Burke—Benj. Davis, Jno. Morrison, Jno. Milton.

Bulloch—James Bird, Andrew E. Wells, Charles McCall.

Camden—James Seagrove, Thos. Stafford.

Chatham—James Jackson, James Jones, George Jones.

Columbia—James Simms, W. A. Drane, Jas. McNeal.

Effingham—John King, John London, Thos. Polhill.

Elbert—Wm. Barnett, R. Hunt, Benj. Mosely.

Franklin—A. Franklin, R. Walters, Thos. Gilbert.

Glynn—Jno. Burnett, Jno. Cowper, Thos. Spalding.

Greene—Geo. W. Foster, Jonas Fouche, Jas. Nisbet.

Hancock—Chas. Abercrombie, Thomas Lamar, Matthew Rabun.

Jefferson—Peter Carnes, Wm. Fleming, R. D. Gray.

Jackson—George Wilson, James Pittman, Joseph Humphries.

Liberty—James Cochran, James Powell, James Dunwoody.

Lincoln—Henry Ware, G. Wooldridge, Jared Grace.

McIntosh—Jno. H. McIntosh, Jas. Gignilliat.

Montgomery—Benjamin Harrison, John Watts, John Jones.

Oglethorpe—John Lumpkin, Thos. Duke, B. Pope.

Richmond—R. Watkins, G. Jones.

Screven—Lewis Lanier, J. H. Rutherford, Jas. Oliver.

Washington—John Watts, Geo. Franklin, Jared Irwin.

Warren—John Lawson, A. Fort, W. Stith.

Wilkes—M. Talbott, B. Talliferro, J. Mercer.

This convention formed a Constitution which was not materially changed until after the war between the States. The ablest men in the State, men of the broadest culture and the strongest minds, were in the body which formed it, and the instrument was worthy of the men who gave it life. The convention was pronounced in its condemnation of what it believed to be a gigantic fraud, and made stringent provisions against a repetition of such an occurrence.

General Jackson having now secured his ends, was elected governor, and the Legislature chosen was in perfect accord with him. He had rather a stormy time as governor. He had denounced many of the leading men in Georgia as conspiring to rob the State. He was devoid of fear, and pursued his foes with ferocity, and they were not disposed to spare him. He was very bitter toward the Watkins family, and had Colonel Watkins arrested and tried by court-martial for having taken, without the consent of the commander-in-chief, Jackson himself, some old Indian guns which were in the arsenal in Augusta, with which Watkins armed his militia on a muster day. John Berrien, the treasurer of the State, who had been a gallant officer during the Revolution, had been victimized by a dishonest clerk who had made way with some of the funds offered to the treasury by the Yazoo purchasers, and which the State had refused to receive. The treasurer promptly made good the loss out of his private property, but he was impeached for embezzlement, and he believed the prosecution was originated by the governor. In neither case was there conviction,* but so bitter was the feeling that there was more than one street brawl and duel resulting in a bloody end.

The conflict between the Federal and Republican parties was now very fierce. It had begun during the latter years

* I found these forgotten facts in an old pamphlet, kindly given me by Mr. Garlick, in Waynesboro, Ga., in which there was an official report of the court-martial and impeachment trial.

of General Washington's rule, and had become very serious during the days of John Adams. The feeling in Georgia was very intense. The governor was a Republican of most decided convictions, and so was the main body of the people. It would seem from the vote of 1796, when Jackson received 6,200, Abercrombie 4,357, Barnett 3,965, Thomas Glascock 2,644, George Walton 2,357, John Milton 1,042, that Jackson, Telfair and Barnett were Republicans, and Glascock, Walton and Milton were Federalists.* The Republicans were largely in the majority, and Abraham Baldwin and James Jackson were elected senators. Governor Jackson then resigned his place as governor and returned to the Senate.

ABRAHAM BALDWIN.

The rush of immigrants to upper Georgia during this period was constant, and the State doubled its population in ten years. The lands were given away and the Virginians and North Carolinians came in great colonies to take up headrights and make settlements. These newcomers were of all classes. Many of them had little property other than they could bring on a pack-horse, but some of them had a few slaves. They built their cabins in the wilderness. A small smoky cabin with a dirt floor was the home of most of them. They came mainly from Virginia, and the

* I am indebted for this fact to my young friend, Professor Phillips, of the University of Georgia.

best blood of England was found in the veins of many an immigrant who had but little education and but little property. There was a very large immigration from middle North Carolina of Scotch-Irish people who came to Warren, Hancock and Wilkes. The farms taken by them were generally small, two hundred acres being, as a rule, the size of a farm. They raised cattle, sheep, hogs and horses, and as a rule aimed only at first to make a living. In our study of the counties the features of every-day life will be more clearly brought out.

During the period under survey the first Catholic church in Georgia was founded by a body of Maryland Catholics who settled in what was then Wilkes, and afterward Taliaferro county. The Catholics had been forbidden a settlement in Georgia during the colonial days, but after the Revolution, when there was freedom of religious worship, they began to come into the seacoast city of Savannah and a number of refugees from Hayti went to Augusta, and in 1802 a church was built in Savannah, but according to Evans, who is very accurate, they had a congregation in Wilkes in 1794.

There was little prosperity in any of the churches during this period. The bitterness of politics, the wild speculation in lands, and the general excitement aroused by the Yazoo sale, with its fierce antagonism, were not favorable to the progress of religion, and the churches all declined.

It was impossible under the circumstances of the pioneers for regular schools to be conducted, and many a man who owned in after time one thousand acres of land could barely write his name, and very many women of the best families were never a day in a schoolroom. The want of education among the better classes in upper Georgia resulted largely from the state of things we have just seen. The same thing was true except in rare cases in Southern Georgia. Governor Gilmer says his first teacher was a vagabond sailor, a cruel disciplinarian who used to whip the children on cold days for exercise. He was a thief and fled the country.

In that inimitable book "Georgia Scenes," there is a graphic picture of the "Turn-out," in which Mr. St. John, the Yankee teacher, after a brave fight with his pupils, came out second best; and Mr. Malcolm Johnston, in his "Dukesboro Tales," presents a realistic picture of the old-field school after the century began. The house of the old-field school was of logs, the seats were backless benches made of split logs. The light came into the schoolrooms from an opening in the logs, closed merely with a shutter of clapboards. The teacher began his school at seven in the morning in summer and closed near sunset, and in winter began as soon as it was possible for the scholars to get to school after the sun was up. There was little studied besides, in the language of the times, the three R's, "readin', ritin', and rithmetic," and it was considered by no means best for girls to study arithmetic. For these services the school-teacher received the full payment of fifty cents per month, payable generally in provisions.

Among the amusements of the people at that period and for a score of years afterward, were gander-pulling, horse-racing, shooting-matches, and country dances. Each man owned a Kentucky rifle with a long barrel, a delicate trigger and accurate sight. Accustomed from his boyhood to shoot the rifle, the frontiersman became wonderfully expert and was proud of his skill. To hit the bull's-eye with every bullet was the aim of the rifleman. The crowds met at the cross-roads, a beef was to be shot for, and each man paid his fair share of what the beef was worth, which was generally about twenty-five cents. The mark was set up and the best shot had the choice of one of the quarters into which the beef was divided.

The quarter race was another favorite sport. Wherever

there was a cross-roads grocery there was a race-track of a quarter of a mile. The races were between the horses from the farms. The bets were small generally, a quart of whisky or peach brandy.

Gander-pulling was another favorite amusement. The feathers were clipped short on the bird's neck, which was then greased or soaped. The poor bird was suspended from a bar between two poles. The horseman dashed under the bar at full speed and caught as he ran the neck of the gander and endeavored to pull off its head. The rider who succeeded in tearing the head from the body of the doomed bird had the body for his pay.

The country dance, so graphically described by Judge Longstreet, was universal until it was driven away by the opposition of the Baptists and Methodists in the early years in the century.

The fight in the ring, for the championship, was as certain as the crowd gathered. In every county there was a best man. He was the champion but not the unchallenged king of the ring. Bob Stallings and Bill Durham were not fictitious characters, and the fight so graphically described by Judge Longstreet was such as was seen on every justice court day for many years after the settlement of Georgia. One of the first laws ever passed by the Georgia Legislature was to punish biting and gouging.

These barbarous customs were not confined to the humbler classes, for in a rough-and-tumble fight between two great politicians, distinguished lawyers both, one of them said, to prevent the other from gouging him, he caught his finger in his mouth and bit it to the bone. Disgusting as these details are, they are history.

Horses were abundant; they were cheap and were indispensable to the farmer, however small his farm, and no man was too poor to own one. Horse-swapping was a fine art, and a horse-jockey was a regular professional who prided himself on his ability to palm off a poor plug on an unsuspecting victim.

The drinking habits of the people were fearfully bad. Everybody drank, many to excess, nearly all moderately. No one condemned drinking except the Methodists, whose general rules forbade all drinking except in cases of necessity, which cases were, alas! too common.

To distil corn whisky and peach brandy was not at all reprehensible, and one of the best men in Georgia, an enthusiastic and liberal Methodist, who, because he thought slavery was wrong, freed all his slaves, left his *still to his son*, who was himself a Methodist class-leader. To get drunk was mildly blamable, but to drink in moderation was temperance.

The people as a body were honest and truthful, and as considerate of women as a knight-errant. They were good husbands and tender fathers. They feared no peril, and shrank from no hardship. Most of them had been brought up on the frontiers of Virginia and North Carolina, or Georgia, and had never known restraint, and were as free as the deer on their hills.

There were now two Georgias—the old Georgia around and below Savannah, and the new Georgia which was above and west of Augusta. In these the social life was very different. The low-country had rallied rapidly after the Revolution, and society had taken on again the features it had borne before the war came. It had not as yet recovered entirely from the devastating effects of the war, but was rapidly doing so. In Columbia and Wilkes life had to begin over again after the war closed, and on the Oconee frontier everything was in a formative state. In the eastern counties of the up-country the rudeness of the first days of frontier life was now gone from some of the homes, and the comforts and even elegancies of life were to be found. The best homes were still double log cabins, but they had tight roofs and stone chimneys, and there was now more than one room for the entire family.

Perhaps the account given of Wilkes and Greene in the last chapter is as accurate a picture of life in the up-country as I can give. The amusements of the people were of a rude kind, but were much the same as were to be found on the border in all the States where Virginians were largely settlers.

There is nowhere else so graphic and exact an account of social conditions of this period as are found in the writings of Judge Longstreet, and in a sketch written by the Judge, and only lately published by Bishop Fitzgerald, there is in his story of the "Rise and Fall of Darby Anvill" a most interesting statement of the condition of things in middle Georgia just before the beginning of the century.

Darby Anvill was an ignorant but thrifty Virginia blacksmith who aspired to a place in the Legislature, and in giving an account of the campaign the Judge brings out a fine picture of the motley company who took up headrights in upper Georgia. Although these plain, uneducated, independent, narrow-minded people had in many cases sprung from the best English and Scotch stock, they had had no advantages of education, and were in the main people of little property, but in every county there were a few people, doctors, lawyers and teachers, and a few preachers, who were recognized because of their culture and position as rightful leaders.

The wise and witty story of the Judge brings out so vividly the two classes that his own account is better than any which another can give.

Darby the blacksmith had become ambitious to go to the Legislature. Some of his friends had espoused his cause, and the intelligent few were shocked at his impudence. The little extracts from the sketch of the Judge gives an accurate rendering of the dialect, as well as a true picture of the rural people of the humbler class.

* * * * * *

"Well," said Jimmy Johns, "may I say you is a candidate?"

"Jimmy, you is a free man, and has a right to say what you please."

"And I am a free man and I'll say what I please, too," said Job Snatch.

"And so am I," said Seth Weed.

"Why, what's got into these boys," chuckled old Darby. "I believe they are gwine to make me a can'date, whether I will or no. I did not know I had so much pop'larity."

* * * * * *

"Darby," inquired Smith, "is it possible that you are a candidate for the Legislature?"

"Why not?" said Anvill, with a blush.

"Why, you are utterly unqualified; you will disgrace yourself."

"I know," said Anvill, "that I'd make a mighty poor out speakin' agin' lawyers, but I reckon as how I could vote as good as them."

"You are mistaken, Darby," said Jones; "it requires a better head to vote right than to speak right."

* * * * * *

"Now, Mr. Smith, you say I'd disgrace myself to go to the 'Sembly, and I reckon it's so, for I'm like my neighbors here, hard-working people, what hain't got no business doing nothin' but workin' for great folks and rich folks, nohow. Now, I want to ax you a few questions, and firstly of the first place, to begin at the beginnin', hain't a poor man as free as a rich man?"

"Certainly."

"And didn't they fight for liberty as well as rich ones?"

"Yes."

"Well, hain't they as honest as rich men?"

"No doubt of it."

"Well, if a poor man is as free as a rich man, and they fit for liberty as well as them, and is as honest, how comes it that some people that's the smartest in the world votes for nobody havin' votes but them that's got land?"

* * * * * *

I have merely made this extract to give a clearer insight into the state of society than could be secured from any description. As the lands were given away all classes found homes in the new settlements, and men of the class of the ambitious blacksmith were side by side and equals before the law with those whose pride of family rose as high in their Georgia cabins as in their ancient Virginia homes.

It was during this period that an invention was made at Mulberry Grove, near Savannah, that had an influence on the world's future greater than perhaps any other invention of that century then closing. It was the invention of the cotton-gin. Eli Whitney, a young New Englander, and a kinsman of Mrs. General Green, had come on a visit to his aunt at Mulberry Grove. At that time the cotton produced on the plantations was generally prepared for the loom by laboriously picking the seed from it by hand. It was a slow process, and what was called a cotton-gin was invented, which consisted of two rollers through which the lint was drawn. It was turned by hand, and was of but little value.

A Mr. Jos. Eve, of the Bermudas, invented a machine of the same order on a larger scale. This was better and was in use for many years on the sea island cotton plantations, still it worked but slowly. Whitney put his head to work, and finally fell on the idea upon which the modern gin is constructed. It has been said that Mrs. General Green made a suggestion which resulted in his perfecting it so as make it useful. He found it somewhat difficult to get a patent, and after filing his application and securing a caveat he put the gins, or machines as they were called, to work in sundry places. The idea of his gin was seized by Jacob Lyons, who made further improvements on it and began to manufacture the machines in Columbia county. There was a long and expensive litigation, and Whitney's claim to the invention was established, but he profited little by it. There were but few machines set up until after the beginning of the new century.

We turn our attention to the counties formed during this period.

ELBERT.

Elbert county was laid off from Wilkes in 1790, and named in honor of General and Governor Elbert. It was one of the first settled parts of Wilkes, and much that has been said of Wilkes refers to Elbert. When laid off it included a part of Hart and Madison. The land was of four sorts: Rich red hills covered with grand forests; beautiful valleys along the streams, and a wide area of what was regarded as almost waste land, the flat woods; and the thin gray lands covered with post-oaks. These red lands and valleys were very fertile and attracted the Virginians, who were seeking homes in a new country, and who were seeking rich lands to grow tobacco.

There was a large area known as the flat woods, where wild grasses grew luxuriantly. The lands were suited for pasturage but not for culture, and for many years were not valued highly. Of late these lands have been among the best in the county, being rendered productive by the liberal use of kainit.

The first settlers, according to Mr. White and others, were:

Dr. Bibb, Wm. Brown, A. Brown, Wm. Barnett, Billy Allen, James Bell, P. M. Wyche, Jos. Deadwyler, David White, Dozier Thornton, Thos. Maxwell, R. Tyner, William

Key, William Grimes, J. Watkins, Colonel Jack Howard, Nehemiah Howard, Peter Oliver, Wm. Rucker, N. Highsmith, P. Duncan, Wm. Haley, Wm. Ward, E. Shackleford, W. Woods, Middleton Woods, Stephen Heard, D. Oliver, J. Cason, W. Brown, W. Moss, Wm. Tait, Enos Tait, Zimri Tait, Robert L. Tait, James Alston, Wm. Alston, Ralph Banks, Wm. Hodges, S. Wilson, Thos. Carter, John A. Banks, Samuel Davis the father of Jefferson Davis, Absalom Davis, S. Nelson, Thos. Burton, Isham Thompson, Wm. Hodges, S. Nelson, J. A. Carter.

Some of these came just before the Revolution, some of them in the early years of it, and many more of them just after its close.

There were but few people of property who came with the first settlers, but there were not a few who had some slaves.

There was much rudeness in the frontier life of those trying days, when the wild Cherokee and the crueller Tory menaced the newcomers. During the Revolution there was a bitter contest with the Tories, and among the more famous of the Whigs of those days was a woman, Nancy Hart. She is the only woman Georgia ever honored so far as to name a county after her. It must be admitted from all accounts that she was by no means comely in features, nor amiable in temper, nor choice in her language, and the report is that she was said by the frontier people to have been a "honey of a patriot but a devil of a wife." This I think is a slander.

The old governor, in an amusing chapter devoted to her, from which most of the stories concerning her are drawn, may somewhat overstate things about her, and make her a ruder woman than she really was; but she certainly was an intrepid Whig, and possibly captured several Tories and had them safely hung. In her old age the governor says she became a shouting Methodist and was recognized by all as a good woman. She married an uncle of Thomas Hart Benton, the famous senator, and the sterling old statesman was always proud of his connection with her. It is certain she was a woman of substance and family and integrity, and her family was among the best.

Land was very cheap and living very simple, and Governor Gilmer has not drawn on his fancy for the picture he has painted of the first years of the Wilkes and Elbert people.

There were few opportunities to secure an education. A large number of the wills and deeds are signed with a mark, and there were but few women whose signatures are attached to legal instruments before 1811 who could write their names.

After the coming of the Broad river people in 1785 there was a steady influx of people of wealth into Elbert, and while wills show much illiteracy and much poverty, they also show that Elbert was now being peopled with a class of substantial Virginians, who brought some culture and wealth with them into what was then regarded as the wilds of Georgia.

The Virginians who largely settled Elbert believed tobacco was the only crop which could be raised to profit, and chose these lands with an eye to its culture, but the first comers were compelled to wrestle with the question of securing subsistence in these remote quarters. They were obliged to have some ammunition and some tools, and they bought them from the traders who had their supplies at Fort James, or perhaps in Augusta, but they had nothing but peltry to rely on for barter. During the war the people of Elbert were reduced to great straits, and after it was over for some years there were few slaves and but little raised for market. The nearest market was Augusta and their visits to it were few. There was little tobacco and no cotton made for market till after 1805. The wealth of the county was in cattle and hogs.

The great rush of immigrants who sought the rich county of Wilkes when the Virginians came in such numbers rapidly peopled that part of it which was afterwards Elbert. The land was granted by headright, and the better sections of the county were soon taken. There was for ten years after peace was declared a constant peril from the Cherokees, who were not fifty miles from the Elbert frontier, but there was nothing that could deter the eager land-hunter, and the country became quite populous.

Petersburg, or old Fort James, was now selected as an inspecting place for the tobacco which was to find a market in Europe. Slave-owners came to the promising country in numbers before the century began. Virginians of wealth settled on Broad river and bought up the valuable lands in the valley of the Savannah. Petersburg became an important and bustling town. The tobacco, which was packed in large hogsheads, was shipped by flatboats to Savannah, where it was sent direct to England. Petersburg merchants were exporters and importers, and goods were sold more cheaply there than in Augusta. Tobacco gave way in the first decade of the new century to cotton, and Petersburg began to decline. With the coming of the steamboats and the growth of Augusta and the abandonment of tobacco planting, its decay was rapid, and now not a house remains.

Elberton was laid out as soon as the county was organized. It had no special advantages as a commercial town, and was overshadowed by the more vigorous Petersburg and Ruckersville, but it was healthy and well located; and while it never before the war between the States became a town of importance, it was the county site and a school center, and had a small and choice population. An academy was established as soon as the county was laid out. It was incorporated and chartered, and the second female academy chartered in Georgia was in Elberton.

With the decline of Petersburg Elberton was still overshadowed by Ruckersville, nearer the river, where there was a bank and large warehouses, and it did a comparatively small business.

The goods sold in the county were brought up the river in flatboats or in wagons from Augusta. The cotton made in the county was sent down the river in boats or carried to Augusta in wagons. The small farmer, as in other sections, gave way in the early part of the century to the large planter who had many slaves, and who could ship his scores of bales of cotton to the Augusta market. By 1830 Elbert had become a county of great plantations, and the richer parts of the county were owned by a few large slave-owners. Some of these men of wealth lived in the village, but most of them in Wilkes on their plantations. It is the same story—negroes increased, lands grew poorer, and the Elbert county planter, finding he could not support his large family of blacks on the red hills of Elbert, removed his negroes to better lands on the rich bottoms of Mississippi, or the black lands of Alabama, or to southwest Georgia. The poorer people went to the flat woods, or the black-jack ridges of what was afterward Hart, or else to the cheap lands of the Cherokee counties. In 1810 there were 7,582 whites and 4,574 slaves in Elbert; in 1830 there were 6,589 whites and 5,765 slaves, nearly as many slaves as white people in the county, and in 1850 the whites were 6,692 and slaves 6,269.

After the war, however, Elbert began, as all the older counties to take on new life. The old planter who had bought but little and who had aimed to make everything at home, gave way to the new planter who traded near home and whose negro employees bought their goods from the country store, and trade began to be brisk. A railroad was a necessity, and largely through the enterprise of the Elbert people a branch road was built from Elberton to Toccoa. Afterward the Seaboard Air Line railroad passed through the village, and Elberton was transformed from a country village into a city.

The Virginia people who came into Elbert at its first settlement were many of them Baptists, and some of them Methodists, and the first Methodist missionaries came into this county, then known as Wilkes, and began their work. Beverly Allen, a scion of a prominent family in Virginia, who was a Methodist preacher, and long but incorrectly regarded the first Methodist preacher in Georgia, had his home in this county. He was a man of rare gifts and of great influence, but become involved in trouble in South Carolina and was expelled from the church. He then became a merchant in Elbert, and incurred heavy debts to eastern creditors. He was sued in the United States court, and when Marshall Forsyth in Augusta, where he was at the time, made an effort to arrest him, Allen killed him and fled to Kentucky. Here he became a prominent physician and a wealthy man.

Some of the oldest Methodist churches in Georgia are still found in Elbert, and the first Methodist conference met at the forks of Broad river, then in Elbert now in Madison county.

The Baptists, the only other denomination of any size in Elbert, have had large success among its people, and the church has sent out not a few prominent preachers to other sections.

There are handsome churches of both of these denominations in Elberton now, and quite a number of each scattered throughout the county.

The Rev. John Andrew, father of Bishop Andrew, lived in this county. He was a soldier in the Revolution, and the first native Georgian who became a traveling Methodist preacher. He was a nephew of Benjamin Andrew, the staunch patriot of Liberty county and speaker of the Assembly. Mr. Andrew was a country schoolmaster when he lived in Elbert.

Wm. Wyatt Bibb, who after having been a senator from Georgia was governor of Alabama, lived at Petersburg.

Charles Tait, also a senator, was from a leading family in this county.

Samuel Davis, the father of President Davis, came to this county, and removed from it to Kentucky. He was a soldier in the Revolution.

When Hart county was cut off from Elbert a large number of the smaller landholders were taken from the old counties, leaving the bulk of the negroes in it.

The first court held in Elbert was held in 1791 at the house of Thomas Carter. George Walton was the presiding justice. This house was about six miles from Elberton, and like most of the larger houses of that day had a cellar. This cellar was used as a prison, and a man named McBride, charged with murder, was confined in it. He was convicted on Wednesday and hung on Friday.

The first grand jury was: Stephen Heard, Moses Haynes, Richard Easter, Isham Thompson, Wm. Aycock, William Hatcher, Richard Gatewood, Ed McGay, James Crow, Angus Johnson, Archer Walker, Edward Ware, James Shepherd, James Patten, John Davis, Cornelius Sale, Oliver White, Wm. Hodge.

At the present time there are few better counties in Georgia than Elbert. The magnificent forests which once crowned its hills have long since been destroyed, and even the forests of a second growth have been cut away, and men cultivate as new ground in cotton land their grandfathers planted in tobacco.

There is in Elbert an inexhaustible supply of the finest monumental granite in America, and the most beautiful granite monuments in Georgia are prepared in Elberton.

The court-house is a very handsome and convenient building, the churches unusually elegant, and the residences and storehouses attractive and tasty.

There is a large cotton factory in the city, and other enterprises of value.

The city is well supplied with water furnished by a bold spring in the city itself.

COLUMBIA.

In 1790 the upper and western parts of Richmond county were made into Columbia, and at a much later period Columbia itself was divided and McDuffie was formed.

The eastern parts of the county along the Savannah river and the northern and western along Little river, and on the Kiokee and near Wrightsboro, were very fertile and were thickly settled before the Revolutionary war. The people distributed themselves into two main groups, one near Wrightsboro and the other on the Kiokee, near where Appling now is. The settlers near Wrightsboro were many of them Quakers from North Carolina, but there were a considerable number of Virginians and Marylanders who settled in that neighborhood as early as 1770.

The list of settlers in St. Paul's parish, which is found in the Appendix, is very largely composed of those who settled in this county. There was a large body of settlers in these neighborhoods before the Revolutionary war. The lower part of the county and the southwestern part was a great pine forest, and for many years after the Revolution was not settled at all except by a few stock-raisers.

The crowds of settlers who had located in this county before the Revolution had been kindly received and encouraged by Governor Wright, and he was so great a favorite with them that they named their principal village Wrightsboro in his honor, and they had little sympathy with the agitators, whether in Boston or Savannah. Many had never seen a leaf of tea in all their lives, and cared little about taxation without representation, as they paid no taxes, and when the Liberty Boys began their revolution, at Governor Wright's request they almost to a man signed their protest against their course.

It is certain that most of these people at the beginning of the war were poor men, who had not as yet done more than build their cabins and open a few fields. They had but few slaves and were as a rule uneducated, but it was also true that there was among them some of more than ordinary culture and people of some property.

The Fews, the Candlers and the Lamars were among these first comers. The Fews came from Wales to Pennsylvania, thence into Maryland and into North Carolina, from which State they removed to Georgia. Of this distinguished family we have spoken elsewhere.*

The upper part of the county was wonderfully fertile, and along Little river and the various creeks which permeated that portion of the county the newcomers made many settlements before the Revolution, and when the British took possession of Augusta this section was at once occupied by their troops, and as a large number of the people were patriots they were driven into exile. After the war ended they returned to their abandoned cabins and soon began to reestablish themselves. The population was very large and the settlers were very thrifty. The best class of Virginians and North Carolinians now came into the growing county. Columbia Court-house became a leading

* See Chapter III.

town in the up-country and held its place for years. The land was given by headrights and two hundred-acre farms were opened all over the upper and eastern parts of the county. The towns of Wrightsboro and Brownsboro were the leading villages in the county.

It was not long after the Revolution before the tide of prosperity began to rise very high. Men with a number of slaves came from Virginia and settled plantations. Stock had unlimited pasturage, and the soil was remarkably fertile. Augusta was a near-by market and tobacco, the staple, found ready sale. By the beginning of the century there was much wealth in the county and an unusual amount of intelligence. It was thickly settled, and when the cotton-gin was invented and the cotton industry began to be an item, Columbia became famous for its rapid advance in prosperity until there were few sections of the State in which there was more wealth and intelligence. The settlers were nearly all from Virginia and were not adventurers, but men of family and means. The Cobbs, Meriwethers, Hamiltons, Dawsons, Applings, Lamars, Fews, Candlers, Napiers, Crawfords, Carrs, Howards, and many others of that class settled in the county, and there was no part of the State in the early part of the century in which there was a more elegant society.

The coming of Daniel Marshall, the first Baptist preacher in upper Georgia, and the formation of the Kiokee church in 1771, we have already noted.

Before the beginning of the century Moses Waddell, a young Presbyterian minister from North Carolina, came into the county and opened a school at Mt. Carmel, where W. H. Crawford and Jno. C. Calhoun were his pupils. There were many separate landholders at that time and a large number of pupils could be secured.

The Methodists came into Columbia as early as they came into Georgia, and found some old Virginia friends awaiting their coming, and had prosperous churches in all sections of the county.

There was an academy at Appling in the early part of the century, and a female school of high grade was established there in the thirties and flourished for a few years, and the usual old-field schools were found in every section of the county.

We have already had a sketch of the distinguished family of Fews, who resided in this county. The grandfather of the famous Howell and Thomas R. R. Cobb died in this county, and his brother, Thomas Cobbs, was said to have been one hundred and ten years old when he died in this county, where he had lived for sixty years.

During the first years of the century Columbia Court-house, as Appling was then called, was a center of wealth, intelligence, and influence. Abraham Baldwin, a young New Englander, who had graduated at Yale College, served as chaplain in the Revolution, studied law, came to Georgia, was admitted to the Georgia bar in Savannah, and came at once to Augusta and then to Columbia Court-house, where he made his home until his death. Few men ever did more for an adopted State, and few men were ever honored more highly than this gifted and excellent man.

The famous Crawford family came to this county from Virginia before the Revolution, and some of its members were soon called to prominent places, and for over a hunered years this family have done the State good service. No county has furnished more families of distinguished Georgians than this old county.

The story told of all these older counties must be told of Columbia. The plantations and negroes drove out the whites; but the red lands and the rich river plantations passed into the hands of comparatively few people, and as the tide of settlement rolled westward Columbia declined in population as far as white people were concerned, but the poorer sections of the county along the Georgia railroad were gradually occupied, first by mill-men who made lumber, and then as places of healthy residences for Augusta people, and Harlem, twenty miles from Augusta, became a thriving village, and still is.

With liberal fertilizing the pine lands have been made productive. The division of the county and the making of McDuffie has reduced it greatly in size and importance, but it is now improving in every way.

SCREVEN.

Screven was laid out in 1793, and called Screven after the gallant general of that name. The county has some very fertile and much very poor land in its borders. On the creeks the land was famous for its fertility, but being what is known as rotten limestone, it was very unhealthy. The pine woods were healthy but very sterile. The population was scant and scattered, and schools were few and churches fewer for many years.

White gives as early settlers in the county: Lewis Lanier, Henry White, Wm. Young, Rowland Roberts, Captain Everett, Paul Black, W. Black, F. Womack, William Blackman, Richard Scruggs, R. Herrington, S. Pearce, N. Williamson, J. H. Rutherford, Jas. Boyd, Jno. Bonnell, H. Bryan, W. Rushing, Benj. Greene, Wm. Shepherd, R. Warren, J. Tanner, Jno. Fletchell, John Nevil, A. Bonnell, B. Lanier, M. Coleton, Wm. Pearce, D. Blackburn, John Jeffers, Wm. Rawls, M. Green.

It is evident from these names that the settlers, like those of Burke, came principally from Virginia and North Carolina. Some of them were people of some wealth, and a few of the settlers on the richer lands were people of culture.

Seaborn Jones, at one time speaker of the House and

long a distinguished lawyer in Augusta, spent his last years here on a large estate known as Mill Haven.

The larger part of the people lived at the first settlement in the pine woods, and were very poor and dissolute. Jacksonborough, the first county site, was so famous for its rough-and-tumble fights that it was said that the children went about the village after a court day with a saucer to gather up the eyes which had been gouged out.*

Much of the county was looked upon as worthless, except as ranges for cattle. The timber near the river could be floated to Savannah, and that which was near the railroad could be made into lumber; but much of the county was not accessible and was unopened.

The building of a branch road has connected the distant parts of the county with the Central, improved methods of culture have made the pine lands profitable for farming purposes, and while the country, which at first was most famous for its fertility and in which there were large plantations and many slaves, is less prosperous, the county as a whole has grown very steadily and is now in better condition than at any previous day. Churches and schools are now found in all parts of the county.

In glancing at Burke and Effingham, from which Screven is taken, we have already largely described this county.

OGLETHORPE.

Oglethorpe county was laid off from Wilkes in 1793. In giving an account of Wilkes I have already glanced at this county, and many of those who are mentioned as citizens of Wilkes in the early days resided on that side of Broad river which was afterward included in Oglethorpe. Governor Mathews, Governor Gilmer's father and uncle, Frank Meriwether, Micajah McGhee, John Thomas, the Stuarts, the Floyds, the Howards, the Popes, and the Hills

* White.

were among the early people who came to this section. A new county was a necessity. It was organized in 1793, and the first court was held three miles from Lexington in 1794.

Oglethorpe has much the same history as the other middle Georgia counties. It was settled at first by men of moderate means; the farms were small, the people thrifty. They prospered and soon acquired negro property; then, tempted by the new lands of the new counties, the small farmers sold out their farms, which were absorbed by the large plantations, and these in turn wore out their lands and went to richer fields. Those who remained in Oglethorpe found themselves in the same condition as the Wilkes, Greene and Burke planters. They had many negroes, much worn land, and but little besides.

There was, however, much good land in the county, and there was a very fine class of industrious people. The old county has rallied to a considerable degree and is perhaps now in better condition than it has been for fifty years. The town of Lexington was at one time a very famous trade center, but its trade has long since been transferred to Athens; but it is a solid town, and perhaps one of the best representatives of the old Virginia county towns left in the State. It has a famous academy, which was the first academy endowed by private bequest in the State. It is a delightful Georgia town of the olden time. Crawford, Winterville and Maxeys are villages on the line of railway to Union Point.

The first grand jury of Oglethorpe was: John Lumpkin, Robert McCord, John Marks, Joel Hurt, Andrew Bell, Jesse Clay, Charles Hay, John Collier, Richard Goolsby, Isaac Collier, John Garrett, John Shields, Robert Beaver, P. Thornton, Jeffrey Early, H. Edmondson, Wm. Pattie, Jas. Northington.

In 1810 there were 6,862 whites and 5,435 slaves in the

county; in 1830 there were 5,670 free and 7,940 slaves, and twenty years afterward there were 4,385 free and 7,874 slaves; in 1890 the entire population was 16,951.

The Baptists came into Oglethorpe in its earliest years, as did the Presbyterians and the Methodists, and the first camp-meeting held in Georgia was held in Oglethorpe county in 1802. It was a union meeting, in which all denominations were represented.

Bishop Asbury, the Methodist bishop, visited this county before the beginning of the century, and after that was often in it. He says in one of his journeys "that as Benjamin Blanton, one of his preachers, was ill, he gave him his place in his carriage, and rode his stiff-jointed horse, that he would only ride to save souls or the health of a brother."

Chancellor Mell, who was a Baptist preacher, during the forty years of his connection with the University was the pastor of a Baptist church in the lower part of Oglethorpe county, and such was the universal favor with which he was regarded that that section was known as "Mell's Kingdom."

The Rev. John Newton, one of the first Presbyterian preachers in Georgia, was the pastor of the church at Bethsalem, near Lexington, in 1788; and on Broad river in 1809, under James Russell, there was a great revival among the Methodists, which brought into the church a large part of that remarkable community. Churches dotted the whole county, and during the days of slavery the Methodists had a missionary for many years, whose work it was to preach to the negroes. Among the Methodist churches is one known now and for a long time past as Cherokee Corner, so called because it was at that very spot that the dividing point between the Creeks and Cherokees was located, and up to a few years past the tree the surveyors marked a hundred years before was living.

Oglethorpe has been long noted for its culture and refinement and for the number of its distinguished men. W. H. Crawford lived at a place called Woodlawn, now Crawford, a few miles from Lexington; and is buried there. He was born in Virginia, and during the stirring days of the Revolution, while he was a lad, his father removed from Amherst county, Va., to Edgefield, S. C., and in 1783 he removed to Columbia county, Ga., which at that time was Richmond. The elder Crawford died before his son was grown and the cares of the family fell on the youth. He taught school for awhile, then attended Hope Hull's school in Wilkes, and then Dr. Waddell's. He was an assistant teacher in the Augusta Academy while Charles Tait was rector. He studied law and settled in Lexington in 1799. He was very handsome, very genial and eloquent, and became very popular with the up-country people, who were largely Virginians. He was sent by them to the Legislature soon after he settled in Lexington, and in 1806, when only thirty-four years old, he was elected United States senator. At the end of the term he was elected again. He soon evinced his great ability as a statesman, and after declining a place in Mr. Monroe's cabinet he was sent as minister to Paris. He returned to America and was secretary of war, and soon after secretary of the treasury. He was a favorite candidate for president in 1824, and the prospects of his election were very bright, when he was stricken with apoplexy. The stroke was not fatal, but his constitution was shattered and his intellect somewhat impaired. He was defeated, and appointed in Georgia to a judgeship. While on the bench, ten years after he received the first stroke, he died. Mr. Crawford was the leader of a party known as the Crawford party, and John Clarke, of whom we speak elsewhere, was his great political antagonist. The war between the two men was bitter and unrelenting until Mr. Crawford's death.

He was a man of brilliant mind, a bitter hater, a fearless fighter. He antagonized Mr. Clay, Mr. Adams and Mr. Calhoun. They differed in everything with each other but agreed in their dislike to him, but he was always the victor over them all.

Governor George R. Gilmer was born in this county and died in it. His father came with the Broad river settlers, and before Oglethorpe county was made in 1790 George Rockingham Gilmer was born.

GEORGE R. GILMER.

The father was a man of sterling character and of moderate fortune. He gave his son the best advantages the country afforded, and sent him to Dr. Waddell's famous school in South Carolina. The governor taught school for a few years in his youth, entered the army, and was five years an officer. He then studied law and settled in Lexington, and entered public life as a member of the Legislature; then he was two years in Congress. In 1828 he was elected governor, and in 1836 was elected again. He then retired from public life and spent the rest of his days in Lexington. He wrote in his old age a gossipy book on early Georgians, in which, with delightful egotism, he tells of himself and of the men and of the times he had known.

Another of the men of distinction who was reared in Oglethorpe was Joseph Henry Lumpkin, long chief justice. He was a man of great beauty of character, whose dignity and suavity of manner was connected with the finest attainments as a lawyer and the highest capacity as a great jurist. He was an humble Christian, a great temperance advocate, and an incorruptible judge, at once the pride of his whole State as well as of the county which gave him birth.

No county in Georgia has had a more distinguished class of inhabitants than Oglethorpe, and no county has sent to other sections of the South a finer class of people.

JOSEPH HENRY LUMPKIN.

Edmond McGhee, who was so noted as a princely planter in Mississippi, and a generous friend of religion and education, who built a handsome church in New Orleans and largely aided both a male and female college in Louisiana and Mississippi, spent his youth in Oglethorpe.

The Gilmers, Meriwethers, Mathews, Marks and Jordans all went from this county.

HANCOCK.

Greene was laid out in 1786, but in seven years its population had grown so rapidly that a new county was carved out of its southern extremity, and from Greene and Washington one was made, known as Hancock, in honor of John Hancock. It was a large county and embraced all varieties of soil. There were the rich red hills, the fertile valleys along the rivers and creeks, heavily timbered with oaks and hickories, and the wide stretches of gray post-oak land and pine-barrens.

The Oconee river with its limpid waters formed its western boundary, and the Ogeechee was on the east. A number of large creeks and sparkling brooks dashed through its forests, and although the Indians were just over the Oconee river and were then hostile, the tide of settlement could not be stayed.

The first settlers of Hancock, according to White, were: General H. Mitchell, Bollin Hall, Charles Abercrombie, General Adams, Henry Graybill, Joseph Bryan, William Rees, Jonathan Adams, John Montgomery, Jacob Dennis, Archibald Smith, T. Holt, T. Raines, J. Bishop, Isham Rees, M. Martin, R. Clarke, R. Shipp, F. Tucker, L. Barnes, W. Wyley, William Saunders, James Thomas, Jephtha Pope, Jonas Shivers, William Hardwick, L. Tatum, R. Moreland.

One who examines this list and the one which follows will find that some of the first settlers of Hancock came from Jefferson, Burke and Columbia, while the bulk of them can be easily traced to the tide-water counties of Virginia and to North Carolina.

In a list of accounts filed by the executor of the estate in Sparta of David Clements in 1801 there were these names:

John Lewis, James Lucas, Jonathan Davis, Joseph Bonner, Simon Holt, John Dowdell, Alex Bellamy, Lindsay Thornton, Isaac Evans, John Shackelford, Robert Tucker, John Hall, William Harper, Thomas Winn, John Trippe, Dr. R. Lee, James Lamar, Thomas Lamar, Peterson Thweat, Captain Samuel Hall, Duncan McLean, R. Respass, Wm. Lawson, Job Taylor, Dudley Hargrove, Dr. John Pollard, Robert Montgomery, Seth Parham, Homer Holt, Jas. Huff, Philip Turner, Dixon Hall, Peter Flournoy, William Hardwick, Thomas Byrd, Frances Lawson, Thos. Glenn, Gabe Lewis, David Lewis, Jos. Lewis, Arch Lewis, Little Reese,

John Freeman, William Lewis, Isaac Dennis, John Dudley, Thomas Jones, William Kelly, Isaac Dunegan, John Dyer, William Johnson, Malachi Brantley, Francis Lewis, Bollin Hall, George Lewis, George Weatherby, John Perkins, Jas. Parnell, Thomas Broadnax, John Cain, Jos. Middlebrooks, H. Jones, R. Tredewell, Woodruff Scott, John Sasnett, Jas. Bonner, Isham West, Thos. Carney, Isaac Wilson, John Brewer, Thomas Carter, Drury Thweat, Jas. Arthur, Daniel Melson, S. Parham, Harris Brantley, William Hatcher, C. Leonard, W. Collier, C. R. Bonner, S. Kirk, Isham Loyd, Andrew Jeter, Isham Askew, James Childs, Joel Reese, Thomas Pentecost, James Hamilton, William Powell, Ben Harper, Robert Simmons, E. Bomar.

There was evidently a much larger white population in the rural parts of Hancock in 1800 than there is now in 1900. There were only thirteen hundred slaves in Greene, of which Hancock was a part, in 1790.

Tobacco had been the staple in Hancock and Greene to 1800, but with the coming in of cotton culture it ceased to be cultivated. Hancock became rapidly peopled after 1800 with the wealthy people of Virginia and North Carolina. The delightful "Dukesboro Tales" of Richard Malcolm Johnston have their location in this county, in the village of Powellton, and the pictures which he gives are portrayals of real people.

The first settlements of Hancock were in the northern and eastern sections of the county on Shoulderbone creek and the Ogeechee river. The hills were heavily timbered, and when cleared were very productive. The county was exposed to the Indians, but it was soon settled.

There were two classes of settlers before the century began—the slave-owner who had a few negroes, a plantation of perhaps four hundred acres, great herds of cattle, flocks of sheep and droves of hogs, and the sturdy yeoman who had little besides his hands and his preempted land of two hundred acres.

At first there was little difference in social features, but as years sped on the division between the classes became marked, and, as in all middle Georgia, the plantation absorbed the farm and the planter took the place of the farmer.

Hancock offered special attractions to the North Carolina and Virginia slave-owners, and they moved into it rapidly after the opening of the cotton industry in the beginning of the century.

Schools became a necessity, and in the thickly settled parts of the county school villages sprang up. Mt. Zion became a center for the Presbyterians, where Mr. Carlisle P. Beman had a famous classical school, and Powellton, where Jesse Mercer had his home and near where Rev. Malcolm Johnston and Governor Rabun lived, was a famous Baptist village with an academy.

Sparta was without a schoolhouse or a church at the beginning of the century, but there was preaching in the court-house, and in 1802 David Clements left a bequest to build a church and gave a lot of ground on which an academy was to be built. This academy was probably where the graded school building is now located.

The Baptists and Presbyterians came with the first settlers, and the Methodists were not far behind them. There were no church buildings in the county for some years. Services were held in private houses. In 1802 there was a camp-meeting on Shoulderbone creek, where there were on Sunday over five thousand people assembled.*

As Hancock was on the frontier it was much exposed to Indian forays. It met them so bravely the county site was called Sparta. Sparta was soon a village of importance.

* Dow's Journal.

It did a large trade for many years and became an educational center. It had its regular chartered academy, and before there was a female college in Georgia Mrs. Warne had a female academy of high grade in Sparta. The Methodist church in Sparta was erected in 1805. There had been services at the home of John Lucas for several years before that, and a conference was held in the village in 1806, and seventy years afterward the Georgia Conference met near the spot where it had held its session seventy years before. Sparta was for a long time a thrifty country town, but with the building of the railroads on each side its commercial importance declined. The wealthy planters in the county had their homes in the village, and, with the lawyers and doctors and country merchants, made a good society of cultured people. As in all these middle Georgia towns, the change of things after the war made a great change in the village. The railroad was completed, the trade in fertilizers was immense and Sparta began to advance, and it has become now a handsome country town, with an elegant court-house, a fine public school building and many charming homes.

The religious history of Hancock is full of interest, but we can only glance at it here. Governor Rabun was a Baptist deacon and lived at Powellton. Jesse Mercer had his home in that village, and there the Georgia Baptist Convention was organized. The Presbyterians had a settlement at Mt. Zion and a congregation at Smyrna, and the Rev. Mr. Gildersleeve published at Mt. Zion the *Missionary*, which was the first periodical of that kind in the South.

Many of the families we have found in Hancock went into Putnam, Baldwin, Jasper and Montgomery, across the Ocmulgee and the Flint into the western counties and to Alabama.

Colonel Chappel, who was born in Hancock and lived in Putnam and Monroe, has given a picture of this county and its first settlers, which is not too highly colored to be true, and upon which I have freely drawn. No county ever was settled by a worthier people, and for enterprise and skill no county ever had planters who surpassed many of those in Hancock. They were men of great moral worth and simplicity of life, and are too many to be mentioned. They formed communities where there was everything to elevate and refine. Bishop George F. Pierce, when a young man, fixed his home in Hancock and called it Sunshine, and here, beloved and honored, he spent all the time he could spare from his exacting labors.

Hancock is still a large county and has the villages of Devereux, Culverton and Jewells in its borders.

Hancock has fine quarries of granite, which have been utilized only in late years, and no county in the State is so rich in "jaspers" of the most beautiful kinds.

This county has been rendered famous by being the first county in which new modes of culture for corn and cotton were applied to the pine woods.

Mr. David Dickson bought a large body that was called Pine-barren and began the liberal use of commercial fertilizers upon it, and began to farm on a new and untried plan. He succeeded and his system of farming excited great attention, and his modes of cultivation were recognized as wise and were adopted in many sections of the country, and that portion of the county which had been regarded as the poorest became one of the best.

The distinguished men of Hancock could hardly be numbered. The Abercrombies, so famous in the early history of Georgia and Alabama, resided here. The Lewises came to this county in its first settlement, and have been distinguished men in a number of different walks of life. Governor Rabun was a resident of this county. Colonel James Thomas and Hon. Eli Baxter were prominent lawyers and politicians in Sparta.

Judge Linton Stephens, judge of the supreme court, colonel in the Confederate army and member of the Confederate Congress, lived and died in Sparta.

Dr. W. J. Sassnett, distinguished as a preacher and a philosopher, was born in this county and died in it.

Dr. Lovick Pierce, so famous as a Methodist preacher throughout the South, died at his son's home in Sparta.

BULLOCH.

Bulloch was laid out from Screven and Bryan in 1796, and named in honor of the excellent Archibald Bulloch, governor of Georgia. The Ogeechee river is on one side of it and the Canoochee on the other. There was some good oak and hickory land on the rivers, but much of the county was piny woods, presenting the usual features of such a section. It had been settled by stockmen, and White gives as the first settlers:

Benjamin Cook, Barnard Michael, John Everett, Jehu Everett, Andrew E. Wells, George Threadcraft, Chas. McCall, Alex Stewart, M. Buckhalter, A. McKenzie, Daniel Lot, Arthur Lot, Wm. Mizell, L. Lanier, C. Lanier, D. Hendrix, N. Sweat, Mr. Oliff, Mr. Shorter, the Groovers and Hodges.

There is very little save in the matter of personal detail to distinguish one piny woods county from another. The physical features are the same, the pursuits of the people are the same, and their features of character are almost exactly alike.

Bulloch was for many years a county where men owned large areas of land, which was valued at not more than twenty-five cents an acre. On this land the cabin was built, and in the wide wire-grass pastures the cattle fed. Every man was a landholder and every man was independent.

There were so few people that schools and churches were

rare, and the children had very limited opportunities for school training.

The larger body of the people of any religious faith were Baptists, and when the division of that denomination took place they were mostly found among the Primitives, but the Methodists had a footing in the county from it first settlement.

Life in these pine woods in the early days when the people found it difficult to go to the markets was very simple. The farmer raised for family use upland rice, corn, potatoes, cattle and hogs. He had his own syrup kettle and sugar-mill. His sheep furnished him with wool. His house was of logs, built by his own hands, and, while plain, was sufficiently comfortable for his wishes. He raised some sea-island cotton and carried a few bales to Savannah, where, with the produce of his hides, tallow and beeswax, he secured enough money to buy some salt, calico, cotton and woolen cards and nails, and these were about the extent of his purchases.

There were in all this section, however, a few families of large wealth who had plantations on the richer lands and lived in decided comfort, but for many years after the county was settled life was very primitive. With the building of the railroads, the opening of the turpentine farms and the setting up of the sawmills, the same results followed of which we have spoken elsewhere, and now Bulloch is one of the best of our inland counties.

McINTOSH.

McIntosh was cut off from Liberty, and in our account of the Scotch settlement about Darien we have given the early history of this county. Away from the coast the land presented identically the same features as Bulloch and the pine woods of Liberty. It was thinly settled by plain stock-raisers, who lived hard and had no social or educational advantages. These people were many of them the descendants of those Scotch people who first fixed their homes near Darien.

Near the coast, however, there were a number of rice plantations, which were owned by planters who had large estates and elegant homes. There was found here, as along all the coast where these planters had their homes, much intelligence, enterprise and hospitality, but nothing to differentiate them from those we have already pictured.

Darien, however, being at the mouth of the Altamaha, was until the railways were built a most important shipping point. The cotton boats from the up-country brought great loads of cotton to this port for shipment to Europe and the North, and Darien was for years a great lumber market. The timber ranger of the up-country rafted his timber to this little city and found a market for it.

It had a small but cultured and wealthy citizenship, and was pleasant and attractive, though somewhat isolated. Like St. Marys, it has had its mutations and has been largely discounted by the decay of its river trade, but it is still a vigorous little city. Outside of Darien McIntosh has but a small body of white inhabitants.

BRYAN.

Bryan, which was named in honor of Joseph Bryan, was cut off from Effingham and Liberty. In the neck between the rivers there was fine rice land and a few planters had plantations in it, but the area of fertile land was very limited, and the main body of the county was flat and sterile pine woods.

In 1850 there were no schools in the county except a few supported by the poor school fund. In common with all that section of the State great changes were brought about by the war, and Bryan has shared in the prosperity the new era has brought in.

WARREN.

The counties of Richmond and Columbia and Wilkes together embraced all the land west of Augusta to the Ogeechee. Much of the land in the northern and western part of this county was very fertile. It was thickly settled with people from Virginia, and it was decided in 1793 to lay off a county to embrace the western section of these counties and name it in honor of Dr. Warren, the hero of Bunker Hill.

The county embraced in its limits all of what is now Warren, a part of what is now Jefferson, and a part of Taliaferro and Glascock.

There was much fine land in the upper part of the county along the Ogeechee, and there was a large colony of Virginians who moved in a body to this new country. Among them were some families of wealth and influence.

The rich valley of the Ogeechee, which was afterward in Jefferson county, was now included in Warren. John Cobbs, the ancestor of General Howell and Thomas R. R. Cobb, who was a delegate to the convention of 1795 from Warren county, lived on a large estate on the Ogeechee, and his son, John Addison Cobb, was a captain of the militia in 1797 in this county.

The first settlers in Warren, as given by White, were:

Sol. Newsome, David Neal, Wm. Johnson, Job Hunter, Cullen Battle, Robt. Abercrombie, H. Peoples, Wm. Hill, A Denton, W. Carson, S. Burnley, B. Upton, S. Perryman, E. Conner, A Brinkley, W. Jenkins, A. Jones, M. English, C. Lowe, Jr., D. A. Simeon, T. Maddux, E. Ivy, J. Burkhalter, E. Wilson, T. Persons, T. Lockett, S. Bell, J. Shivers, P. Newsome, John Newsome.

Many of these were doubtless in Jefferson, Washington, Richmond and Columbia before Warren was laid out.

In 1797 a roll of officers of the militia battalion shows the following:

John Lawson, major; David Neal, Addison Cobb, James Wilson, Chapman Abercrombie, captains; Wm. Landrum, Benj. Mitchell, Jno. Burnes, A. Jones, lieutenants; D. Hutchinson, C. M. Lawson, Moor Carter, ensigns. The second battalion had Major Slatter; captains: Bunkley, Jones, Smith, Hill, Flewellen; ensigns: Carter, Brantley, White, Clower, Cox; lieutenants: M. Womack, Mountain Hill, Burrell Posey, Gibson Flournoy.

The above are nearly all Virginia names, and some of them are found in an after time in Jefferson, which included, when it was laid off, a small part of what had been Warren county.

Before the beginning of the century an iron furnace, among the first established in Georgia, was set up in Warren. It was known as Cowle's Iron Works. Some years afterwards Colonel Wm. Bird, a prominent and wealthy immigrant from Virginia, had another furnace on the shoals of the Ogeechee.

Warrenton was the county site, and was laid off soon after the county was laid out. It became quite a center of trade, and at one time its wholesale trade was quite extensive.

The academy in Warrenton was incorporated in 1812, and Samuel Lowther, Peyton Baker, A. Moncrief, Edward Donahoo, Rufus Broom, Archelaus Flewellen, Turner Persons, George W. Hardwick and Dennis L. Ryan were trustees.

The Methodists came to Warren before it was laid off as a separate county, and had preaching-places in all the thickly settled parts of the county. Some of the leading people in the county were Methodists; among them Judge Stith and his wife and the daughters of John Cobbs, who had married Robert Flournoy and Chesley Bostick. The Methodists had quite a following, and Bishop Asbury mentions a great quarterly meeting at Heath's, where one love-feast lasted from nine o'clock in the morning to three in the afternoon.

While there were thick settlements and considerable wealth in the oak-woods, there was a section afterward included in Glascock which was almost uninhabited for many years.

There was much diversity in the character of the people, and side by side with the wealthy and with people of some education there was much illiteracy, and, as the court record shows, in the early years of the county a great amount of lawlessness.

As a very considerable part of the county was not peopled by large slaveholders and was not the best suited for cotton-growing, there was less of the absorption of small farms than in some of the adjoining counties; but for years there was constant increase in the relative proportion of negroes to whites. In 1810 there were 5,677 free and 3,048 slaves. In 1830, 6,523 free and 4,193 slaves, and in 1850, 6,317 free and 6,108 slaves. The separation of the territory now into Glascock increased this proportion, since Glascock was largely peopled by whites.

JEFFERSON.

Jefferson county was organized in 1796 and named for Thomas Jefferson. There was no part of Georgia which had been peopled longer by white people, as we have seen, than a part of Jefferson. Here the Indian trader had his station before Oglethorpe came, and drew around him Scotch-Irishmen, and all along the banks of Briar creek, Rocky creek, Lambert's creek and the Ogeechee river many thrifty people had their homes before the Revolution.

According to Mr. White the early settlers were: Wm. Hardwick, Jno. Fulton, the Clemmons, Pattersons, Roger and Hugh Lawson, Wm. Gamble, Captain Haden, Captain Connelly, Andrew Berryhill, the Shellmans, John Berrien, the Hamptons, and the Whiteheads. Mr. White has naturally concluded because some of these came from the north of Ireland that all did. It is certain that William Hardwick and John Whitehead were Virginians in their ancestry, and I find a large number of persons receiving land grants before 1800 who evidently came from Virginia, but not a few from north Ireland. They were:

Hugh Alexander, James Harvey, Z. Albritton, Charles Harvey, Thomas Atkinson, Garland Hardwick, Dave Alexander, Jos. Hampton, Henry G. Caldwell, Esq., D. Hancock, Isaac Coleman, Wm. Hannah, Isaac DuBose, W. P. Hardwick, Marth Dorton, G. W. Hardwick, David Douglas, John Ingram, John Evers, George Ingram, John Evans, Wm. Kennedy, R. Fleming, John Land, R. Flournoy, Wm. Lowry, John Finley, Samuel Little, John Green, James Meriwether, R. Gray, John Martin, John Gamble, John Mock, Sherrod Hartley, B. McCutlers, John Maynard, Wm. Peel, Jesse Paulett, Love Sanford, Robert Prior, Henry Tucker, Jesse Purvis, Andrew Thompson, John Reese, Benjamin Warren, Jesse Slatter, John Warnocke, M. Shelman.

All these received grants of land in the county, and there were many whose names are to be found in the Appendix who received grants before the county was formed from St. George's parish or Burke county.

Along the banks of the Ogeechee and on the numerous creeks in the county were large areas of the best oak and hickory land, and away from them were wide areas of pine forests.

Like all the first settlements in Georgia, the first industry of the people was stock-raising, and there was but little else raised for some years. Then some tobacco was planted for market, and there was a tobacco warehouse where the product might be inspected, located on the Ogeechee, in the early part of the century, but after cotton-gins were set up in the county every energy was turned in the direction of cotton-planting. Men made large fortunes raising cotton, and with the usual result—the small farms gave way to the large plantations.

The best lands were very hilly and friable, and as in Wilkes and Greene, the hills soon washed badly and became very much impoverished. In the pine woods, as in Burke, the story was different.

Queensboro* was established during the time of Galphin, and Louisville, which was named in honor of Louis XVI., was selected in accordance with the statute of 1786 by Hugh Lawson, Wm. Few and N. Brownson, commissioners, and laid out in the first of 1796 near Queensboro. An academy was one of the first buildings erected, and it was endowed by the State with £1,000 of confiscated property and the proceeds of the sales of the town lots. The town commissioners of the new city were Rev. David Bothwell, John Shelman, James Meriwether and John Cobbs. Forty acres of land were laid out into lots and they were sold at auction.

Perhaps the most stirring event in its early history was the burning of the Yazoo act spoken of elsewhere.

The capitol was removed from Louisville after it had been there for only seven years, and the modest building which served for a State-house was sold to the county for county purposes, and many of the people of Louisville followed the capitol to Milledgeville.

A State university had been projected, which was to be located in Louisville, but it was never established. The spot chosen by the commissioners at the capital city proved to be unhealthy. The hope that Louisville would be an important city was given up, and it declined, until in 1850

* It has been claimed that this little hamlet was settled long before Oglethorpe came, and was named in honor of Queen Anne, but I can find no trace of it before 1760, and I am confident it was not settled until that time. Galphin's old town antedated it.

there were only two hundred and fifty people in the deserted village. The Central railway was ten miles off. The health of the village was not good. There was no trade, and there was but little hope of any change for the better.

The population of the county in 1810 was 3,775 free and 2,336 slaves; in 1830, 3,062 free and 3,647 slaves, and in 1850, 3,717 free and 5,637 slaves.

The owners of these large plantations in many cases lived in Augusta, Savannah and Macon, and only visited their estates occasionally.

Churches were few and congregations small, but with changes which came with the war a new order of things came in. Sprightly towns sprang up on the railway, and a branch road was made from the Central railway to Louisville. The pine-barrens were filled with a thrifty and well-to-do people. Louisville began to improve and took its place with the progressive towns. Handsome churches were built, a graded school of high order was established, and now there are few villages anywhere more attractive than Louisville, and the county is more prosperous than it has been in fifty years.

The boring of artesian wells in various parts of the county has provided a bountiful supply of the purest water, and the health of the county is remarkably good.

Few counties have sent forth a larger number of good citizens than this old county. Their descendants are found in all the lower and western counties of the State and in all the southwestern States.

The Scotch-Irish Presbyterians had congregations in the county before the Revolution, but churches were not erected. The Rev. Mr. Ronaldson was the pastor, but he was a Royalist and was taken captive, and being released he left Georgia and never returned. After the war ended the Presbyterians sent to Ireland and secured a pastor, the Rev. David Bothwell, and the churches were revived.

The Methodists came after the Revolution, as did the Baptists. The first church in Louisville was built by the father of Roger L. Gamble, and was on the lot where the public school now stands. It was afterward surrendered to the Methodists, but on their securing a lot of their own the old church, much dilapidated, was torn away.

There are now excellent churches in every part of the county and good schools have been established.

At the junction of the railway from Louisville a very sprightly town known as Wadley has sprung up. It has handsome churches, an elegant school building and school, neat residences, and good, solid store buildings, and does a large trade. Bartow, a considerable village, is only a few miles away.

On the railway from Augusta to Tennille there are several villages of some size.

Jefferson has been more famous for its large planters than for its public men, but it has produced not a few men of distinction. Hugh Lawson, whose father came into Georgia from North Carolina before the Revolution, was a captain in the Revolution, one of the commissioners for the sale of confiscated property and for selecting the place for a State-house, and one of the trustees of the university. He was brought up in this county.

Judge Roger Lawson Gamble, who was a member of Congress, long lived in Louisville.

Chesley Bostwick and Littleberry Bostwick, both officers in the Revolution, lived in this county.

The Cobbs, Lamars, Rootes and Flournoys lived here, and at one time no county had so many distinguished people.

JACKSON.

Jackson was laid off from Franklin in 1796, and included in its bounds what is now Jackson, Clarke, part of Hall, and a part of Gwinnett county.

It had, as did most of the up-country counties, three varieties of land. The rich red land, on which grew a heavy growth of oak and hickory wood, was very broken, and when cleared was soon washed away. The fertile bottoms along the creeks and rivers and the gray post-oak lands were level and easily cultivated. The land in Jackson, except a small part of it, was not regarded as good land for cotton culture, and was not in demand by slave-owners. It was settled with white people of moderate means.

Jefferson, the county site, was a very obscure hamlet for many years, but has of late years, since it has been reached by the railroad, become a town of some importance. The Martin Institute, founded and endowed by a Mr. Martin, is located here.

Harmony Grove is a prosperous town in the eastern part of the county. In this little hamlet there was established the first chartered female academy in the State. At that time the Legislature gave a small amount to each chartered academy, but it had refused to charter any academy which excluded males. It, however, abandoned this position, and a female academy was chartered for Harmony Grove.

The first settlers of Jackson, as given by White, were:

Jacob Bankston, Richard Easley, John Smith, Jordan Clark, Abednego Moon, Thomas Hill, Paul Williams, Edward Callahan, Parks Chandler, Andrew Miller, Bedford Brown, Z. Collins, S. Lively, Jonah Strong, Miles Gathright, D. W. Easley.

One of the most remarkable and distinguished citizens of Jackson was John Jacobus Flournoy, a deaf mute. He belonged to a distinguished and wealthy family, was wealthy and intelligent, and often appeared in the press as a writer of force. It was through his agency that the deaf and dumb received State care. At first they were sent to Hartford, Conn., and then to an asylum built for their special instruction at Cave Spring.

The celebrated John W. Glenn, a Methodist preacher of high character in early Georgia, long had his home here.

Jackson has sent out a great many people to other sections, and has been repeatedly cut down to make other counties.

In 1810 the population of Jackson was 8,753 whites and 1,816 slaves; in 1830 there were 6,221 whites and 2,783 slaves; in 1850 there were 6,287 whites and 2,941 slaves; in 1890, 19,176 in all.

The Northeastern railway, from Athens to Lula, passes directly through Jackson, and there is a railway from Gainesville and from Social Circle to Jefferson; the Seaboard Air Line railroad skirts the lower part of the county; so few counties have better railway facilities than this old county, which was for so many years without any.

Where there was the little hamlet of Jug Tavern, there is now the charming little town of Winder, with its fine schools and attractive churches.

MONTGOMERY.

There was a wide sweep of pine woods in the lower part of Washington, which, at the time the county was made, was almost entirely uninhabited. It was considered a barren land, except along the river, which swept along its border and through it. A few people, however, had settled in it as early as 1793, and it was decided to lay out a new county to be called Montgomery, in honor of the brave general of that name.

It was almost an unbroken pine forest, but began to attract settlers because of its value as a pastoral county. In the pine woods of North Carolina there was a settlement of Scotch Highlanders, many of whom had been banished from Scotland because of their adherence to the House of

Stuart. During the Revolution these Scotch people were divided in sentiment, a large number holding with the crown, and an equal body holding with the patriots. After the war was over the colonists divided, and many came to Georgia and settled in Montgomery and what was afterward Telfair and Tattnall. They were a race of brave and sturdy old covenanters. They were the McRaes, McDonalds, McQueens, McDuffies, McCrimmons, McWillamses, and McCramers.

These and many others built their cabins and opened their cattle ranches on the pine-clad hills. They were a thrifty people and were independent from the start. They had their kirk and their schools, and had services in their native Gaelic. They occupied the pine woods, and a few people of English descent opened large plantations on the rivers. Many of these were planters of large wealth.

There was no part of Georgia where there were so many Highlanders, and there was nowhere a more contented and well-to-do people than those who dwelt in these pine forests. A finer type of the people than the Scotch who settled so largely Telfair, Tattnall and Montgomery counties was not to be found in America. They were honest, industrious, religious and successful.

These newcomers were in the main Presbyterians, and they brought their minister with them and had their kirk in this wilderness. Many of their descendants, however, became Methodists and Baptists, and all these denominations are represented in the county now. Nowhere were there better country churches or country schools, and the Methodists established a high school at Spring Hill which was finally merged into the South Georgia College at McRae. The anti-Missionary Baptists have had a strong following in this county.

The county is now being rapidly peopled, and the great ranches of the old Scotchmen, with their herds of cattle and flocks of sheep, are now being turned into turpentine farms and lumber-making villages.

The county has become famous because of its connection with one of the most gigantic land frauds which was ever perpetrated in the United States and of which we have already spoken.

In 1810 there were in the county of Montgomery, which then included a half-dozen of the present counties, 2,207 whites and 747 slaves; but in 1830, when the county had been cut down to its present dimensions, there were only 924 whites and 335 negroes. In 1850 there were 1,541 whites and 613 negroes, and in 1890 there were 9,248. Population is now (1899) largely increased.

The building of the railway from Americus to Savannah has opened up the country, the resources of which were unknown to the outside world, and the county has rapidly advanced.

LINCOLN.

When Oglethorpe was cut off from Elbert on the north and Wilkes on the west, a narrow strip was taken from it on the east, and in honor of General Lincoln, of the Revolutionary army, the county was called Lincoln. It was not a large county, but was in the main a county of most excellent land. The Broad river was on the north, the Savannah river on the east, and the Little river on the south. Much of the land was rich red land, much of it fertile river and creek bottoms. It was very thickly peopled before the Revolutionary war. Mr. White gives as the first settlers:

John Lamar, Peter Lamar, John Dooly, Thomas Dooly, Thomas Murray, John Lockhart, B. Lockhart, Thomas Mitchell, Sterne Simmons, J. Stovall, Stephen Handspiker. M. Henly, Robert Flemming.

Those who are familiar with the names of Scotch-Irish

people will see how many of these first families of Lincoln were of that stock, who came to Wilkes immediately from North Carolina, but more remotely from Pennsylvania and Ireland.

There was a part of this county which was very sterile, but the lands along the rivers and creeks were soon taken up by large plantations.

Lincoln was admirably suited to tobacco culture, and the wealthy slaveholders from Virginia came into it at an early day, and in 1810 there were 2,443 whites and 2,212 negroes in the county. In 1830 there were 2,869 whites and 3,276 negroes; in 1850, 2,218 whites and 3,780 slaves. In 1890 the population was only 6,146.

Much of what is written of Wilkes refers to that part of Lincoln which was in Wilkes up to 1796, and many of the celebrated Kiokee settlers had their homes in Lincoln.

The county was abandoned by many of its best people as soon as the lands in the western counties were opened. The fields grew up in forests, and owing to the distance of the county from markets it has rallied slowly.

Lincolnton was never a large town and is but little changed now from what it was sixty years ago. Goshen was once a place of some importance, but has long since ceased to exist.

The county was the hotbed of Whiggism during the Revolution. Jno. Dooly, the father of Judge Dooly, was a Whig colonel. He was the terror of the Tories and was cruelly murdered by them. His son, Judge Dooly, was famous as a brilliant lawyer and an honored judge, but, alas! as famous for the gross irregularities of his life. The worn-out stories of his coarse wit have been a staple with all writers on early Georgia.

The nearness of the Kiokee church to Lincoln and the influence of Daniel Marshall in this county has made Lincoln largely a Baptist county, and there are some very solid and prosperous churches of that denomination in it now. The Methodists, the only other denomination in the county, have a good following, and it is perhaps somewhat remarkable that the oldest Sunday-school which has had a continuous life in Georgia is in a country church in Lincoln, where for over eighty years a Sunday-school has been held every Sunday.

Judge Longstreet located the scene of the celebrated occurrence when the man was seeing how he "could a fout" in the Dark Corner of Lincoln; but I have been unable to find any part of Lincoln which would consent to acknowledge that it was the part alluded to.

CHAPTER VI.

1800 TO 1812.

The New Century and the New Era—Political Bitterness—Duel between Van Allen and Wm. H. Crawford—Duel between John Clark and Wm. H. Crawford—Jackson Elected Senator—Josiah Tattnall Governor—David Emanuel—John Milledge—Jared Irwin—David B. Mitchell—Sale of the Yazoo Lands to the United States—New Counties Opened—Baldwin, Wilkinson and Wayne Formed—New Settlements Made—The Cotton Gin—Rapid Growth of Cotton planting—Virginia Immigrants—North Carolina Immigration—Removal of the Capital—Flush Times in Georgia—The University Opened—Great Religious Revival—Christ Church, Savannah—The Independent Church, Savannah—The Roman Catholics—The Baptists—Dr. Holcombe—Judge Clay—Jesse Mercer—Mt. Enon Academy—The Methodists—Stith Mead—Camp-meetings—Lorenzo Dow—Jesse Lee—The Embargo—The Alleviating Acts—Establishment of the First State Bank—First Cotton and Wool Factory—First Stage Coach Line—River Communication.

Authorities: Marbury & Crawford's Digest, Sherwood's Gazetteer, White's Statistics, White's Historical Collections, Clayton's Compilation of Georgia Laws, Old Pamphlets, Campbell's Baptists, Smith's History of Methodism in Georgia, Life of Jesse Mercer, Andrews's Reminiscences, Gilmer's Georgians, Bench and Bar of Georgia, Newspapers.

David Emanuel, a Marylander who came to Georgia with John Twiggs, and was a brave soldier in the Revolutionary war, was a member of the Senate from Burke and was president of that body, and became by virtue of his office governor in the interim before a new election took place. He was a man of fine character, who was fully trusted by his fellow citizens.

Josiah Tattnall, Jr., was elected at the regular term as governor. He was the son of the sturdy Loyalist, Josiah Tattnall, Sr., who had stood so firmly for the king and who was now in exile. The old Royalist had sent his bright boy to the Bermudas that he might be kept from doing as the young Habershams and Milledge and James Jackson had done, taking up arms against his king; but young Josiah's heart was with the Whigs, and he made his way back to Georgia as soon as possible and entered the army just as the war closed. He came too late to do more than show his willingness to serve the State. He entered political life and was with Jackson and the Republicans.

The times were times of intense bitterness and Federalist and Republican were at dagger's point. Personalities were common, and the duel was the frequent outcome of the political disputes. Van Allen, of New York, who had settled in Georgia as a lawyer, was killed in a duel with W. H. Crawford. John Clark had a duel with Crawford and shot him through the wrist. James Jackson had a duel with Colonel Watkins and was wounded in the arm, and Judge Tait challenged Judge Dooly and a duel was averted by Dooly's wit. Between the animosities resulting from the Yazoo affair and the political troubles, there was little peace in Georgia in the beginning of the century.

The young governor entered upon his duties, but his health was so broken that he was compelled to resign. He went to the West Indies in a vain pursuit of health and died soon after his return to Georgia and not long after his retirement. He was succeeded by John Milledge, the second of the name. John Milledge's grandfather, Richard Milledge, came with Oglethorpe to the colony, bringing his sons John and Richard with him. The father and mother died soon after they reached Savannah, and upon the son John, whom Mr. Oglethorpe called a worthy and industrious boy, fell the maintenance of the family. He was a fine young fellow and had the friendship of Oglethorpe, and during the Spanish war was appointed quartermaster. He acquired a handsome property, and gave his son John the best advantages for education the colony afforded.

When the Revolutionary troubles began the elder Milledge seems to have been dead. He was a leading man in Savannah but seems to have had no part in the Revolutionary movement, but his son John was an ardent Whig and was connected with those who broke into the magazine. He joined the army, fought through the siege at Savannah, and then with James Jackson made his escape to South Carolina, where he went to Sumter's army, as we have seen, and narrowly escaped being hung for a spy. He was chosen as attorney-general while he was a refugee. When the war was over he married the daughter of George Galphins, and having a considerable estate of his own, and marrying a woman of large property, he became one of the rich men of Georgia. He was very popular and was sent to Congress, first to the House, then to the Senate; was elected governor to succeed Governor Irwin, and then to the Senate again. He retired to private life in 1807.

Mr. Milledge bought with his own funds the seven hundred acres upon which the University and a part of the city of Athens is located, and gave it as a free gift to the trustees of the projected University as a site for the institution, and when the new county of Baldwin was laid out in 1803 the county site was named Milledgeville in his honor.

After his term closed Jared Irwin was chosen governor a second time. He was governor from 1807 to 1809, when he was succeeded by David B. Mitchell. This gentleman was born and brought up in Scotland. He was the nephew of Dr. David Brydie, a physician in Savannah, who was a surgeon in the American army. When Savannah was captured Dr. Brydie fell into the hands of the British and died on a prison ship, having made his nephew and namesake his heir. Young Mitchell came to Savannah, studied law, was admitted to practise, married a Savannah lady, and was rapidly promoted to a place in the councils of the State. He was very popular and was three times elected governor.

He removed from Savannah to an estate near Milledgeville, where he died at a comparatively early age.*

The troubles between the United States and England came to a crisis while Governor Mitchell was in his last year of office. In common with most of the Georgians he was an enthusiastic war man, and cooperated with the general government very heartily. During the financial depression which followed the embargo a bill for the relief of debtors had been passed and approved by Governor Mitchell. Judge Early succeeded him, and while he was governor the Legislature extended the act and he vetoed it. It was passed over his veto, and when the governor offered for reelection he was opposed by ex-Governor Mitchell. Mr. Mitchell was elected governor the third time.

The Legislature in the first years of the century made a sale of the Yazoo territory to the general government, and Governor Jackson, Mr. Milledge and Mr. Baldwin were the parties selected as commissioners by the State of Georgia. After a rather stormy time an agreement between the two sovereignties, as the treaty denominates them, was made and the sale was a fact accomplished.

The United States government agreed to extinguish the Indian title to all lands east of the Chattahoochee, and to pay Georgia $1,500,000 and take the title, with all its shadows, and so Georgia was free from all further care of its western territory.

The United States government went at once to work to negotiate with the Creeks for the extension of the western line of Georgia. Treaties were made in 1802, 1804 and 1805, by which all the lands east of the Ocmulgee river were ceded by the Indians to Georgia. This land was distributed by lottery to the citizens of Georgia, and is now included in the counties of Morgan, Jasper, Putnam, Jones, Wilkinson, Twiggs, Pulaski, Telfair, Laurens, Wayne.

* White.

The first purchase was made in 1802 and divided into three counties—Baldwin, Wilkinson and Wayne. The first drawing was made in 1803, and the country was rapidly peopled by those who drew the lots, or by those to whom they were sold. The people from the eastern counties came in droves into this new country. The upper part of the country was a section of great beauty and attracted a great many settlers from the older counties, and many Virginians now came into this new country.

In the counties along the tide-water in Virginia, where there were many slaves, tobacco culture was now almost abandoned and all farming was unprofitable. The land was worn and poor and the negroes numerous, and the prospect of making fortunes in Georgia raising cotton was alluring, so a great many Virginians and North Carolinians had emigrated and settled plantations in Wilkes, Hancock and Greene twenty years before, and now on the opening of the new purchase they came in numbers to the new lands of Putnam, Jones, Morgan and Jasper, or Randolph, as it was then called. Many of these were men of property who had a number of slaves.

To move from Virginia in the early days of the century was a difficult matter, and often the Virginian came out to Georgia and bought from a dealer in wild lands some fresh, rich land, and prepared for his removal. He brought with him at his first coming a few negroes, cleared some land, and built his houses.

As was the case in first settlements everywhere at that time, these houses were single-roomed log houses, or at best a double log house, with puncheon floor, and stick-and-dirt chimneys. After his houses were built he returned to Virginia for his family. He had a sale and sold out and gave away the larger part of his belongings, and storing the rest in his large four-horse wagon he prepared for his removal.

The women and children of the family were provided with a Jersey or Dearborn wagon. The negroes were mainly on foot driving the cattle before them, and with some of his neighbors who were moving with him he began his journey from Hanover, New Kent, Brunswick, Dinwiddie or Albemarle to "Georgay," as he generally pronounced the name of his new home. He and his sons rode on horseback, and a two-horse wagon was provided for the negro women and the children.

The cavalcade dragged its slow length along until after fifty days of weary travel, camping out at night and cooking by the camp-fire, the families reached the new home. There were years of struggling before the comforts they left behind in the old commonwealth were once more provided, but the lands were productive, negroes increased rapidly, cotton was high, property rapidly increased, and while the loyal Virginian did not forget his old State, and would never admit any land equal to it, he admitted that he found a Virginia almost as good in Georgia.

There was no part of Georgia old, and to all parts immigrants were coming. The poor man with no slaves sought the cheap hills of Jackson and Franklin, or if he was from the pine woods of North Carolina, from Robinson and Onslow and Cumberland, he came generally to the pine forests of lower Washington and Montgomery.

The older counties of middle Georgia had been settled by the same class of people from North Carolina and Virginia, who now came to the new counties, and they had now become quite populous, sending out a number of emigrants, who left the old for the new counties.

The towns in middle Georgia, Warrenton, Washington, Petersburg and Sparta, were towns of large trade, and the streets of Augusta were thronged with wagons from western South Carolina, western North Carolina and upper Georgia. Merchants came to buy goods and farmers to sell produce and buy supplies. Savannah was a busy seaport and fleets of small vessels came in with loads of West Indies produce, and went out laden with rice, tobacco, cotton and lumber. The slave-ships owned in Boston and in England emptied their cargoes on the wharves of Savannah with fearful frequency. These new negroes, as they were called, were generally bought by the rice-planters on the coast, and but few found their way into the interior. This foreign slave-trade was to cease in 1808, and so crowds were hurried to the market before it became a piracy to bring them in.

There was now a demand for the removal of the capital of Georgia further westward. Louisville was too near Augusta, and perhaps not a little unhealthy, lying between the Ogeechee river and Rocky Comfort creek. The capitol had not cost much, and was very unsatisfactory, and so in 1804 it was decided to remove the seat of government from the banks of the Ogeechee to the banks of the Oconee, and to the spot selected as the county site of the new county of Baldwin, which, in recognition of the genuine benevolence of John Milledge, was called Milledgeville. A double log cabin, overlooking Fishing creek just below where is now the railroad bridge on the dummy line, was provided as a mansion for Governor Irwin, and as soon as it could be finished the plain two-story house still standing, and long occupied by Peter Fair, was made the governor's residence. Fifteen thousand dollars was put in the hands of the commissioners to provide public buildings.

The incoming of so many people of means, the fertility of the newly-opened lands, the general healthfulness of the county, the high price of cotton, and the abundance of provisions made these early days of the century flush times. Fortunes were rapidly made, speculation ran wild, cities and villages sprang up like magic, but all at once the embargo came. Then there was stagnation, and reverses began. There was constant agitation and alarm, and then the war of 1812 followed.

The University was located by the commission selected, as we have seen elsewhere, in Jackson county, on the land purchased by Mr. Milledge. The Legislature made a new county named Clarke, and granted an endowment in lands which were afterward sold for $100,000.

Josiah Miegs was chosen as president, and the college had its first commencement, under an arbor, in 1804. In the chapter on education in Georgia I have given a fuller account of this important incident in Georgia history. It was designed to make the institution a university, but it was at this time in its feeblest infancy.

It was during the period under survey that there was one of the most remarkable religious movements ever known in the history of Georgia. It is needless to deny the fact that the morals and religion of Georgia before this time were in a deplorable condition. Crawford, Clarke, Jackson, Tait, Gibbons and Mitchell were duelists, and had each been on the field, some of them more than once. Two of these had killed his antagonist. There was a great deal of deep drinking and gaming among the leading men. John Clarke, the favorite of the common people, was notorious for his excesses. W. H. Crawford was by no means temperate. John M. Dooly was a drunkard and a gambler, although he was a judge. Among the common people the standard of morals was very low. There was a fearful amount of profanity and drunkenness. At their assemblages the people drank freely, and there was never a gathering without a fight in the ring. They raced horses, gambled with cards and dice, and were many of them rude and lawless.

They had many virtues, for they were generous, hospitable, courageous, truthful. There was comparatively little impurity. The marriages were early, and the marriage vows strictly regarded. There were many of the leading men, however, decided in their religious character, and while the lawmaker was somewhat loose in his morals, the laws on the statute book were almost severe in their demands for rectitude of conduct.

The great revival of which I have spoken, which began in 1800, came and swept over the State. Of this I have given a fuller account in my chapter on "Religion in Georgia," to which the reader is referred.

The flush times in the early years of the century were followed by years of financial distress. The wars in Europe had put an end to all foreign commerce. The people coming to Georgia, and the people already here, had been almost crazed by the wild spirit of speculation. Great debts had been made for negroes and land, cotton was becoming the staple, and large plantations were opened. Then the demand ceased, and there was no sale for cotton, rice or tobacco. The United States bank and its branches were the only banks, and they called in their loans. Universal bankruptcy hung over the State. The embargo was threatened, and in 1808 an alleviating act for the relief of debtors was passed. One-third of the debt was to be paid when due, and time was to be allowed for the payment of the rest of the debt.

This provision for relief was renewed during the incumbency of Governor Early, as we have seen, and the act was vetoed by him. The Legislature was very indignant, and the act was passed over the veto, and the people were so resentful that the governor was not reelected.

It was during this period in 1809 that the first bank in Georgia was chartered. It was to be known as the Planters Bank, and was to be located in Savannah, with branches in all the principal towns. The list of commissioners and the places where subscriptions of stock were to be received give us an insight into the important places then in the

State. They were Savannah, Augusta, Columbia Courthouse, Washington, Warrenton, Louisville, Milledgeville, and Hartford (now Hawkinsville).

The plan was a wide, sweeping one. The bank and its branches aimed to reach all sections of the State and embrace a great number of stockholders. No one could hold over fifty shares of stock, and when three hundred thousand dollars in gold and silver was in hand the bank was to begin its work. The scheme was not successful and the bank did not open then, and a new charter was granted in 1810 for one of the same name. At the same time that this new charter was granted the Bank of Augusta, with three hundred thousand dollars capital, was also chartered, and these banks went into operation. The United States Bank had several branches established in the State at this time.

The first manufactory in Georgia was chartered in 1810 and was to be located in Wilkes county. It was to make woolen and cotton goods. The factory was located some twelve miles from Washington and went into operation, but was not successful.

Stage lines were now chartered and established between Augusta and Savannah, and Augusta and Washington in Wilkes. They were to run stages at least once a week. There were of course no railways, nor for thirty years after this, and the first steamboat during this period made its trial trip from New York to Albany; there was as yet none in Georgia.

The people went to market on horseback and sent their produce, when it was shipped by water, on flatboats. The rivers, and even the larger creeks, were utilized as far as possible, and efforts were made by public labor and by the organization of navigation companies to keep them open.

These first years of the century were days of wild trading. Soldiers' warrants, plots and grants of new lands, ancient headrights, confiscated property, all were in the market; and now the eagerness to make money rapidly led to the chartering of lotteries. They had been forbidden by the colonial laws of thirty years before, but were now allowed and encouraged. Christ Church, in Savannah, was to be built by a lottery. The Midway graveyard in Liberty county, near the Congregational church, was to be enclosed by the proceeds of a lottery. Schools in the counties of Washington and Columbia were to be helped by a lottery. The poor of Chatham, the court-house in Savannah and the university all had lotteries for their benefit.*

Joseph Rice, of Savannah, had more jewelry and watches than he could easily sell, and he was permitted to get rid of his goods by a lottery, and was to pay for the privilege ten per cent. royalty to the State. Rivers were to be made navigable and the expense met by a lottery, and a lottery seems to have been the source of supply for all needs.

Josiah Tattnall, Sr., had stood bravely by the king and had been exiled and his property taken. After thirty years his son Josiah was governor, and the Legislature did itself honor when it pardoned the old Loyalist; and when Josiah Tattnall, Jr., affixed his signature of approval to an act pardoning Josiah Tattnall, Sr., he said, "With lively impressions of gratitude I affix my signature to this act."

In those days couples were divorced, murderers were pardoned and natural children made legitimate by the Legislature.

Negro slaves were manumitted by authority of the Legislature, and there were not a few who were made free persons of color by a special act.

The salaries of the governor and of State-house officers were: $2,000 for the governor, $500 each for two secretaries, $200 for secretary of state, $200 for surveyor-general, $1,400 for judge of superior court, and $1,200 for treasurer. The attorney-general and solicitors received $150

* See Clayton's Compilation.

each, the comptroller $600, the clerk of the house $300. The poll-tax was 31½ cents per poll.

A tobacco warehouse was established on the Tugalo, at the mouth of the Seneca, from which it is evident that tobacco was a staple in Franklin at that time. Lincoln, Elbert and Wilkes were the great tobacco-raising counties, and while the change from tobacco to cotton was going on, the Virginia weed still held the highest place, and hogsheads were rolled to the warehouses, inspected and shipped thence to Liverpool and London, and goods were imported direct from England. Thos. Grant and his father, Daniel, who were merchandizing in Wilkes, bought all their goods from England for several years after the century began.

The cotton machines were now erected in all the counties, and the culture of indigo and tobacco was giving way to cotton. The sea island planter still used the old roller-gin and raised his long-staple cotton, which he ginned with it; but what was known as green seed, petit gulf cotton or short-staple was making its way into the up-country as far as the upper part of Elbert, where tobacco was still the staple.

The domestic slave-trade was never regarded with favor in Georgia, and severe laws were passed to restrict it, but the demand for labor to cultivate the cotton farms, and the depressed condition of things in eastern Virginia and Maryland, led to its permanent establishment, and troops of negroes were brought from Virginia and Maryland to Georgia. There were now two decidedly different classes of negroes in Georgia, the pure African, or his immediate descendant, and the Anglo-African from Virginia, North Carolina and Maryland. The blood of the same race belonged to both, but the Virginia negro was removed at least four generations from his African ancestor, and change of climate and of food had greatly improved him in physical and mental features. He was more docile, more intelligent, but perhaps less faithful and more artful than the recent comer. His lips were not so thick, his size was greater, and he was less of an animal in his looks and ways. The pure African on the coast was but little changed from the slave of negro-land or Guinea. He had better food and better government than he had in Africa, but at this time was, while less savage and more tractable, much like in other respects his ancestor across the seas.

The white people of Georgia in the early part of the century presented different features, and these were found in different sections of the State. There were at this time only two cities of moderate size, and so the population was almost exclusively rural.

As the reader has seen, much the larger part of the early comers had been Virginians and North Carolinians, and were a homogeneous body, but those who came from over the sea, and their descendants, were from different peoples and still preserved their original features. The English people who came from 1732 to 1750 belonged to the middle and lower classes of Englishmen. There were few of the gentry and still fewer of the peasantry among them. They were generally those sterling middle-class people who have done so much for England. Very few of them had become farmers; they had either become planters or found a place in the city. The Germans, both the Salzburghers and the later comers, had almost universally continued on the farm, and while they were now distributed largely over southern Georgia, they were still in all their features the same people who had settled at Ebenezer.

The Scotch had among the immigrants to Georgia chiefs of clans and lairds, who were as proud of their Celtic blood and of their Tarleton as "The McIntosh" had been in the Highlands; but the most of the Scotch people, although belonging to the famous clans, were poor peasants, living at first in a very narrow way, and in the beginning of the century were in the main stockmen.

The near seventy years since the coast had been settled had done much to bring about great changes in social conditions there. The estates had become very large and the oneness of conditions had unified society, and whether the low-country rice or sea-island cotton-planters descended from the English, the Scotch or the Huguenots, they had much the same features and formed a society of their own. They were isolated, each man in his own barony, where he was a feudal lord who rarely left his own broad domain and lived among his slaves.

These wealthy, cultured and exclusive people were only a limited number of the white people on the coast. Away from the coast, toward the interior, there were many poor and ignorant people, as well as many thrifty, unpretending, self-supporting and independent farmers who lived on wide stretches of pine land. These people, called crackers by their wealthier neighbors, were descendants in many cases of the indentured servants who had been brought from the various countries across the sea; in others they were the descendants of the thriftless, perhaps profligate, members of good families, or adventurers from the Carolinas or Virginia. They went where land was cheap and where the people lived plainly, and where they could procure a living with but little work.

The overseers have been sometimes confounded with this class, and in Mr. Wirt's "Life of Patrick Henry" the Virginia overseer is written down as a poor specimen of his race, but this was not the case on the coast. It required a man of real parts to manage a great rice plantation, and a good overseer was likely to become in time a wealthy planter.

At this time many of the descendants of the best people

who came in the early days of the colony were managing plantations for their more fortunate neighbors, who sprung originally from the same class to which they belonged, but who had made or inherited fortunes.

I have already given some insight into the life of the piny woods farmer of the better class in my sketch of Liberty county. There were in the first days of the century three distinct classes on the coast who were as distinct in Georgia as the gentry, the yeomanry and the peasantry in England. In the up-country above Burke county there was no such decided distinction in classes. Very many of the people of Wilkes and Greene and Hancock, occupying the same social position, sprang from entirely different stems. Men who had names in the English peerage, or those whose ancestors were Welsh squires and Scotch lairds, were side by side with descendants of Scotch-Irish yeomen, whose almost penniless fathers came from the humblest homes in Ireland to Pennsylvania, and thence down to North Carolina, and had made fortunes by their energy and thrift.

These were side by side with the descendants of the Redemptioners who began their American life in the tobacco plantations of Virginia. There were a great many Georgians who belonged by family connection to the old English aristocracy. Their ancestors had come to Virginia before the seventeenth century. They came to Georgia poor men, and became leading people; and they were not distinguished from the English yeomanry who had also lived in Virginia, and had now removed to Georgia. There was in Virginia and lower South Carolina a very high estimate put upon family distinctions, and the same feeling was found in lower Georgia—especially in Savannah and on the coast; but in upper Georgia there was a strong feeling against this spirit. Family pride was ridiculed and denounced. Popular politicians claimed kinship with the common people.

Milledge, Clarke, Irwin, Jackson, the favorites in political circles, were men who made no claim to ancient or aristocratic lineage, and were loud in their denunciations of such claims. This want of family pride had its origin largely in the principles of the new movement in France and the hostility to the English, which was at its height at this time.

In all the up-country these old family distinctions were lost sight of—at least by the men; and while in the up-country, as in the low-country, there was the "cracker" of the humblest type, as a general thing, where land was so easily secured, the poor man became a landholder, and the thriftless and indolent moved with the ever-advancing line westward. At the time of which we write Georgia society had taken its permanent shape; and there was but little change in it for some time, until the coming in of trading Jews and the Irish and the springing up of populations in the manufacturing villages.

While it is true the constant advance of the settlements into the Indian country brought about a great diversity of social conditions long after this period, and there was much simplicity in life and many hardships, there was in the old counties a great increase in comfort. Burke, Jefferson, Wilkes, and Elbert were now from thirty to forty years old, and convenient to markets, and the comforts of a settled state of things were enjoyed by the people, while the counties west of the Oconee were just being settled and were having to encounter the usual difficulties of the frontier. From the elegant homes of the people on the coast, and in the cities, there was a constant grade to the one-roomed log cabin of the new settler in Morgan or Wilkinson. There were, indeed, almost all kinds of social life in Georgia at this time; but the different kinds became more plainly brought out before the end of the next decade.

There can be no denial of the fact that for the first twenty years of the century there was the same indorsement of dueling that was found in the more Northern States and in England, and no man dared in those days to refuse a challenge; but in 1805 the Georgia Legislature went so far as to forbid the duelist from ever holding public office. Although there was a law against it, it must be admitted that public sentiment in some cases still upheld that cowardly and disgraceful method of settling personal quarrels; but the disapproval set upon it by the Legislature has become more and more a sentiment, until at the present time the duelist is regarded with decided disfavor.

The county towns of Eatonton, Hartford, Warrenton, Lexington, Athens, Madison, Milledgeville and Elberton were all incorporated, and academies were established in each of them.

There was a literary and Thespian society organized in Augusta with the following members: Robert McRae, Richard Wilde, Dan MacMurphey, Samuel Hale, Abraham A. A. Leggett, Henry L. McRae, John W. Shinholser, Zach Rossell, James Wilde, Daniel Savage, Willoughby Barton, Albert Brux, Thos. J. Wray, John R. Barnes. This society was organized in 1808. Among the names of the incorporators is one who won a world-wide distinction as a man of letters. This was Richard Henry Wilde. His little poem, " My Life is Like the Summer Rose," has taken its place beside the choicest gems of lyric poetry, while his discovery of the lost portraits of Tasso and his life of the Italian poet have given him a lasting fame among men of letters. He was of Irish lineage. His father was an Irish merchant who by the perfidy of an American partner was robbed of all he had. His mother a woman of sterling worth, who, when her husband sank under his losses, opened a millinery shop in the young city of Augusta and supported her family. Richard Henry was her oldest son. He labored hard in the counting-room to aid his mother in her efforts to support the younger children, studied law, was elected to Congress when only twenty-seven years old, and held his place there until 1835. He then retired from public life, and spent some time in Europe in literary labors, and on returning to America entered again on the practice of his profession in New Orleans, where he died. He was a man of rare gifts and of very finished culture. There was a literary society of some note in Petersburg, of which Governor Bibb, afterward of Alabama, and the father of Junius Hillyer and Dr. S. G. Hillyer were members.

These middle Georgia towns which had now sprung up were all laid out on the same plan—a plan like that of the old Virginia county sites. A square was chosen. In the center was the court-house, generally a plain square box-house, with a court-room up-stairs and offices down-stairs. On one corner was the village tavern, and around the square the village stores. These country stores aimed to furnish everything the people needed. They sold dry-goods, groceries, hardware, drugs, saddlery, and in all of them there were bars from which whisky was retailed. The county towns were generally small. The county doctor, a few lawyers, the teacher and the court officers generally made up the families in them. The farmers lived on the farms, and the planters at this period were few, and those few lived on their plantations. The country people came in great numbers to the county towns on court days and the days of the general muster.

There was a superior court twice in the year, and an inferior court which met every month. On court days there was a large attendance of the people, especially when the superior court was in session. At that time the whole county was represented, and those who had business in town, as well as those who had business in court, went to town then, and the crowd was increased by those who had no business at all. The most of the people came on horseback. The lawyers from all the country round came in gigs and sulkies. If it was a time of political excitement, a political speech was sandwiched between the morning and afternoon sessions of the court. The ginger-cake wagon with its keg of persimmon beer was always on hand, and the motherly dame who sold a cake for a thrip and threw in the beer was always present. On Tuesday of the first week of the court was horse-swapping day. Whisky flowed freely, and nearly everybody took a dram. Fisticuffs were the result, and they were common. The village was crowded with people for a week, court then adjourned, and all became quiet again.

The militia laws were very carefully drawn and the theory of a citizens' army very beautiful. All able-bodied men between eighteen and forty-five were to be enrolled. They were to be placed in districts, battalions, brigades and divisions. They were to be officered by major-generals, brigadier-generals, colonels, majors and captains. Four times a year the captain drilled his company, twice a year there was a battalion drill, and once a year a general muster. The offices held by the staff were very honorable distinctions. The major-general was elected by the Legislature, and the position was highly valued.

For years after the Revolution there was an earnest and persistent effort made to carry out the scheme of training the militia, but at last it was abandoned because of its thorough inefficiency.

In the first days of the century the militia muster was a very imposing affair. The people came from all the districts in the county. The major-general, attended by his staff, with glittering epaulets and flowery plumes, mounted a magnificent charger. He wore his brilliant uniform and cocked hat, and his staff was elegantly equipped. He was the center of attraction. The brigadiers and colonels and majors were in full force, all uniformed and mounted. The captains, however, were as a general thing in citizen's clothes, with perhaps a feather in their hats. The rank and file were armed with old Kentucky rifles, single-barreled shotguns, sticks and cornstalks. A pretense of drilling and reviewing was made, and after a day of absurdity the mustering militia was discharged until another twelve-month had gone.

There were a few volunteer companies which kept up an organization, the Chatham artillery, the Liberty troop, and perhaps a company in Augusta.

After the muster was over there was generally a time of wild revelry; corn whisky and peach brandy flowed freely, and "Ransy Sniffle" managed to bring "Bill Stallings and Bob Durham" together in the ring. As a general thing there was no more serious casualty resulting from these combats than a bitten ear or a gouged eye. Stabbing was not common, and shooting was almost unknown. No man carried a pistol in those days, and the old-time dirk was regarded as a cowardly weapon.

The sturdy old farmers looked on these muster days with great abhorrence, and looked upon town-people generally as objects of pity. Even the preachers had little hope for the towns.

There was no church in Waynesboro, Washington, Warrenton, Sandersville or Eatonton for years, and then the services held were by no means frequent.

There were made during this time quite a number of new counties—Tattnall, Clarke, Baldwin, Wilkinson, Wayne, Putnam, Morgan, Jones, Randolph (or Jasper), Pulaski, Laurens, and Twiggs.

These counties, which will be glanced at separately, divide themselves into groups, where each county has much the same features.

Clarke, Baldwin, Putnam, Morgan, Jones, Jasper, or, as it was then called, Randolph, form one group known as middle Georgia, or oak and hickory counties.

Wilkinson, Twiggs, Pulaski and Laurens form a second group partly oak and hickory lands, partly pine lands, and Wayne, Telfair and Tattnall exclusively pine woods.

The middle Georgia counties were rapidly peopled, and those who study the names of the first settlers will recognize many of them as Georgians from the eastern counties, though some were Virginians and North Carolinians. The lands were distributed by lottery, and many who drew lots of two hundred and two and one-half acres removed at once to them and began to open farms. The first comers, as in the older counties, were generally poor; they had no negroes, or a very few, and in all new Georgia the wealth of the country for the first twenty years was largely in horses, cattle and hogs. While there were the discomforts resulting from settlement in a new country, these settlers had few severe hardships.

There was for the first twenty years little mental cultivation; very few people had any books. Many of the wills during this period were signed with a mark, and few women could write their names.

In many respects the section which was first called Baldwin presented the same features; and the study of the individual counties will bring out the differences between them. They were all rapidly settled, and by a good class of settlers. It will perhaps be a matter of some surprise that the people of these new counties were less cultivated than those of Wilkes, Hancock or Greene, from which so many of them came; but the surprise will cease when it is remembered that these people came to manhood during the Revolution and the Oconee War, and men of excellent families and of good means had no opportunities for an education, and could barely read and hardly write their names. The features of social life were the same as has been pictured in the early days of Wilkes and Greene. The second group of counties, Wilkinson, Laurens and Pulaski, were partly oak and hickory, but mainly piny woods counties, and were peopled by different classes of people, according to the character of the land.

To these mixed counties two very different classes of people came. To the land on creeks and rivers men of large means came to open plantations. They bought a large area of the best cotton land and settled a score or more of negroes to cultivate it. They then bought a great body of pine land near by, so that their holdings were very extensive. Men like General Blackshear and Governor Troup had establishments like that of an English baron, while the men who lived in the pine woods were such as are portrayed elsewhere.

These two classes of people had little to do with each other. They were on the same juries, and sometimes judges of the same court, but there was no social intermingling. It was the same condition of things that obtained on the coast thirty years before.

In the rich lands of Twiggs, Pulaski, Laurens and Wilkinson there were the same general features that were to be found in the older counties. This was the case in the years following this period; but before 1812 in these counties the forest in many places was unbroken. The cabins were few and far between, and the settler, who thirty years after had an elegant dwelling filled with guests, was now living in a log cabin and carefully seeing after his cows on the ranch and preparing his low grounds to make corn. There was little cotton made by rich or poor; there were few comforts, and there was no luxury.

We shall perhaps get a better idea of the development of Georgia by studying the features belonging to the counties as they come before us one by one.

CLARKE.

Though Clarke was made a county in 1801, it was not then first settled. It was a part of Franklin, then of Jackson, and when the University was established at Athens was made a separate county and called Clarke in honor of Elijah Clarke, of whose distinguished services during the Revolution we have spoken. The county site was Watkinsville, named in honor of Robert Watkins. The original county of Clarke was a large one, and in 1875, when Athens was a considerable town, it was divided into two counties, one of which was called Oconee, the other Clarke. Watkinsville was left as the county site of Oconee, and Athens was made the county site of Clarke.

There was a great deal of first-class land in the undivided county, and a limited quantity in what is now Clarke.

Although Clarke could not present the inducements to settlers which Greene and Hancock did, there came to it some of the same class of people at its first settlement; and the position of Athens as an educational center drew to it at a later day a class of most excellent people, who settled in the village and in the country adjoining. Mr. White gives as the first settlers, Thomas Greer, James Greer, Sol. Craig, Charles Dean, F. Roberson, Wm. Clarke, Wm. Williams, Wm. Jones, Francis Oliver, Thomas Wade, Daniel Elder, Zadock Cook, John Jackson, Hugh Niesler, Thomas Mitchell, James Cook, Wyatt Lee, Robert Barber, Hope Hull, A. Briggs, Jesse White, David Meriwether, Joseph Espey, John Espey.

As we have seen, Athens was laid out on seven hundred acres of land purchased by John Milledge, and was made the seat of the University. It was very healthy, and soon drew to it an excellent class of citizens. It had a good country tributary to it, and soon became a place of commercial importance. The facilities for manufacturing provided by the fine water-powers on the Oconee river, on which the city of Athens is located, were recognized, and at an early date its citizens began to manufacture; and

UNIVERSITY.

some of the most successful cotton mills and other factories in Georgia have been established near Athens. The Georgia railroad early built a branch road to the city, and when the Air Line railway, from Charlotte to Atlanta, was built, the people of Athens built a line of forty miles to tap it at Lula, and when the S. A. L. line reached Georgia it came directly through Athens, and then the Central bought a line from Macon to the city, and thus gave it the best railway privileges, and it has become quite a trade center.

Athens has not only been noted for its culture and refinement, but for the piety of its leading people. Although as late as 1825 there was no church in the village, there was regular religious service in the college chapel. In 1825, or near that time, the Presbyterians built a church on the campus. The Baptists built also on the campus, and the Methodists where the First Methodist now stands. The Episcopalians were somewhat later. There have been great revivals of religion in Athens, in which some of the most distinguished men in Georgia have begun a religious life. The country around is well supplied with churches, mainly Methodist and Baptist.

Clarke was formed in 1801, and by 1810 it had 5,034 free and 2,594 slave inhabitants, and in 1830 there were 5,467 free and 4,709 slaves; in 1850 there were 5,330 free and 5,589 slaves. In 1890 the entire population was 15,186. It has now, in 1899, a very much larger population.

The city of Athens is one of the most attractive and elegant cities in the State. It has a fine electric plant, a street railway, well-paved streets, handsome public buildings, water-works, and all the equipment of a working city. Of the University, with which the history of Athens is so connected, we have spoken elsewhere.

While Athens had always had excellent female schools, and the second distinctively female school in the State was in Athens, it had no female collegiate institute until Thos. R. R. Cobb, as a memorial to a child to whom he was devoted, gave a large donation for a female institute of high grade, which was called the Lucy Cobb Institute in honor of his daughter, and which has held high rank with the best schools for young ladies. The State Normal School is also located here.

In Athens was established the celebrated Southern Mutual Insurance Company, which has been the most successful purely Mutual Fire Insurance Company in the Southern States, and perhaps in America.

The location of the University in Athens has made it famous for its public men. Among the most valuable of the early settlers in the county was Hope Hull, whom we have seen as a young Methodist preacher in Wilkes county in 1788. He had a home near Washington, and established ten years before Athens was founded or the University began its work a classical school and employed teachers to teach it. He was among the heartiest supporters of the proposed college in Athens and was a member of its first board of trustees, and as long as he lived he never lost his interest in it. His two sons, Asbury Hull and Dr. Henry Hull, were like himself men of great worth and public spirit.

Asbury Hull was for several years speaker of the House of Representatives in the Georgia Legislature, a leading banker and capitalist in Athens. Dr. Henry Hull, his excellent brother, once a professor in the State University, spent his long life in Athens.

John A. Cobb settled in a part of Athens which he called Cobham, and here he lived and educated his two sons Howell and Thomas R. R. Cobb, whose fame as soldiers and statesmen is so widely extended.

The celebrated Moses Waddell spent his last days here as president of the State University.

Dr. A. A. Lipscomb, the philosopher and sage, lived here in a charming cottage after he had retired from the presidency of the University.

Young L. G. Harris, famous as a financier and as a philanthropist, lived and died here.

Ferdinand Phinizy, one of the most distinguished capitalists in Georgia, had his home here.

It was in Athens that Dr. Crawford Long used ether as an anesthetic before it had ever been so used by any other person.

Here Dr. Patrick H. Mell, one of the best of teachers and the purest of men, spent his last years as president of the University.

The celebrated Stephen Olin, the peerless preacher, spent several years here as professor of English literature.

Here Dr. Nathan Hoyt, the famous Presbyterian preacher, and Dr. Chas. Lane, who came after him, ended their useful lives, and here Dr. Eustace W. Speer, after having been several times pastor of the church and at one time professor in the University, fixed his home and ended his days; and in this town Henry W. Grady was born, educated and married.

To catalogue the men of distinction who have been connected with Athens would take far more space than I can possibly devote to this famous city.

Clarke was, like all the hill counties, settled by people of moderate means, who raised chiefly corn and other food products. It had in it many stills and made much brandy and whisky, which it sent to the Augusta market, and the records of the county show that the inhabitants were by no means total abstainers; but there is one record on the county books different from any other in Georgia: A man, anticipating that he would be assassinated, made a will, in which he recited his apprehension, and made a bequest to pay the cost of prosecuting the murderer, and suggesting who he would be and how he might be convicted. He was killed. The murderer was arrested and was convicted and hung.

The grand jury in 1806 says: "The college is now opened, and is ready to teach boys from their A, B, C's, up."

MADISON.

Madison was laid out from Oglethorpe, Clarke, Franklin and Elbert in 1811. It is not a large or fertile county, and in very few respects differs from the counties from which it was taken.

There are two forks of the Broad river in the county, and in the fork near to Elbert, in what was then Wilkes county, at the home of James Marks, the first Methodist Conference in Georgia was probably held.

The first settlers as given by White were, Samuel Long, Jacob Eberhart, Samuel Wood, Stephen Groves and General Daniel.

The county site, Danielsville, is a very small village in a hill country. There was for many years no railroad in the county, but the building of the Seaboard Air Line railroad has brought the best part of the county on Broad river into connection with the outer world.

The people of Madison have been a very plain, sober, religious and well-to-do people, and while much of the county is badly worn and washed, there is some good land and many very worthy people in the county.

BALDWIN.

In 1803 Baldwin was laid out from the new territory. It was a very large county when first made, but has been so cut down by forming new counties that it is now quite small. The upper part of the present county, bordering on Putnam and Jones, was the highly-valued oak and hickory land, as was that part of the county of Hancock beyond

Main Building Georgia Sanitarium, Near Milledgeville.

the Oconee, which was put into Baldwin when it was formed. It was at once settled by substantial planters, most of them from the older counties of Georgia.

The lower part of the county, away from the river and the creeks, was in the pine belt, and was considered very undesirable, and was for a long time very thinly settled. Much of it was exceedingly sterile. The lands on the Oconee and the upper part of the county were very fine, and the population was very large in those sections.

In 1810 the population was 3,809 whites and 2,250 slaves; in 1830 there were only 2,753 whites and 4,542 slaves; in 1850 there were 3,546 whites and 4,602 slaves.

Few parts of the State were settled more rapidly and with a better class of people, and none of the middle Georgia counties were more rapidly worn out and sooner abandoned by the large planters. The lands were very rolling and very friable, and under the system of culture then adopted the surface soil was soon washed away.

The first settlers in the oak and hickory lands of Baldwin were many of them people of some means from the older counties. Many of them had their plantations in the county and fixed their homes in Milledgeville. The rapidity with which the county was settled is seen in the first census in 1810, from which it appears that there were three hundred more white people in the county in 1810 than in 1850.

The first settlers were the Howards, Devereaux, Lamars, Bosticks, Sanfords, Joneses, Pierces, Scotts, Hammonds, Kenans, Battles, Holts, Claytons, Byrds, Malones, Napiers and Flukers.

Three thousand two hundred and forty acres were appropriated to the city. John Rutherford, Littleberry Bostick, A. M. Devereaux, Geo. M. Troup, John Harbert and Oliver Porter were the commissioners. Fishing creek, then a bold and limpid stream, made its way to the river along its eastern border. The forests on the hills and along the river were magnificent. Gushing springs and crystal brooks were found in different parts of the tract. The city was carefully laid out and a great square was designated for the capitol. A handsome hilltop was reserved for the governor's mansion, a tract was reserved for a State prison, and the lots were put on the market. After all this was done the county was organized.

The part of Baldwin which lies beyond the Oconee river was in Hancock, and was thickly settled before Baldwin was laid out. Before Milledgeville was located a town called Montpelier was projected on quite a considerable scale; lots were sold, and a few people settled in it. It was located about where the Montpelier Methodist church is now. Another small town named Salem, nearer the river, was also on the east side of the river.

At this time the Oconee was navigated by flatboats, and most of the produce of this part of the county was boated down to Darien, and goods were brought up the river by the same process.

While the pine lands were considered worthless for farming purposes, they were recognized as very healthy, and as Milledgeville at its first settlement was quite sickly, a resort called Scottsboro, on the edge of the oak and hickory woods among the pines, was chosen as a sanatorium, and the people of Milledgeville had their summer homes there, and some of them had permanent residences on these sand hills. There were for many years but few inhabitants of the pine woods, and most of these were very poor and illiterate.

The land in this section was heavily timbered, but was very sterile. When the Central railway built a branch road to Milledgeville sawmills were built along the line to cut the pine timber. Henry Stephens, a sturdy Englishman, planted a large mill ten miles from Milledgeville, and after he had exhausted the timber resources he began another

industry which has done much for that part of the county. He found an inexhaustible supply of most excellent clay suitable for making fire-brick and sewer-pipe and other kinds of terra-cotta products, and he and his sons have built up one of the largest manufactories of these products in the South.

These pine lands have been improved by modern culture, but their chief wealth is in the strata of clay beneath the surface. The history of the cotton belt, as told before, is the story of Baldwin. The stock-raiser, the small farmer, the large planter, the worn-out fields, and the emigration westward, until in 1850 the white population had been reduced from what it was forty years before, and the negroes were twice as many as they were then.

The Legislature, when it decided on making the new city of Milledgeville, as we have seen, laid out three thousand two hundred and forty acres in city lots, and a modest State-house costing, when completed, sixty thousand dollars was built. It was added to at different times until it received its finishing touch in 1837, and presented the appearance which it presents as the Middle Georgia College. The mansion was built during the incumbency of Governor Clarke, and is a very handsome building on a high hill, now occupied by the president of the Industrial College.

The penitentiary was established in 1803, and after the removal of the capital to Atlanta was demolished, and the site is now occupied by the Normal College.

Milledgeville, as the capital city, was, in days gone by, the scene of much gayety and much dissipation, and has witnessed not a few tragedies. There have been several fatal duels arranged for and many bloody street brawls. The fortunes of the little city have been varied, and the number of its population fluctuating.

With the impoverishment of the land near the city, the planters moved to the newer counties, and few of their descendants remained in the county. The capital of the State was for many years a slow-moving and by no means prosperous town. The court-house of the county was burned and many of the early records were lost. The records of the court of ordinary were preserved, however, and an insight into the almost forgotten history of the early settlers is to be found in them. A very handsome court-house has been erected on the old lot.

The first Methodist church was built in 1807; the first Methodist Sunday-school was established in Milledgeville in 1811, when S. M. Meek was preacher in charge. The present Methodist church was built in 1827. It was built on a lot granted by the State on the public square. The Presbyterians, Baptists and Episcopalians had each a lot granted by the State on the same square. The Baptist church having been burned, it was decided not to rebuild on the lot it had, and the church was built on Wayne street. The Roman Catholics built a neat brick house on Jefferson street.

The want of a sufficient supply of water free from calcareous admixture led to the establishment of a system of water-works by which the waters of Fishing creek were utilized.

Near Milledgeville, in Midway, the Oglethorpe University was located. It was a Presbyterian college, of which we speak more at length in our chapter on Georgia colleges. It was nominally removed to Atlanta after the war; but, as it had neither buildings nor endowment, it was never reestablished.

The Georgia Lunatic Asylum was originated in 1837, through the influence of a stranger from New York, who succeeded in getting the first bill passed for its establishment. Dr. Cooper was its first superintendent, but the

McD. + F.
1897
McDANNELL M-VLLE. GA.

asylum was really not an institution until Dr. Green took charge of it. He was superintendent for many years, and died in the office, and was succeeded by Dr. Powell, who has for the twenty years since Dr. Green died been superintendent. It is now the largest and best equipped State asylum of the entire South.

The city of Milledgeville has grown rapidly since the war, and its healthfulness is greatly improved in these late years.

There was an academy in Milledgeville as soon as it was settled, and there have been famous schools in the city and county since that time. There were two incorporated academies in the county which I am unable to locate. Their names were Corinth and Leonora. Dr. Brown established a famous high school for young ladies at Scottsboro, which had quite a patronage for some years. After the war the old capitol was turned over to the trustees of the Middle Georgia College, and a military school was established on the old grounds. Young people of both sexes, however, were admitted to its halls. A few years since the State decided to establish an industrial and normal school for young women, and Milledgeville secured its location in its midst, and the grounds formerly used by the State prison were chosen as a site, and very handsome buildings erected at the expense of the State. The institution has been very popular and largely patronized.

To merely mention a small number of the distinguished people who have resided in this county would take more space than can be given to any one county. The fact that Milledgeville was the capital, as well as the fact that the larger part of the county was exceptionally fertile, led many of the best people from the older counties to make Milledgeville their home. Some of them have been already spoken of. Among them was Dr. Thompson Bird, who was a physician, born in Delaware. He had married Miss

Williamson, a sister of Mrs. Governor Clark, in Washington. He was a very intelligent, public-spirited man. He was the father of Mrs. L. Q. C. Lamar, Sr., and the grandfather of the distinguished Mississippi senator. Colonel Jack Howard, a prominent and influential and enterprising man, who had been a soldier in the Revolution, located in Milledgeville when it was first settled, and removed from there to Columbus. Myles Green, one of the most saintly and devout of Christian men, was clerk of the county courts. Seaton Grantland, who came to Baldwin a poor printer and left behind him a princely estate and a highly honored name, spent the whole of his active life here. Dr. B. A. White, a man famous for his intelligence and his broad views, died in Milledgeville, and was succeeded by his gifted son, Dr. Samuel G. White. Miller Grieve, a sturdy Scotchman, came to the county a youth, and died in it at an honored old age. He was a man of great worth and of strong mind—a Whig of the olden time, when the *Recorder* and the *Federal Union* were the rival political papers of the State. Colonel Richard M. Orme, his associate editor of the *Recorder*, was noted for the sterling excellencies of his moral character as well as for his honesty as a politician. Dr. W. H. Hall, a physician of rare ability and a gentleman of great culture and refinement, was born in this city, and died in it. Nathan C. Barnett, who was Secretary of State for a longer time than any man who ever lived in Georgia, and who was recognized by all as one of the most upright of men, long lived in Milledgeville. Lucius Q. C. Lamar, the father of the governor whose early and sad death deprived Georgia of one of her most gifted and upright men, had his home here. John Hammond, for long years the efficient, careful, trustworthy steward of the Lunatic Asylum, whose name was a synonym for probity, had his home in Midway. Dr. Stephen K. Talmage, one of the distinguished family of that name, who came from New

Jersey to Georgia, and was for many years the president of Oglethorpe University, which, while he lived, was a leading institution among the Presbyterians, lived and died in Midway.

Colonel Broughton, who edited for many years the *Federal Union* newspaper, was a man of fine mind and strong convictions, and exerted a great influence in Georgia politics.

Perhaps no man of his time did more service to his State than Dr. T. F. Green, who for years was superintendent of the Lunatic Asylum. This great charity which has done so much for unhappy invalids, if it did not originate with him, reached its stable place as an institution through his influence and care. He was of Irish lineage. His father was an exile of 1798, who was a professor in the State University. Dr. Green was a physician of fine parts, who gave himself for life to the work of curing lunatics. He had wonderful skill in managing men, and succeeded with all the odds against him.

Judge Iverson L. Harris, a distinguished jurist, whose wealth of intelligence and purity of character and strength of mind made up one of the most valued of men, lived here. These men and such as these, who have all passed away, have made the little county of Baldwin famous in the State for its men of character and gifts.

PUTNAM.

Putnam was laid off from Baldwin in 1807. It was named in honor of the brave old general, and its county site for General Eaton, who had distinguished himself in the war with Tripoli. It had been on the eastern border of the Creek Nation for over twenty-five years.

Hancock, which was originally Greene, had been settled since 1785, and was just across the river, and while the whites had made no permanent settlements in the Nation on the west side of the river, many of them had their cattle ranches, and perhaps not a few had opened farms in the unceded country before the purchase was made in 1803. When the land was distributed by lottery the population in the eastern counties was already considerable, and especially on the good lands in Hancock there were thick settlements. As soon as the new purchase was opened the restless people of the counties near by pressed into it. Other immigrants joined them, many of them from Virginia and a larger number from the eastern counties of the State.

The county was one of the fairest in middle Georgia In the descriptions of the eastern counties we have described this charming country. Grand forests covered the hills, limpid streams made their way through great brakes of cane. The Oconee bordered the county on one side, and Little river made its way entirely through it. Bold brooks and large creeks were in all parts of it. Much of the land was the rich mulatto land, esteemed by the old planters as the best in the world; much of it was in rich valleys on the sides of creeks and rivers, and much of it a less fertile but more easily cultivated gray land. There was but little really sterile land in the county, and none of it was waste. It was not to be wondered at that so fair a land was at once peopled, and it was only a few months after the whites were permitted to settle before the country was teeming with inhabitants and the smoke rose from hundreds of camp-fires before the one-roomed cabin was built. The ferries were kept going night and day and immigrants came rushing in.

The first settlers were:

Wm. Wilkins, Benj. Williamson, John Lamar, John Buckner, Elias S. Shorter, Stephen Marshall, John McBride, Captain Vesey, James Hightower, John Trippe, Isaac Moreland, John White, Benj. Whitefield, Jos. Cooper, Josiah

Flournoy, M. Ponder, Ward Hill, Rev. R. Pace, Rev. John Collinsworth, R. Bledsoe, Wm. Turner, Wylie Roberts, Mark Jackson, Peter Flournoy, Thos. Park, Raleigh Holt, A. Richardson, Tarpley Holt, James Kendrick, Reuben Herndon, T. Woodbridge, Joseph Turner, Warren Jackson, Edward Traylor, Samuel M. Echols, James Echols, E. Abercrombie, Matthew Gage, Thomas Napier, Wm. Jackson, Simon Holt.

None of these new counties, of which Putnam was one, could be said to have had any first settlers. They came in droves, and those mentioned are a few of many. These first people were mainly Georgians, the land being given away to Georgians by lottery. The lots were two hundred and two and one half acres in size, and when Putnam was first settled it was dotted all over with small farms.

Provisions were the only products. Tobacco was not raised and cotton was not as yet planted. Corn, hogs and cattle there were in great abundance. The people were not many of them people of means, and the luxuries enjoyed by the planters of Columbia and Burke were not during this decade found in this new county.

The first people came not only from the older counties of Georgia, but from North Carolina, Virginia and Maryland. There was little to distinguish them from those we have pictured as living in Hancock and Greene. They were much the same, and, as in Greene, the still-house was not far from the church, and in the inventory of estates the psalm-book and the Bible are put close beside the thirty-gallon still.

After the war of 1812, and the wonderful impetus given to cotton production, the people of Putnam increased their wealth very rapidly. Lands were fresh and rich, cotton was high, negroes were comparatively cheap and increased rapidly, and those who settled with a few slaves in the county in 1803 found themselves the owners of a hundred by 1830. There was little elegance but much solid comfort in the county until about 1845, when a number of handsome homes were erected on the plantations or in Eatonton. These mansions, with generally eight large rooms twenty feet square, with broad galleries and wide halls, were handsomely furnished, and the hospitality dispensed was generous. There were fine carriage horses, coachmen, footmen, maid servants and men servants, and there was nowhere a more elegant and luxurious life than was found in many of the families of Putnam.

The population of the county in 1810 was 6,809 whites and 3,220 slaves; in 1830 there were 5,554 whites and 7,707 slaves; in 1850 the free population had been reduced to 3,326 whites, and there were 7,468 slaves.

These figures tell the story of the great changes which passed over this magnificent country. The necessity of providing for so many dependents left the slaveholder but little time to improve his plantation, and when he wore out his lands he opened new forests, until he had laid the whole wood low. He found himself at the end of the war between the States with a yard full of negroes, a sadly impoverished plantation and a heavy debt.

The railroad reached Eatonton as a branch of the Central soon after the Milledgeville branch was completed. It was finally extended to Covington, so that the city of Eatonton has now good railroad facilities.

Putnam early had academies, and the academy at Eatonton was a famous school taught by Alonzo Church, afterward president of the State University. There were some county academies in addition to the central academy, and quite a number of private schools. A famous academy was known as Union academy, near where Philadelphia church now is. Here William H. Seward, a young New Yorker, taught a country school. He afterward returned to New York, became its governer, and was in after time secretary of state. Near this same church Jos. A. Turner, an eccentric, gifted man, published the *Countryman*, and in his country office Joel Chandler Harris learned his trade as a printer and began his career as a writer for the press.

The Baptists, Methodists and Presbyterians came with the first settlers into the county, and there were organizations of these churches before the county was separated from Baldwin.

The first Baptist church was Harmony, which was organized in 1806. The first Methodist church building was Victory, built before 1812. The first Presbyterian church was built near the same time.

Up to 1819 there was no church in Eatonton. The population of the village was small and the church people held their connection with country churches. Then, largely through the influence of Rev. Coleman Pendleton, the ordinary, a union church was built. William Arnold and John Collinsworth, two famous Methodist preachers, lived near Eatonton.

Dr. Henry Branham, a man of large intelligence and wisdom, was a prominent man in Putnam. He was the father of the beloved and gifted Walter R. Branham, who was born in this county, and who was for many years a prominent Methodist preacher in Georgia.

Judge James Meriwether was a scion of that distinguished family which has been so noted for public services in Virginia and Georgia. He was a judge of the superior court, a member of Congress and speaker of the Georgia House of Representatives.

Irby H. Hudson, for years speaker of the House, also lived here.

The Rev. John W. Knight, one of the most gifted and worthy Methodist preachers, whose praise is in all the churches, lived in this county for years, and died while residing in it.

Judge David Rosser Adams, one of the worthiest of men, long lived here.

Josiah Flournoy was in Putnam at its first settlement. He was a pushing planter, an enthusiastic Christian and the first prohibitionist in Georgia. He canvassed the State to secure signers to a petition to abolish the whisky traffic, and made a brave though unsuccessful fight against it. He made a large fortune, gave liberally to all benevolences, and built and endowed a school near Talbotton, which he called in honor of an old friend Collinsworth Institute.

Alexander Reid, famous as an enterprising and public-spirited planter, and as the progenitor of a large and influential family, resided in this county.

These are a few of those worthy people who have made this county famous.

MORGAN.

Immediately northwest of Putnam was Morgan, which was made a county at the same time, 1807, and called Morgan in honor of the brave old general, and its county site was called Madison in honor of James Madison.

In its physical features it is almost the exact counterpart of Putnam. The lower part of the county from Madison southward, and for some miles north of it, was that fine red land so much valued by the Georgia cotton-planter. The Little river, Sugar creek, Hard Labor creek, Indian creek, and the Oconee and Apalachee rivers were all in the county, and on each of them were rich bottoms. The land was heavily timbered with a magnificent forest. It was given away by lottery, and many persons who drew lots of land fixed their homes on them. It adjoined Greene, Clarke and Oglethorpe, and was most rapidly settled. The first settlers came from the older counties, and in the main were people of moderate means.

There were 5,951 free people and 2,418 slaves in the

county in 1810, three years after its settlement; in 1830 there were 5,225 free people and 6,820 slaves, and in 1850 there were only 3,000 free and 6,000 slaves.

These figures show the changes which took place in the county in forty years. The first settlers occupied the rich lands on the rivers and creeks and raised stock. There was very little cotton raised until after the war of 1812. There was one cotton-machine, as the gin was then called, in Madison in 1807, which was owned by Mr. Thomas Jones, who bought the cotton in the seed and shipped it, when ginned, by wagons to Augusta.

The wills made show the people had little property save live stock, but they had a great deal of that. Many of them had a few negroes, though but few of them had more than a half-dozen. Some of the wills are curiosities in the art of wrong spelling. They were evidently written by one acquainted with legal terms, and are prepared in proper form. One of them, made in 1807, reads thus:

"The maker of the will wishes his jeste debtes to be paid, lendes his wife a resenble portien of hogs for family plentee, and towls (tools) suficent to make a crop. Gives his secent child $10, and the value of a negrow gail to be delivered when cold (sold)."

The drinking habits of the people seem to have been very bad, as is evident from the fact that every merchant in the county was presented in one of the courts by the grand jury for selling whisky without a license, and by the number of stills which appear in the appraisements.

The cotton industry received a great impetus after the war of 1812, and men with a large number of negroes began to move in and buy out the small landholders. It is the same story of devastation; lands were worn out and turned out; people moved away into the new country and their places were taken by negro slaves, until in 1850 there were 3,000 whites and 6,000 slaves, and these whites were largely found in the villages and in the thin gray lands of the northern part of the county. The planters lived in elegant homes in Madison, and an overseer took charge of their plantations.

The upper part of the county was more thickly settled with white people, and there were fewer large plantations. The rich planters absorbed the whole of the lower part of the county, and then moved many of their negroes to southwestern Georgia and Texas. A few planters owned nearly all the land and overseers took the place of the independent landowner.

Madison was laid out in 1810 and soon became a town of importance. The first court was held at the house of Fields Kennedy, near Madison, and the first grand jury was composed of:

Nipper Adams, James Brannon, David Montgomery, Eli Townsend, James Mathews, Wm. Noble, Pascal Harrison, Godfrey Zimmerman, Wm. Randle, Wm. Brown, Graves Harris, John Wyatt, S. Noble, G. Bond, A. J. Chadox, Jno. Fielder, Daniel Bankston, William Swift, S. Walker, O. Walker, John Walker, Nathaniel Allen, Thos. Walls, Chas. Smith, John Finley, John Cook, Andrew Nutt, Jos. Peeples, Wyley Heflin, Thos. Heard.

The first sheriff was Joseph White.

The first store in the county was that of Thomas Jones, where Madison is now located.

The first settlers, according to White, were Bedney Franklin, Wm. Brown, Chas. Mathews, Dr. Johnson, Lancelot Johnson, Adam Saffold, R. Mann, and Dr. Wingfield.

To this list might be added a great many more, for it could be said of Morgan, as of Putnam, it never had any infancy. In a few short months after it was settled there were thousands of people building their cabins on its hills. It never had many of the features of pioneer life. Greene was just across the river, and Clarke, which had been peopled nearly twenty years, just north of it.

People of moderate means came into it at first, and the returns from their labors were almost immediate. The hogs and cattle multiplied with great rapidity, and up to 1812 there was almost an excess of the means of support. Good board was only four dollars per month, corn was thirty cents and wheat was seventy-five cents per bushel. Madison was one hundred miles from Augusta, which was the market for all upper Georgia, and became a place of considerable commercial importance early in its history, and when the Georgia railroad reached it, which it did in the early forties, it was for some time the leading cotton market for upper Georgia.

The early citizens of Madison were most of them people of wealth, who had large plantations or remunerative professions or profitable mercantile establishments, and fine living and high living was a mark of the people, but they were not famed for their piety. In 1827 there was no church in the village. There was occasional preaching in the court-house, but the village was destitute of a church building. The Legislature allowed the inferior court to make a gift to the Methodist, Baptist and Presbyterian churches of an acre of ground each, and in 1827 the Methodist church was built. The Baptist church was built soon after on the lot now occupied by the Baptist church for the colored people, and the Presbyterian somewhat later. The bulk of the population was in the rural districts, and before Morgan was a county there was preaching in the county by the Methodists, Baptists and Presbyterians. In 1806 a Baptist church, known as Holland Spring, was built on Hard Labor creek, and another by 1807 on Sugar creek. The Methodists had preaching in private homes, and a strong circuit was formed in which Morgan was included. The first deed of property to them I find was in 1811. Harmony, near what is now Rutledge, Buckhead and Rehoboth are all old churches. There was a camp-meeting in Morgan for a number of years, and in 1827 a grand revival, which resulted in the building of the church at Madison.

Madison early became noted for its elegance and refinement as well as for its wealth, and took great interest in education. The Methodists and Baptists built each a female college, which were prosperous up to the war. The war brought great changes to Morgan. For years the profit of cotton-planting had been diminishing, and in slave times the expense of any kind of large farming in Morgan was greater than its profits, and this fact and the lavish living of planters involved many of them in debt, and when the war ended and their negroes were freed many of them were hopelessly insolvent.

The railroad carried away much of the trade which formerly belonged to the town, and for some time the town and county were in a sadly depressed condition, but a change for the better has passed over it. The building of the Macon and Northern road brought Madison in closer contact with Savannah and opened a new country to it. The building of various factories, and especially the overthrow of the whisky traffic, has given it a new life. One of the handsomest graded school buildings in a town of its size is in Madison. There are four churches for white people and two good brick churches for colored people, and good schools for all classes. The upper part of the county has greatly improved. The lower part is still largely tenanted by negroes.

There are several sprightly villages in the county—Rutledge, Buckhead, Rehoboth, Godfrey and Apalachee.

Morgan has been the home of many noble and worthy men.

Adam Saffold was among her earliest lawyers, as his brother Reuben was one of her earliest physicians. Coming from Washington county in his youth, he lived and died in Morgan. He was a man of pure character, large wealth and great intelligence.

Joshua Hill, who was long a representative in Congress and a senator, who refused to accept the doctrine of a State's right to secede, and remained a Union man to the last, had his home here.

John B. Walker, a great planter, one of the most public-spirited and generous of men, who lived to see his immense estate pass from his hands, and to bear himself with as much cheerfulness and dignity in his poverty as had marked him when he owned five hundred slaves, spent his life here.

Among its other public men were: Thomas J. Burney, the worthy custodian of the funds of Mercer University, whose judgment was as good as his honor was spotless; David E. Butler, the genial and gifted Baptist preacher and lawyer, who was as zealous in his ministry and his devotion to the interests of his church as though State affairs had never engaged him; Samuel A. Burney, whose saintly life was a benediction to the community; John A. Porter, the large-hearted, upright, hospitable friend of all men, whose devotion to the Methodist Church was lifelong, and whose services for its benefit untiring; Wilds Kolb, whose benevolence toward the church is still seen in the returns from his bequests for its benefit. These are some of those who have done much for the county of their residence.

JASPER.

Jasper county was originally called Randolph in honor of John Randolph, who was a great favorite in Georgia because of his denunciation of the Yazoo fraud, as he delighted in calling it; but when Mr. Randolph opposed the war of 1812, and severely denounced Mr. Jefferson, who was immensely popular in Georgia, the Legislature changed the name of the county and called it Jasper, after Sergeant

Jasper. It would be but repeating the description given of Putnam and Morgan if Jasper should be described as it was at its settlement. The same kind of country, the same class of settlers and much the same history marked all these counties which I have joined together as Middle Georgia.

Jasper, like its sister counties, had been rapidly peopled, and mainly by Georgians who moved from the older counties. As was the case in Morgan, they were generally poor people, without culture and with few slaves. The land was very rich, and, as they were an industrious, thrifty people who lived closely and worked hard, they were at once independent, and many made fortunes. The names of the first grand jury, which met in 1808, will give an idea of some of the more important of the early settlers: Jether Mobley, Bolling Smith, Richard Carter, Stephen Lacy, Jesse Evans, Jordan Baker, Henry Haynes, John Morgan, Adam Glazier, Sol Stricklin, Wm. Pate, Spencer Lamb, Micajah Fretwell, Thomas Ramsey, Joshua Hagerty, John H. Whatley, Thomas Gammage, Solomon Patrick, William Lord, Thos. Hooks, Saul Townsend, George Morgan.

The population in 1810 was: Free 5,752, slave 1,821; in 1830, 6,809 free, 6,332 slave; and in 1850, 4,352 free, 7,134 slave. These figures tell the same story as those of Putnum and Morgan. The white people who came in great numbers and opened up the country; who raised hogs and corn; who had few or no slaves, first occupied the land; but when the new purchase across the Ocmulgee was made, they vacated their places and went into the new counties, and their farms were bought by the wealthy slave-owners. Where there was in 1810 a dozen prosperous farmers with an abundance of all necessaries around them, there was, in 1850, only one large planter.

The thrifty village of Hillsboro, near which the celebrated Benjamin H. Hill was born, was in the center of the richest part of Jasper, and there was at one time a thickly settled country around it. It had an academy and a church and quite a number of inhabitants; but the farmers moved west, and the little village sank almost out of sight. It was, however, revived by the coming of the railway.

The Jasper people, like those of the other counties of this section, were mostly eastern Georgians, though some came from Virginia and North Carolina. They were people of very simple lives, and many of them of very primitive manners. The celebrated "horse swap," in which "Yaller Blossom of Jasper" so distinguished himself, had its scene laid in this county, and the actual scene was doubtless before the eye of Judge Longstreet when he came from Augusta to manage a case before the superior court of Jasper county. The people, while not generally educated, put a high estimate on education, and at one time, in the early years of the century, there were five chartered academies in the county. The county underwent rapid changes, and the white population rapidly diminished after cotton-planting began on an extensive scale.

The lower part of Jasper, and much of the eastern part, was remarkably fertile and offered great temptation to the wealthy slave-owners of Wilkes and Hancock to buy lands and remove; and they often bought a half-dozen farms to make one plantation, and thus diminished the white population and increased that of the slaves. This was true of the lands on the rivers and creeks; but the plateaus of thin gray land near to Morgan and Newton were taken by people of moderate means who had small farms and few slaves. As this land did not invite the large slave-owner, it fell into the hands of white people, and the bulk of the whites were in this section. After the war it was the most desirable part of the county.

The first deed for a Baptist church was made in 1810, to ten acres of land near Monticello. At a later period the church was removed to the village. The Methodists had a church in the village as early as 1815, and doubtless one at Hillsboro before that. In 1812, Thomas Grant, one of the first Methodists in Georgia, who, in conjunction with his father, had built the first Methodist church in Georgia, removed to Monticello, to engage in merchandizing. Here he spent the last years of his life. He died in 1827. He was a man of large wealth and of great benevolence, and left a generous bequest to the worn-out preachers of his church.

The remoteness of Jasper from the railway for many years and the exhaustion of its fertility by bad farming led to a large emigration from the county, and the growth of Macon and its proximity to the county were fatal to the commercial prosperity of Monticello; so that, with the exception of a large increase in the negro population and in the fictitious value of the slaves, the county did not get richer, but rather poorer, from 1830 to 1850. It is, however, now in a better condition than it has been for many years past.

Monticello, which was made the county site when the county was laid out, was a thriving county town until the railroads drew off its trade to Macon, Madison and Covington, and it then declined; but it took on new life when the railroad from Macon to Covington and Athens was built; and it is now quite a thriving place, with handsome churches and fine graded schools.

Hillsboro, Machen and Shady Dale are, each of them, neat villages, with good churches and schools.

The county has suffered fearfully from the whisky-making and whisky-drinking habits of its earlier people, but it is now a prohibition county.

Cotton-planting was in its infancy when Jasper was settled, and, as in the neighboring counties, there was but little made. There was no market nearer than Augusta and there was but little trade.

The wealth of the county up to 1820 was sheep, goats, hogs and neat cattle; but in no county were there more abundant supplies of these products. There were, alas! a good many still-houses and much whisky made. At that time the morality of whisky- and brandy-making was not recognized as a question, and in an appraisement in Jasper I find, as in other middle Georgia counties, a Bible, a hymn-book, a still and a puncheon of whisky in close proximity to each other.

JONES.

Jones was named in honor of the Hon. James Jones, a Marylander who came to Georgia to his uncle, Colonel Marbury, when quite young, and was educated in Augusta and settled in Savannah. He was a young senator and died in 1801. (White.)

This county resembles very much the other counties of which we have been speaking, from the pine-belt northward; but in the lower part of the county there was a small strip of rather sterile pine forest. This section of the county was very thinly settled for many years. The strong red lands from Clinton northward, stretching out to the river, were soon taken by immigrants who drew the lots and who settled on the land granted to them. There were few farms of over two hundred acres, and as the land was very rich and the range very extensive, there was in a few years after the county was made a very large and prosperous population. The people came from the older counties and brought with them a few slaves and raised supplies for family use. They were over a hundred miles from Augusta and the roads were almost impassable during the winter, and for over ten years after the county was settled no man raised ten bales of cotton.

The wills and estates taken as they come show as the possessions of the people: Cattle, hogs, a few feather-beds, a wagon, a spinning-wheel, some pewter-plates, some kitchen utensils, some horses, a few articles of plain furniture, some sheep, some geese, and a very few books.

The richer planters, who raised cotton and had many negroes, did not come to Jones and the adjoining counties at an early day.

The first grand jury was John Bond, Daniel Hightower, James Jones, John Mitchell, Geo. Ross, Stephen Gafford, Wm. Calwell, Elkannah Sawyer, Nicolas Ferrell, William Monk, Samuel Calwell, Peter Sanders, Philip Catchings, Eph. Ellis, Elijah Turner, Seymour Catchings, Thos. Seals, Zech. Boothe, Jacob Dennis, Ebenezer Moses, John Harvey, Wm. Jackson, Jno. Bond, Jas. McInvail, James Huddleston, Giles Driver, Chas. Gachet, Wm. Perry, Jesse McPope, Jno. Cooke, Green Winne, Thomas Stephens, Wm. Carr.

Those familiar with Georgia people will see how many of these names are found in Greene, Hancock and Wilkes. There were quite a number of people of intelligence, but the larger number of the people were quite plain and ignorant. Of the thirty-one women who signed deeds before 1818 thirty of them could not write.

Clinton was made the county site when the county was first laid out; but it was then known as Albany, and the first deeds from the commissioners were for lots in the town of Albany.

H. M. Comer, Thos. White, Jno. Cook and Wm. Holton were the judges of the inferior court.

The crowd who came rushing into the county was a motley one, and to some extent a lawless one. In the court of 1808 there were seven indictments for assault, one for perjury, one for larceny. This was the first court held after the county was organized. Six years afterward there were thirteen for assaults, two for cattle-stealing, one for murder and six for misdemeanors.

There came into Jones after the beginning of the great cotton industry a large number of the well-to-do planters, and wealth very rapidly increased.

These wealthy planters were mainly from the eastern counties in Georgia, but there were not a few who came from North Carolina and Virginia. After 1820 many of the smaller landholders went west of the Ocmulgee and their farms were merged into great plantations, until for miles along the highway every acre was owned by one man. No county was settled more rapidly, none worn out sooner, and none deserted by its first settlers more completely than Jones.

Much of Jones is, however, still fertile, and many families abide where their grandfathers settled. The county has been immortalized by the musical pen of Sidney Lanier:

"I knew a man and he lived in Jones,
Which Jones is a county of red hills and stones,
And he lived pretty much by gettin' of loans,
And his mules was nothin' but skin and bones,
And his hogs were as fat as his corn-bread pones,
And he had 'bout a thousand acres of land."

The first settlers, according to White, were Jonathan Parrish, Peter Clower, Henry Low, Wm. Williams, Wilkins Jackson, Jeremiah Pearson, Major Humphries, James Comer, Hugh Comer, Roger McCarthy, Allen Greene, Benj. Tarver, Barley Stewart, James Anthony, George Harper, John Chappel, Jesse M. Pope, Henry Pope, John Bayne, S. Kirk, Wm. Cabiness, P. A. Lewis, James Jones, Wm. Jones, Robert Hutchins, and James Gray. To these might be added George Cabiniss, John Cabiniss, Henry Cabiniss, Robert Ousley, Isaac Moreland, and many others.

The little town of Clinton, before Macon began to be, was a place of much importance, and even after the beginning of Macon a place of large trade and famous as being the place in which more cotton-gins were manufactured than anywhere in the South.

Mr. Samuel Griswold, an enterprising Connecticut man, and Mr. Daniel Pratt, from the same section, established their celebrated gin factory in Clinton. Their agents went all through Georgia and Alabama and the more remote Southern States, and great wagon loads of gins were sent out from Clinton before the railways were built. Then Mr. Pratt went to Alabama and founded the famous town of Prattville, and Mr. Griswold founded Griswoldville on the Central railroad. During the war the works at Griswoldville were burned and never rebuilt.

In the early days of Jones, when the population was large and the white people numerous, there were prosperous country churches and good country schools, as well as an academy in Clinton, but with the changes in population, and especially with the growth of Macon, where there were better educational facilities, and to which many Jones county people removed, the high school was given up and the country schools were few and inferior in many parts of the county, and the country churches suffered from the same causes. The rich lands along the river were at one time populous, but the lands were soon worn out and the people crossed the river and went west, and the few who were left were unable to keep up churches and schools, and where there were scores of families there was left a wide waste of worn-out lands.

In Clinton there was almost from its first settlement an excellent class of Methodists who had at an early day a large and, for those days, a handsome church, and in other parts of the county there were flourishing Methodist and Baptist churches. The growth of the plantations led to the abandonment of these houses of worship except in a few neighborhoods, even before the war. After it was over and new railways were built villages began to spring up, and churches and schools followed, and now no county is better supplied with churches and schools than many parts of Jones.

The negroes in the county are still very numerous. They are generally tenants who rent small farms, for the rental of which they pay a few bags of cotton.

This county was famous for the scene of the Bunkley trial. Jesse Bunkley, a profligate young man of large property, disappeared from Jones and went no one knew where, and for years he was never heard of. At last the conviction became fixed that he was dead and his estate was divided among his relatives. Long after this division was made a man who bore a striking resemblance to him appeared and declared that he was Jesse Bunkley. Many who had known Bunkley swore to their belief that he was not speaking falsely, and many refused to admit his claim. It was finally charged that the alleged Bunkley was a man named Barber, and on the prosecution of Barber as a swindler the case was brought before a jury. It was proven to its satisfaction that he was Elisha Barber, an impostor, and he was sent to the State prison; but many clung to their belief that he was Jesse Bunkley, whose only crime was that he sought to recover property in the hands of others.

The population of Jones in 1810 was 6,000 free and 2,587 slaves; in 1830, 6,516 free and 6,829 slaves; in 1850, only 3,945 free and 6,279 slaves. The relative proportion between the two races has undergone some change since the war, but there are many more negroes than whites still in the county.

The construction of railways to Savannah, Athens and Augusta, all of which pass through Jones, has given the county the best railway facilities, and a number of stations, Griswoldville, James, Haddock, Gray, Round Oak, Bradley and Roberts, have sprung up on the lines of railway and do a thrifty business.

There has been quite an exodus from the country to these villages, in which there have been established good schools and churches.

Jones has been more famous for its successful planters than for its distinguished public men, but it has been the birthplace of not a few distinguished in the various walks of life.

The celebrated Judge Robert V. Hardeman lived and died in Jones.

The celebrated Judge Henry G. Lamar, commissioner to the Creeks and a prominent jurist, was a native of Jones.

H. M. Comer, the celebrated railroad magnate, was born in this county.

WILKINSON.

The lands purchased in 1802 were divided in 1803, as has been already stated, into three counties, Baldwin, Wilkinson and Wayne. Out of each of these many other counties were carved, until each of them was reduced to a small area. Wilkinson is now a county of moderate size and of limited resources. It is named Wilkinson in honor of the general of that name who served in the southwest, and the county site, Irwinton, is named for Governor Irwin. The Central railroad passes through its upper border, and it has two or three small villages along its line. The first settlers, according to Mr. White, were: Chas. C. Beall, S. B. Murphey, J. Hoover, J. Meredith, Abner Hicks, A. Passmore, John Freeman, Joel Rivers, Samuel Bragg, John Lavender, Isaac Hull.

The population of Wilkinson in 1810 was 1,836 whites and only 318 slaves. In 1830, when it was much reduced in size, there were 5,591 whites and 1,922 slaves; and in 1850 there were 5,467 whites and 2,745 slaves. In 1890 there were, in all, 10,781. The county is not a fertile one, and has not been thickly settled, and its religious and educational advantages have not been of the best. There has, however, been a good academy at the county site for many years, and the county has shared in the advantages of the public school system. The Methodists and Baptists have provided the people with what religious instruction they received, and there are churches of these denominations in all parts of the county.

The county has been almost purely an agricultural one, and there has not been a single manufactory in its borders. Much of the land is quite poor and inhabited by poor people who furnish to the Macon cotton mills a large part of their operatives. There is little to distinguish Wilkinson from the other counties that have been classified with it, and it is at present less important as a county than it was sixty years ago.

TWIGGS.

Twiggs was formed from Wilkinson, and is directly west of it, and it has the same features as the county from which it was made. The Ocmulgee is on its western border, and some very large creeks flow through it. Much of the land is a poor flat woods, but much of it near the creeks is of a very superior grade. The rich land was bought up by large planters; some of whom owned thousands of acres and had hundreds of negroes.

The county was largely peopled by immigrants from the eastern counties, but drew some of its wealthiest settlers from eastern Virginia. Its first settlers, according to Mr. White, were: Arthur Fort, Ezekiel Wimberly, Wm. Perry, Wm. Crocker, Ira Peck, Henry Wall, General Tarver, John Everett, D. Williams, Joel Denson, S. Jones, Willis Hodgins, Milton Wilder, Josiah Murphy, D. Lowrey, C. Johnson, C. A. Tharpe, John Davis, C. W. Milton, B. Ray, S. Harrell, T. Harrington, H. Sullivan, Colonel Hughes; and the first grand jury, which was drawn at the superior court in 1811, was, according to the same careful authority: Frances Powell, M. Buzby, A. Wood, Wm. Ford, I. Wilkinson, T. C. Heidelburger, B. Joiner, S. Barnabee, W. Herrishell, T. Pearce, Wm. Carr, W. Grimes, Robin Andrews, Wm. Cloud, John Matthews, John Young, Arthur Fort, Jr., John Hawthorne, Ashley Wood, S. Belk, John Evans.

The population of Twiggs in 1810 was 2,763 free and 642 slave; in 1830 it was 4,524 free and 2,507 slave; and in 1850, 3,559 free and 4,620 slave. This slave population was, as in the counties of Laurens and Pulaski, not generally distributed, but confined to one section of the county; and while many people had no negroes, others had a large number; and while the white population was increasing in some parts of the county, it was growing less in other sections. The rich lands of Twiggs were settled very soon after they were opened by a sturdy people of small means; but they soon gave way, and the great plantation, as usual, absorbed the farms.

The town of Marion, which was the county site for years, was a bustling, stirring place, with its lawyers and its merchants; but, as Macon grew, Marion lost its importance as a trading point, and the county site was changed to Jeffersonville, and nothing now remains to mark the place where it stood.

The planters of Twiggs were men of broad views, who conducted great planting interests and gave their families all the advantages that wealth could procure. They were generally men of intelligence and enterprise, while their fellow countymen living on the poor ridges and in the flat woods, tilling their own farms, were poor and illiterate.

There were but few schools in the county, and the planters congregated at Jeffersonville, where they could keep up a good school. In all the county, in 1850, there were only seven schools, with 309 pupils. There was a great deal of wealth in some parts of the county, and near the great plantations there were rich churches well supplied with an intelligent ministry; but in the poorer sections the churches were very poor. The Baptists were a very wealthy and strong denomination in Twiggs, and the celebrated Charles D. Mallary resided on a large plantation in Twiggs for several years, and preached in the county to a Baptist congregation of remarkable intelligence and large wealth. The Methodists shared with the Baptists in the religious care of the people, and had several churches and a camp-ground in Twiggs in the days of its prosperity. They still keep up a circuit in that county.

The building of the railway to Dublin has brought a new era into the county, and while there are many abandoned plantations where once there was great fertility, in other sections of the county, where there was but little prosperity in days gone by, there is a great change for the better.

LAURENS.

Laurens was laid off from Wilkinson in 1807 and named Laurens in honor of Lieutenant-Colonel Laurens, the gallant South Carolinian who was killed in one of the last skirmishes of the Revolution.

The first court was held at the house of Peter Thomas, not far from Dublin.

The place selected as a county site in 1809 was called Sumterville, and was between Rocky and Turkey creeks, in the most thickly settled part of the county. There was a considerable settlement in this oak and hickory part of the county.

The first grand jury was: John Speight, Benj. Adams, Andrew Hampton, Leonard Green, Jesse Wiggins, Benj. Brown, Chas. Stringer, Nathan Weaver, Wm. Yarbrough, Wm. Boykin, Jno. Gilbert, Jos. Yarborough, James Sartin, Wm. McCall, Edward Hagan, Jno. Stringer, Simon Fowler,

Jesse Stephens, Henry Fulgham, Thomas Gilbert, Robert Daniel, Chas. Higdon, Sam'l Stanley, Sam'l Sparks, Joseph Vickers, Mark May, George Tarvin, David Watson, Joseph Denson, Geo. Martin, Gideon Mays, Ben. Dorsey.

In 1809 a part of the county was added to the new county of Pulaski, and a part of Washington and Montgomery was added to Laurens. No public buildings had been erected at Sumterville, and when this new addition was made to the county it was decided to put the county site at a point nearer the river, and an Irishman who had a sawmill offered land for the public buildings, provided he was permitted to give the county site a name. This was agreed to, and with the remembrance of his native isle present, he called the coming village Dublin.

The county after the addition was made to it was very large and thinly settled. There was some very fertile land in the western part of the county and along the river and in the Buckeye section, which was soon taken up by planters from the other parts of the State and by immigrants from North Carolina and Virginia. The larger part of the population consisted of poor people, who bought their lots of land in the pine woods for a song, or simply squatted upon them. There were thus two widely divided classes at the first opening of the county.

Governor Troup, whose ancestral domain was on the river, had two large plantations in Laurens, and General Blackshear, whose home was taken into Laurens from Washington, had a princely estate. The lands were cheap, the best selling at two dollars per acre, and the pine lands at from ten dollars to one hundred and fifty for a lot of two hundred and two and one half acres. These piny woods settlers were many of them very illiterate and rude in their manners.

Peter Early, the judge, was a courtly old Virginian, and when his court held at a private house, being disturbed by a drunken man, he ordered the sheriff to put the fellow *in the fence*, by which he meant to put his neck between the rails of a high fence and confine it there. The sentence was carried out, much to the displeasure of the man's neighbors. Another man who had sworn profanely in the judge's presence was sent to jail in Sandersville for three months. Another who had stolen some cattle was sentenced to be forthwith tied to a tree and given thirty-nine lashes on his bare back for three days in succession, and then branded with the letter "R," and after he paid the costs to be discharged.

Of the first twenty-five persons signing deeds and other instruments in the county, only five were able to write their names.

There were but few negroes except on the large plantations, and up to 1820 nothing was produced in the county for market except horses, cattle, hogs and whisky. The remoteness of the county from market and the ease with which stock was raised made it a great stock-raising county.

After 1820 the cotton production on the oak and hickory lands was very great, and negroes were brought into this section in large numbers. The Savannah market was reached after 1840 by the Central railway, which the Laurens planters tapped at Tennille, and cotton was largely grown by the wealthy planters; but for many years the pine woods farmer continued to raise sheep, goats and cattle almost entirely.

No county has undergone greater changes or has improved more rapidly than Laurens since the war. A railroad has been constructed from Dublin to Tennille, one from Macon to Dublin, and one from Hawkinsville to Dublin, and the village has become a handsome city. The court-house is an elegant building, the churches are neat and commodious; there are banks, storehouses, warehouses and handsome residences. There are excellent schools in the city and its vicinity, and the moral tone of the county is of the best type.

For many years there was but little attention given to religion or education in the county. The rich planters sent their children abroad for an education, and the children of the poor had no school privileges. Churches were scattered and congregations were small, but a great change has passed over the county.

Laurens has had her share of distinguished citizens. Governor Troup had his home here. He had two large plantations in this county, on one of which he lived. He called it "Valdosta," another he called "Vallambrosa." He lived a right lonely life, seeing few people and spending his time in his unpretentious home with his books, or in fishing and hunting.

General David Blackshear, who came from North Carolina and settled on a grant of land he received for his services as a young soldier in the Revolution, was one of the first settlers in this county. He was, according to his biographer, the accurate Colonel Miller, a descendant of those Germans who came with Baron de Graffenreid to North Carolina. While a boy he served in the Revolutionary army, and when it was over he came to Georgia and received a soldier's warrant for a lot of land in Washington county. In 1802, when the country west of the Oconee was purchased, he went as a surveyor into the woods, and not only surveyed the land but succeeded in securing a large body of it. He was a man of unusual sagacity and of great energy, and soon became a very wealthy and prominent man. He was made a brigadier-general in the war of 1812 and put in command of a department. He occupied high positions in the State and was a man of great worth.

The Guyton family was a prominent one in Laurens.

They were of Huguenot ancestry, who came first to South Carolina and settled on the Santee in 1862. Some of them come to Georgia when Laurens was a young county and purchased large holdings in the Buckeye neighborhood. Colonel Charles Guyton, one of this family, reached distinction during the war between the States, and was for a number of sessions in the Legislature.

Many of the first immigrants to Laurens came from North Carolina and settled in a colony, and when Early county was settled, drawn by the rich promise of the new land, they formed another colony which settled in that section, and when Early was divided and Thomas was made the Laurens colony was quite a large factor in its population.

In 1810 the population of Laurens was 1,725 free and 485 slaves; in 1830, 3,214 free and 2,375 slaves; in 1850, 3,468 free and 2,974 slaves.

PULASKI.

Pulaski, as it was first laid out, was on the east side of the Ocmulgee river, and was formed from Laurens. After 1820, when the new lands west of the river were opened to settlement, a considerable body south of what is now Houston was placed in Pulaski. It was named Pulaski in honor of the gallant Pole who fell at the siege of Savannah. The first county site was Hartford, but it proved to be very unhealthy, and a new town named in honor of Colonel Benjamin Hawkins, the Indian agent, was established on a high bluff on the west side of the river, and in 1836 the courthouse was removed to that flourishing young town.

The upper part of Pulaski was broken red land, covered originally with a fine growth of oak and hickory. It was very fertile and was soon settled, as had been Wilkinson, Laurens and Twiggs, with large slave-owners from the older counties. The pine lands were settled by poor people who had their ranches and farms in the wire-grass.

When the new purchase on the west side of the Ocmulgee was made a part of it was added to Pulaski. It presented the same features as the older territory. The upper part of the county soon became a great body of plantations. The cotton was boated to Savannah, and the boats brought the luxuries of the city to the homes of the planters. The planters sent their children away to college in Macon, Oxford, Penfield and Athens, and often fixed their own homes in some of the up-country towns and left their interests in the charge of an overseer.

The piny woods farmer lived in his log cabin on what his fields and flocks furnished him, and went to Hawkinsville at rare intervals for his few needful supplies. His home was remote from the home of his neighbor, and in such a state of society good schools and good churches were impossible.

With the building of the Macon and Brunswick, now the Southern railroad, a change for the better took place, and this beneficial change became much greater after the war ended. There are now fine schools and good churches and good communities in Pulaski, where a score of years ago there was only a wild unbroken pine forest.

The first settlers of Pulaski were Joseph Reeves, S. Colson, Edmond Hagan, George Walker, Wm. Hathorn, J. M. Taylor, Edmond Blackshear, Mack Mason, Thos. Mitchell, Joseph Bryan, John Rawls, the Jordans, Lamars, Phillipses, and others.

The population in 1810 was 1,585 whites and 528 slaves. These slaves were confined to the richer sections and in the pine woods there were very few. In 1830 the white population was 3,141 and the slaves were 1,765; in 1850, the free population was 3,823 and the slaves were 2,804. The slave population increased much more rapidly in proportion than the free, and yet the inhabitants of the pine woods were increasing steadily. While they increased, the whites from the oak and hickory lands were growing fewer.

For nearly twenty years after Pulaski was settled there was a large trade, first at Hartford, and then at Hawkinsville. These two towns had steamboat connection with Darien, and to these points cotton was brought for shipment from the near-by counties. Hawkinsville gradually absorbed Hartford. It had a bank and large warehouses and a Methodist church before it became the county site. It was the point to which the piny woods people of the lower counties brought their hides and other products for sale; and the Hawkinsville merchant did a large business with the planters of Twiggs, Houston and Dooly. With the growth of Macon and the building of the railroads Hawkinsville declined in importance until it became an insignificant hamlet; but after the building of the Macon and Brunswick (afterward the Southern) railway it revived, and is now a much more flourishing town than it ever was. It has now (1898) elegant churches, a very handsome public school building, an excellent court-house, a supply of the purest artesian water, railroad and river communication, and has a very fine trade with the country near by.

WAYNE.

Wayne county, when reduced to its present dimensions, was long regarded as one of the poorest counties in the State. It had neither court-house nor jail in 1850, nor was it able to support a single school.* There were in it at that time, according to White, a few poor people who lived at long distances from each other and raised a few cattle and some sheep, and lived with the aid of their guns and fishing-tackle.

* White.

In 1810 there were in the then large county 422 free and 554 slaves; in 1830, 687 free and 276 slaves; and in 1850, 1,093 free and 406 slaves. Since then the county has been reduced in size, but the population in 1890 was 7,485. The railways had then passed through the county, and mills, turpentine farms and flourishing towns had followed; and, while for many years there was no part of the State so destitute of religious or educational advantages, under the new order of things the country became well furnished with schools and churches. The new methods of farm culture have developed what was apparently hopeless sterility into moderate productiveness.

TELFAIR.

Telfair was formed from Wilkinson in 1807, and named for Edward Telfair. We have, in our account of Montgomery county, drawn a picture of Telfair. In all this region known as the pine-barrens there was so much general resemblance, that the impression that there was no difference in land where pine trees grew was a common one with those who did not know better; but this was quite an error The great pine belt was in that geological formation known as Quaternary, and a small part in what was known in Georgia as the rotten limestone country and by the old geologists as the Tertiary, where there are many fossils. Much of the pine land near the coast consisted of barren sand dunes, and is now, and probably always will be, worthless, and much that might have produced well is too flat for drainage; but in Montgomery and Telfair and the adjoining counties there is a large body of pine land high and dry, with a good foundation of yellow clay, where the water is pure and free from lime. This land is not naturally fertile, and when manured does not hold its fertility; but by liberal fertilizing it can be made to produce largely. The Scotch immigrants of America (Scotchmen from

North Carolina) saw the worth of these lands, and, as they cost but a trifle, they secured large bodies of them and built up good homes. Much of this land, however, was not taken up by home-seekers, but by speculators who secured the titles to it for a very small price. It was thought to be worthless; and many of those who drew lots would not pay the five-dollar fee demanded for a plot and grant. The speculators took this reverted land for the price of the warrant, and secured the title. They then put the lands on the market. There were not a few lots which were held under forged deeds, and innocent people were inveigled into the purchase of lands which were worthless, or for which the seller had no title. A company of Maine lumbermen, who thought they saw large possibilities in lumbering in Georgia and in working up the pine forests of the South, bought from the real owners who had bought them from the State, for an insignificant sum, many thousand acres of land in Telfair and the adjoining counties. They paid for the land, and received good titles to it. They built large sawmills on the Ocmulgee river, and founded a city which was called Lumber City. The venture was not successful, and they abandoned the country. They held to their deeds, however, and paid the trifling taxes which were demanded. The mills rotted down. The lands were unoccupied, and were taken possession of, in many cases, by land thieves. They sold the lots to *bona-fide* purchasers and gave bogus titles. In some cases the lots were sold for taxes and bought in good faith; and, in blissful ignorance that the Maine company existed, these simple-hearted purchasers took possession of the lands and improved them. They never dreamed that the Maine company had any successor or representatives. For decades of years matters went on in this way, until after the war, when the great lumber firm of W. E. Dodge & Co. appeared on the scene and presented titles to the land, which were recognized as good, and presented tax receipts which showed that the tax sales had been illegal. They demanded that the owners should vacate their holdings. There was much litigation, and men were ejected from their homes by violence, and in turn there was murder and lawless proceedings against the agents of strangers. The courts came in; false titles were exposed, and blood-stained criminals were punished by lifelong imprisonment in distant prisons. There was, of course, a great deal of the county not involved in these troubles, and the railways opened it up; the turpentine and lumber men came in, and few sections of the State have developed so rapidly as this section of the once despised pine-barren of Telfair.

The lots of land were large—490 acres in a lot, and a lot of land was often sold for twenty dollars. The result was the securing of large bodies of land by comparatively poor men, who relied upon the wild pastures for feeding their cattle, and upon a small area of well-fertilized land for their breadstuffs.

Montgomery, Telfair and Tattnall were all peopled in the main by thrifty Scotch people, and cattle- and sheep-raising was the great industry. And in no part of Georgia was there a better type of people than in these pine forests. These people had the virtues and the vices of the Scotch. They were clannish and somewhat narrow, and many of them were too fond of whisky; but they were plain and honest, and shrewd and religious. The school was found in every section; but the county was thinly peopled, and kirks of their fatherland were few and often remote, and so many of the Scotch Presbyterians became Methodists and Baptists. The Methodists had missionaries and camp-meetings and organized churches among them at an early day, and built up quite a church from the descendants of the Highlanders.

The population of Telfair in 1810 was only 526 whites

and 288 slaves; in 1820 it was 1,571 whites and 561 slaves. Twenty years later it was 2,396 whites and 831 slaves. These slaves were almost entirely confined to a few plantations on the river, where there was sometimes a large number, amounting to scores, on a plantation.

The first settlers were: Jos. Williams, A. Graham, D. Graham, John Wilcox, Thos. Wilcox, G. Mizell, A. McLeod, Robert Boyd, Moses Rountree, James Mooney, Wright Ryall, McDuffie, J. A. Rogers, N. Ashley, C. Ashley, John Coffee, W. Ashley, A. Brewer, J. Herbert, S. Herbert, J. MacCrea, Duncan MacCrea, O. Butler, Lachlin Leslie.

Of these the Ashleys, Coffees, Brewers and Rogers were English, and had large plantations on the river. The others were pure Scotch.

The Southern railway passes through Telfair and the steamboats ply the river.

The people of Telfair always valued education, and the country school was in every neighborhood from the first settlement. They were, however, a poor, plain people and were content with the elements of an English education; but as the railroad came the desire for better culture was developed, and high schools were established, and in McRae there is a collegiate institute known as the South Georgia College, which is quite a flourishing school and is doing much for higher education.

TATTNALL.

The immense county of Montgomery was divided in 1801 and a new county was made. Josiah Tattnall, the patriot son of the staunch old Loyalist, had been governor and his health had given way. It was evident that death was not far away, and he resigned his seat and fled to the West Indies. In delicate compliment to him the new county was called Tattnall.

There were in it in 1810, scattered over a large area, one thousand five hundred and twenty-four white people, and five hundred and twenty-four negroes. The Altamaha was on its southern and western border, and there were some large plantations on it, and the negroes were probably found on a few estates.

The first settlers, as given by White, were: Ezekiel Clifton, Ezekiel Stafford, Henry Holland, Stephen Mattock, Wm. Coleman, Wm. Eason, George Lewis, Joseph Collins, Nathan Brewton, Moses Jernigan, Jones Temples, B. Stripling, A. Daniel, Jno. Mattox, Step. Bowen, E. Bowen, A. McLeod, John McFarland, James Turner, James Jones, M. Jones, Jesse Collins, David Boyd, Allen Johnson, Elisha Parker, Elisha Curl, James Tillman, Dan'l Highsmith, Jno. McArthur, Alex. Gordon, John Jones, Joshua Dasher, Reuben Nails, Luke Sapp, Benjamin Sapp, John and Grove Sharp, Levi Bowen, Lewis Strickland, John Anderson, James Underwood and John Dukes.

The students of this list will be able to pick out sundry Scotch names from it, but the bulk of the people were of English and American origin.

The lands, save on the river, were purely pine woods, and like those of Montgomery, were valued for their pasturage alone, and although the landholders had much land, they lived in a very simple way.

For thirty years there was no fixed place for a courthouse, and it was 1832 before Reidville was fixed on as a county site.

The county was very thinly settled, and being so remote from markets and so isolated, it was largely dependent on its own resources, and perhaps no people were more prosperous and independent.

The railroad which came through the pine woods to Brunswick did not pass through Tattnall, but the Central and the Savannah, Americus and Montgomery railroads eventually reached it, and now the county has good railroad facilities and has rapidly improved.

The immense pine forests have been a source of large revenue for years and are still richly productive. There is but little to differentiate this county from that of Montgomery, from which it was taken, and in describing Montgomery and its people we have described Tattnall.

The Baptists and Methodists have been the ruling Christian denominations, and the Methodists have had a campground here for over sixty years.

There has always been some attention paid to education, and the county had an incorporated academy at an early day, but education, except by a few families of large means, was for a long time sadly neglected.

The county is one of the best of the pine woods counties and is being rapidly developed. The Altamaha river is its southern boundary, and, being always navigable, it has given the lower part of the county easy access to Darien, and there has been considerable trade in lumber and cotton, and of late years in naval stores.

CHAPTER VII.

1813 TO 1820.

Peter Early—William Rabun—Matthew Talbot—Great Increase in Production—Advance in Population—First Steamboat Line—Improvement of Rivers—First Transatlantic Steamship—Roads—Character of the Productions of the State—Inflation—Change Bills—New Banks—Bank of Darien—Academies—Religious Progress—Social Conditions—The Low-Country People—The Low-Country Slaves—Life among the Cotton-Planters—Drinking Habits—The Cross-Roads Whisky Shop—The Georgia Yeomanry—The Georgia Cracker and his Origin—Trouble with the Creeks—Massacre of Friendly Indians—Political Antagonisms—Newspapers in Georgia—New Counties—General Description of the Mountaineers—The Hill Country and its People—The Piny Woods Counties and the People—Emanuel—Irwin—Appling—Early—Walton—Habersham—Rabun.

Authorities as in last Chapter, with the addition of Andrews's Reminiscences of a Georgia Lawyer, Clarke & Mitchell Pamphlet (very rare), Lamar's Compilation of Georgia Laws, and the newspapers of the period.

Judge Peter Early succeeded Governor Mitchell as governor in 1813. He was one of the illustrious family of Virginia Earlys who had descended from an Irish immigrant who came to Virginia in 1661. His father was Joel Early, an eccentric Virginia gentleman who settled a large manor on the Oconee river in what is now Greene county. The father was a man of culture and gave his son the best advantages the country afforded, and he was graduated at Washington College, in Virginia.

He studied law and was soon made a judge. He was a man of fine attainments and strictest integrity. As we have seen, he vetoed the bill to extend the stay law, and it was passed over his veto, and when he offered for governor at the end of his first term he was defeated by Governor Mitchell, who, for the third time, was chosen governor. He was disgusted at this treatment and returned to the seclusion of his country home in upper Greene, but his fellow citizens insisted on his accepting office again, and he was chosen State senator. While holding this office he died.

Governor Mitchell, of whom we have already heard, who was now elected to take Governor Early's place, did not serve out his term of office, but resigned to take the position of Indian agent.

William Rabun was president of the Senate and became *ex officio* governor. Governor Rabun was born in North Carolina, and his father removed to Georgia while he was but a lad and settled first in Wilkes and then in Hancock county. The governor had few educational advantages, but was a man of fine sense, a laborious student and a man of highest character. He had been for years a member of the State Legislature, and was president of the Senate when Governor Mitchell resigned. He was elected to succeed himself, and while in office, in the vigor of his manhood, he died.

Matthew Talbot, at the time of Governor Rabun's death, was president of the Senate, and succeeded to the office of governor. At the election John Clarke was chosen as governor.

Governor Talbot was a native of Virginia, a son of John Talbot, one of the early immigrants to Wilkes county. He settled in this county, but afterward removed to Oglethorpe. He was a member of the Assembly for a considable number of years, and president of the Senate from 1818 to 1823. He was a leading man in the Clarke party, and came within two votes of being elected governor over George M. Troup. His character for probity and strong common sense was very high. He was succeeded by General John Clarke, of whom I shall speak in the next chapter, at the close of the period now under survey.

During this period Georgia was rapidly developing. There was then no part of the State in which the lands were worn out, and into the first counties there was a constant immigration and a rapid increase in population. The multiplication of cotton-gins and the demand for cotton abroad had given a great impetus to cotton-growing. The embargo and the non-intercourse acts and the disturbances resulting from the Napoleonic wars had almost put an end to cotton production for some years, but now that the war was over the demand was lively.

The list of exports from the Georgia ports were: 1810, $2,557,225; 1811, $1,066,703; 1812, $1,094,595; 1813, $2,147,449; 1814, $4,146,057; 1815, $7,436,692; 1816, $8,530,831; 1817, $10,977,051; 1819, $6,525,011.

The population, which in 1790 was 82,000, in 1810 was 252,000, and in 1820, 340,947. With this growth in population and in commerce, the question of transportation became a very important one. The rivers into the interior offered the best facilities within reach of the people for moving produce, and after the introduction of steamboats, where the water was deep enough to float them, they were brought into general use. In 1814 Samuel Howard of Savannah received a charter for a line of steamboats, and a little later a large company was chartered to put a line of boats on the Altamaha and Savannah route. A great deal of freight was carried by the flatboats on the various rivers beyond the limits of steamboat navigation. The State made sundry appropriations for cleaning out the smaller rivers, and even the larger creeks, in order to make them navigable for steam and flatboats. Some adventurous Savannah merchants deserve to be immortalized for leading in the great work of transatlantic steam traffic. They were Wm. Scarboro, A. B. Fannin, I. P. McKinnie, Samuel Howard, Charles Howard, John Haslett, Moses Rodgers, A. S. Bulloch, John Bogue, Andrew Low & Co., Robert Isaacs, I. Minis, S. C. Drummond, J. P. Henry, John Speakenan, Robert Mitchell, R. & Q. Habersham, John S. Bulloch, Gideon

Pott, W. S. Gillette and Samuel Yates, who formed the Savannah Steamship Company, and who had built for them the first steamship which ever crossed the Atlantic ocean. The ship was named Savannah, and sailed from Savannah for Liverpool in 1819.

The roads were wretched. All the repairs upon them were made by a contribution of labor levied on the people living near the roads, which was paid during the summer-time when there was a rest from farm work. There was no art of road-building known to them, and when the rains began in the fall and winter and the heavy loads of cotton were conveyed to market and goods were brought from it, the highways became almost impassable. Augusta was the point to which the cotton from Middle Georgia and the produce from upper Georgia were sent, and the roads through the hill country of Middle Georgia were in an execrable condition during the entire busy season; and the roads to Savannah were almost as bad. It was a matter of serious concern, after the crops were made, as to how they could be marketed.

The agricultural interests of all parts of the State were rapidly advancing. The rice culture of the coast was now very profitable, and the rice-planter had none of the difficulties to encounter which his up-country fellow citizen met with; and the sea-island cotton-planter was as fortunate. The produce of the pine woods was almost entirely cattle, which could be driven, or ranging timber, which could be floated to market. The up-country people sent very little produce to market except cattle and whisky, but the middle belt was seriously embarrassed to get its main crop—cotton—to market.

The cotton machines had now taken the name of gins, and were becoming quite common in the middle counties of the State. They were not at this period, as in after time, owned by the planters themselves, but were set up by the merchants in the small county towns, who took the cotton in the seed, ginned it and sent it to market packed in round bales, which were of about three hundred pounds weight. The cotton-screw and cotton-press were as yet unknown. From Elbert, Wilkes and Lincoln a considerable quantity of cotton was sent by flatboats to Augusta; but even from those counties in which there was access to the river much of it was sent in wagons to the same market.

The demand for labor to make cotton caused a great influx of negroes, who were brought out by the negro traders in large numbers. From 1815, and for over twenty years thereafter, there was great activity in all circles and much inflation. Land was cheap, selling at from one dollar to two dollars per acre. Cotton was from seventeen to twenty cents per pound; and men bought plantations in Morgan, Jasper and Jones, and paid for them with the proceeds of one crop.

Money was necessary to meet the demands of these busy days; and as there was not sufficient specie, and as neither the State banks nor the United States bank met the demand for small currency, change-bills called "shinplasters" were used. These grew to be such a nuisance that the Legislature adopted the same method to suppress the floating of them that the United States adopted to suppress the issue of State banks: it taxed the "shinplasters" 25 per cent. The Planters Bank had been chartered in 1810, the Bank of Augusta at the same time. In each of these the State had a block of stock. The Bank of the State of Georgia was chartered in 1815, and the Bank of Darien in 1818. The latter was largely owned by the State, and the Legislature agreed to guarantee the redemption of the notes. The bank was to have its nominal home in Darien, but an office for discount was to be in Milledgeville, and it was to have branches in all parts of the State. At Darien, Milledgeville, Dublin, Clinton, Watkinsville, Hartford, Macon

Greensboro, Columbia C. H. (or Appling), Eatonton, Monticello, Madison, Sparta, Sandersville and Lincolnton stock was to be subscribed for. The State was to own a majority of the stock, and it was to be a State depository.

The efforts to open manufacturing establishments had not been successful, and so a charter was granted for a lottery, whose profits were to be applied to the building of a woolen factory in the up-country.

There was a good deal of interest taken in the education of the higher classes. Academies were chartered in all the principal towns, and each received a stipend from the State. The academies at Sunbury, Augusta, Washington, Waynesboro, Greensboro and Savannah, which had been long established, were now flourishing, and during this period academies were incorporated in Powelton, Madison, Monticello, Eatonton, Warrenton, Elberton, Sardis, Hillsboro, Dublin, Jeffersonton, and in the counties of McIntosh, Jackson, Jasper and Camden.

Some of these academies, as they were called, were merely ordinary schools in which the English branches alone were taught; but in most of the villages the elements of a classical training were given. The Mt. Enon Academy, founded by the Baptists, had suspended, and the college at Athens was sadly crippled by the war and was still not flourishing.

The masses were only provided for by what was known as old field schools. There was no provision made by the State up to this period for the establishment of free schools, and those who were not near enough to the academies to attend them were largely without any school facilities at all. This was the case even in the older counties, while in the newer there was almost an entire absence of any provision for even primary education. The old field school was not much changed from what it had been twenty years before, and it underwent little change for twenty years after this.

The great religious interest which had continued from 1800 to 1812 had somewhat lost its vigor, but still the advance of the leading churches was steady, if not rapid. The evangelical preachers still went with the new settlements, but their number was too few to do more than give a very unsatisfactory service.

In my sketch of the counties and in the special chapter devoted to the subject, I have endeavored to give a fuller account of the religious movements of the period than I can give in this summary.

The Baptists and Methodists were now the leading denominations in middle and southern Georgia; but the Presbyterians were influential and wealthy. The Baptists had a high school in Powelton and the Presbyterians one at Mt. Zion.

The Methodists were steadily growing, especially through the agency of the camp-meetings, which were now held in every county. In the older counties there were log churches in the country for the Baptists, Methodists and Presbyterians, and in some of the towns there were plain frame churches, but in most of the county towns there were no churches of any denomination. Except in Ebenezer, Savannah, Augusta, Milledgeville, Midway and Mount Zion, there was preaching only once a month in any church.

During this period there was, as far as I can discover, but one Sunday-school in the State and that was in Lincoln county at a church called Pine Grove, and it has had a continued existence to the present time without a break.

Camp-meetings were very necessary and were very needful in those days. They were not confined to the Methodists alone, but were held also by the Presbyterians and Baptists.

As yet society in new Georgia had most of the features

which belong to all newly settled countries. The houses were still in the main of logs, and most of the people very plain in their style of living. Nearly all the people of family owned their homesteads, and while many of them were in humble circumstances, they were very independent.

The farms at this time were generally small, not over two hundred acres, and there were many more separate homesteads in 1820 than there were twenty years after that date, and after 1840 the number decreased with fearful rapidity.

Washington, Warrenton, Sandersville, Eatonton, Madison, Monticello and Sparta were towns of considerable trade. At that time a few merchants carried very large stocks of all kinds of goods, which were sold on twelve months' time, and generally at one hundred per cent. above cost. The merchant went to market twice a year. A few went to New York, the larger number went to Charleston, and many went no farther than Augusta. Here they bought dry-goods and hardware. Groceries were generally purchased in Augusta. The goods bought in New York were generally shipped by sailing vessels to Savannah, and thence boated up the river to the nearest point to the wagon-train. There were regular wagon-trains to Baltimore and Philadelphia.

There were few stores in which liquor was not sold. The profits were very large and the risks very great. The laws for the collectien of debts were very severe. Men were sold out relentlessly by the sheriff, and imprisoned for debt when they could not or would not pay. Absconding debtors were frequent, and to run away between two days was a common thing. Fortunes were being rapidly made during this period. Men who came to Georgia in the first of the century with a few negroes, who bought land at one dollar an acre, now found their slaves largely increased in number and their land worth tenfold its cost. Men who had taken a headright in the latter part of the old century, and who were poor and illiterate, had now become owners of large plantations. They were, many of them, unable to read or write, but they knew how to make cotton.

Extravagance and luxury was at a discount; simplicity and plainness at a high premium.

The people of middle Georgia were no longer frontiersmen. Even the newly settled counties had none of the rugged features of the frontier, but they were still unlike their low-country fellow citizens.

The coast had been settled for near a hundred years before this epoch. The planters had constant intercourse with the city. The wealthy among them were very wealththy, and the poor very poor They had no middle class. The up-country people had no intercourse with their low-country fellow citizens. They were alike Georgians. Their ancestors came from the same parts of Europe, but peculiar environments had affected each class; and there was as much difference between the sturdy farmer of Greene and Hancock and the rice-planter of Liberty, as between a sturdy Irishman and a canny Scotchman. In many respects the Yorkshire man and the cockney differed no more in their vernacular than the up-country rustic and the low-country planter. Their manners were as different as their pronunciation. The up-country man was brusque, independent and unconventional; the low-country man fastidious, considerate and mild-mannered. These people did not coalesce when they came together.

The social life of Georgia had now taken the features which it wore for many years afterward, and at the risk of some repetition I ought now to portray these different types of Georgians with some care.

The low-country people in many cases were large slaveholders. They lived on their plantations during the winter and at their city homes, or homes on the islands, during the summer.

The planters and their families were generally people of finished manners, of good culture and of literary taste. They were very exclusive in their social relations and distant to strangers, but exceedingly genial to those admitted into the charmed circle. Their houses were airy and comfortable. Generally they were of one story, with very wide verandas and roomy halls. Their tables were well laden with the products of their own fields, and when near the coast, with fish and oysters. There was careful attention given to table furnishing, and silver fifty years old, and china which had been imported by the Savannah merchants from Hongkong, were brought out whenever there were guests.

The best periodicals, of which there were few in America, came to their homes, and the best books of the old English writers were on their shelves. Servants were well trained and were polite and attentive. The planter's wife and daughters had little to do except to see to the proper care of the little children or aged and helpless slaves, and entertain the guests who came at all hours.

The rice-planter and the sea-island planter were active, money-loving, energetic men. They were sometimes men of broad culture, like Mr. Cooper or Mr. Spalding, who lived among their books, and sometimes men of pleasure who followed the hounds with a sportsman's zest; but generally they were intent on the one point of building up the fortunes of the family. They had generally large increase every year in their negro property. Their cattle multiplied in large numbers. They had unbounded credit with their factors. They were generally Episcopalians in religion, except in Liberty, and while Democrats in their political faith, were socially aristocrats in feeling and manner. They were men of a high sense of honor, guileless and unsuspicious, true husbands, good masters, delightful friends; not always temperate, and always ready to fight.

The negroes on the rice-fields and on the sea islands did not differ from each other; and while to those who had never known them they seemed unhappy savages, they were the best satisfied laborers on earth. This negro was but one remove from the African savage. He revered his master as a prince royal and his mistress as a queen, and dreaded the overseer, and especially the black driver, with a holy dread. As yet but little intelligent effort had been made to Christianize him. The traditions, the folk-lore, the superstitions his father had brought with him from Africa, he still held to. He had his fetish and feared with holy fear the conjurer or hoodoo. He had no world beyond the island on which he made cotton, or the quarter of the rice plantation where he had his cabin.

The rich and poor whites living in this section of Georgia had drifted farther and farther apart. The overseer was the trusted employee of the planter, and his family was treated with great kindness and respect by the ladies of the big house; but there was no social intercourse.

The life of the planter of Burke, Jefferson, Wilkes, Columbia and other middle Georgia counties was like and yet unlike that of the rice-planter or sea-islander. This Georgian was an American of long descent. His ancestors were Virginians; he had the proudest blood of America and England in his veins, but he was disposed to ignore that fact, and boasted of his contempt for such claims.

The middle Georgia planter had in most cases made his fortune, and, as he was generally from Virginia, enjoyed it in a Virginia way. He had come to Georgia thirty years before, and for a considerable time had lived in his log cabin on the frontier, where the angry Creeks threatened the settlements with their raids. He had ridden with

Clarke and Irwin in pursuit of the robber horde, and housed his family in the blockhouse on Fort creek while he and his slaves made corn on the rich bottoms of Shoulderbone, But the Indians had been long gone; the war for free trade and sailors' rights was over; the cotton-gin had been set up; and wealth had poured in upon him. So he built his great square house with eight rooms twenty feet square, with broad piazza and wide halls. He bought a gig for his wife, and sent his sons to Dr. Waddell and his daughters to Mrs. Dugas to school. His fields were broad; his slaves were many; his flocks of sheep and goats were large, and his cattle were in great herds. His hogs were numerous, and, alas! his still turned the produce of his orchard into peach and apple brandy, which he always kept on his sideboard. He was a just master. He gave his negroes a peck of meal and three pounds and a half of bacon a week, and in after years a quart of muscovado molasses in addition. His negroes also had their three suits of clothing and a stout pair of shoes every year. He gave them their holidays on every Sunday and on Christmas week The old planter generally dressed in homespun, and counted no man his better.

The good women of middle Georgia society at this period and for twenty years afterward were the best and busiest of their kind. They had married in the early years of the century, and had known but little of the schoolteacher and had never seen a dancing-master. Reaching womanhood before they ever saw a town or city, they had the simple, genial manners learned from their old Virginia mothers. They had culture, but it had not come from books. They knew all kinds of domestic work; they could weave and spin and knit, and, if need be, cook and wash; but they had too much to do to attend to these homely duties themselves. They saw to the welfare of the negroes, especially the ailing women and the little children. They knew the virtues of boneset and sage and catnip; they could dress a blister or make a poultice or bind a bandage with the skill of a physician. These matrons led busy lives; to see to the making up of negro clothing; to see after the kitchen garden and the flower garden; to go to week-day meetings and to get ready for camp-meeting; to spread a generous table every day, and especially when Brother Pierce or Brother Mercer or Dr. Cunningham came—kept them constantly employed. They were proud of their Virginia lineage, and spoke of the old commonwealth as if no spot on earth could ever be like that. They had read no books but the Bible and "The Pilgrim's Progress," and possibly "Charlotte Temple" or "Alonzo and Melissa"; took no magazines, and had no fashion plates. Their carpets were made of rags; and they had cut the rags themselves, and had them woven by their own trusted weavers. Their household furniture was plain; but the splint-bottomed chairs were immaculately white, and the beds were covered with the snowy white counterpanes in summer and the red or blue-check counterpanes in winter, woven by their own handmaidens. They ruled their households with a kindly rule, and the old squires bowed submissively to their mandates.

The hardships of the frontier, by 1820, were left behind in all the older counties, and wealth and plenty was in the land. The lavish living of the old Virginian was reproduced in all parts of middle Georgia.

The home of Ralph Banks still stands in Elbert county, where it was built by his own carpenters nearly seventy-five years ago. It has fourteen large rooms above ground, cellars beneath. The inventory of his estate shows scores of slaves, thousands of acres of land, horses, sheep, cattle, goats, wheat, oats, barley, and, alas! good Methodist as he was, one hundred gallons of peach brandy, sundry barrels of hard cider and a barrel of wine. On the estate all the clothing was woven by hand; the leather was made by the planter's own tanner, and the shoes by his shoemaker.

It must be admitted that in the early part of the century there were stills on most of the large plantations, and that apples and peaches, which were produced in great quantities, were turned into brandy, which was to be drunk moderately and thankfully. Everybody drank in those days, except a few very strict Methodists. On every sideboard there was a decanter, and the host invited each guest to help himself—which he generally did, sometimes asking a blessing from heaven on this good creature now provided. No one was considered to be genuinely hospitable unless he passed the decanter.

The picture I have just drawn is of the planter who belonged to the wealthy class; but these were by no means the majority of the people. There was still in all the older counties a much larger number of small farmers than of planters. Many of them had no negroes at all; a great many only a few. They owned land and live stock, and by hard work made an abundant living. They lived in great simplicity. Their cabins were still of logs, and were oftentimes the same which they built thirty years before, save that a few sheds had been added to the main room as the family increased, and that a kitchen and dining-room were in another cabin in the yard. These people were the Georgia yeomanry. They had but little education; many of them could not read, and but a few of them could write their names. They were not hirelings or tenants; they were proprietors, and were as proud and independent as if they had owned princely domains. As a body they were honest. Marriages were early, and children were many. They had but few luxuries; they worked hard and lived hard, but they had an abundance of plain food and cared for nothing more than their farms produced. They did not hesitate to take a dram on all proper occasions, and when they went to town they often came from it "disguised in liquor," which was a venial sin to be acknowledged at the next monthly meeting of the church. They had little intercourse with the rich people and the town folks, and were generally at dagger's point with the rich man's "niggers," who regarded them with great contempt and called them "poor buckra." They dressed in homespun fabrics, and many of them, men and women, went barefoot during the summer, except when they went to town or to meeting.

These middle class people have been confounded with those below them who were known as "crackers"; but they were an entirely distinct class. It cannot be denied that scattered over Georgia there were to be found the unquestionable "cracker"—the humblest of Georgians. He was not a yeoman, nor was he a landholder: when land was granted freely he would not pay office fees; but rented or "squatted." He was lazy and shiftless; and, while he had not a few good qualities, he was rather a poor citizen. He seemed to have a fondness for poor land and whisky, and wherever there was a post-oak ridge he built his cabin there. He never had a comfort, nor ever cared for one; he had but little, and seemed to want but little. He was not proud of anything but his independence and his ignorance. He was but a reproduction of the humblest English laborer or Irish peasant, from whom he was descended. He had no aspiration, and rarely rose to a better place. He was not, by any means, only a Georgian, for his double was found in every section of the United States. The pioneer farmers were in appearance like "the poor white," the "moss-back," the "sand-lapper," the "cracker"; but it was in appearance only. The genesis of this race of "crackers" must be sought for beyond the seas, and his first American ancestor was likely a vagrant lad picked up in the English or Scotch seaport and brought over by a sea captain who sold him to a tobacco-planter for five years. When his time was out he began to move and his descendants have kept moving ever since. He was always found where there were new settlements, and where land was poor and life was hard. In many respects he has in 1900 the same features which belonged to his class two hundred years ago; he has not degenerated—he has simply never advanced. Apparently he has disappeared; but start a cotton mill, or open a mine, or settle a new country, and he comes. He is scattered through the mountains, in the pine woods, or is now working at the poorest paid labor in the cotton mills.

The Creek Indians were never reconciled to the cession of their lands, and were disposed to depredate on frontiersmen, and, through the agency of Ambrister and Arbuthnot, in 1818 the Seminole part of the Creeks rose against the whites, and General Andrew Jackson was sent to suppress them. The war was a short one; the Indians were quickly conquered; Ambrister and Arbuthnot were hanged, and a body of friendly Indians were cruelly massacred by some Georgia troops. The Seminoles were driven to east Florida, and for twenty years there was peace on the frontier.

Political excitement ran very high between Clarke and Crawford, and was the more rancorous because the issues were personal rather than political. These parties were in the height of their antagonism, and the Clarke party had, just as this period closes, won a signal victory by electing John Clarke governor. The animosity felt toward him and his adherents was intense, and they paid it back with interest.

There were now in Georgia six newspapers: Augusta *Chronicle*, Savannah *Republican*, Washington *News*, *Georgia Journal* (Milledgeville), Savannah *Georgian*, and the *Recorder* (Milledgeville). These papers were about evenly divided between the two parties. It had not been a time for book-making, and not a book (save a book of laws) had been published in the eight years.

The war between England and the United States, to which we have alluded in the last chapter, did not for some time seriously involve Georgia. There was some little alarm felt on the coast, and a few troops were stationed in Savannah and St. Marys; but the restless Seminoles and bitter Creeks were on the war-path in both Southern Georgia and Alabama. A body of Georgia troops under the command of General John Floyd, who had come to Georgia a Virginia ship-carpenter and acquired a large estate, and who was a man of real parts, marched into the Indian Nation beyond the Ocmulgee, near Columbus. Here he built Fort Mitchell, and, marching westward, fought the battle of Autosee, in which he was wounded. The general was the first man to march through the great Okefinokee swamp, where he cut a road known as Floyd's trail. He recovered from his wound, and was in command at the battle of Challibee, where the whites were again victorious. The war ended with the battle of New Orleans early in 1815.

During this period the war with England and the war of the Creeks came to an end.

By the treaty made by General Jackson with the Creeks all of the southern and southwestern parts of the State still held by the Creeks was surrendered to the State of Georgia; the Cherokees relinquished their control over a part of their country; and by a second treaty by ex-Governor Mitchell the Creeks surrendered their control over that country between the Ocmulgee and the Flint, which was afterward divided into Walton, Gwinnett, Hall, Habersham, Appling, Early, Irwin, Emanuel and Rabun counties.

In giving an account of these new counties it may be best to divide them into groups. There were three kinds of country represented: The mountains, including Rabun and Habersham; the hill country of Gwinnett, Hall and Walton; the pine woods of Emanuel, Early, Irwin and Appling.

The mountain country of upper Georgia was largely occupied by the Cherokee Indians. Only two counties were now formed in this territory. The country was very wild and very sparsely settled. It was exceedingly rough, and the few inhabitants at that time were perhaps the most thriftless of the Georgia people. They had gone into the mountains, where they built log cabins of the most primitive sort, with dirt floors and leaky roofs. They planted some corn and had a few cows. The country was full of game, and they depended largely upon their skill with the rifle to secure food for their families. Clothing was hard to get and money they never had.

The pioneer went once a year to the new town of Athens or Clarksville and traded his peltry for a little powder and lead, an axe and a hoe and some iron, and a little "spun truck," as he called cotton yarn, and went back to his mountain cabin to stay there for the year.

During the summer life was not so hard. The crofter in Scotland, the peasant in Ireland and the English farm laborer, from whom in all likelihood the first mountaineers came, had in many respects a harder life than their Georgia descendants, for their woods were not full of game, nor did they have fuel furnished them without stint, nor had they as rich pasturage for their cattle.

It cannot be denied that at this early day and for many years afterward, that not a few of the lonely denizens of these mountain coves were fugitives from the penalties of the law. In South Carolina, or North Carolina, or Tennessee, in a rough-and-tumble fight he had gouged out an eye, or bit off a nose, or mayhap have been guilty of some act more disreputable, and had fled to this lonely corner of a new State and hid away.

Sometimes the poor settler was averse to steady work

and sought to find some place where he could as far as possible live without it. In these wild mountains he lived as free as an Indian and had as few comforts. He had a little patch of corn and he pounded it in a mortar or made it into hominy. He went barefoot in summer and wore Indian moccasins in the winter. A coon skin made him a cap, and his wife wove the cotton cloth which he wore in summer and the jeans he wore in winter. He had no education. He could not read, his wife could not read, the peasant from whom he had descended could not read. He lived in the same kind of house his over-the-sea forefather had lived in, only the cottage of that peasant was made of stone and covered with peat and he paid rent for it, and the mountaineer paid no rent and lived in a cabin of poles covered with boards. He kept his hearth ablaze with wooden logs, while his progenitor hovered over a fire of peat. He had never known any other life than the lowly one he lived, and was satisfied with it. No landlord asked for rent, no tax-gatherer for taxes, and in those days not even an office-seeker came near him.

These were some of the first mountaineers but by no means all. There in the mountains were valleys idyllic in their beauty. They had been the home of the Indians, and when they vacated them, men of some culture, who had known something of society but who had become weary of the bustle of life, sought a secluded home here, and more frequently the bustling North Carolinian, landless and enterprising, led by the fertility of these valleys, built his cabin in one of them and planted his orchard.

These mountaineers who eighty years ago and those who succeeded them for twenty years afterward were as distinct from other Georgians as the Scotch Highlanders were from their Lowland kinsman. They were not like the upper Georgia yeoman, the middle Georgia planter, or even the piny woods rustic. These were not themselves all alike, and a description of one person, however exact, would be entirely unsuited to another who lived near him.

The same class of people who came into the mountains of upper Georgia settled in North Carolina, Tennessee, Kentucky and western Virginia. The north Georgia mountaineer came generally from the mountainous parts of North Carolina, as the piny woods stock-raiser came from the pine woods of eastern North Carolina.

As a rule the people were for many years poor and illiterate. They were fearless, sensitive, prejudiced, but hospitable, kindly and sincere. They were not as a general thing enterprising, and seemed too content with privations which industry would have removed. At the time which this period covers there were all the discomforts of the earliest frontier, and everything was in its pristine wildness.

The hill country of Walton, Gwinnett and Hall presents such uniformity of feature that it is difficult to give an account of any one of the counties without saying what was true of another adjoining.

The country lies at the foothills of the Blue Ridge, and while none of it is remarkably fertile, it is nearly all arable. There are some rich valleys along the rivers and on the many creeks and branches, called in Georgia parlance "bottoms."

The country produces corn, wheat, oats, rye, potatoes, cotton and tobacco; apples, peaches, pears, cherries and plums grow in great abundance. It is not, however, generally a fertile country, and needs careful culture and generous fertilizing in order to produce good harvests.

The water is cool and the air pure.

The rich cotton lands of middle and southern Georgia were more attractive to the Virginia slaveholders than these sections, and they turned their steps thither, and left all this country to people of small means who had few or no slaves. I doubt if there was in all this section in 1820 a farmer worth twenty thousand dollars. Perhaps not one was worth half so much. Land was sold as a general thing for a dollar an acre, or less, except the exceptionally fine land on the rivers, which brought from two to five dollars.

The people who settled here were mainly Carolinians, either from upper South Carolina or western North Carolina. They came from the hill country to the hill country. They were very plain and very simple in their lives and had very small estates; but were thoroughly independent and self-reliant. They were landowners and had their farms stocked and made a good livelihood, and while not generally people of culture, they believed in churches and schools, and though there was much ignorance and much drinking among them, there was much good sense and piety. As a class they filled the place between the middle Georgia planter and the ignorant mountaineer. There were many very poor and ignorant people among them, and the inimitable "Bill Arp" (Colonel Charles H. Smith) has drawn a picture of one so graphic that I transfer it to these pages as presenting in a more satisfactory way a picture of a class of people who have been sadly misread by those who have merely caught a glimpse of them and noted their striking and peculiar traits.

* * * * * * * * *

"So I did not rob Bill Arp of his good name. * *

"He was a small, sinewy man, weighing about 130 pounds, as active as a cat, as quick in movement as he was active, and always presenting a bright, cheerful face. He had an amiable disposition, a generous heart, and was as brave a man as nature makes.

"He was an humble man and unlettered in books; never went to school but a month or two in his life, and could neither read nor write; but still he had more than his share of common sense, more than his share of ingenuity, and plan and contrivance, more than his share of good mother-wit and good humor, and was always welcome when he came about.

"Lawyers and doctors and editors, and such gentlemen of leisure who used to, in the good old time, sit around and chat and have a good time, always said, 'Come in, Bill, and take a seat;' and Bill seemed grateful for the compliment, and with a conscious humility squatted on about half the chair and waited for questions. The bearing of the man was one of reverence for his superiors and thankfulness for their notice."

* * * * * * * * *

There were, however, in these new counties not a few who were people of real culture and refinement, and who were led to fix their homes in them by the inducements which new settlements always hold out. They came to these new villages to teach school, practice law or merchandize, and oftentimes settled plantations on the rivers and creeks. The section was very rapidly filled up with a hardy, industrious, pushing people, and the county sites soon became thrifty villages.

The lands were very hilly, light and easily washed away, and there was after the period of which we write the usual result of the culture of those times—desolate fields given up to broom-sedge and to scrubby pines; but this did not come until twenty years later.

Those who came at first were generally people of very moderate means, but they were independent from the beginning. Religiously they were Baptists, Methodists or Presbyterians in their affiliations. Their creeds were short ones and they believed in them fully. The Bible, as they understood it, was the final arbiter on all questions.

The picture I have given of the Georgia yeoman and the picture drawn by Colonel Smith of the Georgia cracker are, I am sure, correct portraitures of the two main classes of settlers in upper Georgia in 1818.

The picture we have had of the pine woods elsewhere belongs to this large section which now comes under survey, and which was at this time opened for settlement, except a part of the county of Early. Great pine forests stretched from the Altamaha to the Chattahoochee, only broken into by a few hammocks and some river and creek swamps. Much of this pine land was too wet for culture, much of it a barren sand bed; but much of it only needed to be manured to make it productive. At that time all was regarded as hopelessly sterile and as only fitted for grazing land for some small black cattle, such as had been imported from the Highlands. The people who came into these pine woods in their earlier settlement were mainly from the eastern counties of North Carolina and Georgia and lower South Carolina. The Scotchmen settled in Telfair and Montgomery, but descendants of Americans in Irwin and the counties springing from it. At first the newcomers were merely ranchmen. They lived at great distances from each other, and lived very plainly. In many respects they were like the better class of monntaineers; but they had fewer hardships to endure, owing to the greater mildness of the climate. Many of these people were of Scotch or Scotch-Irish ancestry, and many were descended from the Highlanders who came to Georgia near a hundred years before. The settler in the pine woods in 1820 lived almost entirely within himself. He had little to sell, and had far to go to market; and he knew nothing of foreign luxuries. He made some long-staple cotton; his wife and children picked out the seed with their fingers, and his wife spun it and wove it into cloth. His sheep furnished him with wool, and he made his own leather and his own shoes and his coonskin cap. He had no mill nearer to him, often, than forty miles, and no store nearer than Centerville in

Camden or Hartford in Pulaski; but he had a country where the climate was mild and where he could raise corn and potatoes and sugar-cane, and where deer and turkeys were so abundant that no skill was necessary to kill or capture them. He had an abundance of hogs and cattle, and, while it was somewhat difficult to get salt to cure his meat, he had learned the art of jerking beef, and was not too particular about a gamy flavor to his meat. He was a great hunter. The panther, which he called the "tiger," was still in the swamp, and the bear gave him trouble by seizing his pigs and ravaging his corn patches. The isolation and discomforts of this life, and the apparent sterility of the country, did not invite immigrants, and for years after this time the country was very sparsely settled.

In this new country, though they had few schools and churches, yet the traditions of a religious people still influenced them, and, while they were not intelligently religious, they were not grossly immoral. Unlike their up-country kinsmen, the piny woods "cracker" was not near a still, and was a long way from a drinking-shop; and, while he had no more objection to a drop of whisky than the mountaineer, he was less likely to drink to excess. One of the largest of these new counties was called

EMANUEL.

It was made in 1812, and named in honor of that staunch Maryland Whig, David Emanuel. It comprised a large body of almost exclusively pine woods. There were a number of streams running through it: the Ohoopee, the Canoochee and Ogeechee rivers and a number of large creeks. Though there were large swamps, the lands bordering the rivers were not arable, and there was no attention paid to agriculture. The one industry of the country when it was first settled was stock-raising. On account of its large size it was called the State of Emanuel. The first settlers were generally poor, but were able to make a good living, and were independent. They were of that class of piny woods people which occupied nearly all this section of the State, and whom we have so often described.

The first settlers were, according to White: James Moon, Wm. Stephens, Henry Darden, George Roundtree, Richard Edinfield, M. Thigpen, A. Gardner, N. Rowland, E. Swain, James Tapley, John Small, James Hicks, Wm. Phillips, I. Sutton, E. Lane, B. Johnson, John Wiggins, P. Newton, Wm. Rowland, Wm. Norris, I. Norris, Wm. Douglas, S. Powell, John Rhiner, M. Curl, S. Kennedy, E. Coleman, D. E. Rich, E. Wilkes, S. Williamson, B. Keys, J. C. Sumner.

There was much about Emanuel and all these pine-barren counties to attract men of small property who loved a free and independent life. The first settlers were mainly cattle-rangers. In the latter days they were timber-rangers, sending their fine timber to the Savannah market. They spent the summer in hewing logs for their rafts, and in the winter floated them to the Ogeechee canal and to Savannah. They had few wants, and the money they received for their timber was, much of it, laid aside for future use. Next to timber the main resource was cattle- and sheep-raising. There were a little corn and sugar-cane and some oats raised; but the agricultural value of the lands was overlooked until the war ended and the commercial fertilizers were found suited to the land and cotton was cultivated to profit. The railroads penetrated the county in search of timber for the mills, and the turpentine farmer leased the land and bled the trees and set up his still. Emanuel then began to improve in every way, and has gone steadily forward until there are several flourishing towns in the county.

For many years the only denominations of Christians were the Methodists and Primitive Baptists.

Swainsboro and Stillmore and Adrian are thriving towns with good churches and good schools.

IRWIN.

The story of Emanuel is the story of Irwin, which was laid off in 1818, and named in honor of Governor Jared Irwin. It was an immense county.

The first settlers were:

John Dormany, R. H. Dickson, M. McDuffee, L. Mobley, John Henderson, Thos. Bradford, Lott. Whiddon, Redding Hunter, John Joyce, Wm. Bradford, S. Griffin, James Wallace, James Allen, John Ford, Saul Story, Thos. Gibbes, John Gibbes, Wm. Frissell, J. C. Sumner.

These first settlers were scattered over an immense area and the homes were far apart. As late as 1866 the writer, passing through this county, rode seventeen miles on the public road without seeing a single house.

There were in 1820 only four hundred and eleven people in all this county, which then included Wilcox, Lowndes, Brooks, Thomas, Colquitt and Worth counties. The social condition of the people was for many years such as we have presented as that of the pine woods frontiersman.

The railroads, however, passed through the county. Turpentine farms were opened, lumber mills erected and villages sprang up, and in 1895 a large colony of Northern people, drawn by the climate and the possibilities of the county, founded a city called Fitzgerald in the heart of the pine-barrens. Farms were opened, railroads were built, manufactures started, and the young city is being peopled with a good class of settlers from the northwest and other parts of the country.

The county was so thinly settled that for many years schools and churches were very few and the people were quite illiterate. They were, however, people of great simplicity of character and were sterling in their integrity. Few sections have developed more rapidly than Irwin and few give promise of greater development.

APPLING.

The county of Appling which, when laid out, included in its boundary several very large counties, was laid out in 1818, and was named in honor of Colonel Daniel Appling, a worthy citizen of Columbia county.

The first settlers, as given by White, were: Nathan Dean, John Taylor, Henry Taylor, Silas O. Quinn, Moses Vick, John Johnston, John Hawkins, J. Smith, D. Redish, D. Summerall, R. Strickland, Samuel Sellars, John Purvis, A. Eason, G. Moody, John Roberson, Jesse Carter, Samuel Carter, Thos. Wood, R. Swilley, S. Swilley, B. Grogan, the Mobleys, Halls, Overstreets, and Wilcoxes.

It was almost an unbroken plain of pine forests. The Altamaha was on its northern and eastern border. There was some good land on this river and some large plantations were opened there by large slave-owners at an early day, but much of it was a wide, wild swamp, too low for cultivation, while away from it there was an unbroken pine forest.

There were some large cattle ranches and many sheep, but there was little attention paid to agriculture for many years. The people were sheep-raisers and cattle-men and timber-rangers.

The same story told of Irwin and Emanuel after the war is true of Appling. Railroads came, the lumber mill and turpentine still followed. Handsome towns sprang up and the population has largely increased. The first settlers in Appling were frontiersmen, and but little attention was paid to schools or churches.

With the first opening of the country the Methodists sent Missionaries into these wilds and the Baptists came with the first settlers. The churches, however, were few and far apart, and the school advantages for many years exceedingly meager.

The population of this county in 1820 was 1,264; in 1830 there were 1,289 whites and 179 slaves; in 1850 there was a free population of 2,645 and 405 slaves. These slaves were confined to a few plantations on the banks of the Altamaha. At the time this census was taken Appling covered the ground now occupied by a half-dozen counties.

There was much of the county peopled by North Carolinians, who were timber-rangers, but after the war a different class of North Carolinians came in, who were turpentine distillers, and now there are in the county several thrifty towns along the railway.

EARLY.

The other of these counties into which all of southern Georgia was divided in 1818 was called Early in honor of Governor Early. It included a large part of southwestern Georgia, and, though a number of other counties have been carved from it, it is still a large county.

Blakely was made the county site in 1826.

The first settlers were, according to White: Isham Sheffield, Arthur Sheffield, West Sheffield, James Bush, John Hays, Jos. Grinsley, Richard Spain, Fink Porter, Jos. Boles, Jno. Rae, Abner Jones, Nathaniel Weaver, James Jones, S. V. Wilson, Jno. Dill, Alex Watson, James Carr, Jno. Tilley, Wm. Hendricks, John Floyd, D. Roberts, Andrew Bird, B. Collier, J. Fowler, Martin Wood, Geo. Mercier, W. Dixon, A. Hayes, James Brantley, and E. H. Hayes.

These first settlers in Early were scattered over a wide area, which is now in several counties. The county of Early proper was slowly settled.

There was along the banks of the Chattahoochee and its tributary creeks a great deal of rich cotton land of the rotten limestone formation, with forests of oak and hickory, but it was sickly and hard to open.

The larger part of the county was pine woods, and it was settled by plain, poor people who raised cattle, but to these fine oak and hickory lands some eastern planters, as soon as the Indians were finally removed, came with many slaves. They were people of culture and wealth, and settled large plantations and lived in great elegance. Their homes were not far from the Chattahoochee river, and they had all the luxuries of the cities brought from Columbus and Apalachicola by the steamers which came weekly.

The larger part of the population, however, was the same class of pine woods people we have seen elsewhere. Immigrants came from the eastern counties in Georgia and from South Carolina and North Carolina. The pine lands of Early were more productive than the lands further east and there was more extensive planting.

In the first days of the county the people had access to the outer world by the boats which went up and down the Chattahoochee.

In 1850 there were as many negroes as whites in the county, but the negroes were almost entirely confined to one section of it, to the plantations on the river or on the creeks flowing into it. Some up-country people had their plantations in this county and spent their winters on them, but their homes were far away, but some of the wealthiest of the people lived in the county all the year round.

The educational advantages of the people were not good. The wealthy had their private teachers and their children were taught at home until they were old enough to go from home to school. They were educated in the best schools of the South, and when they returned to their isolated homes they brought with them as visitors their friends and kinspeople and had a society of their own. In the summer-time and in the malarial season they sought the up-country or their piny woods retreat.

The lands on the river and the creeks were very fertile, and a bale of cotton per acre was often produced.

The churches were not many and were far apart, and for many years the ministers were poorly supported and were of inferior grade. After the war railroads were made, and the changes brought about were very marked in church and school matters.

The wealthy planter whose great plantation was on the river had put all his earnings into young negroes whom he had brought up, and he had no money laid away. When his negroes were freed the bulk of his estate was gone. The plantation negroes were not willing to remain longer in the swamps, and left the plantation for the towns and for their old homes in the up-country and Carolina. The old planter found himself unable to cope with his difficulties, and abandoned his plantation and sought another home, or else, trying to recruit his shattered fortune, he mortgaged his land, bought mules and supplies on a credit, and when disaster to his crop came, as it did, he found himself a bankrupt.

In the picture of the southwest Georgia planting country, which is found in the future chapters, the condition of things in that part of Early in which the planters made their homes is given.

WALTON.

When the first effort was made to settle the Cherokee country in 1802 a new county was projected to be called Walton, and a bill was passed to lay it out. The act was never carried into effect, but in 1818 a new county bearing the same name was provided for, and it was organized.

White gives as the first settlers in this county: Charles Smith, R. M. Echols, P. Stroud, Jno. Dickerson, Warren J.

Hill, Jesse Arnold, Walter T. Colquitt, Jonas Hale, V. Haralson, J. M. Well, A. W. Wright, C. D. Davis, W. Briscoe, R. Briscoe, R. Milligan and J. Richardson.

The county was a very large one, and, in the main, not a fertile one. The larger part of the land was a light gray soil, moderately productive at first but soon exhausted. There were, however, some bottoms on the creeks and rivers which were very fertile. The climate was good, the country healthy, the land cheap, and there soon came into this section a very large number of immigrants. Many of them had been the fortunate drawers of the lots of two hundred and fifty and one-half acres and were from other parts of Georgia, and many of them were from the upper part of South Carolina.

So rapidly was the county peopled that in twelve years after it was opened for settlement there were nearly ten thousand people living in it.

Land was sold in lots of two hundred and fifty acres and generally brought about one hundred dollars per lot, or less than fifty cents per acre. A lot sold at sheriff's sale brought five dollars and a quarter, another brought twenty-five dollars, but land on the rivers even as early as 1821 brought seven dollars per acre.

The first place at which court was held was the Cowpen, which was two miles from Monroe.

Judge John M. Dooly held the court. As was universally the case in new counties the larger number of cases was for assaults. There were, however, bills for hog-stealing, perjury, adultery and mayhem, and a group of men were charged with gambling at seven-up, three-up and faro.

There was loud complaint against illicit liquor-selling where men sold less than a quart without license.

One man was presented and finally punished for cruelly whipping his slave, and one was condemned to be hung for murder. He was, however, pardoned.

While there were few people among the first settlers of Walton who were wealthy, and many quite poor, there was a large number of well-to-do people with from five to ten negroes and an abundance of cheap but productive land. To illustrate the general condition of the well-to-do people one estate shows: 10 negroes, 33 hogs, 17 cattle, kitchen and household furniture, and, what was rare, forty-five dollars' worth of books, while some of the estates indicate abundant means. Theophilus Hill had 42 negroes, 22 sheep, 350 barrels of corn, 12 beds and bedsteads, $100 worth of hogs, 2 cotton-gins, etc.

The bulk of the people had only their land and a small number of cattle, horses, hogs, and a scant supply of furniture. There was but little cotton and very little of anything was made for sale. Corn, hogs and cattle, as in all the new counties, were the products. The coming of new settlers into the county provided a market for the surplus the farmers might have.

Monroe was selected as the county site, and named Monroe after the then president. It soon became a prominent up-country town and the center of quite a coterie of prominent men.

Walter T. Colquitt, then a young lawyer, settled in this little village and made his first reputation as a brilliant lawyer in the courts of this new country.

Judge James Jackson, so famous for the purity of his life and his ability as a jurist, and Judge Junius Hillyer, a prominent lawyer and a member of Congress, were among its citizens.

Governor Henry D. McDaniel, famous as being one of the best governors Georgia has ever had, began his professional life in Monroe, and after his term was over returned there to spend his last years.

Monroe was long a secluded country village with small trade and a small population, but since it has been reached by the railway has become quite a thrifty town, with a fine court-house, a good graded school and some prosperous cotton mills. Social Circle, on the Georgia railway, is a

WALTON COUNTY COURT-HOUSE.

sprightly and enterprising village; and Logansville, in the northwestern part of the county, is a village of considerable trade. Bethlehem is a small hamlet north of Monroe.

The educational advantages of the county for many years

were quite poor, but they are better now than they ever were.

The people who came into Walton were mainly Methodists and Baptists, and the Walton circuit of the Methodist preacher was a very large and important one in the early days of the county's settlement. In 1827 there was a great revival in Monroe, at which Walter Colquitt, a young lawyer, was converted; and a number of years afterward, in the same village, young James Jackson, afterward judge of the superior court and member of Congress, and finally chief justice of the State, was converted and became a lay preacher.

The Baptists were among the first Christian workers in the county, and perhaps the oldest church in the county is a Primitive Baptist Church.

GWINNETT.

Gwinnett county, named for Button Gwinnett, was laid out in 1818, and its county site was, in honor of the brave sea captain, called Lawrenceville. Like all these up-country counties, it was very rapidly settled. Its population in 1830 was 13,289, and twenty years afterward, in 1850, was only 11,257. There was a considerable part of the county cut off into other counties; but it is evident that the population did not increase after the first few years. The people in those days were very migratory, and the opening of better lands to the west led to quite an emigration from the county. The history of these foot-hill counties is much the same. The settler came, built his cabin, opened some fields, and then, hearing of better lands in Carroll, Campbell, Heard, or in Alabama, he sold his farm at what he thought was a fair price, and went to this new country to begin life again. There were but few of the hardships of the frontier to encounter now in the country to which he was going, and there was little difficulty in moving when all he possessed could be put in an ox-cart; and the prospect of bettering himself by finding a larger range and cheaper land led him to move on. There were some very fertile lands on the river in Gwinnett, especially on the Chattahoochee; but the main body of the land was thin and easily worn out. With the exit from the country of the first proprietors the land was taken up by the large landowners, and the plantations took the place of farms. But a new era came to the country when the railways were made, and along the line of the Southern the flourishing villages of Norcross, Buford and Suwanee sprang up. Cotton was cultivated largely, and the county began to improve rapidly. A railroad was built to Lawrenceville, and when the Seaboard Air Line railroad came through the county it passed through Lawrenceville.

The early settlers of Gwinnett were the Winns, Hutchinses, Baughs, Howells, Stricklands, Simmonses, Anthonys, Baxters, Grahams, and many others.

The religious denominations in the county are Presbyterians, Baptists and Methodists, and for many years the Methodists have had within three miles of Lawrenceville a camp-ground, where the most distinguished preachers of Methodism have preached.

The style of life among the rural people of Gwinnett has always been a very simple one. There was but little wealth, so there was but little show. The schools were very ordinary affairs, and education out of the village was not at a premium. Industry and close economy were the sterling virtues of the people.

Dr. Jesse Boring, the celebrated Methodist divine, and his brother Isaac began their lives in this county when it was Jackson, and their father, a man of sterling worth, was for a long time representative from it. Samuel Anthony, another distinguished and famous Methodist preacher, spent his boyhood in this county. James P. Simmons, a lawyer and an author, lived in this county; and the Howell family, who have been so prominent as connected with the Atlanta *Constitution*, came from Gwinnett. The Winn family and the Hutchins family, distinguished as lawyers and judges, lived in Lawrenceville; but no man has cast a greater luster on Gwinnett, the place of his birth, than the Philosopher of the Etowah, Colonel Charles H. Smith, who, under the name of "Bill Arp," has won a high place among literary men as a wise and witty writer, and who has secured the strongest grasp on the hearts of the common people as their adviser and friend. Men everywhere have read with eagerness his letters to the press, in which there is such a wealth of sterling common sense and such a perfect purity of teaching.

HALL.

Hall county was laid off in 1818, and named in honor of Lyman Hall. It was very rapidly settled by a class of worthy but poor people.

The land is not generally fertile, but most of it repaid the tiller's toil, and there are some beautiful and productive farms on the creeks and on the Oconee and Chattahoochee rivers.

It was, like Habersham, famous for the salubrity of its summer climate, and early drew to it a class of wealthy people from the low-country, who fixed their summer homes in Gainesville. The celebrated New Holland springs and the White Sulphur springs were excellent summer resorts near Gainesville, and when the Southern railway was built Gainesville developed into an excellent market for the mountain counties bordering it, and became a place of large trade. The manufacturing of shoes became a leading industry, to which has since been added the manufacturing of cotton.

It has been an educational center, and the Gainesville

Female College has become famous as a school for young women.

Gainesville has now grown into a city of considerable size, populated by a class of enterprising and intelligent people, and has become the leading summer resort of the up-country.

The celebrated Glade mines are in this county. They were owned by Dr. Richard Banks for many years, and while working the mines some beautiful diamonds were found which are still in the family of Dr. Banks. The mines are now owned by a northern company.

Dr. Richard Banks was long a citizen of this county. He was a member of that distinguished family who sprang from Ralph Banks, one of the first settlers of Elbert county, and was long noted for his sterling worth and his tender philanthropy.

The celebrated banker, Richard T. Wilson of New York, began his life in this county as the son of a Scotch tanner, and made his first money as a boy on a Hall county farm.

The religious character of the people has always been good, the Methodists and Baptists being the leading denominations.

The villages of Flowery Branch and Belton, considerable little hamlets, are in this county.

The city of Gainesville, with its handsome court-house and its neat churches and handsome private residences, as well as its well-built stores, is the most important point of northeast Georgia.

The population of Hall as early as 1830 was nearly twelve thousand, but in 1850 eight thousand seven hundred and thirteen.

The first settlers of this county as given by Mr. White were: W. H. Dickson, E. Dunnegan, Jos. Wilson, John Bates, B. Reynolds, R. Armour, Jos. Gailey, T. Terrell, John Miller, D. Wofford, M. Moore, W. Blake, Jos. Read,

R. Young, J. McConnell, R. Wurm, Thos. Wilson, William Cobb, Joseph Johnson, John Barnet, E. Cowen, A. Thomson, Jesse Dobbs, James Abercrombie, Solomon Peake, Richard Banks, Wm. Cotter.

HABERSHAM.

The county of Habersham lies north and northwest of the county of Franklin. It was originally owned by the Cherokees and was surrendered by them to the United States commissioner in 1818. It is in the main a very poor county. Along the Tugalo, the Sequee and the Chattahoochee there are some beautiful valleys, but in the main the land is a thin red land which is soon exhausted.

It has, however, such an altitude, being from fifteen to eighteen hundred feet above the level of the sea, and at Tallulah falls over two thousand two hundred and fifty feet, that it has almost unrivaled advantages as a summer climate; and before the railroad system was fairly opened, and when it was necessary to find mountain resorts as near home as possible and reach them by private conveyance, the people from the low-country and from the cities of Savannah and Augusta fixed their summer homes on these foot-hills. They came to the up-country in June and remained until November. They built neat villas and surrounded themselves with many comforts, and formed a delightful if somewhat exclusive society. The population, however, was largely of those sturdy yeomanry who have done so much for Georgia; and in 1830, when Habersham included White, there were ten thousand people in the county. The most of these were poor people, and life among them was very primitive.

There was much inducement for the landless South Carolinian and North Carolinian, or Georgian, to settle when he could get one hundred and sixty acres of land, much of it arable, for one hundred dollars; so the tide of settlers poured into the country, and one-roomed cabins sprang up like magic in the forests. The rich lands on the rivers were soon occupied by the well-to-do immigrants from North Carolina.

The beautiful Nacoochee valley, one of the fairest spots of earth, comprising a narrow strip of land on the Chattahoochee, at the foot of Mount Yonah, had been bought at the first settlement of the county by Major Williams and by a few other North Carolina settlers. It was evident that in the days of De Soto the Spaniards had mined for gold in this valley, and in the garden of a local Methodist preacher, a Mr. Richardson, a rich placer mine was discovered in 1829. This was the beginning of the wild gold excitement which made the unpeopled mountains of upper Georgia for a long time as populous as a city full. Along the Chattahoochee and on Duke's creek, after the placers were washed out, the veins were opened and stamp-mills were put up. While digging for gold a subterranean town, evidently of De Soto's time, was discovered.

The county was early a favorite with tourists, and the railroad from Atlanta to Charlotte opened up the country to them, and the marvelous beauty of Tallulah Falls in this county, began to draw visitors from all sections. This wonderful freak of nature has but few equals east of the Rocky mountains. The Tallulah river, a limpid and rapid stream, dashes its way through the hills into a deep cañon, and then over sundry precipices until it reaches the grand chasm, where it is eight hundred feet below the surface of the earth. A pool at the base of one of the cascades is called "Hathorn pool," in memory of a Presbyterian minister who many years ago lost his life while bathing in it.

There is a beautiful cascade of one hundred and eighty feet near the city of Toccoa, also in this county.

There was quite an immigration of Swiss people to these

foot-hills some years ago. They have been thrifty people and have done well raising grapes and other fruits and cultivating small farms.

Although Habersham has been remote from the center of population in Georgia, and has, in the main, been inhabited by a very plain, uncultured people, no county has had in it a finer class of cultured men and women, Most of these have, however, only resided here a part of the year, but some have been permanent residents.

Among the distinguished citizens of the county was Dr. George D. Phillips, long a prominent physician and a distinguished member of the Senate of the State. He was a Virginian by birth, who came from the mountains of North Carolina to Georgia, and won by his probity and ability the highest place in the confidence of the people. His three sons, General Wm. Phillips, Colonel Charles D. Phillips and Major Jas. P. Phillips, were distinguished officers in the Confederate army.

Colonel McMillan, who lost his life during the war, was from this county. He was a gallant Irishman by descent, and led a regiment.

The county has always been a religious one, and the Mossy Creek camp-ground has been in existence for over seventy years. The Baptists have a strong hold in this county, and the Presbyterians and Episcopalians have each of them churches in it.

The mining interests of the county have been more or less prosperous since the first opening of the mines seventy years ago.

In the last few years the manufacturing interests of the county have been greatly developed, and the prospect of rapid advance in this direction is bright.

Among the early settlers were: Gabe Fish, Major Williams, Alex Walden, B. Cleveland, John Whitehead, John Grant, Jesse Kinney, Chas. Rich, Mr. Vandiver, H. Moss,

Wm. Herring, Mr. Richardson, Mr. Lumsden, Mr. Logan, Josiah A. Kees, James Quillian and General Wofford.

RABUN.

Rabun was formed from the Cherokee country in 1819, and was named in honor of Governor Rabun. It was in the extreme northeast of Georgia, with South Carolina, North Carolina and Tennessee bounding it.

The county was a wild one. There was one beautiful valley of considerable extent, known as the Tennessee valley, and some smaller valleys on the creeks and on the Tallulah river. The larger part of the country was exceedingly mountainous, and the mountains, while covered with timber, were unsuited for pasture lands or farms.

The remoteness of the county from any market and the general sterility of the soil prevented its rapid settlement; and the fact that it was possible for a fugitive from justice to hide in these mountains of another State led not a few men of shadowy character to hide in Rabun. But there were many excellent people who came at an early day and fixed their homes in the then wild valleys and in the county town Clayton. The first settlers were generally from North and South Carolina, and in the main were very poor and uncultivated people. There was but little hope, out of the few small valleys, for remunerative farming; but the range was wide and wants were few, and the hill farmer managed to live, while the valley farmer was often well-to-do. The county was slowly peopled, and a part of it is even now uninhabited.

The celebrated senator, Dr. H. V. M. Miller, was born in this county and brought up here, and from here went out to win a place among the great men of his State. Judge Logan E. Bleckley, the many-sided sage, who, as a philosopher, a wit and a lawyer, has been equally distinguished, was born in Rabun and reared under the shadow of these mountains.

The county has never had a railway in it; but when one comes and the taste for mountain-ranging becomes more common in Georgia it will be the tourist's favorite resort.

CHAPTER VIII.

1820 TO 1829.

John Clarke—George M. Troup—The Treaty—John Forsyth—Purchase of the Lands between the Ocmulgee and Flint—Great Purchase between Flint and Chattahoochee—The Opening of the New Country—Banks—Education—Lotteries—Macon—Columbus—The Newspapers—Dueling—Religious History of the Period—Great Revival—Jos. C. Stiles—John E. Dawson—C. D. Mallary—Stephen Olin—John Howard—Lovick Pierce—Settlement of the New Country—Flush Times—Education—Factories—Anti-Tariff Feeling—Counties Formed—Newton—Houston—Dooly—Monroe—Henry—Fayette—Dekalb—Bibb—Crawford—Pike—Upson—Decatur—Ware—Taliaferro—Butts—Baker—Lee—Troup—Meriwether—Harris—Coweta—Campbell—Carroll—Talbot—Marion—Thomas—Lowndes—Muscogee—Randolph.

Authorities as in last Chapter, with Dawson's Compilation of Georgia Laws, Prince's Digest for the history of the counties, United States public documents referring to the troubles of Georgia and the general government, Newspapers of the period.

John Clarke was elected governor by the Legislature in the fall of 1819, and was governor when the period which is covered by this chapter began.

He was the son of Elijah Clarke, the great partizan chief, and was with him in his Revolutionary campaign and in his forays against the Indians after it. He had won his spurs as a fearless, able soldier before he was a man, and was especially distinguished in the last severe conflict between the whites and the Creeks at Jack's creek.

The accounts of John Clarke differ, as they come from his friends or his foes. That he was a man of fine mind, that he was a brave soldier, that he was a man of generous heart when his passions were not aroused, that no charges of dishonesty were justly laid at his door, none deny. That he was unsteady in his habits, that he had little education, that

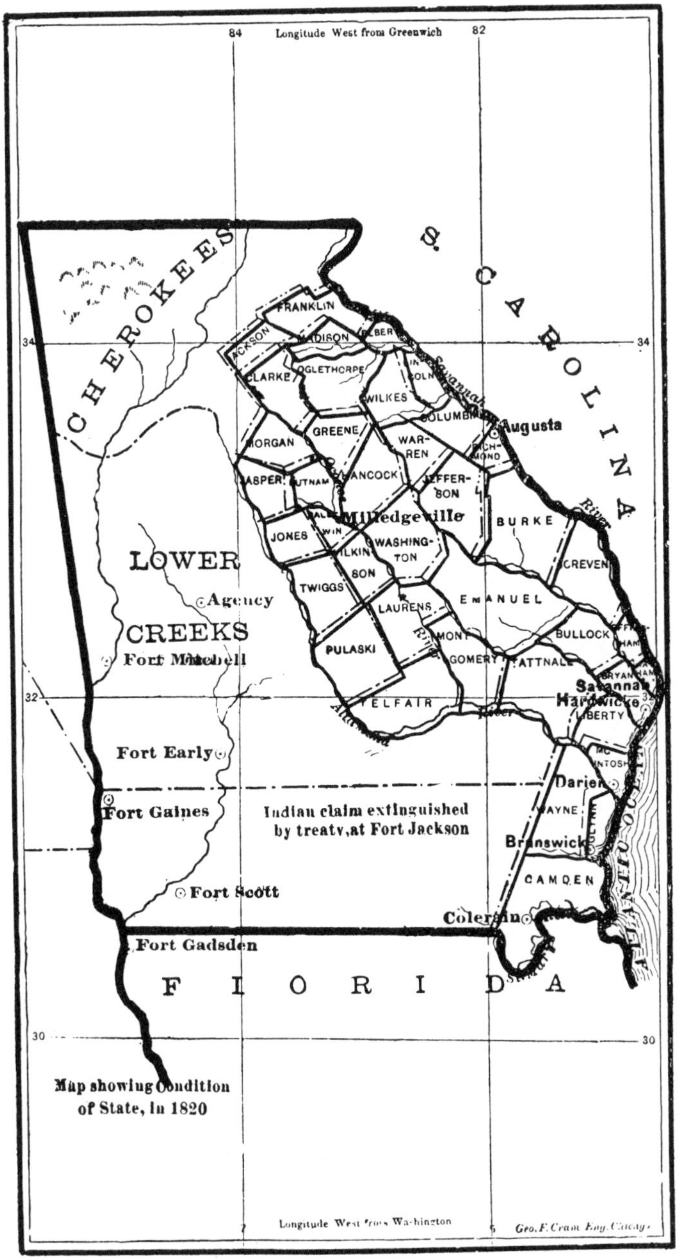

Longitude West from Greenwich
84
82
34
32
30
CHEROKEES
S. CAROLINA
FRANKLIN
JACKSON
MADISON
ELBERT
CLARKE
OGLETHORPE
LINCOLN
WILKES
Savannah
COLUMBIA
Augusta
MORGAN
GREENE
WAR-REN
RICH-MOND
JASPER
PUTNAM
HANCOCK
JEFFER-SON
Milledgeville
BURKE
River
JONES
BALD-WIN
WILKIN-SON
WASHING-TON
SCREVEN
LOWER
Agency
CREEKS
Fort Mitchell
TWIGGS
LAURENS
EMANUEL
BULLOCK
EFFING-HAM
PULASKI
MONT-GOMERY
TATTNALL
BRYAN
Savannah
Hardwicke
LIBERTY
TELFAIR
Altamaha
Fort Early
MC INTOSH
Darien
Fort Gaines
Indian claim extinguished by treaty, at Fort Jackson
WAYNE
GLYNN
Brunswick
ATLANTIC OCEAN
CAMDEN
Fort Scott
Colerain
Fort Gadsden
St. Mary's
FLORIDA
Map showing Condition of State, in 1820
Longitude West from Washington
7
5
Geo. F. Cram Eng. Chicago

he had a violent temper and was an unrelenting foe, his best friends are forced to admit.

There was a bitter feud between him and Wm. H. Crawford, and the Clarke and Crawford parties divided the State into hostile camps for years.

He had a fierce hatred for Judge Charles Tait, who was a warm friend to Crawford, and whom Clarke suspected of having made an effort to defame him. His animosity to him reached such a height one day, while heated with drink, and while Judge Tait, the judge of the circuit, was riding quietly along the streets of Milledgeville, he attacked him with a horsewhip. Judge Tait was not only a judicial officer but a lame man, and Colonel Clarke's attack was loudly condemned. He was fined two thousand dollars for the assault, but the fine was remitted, though the verdict stood.

He assailed Crawford so virulently that Crawford challenged him and went on the field. Crawford was shot through the wrist.

Clarke was said to drink to very great excess, and to be very violent when in his cups, and was in great disfavor with many, but he was the idol of the common people and was the favorite with many of the leading men of the State.

By this time political parties had divided mainly on social lines. The rich Virginians, the city people, and the low-country planters were antagonized by the plain and uneducated denizens of the small farms. Crawford was a classical scholar of excellent family, ot commanding presence, and had been successful, while Clarke was the leader of the *sansculotte*, as well as a large party of respectables.

He wrote a very bitter pamphlet against Crawford, Tait and Mitchell, in which he labored to show that there was a shameful conspiracy between Tait and Crawford to rob him of his character as an honest man. He accused Mitchell, who was a friend to Crawford, of uniting with him in smuggling a cargo of African slaves into the State. The impartial reader of this pamphlet, while he can but admire the vigorous English in which it is written and the evident sincerity with which Clarke makes his damaging charges, is obliged to decide that the angry man's charges were baseless suspicions; but there were a great many people in those bitter days who did believe that their political idol, the intrepid soldier, who had fought for them against Tories and Indians, who was an up-country yeoman and not a low-country aristocrat, who was a poor man and not a large slaveholder, and who had few advantages of education and was not, like his antagonists, a Latin scholar, which, to them, was the highest culture, was a victim of a malicious persecution.

He was a candidate for governor against Governor Troup and defeated him, and a second time he ran against him, with the same result. When Troup, who defeated Talbot by a very small vote, stood for reelection in 1825, Clarke was again a candidate. The two men were in many respects alike, and in many others very unlike. Both were fierce in temper, unrelenting and fearless; both fond of wine and always ready for a fray; but Troup was a man of gentle blood, an English aristocrat in every fiber of his being, although he was a decided Democrat politically. He had had all the advantages of a liberal education, had spent his life in the best social circles of the cities, and the culture and wealth of the coast and of the low-country was at his back, and the Crawford party, containing the wealthiest element of the up-country, supported him warmly. He had been elected to the Legislature from Chatham county before he was of age, and was sent to Congress as early as he could be admitted a member. Like his opponent he was a pronounced Republican and States' rights man, going beyond Mr. Calhoun or Mr. Jefferson in his States' rights views. General Clarke had opposed him before the Legislature, and, as we have seen, defeated him twice.

The proud and taciturn patrician would descend to none of the arts of a politician, and so he was no match for his wily antagonist, and Clarke triumphed; but in 1823 Troup ran against Talbot, a Clarke man, before the Legislature, and was elected by two votes.

The method of electing the governor by the Legislature was changed, and the election of 1825 was before the people. The Clarke men again called upon John Clarke to lead them to victory, and the fiercest strife Georgia had ever known was the result. The newspapers had become more numerous, and the style of writing was more vigorous than polite. The election was, however, won by Troup by a majority of about seven hundred. Governor Troup's second term was perhaps the most notable, and it was the most stormy of any that up to that time had been known in Georgia, and the story of Troup and the treaty is in place here:

The Yazoo fraud was indirectly the cause of the most threatening collision which had ever taken place between the general government and any one of the States, for the famous conflict of Governor Troup with the president, John Quincy Adams, which put Georgia in positive rebellion against the general government, resulted from it. That the sale of the Yazoo lands would be recognized as a fact accomplished by any impartial court was apparent, and the Georgians were very willing to shift the issue and let the United States government meet the question. The cession of the lands in dispute was made, therefore, in the first years of the nineteenth century to the general government, and it agreed, among other things, to extinguish the Indian title to all lands held by the Creeks and Cherokees in Georgia and put Georgia in peaceable possession of them. The Georgia settlements by 1802, when the agreement was entered into, extended to the banks of the Oconee on the west and to the Cherokee nation, which occupied still a considerable section on the north and northwest. As we have seen, this line was advanced to the Ocmulgee.

The opening of the new lands in middle Georgia, the invention of the cotton-gin, the decline of tobacco-planting and the large increase of negro slaves in the older States had led to a very large immigration of Virginians and North and South Carolinians into Georgia, and the new counties east of the Ocmulgee had become thickly peopled. There was a large area of most excellent cotton land between the Ocmulgee and the Chattahoochee which was still occupied by the Creeks as a hunting-ground, but was otherwise untenanted. The Georgians cast a longing eye on the beautiful domain, and persuaded themselves they had a good title to it and were kept out of it by the perfidious Creeks. The Creeks were now reduced to about twenty thousand. Of these fifteen thousand lived in Alabama and five thousand were scattered through Georgia. During the war of 1812 some of them had been friendly to the whites and some had been hostile. Among the friendly Indians was Colonel William McIntosh, a half-breed. He was the son of Captain McIntosh, who was an uncle of George M. Troup. Captain McIntosh was a British captain and had lived among the Creeks and had an Indian wife. Colonel William McIntosh, his son, was now a man of large property and of considerable intelligence, and was a chief among the Creeks. The hostile party had been perfectly subdued and had relinquished all the land they claimed in Alabama and Georgia except that which had been reserved to them by treaty. The United States government now proposed to them to buy all their possessions in Georgia and Alabama and give them acre for acre of better land across the Mississippi, in addition to a liberal payment for improvements. There were two parties in the tribe, one led by McIntosh, who thought it best to sell their lands and remove, and a much larger party who were opposed to any trade whatever.

The Georgians were growing very restless. They stood on the banks of the Ocmulgee, an impatient, anxious horde, and made a loud clamor for *their* land. The parties of Crawford and Clarke were bitterly antagonistic to each other, but on this question they were both agreed. Georgia ought and should have her land. Governor Troup had defeated John Clarke for governor and was in the executive mansion. John Crowell, a bitter antagonist of Governor Troup and a warm friend of John Clarke, was in the nation as Indian agent; Mr. Monroe was in Washington spending the last year of his presidency; Mr. Calhoun was his secretary of war. There was to be of necessity a change in the administration early in 1825, and Mr. Monroe and his secretary decided it was necessary that the Georgia matter should be settled before the new administration came in, and if possible the Indian title to all land east of the Chattahoochee should be extinguished. Before taking anything like coercive measures, Duncan G. Campbell and James Meriwether were appointed as commissioners to treat with the Creeks and get their consent to the sale.

Campbell was a Clarke man. He was a friend of Crowell, the Indian agent, and a man of unquestioned integrity and good sense. James Meriwether, his colleague, was a member of an old and distinguished Virginia family, famous for sterling virtues and clear heads. These two men were selected for the purpose of making a treaty and went at once to the nation to confer with John Crowell, the Indian agent. It was clear to them that Crowell could do much to defeat the treaty, even though he might not be able to secure its ratification. Crowell was a wily and determined man, and Campbell, who was his friend and his party associate, was anxious to secure his help. Crowell was a good hater and Governor Troup was the object of his deepest animosity. Campbell feared that this animosity might lead him to oppose the treaty which Governor Troup was so anxious to have made, and which would certainly bring to the governor such popular favor. So he used all his influence with Crowell to lead him to help forward his mission. The agent did not commit himself one way or the other, but in accordance with his instructions from Washington he ordered the Indians called together and made arrangements for their maintenance while they were in council. The Indians came at the call of the agent to Broken Arrow, in Alabama, and met the commissioners. It was soon evident that they were in no humor to make any treaty whatever. McIntosh was in favor of the nation selling its Georgia lands, but he was almost alone. The commissioners found themselves antagonized at every point. It was evident that some secret influence was at work to defeat them. Crowell said he was neutral, and that while he favored the removal of the Indians, he did not, as their agent, feel at liberty to use his influence to bring it about. Walker, however, the assistant agent, who had married an Indian woman, was bitterly and avowedly opposed to the sale, and used all his influence against it, even writing the replies which the chiefs made to the commissioners. With Crowell doing nothing to help them, and Walker openly and secretly opposing them, their only hope was in McIntosh. Since the death of McGilveray there was no man among the Creeks that could compare with McIntosh in ability. He had visited the new land and came to his tribe with a favorable report, but it was in vain. The Indians were fixed in their determination not to sell an acre of their land in Georgia or Alabama, and the commissioners, defeated at every point, left the nation and returned to Washington city.

The government was determined the treaty should be

Gov. G. M. Troup.

Geo. W. Crawford.

W. H. Crawford.

John Forsyth.

made and that nothing should be allowed to stand in the way, and so Walker was dismissed and Crowell was reprimanded, and a new council was called to meet in February at Indian Springs, on the Georgia lands, and Crowell was ordered to summon the chiefs and provide for them. They were summoned and provision was made and some of them were present. McIntosh was there favoring the treaty. Big Warrior and Little Prince were there to declare their opposition to it, and when they had protested they returned at once to the nation. McIntosh, however, and several other Indians, claiming to have authority, signed the treaty. There was no delay in conveying it to Washington. It was hurried to the Senate, and was there ratified. The day after it was ratified the protest against it came from the nation, but it was too late.

Up to this time the State of Georgia had had nothing to do with the matter. The United States government had been the sole actor; but now that the treaty was made Governor Troup decided as soon as possible to get possession of the ceded lands. It had been agreed in the treaty that the Indians in the ceded territory should not be molested for twelve months; but in a few weeks after the treaty was made Governor Troup made an agreement with McIntosh by which he secured permission to begin the survey at once. Governor Troup was a good hater, and regarded with a Scotchman's antipathy the new administration with John Quincy Adams at its head and Henry Clay as secretary of state, and he had no disposition to consult this new government about what he, the governor of a sovereign State, should do; and so he made arrangements at once to send his surveyors into the field to run off the lines and form the new counties.

McIntosh, who gave his ready assent to this course, was apprehensive of trouble and asked the protection of the governor. He was, however, a thoroughly fearless man, and took no steps for his own safety. The chiefs among the Creeks claimed that they had a well-known law that any chief selling lands without the consent of the council should forfeit his life. If McIntosh knew of this law or feared its execution, he took no precautions to protect himself; and, while he expressed his fear that he might be molested, he remained quietly and unprotected at his home on the Chattahoochee, in what is now known as McIntosh Bend, in Carroll county. Here he had a large plantation well stocked with cattle and a number of negroes. He had two plantations and three wives, and was the only chief of prominence this side of the Chattahoochee. The Indians in Alabama determined that he, whom they said had betrayed them, should die, and they made all their plans for his assassination. A body of picked men quietly glided up to his house at the bend in the night, and after a brave fight on his part he was shot down, and two other chiefs were killed at the same time, and his house burned and his cattle slaughtered. The executioners of the edict of the secret council then returned to Alabama without doing further harm to any one.

The killing of McIntosh and his sympathizing chiefs produced an intense excitement in Georgia, and wild rumors of an Indian war were afloat everywhere. Governor Troup was greatly outraged at the death of his relative, and laid the blame on the general government, and especially on Crowell, whom he accused to the president as being accessory to this foul murder, as he called it.

The United States government had been very tardy in indorsing the procedures of the commissioners, and especially Governor Troup's haste in beginning the survey, and now sent out T. P. Andrews, Esq., from Washington City, to look into matters. Andrews came at once to Milledgeville and had the case laid before him, and especial emphasis given to the charges against Crowell. To one who reads the voluminous correspondence between Major Andrews and Governor Troup it will plainly appear that if Andrews had not prejudged the matter before he came to Georgia, it did not take him long to come to the conclusion that the treaty was a fraud, that McIntosh was a traitor, and that Crowell was an innocent man.

The correspondence between Major Andrews and Governor Troup was very fiery. The surveyors were getting ready for the survey when General Edmund P. Gaines, then in command of the division, was ordered by the secretary of war to go to the nation and to keep the surveyors out of the ceded lands. While matters were in this condition Andrews, who had definite charges made to him concerning Crowell, suspended him for the time being. Governor Troup sent Henry G. Lamar into the nation to find out and report the temper of the Indians, and then sent three commissioners, Messrs. Jones, Jordan and Torrance, to examine witnesses and see if it was possible to convict Crowell of the crime charged against him. The bitter hostility of the commission was at once manifested. They bullied and badgered and abused and insulted the old missionary, Isaac Smith, and his Baptist associate, Mr. Comprere, and all other witnesses, and made every effort to force a conviction; but their failure was pitiful. While one may well believe Crowell, who was a bitter foe of McIntosh, shed no tears over his death, yet it was evident that he had had no part or lot in it.

General Gaines was now in charge, and it was soon manifest that there was to be war between him and Governor Troup. General Gaines and Major Andrews were disposed to open the question as to whether the treaty ought to have been made, and Governor Troup was determined that it should not be opened. He would go forward with the survey. The secretary of war took sides with General Gaines and Major Andrews. Then it was that Governor Troup said: "We have exhausted the argument.

We will stand by our arms," and ordered the militia to be in readiness to march into the nation. Congress was, however, in session, and the president referred the question to it for a settlement. The secretary of war, while he repudiated the treaty of February, immediately made another which gave the Georgians all they asked; and although the stern and intrepid governor refused to recognize this second treaty, the United States allowed the survey to go on; and so the great issue was settled. The Creeks went over the Mississippi; the McIntosh party got $100,000 damages; Crowell was acquitted, and Governor Troup was rewarded with a seat in the United States Senate. So ended without bloodshed the fiercest contest, up to that time, ever known between a State and the central government.

After Governor Troup was elected Senator John Forsyth was chosen as Governor. He was born in Virginia, but came to Georgia a child. His father, the United States Marshall, was killed in Augusta. Young Forsyth had a classical education, and was graduated at Princeton. He was a man of fine mind and high principles. He received many honors from Georgia, and served her faithfully.

In 1821 a treaty had been made by the United States commissioner with the Creeks, and that magnificent country between the Flint and the Ocmulgee had been ceded by them and distributed by lottery among the people. In 1825, as we have seen, the State secured possession of that section between the Flint and Chattahoochee, and in 1827 the Creeks ceded the last acre of land held by them and withdrew from the State.

The Creeks were the most powerful of all the Indian tribes in Georgia, but they had no very extensive settlement in the State. Their main towns were in Alabama, and, while they laid claim to all Georgia, comparatively few of them lived on this side of the Chattahoochee. By successive agreements they had surrendered first one part of the country and then another, until, after nearly a hundred years had passed since Oglethorpe made his first treaty with them, they were entirely removed from the present territory of the State.

Georgia now made great strides forward. Planting cotton was never so profitable, and the tide of immigration into the new lands was at its flood. The immigration from Virginia and North Carolina of people of means, such as those who settled in Jones, Jasper, Putnam and Baldwin, had now diminished very considerably, and the current from Virginia was flowing to the black lands of Alabama and Mississippi; but a great crowd of worthy people of small means was moving from central North Carolina and upper South Carolina into Walton, Gwinnett and Newton, while from the pine woods of eastern Georgia and the southern part of South Carolina the restless cattlemen were moving into Ware, Appling and Irwin.

The rich hummocks of Thomas and Lowndes and Decatur were attracting large slave-owners from Burke, Bulloch, Screven, Laurens and Montgomery, and the rich lands of Baker were settled by the large planters from Jones, Twiggs, Putnam, Burke and Liberty.

Cotton was now worth fifteen cents a pound, and was, to a large degree, a surplus crop, since the thrifty planter made all his provisions on his plantation. The opening of cotton lands in southwest Georgia, where large bodies could be easily bought, led to the making of many very large plantations, and what had been occasional in the older counties became the rule in this new section, and throughout Lee, Baker and Early the same system of planting obtained which was found on the large cotton plantations of the older counties. It grew up as the negro population increased, and had reached immense proportions at the beginning of the war. Many men who began life with a family of negroes of perhaps five or six found themselves at sixty years old possessed of a hundred slaves, and had never bought any, but many more bought negroes and land with every ending year, until their slave property was very great and their lands were baronial in extent.

They wore out the hills of eastern Georgia making cotton, and then came to southwestern Georgia and bought large bodies of land and opened plantations. They did not live on their places themselves in many cases, but employed an overseer and fixed their negro quarters on them. Their plantations were managed with a great deal of skill and with a complete organization. A large plantation was a little kingdom. The overseer was in charge, a black driver was under him, there were hoe-hands, plowmen, quarter-masters, cooks, gardeners, blacksmiths, carpenters, shoe-makers, a midwife, nurses, dairy maids, spinners, weavers, seamstresses, chicken- and turkey-raisers, and even a gang of little negroes, called the "drop-shot gang," who carried water and food to the hands in the field. The system of working was exact. There was a horn blown, or a bell rung, as early as it was possible to see, and by sunrise the hands were in the fields. The work was steady until noon, then the mules were fed and the hands ate their midday meal; work was then resumed and continued till dark. On Saturday the rations of three and a half pounds of bacon, one peck of meal and one quart of molasses were given to each adult. Twice a year each negro received a suit of cotton clothing and once a year one of woolen kersey, and in winter had a pair of strong, well-made shoes. At the quarter each negro family had a cabin, a garden or patch, some chickens, and often a pig.

Plantation discipline was very strict and punishment for any dereliction was very sure, and for grievous offenses sometimes severe, but rarely cruel. Young negroes were punished with a few strokes of a cowhide, and more serious offenses by bucking and strapping the offender.

The overseer's orders were imperative and absolute, and were never resisted. He knew his own interests too well to punish injuriously a slave or to overwork him or neglect him. He was always a man of good sense and of energy, and was often a good practical physician, who made his own prescriptions for ordinary ailments. He received a good salary and always made money.

There was never a time when fortunes were so rapidly made as by the Georgia planters from 1820 to 1835, and there never were a people more eager in their pursuit of wealth. The old restriction on the domestic slave-trade was removed, and the negro speculator, as he was called, brought great troops of negroes from Virginia and Maryland and sold them to the Georgia planters. The lands of the older parts of middle Georgia were not worn out, and the lands in the west of Georgia were now new and unopened. Cotton was bringing a high price and had ready sale. Negroes rose in value every year, and the rich planter bought a number every winter and opened new grounds.

No business was in greater disrepute than negro speculating, but it was profitable. The eastern Virginian found himself with worn-out lands and many slaves on his own estate, and was compelled to sell some of his slaves or move from his ancestral halls. The Richmond slave-dealer bought his negroes and sent them to Georgia, and bought also those who were sold by guardians and administrators, and many of them came to Georgia.

The planter spent his own money and borrowed from the bank that he might buy more land and more negroes. There was nothing thought of but making cotton. The planter bought more land to make more cotton to buy more negroes to make more cotton. There was no attention paid in many cases to any improvements in the condition of things around his home. A man with an income of $5,000 per year from his cotton crop, and that clear profit, often lived in a log cabin and fed his family on fat bacon and corn bread. The rich lands of the western counties enticed the well-settled planters in the east to sell out their homes and begin life again in a log cabin. All was bustle and hurry. Forests were felled, fields were opened, cotton-gins and screws were erected, and now, for the first time, mules were largely bought.

The system of making cotton and buying supplies was not yet in vogue. The planter made what his plantation required—in many cases economizing in what his family needed that he might buy a new lot of negroes and a nearby plantation. The pine lands were still neglected; but there were extensive ranches in Thomas and Lowndes, and rich planters had thousands of cattle on their stock-farms in these barrens. Money was easy, and the planters could get almost unlimited accommodations at the various banks. Macon had sprung up like magic, and cotton from all these new counties and some of the old was being emptied into the warehouses on Walnut street and Bridge row. A line of steamboats had been put on the river, and barges loaded with cotton were towed down the Ocmulgee to Darien. Hawkinsville, which had absorbed old Hartford, was the center of trade from the counties south of it, and Houston and Dooly, and the cotton-producing counties on the west shipped their cotton to Columbus. Augusta and Charleston were the markets of the up-country merchant, who bought his groceries in Augusta and his dry-goods in Charleston, and sent his cotton in wagons to Augusta and Savannah.

The planters who did their work on a large scale were not more eager after money than the prosperous cotton factor, the merchant, or the small farmer who cherished now the hope of becoming a large planter himself in time.

During the early part of the period of which we write religion was sadly neglected, and little attention was paid to education; but there was not an entire cessation of interest in the matter of academies. The education of girls began now to attract a considerable amount of attention, and, although the Legislature had refused to charter any female academy and give it a part of the appropriation (as we have seen in the account of Jackson county), in 1827 a charter was granted for a female academy, and it received a small appropriation. There were few exclusively female schools, but all the schools aided by the State up to this time were mixed.

The matter of transportation was now, in some sections, more satisfactory, as steamboats had been put on most of the rivers.

In the cities the banking facilities were much increased, and there were now the Planters Bank, with a circulation of $214,922; the Mechanics Bank, with a circulation of $456,621; Marine and Fire Insurance, with a circulation of $155,000; Bank State of Georgia, capital $1,500,000; Bank of Darien, with a circulation of $329,000; Bank of Augusta, with a circulation of $437,764; Central Bank of Georgia, with a circulation of $223,125—this bank had a capital of $2,485,753.51. Just as this period drew near its close the Bank of Macon and the Bank of Columbus were established. These banks claimed a specie basis for their circulation, and at this time were all specie-paying banks. The State had large interests in several of them, as it had in some of the transportation companies.

At this period the number of chartered academies in the State was very large. There were but few county towns in which there was not one; and in the thickly settled counties there were a number in various parts of each. There was a small fund given by the State for the education of poor children, but it was very meager, and in the poorer sections the people had very few educational advantages. The subscription school (as the private school was called) was still the only reliance of many of the people, and it was a poor and uncertain one. The University had Dr. Waddell now at its head, and was becoming prosperous. The thriving city of Milledgeville was the first city in Georgia to attempt a school on the modern plan, and endeavored to establish a common school system; but evidently the effort was not successful. The lottery was still popular. The Salem Academy in Clarke (in after time under the care of the Methodists) was now to have the benefit of a lottery; Augusta, Macon, Milledgeville and Monroe were to build Masonic halls with a lottery to help them. The male and female academies in Greensboro, the Eatonton academy, the poor in Burke county, the Wrightsboro academy, the DeKalb county academy, the Washington county academy, the Madison academy, the Clinton academy, the Fayette county academy, the Madison county academy, all were to be helped by lotteries.

Up to this time there had been nothing on the statute books prohibiting the learning of a negro to read or write. But the abolition question was beginning; there was an insurrection of negro slaves in Virginia; so the Legislature passed an act prohibiting all persons from teaching negroes to read or write.

The newspapers established during this period were *The Constitutionalist* (Augusta), *The Macon Telegraph* (Macon), *The Enquirer* (Columbus), *The Athenian* (Athens), *The Statesman and Patriot*, *The Courier* (Savannah), *The Advertiser* (Mt. Zion, Hancock county), *The Republican* (Jackson), *The Cabinet* (Warrenton), *The Phœnix* (Darien). There was no daily, but the *Constitutionalist* and *Courier* were published semi-weekly.

During this period Georgia was visited by the greatest religious awakening in her history. The Georgians were, as far as their every-day conduct was concerned, far from being exemplary, but the common people were very sound in their faith. There were a few skeptics among some of the leading public men of the older cities, but the plain people believed in the Bible and reverenced religion. The camp-meeting had now become a fixture in nearly all the counties. There was no county in which there was not a camp-ground, and in many there were several.

The settler had not built his cabin in the new purchase before the circuit-rider was at his door. Soon a suitable place near a spring was chosen for an encampment, a bush harbor was made, logs were provided as seats, and a camp-meeting was announced. In the older counties where camp-meetings had been held for twenty years comfortable little tents made of rough plank or logs had been built and a large board-covered tabernacle provided. Crowds came from a score of miles, preachers by the dozen assembled, and the most gifted men of the churches preached their most earnest sermons. There were often, during this period, one hundred tents on the ground, and sometimes five thousand people were in the congregation.

The religious awakening extended to all sections and embraced all classes of people, and largely changed the face of Georgia. The rough brutality of the ring, the horse-race and the shooting-match ceased in middle Georgia; children grew up to manhood who had never seen a playing card, and even dancing was given up in the country neighborhoods. Churches sprang up everywhere, and in villages and in county towns where there had been none houses of worship were built.

Judges like Colquitt opened their courts with prayer and preached to the people during the recesses of the court. Many deplorable things were left, but in the Georgia of 1830 there was a vast change for the better.

It was during this great revival that the distinguished Judge Longstreet became a Methodist, and afterward a Methodist preacher. He never lost his individuality, and was the same humor-loving man after his conversion as he had been before. It was while he was a leading layman in his church that he wrote "Georgia Scenes." It has been absurdly said that he was greatly ashamed of this book and endeavored to suppress it. On the contrary, he recognized it—as it was—as the truest picture of certain phases of Georgia life which had ever been painted.

Walter T. Colquitt, the great Democratic lawyer, was another who became a Methodist.

Dr. John E. Dawson, a cultivated and wealthy physician, was converted and gave up his practice and became one of the most distinguished Baptist preachers in the South.

George F. Pierce, then a boy at college in Athens, who afterward was the bishop of the Methodists, and Dr. John Jones, long one of the most noted of Presbyterians, were converted during this great awakening.

Among the Baptist workers were Dr. Adiel Sherwood, young Dr. Dawson, Jonathan Davis and Dr. Charles D. Mallary, one of the most cultured of their preachers, who had been brought up and educated in Vermont, and was the associate of Stephen Olin in college and his lifelong friend.

Stephen Olin, who was also a Vermonter, a man of magnificent intellect and fine culture; John Howard, famous for his eloquence and his fervor; Lovick Pierce, then in his vigorous young manhood, and James O. Andrew, afterward bishop, were among the Methodists; while Jos. C. Stiles and Dr. Hoyt, who had just come to Georgia, were among the Presbyterians.

As we have seen, there was quite a large and fertile section of land opened to settlement, and the rush of immigrants was immediate and continuous. There were some of the older counties now divided and all the new purchase was mapped out into counties. The land was granted by lottery. Many who drew the lots removed at once to them and settled. Some sold their grants to others, who moved, and in many cases the land speculator bought the plot and grant for investment. There was quite a diversity in the quality of the land opened to settlement. Some of it was what was known as land of the first quality. Much in the counties of Coweta, Troup, Meriwether, Harris and Talbot was not surpassed by any in the State. It was healthy, fertile and accessible, and brought good prices for those times.

The lands in the low-country pine woods varied much in fertility and were very cheap, while the lands of Carroll and Campbell were sold at very low prices, and, at that time, were regarded as only desirable by those who wanted cheap homes and an extensive range.

There was no part of Georgia as yet exhausted, and the tide of prosperity which had set in just after the war with England had not ebbed. The counties formed during this period divide themselves into groups closely resembling those mentioned in previous chapters. Henry, Fayette, Dekalb, Newton, Pike and Butts made one group. The land, as a whole, was not fertile, but, in the main, arable. The price at which the land was sold was generally not more than one dollar per acre, often much less.

Cotton was not the chief product, and few men had many slaves. The account given of each county will show such a similarity of nature and conditions as will render the story of one county the story of all, except in certain individual features. Troup, Meriwether, Harris, Coweta, Talbot, Monroe, Houston, Bibb and Upson were great cotton-raising counties in which there was little diversity of feature. The people who occupied the lands were largely cotton-planters, and the land was famous for its fertility. In Marion, Decatur, Baker, Randolph and Thomas there was a country of mixed features, in which there were large cotton plantations and many slaves, or wide unsettled ranches in the pine woods; while Lowndes, Ware, Crawford, Dooly and Muscogee were almost exclusively piny woods counties, in which there was little raised for market besides cattle. The people who occupied these counties varied in accordance with the nature of the soil and the character of its products, running all the way from the most ignorant rustic who lived in a one-roomed cabin to the wealthy planter with five hundred slaves and an elegant mansion.

Manufacturing had been almost entirely abandoned, and the people were intense anti-tariff men, and for years after this the word "tariff" was sufficient to rouse any average rustic to wrath. Judge Longstreet used to tell of a traveler from the up-country who came suddenly upon a railway, the first he had ever seen. Directly, to his alarm and that of his boy, the train came rushing by. "Dad," said the thoroughly frightened boy, "what is that ar thing?" "I dunno, son," said the father; "but I 'spect it ar the tariff." And this was over ten years after this time. The passage of the tariff act of 1828 aroused great alarm and resentment, and Georgia was in a fever of political excitement when Governor Gilmer, in 1829, took the gubernatorial chair.

We turn now to the study of the counties:

HENRY.

Henry county, which was laid off in 1821, was rapidly populated. It was named in honor of Patrick Henry and its county town after the gallant McDonough. In 1830, not ten years after it was made a county, there were over 10,000 inhabitants in its borders. It was a healthy county; land was cheap, and settlers from South Carolina and the older counties in Georgia crowded into it. They were very plain, good people—industrious, economical and religious. Much of the land was hilly, and much of it very thin; but it produced those things that were needed for the support of its inhabitants, and there was no want among them.

The first superior court, according to White, was held in

1822, at the house of Wm. Ruff, and the names of the first grand jurors were: Wm. Jackson, Wm. Malone, James Sellers, James Pate, Thomas Abercrombie, C. Cochran, G. Gay, Wm. Wood, Willie Terrell, Jether Barnes, Robert Shaw, Jas. Colwell, John Brooks, F. Pearson, Wm. McKnight, Jacob Hinton, Jackson Smith, S. Strickland.

The first settlers, according to the same authority, were: Wm. Hardin, Jesse Johnson, James Sellers, H. J. Williams, Wm. Pate, D. Johnson, W. H. Turner, M. Brooks, S. Weems, W. Herbert, Roland Brown, R. M. Sims, Wm. Crawford, E. Mosely, John Brooks, Reuben Deming, Jacob Hinton, E. Brooks, John Calloway, R. Jenks, Colonel S. Strickland, Parker Eason, Jos. Kirk, Wm. Griffin, John Griffin, Daniel Smith, Wm. Tuggle, John Lovejoy.

Henry was drawn upon very largely by Griffin on one side and Atlanta on the other; but its population, which was over 10,000 in 1830, was 14,726 in 1850. Of these there were nearly 5,000 slaves.

When the Southern railway from Macon to Atlanta and the Midland from McDonough to Columbus were opened, the country was furnished with the best railroad facilities, flourishing villages sprang up along the line, and McDonough, which had declined until it was a very small hamlet, began to take on the proportions of a considerable and prosperous county town.

The people of Henry have always been noted for their moral and religious excellence. The Baptists and Methodists have been the main bodies of Christians. The Methodists for many years had a very prosperous camp-ground in the county, and at one time more than one.

Hampton is a small but sprightly village on the line of the M. & W. R. R., and Locust Grove and Stockbridge flourishing towns on the Southern.

NEWTON.

Newton county was formed from Henry, Walton and Jasper. The land was cheap and healthy, and, like Henry, it was soon settled by a very good class of plain people, most of whom came from the older counties. It was organized in 1821, and named in honor of the companion of Jasper, who assisted him in capturing the British guard near Savannah. The county site was called Covington after a brave officer in the war of 1812.

The people who settled Newton were in the main a very plain, uncultivated but worthy people. There were some persons of large wealth who took up the best lands in the lower part of the county, and near Brick Store there was a very famous settlement of elegant people. They were wealthy, highly educated and refined. They had a handsome church and an excellent school. In the neighborhood of Sandtown, Newborn and Starrsville there were other excellent settlements with good schools; but in the larger part of the county churches were small and schools were few and poor.

Newton was selected as a seat for the manual labor school and of Emory College, and there were some improvements in the section near the college and in the county around Covington; but the religious and educational advantages of the county on the whole were for many years very limited.

A number of very distinguished men have sprung from this county, to some of whom we have alluded.

Covington, the county site, was laid out in 1821, and was for many years a country town of respectable proportions, with good churches and good schools, and was at one time the seat of the Georgia Masonic Female College, which was quite a prosperous institution. The town has greatly improved in late years, and has an excellent graded school, two railways and a street railway. It is a prohibition town and has an excellent population.

Oxford, the seat of Emory College, is a beautiful village among the oaks, and is noted for the piety and intelligence of its people.

The county of Newton was one of the first to enterprise cotton mills, and at Newton Factory and at Cedar Shoals there were mills fifty years ago, and at the present time there is quite a large and prosperous factory at Porter Dale, formerly Cedar Shoals.

The county is rich in its quarries of most excellent granite.

The G. R. R. and the Middle Georgia and Atlantic road are in Newton, and the people of the county have the best railroad facilities.

The Methodists, Baptists and Presbyterians have each a good following in the county. Newton is a prohibition county and is noted for the moral worth of its people.

The county was opened for settlement in 1821, and in 1830 there were 11,815 inhabitants; of these 3,003 were slaves. In 1850 there were only 8,109 whites and 5,187 slaves.

The first court held in the county was in 1822, and the first grand jurors were: Solomon Graves, C. A. Carter, James Johnson, L. Dunn, R. J. Lane, Wm. Jackson, W. Whateley, H. Jones, Thos. Jones, Jno. Stocks, S. D. Echols, W. Fannin, F. H. Trammell, J. Bloodworth, Henry Lane, David Hodge, Robert Leake, John Stephens, G. B. Turner, Geo. Cunningham, Jno. F. Piper, James Hodge.

Newton, as we have seen, was selected as the seat of the manual labor school established by the Methodists, of which I speak more fully in another chapter. When it was decided to establish a college a large body of land was purchased by the trustees and Oxford, a college village, was laid out. It naturally drew to Georgia a fine body of people, among them Dr. Few, of whom I have already spoken, Judge Longstreet and Dr. Means, all of whom had connection with the college. The mother of Justice L. Q. C. Lamar resided here; Judge Longstreet, wise and witty, Bishop Geo. F. Pierce and Bishop James O. Andrew had their homes here.

While Bishop Andrew was living in this village he lost his first wife and married Mrs. Greenwood, who was a slaveholder. By circumstances beyond his control he had already become a slaveholder before his marriage with her. The laws of the M. E. Church forbade slaveholding on the part of its ministry if it could be avoided, and there had been no slave-owning bishop before this time. When by this marriage he became the husband of one who had a number of slaves there was much feeling aroused in the North, and he was arraigned, not for any wrong-doing, but for being connected with slavery. He wished to resign, but the Southern members would not permit him to do so, and eventually he was virtually deposed, and as a result of this the M. E. Church was divided and the Methodist Episcopal Church, South, was organized.

FAYETTE.

Fayette, named after General Lafayette, was, at its laying off, a large county. It was in many respects the counterpart of Henry. It was settled rapidly, but not so rapidly as Henry or Monroe. It had, however, 5,000 people in it by 1830, and near 9,000 in 1850, nearly 2,000 of whom were slaves.

The people who settled in the county were generally plain, poor people, who were industrious and economical and made a good livelihood, and, while many of them were primitive in their manners and illiterate, they were a worthy class of people, who led simple and unpretending lives.

Fayetteville, the county site, was long a small village

Court House, Decatur.

without railroad connections, but when the Atlanta and Florida road was constructed it was connected with Atlanta by rail, and is now (1898) a prosperous county town.

White gives as the first grand jury: James Strawn, Wm. Morgan, Matthew Burge, Wm. Watts, Jos. Shaw, John Levi, Chas. Lisles, Jno. Hamilton, James Head, A. Tilghnam, Wm. Gilliland, William Powell, Larkin Lardner, Stephen Smith, Wm. Harkess, James Garrett, M. Glass, R. Barrow.

Much of Fayette county is very poor, but there are some excellent farms on the Flint river and on the creeks, and while the people are not wealthy they live in comfort.

The Baptists are perhaps the largest denomination of Christians, but the Methodists come close to them.

DEKALB.

There is such a general resemblance between the up-country counties which adjoin each other that it is difficult to describe one without describing the other. Dekalb, which was laid out in 1822 from Henry and Fayette, presents almost the same features as we have found in those counties. It was laid out in 1822, and had over ten thousand people in it in 1830.

Lands were cheap, and the homeless people in Georgia and other States were many and they crowded into these hills. As a general thing the lands were very poor and cheap, but along the creeks and brooks there were some fertile tracts, and along the South river some first quality lands.

The village of Decatur was an important little town, inhabited by substantial people almost from its first settlement.

Fulton county was made from Dekalb, and the size of the county was lessened and the population much reduced. The first settlers in Dekalb, some of whom lived in what is now Fulton, were, according to White: Wm. Jackson, James Montgomery, Jno. R. Brock, Wm. Ezzard, Wm. Hill, Stephen Mays, Reuben Cone, J. M. Smith, Wm. David, Mason Shewmake, John Simpson, Amos Towers, Jno. W. Fowler, Edward Jones, Andrew Johnson, Jno. Turner, I. P. Carr, James W. Reeves, William Murphy, George Clifton, James Jones, Jesse Lane, Lachlan Johnson, William Terrell and George Brooks.

Stone mountain, one of the wonders of Georgia, an immense pile of solid granite, is in this county. It is three

STONE MOUNTAIN.

thousand feet high and six or seven miles in circumference, and from its summit can be secured the most entrancing view of all the country round for sixty miles. The mountain is of granite, a peculiarly valuable kind suited for paving and building, and has greatly enriched those who own it.

The growth of Atlanta and its proximity to Dekalb county have caused a number of villages to spring up in this county. Kirkwood, Clarkston, Stone Mountain, Lithonia and Ingleside are all flourishing villages, while Decatur has reached the proportions of quite a city.

Dekalb has been the home of many excellent people,

who have done the State good service. The Rev. John S. Wilson came to it a young man, and never left it, except to remove a few miles to Atlanta, till his death in old age. He was a teacher and a minister of the Presbyterian church. He was a man of great worth and of great influence.

Charles Murphy, long a member of Congress and a lawyer of great ability and integrity, lived in Decatur for many years, and died there.

James M. Calhoun, a sterling Whig, a worthy and gifted lawyer, lived here for many years.

William Ezzard, once judge of the circuit court, a pure and upright man, and Dr. Calhoun, a physician of the old school, were among the prominent citizens of the little village in its early life. Gov. A. H. Colquitt, famous as a soldier, statesman and a Christian, lived and died in this county.

Among its present citizens are Colonel Scott, who has, at his own expense, built the Agnes Scott Female Institute, a Presbyterian school; Colonel M. A. Candler, who has represented his district in Congress; General J. B. Gordon, famous as a soldier and a statesman and senator.

The Orphans Home of the North Georgia Conference is located near Decatur. There are over one hundred children who are being cared for by the North Georgia Conference. It is now under the care of the Rev. Howard L. Crumley, as agent, who has done much for it. It was the first orphanage of the Methodists, and its founder was the great Dr. Jesse Boring, who, in his old age, aroused the church to a sense of her duty to her orphans, and caused, by his earnest pleadings, at least ten homes to be erected in the various conferences.

PIKE.

By the same act which made Henry and Fayette separate counties the county of Pike, north of Monroe and south of Fayette, was provided for. No two counties could have resembled each other in every feature more than Pike and Fayette. In Pike there was a large area of pine woods, some fine land on the river and on the creeks, and in the west of the county some excellent bodies of red land, but the larger part of the county was gray land of moderate fertility.

It was rapidly peopled and was settled, in the main, by people of moderate means, of whom, in 1830, there were six thousand, and, unlike the richer counties, it continued to grow and more than doubled its population in twenty years. In 1850 there were only four thousand negroes in the county, and they were equally distributed throughout the county, which then included Spalding. In 1890, after Spalding had long been given off, there were over sixteen thousand inhabitants still in the county.

The early settlers, according to White, were: John Marshall, Isaac Cooper, B. Jordin, J. Gilder, S. Stephens, T. Mathews, E. Phillips, B. Grace, J. Weaver, W. Mobley, E. Mabry, W. Amos, E. Walker, W. Taylor, J. Farley, I. Gilbert, J. Johnson, R. Myrick, J. Moore, General Daniel, Jas. Neal, Jno. Neal, J. B. Read, James Williamson, H. G. Johnson, W. E. Mangum, Gideon Barnes, W. J. Milner, William Ellis and B. Orr.

Perhaps no county in Georgia ever had a better class of settlers than those who came into Pike. But few of them were people of large means, but they were industrious, pious and thrifty. The country was healthy and the land was productive, and there was a general prosperity from the first settlement.

Its first county site was called Newnan; but in 1825 Zebulon was laid out and made the county site. It was at one time a town of some importance. After the railroad skirted the county and Griffin was built up, the little village declined and never recovered its position. A railroad now

passes through it from Atlanta to Fort Valley, and it is improving.

Barnesville is quite an enterprising and energetic little city on one side of Pike. It has long been famous for its excellent schools, and Gordon Institute is one of the largest and most successful of high schools. The school is coeducational; it has an elegant equipment and a very large patronage. There are excellent churches in the city for white and colored people, and a very admirable population. In addition to its school advantages, it has become a manufacturing town of some importance. Its famous carriage factories, its knitting-mills and its cotton-mills give employment to many hands.

Milner is a respectable village not far from Barnesville, on the Central railroad.

The Midland road, which passes through the western side of Pike, has developed a new section of the county, and there are some thriving villages on it.

Pike has been the home of a sterling class of business men, but has not been famous for its men of political eminence. It was the residence of an Irish merchant, Samuel Mitchell, who bought the lot upon which Atlanta stands and laid out the city.

BUTTS.

Butts, which was named from a brave captain of that name who lost his life in a fight with the Indians in Alabama, and whose county site was named in honor of Andrew Jackson, was laid off from Newton and Henry in 1826, and four years afterward had in its boundary 4,000 people. It has thè Ocmulgee on its eastern border, and has some good, strong red land on the river; but the larger part of the county is of light, gray soil. It was never, except near the river, a very fertile country; but the land was easily tilled and cheap, and the county was peopled by a class of industrious, plain people who worked their own farms and led independent lives.

For many years Butts was some distance from the railway and was very far behind some of the contiguous counties in its advancement; but the building of the Southern railway gave new life to the county. Jackson, from being an insignificant hamlet, has become a sprightly county town; and Flovilla, near Indian Springs, a place of considerable trade.

The churches for a long time were very few and very much neglected, until the railroad came; but since that event and the establishing of the public school system the change for the better has been very decided.

In 1830 there were nearly 5,000 people in Butts; in 1850 there were 6,000, and in 1890 there were 10,500.

Indian Springs, the most noted watering-place in Georgia, is located in Butts. A small stream of pure, strong sulphur water trickles from a rock, and is said by many who have tested it to be invaluable as a remedy for divers diseases, and has been so regarded for over seventy years. It was at this place that the treaty of 1818 was made, and the famous treaty between McIntosh and his followers and Messrs. Campbell and Meriwether was made in 1825.

Butts, in its most fertile part near the river, has had the same history as Jasper and Monroe. It was very productive and became the property of large planters, and is now largely in the hands of negro tenants; but the poorer lands are still held by white owners who live on them, as the white population has never diminished but steadily increased.

There has been no county in which there has been a more gratifying improvement in the building of churches and the founding of schools. In Jackson, Indian Springs, Flovilla and in the rural parts of the county there have been established good schools, and handsome and convenient churches have been erected.

The county was first a part of Monroe and was settled as early as any part of its mother county. The first inhabitants must, therefore, be found among those who came to Monroe.

The Hon. David J. Bailey, long a member of Congress and a man of influence, for many years had his home in Jackson, but the county has been so small and remote that it has had few noted men.

CAMPBELL.

Campbell county was named in honor of Duncan G. Campbell, and was laid out in 1827. It was not thickly settled for some time, and in 1830 had in it only 3,000 people. In 1850 its population had but little more than doubled, and of these 1,500 were slaves. The value of the lands was not great. The hills were many and were sterile; but on the creeks and the river the land was fertile. While the land was poor, it was moderately productive, and the people were plain and industrious, and so made a good living.

There was some excellent land near Palmetto, and a very prosperous village was built up there; and at Fairburn, nearer Atlanta, there is another sprightly village.

The water-power on the Sweetwater was very fine, and one of the most successful factories in Georgia was built on that stream.

The early settlers, as given by White, were the McClartys, Stewarts, Lathams, Beaverses, Longinos, Davenports, Wattses, Cochrans, Whites, Kolbs, Pauletts, Skeenes, Penningtons, Bullards, Bryans, Hightowers, Hopkinses, Smiths, Jenningses, Silveys and Thorntons.

The first grand jury, which met at Campbellton in 1829,

was composed of Fulton Sheats, Jere Sampler, I. D. Crumpton, D. Hall, S. Baggett, H. Bird, J. Turner, Q. Dawson, S. Green, C. Field, George Haines, M. Anthony, T. Hill, I. Crow, D. D. Smith, I. West, E. Dorsett, I. Wise, I. Gresham, I. Hayne, I. Dorsett, I. Gray, Moses Benson.

The fact that the larger part of the county was some distance from the railroad and there was no considerable town in it has had the effect of drawing to Atlanta quite a number of the leading families of Campbell. There has been too little attention paid to education; but there has been for years a high school at Fairburn and one at Palmetto, and the usual common schools are found in the rural parts of the county. The people are generally religious and moral, and generally belong to the Baptist and Methodist Churches.

CARROLL.

On the west of Campbell is the county of Carroll, named for Chas. Carroll of Carrollton. It was laid out in 1826.

It is in the main a county of second-class land, but there is some excellent land in it, and early in its history there was discovered a rich deposit of gold in a part of the county, and a village sprang up which was known as Villa Rica. A large number of those who came to dig gold remained in the county as permanent citizens and opened farms.

There was but little inducement for men with many slaves to turn from the rich cotton lands south of Carroll to settle in it, and so as late as 1850, when the county was very large, there were only one thousand one hundred slaves in its borders. The larger part of the people owned their own homes, but owned no slaves. The population grew rapidly from natural increase as well as from immigration, and in 1890 there were twenty-two thousand inhabitants.

The opening of the railroad from Griffin to Carrollton was followed by the building of the railway from Carrollton to Chattanooga, and then by the Georgia Pacific, which runs through the county. These have given it the best railway advantages, and perhaps no county in the State has advanced more rapidly in every respect than Carroll since the war. Carrollton, from being a small village, has become a town of considerable importance.

Religion and education have advanced with the progress of the county, and now there are good schools and good churches in every part of it.

Whitesburg is a village in the east of the county, near to the Hutchinson cotton-mills, where there is a high school largely attended. The school is under the control of the Methodists, and has a small endowment left by Arthur Hutchinson, an Irish manufacturer. There are excellent schools in Villa Rica, Carrollton and Bowden, and along the lines of railway in a number of villages there are good schools.

Carroll is on the border of the State, and at its first settlement was very remote from market; land was very cheap and the population very small.

In 1830, when the county was much larger than it is now, the population was only three thousand four hundred and sixteen, of which only four hundred and eighty-seven were slaves.

It was the center of a mining excitement, and many wild and lawless men came into it. There was an organized body of horse thieves known as the Pony Club, at one time in the county, who carried on their nefarious work with impunity, and murders were fearfully common near the mines, while gambling and drunkenness sought no concealment; but with the establishment of the courts and the faithful work of the churches the lawlessness of the people has long since disappeared, and no county has a higher standard of morality and religion than this county at the present time.

HOUSTON.

In 1821 a county was formed adjoining Pulaski, Bibb and Crawford, which was called Houston, in honor of the distinguished governor of that name. The county site was called Perry, after Commodore Perry.

There was a large part of the county in the pine woods, and much of it in the rotten limestone region known as the black lands. The lower part of the county was remarkably fertile, and while to white people it was very unhealthy, it was not specially so to negroes, and it drew to it at its first settlement many of the wealthy planters from the older counties, who opened large plantations and who were very prosperous. They often had their homes in Bibb and Monroe, or in the pine belt of the county. Much of this pine belt was productive and the valley of the Flint river adjoined it, and it soon had a settlement of excellent people, who formed a village called Fort Valley, probably because of its having been the site of one of the early Indian forts. The land about the village lay well and was quite productive, and when the railroad reached it the section was thickly settled.

It was discovered that the country around the village was admirably adapted to fruit culture, and many acres have been put in fruit trees, and fruit is raised in great quantity for distant markets. The desirableness of the land to the orchardist has led many settlers from the west and north to buy fruit farms, and the need of crates and baskets for shipping fruit has led to the founding of factories to provide them, and the little city has become the center of a number of small factories and has a good trade in a variety of lines.

Flint river is within a few miles of the city, and there are large plantations and stock-farms on it, and in proximity to it large cotton plantations.

The building of the South Georgia and Florida railroad, which passes directly through the county, has developed some flourishing villages, in which there is considerable trade.

The population in 1830 was 5,175 free and 2,194 slaves; in 1850 there were 6,526 free and 9,924 slaves. The free population in 1830 was almost as great as it was twenty years after.

The people of Houston have always put a high estimate on education. There were chartered academies at Perry, Fort Valley, Henderson and Hayneville at an early day, and many of the sons and daughters of the planters were sent abroad for an education.

Mr. Everett, of Fort Valley, a very wealthy Methodist, came to the rescue of the Wesleyan Female College when it was in distress, and by a generous contribution, or rather by the purchase of scholarships, succeeded in saving it from sale and, possibly, failure. Since the war the villages along the line of railway have become centers for good schools, while in Fort Valley there is a graded school of excellent character.

The Methodists and Baptists are the principal denominations of Christians, and they came to Houston with its first settlement, and during the pastorate of Rev. Samuel Anthony, on the Perry circuit in its early days, there were sixteen hundred additions to the Methodist church alone in one year in this and the adjoining counties of Dooly and Pulaski.

The county had become by 1850 one of the largest cotton-growing counties in the State, and there were very large plantations and a great many slaves. The rich bottoms on the Flint and the black lands below Perry were occupied by large planters who had a large number of negroes, but after the war the negroes deserted these black lands and they became unprofitable to the planter and declined in value, until plantations which were worth before the war ten thousand dollars were not salable at one-tenth the price.

It is hardly possible to give a list of early settlers in any of the counties of this period, since they were settled by such a number at near the same time, but Mr. White gives as among the first settlers: Abner Wimberly, James Clark, David Clark, Allen Sutton, Allen Williams, M. Joiner, Thomas Gilbert, Mr. Kelly, Colonel Howell Cobb, Lewis Hunt, Daniel Dupree, Jacob Little, James Everett, Rev. D. McKenzie, Thos. Scott, D. W. Mann, H. W. Kaley, J. Pollock, A. Wingate and F. Pattillo.

These were among the first, and there was at an early day a large immigration from South Carolina of wealthy slave-owners, who settled in the black lands of the county and who made very great fortunes.

After the war, as we have seen, the rich country of the prairies and rotten limestone region was, to a large extent, deserted, and the pine woods sections greatly improved, but in late years there has been some improvement in the black land country.

There was a cotton-mill of small size established in Houston at an early day which has now been abandoned, and there are now no cotton-mills in the county.

There are few counties with better railroad facilities and in which there has been greater development than in Houston during the last few years.

DOOLY.

Dooly was in the upper part of the purchase of 1818 and was included in Early, but was made into a separate county in 1821 and named in honor of Judge Dooly. It had in its bounds what are now several large counties.

There were sundry rich hummocks on the creeks and some fine bottom land on the river, and these were soon occupied by cotton-planters. The pine woods were regarded as barrens, and when oak and hickory lands were worth ten to twenty dollars an acre the pine lands were held at from fifty cents to one dollar.

In 1887 a new railroad was constructed from Macon, Ga., to Palatka, Fla., and one from Americus to Savannah. These railways opened up the pine woods, mills were erected, turpentine farms opened, and prosperous towns sprang up. Farmers began to cultivate the land from which the saw-mill men had cut the timber and opened productive farms.

The story of Dooly is much the same with all the wire-grass counties, only modified by the fact that Dooly had a larger area of rich land on its creeks than most of them, and there was from the first a larger number of wealthy people, and the growth of the towns had been greater. Vienna, Ashburn and Cordele are places of considerable business.

While the upper part of Dooly has long been settled, and while there were churches and schools in Vienna and Drayton from the early twenties, the pine woods were sadly neglected by the preachers and teachers for many years. The Primitive Baptists and a few scattering Methodists were all the religious people in this section, and a few log churches the only houses of worship; but with the coming of the railroad and the influx of new people churches and schools sprang up in all directions, and now Dooly is abreast with any of the counties in the provision she has made for the improvement of her people.

MONROE.

The county of Monroe, which was named in honor of James Monroe, was laid out in 1821 and the land distributed by lottery. It lay abreast of Jones and Jasper, which had been settled for nearly twenty-five years. They were already crowded with inhabitants and the first settlers had grown restless and longed for new lands, and when Monroe was opened they came rushing into it in great troops.

It was a magnificent domain when it was first laid out, stretching from above Griffin to below Macon, but was soon divided into sundry counties; indeed, they were ordered before Monroe could be organized, and the county stands at present almost as it did when it was organized in 1822.

It is now bounded on the east by the Ocmulgee river; the Towaliga, a river of some size, flows through its north-eastern corner, and it is well watered with large creeks and many brooks. It does not differ from other middle Georgia counties, and, as is common in them, it has fine red land, rich bottoms and some gray thin land, and in the northern part a considerable pine belt.

The county when opened was accessible and healthy. The land was given away to Georgia people, and it was soon very thickly settled. The fortunate drawer of the land in most cases moved directly to it, or sold to one who did.

Monroe was settled largely by Georgia people. It never had any of the features of the frontier, except the single one of log cabins, which were a necessity in all new counties in those days. The people who came to Monroe were so many that it was more thickly peopled a few years after it was settled than it is now. In seven years there were 16,000 in the county. In 1850, thirty years after it was settled, there were a thousand more negroes than whites in the county.

The history of agriculture in Monroe is but the same story told of the older counties east of the Ocmulgee. It was at first settled by people of moderate means who had but few slaves and small farms, and oftentimes there were several families on one lot of land. Then these small farmers sold out their possessions and went westward, and the wealthy slave-owners bought their farms and made large plantations. Negroes increased; for the country was healthy, and they were well cared for. As the planter was anxious for quick returns from his fields, the grand forests were cut down and large cotton fields opened. The land was hilly and the soil easily washed away, and many of the large plantations were soon reduced to a state of almost barrenness. Fields were worn out and washed into huge gullies and then given over to the old-field pine and the Bermuda grass. The planter found it difficult to make any clear profit on his products, but comforted himself with the thought that he had such a valuable lot of young slaves. He found himself, when they were freed and commercially valueless, with his old fields and his decaying buildings as his only estate. There were years when it seemed as if the old county, once so rich, would never rally; but there came a better day. The lands were divided into smaller bodies, the hills terraced, the farming diversified, and the old pine fields were brought into cultivation; and now perhaps Monroe is really more prosperous than ever. But much of what was once the best part of the county when white people had beautiful country homes is given up to negro tenants; and, as is the case in all the middle Georgia counties where the landed estates are large, there is a tendency to leave the country for the town. This, however, is only true of that part of the county in which there were plantations and not farms. In the pine woods and the gray lands the farms were small and the inhabitants many. The people had but few slaves, the larger number none. They lived in log houses and in a very plain way. They spun and wove their own clothing and worked their own fields. They had not been cotton-raisers before the war except on a very small scale, and their main effort was to raise supplies for home use. When the war ended and the negroes were freed and commercial fertilizers were introduced largely, it was in Monroe as it was elsewhere, and these poor sections of the county became the best.

The county was a very large one and was thickly peopled, in the rich red lands by negro slaves and in the pine woods and gray lands by white people. It was very rough, and roads in the early days were very bad; and, as there was no navigable river, it was decided to build a railway.

The first railway projected in the State was the one from the new city of Macon to the new town of Forsyth. After much struggling it was built. Years afterward a part of the county on the eastern side was traversed by the Southern railway, and a section which had been thickly settled but which had become thinly peopled with white people was brought into communication with the outside world. Some sprightly villages, with good churches and schools, have sprung up beside the new railroad.

Forsyth, named in honor of John Forsyth, was made the county site when the county was organized. It was too near Macon to become a place of great commercial importance, but up to the war was a thrifty town with three churches for white people and as many for negroes, a high school for males and a female college. The Monroe railroad, now the Central, reached Forsyth in the early forties, and it was the first interior town in the State to have a railway connection with a navigable river.

After the war, in common with all middle Georgia towns, Forsyth began to make a forward movement, and it is now a very prosperous little city. There is a very fine courthouse. The Baptists have a handsome college. There is a large graded school. The Baptists, Methodists and Presbyterians have very neat and comfortable churches. There is a cotton-mill, an oil-mill and other enterprises. The planters have moved in from the country to get school privileges, and the population has largely increased.

The county is a prohibition one, and is noted for its sobriety and morality. In the extreme southwest of the county the lands were very fine, and a body of wealthy planters settled a village where they could educate their children and named it Culloden. They were mainly Methodists, and were rigid advocates of total abstinence. They had an act passed forbidding the sale of liquor within a mile of the village. They erected the first brick church built by Methodists in Georgia. They established a high school and opened the celebrated Culloden Female Seminary, over which Dr. John Darby presided. The little village was sixteen miles from a railway, and sank into a decline; but the building of the Macon and Birmingham and the Atlanta and Florida railroads, both of which pass through it, has given it a new vigor.

The people of Monroe were of the best class of Georgia people. They came from Hancock, Baldwin, Greene, Morgan, Jones and Jasper.

The settlers of Monroe were a truly religious people, and the first thing they did when they reached their new homes was to build log houses of worship.

The Baptists were very numerous among the first comers, and as they had not divided at that time into the Primitive and Missionary bodies, they were possibly the most numerous body of Christians in the county. They established churches in all sections of the county and had a large following.

The Methodists came with the first settlement and soon had churches in every part of the county. At one time there were three camp-grounds belonging to these in different parts of the county. They had a missionary to the negroes, a stationed preacher in Forsyth and two circuit preachers in the county in 1860.

It was in Monroe that the Congregational Methodist

church, which is Methodist in doctrine and Baptist in church government, was organized.

The Presbyterians had two churches in the county, but were not numerous.

After the division of the Baptist church the Primitive branch was very strong and wealthy and so continues to the present time.

Monroe has produced some very distinguished Georgians. Her list of public men in church and State is a long one for a county which has been more a county of plain, thrifty, energetic planters than of lawyers or politicians, and few villages have sent out so many distinguished men as the little village of Culloden. Here Governor James M. Smith was born and received his early education. In this village the Hon. Alexander Speer, formerly the secretary of state in South Carolina and a famous Methodist preacher, had his home, and from this village his two gifted sons, Judge Alexander M. Speer of the Georgia Supreme Court, and Dr. Eustace W. Speer, one of the most distinguished of the preachers in Georgia, went out to begin public life. Colonel N. J. Hammond, so famous as a lawyer and a statesman, began life in Culloden, and Dr. W. F. Cook and his brother Dr. J. O. A. Cook were brought up here. Judge E. G. Cabaniss, long a judge and one of the most gifted and excellent of men, lived in Forsyth. Judge R. P. Trippe, long a judge in the supreme court, a member of Congress, lived in Forsyth for many years.

The county has been noted for her excellent schools. The Baptist Female College in Forsyth has been for fifty years a good school, and some of the most distinguished Baptist preachers in Georgia have been professors in it. There was a Methodist male school, Hillard Institute, in Forsyth.

Early Cleveland was famous for the excellent private

academy which he conducted for many years in the county, and the Rev. Thomas G. Scott, either as teacher or as county school commissioner, spent his life in educational work in this county.

The celebrated seminary in Culloden had a fame which went beyond the State.

BIBB.

When it was decided in 1822 to lay off a city opposite Fort Hawkins, a new county was a necessity, and Bibb, to contain a part of Jones and a part of the projected county of Monroe, was decided on. It was to be called Bibb, after Senator Wm. Wyatt Bibb of Elbert, and the county site Macon after that staunch Republican, Nathaniel Macon of North Carolina.

This new county when made had in it some very excellent land and much whose agricultural value was very small. The upper part, bordering on Monroe and reaching down to within a few miles of Macon, while very hilly, was very fertile. This was soon taken up by large slave-owners who came from Baldwin, Putnam and Jones. They formed a community of wealthy planters, many of them kinspeople, and were of the best class of Georgians. There were but few small landholders among them, and they soon sold out their farms and went west.

The same story told of these people elsewhere is true of Bibb. Plantations grew, lands were worn, and planters took the place of farmers. As their wealth increased, in many cases they removed to the city and left their plantations in charge of overseers. When the railroads reached southwestern Georgia many of them settled plantations there and removed the larger number of their slaves to these new fields. The usual changes passed over the social features of the county: negroes and plantations took the place of white people and farms, schools went down and churches were thinly attended.

The pine lands south and west of Macon were for a considerable time thinly settled and by poor people; but the lands were healthy and the products of small crops found a ready market in Macon, and even before the war there was much thrift in a number of the piny woods homes. After the war and the building of the railways these people prospered more largely and some good villages sprang up where a few years before there had been only sterile pine woods.

The prosperity of Macon has had its effect on the country around it, and market-gardens and dairies have been numerous.

As I shall give in a future chapter a sketch of Macon there is much which concerns the country which will be then brought under review. The first settlers could hardly be given, for the county was scarcely laid out before it was thickly settled.

The religious privileges of the Bibb county people have always been good. The Baptists, both Missionary and Primitive, have had a large following, and some of the best country churches in Georgia have been found in the rural districts of this county.

While the city of Macon has always had the best of schools, the country around it was not for many years so well favored. In the first settlement of the county there was an academy in the Holt and Myrick settlement, nearly four miles from Macon, known as the Lake academy; one in the northern part of the county, in the Lamar settlement, known as Washington academy, and one near Liberty chapel in the pine woods.

There were besides these a few schools which were of inferior grade, but when the common school system was adopted by the county school facilities were provided for all classes,

Fort Hawkins.

black and white, in every section of the county; and now in no part of the State is there better provision made for the education of all classes.

The nine railroads which terminate at Macon have led to the establishment on their lines of sundry small villages, until the country has been well dotted with them—Holton, Mims, Rutland, Walden and Lizella are hamlets of small size on the railroads.

CRAWFORD.

By the same act in 1822 by which Bibb was made a county another was ordered in the new purchase, which was called Crawford in honor of the celebrated William Harris Crawford.

The county site was called Knoxville, in honor of General Knox, Washington's secretary of war.

It adjoined Monroe on the north, and a limited part of its upper territory was of the same kind of land as that which belonged to Bibb and Monroe. There was a valley of rich land along the Flint, and some rich bottoms on some of the creeks; and there was a remarkable hill known as Rich Hill, which, rising in the midst of a pine forest, was itself a great deposit of fossils and was the richest of limestone land. The rest of the county was all pine forest, and much of it richly deserved the name of pine-barrens.

The population varied with the land. Along the river were extensive plantations, and planters with many slaves owned them. These plantations were rarely occupied by the planters themselves, but were in charge of overseers. From one hundred to five hundred negroes were often on a single estate.

The land was very fertile, but was subject to overflow, and was leveed for miles; but during the war the levees broke, and after it was over the negroes moved out of the swamps, and the river floods were so common that after a vain effort to cultivate the rich lands profitably, they were at length to a large extent given up to cattle ranches.

The people in the pine woods section of Crawford were, many of them, poor people living on poor land and in a poor way. They had but few religious or educational advantages. Knoxville was a very small hamlet, with a few families of cultivation and wealth residing in it; and its proximity to Macon, its distance from a railroad and the general poverty of the country around it prevented anything like growth until the railroad came close to it. It is now somewhat improved.

Crawford had in it in 1850 as many negroes as whites, but they were owned very largely by the wealthy people who owned the river plantations.

The strong red lands north of Knoxville and adjoining Monroe had the usual history of such lands at this period. They were at once occupied and soon impoverished and sold by the owners to some near-by planter who absorbed them into his great plantation, until much of the land was owned by a few people.

It was in Crawford that remarkable man Colonel Benjamin Hawkins, the famous Indian agent, lived and died. The old agency on the Flint river was for many years his home, and here he ruled the Creek nation with an imperial but kindly sway. Descended from an aristocratic English family who resided in North Carolina, he was educated at Princeton College, and while there became a proficient in the French language. He entered the army during the Revolution and became a member of Washington's staff, where his knowledge of French made him useful. He was elected after the war senator from North Carolina, and Washington, when he was president, selected him as commissioner to treat with the Indians. He became fascinated with Indian life, and accepted the position of agent of the Creeks and settled among them. He was a man of great wealth and large enterprise as well as of fine culture, and conducted extensive farming and pastoral interests in the nation, at the same time directing his efforts to elevate the people among whom he lived. He had large interests in Crawford and a comfortable residence at the old agency on the Flint. Here, as a kind of satrap, he lived for many years, revered and beloved by the wild tribes who knew how implicitly they could trust him. While his home was here he died.*

Judge Samuel Hall, judge of the supreme court, was from this county, and Judge Simmons, at present chief justice, was born and brought up here.

The religious and educational advantages of the county before the war were few. The leading denominations were the Missionary and Primitive Baptists.

UPSON.

Upson county, which adjoins Monroe and Crawford on the west and Pike on the north, was laid out from Crawford and Pike in 1824 and named in honor of Stephen Upson, a distinguished lawyer of Oglethorpe county.

Thomaston, its county site, was laid out in 1825.

Upson has a good deal of fine bottom land immediately on the Flint river and some fertile bodies on the various creeks; but the main body of the land is like that of Pike and Monroe—very hilly red land easily washed away. It was productive when first cleared; and, as the climate was good, soon after the county was laid out it was settled by a body of pushing planters. The red lands were cleared of their magnificent trees. The hills were high, and the washing rains denuded them of their soil, and much of the land became sterile; and while Upson had 7,913 people in it in 1830 (only six years after it was made a county), in 1850

* Wheeler's History of North Carolina; Chappel's Pamphlet.

the population had only reached 9,000, and in 1890 there were only 12,000 in the county of all races.

Much of the land was badly worn, and many of the landowners after the war sought the villages and towns as places of residence, and the negroes were tenants in the country where their fathers had been slaves. The rural white population, as in all these middle Georgia counties, decreased, but the villages all increased in the number of inhabitants.

Upson was one of the first of the middle Georgia counties to enter upon manufacturing on an extensive scale, and there was established in the county several large cotton-mills at an early date. The Waymanville factory, Rogers factory and Respess factory were cotton-mills of considerable importance long before the war. Some of these were burned by the Federals who desolated Upson on a raid, but some escaped. The Waymanville factory is still standing, and has been for fifty years a prosperous mill.

The town of Thomaston was, like most of the interior towns, a place of little importance until after the war, but is now a thriving and prosperous little city. It has two railways and is an educational center, with an excellent institute and two handsome churches, the Methodist and Baptist.

The county has always been noted for its decidedly religious character. The Primitive and Missionary Baptists are strong, but the Methodists are, perhaps, most numerous. There are good churches all over the county, and a successful camp-meeting has been held for many years near or at the Rock, a village eight miles from Thomaston.

TALIAFERRO.

The counties of Wilkes, Warren and Hancock, which adjoined each other, were all large counties, and in 1825 it was decided to take a corner from each and make a new county. This was done and this new county was called

Taliaferro, after Colonel and Judge Taliaferro, and the county site was called Crawfordville in honor of W. H. Crawford.

This very small county has had the same history as its parent counties and it is needless to repeat it here.

The first Roman Catholic church in a rural section, and perhaps the first in any section of Georgia, was built at Locust Grove, afterward Raytown, in this county, then Wilkes.

Taliaferro has been rendered famous by being the county in which Alexander H. Stephens was born and the county in which he is buried. He bought the little farm his father, who was a country teacher, owned, and it was his residence when he died. His father was a Pennsylvanian of a correct, if of limited, education; a country school-teacher, a man of great integrity and of very small estate. He was living on this little farm of one hundred acres when he was taken violently ill, and died, leaving his son Alexander an almost penniless orphan. The guardians of the boy gave him his first schooling in this county, and his academic training in Washington. He was graduated at Athens. When he began the practice of law he settled at Crawfordville. It was then a new village in a new county. He was soon sent to the Legislature, and early evinced his wondrous power as an orator and his astuteness as a statesman. His career as the great commoner, both before and after the war, is too well known to be told here. He died in Atlanta while governor of the State, but was buried at his lifelong home.

The little county was a healthy one, and negroes increased very rapidly, with the usual result, and in 1850 there were more negroes than whites in the county.

TROUP.

When the lands secured by the Indian Springs treaty in 1825 were opened for settlement a large county was formed on the western border of the State, including what is now a number of counties, and was named Troup in honor of the fiery governor, and its county site was called Lagrange after the home of the Marquis de Lafayette, who had but recently made a tour through the United States.

This county has been repeatedly divided until it has reached its present size. There were few sections of the State superior to it in attractiveness and fertility. The oft-told story of middle Georgia is applicable to Troup. Much of it was very rugged and very rich. The water was pure, the air free from malaria, the forests magnificent, and on the Chattahoochee and the various creeks there were bottoms of great fertility. There was no part of the county sterile and it was rapidly settled, not by poor people, who are generally the first in a new country, but by well-to-do planters from eastern Georgia, who opened large cotton plantations at their first coming.

Although the first settlers came into Troup in 1826, by 1830 it had a population of six thousand. Lagrange, when Sherwood published his first gazetteer in 1829, had only a court-house, a jail, a Methodist church and seven residences, and in 1833 was large enough to entertain the Georgia annual conference.

The lands were so productive that they were at once occupied by large planters, and soon after the settlement of the county cotton was sent in wagons to Columbus and Montgomery by hundreds of bales.

The log house, the first in all new counties, soon gave way, and a few years after the settlement of the county there were handsome residences in all sections of it.

The same methods of planting which had resulted in the almost desolation of the older counties of Georgia were at once adopted in Troup. The people of moderate means were soon bought out by the large planters, the forests were cut down, cotton was planted largely and almost ex-

Dormitory Southern Female College, Lagrange.

clusively, and the lands washed away until, when the magnificent county ought to have been in its prime, much of it was counted as worn out.

Many of the planters lived in the town of Lagrange and their great plantations were in charge of overseers.

There were in 1850 seven thousand eight hundred and thirty-one whites and over nine thousand negroes in the county.

In no county in the State was there so much attention given to education, especially to the education of girls. A female high school, from which sprang the Lagrange Female College, was established by Thomas Stanley in Lagrange as early as 1833. The Montgomerys afterward built from this foundation the Lagrange Female College, which became in the course of time one of the most famous schools in the State. It was afterward sold to the Methodists and is still a flourishing institution.

The Rev. Milton E. Bacon established a female college under Baptist auspices not long after the Lagrange Female College was chartered, and carried it to a high degree of success. Both of these colleges were destroyed and both rebuilt.

The education of males attracted as much attention at an early day, and the Rev. Carlisle P. Beman, the famous teacher, taught a male school in the village, and the Rev. Otis Smith had a classical school for boys at Brownwood, where Dr. Brown had at one time his female seminary.

The religious privileges of Troup have always been of a very high order. The Methodists were early in the county, and a Methodist church was one of the first buildings in the then village of Lagrange. The Baptists had a large membership and the Presbyterians a strong church. Each of these denominations had good churches in Lagrange as early as 1835. The wooden churches of the Baptists and Methodists have long since been replaced by neat brick structures, and the Methodists have a third church on the same lot. The most distinguished preachers of each of these three denominations have filled the pulpits in Lagrange.

The city has become in late years quite a manufacturing town, and with its two railways, its colleges and its commerce, it has become one of the leading cities of that section of Georgia.

West Point, immediately on the Chattahoochee river, is a town of considerable importance. It has a large graded school, several churches and some large factories near by, and does considerable business.

Hogansville, on the other side of Lagrange, is a village of some size, with an excellent population.

The county of Troup has long been famous for its public men and its brilliant and beautiful women. It drew to it at its first settlement men of culture and influence. Julius Alford, known as the war-horse of the Democracy; Walter T. Colquitt, the great stump-speaker as well as advocate and judge; Hugh A. Haralson, a leading Whig and congressman; Edward Young Hill, the great jurist; Benj. H. Bigham, the lawyer and judge, all lived here; but no man perhaps has shown with such brightness as Benjamin H. Hill, who spent his boyhood in the county and his youth in the town of Lagrange, and won his first laurels as a great orator while living there. Mr. Hill was born in Jasper county, but his father moved at an early day to the county of Troup. The father was a man of fine intelligence, of pure character and of large means. He gave his son the best of opportunities, which he faithfully improved. He began the practice of law in Lagrange and soon was at the head of the bar in Georgia. He took ground against the measures of the leading party in Georgia, the Democrats, and when the excitement concerning secession began was a decided Union man. When the State seceded he took his place as advocating a Southern Confederacy, and was a senator to the Confederate Congress and a close friend of President Davis. After the war he was in the House and finally in the Senate, when, in the vigor of his manhood, he passed away.

Dr. R. A. T. Ridley, famous as a physician and a public man and noted for his philanthropy and his piety, lived here.

Troup suffered fearful reverses from the war. The Troup people were free livers and somewhat careless financiers. Their wealth was largely in their slaves, and all they had made was invested in the negroes they had reared. They were kind and careful masters, the country was healthy, and their negroes had increased largely and rapidly. Many of them were in debt for slaves they had bought, as well as for expenses incurred in supporting those they had raised. When their property was rendered valueless by Federal fiat many of them were hopelessly bankrupt. The planters, as in Middle Georgia, found it impossible to manage as they had done, and many of them removed from their country homes and went to the towns, renting their plantations to their ex-slaves. The towns prospered at the expense of the country, and for a time it seemed as if the country would be deserted. But now the current is turning, and there is a tendency to build up homes in the rural sections.

The building of the Atlanta and West Point railway over forty years ago brought Troup into connection with the seaboard, and the building of the Macon and Birmingham road to Macon has brought it into closer connection with Savannah.

MERIWETHER.

Meriwether county, named in honor of General Meriwether, kinsman to James Meriwether who made the treaty, was cut off from Troup in 1827. The description I have given of Troup is applicable to Meriwether in almost every feature. Like Troup, it was settled from the eastern counties, and in 1830, only three years after it was laid out, there were nearly 4,500 people in the county. Much of the land in Meriwether was like that of Troup, and the same wasteful agriculture exhausted the lands as rapidly. There was, fortunately, some poor land in the county tenanted by poor people, and this has not been worn out, but has improved.

This county is famous for the only thermal spring in Georgia. It is known as Warm Springs. It sends forth 1,400 gallons per minute at a temperature of 90°. It is 1,200 feet above sea level. The improvements are very handsome, and the watering-place is very popular. There are also chalybeate and sulphur springs in the county.

The people of Meriwether have always been noted for their morality and for their attention to education. There are now schools of high grade at Greenville, Stinson, Senoia and Woodbury. A camp-meeting attended by immense throngs has been held in Meriwether near Warm Springs annually for over seventy years.

Meriwether has had her share of distinguished men.

The Hon. Hiram Warner came from Massachusetts to Georgia and settled in Houston county as a teacher. He studied law, was admitted to the bar, elected to the Legislature, and made a judge of the Western Circuit. He fixed his home in Greenville and never changed it. He was placed on the supreme bench as soon as the supreme court was established, and retained his place there until his death, except during the period in which he was a member of Congress.

Colonel Henry R. Harris, for several terms a member of Congress and an assistant postmaster-general under Mr.

Cleveland's administration, was born in this county and has resided here all his life.

Governor Atkinson was a native of this county, and was brought up and educated in it until he went to the University.

For many years after the neighboring counties were supplied with railroad facilities Meriwether had none. The road from Griffin to Newnan skirted the upper part of the county, and the West Point road passed through a corner of it. But a narrow-gage road was built from Columbus to Greenville, and the Macon and Birmingham crossed the county from east to west, and the Midland from the northeast to the southwest. No county has now better railroad facilities, and no county has made more rapid progress since the advent of the roads.

Greenville is a prosperous county town with an excellent people, good churches and good schools.

Stinson, Woodbury, Warm Springs, Senoia and Harris City are all promising villages.

The preachers came into Meriwether with the coming of the people, and had but to gather the members of their various churches together. A plain church was among the first buildings in every neighborhood. The Methodists and Baptists are the leading denominations, and they have been in the county since its first settlement.

HARRIS.

From the south of Troup and the north of Muscogee a county was cut off in 1828 which was called Harris in honor of Charles Harris of Savannah, a distinguished lawyer who died about the time the county was laid off. It was a county of varied resources, and was, like the neighboring counties, rapidly settled. In 1830 there were 5,000 people in it, although it was but four years old, and in 1850 there were nearly 7,000 whites and 8,000 slaves. The county was settled, as were all these western counties, from the eastern and middle parts of the State.

Many of the people, when they came to Harris, were large slaveholders, and were well supplied with all the requisites for planting; so the best red lands were taken up in large plantations, while the poorer lands were occupied by people of limited means.

Hamilton, the county site of Harris, was named in honor of that staunch anti-tariff Democrat of South Carolina, General J. W. Hamilton. Hamilton was too near to Columbus to ever become a town of much commercial importance, but has been from its first settlement a pleasant place of residence. The schools in the town have been good, and education has been carefully attended to.

When the narrow-gage road was completed to Greenville, across the Pine Mountain, a village of some importance named Chipley was built up.

The first court was held in Hamilton in 1828 and was presided over by Judge Walter T. Colquitt.

There is so little to distinguish one of these western cotton-raising counties from the other that anything like an elaborate account of any one is out of place, and Harris is no exception to the rule. It was largely settled by eastern Georgians—an intelligent, moral and religious people. The chief denominations were Methodists and Baptists and the churches were established as early as the county.

The city of Columbus, being so near to Harris, has drawn to it a large number of Harris county people. The county has not been famous for distinguished public men, but as a rule the citizens of Harris have been noted for their intelligence and morality.

COWETA.

Coweta, which adjoined Troup on the east, was a large and, in the main, a fertile county. It was named Coweta after the old Indian town two miles below Columbus, and its county town was named Newnan in honor of General Daniel Newnan, a brave soldier in the war of 1812.

The county was in all respects like those already described which adjoined it. There was no waste land in it, but the fertility of its various sections differed much, and according to the nature of the soil was the class of settlers who made their homes in the county.

In the rich red lands there was the slave-owner, and on the poorer gray lands the men of smaller means. The lands, having been granted by lottery, were very rapidly occupied by Georgia people, and in three years there were 5,000 people in the county, of whom 1,372 were slaves.

There were but few people of anything like considerable property, and the larger number of the first comers were men in very moderate circumstances.

There was, however, as in Troup, quite an immigration of people of some property from the eastern counties. After the county had been settled some time there came to it a fine body of people who moved in a body from Virginia, and, besides these, a colony of German origin from South Carolina, but the larger part of the people came from the eastern counties of Georgia.

They had few hardships to encounter and found land very cheap and a wide range for their cattle and hogs, and were soon comfortably fixed in their log cabins.

The first court-house was at Bullsboro, about two miles from the present city of Newnan, and the first court was held there by Judge Walter T. Colquitt. This place, which was chosen as a county site, was not satisfactory, and no public buildings were ever erected there. At that time Coweta included Heard and Carroll and was an immense county.

The early records show that there was a great deal of fraud in taking up the lands, which were distributed by lottery, and that, as is common in newly settled counties, there was a great deal of drinking and fighting. There was, however, never a reign of lawlessness in the county.

The people were generally poor and generally moral. They were from the best families east of Coweta, and were substantial, industrious and unpretending people.

The price of land at the first settlement of the county ranged from fifty cents to two dollars and a half per acre, only the very best lands bringing more than one dollar.

The chief property of the first comers was cattle. Cows and calves sold for twelve dollars; cattle, as they came, at six dollars per head. There was much bacon made, which found ready purchasers in the newcomers.

It was, however, only a few years after the county was settled before it became famous as a cotton-growing county and the plantations were greatly enlarged.

Coweta was no exception to the general rule in middle Georgia. Farms were absorbed in plantations, and the same condition of things noted elsewhere followed the reverses of the war. The planters abandoned the plantations and negro tenants alone were left. A gratifying change is now passing over the county. The great estates are being divided and the number of smaller landholders is increasing.

Newnan was made the county site in 1827, and has been one of the leading towns in western Georgia since its first settlement. It soon became a place of commercial importance, and, being the site of the public buildings and of the academies, it drew to itself a population noted for its intelligence and refinement. The ante-bellum homes, some of which still stand, were commodious and imposing, with large grounds about them, mainly owned by planters who had large estates in the county.

The citizens took great interest in education in all sections of this county. Mr. M. P. Kellogg, a northern teacher of great ability and enterprise, built up a female institution of high grade, which he called College Temple, and which was a noted school for girls for many years. There was, from the settlement of Newnan, a classical school for males, and in the country neighborhoods there were some excellent schools. The Longstreet Institute, the Rock Springs Academy and the Senoia Institute were all fine schools.

The Methodists, Baptists and Presbyterians came with the first settlers, and the Methodists and Baptists each had a log church in Newnan in 1827. The Presbyterians came next, and the Episcopalians have now a church in the city. These first churches were of logs, but they soon gave way to better buildings, and these in turn to those which are still better; and now in Newnan there are elegant churches which would do credit to any city, while all over the county there are comely and comfortable churches of various denominations. In addition to these the colored people have a number of neat and attractive buildings.

This county has been the home of many prominent and useful men who have been distinguished in the history of the State.

Rev. Dr. Luther M. Smith, president of Emory College and of the Southern University, was born and brought up in this county.

W. B. W. Dent, a congressman, was a useful resident of this county in its earliest settlement.

Hugh Buchanan, a gifted Scotchman and true soldier, and who was severely wounded in the war between the States, came to Coweta a young teacher and studied law. He became at once prominent, was sent to the Legislature, elected a judge of the circuit court and a member of Congress, and died here greatly esteemed.

The celebrated Dr. Calhoun, the famous surgeon of Atlanta, whose reputation as an oculist has become world-wide, was brought up in Newnan.

Perhaps no town in the State has had a better class of enterprising citizens than Newnan. The Messrs. Cole, natives of Coweta, built up a famous foundry and machine shop, whose work took the highest prize at more than one State exhibit, and in common with others built up a cotton-mill, which has been successful from its beginning.

There is now no town in western Georgia in which there are evidences of more genuine prosperity than Newnan.

TALBOT.

Talbot was named in honor of Matthew Talbot. He was one of the prominent men of Wilkes and was senator from that county and president of the Senate when Governor Rabun died. The death of Governor Rabun made him ex-officio governor. He ran for the governorship, but was defeated by G. M. Troup by two votes.

The county of Talbot was ordered in 1826. It was a very large county and of very varied features. Some of the land was remarkably fine, and the Talbot valley, lying between the Oak and Pine mountains, is a valley of great beauty and fertility. Much of the county was very rugged, and though the hills were fertile, they were easily washed away. There was some valley land on the river and a large body of pine woods.

The county was speedily settled, and in 1829 it had 3,841 free inhabitants and 2,099 slaves. The wealth of the neighborhoods varied according to the character of the soil.

The same story told of Meriwether and Troup can be told of Talbot. Eastern planters moved all their interests to the new country. The proximity to Columbus enabled the settler to secure all the comforts he had left behind. Schools were at once established, churches built, and so Talbot became a great cotton-raising county. In 1830 there were 7,811 free and 8,723 slaves.

The population of Talbot differed but little from the

best population of the adjoining counties. It was largely settled by eastern Georgians, and the oak and hickory lands by cotton-planters. They had been neighbors in Morgan, Putnam and Hancock, and there was but little change in their lives in this new county.

As was always the case the pine lands and the poorer sections were neglected and thinly peopled for a number of years; but when the railroad to Columbus passed through the county mills sprang up and farms followed. The Midland road from Griffin to Columbus passed through Talbot, and a branch road from Talbotton to Bostwick connected Talbotton with the Central railroad.

The history of Talbot is simply that of all the slaveholding, cotton-planting country. It suffered much from the reverses which followed the war, but is now perhaps as prosperous on the whole as it has ever been.

Talbotton, the county site, was settled as soon as the county was made. It has been famous from its settlement for its culture and refinement, and while it has suffered, as all the near-by towns have done, from the attractions of the large cities which have drawn its people away from it, it is still a thrifty town, with a good trade and an excellent population.

Geneva and Bostwick are small villages on the Central railway.

The Collinsworth Institute, now suspended, was built and endowed by Josiah Flournoy, and was long a famous high school among the Methodists. The LeVert Female College, now the graded school, was a famous female college.

From Talbotton Allen F. Owen was sent to Congress and made minister to a foreign court, Geo. W. Towns was made governor and Barna Hill was made judge.

Leonard Rush, one of the ablest of Georgia preachers, long had his home in the Talbot valley.

BAKER.

A very large county in the northeastern part of Early was cut off from that county in 1825 and named Baker in honor of Colonel Baker of the Revolutionary war. It was, when laid out, almost an unknown land to the people of Georgia, and few had any appreciation of the immense value of the as yet untouched soil. It was not a pleasant country to the eye, nor did it seem to promise good health. It was in what the old geologists called the tertiary formation; the water was strongly impregnated with lime, and the air was laden with malaria. It was soon discovered that the hummocks were exceptionally fertile, and adapted especially to cotton.

It was at first taken possession of by the stock-raiser and was a fine land for grazing, but as soon as the fertility of its soil was recognized it was bought up by the large slave-owners of middle Georgia and plantations were opened.

While the climate in winter and the early spring was very fine, it was very unfriendly to white people in the later summer and fall, but it was not so to negroes, and they breathed the malarious air with greater impunity.

As soon as the great value of the cotton lands was discovered, and all danger from the Indians was removed, the county became very attractive to men of large means, and it was soon turned into a great plantation and negro quarter.

In no part of the State was planting carried on on so large a scale. From one hundred to two thousand bales of cotton was the ordinary crop of a Baker county planter. The cotton was sent by steamer down the Flint and Apalachicola to Apalachicola in Florida, and thence shipped to New York and Europe.

The plantations were very large and the pine woods adjoining were almost unpeopled, and in 1830 in the entire county, now divided into several counties, there were only 1,253 inhabitants of all kinds, of whom the larger number were whites, but in 1850, after the planters had begun their settlements, there were 8,000, of whom 4,000 were negroes. The pine lands were at first regarded merely as grazing land and were not valued by the cotton-planters, but when cultivated were found to be almost equal to the hummocks in fertility, and they too were put in cotton fields.

Baker received quite an uplift when the Central road, then the Southwestern, reached Albany and there was quick transportation. The transfer of the cotton-planting interest from the upper counties, from Liberty, Burke, Baldwin and Putnam, to Baker was made rapidly after 1850 and there was quick transit to Savannah. Albany became quite an important cotton market. The county was then divided into Baker and Dougherty.

There was little likelihood that a county of large plantations and absentee landlords would be a county of good schools or prosperous churches, and this county, outside of Albany, suffered for the want of them for many years. Schools were few and churches were fewer. The planters did not live on their estates in many cases, and those who did were too few to keep up good schools. So they sent their children abroad or employed private tutors. There were too few people to form good congregations, and although Methodist and Baptist preachers were in the county from its settlement and had churches and many members among the slaves, they had small following among the whites.

LEE.

Lee county adjoins Baker on its northern side. It was laid out in 1826 and was named Lee in honor of "Light Horse Harry." This county was the exact counterpart of Baker. It was very fertile, but was considered quite unhealthy, and was but slowly settled. In 1830 there were but 1,680 people in a very large county; but when its resources as a cotton country were discovered it had the same history as Baker. It was bought up by wealthy planters and turned into a great cotton plantation. The planters of Bibb, Baldwin, Jones and Putnam transferred the larger part of their working force to Lee and put them in charge of overseers; and the history given of Baker tells the story of Lee in all its details.

There was for years after the county was settled very bad drinking water, many ponds and much ill health. Whites deserted the country, and the plantations became immense, for Georgia negroes by the hundreds were settled on them in charge of overseers.

Captain Fort succeeded in solving the water problem by boring a deep artesian well. His example was followed by others, and now there is, as in Baker and Dougherty, good water everywhere.

Before the war the county was so thinly settled by white people that the conditions usual in such sections were found here. Schools were few and churches fewer. After the war, with the building up of the villages along the railway, there was improvement on all these lines.

DECATUR.

The immense county of Early was made into a number of new counties, and among them one on its lower border extending to the Florida line was made in 1823. It was called Decatur after the gallant Commodore, and its county site was named Bainbridge in honor of Commodore Bainbridge.

The description given of Early county in the preceding chapter is applicable in almost all respects to Decatur.

It contained a great body of pine land, through which the Flint river ran diagonally into the Chattahoochee. There were a number of large creeks in the county, and on these rivers and creeks there was much rich hummock land timbered with oak, hickory and other hardwood trees. The main body of the land was pine land, and, as was universal in the first settlement, it was regarded as mere grazing land and was esteemed as of little worth. The lands on the rivers were fertile and accessible, and were soon taken up by the wealthy cotton-planters, many of whom moved from the eastern counties of Georgia, and some from South Carolina. These cotton-planters bought large bodies of pine land in connection with the land they cultivated and had very large estates.

For convenience of access to the outside world the larger planters lived near the Chattahoochee or Flint rivers, and really had but little intercourse with the stock-raisers scattered over the pine-barrens of this county. These Chattahoochee and Flint river planters lived, as did those who were near them in Early, in a community of their own. They had many slaves and splendid mansions, and no people in Georgia lived with greater elegance. The history of the great Munnerlyn estate will perhaps give a better exhibit of this one phase of this southwestern Georgia life than any general statement:

Mr. Munnerlyn went from South Carolina to Florida; but not being pleased he bought the famous Fowltown tract in Decatur county. It lay between the rivers, where the Indians had a town. Here he settled a large plantation. There were thousands of acres in the tract. He built a large and comfortable mansion house with broad verandas, wide halls and airy rooms. There was about it a large park, a well-kept flower-garden, a large kitchen-garden and all the needful equipment of a gentleman's home. The plantation was on the river, the fields stretching out along its banks for miles. There were several settlements known as negro quarters, each with scores of negroes and each in charge of an overseer. The discipline spoken of elsewhere was observed on the estate, and for many years there was great prosperity. Mr. Munnerlyn was merely one of many; but after the war it was no longer possible to keep up the admirable discipline that had brought success, and the great estate was abandoned.

On the banks of the Chattahoochee, isolated and remote from all people of like kind, there was, up to 1860, an elegance, a refinement and a style of living equal to any in the land. There were books, periodicals, newspapers, musical instruments, and all the comforts and many of the luxuries of life. The fine fish and oysters of the coast, fruit from the West Indies, flour from Baltimore, and all the table comforts furnished by the city market were at the planter's call, while his own plantation supplied all the poultry, the mutton, the beef and hams demanded by the generous housekeeper. There was a lavish hospitality, and during all the winter a houseful of guests. The life of the James river planter of the last century and of the sea island planter of the first part of this was reproduced in the western border of Georgia, where for scores of miles east of the river there were only log cabins and poor, plain rustics. The main body of the Decatur people lived in the pine woods and had the same features of character belonging to these stock-raisers everywhere.

Then the railroads came, with the usual result.

There were in the county in 1830 3,850 people, and in 1850 about 8,000, of whom there were 3,639 slaves.

In a county like that of Decatur, where there was such inequality in social conditions, there was, of course, great inequality in the school and religious privileges. In certain wealthy neighborhoods there were congregations of select people, while in the pine forests the churches were few and far apart and were attended by the poor and illiterate. The results following the war produced great changes in this direction. The building of the railway from Savannah to the Chattahoochee, and from Montgomery, Ala., to Bainbridge brought all parts of Decatur into notice.

Bainbridge, the county site of Decatur, was for some years, on account of its location on the river, the most important town in this section of southwest Georgia. With the building of the railway to Albany and the decline of Apalachicola it suffered a temporary decline, but with the extension of the railroad and the building of the line from Montgomery it was provided with excellent railroad facilities, and has become quite a busy and prosperous city.

There are sundry small villages along the railways in the county which are centers of a good trade.

THOMAS.

Thomas county, on the line of Florida, was laid out in 1826. It was named in honor of General Jett Thomas, a soldier of 1812. It was in the main a pine woods county in which there were a few bodies of fertile hummock land. In common with all sections of this kind, it drew to it two very different classes of settlers, the cattle-raiser and the cotton-planter; but it was very thinly settled for a long time. It had in 1830 only 3,000 inhabitants when it embraced what are now several large counties; and at this early day 1,168 of these first comers were slaves. Although the size of the county was greatly reduced, in 1850 there were 9,000, of whom 5,155 were slaves.

Many of its first people emigrated from Bulloch, Screven, Burke, Laurens and Montgomery, and brought with them a number of slaves. The planters located on the rich hummocks near the Florida line, and raised cotton. Large fortunes were rapidly made. The cotton was sent by wagons to Magnolia, St. Marks and Newport, Fla., and shipped by sailing vessels to New York. The land was very fertile, and the cotton product was very large. The planter, being remote from markets, depended largely on his own resources, and few planters were so independent or so prosperous.

The pine woods furnished a range of wide extent, and the cattle fed on the wild pastures and increased to large numbers.

The county was healthy and negroes increased rapidly, and as land was abundant and cheap the first comer secured a large body of it, and although he lived a long way in the interior, he was only a three-days' journey from the Gulf coast and found a ready market for his cotton there, and so his property rapidly increased.

The poorer class lived in great simplicity and did not differ from the ordinary pine woods people whom we have so often described. Those of them who first settled near the plantation of the rich planter, whose favorite maxim was "poor land is the best neighbor," sold out his small lot of two hundred and fifty acres and went to Florida.

The homes of some of the wealthy planters just before the war were very elegant. They generally lived on or near their plantations, and as they had access to the city markets through St. Marks or Newport, and as they had money to their credit in New York, they bought oftentimes handsome furniture, and as they had abundant timber and often a lumber-mill of their own, and their own carpenters and brick-makers, they built themselves commodious and handsome residences. The plantation furnished them with all the comforts they needed; the most beautiful flowers, exotics elsewhere, grew in the open air. The water-oaks were of great size, the magnolia was indigenous and the yellow jessamine and the red woodbine festooned the forest trees.

The good women were famous as housekeepers and labor was abundant.

The young people were sent abroad for an education and

had the advantage of the best schools. As the wealthy cotton-planters lived remote from the seaboard, shut up to themselves, they formed an exclusive circle, but one sufficiently extensive for pleasant society.

There was no sale for the smaller products of the plantation, and so the planter's table was laden with the most toothsome viands from his own estate, and his hospitality was boundless.

Thomasville was a quiet little village for many years after it was settled, but with the building of the railway it became quite a mart of trade. When the war ended attention was drawn to its matchless winter climate. Great hotels were built and visitors came by the thousands. Many of these visitors were so well pleased with the county that they decided to establish winter homes in it, and in Thomasville and in the country roundabout some of them built very handsome homes and purchased large bodies of land as hunting lodges. These winter visitors form a society of their own and have little to do with the people of the city or county in which they sojourn for a little while. They spend only a few of the severest weeks of the year in this climate and then return northward.

The sand pear, or LeConte pear, was found so admirably suited to the soil around Thomasville, that until the blight reached the trees, it seemed as if the whole county would be a pear orchard; but while the blight checked, it has not entirely destroyed the fruit-raising industry.

The little towns of Boston and Cairo, one on the east and the other on the west of Thomasville, are both sprightly towns, with a good trade.

Thomasville, by the bequest of Remur Young, has a small and feeble chartered college for girls, called by his name, and there is a male school which is owned by the city, known as the South Georgia College, and the usual county public schools in all sections of the county.

Few parts of the State have grown with greater rapidity than Thomas has since the war, although its progress has been retarded by the purchase of large bodies of land by the rich men of the north and west, which have been turned into game preserves and which are owned by absentee landlords who only visit the county once a year, and take no interest in its development and have little intercourse with its people.

WARE.

In 1824, out of the great county of Irwin, which embraced so much of southern Georgia, several counties were formed. One of these was the county of Ware, named in honor of Nicholas Ware of Augusta.

We have already seen the county from which it was made, Irwin, and there was but little to distinguish this part of the county from any other part of it. It had, however, in its borders one of the largest swamps in America, the Okefinokee, which has no rival in America except the Dismal Swamp in Virginia and the Everglades in Florida. This swamp has been explored but partially, and has been found to be a vast marsh, with occasional lakes and islands. There is in it some good timber of various kinds. The swamp was purchased from the State a few years since by a land company, and an effort was made to drain it by a large canal. The promoters hoped not only to drain the swamp, but by the canal to provide a means for floating the timber found in it to the Satilla river, and thus recover much land for cultivation and secure timber for the mills. The effort, however, has not been a successful one. The great swamp was a hiding place for deserters during the war. It is famous for its fish and its vast number of wild bee-trees with their stores of honey and beeswax.

The county of Ware had few advantages for agriculture, and was almost entirely given up to cattle-raising until the building of the Atlantic and Gulf railroad, when the vast timber resources of the country were first developed.

After the war the turpentine farms were opened, and when the great Plant System of railways decided on a direct line to Florida, to provide for its Florida travel, it made the point of departure from its main line a little village in Ware called Waycross, where the Brunswick and Western railroad crosses the Savannah, Florida and Western. Here it resolved to build large shops and have a hospital. A city sprang up, and now there are three fine school buildings, electric lights and water-works.

For many years the country was thinly settled. Churches were few and schools were rare. The people were good, poor people who were isolated and illiterate and had little ambition to improve their condition. But perhaps in no part of the State is there now more intelligence or a better type of piety.

Waresboro has become quite a prosperous little town, and there are churches and villages all along the various railroads which permeate the country. The artesian well has opened up inexhaustible fountains of pure water, and the health of the country and city is now remarkably good.

LOWNDES.

Lowndes county was laid off from Irwin in 1825, and was named in honor of the free-trader Senator Lowndes of South Carolina. Its first county site was Troupville, named for Governor Troup. When it was decided to move the county site to where it is now the name chosen was Valdosta, which was the name of Governor Troup's country home.

It has a wide stretch of pine woods, broken into by a few hummocks. The rivers which traverse the county have no swamps, but make their way through banks of sand. There is some pine land which is productive, some that is very sterile, and some that is too flat for good drainage. The hummocks are productive, and the county as a whole is a good one.

The land was laid off originally in large lots of 490 acres, and those who had only one lot were accounted as having a very small holding.

The people generally were independent and contented. They had no slaves, or but few; had little and wanted little. But there were almost from its first settlement a few large planters who had extensive plantations and many slaves. Their homes were plain but comfortable. But the most of the people were mere stock-raisers who lived at home. They were, like the other piny woods people, comfortable and contented. They lived on the large land lots remote from each other, and made no other effort than to live comfortably and independently.

The railroad came, the little hamlet of Valdosta began to grow, and trade from the counties roundabout began to come into it. The mill man came to make lumber, the turpentine distiller to make turpentine, and the little town became a city, with banks, factories and wholesale stores and handsome churches and other public buildings.

The county of Lowndes was near no navigable stream, and had no railroads, and was for many years settled only by those who wanted to lead a quiet life and who had little hope of making fortunes.

There came into the county at an early date many descendants of the old Salzburghers, who made a most admirable class of settlers.

There was some cotton raised in the county, which found a market at St. Marks; but there was little bought or sold.

But little attention was paid to religious culture or education until the railway reached the county, and for a number of years afterward; but now there is a fine graded school in Valdosta and good schools in all sections of the county.

Andrew Female College, Cuthbert.

RANDOLPH.

The county of Randolph was the second county in Georgia named for John Randolph. It lay on the Chattahoochee, and when laid out in 1828 the Indians were on the Alabama side. The county was a pine woods one, was very remote from the center of population, and did not attract settlers rapidly; but it had a considerable number of people scattered over it who were engaged in raising cattle.

After the last Indian trouble in 1836, when the town of Roanoke was burned, the value of the lands in Randolph was discovered and the county began to improve. The opening of the Southwestern railroad brought into it a large body of new immigrants.

There is but little to distinguish this county from the other piny woods counties of the southwestern part of Georgia; but it has been exceptionally fortunate in the class of people who have settled it.

Cuthbert, the county site, is a beautiful, enterprising and prosperous city. Its citizens have taken great pride in its educational advancement, and before the war the Baptists and Methodists had each a college for girls located here. The Methodist college was burned a few years since, but has been rebuilt. It is an elegant building and the school has a large patronage. There are good churches and schools in every part of the county, which is steadily improving.

MARION.

Marion county was named in honor of the great partizan chief, and was laid off from Lee and Muscogee. Much of it was sterile pine woods, but there are sundry bodies of good land scattered through it.

It had in it in 1830 only about 1,300 people all told, but in 1850 the population was over 11,000, of which 3,600 were slaves.

Buena Vista, which was made the county site in 1847, since the railroad reached it, has become a prosperous town.

The inhabitants in the county are a plain, good people, and there are churches and schools in all parts of the county.

As in all the pine woods counties, there has been a decided advance in all material interests since the war and since the introduction of fertilizers; but as the county has been reduced in size by its giving of territory to contiguous counties newly formed, there has been no increase in its population, which in 1890 was only 7,000.

MUSCOGEE.

The present county of Muscogee is not a large nor is it agriculturally a rich county. It derives its importance from being the county in which the city of Columbus, with its valuable manufacturing interests, is located.

As we shall speak of the city in another chapter, we have little to say of the county now. It is largely of pine woods and the pine lands are thin and generally sterile. There are sundry creeks in the county and there are some good bottom lands upon them, but the country around the city is not generally fertile.

The Chattahoochee in Muscogee flows over great beds of rock and forms an immense shoal and gives an almost unlimited water-power. South of the shoals the river is navigable to the Gulf, and along it are some fine productive bottoms.

The county was not thickly settled, the attention of the people being turned almost entirely to the city, and the proximity to the Indians across the river making it somewhat perilous to live isolated. After the city grew and the Indians were removed the planters chose the rich lands of Alabama. There is but little outside of Columbus and its vicinity of interest in Muscogee as it at present stands.

CHAPTER IX.

1829 TO 1837.

Governor Gilmer—Gold Discovery in Habersham—The Rush of Intruders—Troubles of the Governor with them and with the Indians—Extension of Georgia Laws over the Cherokee Nation—Recusant Missionaries Arrested and Convicted—Their Imprisonment in the State Prison—Governor Lumpkin—Governor Schley—Flush Times—Banking Mania—Wild Speculation—List of Enterprises—Manual Labor Schools—Mercer University—Emory College—Oglethorpe University—Wesleyan Female College—Mission Work among the Cherokees—Final Removal of the Cherokees—New Counties Laid Out—The Mountains and the Mountaineers—The Settlers in the Hill Country—State Benevolences—Asylum for Deaf and Dumb—Asylum for Lunatics—First Public Move towards Securing a History of Georgia—The First Geological Survey—Dr. Cotting—The Gold-seekers—Salting Mines—The Blue Limestone Country—Political Strife—Newspapers—Education—Religion—The Great Railroad Movement.

Authorities as in last period, with Prince's Digest, files of newspapers, Gilmer's Georgians.

George R. Gilmer, who was elected governor, has already been sketched in my account of Oglethorpe county. He was born in Georgia, but in a settlement of Virginians. He married a Virginian and spent much time in that State. He was nominally a Georgian, but really a Virginian in all his sympathies. He had been an adherent of Mr. Crawford, but was somewhat of a free-lance in politics, and was brought out by the Clarke party, who had been defeated by Troup and Forsyth. He was opposed by Joel Crawford, but elected over him.

He came to his office in a troublous time, for it was during the gold mania. In a garden in the Nacoochee valley the spade of a workman had turned up a nugget of gold, and there was a discovery of rich deposits of the precious metal in other parts of Habersham county, and the discovery had brought into the up-country a vast horde of gold-seekers. The Indian country, in which white men were not allowed permanent residence, was in this section of country, and the gold-seekers poured into it. The governor issued a proclamation commanding the intruders to depart; but "these paper bullets," he says, "had little influence over a people who could not read."

The gold-hunters dug the gravel from the bottom of the streamlets and the banks and valleys near by, rocked their long-toms in the daytime, gathered their nuggets, and spent the nights in drinking, gaming and fighting.

In addition to the annoyance the governor had from the intruders, he had more serious trouble from the Cherokees themselves. They were a somewhat weak tribe, who had shared with the Creeks the possession of Georgia. They had been so often defeated by the "Long Knives," as they called the Virginians, the Georgians and the South Carolinians, that there had been no open war for a long time, and they had lived quietly in their beautiful valleys.

The Moravian, the Presbyterian, the Congregationalist, the Methodist and the Baptist missionaries were at work among them, and with good success. Many of the Scotch traders lived in the nation during the last century, had married Indian wives and their children were now in control of the tribe.

The United States government, after having agreed with Georgia to extinguish the Indian title, had granted a title in fee to many of these Indians, and a reservation had been secured to them; and one of their chiefs, John Ridge, acting under the instructions of another chief, John Ross, in the dead of winter, after having warned off some white intruders and after their refusing to leave, had burned the cabins of the intruders and drove their families from the nation.

The indignation among the whites was very great, and

it was all the governor could do to restrain the angry frontiersmen from taking summary vengeance and precipitating a bloody conflict. In vain had the appeal been made to the president to carry out the agreement with the State to extinguish the Indian title. So the Legislature was called together, the laws of the State were extended over the territory, and all the white men who were in the nation were required to take the oath of allegiance to the State government. An Indian having committed a murder, was tried for the crime in Hall superior court, which had jurisdiction over the entire nation, and he was convicted, and, despite the interference of the Supreme Court of the United States, he was duly hung. There were a number of white missionaries from the North who refused to vacate their places or take the oath; and they were arrested and tried on the charge of contemning Georgia laws, and they all purged themselves of contempt and were discharged but Messrs. Worcester and Butler, who refused positively to do so. They were arrested and were treated very brutally by General Nelson, who was the officer in charge of the militia forces, for which, much to his indignation, he was called to account by the governor. These missionaries were brought before the civil court and tried for contumacy. They were ably defended, but being unwilling to make any concessions, were finally sentenced to confinement in the State prison. They were offered a free pardon on condition that they would comply with the law or leave the nation. They refused to do either, and went submissively to the State prison. Their punishment was more nominal than real, and after a short time in prison they gained their consent to make the submission demanded, and were released.

The governor was roundly abused for the persecution of these good men, but it is evident that the missionaries were unwilling to do anything to relieve the situation and that he reluctantly consented to allow the law to take its course;

and it is evident there was no disposition on the part of any of the civil authorities to throw any impediment in the way of proper missionary work. The two imprisoned missionaries were doubtless honest in the course they took of rebellion against the State, although they took a course which none of the other missionaries felt called upon to take. The rabble who had gone into the territory to dig gold was removed out of the nation by the Federal troops, and steps were taken by the president to secure the removal of the Indians from Georgia. This was not finally accomplished until Governor Gilmer's second term, which began in 1837.

The course of the governor in not at least winking at the course of the intruders made him so obnoxious to many that he was defeated when he offered for reelection in 1831, and Governor Wilson Lumpkin took the vacated place. Governor Lumpkin was a Virginian by birth, who had spent his youth in the clerk's office in Lexington, where his father was clerk. He entered early into public life, was a member of the Legislature and filled important county offices; and now, as candidate of the Crawford party, defeated Governor Gilmer.

While he was governor the Cherokee lands were surveyed and laid off and distributed by lottery, although the Indians were still in the territory. The lots were of forty and sixty acres, the small lots being in the gold region.

Governor Lumpkin finished his term, and was succeeded by Governor Schley. Governor Schley was a Marylander. He came to Georgia when a boy. He studied law and became a leading lawyer in Augusta. He was then a member of Congress and a judge of the superior court, and was elected governor in 1835.

While he was governor the Seminoles in Florida, who were kinspeople of the Creeks, rose against the whites; and the Creeks in Alabama having heard of this insurrection, resolved to make one more effort to recover their Georgia lands. They invaded Georgia in May and June of 1836. The settlers fled, and Governor Schley ordered out the militia and took the field in person. The Indians burned the little village of Roanoke in Stewart county and killed twelve persons. They burned a steamboat which was at anchor at the village and attacked another which was ascending the river and succeeded in capturing it. They had a sharp fight with a small body of whites on Sheppard's plantation. They then took position in a dense swamp, from which they were finally routed. Another band of Indians making an effort to reach the hostiles in Florida were attacked by the whites and defeated, and the disheartened tribe at last made a full surrender and consented to remove in a body to Arkansas, and the last Creek left Georgia. There was no further disturbance with the Indians in the State, and the wild Seminoles were driven into the Everglades of Florida and from thence removed to the west.

The Cherokees, as we have seen, were somewhat tardily accepting the situation and were peaceable, and then the wise, far-seeing governor gave himself to the work of advancing the general interests of the State. He was a man of great sagacity and broad views, and recommended in his message to the Legislature the building of the Western and Atlantic railroad, a geological survey, and what was sadly needed, an asylum for the insane. He was a man of affairs, and when his time was out as governor and Governor Gilmer was elected in his place, he retired from public life and became a manufacturer.

Governor Gilmer was elected governor the second time in 1837. The first part of the period now under survey was a time of great inflation. New plantations were being opened in all sections of the State. Villages and towns were springing up like magic. Macon and Columbus, which were not ten years old when this period ended, and which were but founded when it began, were now considerable cities.

The banking interest had taken a new impetus and rose, according to Governor Gilmer, to a mania. The State, which had a large block of stock in the Planters Bank, the Bank of Darien and the State Bank, now chartered a new bank, called the Central Bank of Georgia. The capital stock was to be the balance in the State treasury, the State's shares in the Bank of Augusta, in the Planters Bank, the Bank of Darien and the Bank of the State of Georgia. The purpose in establishing this bank was to make money easy for the planters, and the ease with which discounts were secured was in inverse ratio to the ease with which collections of the notes were made.

Four banks were established in Columbus, five in Macon, one in Milledgeville, one in Brunswick, one in Rome, one each in Hawkinsville, Irwinton, Florence and other small towns.

The notes of these various specie-paying banks were legal tender, and they were all specie-paying when there was no extensive call for redemption. Notes were issued freely and paper discounted readily, and there was a wild era of speculation. The rich lands in the newly opened western counties in Georgia and in the Cherokee country were bought and sold in many markets.

The Georgia land speculator crossed the Chattahoochee river and bought land in Alabama. Land-trading was universal. Lawyers, preachers, doctors, merchants and bankers were all buying plots, grants and soldiers' warrants and selling them at an advance. Money was easy, and when the trader had no money of his own he went to a bank and secured a loan.

Negroes came in droves from Virginia and Maryland, and were bought on nine months' time, and large fortunes were apparently possessed by men who were in debt for everything they held.

The growth of the cities made speculation in town lots a prominent feature of the times, and many men trading in town lots became rich by repute in a few weeks. There was what is called in modern language a "boom" in real estate in town and country.

The growth of cotton in the western counties made the question of transportation one of prime importance, and schemes of various kinds were entered upon to provide for the carrying of produce to the seaports. Railways were now attracting attention and charters were granted to quite a number. The Central Railroad and Canal Company was to connect Macon and Savannah, and the Georgia Railroad and Turnpike Company to connect Augusta with Eatonton, with branches to Madison and Athens. The Monroe railroad was to run from Macon to Forsyth, the Western Turnpike Company from Rome to Chattanooga, and Thomas Spalding was given a charter to dig a canal and build a railway from Brunswick to Albany. It was to be a railway of wood, or a canal. Mr. T. Butler King and his associates were to construct the great Western road from Brunswick to Macon, and thence to Tennessee. A road was to be built from Brunswick to Florida, and a railroad from Macon to Columbus and Lagrange. Steamboat lines were to run from Augusta to Savannah, and from Macon to Darien; the Western and Atlantic railroad from some point near Rossville, on the Tennessee line, to some point in middle Georgia, either Athens, Madison, Milledgeville, Forsyth or Columbus. This was to be built by the State. A railroad was also chartered from Madison to the Chattahoochee, and from St. Marys to Columbus.

These were some of the railway and steamboat lines chartered, and then there were sundry other corporations and joint stock companies. Among them the Macon Insurance Company, the Flat Shoals (Dekalb) Cotton Mill, the Augusta Mining Company, the woolen and cotton mill in Augusta, a woolen and cotton mill in Upson, the Franklin factory in Upson, the Camak factory in Clarke, the Richmond factory in Richmond, the Scull Shoals Company in Greene county, the Pigeon Roost Mining Company in Lumpkin, the Auraria and Blue Ridge turnpike, the Eatonton Manufacturing Company, the Georgia Mining Company, the Flat Shoals Manufacturing Company in Harris county, the Oglethorpe Insurance Company in Macon.

This long list of companies shows the character of the times. Stock companies of all kind sprang up in every direction. This state of things continued until the sudden burst of the panic of 1837, when the whole country was swept by a cyclone of disaster from which there was no recovery for near ten years.

In these flush times there was a new impetus given to the cause of education. The people in Georgia were mostly planters and farmers and had made their property by hard work, and the one sin in their eyes was laziness. The rapid increase of wealth and the multiplication of slaves had led the planters to fear that their sons might grow up in indolence and become worthless. The scheme of manual labor schools, some of which were established in the North, struck them favorably, and led to the establishment of several in Georgia. Of these more is said in a succeeding chapter. From these schools the advance was made to the chartering of new colleges. The Mercer University among the Baptists, Emory among the Methodists, and Oglethorpe among the Presbyterians were all chartered and established. The Macon people of all denominations secured a charter for the Georgia Female College, and the Baptists in Washington one for a Baptist female college, which, however, was never founded.

The last of the Indians were removed from Georgia

during this period. The Creeks and other tribes had gone years before, and now the Cherokees (in 1837) were removed. They were a weaker but more civilized tribe than the Creeks, and, as we have seen elsewhere, had a number of villages in upper Georgia. They had large towns in Murray, Polk and Gordon, and had schools and churches; and when an effort was made to remove them they stubbornly resisted it. The sympathies of the Northern people, who had freed themselves from the presence of the Indians, were now with the Cherokees. The Georgians wanted the land the Indians held, and claimed it by virtue of the same title with which the New England and all the older States held their Indian land. The United States had agreed to extinguish the Indian title nearly forty years before this period, and had provided a better country for the Indians in the West and offered them free transportation to it, a year's supply of provisions and full pay for their belongings in Georgia; but the Cherokees were not willing to go. They appealed to the supreme court of the United States, and gave Wm. Wirt a fee of $20,000 to defend their right to their old homes. The State had, as we have seen elsewhere, extended her laws over that part of the nation which was in her boundary and had forced all the white people in the Indian country to take the oath of allegiance to Georgia or to remove, and had punished those who had refused to do so. It had surveyed the country and granted to its citizens land of the Indian nation; but still the Indians lived in their old homes. Governor Gilmer, who was a political foe of President Van Buren, found that Ross, the Indian chief, still pressed the case of the Cherokees before the supreme court of the United States. The president still delayed action, and apparently purposed to give the Indians two years longer in which to decide whether they would remove or not. So Governor Gilmer took matters in his own hands and ordered General Chas. Floyd to march with his militia to the nation.* General Scott was in charge of the United States troops in the nation, and was now ordered to gather the Indians into forts. Still the poor Cherokees thought they would be permitted to return to their cabins again; but they soon found the decree was irrevocable, and that they must go to a new land and one to them unknown. It was a pitiful scene. The land they were to leave was theirs and had been the land of their fathers. For it they had fought against the Creeks and the Long Knives; they had not sold it, nor had it been wrested from them in war, nor had they given it away; but by a law which they could not understand they were compelled now to go to an unknown land far away and leave behind them all the little property they had accumulated, or to sell it at such price as the whites in authority chose to pay. Some of these homes were very humble, for most of the Indians were very poor; but the ruling chiefs, who were generally half-breeds, had large plantations and, for those days, very handsome brick residences and many slaves. The edict went forth, the poor Indians were obliged to submit, and the Cherokees left Georgia forever in 1837.

Five years before this the land had been surveyed, divided into lots and distributed by lottery. This new territory was divided into the counties of Cherokee, Cass, Cobb, Forsyth, Gilmer, Lumpkin, Murray, Paulding, Walker and Floyd. These counties divided themselves into groups: there were the gold-producing counties, the hill counties of the freestone group, and the blue limestone counties. In the mountain gold-producing group were Lumpkin, Union and Gilmer; in the hill country were Cobb, Forsyth and Cherokee, while the blue limestone counties were Cass, Paulding, Floyd, Walker and Murray. Each of these groups had its distinctive features. In Lumpkin and the adjoining coun-

* These facts are largely presented in Governor Gilmer's "Georgians," in his autobiography.

ties there was gold, but only in Lumpkin did mining have prominent place.

The lottery which divided the land was drawn in 1832. It was a time of absorbing interest. The discoveries of gold in the nation had been just sufficient to arouse the highest hopes of richer discoveries, and men expected to find mines of untold wealth on the newly granted lands. There was one lot which the intruders had found very rich. It was known as lot No. 42, and it was supposed that it would give its owner a princely fortune. When the drawing came off men waited eagerly to hear who would draw it. The speculators were on hand, prepared to hurry to the lucky drawer and buy it from him. When the fortunate drawer was known one man, by the aid of a relay of horses, reached the owner and for a fabulous sum succeeded in buying it. When he went to the mine and began work he found its *treasures all gone.* There were many such cases. Men sold their estates in Middle Georgia, bought gold lots and attempted gold-mining, and in many cases lost all they had invested. There was little besides the mines to lead men to settle in the mountains of northeast Georgia. The valleys were narrow, the hills were not naturally fertile, and when cleared of timber soon washed away, and the mountains were too rugged and barren for profitable culture. But the scenery was charming and the healthfulness of the country perfect; the products were such as were necessary for family use, and so to the hard-working man there was a chance for a livelihood.

We have already in a previous chapter given an account of the first mountaineers; and while the lapse of twenty years had made many changes, and the class of people who had come into this section were superior to the first settlers, there was much that was very rude. The people had no money crop and so money was scarce. The winters came early and went late. Roads were few and poor and the people necessarily scattered. Those who were fond of ease did not find it in the rugged land, and there was little to attract the man of means. So settlements were slowly made. There was no considerable change from the mountains of twenty years before, except that there was less game and a less luxuriant pasturage. There were some valleys which were so fertile that they drew substantial farmers from North Carolina, but in the main the people were still poor and illiterate. The settlers were mainly from the mountains of North and South Carolina, and the country was settled slowly. The gold mania, however, had made the mountain country known, and many who came to dig gold bought little farms and built cabins and raised large families of sturdy children.

The hill country of Cobb, Forsyth and Cherokee has been already described in telling of the foot-hills of the Blue Ridge in the eastern part of the State. Indeed, these hill lands of Cherokee and Cobb and Forsyth were largely peopled by those who came to them from Franklin, Jackson, Hall and Madison—eastern counties of the same kind. Gold was looked for in all these Cherokee counties, and so the lots were only forty acres in size. When gold was not found and there was no indication of it the lands were very cheap; from $10 to $20 was the price of a single lot, and many a man bought a small farm for the price of an Indian pony. The cheapness of the lands led to rapid and thick settlement. The country was soon filled up with enterprising young people, and numbers who became substantial farmers on large farms began life in one of these Cherokee counties on forty acres of poor land.

While the homes of the planters in eastern and middle Georgia were elegant and well furnished, there was much of upper and lower Georgia in which there was the same simplicity of life which had belonged to the settlers in eastern

Georgia a hundred years before. The people in all this hill country were a sturdy, brave and self-reliant people.

Their literary culture was very limited. It is likely that, outside of the mines and the country towns, there were in none of these new counties a half-dozen classical scholars, and but a small number had had any training in English, many could not write and some could not read.

For some years there was not an academy in any of these counties where the classics were taught. There was not a piano in them outside a few in the villages. There were few negroes and little wealth, but there was no pauperism. The men plowed, and the women did the household work and often helped in the field. The people had never known luxury and were independent of it.

The country was not an easy one to subdue. The land was stony and often sterile, but the water was cool, the air bracing, and, though the land was not rich, it produced enough to give a comfortable support. A worthier people never lived.

While the class who had settled this new country were, as a general thing, men of little property and of little culture, and while there were many of them rude and disposed to wild revelry, there were many of a different class. They lived in cabins, but their cabins were clean and neat. They were pious and industrious, and the camp-ground and the log schoolhouse and the log church were sure to be near their homes. The Baptists had churches, often cabins of logs, in every nook, and the Methodist circuit-rider reached every settlement. The most gifted men of the Methodist Church were presiding elders in this section. There were scattered through these counties, chiefly in the country villages, some highly educated Presbyterian ministers, men of cultivation, who were preaching or teaching.

There was much intemperance still in the country, but during this period the great total abstinence movement was being pressed. Men like James O. Andrew, Adiel Sherwood and Jos. C. Stiles were ardent friends and workers for total abstinence; and Josiah Flournoy, one of the wealthiest men in Georgia, was canvassing Georgia for signatures to a petition against allowing liquors to be retailed. He was bitterly opposed and his life was threatened, his gig was smeared, his horses' tails were shaved, and every annoyance that could be heaped on the good man he was called on to encounter, but he kept bravely on. He had many backers, but the politicians were against him and his advance movement was defeated.

There was now every variety of life to be found in Georgia. The uneducated, uncouth farmer from the mountains was in the Legislature side by side with the aristocratic sea island planter and the cultivated, college-bred lawyer from the city; or the educated, wealthy planter from Wilkes or Hancock—men like Colquitt and McDonald and Stephens and Toombs—were the political friends of men who lived in log cabins and could barely read and were unable to write their names, but who could carry their counties in any election.

While some parts of Georgia had been settled a hundred years, this new country had just been opened, and there was found in it all the features of frontier life. There were but few slaves and few comforts as yet in it. The log cabin with one room was still the home of the settler. Governor Gilmer, after he left his place in Congress and before he was elected governor, in 1837 made a tour from his home in middle Georgia to Montgomery, Ala., and back in his private carriage. In returning he says: "We arrived a little before night at the home of a man in Carroll county who had sixteen children. The family lived in one room without a loft. There were three beds in the room, and I and my wife occupied one. The next morning when I wanted a towel for my wife, the hospitable hostess took a a shirt of one of the boys and tore off a part of it and gave it to me for my wife to wipe her face and hands on." The aristocratic Virginia lady was asleep when this provision for her comfort was made, and was in blissful ignorance of whence the rag came which she used as a towel. The next night, he says, they spent in a house located in a potato patch and for supper ate "'sobbed' Irish potatoes and coffee with one grain to the gallon, without milk or sugar." These frontier hardships were found only in the newly settled counties, where houses were few and far between.

In the mines there was a shameless disregard of all moral requirements. Men were a law unto themselves, and even in so old a county as Murray the courts were often broken up by a lawless mob.

At the great gatherings on court days and muster days there were in nearly all the county towns scenes of wild revelry. In all these there was a grog-shop and a country fiddler, and the drinking crowd had a shake-down dance, a fight or a horse-race, and sometimes all of them.

"In Cobb," White says, "Judge Warner, being greatly annoyed by a drunken man, as there was no jail, ordered the sheriff to put the head of the culprit between the fence-rails of a horse-lot near the cabin in which the court was held. The sheriff did not return to the court-room, and when sent for was found sitting on the fence to keep his prisoner from escaping." Another judge, who had no jail but an old stable, was annoyed by a drunken man who boasted loudly that he was a "hoss." "Mr. Sheriff," said the judge, "put that horse in the stable."

The curse of the land was the cross-roads groggery, which was found in every neighborhood.

The old field school, which had ceased to exist in the older parts of the State, had been transferred to the newer counties in the north and west of the State; and schools were found only in a few places and for a few month in the year.

The roads were still execrable in winter time in all Georgia, and the heavy stage and great wagon in the cotton region made their way over rough causeways and plowed through oceans of mud.

During this period the State made its first benevolent movement by making an appropriation for the relief of the deaf and dumb and for lunatics.

John Jacobus Flournoy,* a wealthy man, was deaf and dumb, and his sympathy for those who were suffering like himself led him to his active work to secure some help for them. The legislature made a liberal appropriation for their education, and they were sent to New Haven, Conn., until an asylum for their relief was established at Cave Spring.

A Mr. Bevan, who unhappily died before he began his work, received an appropriation of four hundred and fifty dollars to enable him to collect materials for a history of Georgia, in which there was to be an account of (1) the original settlement, (2) trade, manufactures and natural history, (3) peculiar settlements, (4) academies, (5) various religious sects, and (6) manners and customs.

An effort was made to provide a State library, but the bill failed.

By Governor Schley's suggestion ten thousand dollars were appropriated to a geological survey, and Dr. Cotting, to whom White is so largely indebted for his mineralogical and geological information, made a careful survey of the various counties in the State, and gave the first full account of its large mineral resources.

There was great excitement in gold-mining. Now and then a rich pocket would be opened, and thousands of pennyweights would be taken in a few days; and then it would

* See sketch Jackson county.

be emptied, and all that had been made would be lost in a vain search for another. There were, of course, great frauds perpetrated on the inexperienced prospector. Mines were salted and sold; brass filings, and even gold dust itself, was used to mislead. The most innocent looking rustic was wise in the art of deceiving the unwary. A prospector heard of a discovery of gold in an obscure part of one of the counties. He and his associates rode out to see about it. They met the rough farmer who was the owner of the reputed mine on his way to mill. He said he did not know much about it; but "thar mout be gold in the branch bottom; he had seed what they told him was signs. He was obleedged to go to mill; but they would find his leetle boy at the cabin, and he would show 'em whar to dig." They went to the cabin, and the little tow-headed boy led them to the branch bottom. They began to wash the dirt, and sure enough they found some grains of gold. They were delighted at the prospect, when the little fellow said: "You uns had better dig over thar. Dad put most of it in that ar place." That mine was not sold to those prospectors.

The mines were scattered all through the country—in Gilmer, in Union, in Lumpkin, in Habersham, in Hall, in Cherokee, in Pickens, in Cobb, in what is now White, and Towns and Rabun. No one could tell where the rich find might be; so the prospectors were scattered over the hills and in the valleys in every direction. There was but little produced in the way of food crops, and the wagons from Tennessee and North Carolina came laden with supplies for the miners.

There was not always failure in mining. The first mine was found in the garden of a local Methodist preacher near Nacoochee, the Rev. Mr. Richardson. It was very rich, and the owner reaped a large return from it. When Dr. Mitchell, the agent of Emory College, visited him, to ask a subscription to the college, he gave him an astonishingly large one. The agent proposed to take his note for the amount. "No," said the old miner; "I had as well pay it now." And he counted out the amount in gold eagles.

An Englishman by the name of Hockenhull had been digging gold with some success in the mines. His Yorkshire sweetheart had crossed the sea to meet her lover and had joined him in the mountains of Georgia, where they were wedded. The thrifty little Englishman and his fair bride prospered, and they had laid by a snug sum when he ventured to open a new mine. The shaft was sunk at large expense and weary days went by, but the gold was not found. At last the savings were all gone and the miner was out of heart.

"Mary dear," he said, "we are ruined. I have spent every dollar we had and we have not a color yet."

"Be of good heart, Johnny dear," she said, "dig on a little while longer and by God's blessing you'll come out."

And so he did. She said:

"The very next day he struck it 'rich,' and that mine made his fortune."

The placer miners were a wild race.

"Oh yez! oh yez!" one said, "Brother Jackson will preach at Bill Jones's shack to-night at early candle-light."

"Oh yez! oh yez!" said another voice, "I will run my faro bank to-night, beginning at early candle-light."

There was but little to attract men to the farms when the land was so poor and the prospect for a fortune in mining was so bright, and so most of the people were gold-diggers. There was much gold dug, but it was a question whether each gold nugget had not cost more than it was worth.

This Cherokee country now opened to the whites embraced in its boundary the only body of blue limestone land in the State. In the area in which is now Murray, Whitfield, Walker, Dade, Chattooga, Gordon, Cass (now

Bartow), Floyd and Polk counties, there was a magnificent body of limestone land along the banks of the Coosawattee, the Oostanaula, the Connesauga, the Etowah rivers, the Euharlee and Cedar creeks, and there were some beautiful valleys in which the Cherokees had their town. These lands had been cultivated by them in corn almost exclusively. When the whites occupied them their great value as wheat and cotton lands was recognized. Some of the improvements which the Indians had made on them were of a superior kind, and when the country was opened to white settlers they found fields already cleared and houses already built, and these were bought by men of means, and large plantations were at once secured. The country was a magnificent wheat and corn country, and this part of the State soon became the granary of Georgia.

It was not long after the opening of this country and the removal of the Indians before the Western and Atlantic railroad began to make its way towards Ross Landing on the Tennessee river.

The prospect of rapid transit to the Atlantic and the fact that there was a certainty that steamers would be put on the Coosa at Rome, opening up a fine country in Alabama, led enterprising men to make large ventures in this section.

During the days before 1840 there was a steady influx of wealthy settlers from middle Georgia and from South Carolina, and this section became populated at a very early date with a body of most enterprising and thrifty people. Its rich mineral resources had been even then discovered, but were not developed. No part of the State was settled more rapidly and by a worthier people.

There had been a period of great inflation in every part of America, and nowhere to a greater extent than in Georgia, but the time of liquidation had come. The banks had issued millions of notes, and had but little specie with which to redeem them. They had loaned their notes freely to planters and taken personal security for them. The State had gone largely into the banking business. The Great Central Bank of Georgia was resorted to by all who needed discounts and who were in political favor, until it had millions of notes in circulation, which were protected by the credit of the State.

When President Jackson removed the government deposits from the United States bank and placed them in the State banks the panic of 1834 followed. This panic did not affect Georgia perceptibly. The price of cotton kept up, the local banks furnished money freely, and, while in the North and West there was a time of great financial distress, in the South money was easy.

It has been the rule with all writers on this great panic of 1837 to attribute it to General Jackson's arbitrary order and to the failure to recharter the United States bank. This Mr. Benton denies, and seemingly with good reason. Mr. McCullough, however, holds to that position, but gives as a reason for it that the banks were led by the holding of United States deposits to encourage wild trading and prepare the way for disaster.

The financial crash of 1837 began in England, and caused the suspension of scores of banks and the downfall of hundreds of factories in that kingdom. The banks in the eastern American cities were forced to the wall, and as the tidal wave swept on it reached Georgia and all the banks except two suspended. Up to this time, although there had been all the commotion excited by the Jackson panic of 1834, although there had been some few failures in Macon and Columbus, there had been no distrust of the soundness of the State banks generally; but now they nearly all suspended. Cotton had been very high, running in 1836 as high as 17 cents a pound. Money was easy. Speculation was wild. The banks were engaged in a bitter war with each other, and there was not the slightest indication of the coming storm; but it burst suddenly and swept England, desolated the cities of North America, and for ten years raged with fury in Georgia.

The character of the calamity it brought and a fuller history of it will be given in the next chapter.

At no time, perhaps, in Georgia history was there a fiercer political strife than at this time. The long and bitter war between the Clarke and Crawford parties, which only ended in the death of W. H. Crawford and the retirement of John Clarke from Georgia, had been almost entirely personal. There was no political principle involved, and it was merely a strife between leaders. The tariff question of 1828 found all parties in full agreement, all opposed to protection; but when the nullification measure in South Carolina was proposed parties became fiercely antagonistic and were divided by plain lines. The Troup party was an anti-Jackson nullification party in the main. The Clarke party was generally for Jackson and the Union. The celebrations of the fourth of July were still observed, and a great dinner or barbecue always attended them. The political banqueters found these occasions a good time to toast the nullifiers or roast Andrew Jackson or Martin Van Buren, or *vice versa*. As is well known, the compromise measure of Mr. Clay averted a strife which at one time seemed inevitable. The blue cockade had been worn by defiant nullifiers, and the Jackson men cried "Treason!" vociferously. The scales were evenly balanced in Georgia.

The congressional delegation was about evenly divided. Mr. Berrien and Mr. Forsyth were pronounced Jackson men; Governor Gilmer was opposed to nullification but not an adherent of Jackson.

It was during this time that young Robert Toombs, hearty, genial, fearless and gifted, first made his power as a young orator felt, and "Little Aleck," as Mr. Stephens was called, first caught the admiring ear of the Georgia people. They were anti-Jackson, States' rights men. Out of these two parties, known as States' rights men and Union men, sprang, during the next decade, the Whigs and Democrats.

The newspapers had now increased in number and influence, and they were intensely partizan. There were now leading papers in Savannah, Augusta, Milledgeville, Macon and Columbus. The list, as given by the Macon *Telegraph*, in 1832 was:

The *Athenian*, Athens; the *Chronicle*, the *Constitutionalist*, the *Courier*, Augusta; the *Enquirer*, Columbus; the *Georgia Messenger*, the *Advertiser*, Macon; the *Recorder*, the *Journal*, Milledgeville; the *Advertiser*, Mt. Zion; the *Republican*, the *Georgian*, Savannah; the *Cabinet*, the *News*, the *Christian Index*, Washington; the *Christian Repertory*, Macon; the *Miners' Journal*, Dahlonega; and papers in Cassville, Covington, Darien, Brunswick and Bainbridge.

The *Georgian* and *Republican*, Savannah, and the *Chronicle* and *Constitutionalist*, Augusta, were the dailies.

The strict construction views of the majority of Georgians had made any movement toward establishing a common school system of education abortive. There had been, however, some provision to advance the cause of education. There had been appropriated $500,000 to poor schools and academies, the interest of the sum to be equally divided between them. No academy could get a share of the fund unless it was chartered, and this led to their being very numerous. They had the names of academies and a large board of trustees and a charter, but had few other features of a school of high grade. In 1834 there were forty-seven counties in which there were academies, in some several. The number increased annually until there were few counties in which there was not at least one. In many of these only the English branches were taught, and but few of them had a hundred pupils. The amount granted to them was divided according to the number of pupils. The poor school fund was very small, and was carefully dispensed.

An application was made to the comptroller setting forth the number of children who attended school and the teachers were paid five cents a day for each pupil. Often the teachers did not render any account, and in 1834 there were forty-two counties who received nothing from the fund. Schools were established mainly by private effort, and in every neighborhood where there were well-to-do people there was a good grammar-school or an academy. In several of the counties there were female academies. There was no general system of education and there was much illiteracy in the State, and $2,000 was appropriated by the Legislature to pay the cost of a commission, who should look closely into the common school system of New England and see if it might not wisely be introduced into Georgia.

The plan of manual labor schools came before the Legislature and received its indorsement.

While the State did something for academies and poor schools, it did nothing for the university, which depended on its tuition fees and the rental of the lands which had been given long before.

The religious history of this period has no such story of great advance as had that of the decade which preceded it. There was too much political strife and too much eagerness after money to favor religious movements, but the great revival of the last years of the twenties had left its effect upon all the churches. The Baptists and Methodists had mainly profited by the great awakening, though the Presbyterians had shared with them in the ingathering. The Georgia Conference of the Methodists had now been cut off from the South Carolina and was making an earnest and to some degree successful effort to send the gospel to all parts of Georgia and Florida. The war in Florida with the Seminoles had to some degree disturbed things in the newer counties in southern Georgia; but in the up-country among the Indians there had been a good work done and circuits already laid, and so when the Indians were removed the itinerant preachers were on the ground. The circuits were very large, but the preachers preached nearly every day, and the people attended a week-day service almost as well as they attended one on the Sabbath. The camp-meetings were still a great influence for good, and were found in all the counties, new and old. We will get a more satisfactory account by glancing at each county in detail.

It was during this period that the great railroad system which has grown to such proportions in Georgia had its beginning. Railway building was in its infancy in the United States, but a line of road had been built out from Charleston reaching towards Augusta, and now, as we have seen elsewhere, plans were made to reach the interior of Georgia by railways. Many of these were chartered but never built, others chartered were never begun, but some were successfully carried through.

The first of these was the Central, which was to run from Savannah to Macon. It was chartered as the Central Railway and Canal Company, and an experimental survey was made under Colonel Cruger in 1834. There were two routes under consideration, one going through the hill country and making an air-line from Savannah to Macon; the other following the rivers and keeping near the water-courses. The last route was the one selected. The country through which the road made its way was very flat and swampy, and while heavy grading was not necessary, much bridging was demanded. There was an abundance of yellow pine along the way, and railroad building in those days demanded much timber. The iron was a flat bar which was laid on a stringer and the stringers laid on cross-ties. Railroad building was in its infancy and the construction was very difficult and slow. There were no labor-saving machines and all the excavation and fillings were made with the shovel, the hand-barrow and dumping-cart. There was no town on the entire line of two hundred miles between Savannah and Macon, and all hope of a revenue depended upon the completion of the line. A bank was chartered to furnish funds, and the bills issued by it were used to pay the expense of construction.

The panic of 1837 came, with its desolations, soon after the road was begun, and the road was just completed when the depression ended. The first president of the road was W. W. Gordon, and its first chief engineer L. O. Reynolds, Esq.

The Georgia Railroad and Turnpike Company was chartered in 1833, but the work was not begun until 1835. It was to run from Augusta to some undesignated point in middle Georgia. It had the same difficulties to encounter that had been met by its associate the Central, except that as it went westward it entered the hill country sooner and heavy grading was necessary. The laborers were imported Irishmen, and the engineer corps came from Pennsylvania. The Georgia Railroad Bank was chartered to give help to the construction, and in ten years from the time the work was begun in Augusta the road reached the village of Marthasville, in Dekalb county, where is now the city of Atlanta.

There was a decided objection on the part of the villages and towns along the line to having the road pass directly through them, and while the Georgia passed near the towns it left some of them a mile or more on one side.

Perhaps the most daring venture at this period was the enterprise entered into by the young city of Macon and the surrounding country to help it reach the west by a line of railway built largely by its own capital. It was at first designed to connect Forsyth in Monroe county with Macon and give the cotton-planters an easier way of conveying their cotton to market. It, too, was to be built by a bank, and an elegant building, now occupied by the city authorities in Macon, was erected for a banking building and railroad offices. The heaviest work on the line was at the beginning of the work near Macon in cutting through the river hills; but the undaunted president, Mr. Griffin, despite the heavy outlay, did the work and declared a dividend of ten per cent. as soon as the first few miles were completed. The road had great difficulties to overcome, and, as we will see in the next chapter, the bank upon whose support it rested was forced at last to suspend for an indefinite time. Then the bank failed, and the road was sold and completed to Atlanta under another name. The banking house was sold, and after having been a medical college and a warehouse, it became at last a city hall. When the road became involved the directors worked hard to save it. They issued bank notes of all denominations and even change bills as low as 6¼ cents. They made the loudest boasts of their progress, and called for new subscriptions to stock. In 1842 the road had an engine, the "Ocmulgee," and a passenger coach with three compartments capable of accommodating sixty-seven passengers. It had a line of stages at its terminus, which was Barnesville, to convey passengers northward, and in 1842 one could ride in the handsome new car forty miles for $3.15; and the total receipts for six months were for freight $6,162, and for passengers $12,451. For years the bills had been under suspicion, and were hard to circulate out of Macon; but the bank pluckily attempted to resume specie payment. It made a pathetic effort to furnish what it did not have, using all kinds of delaying artifices; but the inevitable came. The bank failed hopelessly, and the railroad had to be sold. It had reached

Griffin, and a part of the line was laid with wooden rails and the cars were drawn by mules. The brave Griffin had made a hard fight and gone down and carried his friends with him. The road was bought by a Northern company for a song and reorganized as the Macon and Western, and for years was the best railroad property in Georgia.

The Western and Atlantic railroad was to run from some undesignated point in DeKalb county to Ross Landing on the Tennessee river. It was one of the most difficult enterprises ever ventured on in Georgia. The other two great lines had some connection by water with the outside world, and could secure material for building with but little difficulty; but this road was to begin in the wilderness, over one hundred miles from the nearest point to a navigable river. There were rivers to bridge, great hills of stone to be cut through and mountains to tunnel. Every pound of iron and every working tool had to be brought from Macon. The work had no financial backing but the credit of the State, and had but begun when the financial crash of 1837 came on. But, despite all these difficulties, ten years after the first dirt was broken the cars ran from Ross Landing to Marthasville, or, as they are now known, from Atlanta to Chattanooga.

When one considers that railroad building in the United States was just begun, and that these roads were built by money furnished by stockholders and not on money borrowed on bonds, the work of building them will appear to be, as it was, a remarkable achievement. The roads were long in process of construction, and all of them were built on the same plan, with long stringers and flat bars, and all had the same small wood-burning locomotives.

I have, in order not to break abruptly the continuity of the story, anticipated the events of the next decade.

We turn now to the study of the counties.

HEARD.

Heard county was laid out in 1830 from Troup, Carroll and Coweta and named in honor of that brave patriot Stephen Heard.

The eastern part of the county was very rugged, a part of it near Coweta very red land, and a great deal of it gray land broken into many hills. There were some good plantations on the Chattahoochee river and on the creeks. The western part of the county was a great pine forest, and had in it one of the largest quarries of monumental granite in the State. There is some fine land in the county, but much of it is only moderately fertile.

It was settled in the main by men of small means and plain ways. They were of the best class of Georgia yeomanry, and in no county is there less pauperism or a better standard of morals than in the larger part of the county. There are some sections of Heard, on the hills near Alabama, as in all these western counties, where there is a great deal of illicit distilling and a rude people.

Franklin, the county site, is a small village on the river. The advantages possessed by the railroad towns have prevented its becoming a place of importance. Corinth and Houston are two small villages in other parts of the county.

STEWART.

In 1830 the county of Stewart was formed from Randolph, and was named Stewart in honor of General Daniel Stewart.

Its topographical features are very much like those of the county from which it was taken and which have been described. In one part of it the pine woods give way to lofty oak-clad hills of rich red soil, but land easily washed away. Along the river there are fine cotton lands on which at one time there were large plantations.

The county was rapidly peopled, and was a populous

county soon after its settlement, but was for a long time dependent upon the boats and the wagon-trains alone for communication with the outside world.

It was in Stewart, at a village called Roanoke, that the Creek Indians made their last serious attack on a white settlement in Georgia. The little village was on the Chattahoochee river, and the attack was made in 1836 by, as was supposed, three hundred Indians. There were few people then in the fort; but of the number twenty were killed and wounded. There was another more serious battle with this same body of Indians at Dr. Shephard's plantation a short time after this in which the Indians were defeated and twelve white men killed and as many wounded.

Lumpkin, the county site, has long been famous for its refinement and morality.

Two railroads have been built through Stewart in the last few years, and the county has taken on new life and promising little towns have sprung up along the lines.

Stewart had in it bodies of fertile land suitable for large cotton plantations, and these sections were appropriated by the wealthy slaveholders, and were owned in many cases by absentee landlords, who only occasionally visited their plantations. But much of the land was admirably suited for homes, and many of the neighborhoods were the abode of farmers who lived on their plantations and built up a good community.

SUMTER.

Sumter county was laid out in 1831 from Lee, and was named in honor of General Thomas Sumter, "the Game Cock of Carolina," as he was called. Its county site was called Americus. The physical features belonging to all this section of Georgia, and of which we have written, were those of Sumter. The rich cotton lands which were found in the hummocks along the creeks and rivers early drew the attention of the planters of Bibb, Jones, Jasper and Monroe, and large plantations were opened by them. There was a large section of the country which was a pine forest and was for a long time a cattle-range, but which is now an excellent planting section.

The county has been almost latticed with railways, and Americus has become quite a railroad center.

The county has been noted for the high character of the people, who were mainly immigrants from the older counties. There were some large plantations owned by up-country people, but the larger number of the planters lived on their plantations or in the city of Americus.

Americus, the chief town in Sumter, is a beautiful little city, in which there has been much enterprise and public spirit. It built the Americus Female College before the war, and was noted for its handsome churches and intelligent congregations at that period. It was, before the war, the center of much wealth, and after it was over it took on a new life. Aiming to get into closer connection with Savannah, it enterprized and, largely by its own capital and almost entirely by its own energy, built the S. A. M. road, first to Savannah on the east and then to Montgomery, Ala., on the west. It has established factories for the manufacture of fertilizers and ice, sash, blinds, etc., and has an elegant hotel, a fine system of public schools, sprightly newspapers, and is otherwise a stirring, prosperous city.

It was in this county, on a high pine hill, that the old prison camp of Andersonville was located, and there is at Andersonville a national cemetery under care of the United States government.

The Methodists, Baptists, Presbyterians and Episcopalians have all churches in Americus and through Sumter county, and there are good schools and good churches in every neighborhood.

COBB.

The county of Cobb, which was named in honor of Judge Thomas W. Cobb, was laid out from the Cherokee purchase in 1832. It was the most southerly of the counties of the purchase. As gold had been found in the county the lots granted comprised only forty acres, and as they were quite cheap in price, Cobb was soon thickly settled by a very excellent though, in the main, a poor people. There were but few slaves, and they were almost entirely confined to the plantations along the river and larger creeks, or were household servants in Marietta. The immigrants to the rural districts came from the older counties of northeast Georgia and from upper South Carolina. They were an industrious and hardy race of small farmers. The town of Marietta derived importance from being the terminus for a long time of the newly projected Western and Atlantic railroad, and its charming climate soon drew to it quite a number of settlers of refinement and wealth from the low-country.

The people had small farms which were not very fertile, and they were forced to live very economically. For years they raised only family supplies, spun and wove their own clothing, and handled but little money. Toward Powder Springs, on the Chattahoochee river and Sweetwater creek, there were some cotton plantations, but the number of negroes in the county was not one fifth of the population.

Mr. Roswell King from Darien, when cotton manufacturing began on a large scale in Georgia, established the Roswell cotton-mills, and founded a charming village around them, which is now known as Roswell. This factory was well managed from its foundation, and has been one of the most profitable mills in the State. It is still in active operation. For years it was remote from the railroad, but on the building of the Southern a branch road was built to it.

The Western and Atlantic railroad goes through the center of Cobb, one branch of the Southern through its western side and another through its eastern, and the North Georgia Railroad goes from Marietta northward to Knoxville, Tenn., and thus all parts of the county have railway advantages.

Marietta, charmingly located at the base of the Kennesaw mountain, has an unrivaled climate and a considerable population of the best people. It commands a good trade from the county and from those which adjoin.

From the mountains of Cherokee and the hills of Paulding, through the great enterprise of General William Phillips, a citizen of Marietta, a railroad was projected and finally completed from Marietta first to Murphy, N. C., and then to Knoxville, Tennessee. It passed directly through the great marble region of upper Georgia. The rich quarries were opened and polishing mills were erected near Marietta, and the marble prepared for ornamental, monumental and building purposes. These mills have been very successful and prosperous. A paper-mill is also in the county, and a woolen-mill, and there are quite a number of other enterprises.

The convenience of Marietta to Atlanta, and its great attractiveness as a place of residence, has made it a place for the homes of some who do business in Atlanta.

Acworth is quite a sprightly town above Marietta, and Smyrna a place of some attractiveness south of Marietta. Powder Springs on the Southern road is a very sprightly town.

During the war Marietta, which was near the Kennesaw mountain, was a focal point, and on all sides of it the war raged. On the Kennesaw General Polk was killed, and in Marietta the great burial ground of the thousands of Federals who fell between Chattanooga and Atlanta is located.

It was in Marietta that the Rev. George White, an Episcopal minister, to whom Georgia is so much indebted for preserving her records and for giving an account of her resources and sketches of her people, lived for many years; and "White's Statistics" and "White's Historical Collections" were prepared here. Mr. White was a Georgian by birth. He was at one time a Methodist preacher, but while a young man joined the Episcopal ministry. He was a man of fine parts and was very industrious. He was enthusiastically devoted to Georgia history, and, having resided for many years in Savannah, had excellent facilities for its study. He published "White's Statistics" in 1850, and five years afterward a much more expensive and extensive work, known as "Historical Collections." His work has been of inestimable value to me in preparing this history. After publishing the "Historical Collections," which was probably not a remunerative work, he reentered the ministry and while in charge of a church in Memphis died.

To Adiel Sherwood, the Baptist preacher, to Wm. Bacon Stevens, the Episcopal bishop, to Mr. White, the village parson, and to Colonel C. C. Jones, Georgia is largely indebted for a knowledge of her resources and her history.

Governor McDonald lived for many years in Marietta, and died there. He was governor of Georgia in the trying times of the great depression which began in 1837 and continued during all the days of his administration. He was an upright man and a wise counselor.

Judge David Irwin, who lived here, was a famous jurist and one of the first codifiers of Georgia laws. He began life as a shoemaker, but by dint of real talents and great energy became one of the leading lawyers in upper Georgia and a judge.

General Hansell, a descendant of the distinguished Harris family, a lawyer of note and a man of affairs, resided here and was for many years president of the Roswell cotton factory.

But no man ever cast a brighter luster on the county of his birth than W. D. Anderson, D.D. He was a gifted young man, the son of a distinguished father who had been a judge of the superior court in which the son practiced, but who had died when his son was an infant. Young Anderson had the best of stepfathers and had every advantage of education. He graduated with honor in Athens; went from his college class to the army and won his laurels there; returned to Marietta, studied law and rose to a high place; entered politics, was in the convention which framed the constitution of 1868, and was elected speaker pro tem. of the House of Representatives; but laid all his honors down for the Methodist ministry. Few men were ever more beloved or more useful or more gifted. The degree of D.D. was conferred on him by Emory College, and the highest honors of the church awaited him, when he was suddenly called away, dying in the brightest bloom of life.

George N. Lester, a lawyer of great ability, attorney-general of the State, a warm-hearted, impetuous, fearless soldier and an orator of no mean parts, who began life in the hills of Forsyth and ended it in the vicinity of Marietta, long lived here.

While Cobb was long regarded as one of the poor counties of Georgia, such has been the character of her people and their industry and enterprise, that for successive years she bore off the prize of one thousand dollars which the State Agricultural Society offered for the county furnishing the greatest variety of products.

Cobb has always been a religious county. The rural people, while not cultured, have been noted for honesty and simplicity of life. The Methodists are perhaps the leading denomination, but the Baptists are very numerous and influential. The Presbyterians and Episcopalians have quite a large membership in the city of Marietta.

The city of Marietta was for a number of years the seat

of the only military institute Georgia then had, the Georgia Military Institute, which was burned during the war and has never been rebuilt.

The city has now a good system of public schools, and the county is well supplied with schools supported by the common school fund.

There are some very handsome churches in Marietta, and its proximity to the marble quarries has enabled the church builders to use this costly material very lavishly.

The city of Marietta is famous for the beauty of its homes, and it has been a favorite place of residence for distinguished men. Senator Clay has his residence here, and has been a prominent lawyer here for years. The city is quite a favorite resort for those who want a dry climate in winter and a bracing one in summer.

CHEROKEE.

When the Cherokee country was laid out a county called Cherokee, of great size, which has since been much cut down, but is still a very large county, was formed. The county site was called Canton. As in Cobb, the lots were only forty acres each, and as land was cheap the county was rapidly settled by white people who had very few slaves. In 1850 there was one slave to every ten white inhabitants.

There were some rich lands on the Etowah, and some good gold mines near to it, and there were some few people of considerable means who fixed their homes in the county, but Cherokee was, like Cobb and Forsyth, settled mainly by those who had little besides their cheap homes and their strong arms.

When Cherokee was first settled it was very remote from any market town. The railroad did not reach the interior for ten years after it was thickly settled. There was but little produced for sale and the people lived within themselves. They had but few schools and they were inferior, and their churches were small log houses. The people lived plainly and cheaply, but were free from want. Many of them were Scotch-Irish and many belonged to the best English stock. They had few slaves, lived hard and closely and developed a sturdy manhood. That these people were mainly provincial could but be expected. Their wants were few and their aspirations not high; but they were a strong, self-reliant people, in no respect differing from those of Cobb and Forsyth. There were a few wealthy people on the Etowah and Little river, and in the villages, but as a general rule they were those worthy yeomanry we have so often described.

The county was a score of miles from the nearest railroad until the North Georgia railroad traversed it. It is now in close communication with the northern part of Georgia and with Tennessee and Atlanta.

It was in this county that young Joseph E. Brown began the practice of law. Here he married his excellent wife, the daughter of a prominent and wealthy Baptist preacher; here he was living when he was elected judge, and was reaping wheat in his fields when he received the news that he was nominated for governor.

During the early days of the county a family of German origin, the Reinhardts, settled in Cherokee, and a scion of this family is now living in Atlanta. In 1885 Colonel A. M. Reinhardt established a school which bears his name and which has since been raised to a country college and is doing most excellent work in training teachers and educating young people. It is under the patronage of the M. E. Church, South.

The town of Canton, located on the banks of the Etowah, is now a sprightly mountain town, with its churches and schools, and is becoming a desirable up-country resort for low-country people.

One of the most productive gold mines in Georgia is in Cherokee, the Franklin mine, from which an immense quantity of gold has been taken during the last sixty years.

There were discovered some traces of copper which were sufficiently promising to lead to the opening of a large mine, and an effort was made to smelt the ore, but it was not successful. The only rich return was to those who sold their holdings to sanguine prospectors.

FORSYTH.

Forsyth lies abreast of Cherokee, with Cobb on the east; and it is impossible to describe Cherokee and Cobb without describing Forsyth. It has the same physical features and was peopled by the same class of inhabitants, but had a few more slaves in proportion to the white population. In Cherokee and Cobb there was about one in ten, in Forsyth one in eight.

Many of the people of Forsyth bear the same names as those of Franklin, and the first settlers came from the foot-hill counties in the eastern part of the State. There were a few northern people among these early settlers, who came to this county as merchants. There was not much first-class land in the county, but not a great deal that was not arable. Land was cheap and easy to be secured, and, as we have seen in Cobb and Cherokee, there were many separate landholders and a large number of small farms. The Southern railway now skirts Forsyth but does not pass through it, and the Forsyth people are still out of the busy whirl of life.

Cumming, the county site, was named for Wm. Cumming, who was a townsman of John Forsyth, and, like him, a staunch Jackson Democrat. It is a quiet country village, with a good school and good churches.

There is little to distinguish this county in any way. It was populated with a sturdy, thrifty, religious people, very simple in their ways and thoroughly independent. There was but little mining interest in the county, and the wild population which belonged to Lumpkin found no abode in Forsyth, and society from the first was good.

GILMER.

Gilmer county, named in honor of Governor Gilmer, is one of the mountain counties, and at the time it was laid out was a county of very great size, including what is now a very large part of Pickens and Fannin and portions of other counties now contiguous. With the exception of a few small and beautiful valleys it is a county of mountain ranges. The mountains are covered with timber and are not arable. The grass, which grows luxuriantly on some of them, gives good range for cattle for a short part of the year, but the mountains are too steep for good pastures. The streams are many, and on their borders are narrow strips of moderately good land. The timber resources of the county are very fine, but the white pine, hemlock, oak and poplar are too far from any market to make lumbering profitable. The valleys of the Coosawattee, the Ellijay and the Cartecay are very beautiful and fertile, but limited in area.

The lands were granted in lots of 160 acres, and many of these lots fell to men living in the lower counties of the State, and were counted as of so little value that they were never claimed, and some of them were taken by squatters from Georgia and other State. There were some very profitable gold mines in the county when it was first settled, and the White Path mine was said, when first opened, to be fabulously rich. Many of the people who settled in Gilmer were very poor and illiterate, but there were quite a number of excellent families who occupied the valleys. The ruling element, however, was a wild one; and, with few schools and churches and with whisky distilleries in all portions of the county, advance for many years was impossible. Many of the Gilmer people sympathized with the United States in the war between the States, and after the war were pronounced Republicans. Many of them connected themselves with the M. E. Church (known as Northern Methodists), and the church established a high school among them. Then the sale of whisky by retail was forbidden, the railroad came, the common school was put into efficient operation, new churches were built and new high schools opened by the Southern Methodists at Cartecay and Blue Ridge, and the general interests of the county are improving everywhere.

LUMPKIN.

There is perhaps less arable land in this county than in any other county in the State, and it derives its prominence from the extent of its gold fields. Dahlonega, which was selected as its county site, was called by the Indians "Yellow Money." In all parts of the county were found placers in which some gold was to be found, and when the gold fields were opened an immense horde came rushing in.

There were very few slaves in this section, and in 1850, when the county embraced what is now three or four counties, there were only 200.

The large yield of gold led the United States government to establish a mint in the growing town of Dahlonega, where for a number of years gold was coined. The placers were exhausted to a great measure after a few years, and the gold fields of California began to attract the miners. For some time after they were discovered mining in Lumpkin seemed to be at an end. Then was introduced the sluicing system, and the hills were washed down, the veins exposed, and the quartz, which had a small quantity of gold, was powdered in the mills and the gold collected by quicksilver. Much northern capital was employed, and there has been as much gold gathered as in the early days of large nuggets.

The intelligence necessary to successful mining has always brought into Lumpkin people of broad views and culture, and working in mud and slush has called for cheap labor of the poorest class, and so the extremes of people have been found in this county.

Through the influence of Colonel Price, a member of Congress, who lives in Dahlonega, the United States government granted the use of the mint, which had been abandoned as a mint, for a college; and the State, which had appropriated the large amount given by the United States government for an Agricultural and Mechanical College to the University and its annexes, made an appropriation to this North Georgia and Agricultural College, and it has been quite prosperous and has done great good.

In a county so mountainous and so sterile as Lumpkin, whose chief resources are its minerals, the advantages of common schools and the blessing of good churches were at first sadly lacking. There was, however, on the part of the stirring Baptists and the ubiquitous Methodists an effort made from its first settlement to do religious work in every section. There were three camp-grounds in the county, and in every part of it there was a homely log house in which the gospel was preached.

The changes in this section are many and for the better. Prohibition obtains throughout this section, and while there are still drunkenness and other immoralities, there is a vast advance. Some day a railroad will open up the wondrous beauty of this mountain country, and it will be filled with delighted tourists.

On the summit of the mountains there was discovered some years ago a fine spring of mineral water, and Colonel H. P. Farrow built a handsome hotel on the spot and opened it for guests. It has become a noted summer resort which is very popular with those who are seeking a restful place for the heated term. It is located over thirty miles from the railroad, but is a charming retreat from the dust and heat of the low-country.

UNION.

At the time Union county was formed there was a fierce political strife between the nullifiers and the Union men, and the new county was called Union because of the devotion of its people to the union of States and the sympathy of a Union Legislature with their views.

The account we have given of Gilmer is suited to Union, for there is but little difference between the two counties. Mountains, only broken into by small and narrow valleys, cover the county.

The people were mainly emigrants from North Carolina and generally poor, and the farms are generally sterile. Along the river there are some beautiful valleys and some bodies of excellent land.

Blairsville, the county site, is quite a small village peopled by some very good people.

There are a few gold mines in the county which have now and then produced a good yield of gold, but the mining resources of the county are limited.

There were only a few slaves in the county when the emancipation proclamation was issued.

The settlers in Union are of the same class as those who inhabit the other counties written of. They have the best Virginia and North Carolina names. There are no people in Georgia of better blood than these mountaineers, and from the families of this hill country have gone men of brawn and brain to all sections of the southern country.

Union has been long difficult to reach. Lying in the lap of the Blue Ridge, with mountains on all sides, it has been out of the lines of travel. There was little for its first inhabitants to do save to make a plain livelihood by farming, and they have been content with small returns from their labors. They made but little for market. Some cabbages, some apples, a few cattle and a little bacon were about all they had to sell. They lived among themselves and by the aid of their own resources. There has been a steady improvement among them for some years, and when a railway opens a market for the fine timber, and when fruit is grown for market and the charming scenery of the country draws the tourist, Union will be appreciated as it deserves to be.

MURRAY.

On the west of Gilmer is Murray county, named for Speaker Murray of Wilkes. This county was on the west side of the Blue Ridge and in the blue limestone country. Much of it was very fertile, and perhaps, take it all in all, the most beautiful farm in Georgia is located in Murray. Where the Coosawattee and the Talking Rock come together and form the Connesauga, at the base of the mountains, are 1,700 acres of beautiful valley land in one body, all taken up by one owner, Colonel Carter. But in various parts of the county, on the creeks and in the coves, there are fertile valleys where clover and timothy grow in great luxuriance. This county was a favorite home of the Cherokee Indians, and at Spring Place and near-by were the mission schools. The well-built brick houses of some of the Indian chiefs are still standing.

Although the county is new, the country has been inhabited a very long time, and much of the best land has been cultivated over a hundred years. There is in the county much sterile land, but there is also much that is productive.

The people who settled Murray were among the best people who came to the mountains, and there was an unusual amount of wealth for a mountain county.

Spring Place, the county site, was a famous up-country town before the railroads came; but since the building of railways it has been overshadowed by the towns on the line and has declined. There has been quite an exodus from the county to the railway, but the best valleys are still well peopled.

The religious concerns of the county have been seen after by the Baptists, the Methodists and the Cumberland Presbyterians.

The school advantages have been very limited. The common school system of the State has provided for the people of moderate means, and those in better circumstances send their children to Dalton and other railway towns.

The county in its first settlement was noted for its lawlessness, and at one time the judges were prevented from holding court by the mob. But by the nerve and determination of Judges Kenan and Warner the lawbreakers were subdued, and now few counties have a better class of people in the main than Murray.

Spring Place is the county site. The little village was famous as a place where the Moravian mission among the Cherokees was established and where Mr. Gambold, who for so many years gave himself to the work of civilizing this tribe, had his home. The American Board of Missions also established a mission near here. The chief Vann lived in a substantial brick house and cultivated a large plantation proximate to the village and the mission. He had a number of slaves. The remoteness of this mission from all demoralizing influences made the work of the missionaries wonderfully successful. Mission stations with Spring Place as a center were established all through the country adjacent, and long before the Indians were removed there were the circuits of the Methodists and churches of the Baptists.

When the Indians were removed their improvements were bought by white men, many of whom were by no means as worthy people as the Indians whom they displaced.

It was in this county that the celebrated J. Howard Payne, author of "Home, Sweet Home," at that time a correspondent of a New York paper, was arrested and treated with such indignity by the guard under a Captain Bishop that the Legislature expressed its profound regret for the outrage.

PAULDING.

Adjoining the county of Cobb in the west of the newly acquired country was Paulding county. It was named in honor of one of the captors of Major André, the British spy, and was when first laid off a very large county, reaching from Floyd to the Chattahoochee, in what is now Douglas county. It was afterward reduced until it has reached its present size.

The county as it now stands is not a fertile one. It is very rolling and the land is thin.

Up to the building of the Southern railway from Rome to Atlanta it was shut up in its own hills and was very slow in development, but since the coming of the road its improvement has been marked and rapid.

The settlers of Paulding were of the same people who settled Cobb, and life in the rural districts of the two counties was much the same.

Bauxite is found in large quantities in this county, and much of it is mined and shipped to the North, where it is prepared for manufacture into aluminum.

Mr. White, who lived in the county adjoining Paulding, gives only a very short list of early settlers. The settlers were few and their circumstances very humble. They lived, as did most of these people of these sterile hills in upper

Shorter College, Rome.

Georgia, in a very poor way, and when they had no markets and raised no cotton, they had but little money and few comforts; but when slavery was abolished and fertilizers brought in, the people began to raise cotton, and being near Atlanta, where they find a ready market for their poultry and smaller products, they have been rapidly improving in population and in their circumstances.

There are some fine lands and some well-to-do farmers on the creeks in some parts of the county. The Sweetwater valley has long been noted for its fertility and its excellent class of people.

The proximity of Paulding to Atlanta and Rome and the general ruggedness of the country will some day result in its becoming a grazing and dairy county, famous for its fruits and poultry, and cause it to grow largely in population.

There has been decided improvement in the educational and religious conditions of the county since the war. The Methodists have always preached in some parts of the county, and now their circuits and missions have reached all parts of it; and the Baptists are in it in large numbers.

The people were for a long time very rude and unlettered. There was little chance for them to be otherwise where settlements were so scattered and people so poor; but with the system of common school education, in common with all counties similarly situated, Paulding has rapidly advanced.

FLOYD.

Floyd, which was also a large county, containing several which now adjoin it, was laid off as soon as the country was opened. It was a very fertile country, through which ran the Coosa, the Oostanaula and the Etowah. The Indians had placed a high estimate upon it, and it is supposed by Pickett, the Alabama historian, that the "Chiaha" of

De Soto's chronicler, where the Indians had their chief city, was in Floyd.

The great fertility of this county led at an early day men of wealth to remove into it and settle plantations, and among them was Colonel Mitchell, from middle Georgia, through whose influence the county site was changed from Livingston, ten miles below, to what is now the city of Rome, lying at the junction of the Etowah and Oostanaula. Rome had great advantages in its location, and soon gave evidence of the fact that it was to be a city of no contemptible size.

Many of the rich bottoms on the Etowah and Oostanaula had been cultivated by the Indians for a long time, but only in corn. They were found admirably suited to cotton culture and productive wheat lands, and to be very valuable.

There was much broken land in the county and not a little that was quite sterile, but there were some beautiful valleys in different parts of it. Vann's valley, named after an Indian chief, where the Indians had lived, was a fine section of the county, adjoining the famous Cave Spring valley.

Cave Spring is the name of a beautiful hamlet, so called because of the existence of a bold spring which rushes from the heart of a mountain which overlooks the village. The fertility of the country roundabout and the beauty of the location drew to it an excellent class of people. The Baptists established a high school here, endowed by a Mr. Hearn, the Methodists the Wesleyan Institute, and the State has here its Asylum for the Deaf and Dumb.

Rome, the chief city of Floyd, is surrounded by a very fertile country, and is at the head of navigation on the Coosa river. The falls of the Coosa in Alabama preventing the passage of boats to the gulf gave Rome the control of the rich valley of the Coosa; and as soon as the Western and Atlantic railroad was completed a branch road connecting Rome with it was built. So Rome became the chief cotton market of upper Georgia. The Messrs. Noble, a family of enterprising Englishmen, settled in Rome and erected extensive machine shops. The Southern railway connected Rome with the northwest and the southwest, and the railroad from Chattanooga to Carrollton opened an excellent country north and south of the city. The growth of Rome has been very rapid, and it is now the chief city of upper Georgia. The Methodists have a very handsome church in Rome and a number of suburban churches; and the Baptists, Presbyterians and Episcopalians are all represented by good churches. There is located in Rome the celebrated Shorter Female College (Baptist), which was built and endowed by Colonel Shorter, who was one of the first settlers in the county and a man of very great wealth. There is also a fine system of graded schools kept up by the city.

WALKER.

In 1833, in the extreme northwest of the Cherokee country, the county of Walker, named in honor of Freeman Walker, a distinguished lawyer and politician of Richmond county, was made. Its county site was called Lafayette.

This county, like most of the up-country counties, was very large when it was laid out and is still a county of considerable size. It had been a favorite country for the Indians, and when they went west the rich lands on Chickamauga creek, in McLemore's cove and on Broomtown creek drew from the low-country of Georgia and from the neighboring counties in Tennessee a body of fine settlers.

Lookout mountain was in the west of the county, and was an excellent stock range, and in time was found to be well suited to the growth of various small fruits and vegetables.

For years Walker was cut off from the outer world. Chattanooga and Dalton on the railroad sprang up and took the trade of the Walker people from Lafayette. The little county site languished for years; but the building of a railway from Chattanooga to Carrollton, which passes through Lafayette, has given new life to it, and the prospects of its rapid advancement are very bright.

Some ten miles from Chattanooga is what was long known as Crawfish Springs and what is now known as Chickamauga. A subterranean river comes bursting out of the side of a hill in great volume, becoming a stream of 180 feet in width a few yards from its exit from the cave. It is as clear as crystal and has in it a great quantity of fish which can be seen with the naked eye. This beautiful spot was owned by a Mr. Lee, who had a large estate around it. It was settled on as a place for a young city, and Chickamauga was projected and, in the language of the times, was vigorously "boomed." This boom was moderately successful, and an attempt was then made to build another city, Kensington, near McLemore's cove, which did not succeed. This cove, in the heart of the mountains known as McLemore, has long been famous for its fertility and beauty. The extent of its land is not great, but the quality is very good. The Hon. Wm. Dougherty had a summer home here, and Rev. Charles Wallace Howard, who was distinguished as a careful student of Georgia history and as a developer of her resources, spent his last days in this county on Lookout Mountain, where he had a ranch and a garden.

Moore and Marsh, the famous wholesale dry-goods men of Atlanta, began their mercantile life in Walker, and many of Georgia's distinguished men have resided in this county.

For years before the war the educational advantages of the county were very few. There was a classical school in Lafayette and some of inferior grade in other parts of the county from the first settlement; but until the common school system was inaugurated there was little intelligent effort made to educate all the people. As in all the country, there have been great improvements.

From the first opening of the county the Methodist circuit-rider and the Baptist elder have been at work in Walker, and the people are in the main a religious people.

CHATTOOGA.

From the lower part of Walker and the upper part of Floyd a county was formed in 1838, known as Chattooga. The face of the country is broken by ridges and ranges of low mountains. There are in it some very beautiful valleys and some very excellent land.

Summerville, the county site, is a neat and pleasant country town with good schools and churches.

There is in the county one of the most successful cotton factories in the State, known as Trion Factory. It is located on the Chattooga river, and not only has good water-power but is also run by steam.

There is a settlement in this county known as South Carolina, because of excellent well-to-do South Carolinians who settled in it.

The county has had an exceptionally good reputation for its morality and its religion, and has paid unusual attention to its schools.

It was for many years secluded, but by the building of the railroad from Chattanooga to Carrollton its entire length has been traversed by a railway.

DADE.

Lookout mountain, which passes through the upper part of Walker, cuts the extreme northwest corner of Georgia into a small county known for many years as the State of Dade. It was named in honor of Major Dade, who was killed, with his whole command, by the Seminoles in Florida.

There were only 2,500 people in the county in 1850, of whom only 148 were slaves.

In this county is the only deposit of coal in the State, and ex-Governor Brown opened the mine and operated it with convicts leased from the State, and built a large iron furnace.

The people of the county are isolated from Georgia and have their associations with Chattanooga. They are a plain, good people, of simple tastes and habits, and are moral and religious.

BARTOW (ONCE CASS).

Among the new counties laid out in 1832 was Cass, named in honor of Lewis Cass. When General Cass took decided anti-southern ground in 1861 the indignant Georgians changed the name to Bartow, after the gallant general of that name who lost his life at the first Manassas.

There is no part of Georgia in which a finer body of land is to be found than is included in this county. It had been a favorite section with the Indians, and the lands on the Etowah, Pine Log and sundry other creeks were famous for their fertility and had been cultivated by them. In addition to these agricultural resources there are large quarries of limestone and large deposits of iron ore and manganese.

When Cass was first opened it was somewhat remote from the older counties and difficult to reach; but it was rapidly peopled by the best class of settlers. Many of them came from the older counties, and some very substantial people came to it from South Carolina. It was so rapidly peopled that in ten years after it was settled it had in it nearly 13,000 people, of whom over 2,000 were slaves.

The land is largely in the blue-limestone region and produces wheat, corn and cotton very abundantly.

The county site was called Cassville, and few villages anywhere had at their first settlement a finer class of people than this little hamlet. When the Western and Atlantic railroad reached the county Cassville was off the line of railway, and during the war the village was burned and the county site removed to the city of Cartersville, on the railroad.

In Cass county the first extensive foundry and rolling-mill in Georgia was established by Cooper, Wiley & Co., and the first railway iron made in Georgia was made at this mill. These iron works were destroyed during the war. Cass was overrun by the Federals, and no part of Georgia suffered more from their ravages.

This county has been famous for its men of distinction. Warren Aiken, once a candidate for governor and long a leader of the Whig party; Colonel W. H. Stiles, the accomplished minister to Austria; Charles Wallace Howard, one of the most accomplished of Georgia writers; Judge Turner Trippe, a prominent jurist; Colonel Lewis Tumlin, a member of Congress, all lived and died in this county.

The county has always been noted for its attention to education and religion, and there is a large graded school in Cartersville and excellent schools in all the country neighborhoods.

Cartersville, the county site, is a city of considerable size and enterprise, noted for its handsome buildings, its fine climate, and its excellent citizenship.

Kingston is a hamlet of some importance, at the junction of the Rome railroad.

The county is well supplied with Methodist, Baptist and Presbyterian churches.

There is no county in the State where there are handsomer country homes than are to be found in this county.

The rich beds of manganese and hematite iron ore have added much to its wealth.

As is always the case in a county of rich valley lands, there are also sterile hills inhabited by poor and ignorant people; but taking man for man, there are few sections of the country where there is a better grade of people than is to be found in this county.

MACON.

Macon county, named for Nathaniel Macon, was formed from the adjoining counties. It had in its borders some very excellent land on the Flint river and on the creeks, and some beautiful and extensive plantations of the best red pine land in the eastern part of the county. The best of this land was taken up at an early day in large plantations, on which there were placed many slaves. In 1850 there were about 4,000 white inhabitants and 3,000 slaves. Oglethorpe is the county site, on the west side of the Flint. It is a village of respectable size, with a very fine court-house. Two miles west of it is the flourishing little city of Montezuma. It is located very near the river, and was for some years considered quite unhealthy; but the boring of an artesian well opened a vein of the purest water, which came gushing to the surface in inexhaustible quantity, and has removed the source of disease, and now no village in the State has a better record for health. The most remarkable industry of this county is its fruit-growing and its famous nursery business. Mr. Samuel H. Rumph conceived the idea of a great nursery on the red hills of Macon, and devoted himself to the work of planting one and having large orchards; and finding a demand for his choice fruit in the northern States, he began the shipment of peaches and plums to New York and other northern cities. The business of fruit-raising and fruit shipment thus begun has become an immense one, and hundreds of car-loads of peaches

Gov. Chas. J. Jenkins.

Gov. A. H. Stephens.

Gov. H. V. Johnson.

Gov. Howell Cobb.

are shipped from this section. The famous Elberta peach originated in his nursery, and has spread all over the land. The cotton industry has given way to the raising of fruit and fruit trees.

CHAPTER X.

1837 TO 1847.

Governor Gilmer—Governor McDonald—Governor Crawford—The Beginning of the Great Financial Crash—List of Banks—Low-price Cotton—Condition of State Treasury—Contraction of the Circulation—Troubles in the State Finances—Governor McDonald's Nerve—The Central Bank of Georgia—Cherokee County Populated—The Monroe Railroad Failure—Completion of the Central Railroad; of the Georgia Railroad; of the Western and Atlantic Railroad—The Effect of the Depression—Political Excitement—"Tippecanoe and Tyler too"—The Opening of Mercer and Emory—Settlement of the Western Counties—Features of Middle Georgia Life in 1840—The Mountaineers—The Wire-grass Country—The Religious Condition of Georgia—The Camp-meeting—Georgia Talent in the Pulpit and on the Platform.

Authorities: Acts of Legislature, White's Statistics, White's Historical Collections, Gilmer's Georgians, Miller's Bench and Bar of Georgia, Sherwood's Gazetteer, Campbell's History of the Baptists, Smith's History of Methodism, History Bank of England—Benton's Thirty Years' View, newspaper files.

Governor Gilmer was elected as the candidate of the States' rights or anti-Jackson party in 1837. This was the second time he had been chosen as governor. Once he was elected by the Clarke and now by the States' rights party. He entered his office after the great panic of 1837 had begun, and left it broken in health when it was at its height.

This panic was not, as many have supposed, the same as that brought about from the removal of the deposits by General Jackson.* That panic began in 1834 and ended in

* In making the above statement I am aware that I am not in accord with the general opinion as to the cause of the panic. Colonel Benton takes the ground I have taken above; and, indeed, until I had read his discussion I had never questioned the fact that General Jackson's vigorous measure brought about the calamity. I was, however, satisfied, after further research, that the old senator was correct, and the History of the Bank of England, referred to in the list of authorities, fully establishes his position.

1835. This was far more wide-spread than that, and had an entirely different origin. There had been a time of great inflation in England. Many private banks had been established. Money was easy and many new cotton-mills had been erected. Suddenly, and apparently without cause, a general distrust of the stability of these country banks was aroused, and there was a general call on them for specie; they in turn demanded the payment of obligations due to them. They were forced to suspend, and the American banks in the larger cities suspended also; and in May of 1837 every bank in Georgia but two suspended specie payments. This was done avowedly as a matter of precaution and not of necessity. The banks in New York, Philadelphia, Baltimore and Charleston had suspended, and the Georgia banks were forced to follow their example or be drained of specie. In 1834, according to Sherwood, there was in Georgia:

	Capital.	Circulation.	Specie.
Planters Bank, Savannah	$ 535,000	$214,922	$147,132
Mechanics, Augusta....................	200,000	456,621	183,497
Marine and Fire Insurance, Savannah....	170,000	165,485	118,521
Insurance and Banking Co., Augusta....	150,000	191,092	86,150
Commercial, Macon	100,000	73,376	53,229
Columbus............................	203,333	132,790	86,492
Columbus Insurance..................	150,000	111,496	72,412
Bank State of Georgia, Augusta	1,500,000	......	......
Bank of Darien, Darien................	469,017	329,942	73,186
Farmers Bank, Chattahoochee	119,825	72,063	8,972
Bank of Augusta......................	600,000	437,764	353,405
Hawkinsville.........................	100,000	179,852	78,870
Central Bank of Georgia, Milledgeville ..	2,485,733	237,725	135,186

The mania for establishing banks was wide-spread, and before 1834 a large addition had been made to this list. There was the Monroe Railroad and Banking Company, Macon; the Georgia Railroad and Banking Company, Augusta; the Central Railroad and Banking Company, Savannah; the Planters and Mechanics, Columbus; the Bank of St. Marys; the Ocmulgee Bank, Macon; the Irwinton

Bridge Co., Irwinton; the Florence Bridge Co., Florence; the Western, Rome; the Brunswick, and sundry others.

Money had been for some years an easy thing to obtain. Planters indorsed for each other and banks freely discounted the paper. Political favorites secured at the Central Bank of Georgia an almost unlimited credit. Cotton in 1836 was 17 cents a pound, and cities were springing up like magic. The crash of 1834 had not affected Georgia, but now came the day of settlement. England had become fearfully involved, and the English manufacturers went down before the storm by hundreds. The Bank of England found itself seriously embarrassed and suspension of specie payments seemed to be absolutely certain. Cotton, which was 12 to 15 cents in January, 1837, began to decline, and by 1839 was down to 7½. In 1840 it was 6 to 7, in 1841 best grades 7½, in 1842 4 to 7, and the lower grades as low as 3. The banks called in their loans and contracted their circulation. Specie could not be secured and change bills were issued by banks and private parties. Negroes declined to one half the price they had been held at in 1837, and lands were almost worthless. The railroads which had been projected had suspended banks at their backs as their only reliance. The Western and Atlantic railroad was built with bills of the Central Bank of Georgia, the Monroe railroad with its own bank bills, and so the Georgia and the Central. The iron was imported from England and paid for in cotton purchased by Georgia bank notes. The antagonism to the banks by the Jackson party was fearful, and the banks fought against each other savagely; and to fill the cup of misery, the United States bank, which had been working under a Pennsylvania charter, became hopelessly insolvent, and a new panic set in.

The State treasury was empty. The State bonds were protested, and its credit was worthless. The Central Bank, which the State had fathered, was hopelessly involved; the

Bank of Darien, in which it had much invested, went into bankruptcy; the Monroe Railroad and Banking Company was insolvent; there was a general crash in every direction.

In 1841 the exhibit of the banks showed: Planters, capital $535,000, circulation $70,000; Planters and Mechanics, capital $270,000, circulation $178,000; Commercial, capital $347,000, circulation $7,000; Georgia Railroad, capital $600,000, circulation $428,000; Central Railroad, capital $406,840, circulation $370,000; Monroe, capital $400,000, circulation $90,000; Augusta Insurance, capital $500,000, circulation $41,000; Hawkinsville, capital $160,000; circulation $77,000; Columbus Insurance, capital $600,000, circulation $4,669; Darien, capital $419,000, circulation $194,000; Ocmulgee, capital $337,000, circulation $10,000; Western, capital $163,000, circulation $127,000; State of Georgia, capital $1,500,000, circulation $288,000; Brunswick, capital $200,000, circulation $54,000. This exhibit shows the extent of the contraction. There was for seven years no permanent improvement in the price of cotton. Thousands of solvent farmers had indorsed for their neighbors and were now forced to sell everything to pay their debts.

During this period, after Governor Gilmer's term had expired, Charles J. McDonald was chosen as governor. He was a South Carolinian of Highland Scotch parentage. He was educated in Columbia, S. C.; came to Macon and began the practice of law, and was at one time mayor of the city. He was living in Macon when he was elected governor. He was a man of fine person, sound sense and invincible courage. He found financial matters in a terrible condition, and had a Legislature afraid to confront the difficulties by taxing people who were almost driven to desperation by the State of affairs. The staunch governor did not approve of any dodging. It was absolutely necessary to increase the tax assessment or go to the wall. The Legislature refused to levy a higher tax. The governor promptly suspended all orders on the treasurer and forbade him to pay any new appropriations until funds were furnished to pay the old ones. He finally carried his point, but matters were still in a chaotic state when Governor Crawford was elected in 1843.

Governor Crawford found the panic had about exhausted its fury. It had continued for near six years, and had left behind it ruin and desolation; but the time for reaction had come. As will be seen, he restored the credit of the State. The depression may be said to have ended when he came into office. A number of banks had failed; many wealthy men were paupers, and not a few who were poor at the beginning of the troubles came out of the ruins enriched with spoils. It was the second great panic Georgia had passed through, and in its results the most injurious of any until the crash of 1865.

George W. Crawford, the Whig who succeeded Governor McDonald, was a native Georgian, the son of Peter Crawford, long a famous politician of Columbia county. He was born in Columbia county and was educated at Princeton College. He was a man of great practical sense and of fine business capacity. He entered on his office when the financial tide had reached its lowest ebb and was just about to turn. He redeemed the credit of the State, and by pledging his private fortune and using his personal influence he gained the consent of the banks to receive the State's obligations at their face value. Mr. Crawford was afterward in General Taylor's cabinet. When his term had ended he returned to his home near Bel Air in Richmond county. He came into office when the railroads were unfinished, the banks suspended, business depressed, and lived to see a line of railway from Savannah to Chattanooga and a general revival of prosperity.

In order to protect the note-holders of the Central Bank the State issued bonds payable in five years and ordered the stock it had in the various banks sold and the Central Bank bills taken in payment, and finally, in 1842, the bank was put in process of liquidation, but remained nominally in existence till after 1850, when its charter was again extended that it might wind up its affairs.

The general disturbance in financial matters, the constant contraction of the circulating medium, the painful fall in the prices of real estate and negroes affected most seriously middle Georgia and the cities, but it had little effect upon upper Georgia and the grain-growing portions of the State. These independent farmers had but little concern about banks, for they had but little to do with them. They made all their supplies and lived contentedly at home. There was a constant influx of the best people into this newly settled part of Georgia. The gold product had reached its highest point and was declining; for the old methods of placer-mining had not as yet been replaced by the great flumes and stamp-mills. The Cherokee country, from which the Indians had now been finally removed, was rapidly peopled, and crowds of immigrants were on the roads from the eastern counties and from South and North Carolina to open farms in Cobb, Cass, Cherokee, Floyd, and others of the new counties. There was no railway communication, no telegraph, few mails; and while the older parts of the State and the black belt, as it was called, were in such financial distress, there was little of it known in these sections, and the tide of advancement rolled on.

The railroad mania which seized the State between 1833 and 1836 had resulted in beginning and abandoning sundry wild schemes. The ideas entertained of the expense and difficulty of railroad-making were very crude, and it is almost ludicrous to see with what confidence men embarked in the wildest schemes. There was a fearful collapse in many of them and in many other schemes. Insurance companies, mining companies and manufacturing companies failed. But perhaps the wildest scheme of all these wild times was the *Mora multicaulis* speculation. The *Mora multicaulis* was the mulberry which fed the silkworm, and fortunes were to be made in rearing trees of this kind. Many went wildly into it. Orchards were planted, silkworms were bought, cocoons were imported and silk was spun. The State offered a bonus, and Georgia, which had failed a hundred years before in raising silk, was now to succeed. It was, however, but the delusion of an hour. Georgia repealed the law offering a prize for raw silk, mulberry orchards were cut down, and in a little time the wild *Mora multicaulis* mania was relegated, like that of the tulip mania in Holland, to almost oblivion.

From the opening of the new purchase in 1825 to 1837 there had been a marvelous growth in the two new cities of Macon and Columbus. There was a line of steamers from Macon to Darien, and they towed down barges laden with cotton. Magnificent mansions crowned the hilltops in Macon. The new Georgia female college was erected. Vineville had been settled and handsome homes built in it, and there were great enterprises projected by the young city. Columbus, too, had grown with great rapidity and there was, as always is in new towns, a boom in both cities, and then came the crash. The calamity did not come at once and disappear in a short time, but was a succession of disasters until the whole community was involved. In these new cities there was not an important cotton house that did not suspend, and many of them were hopelessly bankrupt. The country, however, was fresh and productive and the large planters were in the habit of making all their supplies, and the smaller farmers were compelled to do so or suffer, and so, despite the scarcity of money, the country people who were not in debt lived in comfort.

Political excitement in Georgia was very high during this period. Mr. Calhoun had many followers and Mr. Van

Gov. McDonald.

Gov. Wilson Lumpkin.

Buren was bitterly hated. The States' rights men and the old party lines of Crawford and Clarke were still drawn. There were no Federalists and no protectionists in Georgia, but there were Troup men and Clarke men, bank men and anti-bank men, and Jackson men and Calhoun men. These parties were known as Whigs and Democrats after 1840.

Then came the unique campaign of "Tippecanoe and Tyler too," of "hard cider and log cabins," and the election of General Harrison and Mr. Tyler. The Troup States' rights, anti-Jackson men were generally Whigs, the old Clarke men Jackson Democrats.

There had been a steady advance in the interest of education. As incorporated academies received some aid from the State, all the schools of any size established in any of the counties were academies.

Three new colleges, Mercer University at Penfield, established by the Baptists, first as a manual labor school; Emory College, at Oxford, which had sprung from the manual labor school at Covington, and the Georgia Female College at Macon, the first institution in the world to grant diplomas to women, had opened. Despite the pressure in the financial world and the bankruptcy of many who had promised large subscriptions, all these schools were opened during these depressing times and had from the first an encouraging patronage. The depression was so long-continued that the country gradually adjusted itself to it, and in spite of its existence and its effect on the cities, there was steady advance in all directions in the newer parts of Georgia. This advance had been at the expense of the older counties. The eastern counties, now nearly one hundred years settled, sent off large colonies to the western counties, where land was fresher.

The rich planters, who had estates in Twiggs, Laurens, Wilkinson and other middle Georgia counties, opened large cotton plantations in Thomas, Decatur, Early, Lee and

Baker. The planters of Greene removed to Troup, Meriwether and Harris. The towns of Greensboro, Warrenton, Washington and Madison had begun to wane, and the towns in the western part of the State, Lagrange, Newnan, and Greenville, to grow. As the plantations in the older counties were sold they were generally purchased by planters who already had large holdings near them, and, if not absorbed, were put in charge of overseers; and so the white proprietors diminished in number, and the country communities, once thickly peopled, became merely large cotton plantations. Where there were at one time farms of often a dozen separate and independent landholders, there was now but one plantation. All those features which had belonged to the life of forty years before had disappeared from the heart of middle Georgia. The white people who held their places in these old counties were of the finest type of sturdy, pushing, intelligent planters, and there was now a transfer of old middle Georgia to the cotton belt of the western counties, and the life we have portrayed as being found in Wilkes and Greene in 1820 was reproduced in the new counties in 1840. Lagrange, Greenville, Newnan, Hamilton and Thomaston had all the freshness and vigor of youth. The flush times had been times of great improvement in architecture everywhere, and the large mansion with its beautiful Corinthian columns, its broad verandas, its wide galleries, its large rooms and green Venetian blinds, was found alike in city and in town, and at some places in the country neighborhoods. There were among the wealthier classes of middle Georgia the same features of life found in the older counties in Virginia and which had come by direct descent from the English country gentleman.

The railroads had but now been built, and there was still a necessity to use private conveyances very largely. The old gig and chair now gave way to the new covered buggy and the comfortable traveling carriage and barouche or Jersey wagon. The equipages found in the county assemblages were sometimes very handsome and the dressing was extravagant. Wealth had wonderfully increased and luxury came in its wake.

The low-country people lived among themselves, and social life on the coast had undergone little change for fifty years. The political influence of the coast people, which had once been controlling, had now to a large degree lost its power, although Senator Berrien, a Savannah man, held his own against all comers.

The up-country presented at this time some very different features of social life. In Cass, Floyd, Murray and Chattooga there was quite a large number of middle Georgia and South Carolina slaveholders, who were cotton-raisers, and there were among them the same features of society which were still found in the older counties; but in the mountains proper, in Lumpkin, Union, Gilmer and Rabun, there was an entirely different type of people. The fearful illiteracy of the Georgia people, as shown by the census of those days, was mainly found in the mountains, and in what was known as the pine-barren or wire-grass country.

In the sketches of the various mountain counties I have endeavored to picture as accurately as I could the features of rural life in the Georgia highlands. Life in the mountains was very hard, and the drinking habits of the people were like those pictured by Ramsey as in Scotland eighty years ago. The farmers made only corn, and much of that they had distilled into whisky and drank the whisky.

The amount of taxes paid by some of these mountain counties was not equal to the receipts from the poor school fund, small as it was at that time. There were, however, in every mountain county some good bodies of land which were settled by those who valued education and sought it for their children.

At this period, however, nearly sixty years ago, the country was almost entirely new and the settlements of the people few and far apart. They were a kindly, hospitable and honest people, and the traveler who came to the cabin in which they made their homes shared their simple fare of corn bread and bacon and rested securely on a bed of straw in a home on which there had never been a lock. Robbery and murder were almost unknown, although when the people met on muster and court days and drank freely of corn whisky, there was much rough-and-tumble fighting. The features of middle Georgia life of 1800 were found in the mountain country in 1840.

The wire-grass country in some of the southwestern counties had much less of uniformity and many more striking contrasts than were to be found in middle or upper Georgia. In this section some habitable land sold for less than $50 for 490 acres; other lands were sold at $500 for 250 acres. The cotton-planter with one hundred negroes lived not far from the poor ranchman who had never owned a negro. Men who had graduated at the best colleges and whose libraries were filled with choice books, and men who could not write their names and who had not even a Bible in their cabins, were members of the same grand jury.

The cultivated and wealthy classes were but few. In examining a large number of wills and appraisements in Thomas, I find in its early day, in the careful enumeration of everything owned by the settler, no mention of any books at all save in two or three instances, and then the books were very few. The mountain people lived in settlements close together, but the ranchmen and large planters lived at great distances apart. So good schools were almost impossible.

There was still much game in the woods, and hunting was a source of profit as well as a pastime, and the children grew up keen woodsmen though poor scholars. In the pine woods the people were of great shrewdness, as many a trafficker found to his sorrow; and while the settler was in the main an honest fellow, he was a trifle careless as to whose calf he put the branding-iron on, and, like his Scotch ancestor, he was careful of the "siller" and a little too fond of a "wee drop." The prevalence of the prefix "Mac" or "Mc" in all this wire-grass country will show the Highland origin of most of these people.

The religious condition of Georgia was never the same after the revival which began in 1827. The camp-meeting had become the great revival agency, and camp-meetings were held by the Methodists and Baptists and Presbyterians. In middle Georgia there were great lavishness and almost extravagance displayed at these meetings. For weeks before arrangements were made for tenting. The tent was a large sheathing house, with a dirt floor and a board-covered roof. The floor was covered with wheat straw, and the beds placed either on scaffolding or on the straw. The great log fire behind the tent served for a cooking place. Pigs and lambs were barbecued, and chickens by the score were prepared for the hosts of guests who received free entertainment. Every one was welcomed, and for all an abundant feast was provided. The tabernacle was generally a large shed covered with boards. There was preaching four times every day, and the preacher had full swing. These open-air meetings were the field services of this century. The negroes had their place reserved and came in great numbers to the meetings. These meetings were of all grades, from the humblest in the mountains to the elegant encampments in Burke or Warren or Greene. But the regular protracted meeting, or four days' meeting, as it was called, was becoming an institution among Methodists and Baptists. Each of these churches was energetically pressing its work as the tide rolled westward, and was winning large numbers of adherents, native Georgians.

Pierce, Mitchell, Dawson, Bacon, Few, Key, Longstreet and Warren, who had liberal educations, were in the pulpit, while George W. Crawford, Toombs, Stephens, Herschel V. Johnson and Colquitt, all native Georgians, were among the great stump-speakers of the day.

The notable men of the first era, Baldwin, Few, Jackson, Glascock and Walton, had all passed away, and those of the second, David B. Mitchell, Clayton, L. Q. C. Lamar and Oliver H. Prince, had now given way to a group of brilliant young men who were on opposite sides of local issues and who were to win fame in the future. During this era appeared that phenomenal book "Georgia Scenes." No American before Longstreet attempted a realistic and accurate story of American life. The "Sam Slick" of Haliburton was a caricature, and the stories of Cooper were romances; but the "Georgia Scenes" told of Georgia life as it really was. It has had many imitators but no successors, and is worth more as a true history of a class of Georgia people than any record of the time.

During this period Texas was admitted into the Union, and the war with Mexico resulted. Georgia sent a regiment into the army commanded by Colonel Henry R. Jackson, and a company of cavalry under command of Captain Loyall. The infantry was not actively engaged, but the cavalry troop did efficient service, and young Lieuteanant Thomas, afterward General Thomas of the Confederate States army, captured General La Vega with his own hand.

CHAPTER XI.

1847 TO 1860.

Governor Towns—Howell Cobb—Herschel V. Johnson—Joseph E. Brown—The Completion of the Main Railroad Lines—A Picture of the Georgia People in the Middle of the Century—The Sea Island People—The Middle Georgia Planters—The Georgia Yeomanry—Introduction of Commercial Fertilizers—Manufacturing in the Rural Districts—Educational Facilities—The Middle Georgia Negroes—The Middle Georgia Towns and Villages—Religious Improvement—The Blue Limestone Country Developed—The Piedmont Country—Wonderful Development of Southwest Georgia—The Wire-grass Country again—M. & B. and A. & G. R. R.—Features of Every-day Life—Days of Prosperity—Banks—The Panic of 1857—Suspension of the Banks—Passage of the Stay Law—Illiteracy of the People—Measure of Thomas R. R. Cobb to Dispel It—The Daily Press—The *Southern Cultivator*—The Agricultural Society—The First Agricultural Fair in Georgia—The End of the Current History—General Account of the Origin of the Georgians—Coming of the Catholic Irish and of the Jewish Traders—The New Counties Glanced at: Banks, Hart, White, Milton, Dawson, Towns, Pickens, Fannin, Spalding, Clayton, Fulton, Whitfield, Polk, Gordon, Dougherty, Terrell, Clay, Chattahoochee, Schley, Clinch, Coffee, Echols, Dodge, Johnson, Pierce, Worth, Brooks, Glascock, Charlton, Haralson, McDuffie, Rockdale, Oconee.

Authorities as before. Acts of the Legislature for period under survey, newspaper files, personal recollections and personal investigations into county records.

Governor Crawford, after four years of efficient service, left the executive mansion to Governor Geo. W. Towns, who had been chosen to succeed him.

Governor Towns was born in Wilkes county and admitted to the bar in Alabama. He removed to Talbot county, and while living there began his political career. He was elected to Congress for three terms and then elected governor. He was a man of great suavity and exceedingly popular with his party. During his administration peace with Mexico came, and the complications which followed brought about strife between the fire-eaters, as the secessionists were called, and the Union men. This strife was very bitter, and ultimated in a division of the Democrats into Southern rights and Union parties; and when Governor Towns's term was ended Howell Cobb was nominated by the Union party, and was elected by a large majority. Mr. Cobb was born in Jefferson county. He was a man of fine native gifts, and had had the best advantages for education that the State afforded. He was genial and popular, and had been elected to Congress when quite young and had served four terms, and had served as Speaker of the House of Representatives.

On the election of Mr. Buchanan in 1856 he was given a seat in his cabinet, and was occupying that position when Georgia seceded. He then resigned from the cabinet and returned to Georgia, and was elected a member of the Convention which formed the constitution of the Confederate States. When the war began he entered the army as colonel, and was made a brigadier-general, and then placed in command of a department.

After the war was over he again entered upon the practice of law with his kinsman Judge Jackson and removed to Macon. While on a visit to New York he died very suddenly.

Herschel V. Johnson, who succeeded him as governor, was a native of Burke, was graduated at Athens, and was admitted to the bar when quite young. His advancement was very rapid; and while Governor Towns was in office he was appointed by him to a vacancy in the office of senator of the United States. After his term in the Senate expired he was elected a judge of the superior court. He was then nominated a candidate for governor; and after a very hotly contested election, by the narrow majority of 500 he was chosen governor over Chas. J. Jenkins.

He served as governor two terms. He was an intense Southern rights man. But when the Democratic party repudiated Stephen A. Douglas and nominated Breckinridge,

Jos. E. Brown.

Ben. H. Hill.

Gov. A. H. Colquitt.

Dr. G. J. Orr.

he took the side of the Douglas party, and was placed as second man on the ticket. He doubted the wisdom of secession, and took no active part in affairs during the war. He returned to his estate in Jefferson county and died there while judge of the superior court. He was famous for his great power as a platform speaker, for his deep devotion to his friends and intense hatred of his foes.

He was succeeded by Joseph E. Brown, to whom we have alluded in our sketch of Cherokee county. Mr. Brown was born in South Carolina, but his father, soon after his birth, removed to Georgia and settled near Gaddistown in Union county. He was a worthy man and, while in humble circumstances, was an independent farmer. Joseph his son resolved to secure an education, and went over to Pickens county in South Carolina and spent a few years in a good country school. He then studied law; and attracting the attention of Dr. Lewis, a man of means and of broad views, he was provided by him with money to go to the law school of Yale College. He was successful from his beginning as a lawyer in Canton, was elected to the senate of the State when a young man, was then a judge, and now he was chosen governor.

He was governor for four terms, and was regarded as one of the most astute men in the land. He had many bitter enemies and many ardent friends. His life has been written by his friend Colonel Fielder, and the story of the events and times in which he bore so large a part has been well told by another warm friend, Colonel Isaac W. Avery.

I have now given a short sketch of every governor of Georgia from 1732 to 1860, and a rapid recital of the main events in Georgia history up to 1847, and it now remains for me to put in one chapter the story of those last years which marked the close of an epoch such as can never be found again when the great revolution which made a new Georgia began.

The period between 1847 and 1860 was an era of rapid development. The Central railroad had reached Macon and joined the Macon and Western, which had been completed to Marthasville in DeKalb county, and the Georgia railroad from Augusta and the Western and Atlantic railroad from Chattanooga had reached the same point. It was now possible to transport cotton unloaded from north Alabama boats at Chattanooga to Savannah, and grain from East Tennessee to Charleston by continuous railways. The village of Marthasville had become the city of Atlanta—a name selected for it, or rather made for it, by Mr. Garnett and Mr. Peters, who were civil engineers on the Georgia railroad. A road was projected and completed from Rome to Kingston to join the Western and Atlantic railroad; one from Athens to Union Point on the Georgia; one from Augusta to Millen to tap the Central; one from Atlanta to West Point to join the road from Montgomery; one from Macon to Columbus; one from the Central at Gordon to Milledgeville and Eatonton; one from Macon to Albany, and, later, roads from Macon to Brunswick and from Savannah to Thomasville. These railways brought all parts of the State into connection and led to the rapid development of every part of it.

In endeavoring to get a view of the industrial condition of the State during this period it will perhaps be best to glance at its various sections as they present themselves.

The rice plantations and sea islands were now owned by a few wealthy and aristocratic people who had a large number of slaves; and rice and cotton were the chief products. There were raised besides, for home consumption, cattle, hogs, potatoes, turnips, and all kinds of garden supplies. There had been little change in this section for sixty years, and the pictures we have of the people in the previous pages were as true of them in 1860 as in 1820. The larger rice plantations were on the Ogeechee, the Savannah, the Satilla, Hutchinson's Island and in Liberty county and Bryan's Neck. The negroes had increased till they were counted by the hundred. The richer planters had their winter houses among the live-oaks near the rice-fields, and spent their summers and the early fall in the Northern States or on the sea islands. They still pursued much the same methods of culture their fathers had used, save that the improved methods of hulling rice were now adopted, and the rice, instead of being prepared for market on the plantations, was shipped by the schooner-load to the rice-mills in Savannah. The social life among them was such as we have before portrayed. They were hospitable, refined and self-indulgent. Their wealth was largely in their negroes, and as their plantations furnished all they needed, and their factors were ready to attend to all their wishes, they went on their even way and cared little about accumulations other than that from the natural increase of their slaves. Life was about as fixed among them as among the English gentry whom they so much resembled.

The middle part of Georgia was becoming more and more a great cotton plantation. The poorer landholders had removed from the older counties; and in these counties and as far west as the Ocmulgee one rode for miles through the lands of some great proprietor. A group of cheap cabins, an overseer's house, a large barn, a cotton-gin and screw, with now and then an elegant, roomy mansion in a grove of oaks and hickories, were presented in all sections of the old counties. Cotton was the main product, but among the best planters the raising of meat and breadstuffs was still carefully attended to. The social life of twenty years before was now almost unchanged, except that the young people were better educated. There was, however, a sad destruction of the beautiful woods, and the evidence of careless culture was seen in the many old fields on the plantations. Wilkes, Lincoln, Elbert, Greene and Columbia were now counted old and worn-out; and many large planters had moved their slaves to southwestern Georgia and even to Louisiana and Texas, and were opening plantations in new lands. They still held to their old homes, and these changes in the location of their laborers were made during the period of which we are writing. All the rude features of life in middle Georgia had now disappeared, and there was nowhere a more dignified society or a more religious, worthy people than there was now in this part of the State. But no one could fail to see that the white population was becoming more and more reduced, and that there had been a real devastation of the splendid country which had been settled but little over fifty years. The fields no longer produced remunerative crops, and there seemed but little prospect of improving them, when Mr. David Dickson of Hancock county, by the wise use of commercial fertilizers, opened the way to a wonderful change in planting and of making the ridges and pine woods which had been considered worthless good cotton land. This was by the liberal use of commercial fertilizers. Mr. Dickson was the first planter in Georgia to use the then newly introduced Peruvian guano and to adopt a new method of cultivating both corn and cotton.* There was considerable interest aroused in cotton-spinning, and mills were constructed in Butts, Greene, Newton, Putnam, Wilkes and Elbert. These factories were run by water-power and paid good dividends. There was now much wheat raised, and in every county there was a merchant mill where good flour was made, and in the grist-mills there were often bolting-cloths for wheat flour. There was a constant advance in education, and in every neighborhood there was an academy. Mercer, Emory, Oglethorpe and the State University were the male

* Hancock County, Chapter IV.

colleges, and there were a number of female colleges, chief among them the Wesleyan in Macon and Lagrange College.

The negroes had greatly improved since they were last glanced at. On the large plantations there was much careful missionary work, and in the interior much attention had been paid to their moral as well as temporal welfare. It is doubtful whether there was any part of the world, except perhaps Scotland and New England, where ordinary laborers on farms were the equals in all respects to the negro slaves in middle Georgia just before the war, where they were so well fed, so well housed and their health so carefully looked after. They were not free from vices, but the interests of the owner led him to guard them carefully against all those vices which reduced their value commercially. Murder was rare, and drunkenness almost unknown. They married early, and while they sometimes married often, they had their wives and children. That they were honest as a class or put a high estimate on social purity or the bond of marriage no one could justly say. They could not read, as a rule, but they were oftentimes good farmers and skillful mechanics. While not strictly moral, they were very religious.

The villages and county towns grew slowly during this period. The large planter went to the city for his heavy groceries, and he bought comparatively little at his county town. In Washington, Madison, Covington, Eatonton, Forsyth and other county sites there was considerable trade, and these county towns were becoming more generally markets for cotton and depots for supplies.

Through all the country there were the same churches which had generally been built of unplaned plank or logs thirty years before, and the old plan of monthly meetings was still followed; but now the churches in the towns were beginning to secure pastors who gave them weekly services, and the plain, uncomely country churches were being now replaced by neat and attractive buildings.

The drinking habits of the people had undergone a great change. The decanter was no longer on the sideboard and the still had disappeared from most neighborhoods, though it was likely to appear again if there was a good peach crop; and while there was still the cross-roads groggery, it was under the ban.

The up-country, as it was called from Atlanta northward, had very rapidly and steadily improved. There was but little cotton raised except in a very few counties. In Cass (now Bartow), Floyd, Chattooga and Polk there was some cotton planted, but the main products were corn, wheat and bacon.

Marietta had become quite an important town, Cartersville was still but a hamlet, Kingston was a considerable village, and Dalton (or Cross Plains) was becoming a city of some importance. Ringgold was a rather large depot where wheat was purchased in large quantities, while Rome had become a bustling city. The country all along the line of the new railroad was rapidly filling up with a sturdy and industrious people. There had been a gratifying improvement in the morals and culture of all this section, and an excellent class of people had now fixed their homes in it, and all the rude features of frontier life had disappeared. Along the Etowah in Cedar Valley and along the Chattooga there were now elegant homes.

There were good schools established in most of the towns and villages, and there was much more attention given to common schools. During this period a Baptist college was established at Cassville, and the Georgia Military Institute had been opened at Marietta and had a large patronage.

That part of Georgia known as the Piedmont country, on the foot-hills of the Blue Ridge, Franklin, Madison, Hall, etc., had lost many of its people, who had removed to newer counties, and being remote from the railroads that section had retained many of its early features, but these old counties had not seriously deteriorated.

The greatest changes in Georgia had, however, passed over the rotten-limestone land of southwestern Georgia, which at the beginning of this epoch was attracting a large immigration. As the railroads reached southwestern Georgia the planters living on the worn lands of middle Georgia, whose slaves had rapidly increased, were led to make large plantations in these counties, and in Macon, Lee, Dooly, Sumter, Dougherty and Baker they settled a large number of slaves. In the history of the counties which preceded this chapter I have already spoken of the opening of these plantations. The country was wonderfully fertile, and for a time was strangely free from the ravages of the caterpillar and the boll-worm. Crops were nearly always sure, prices during all this period were good, and the property of the southwest Georgia planter increased with marvelous rapidity.

During this period there was constructed the Macon and Brunswick railway from Macon to Brunswick, and the Atlantic and Gulf from Savannah to Thomasville, connecting Macon with the coast and the Savannah with the Chattahoochee. Both lines went through an almost unbroken pine forest, and there was little development along them before the war began, but the beginning of the great development of this pine country was made at that time.

In the history of the counties which comprised this section I have told of the wonderful changes which have passed over this entire wire-grass country, but at this time there was but little change to be seen from what had been thirty years before: the same scattered houses, the same simple habits, the same want of educational advantages, were found in 1860 as were found in 1830. The story of the cities will give an insight into the condition of things as presented by them during this era. After the terrible depression from 1837 to 1843 the whole country was wonderfully prosperous for some time. The old banks were solid and reliable; and, save the bank of St. Marys, which was managed in Columbus and which was the last bank in Georgia to issue shinplasters, all the old banks were recognized as perfectly solvent. They had large circulation, large resources and the full confidence of the people. Their branches extended all through the State, and they gave liberal accommodations. When specie was demanded for their bills it was promptly furnished. A few wildcat banks were opened, but these were soon discontinued. In 1857, however, when the cotton had just begun to move, a sudden financial crash came upon the country, and there was a run upon the Georgia banks for which they were not prepared. They suspended, and their suspension was legalized by the Legislature. The suspension was temporary and business went on, and up to the beginning of the war in April, 1861, there were no serious results from the panic. The Legislature passed what was known as the stay law, and no debts could be collected by legal process.

The wretched illiteracy of many of the Georgia people and the inefficiency of the private school system, supplemented by a pitiable sum doled out for pauper education to remedy it, had been a source of deep mortification to many Georgians. The political theories concerning paternalism which dominated led the people to oppose vigorously anything like a common school system, and for years the progress of primary education where it was most needed was sadly slow. But Thomas R. R. Cobb, the gifted brother of Howell Cobb, formulated a plan for a school system which he hoped and expected, if adopted, would secure the education of the masses and at the same time avoid anything like socialism. His plan, however, was never given a fair trial; and with the overthrow of the old State government and the formation of the new constitution after the war, the common school system displaced it. It might, however, safely be said that as far as much of Georgia was concerned, there had been for years few children who were forced to remain in ignorance because there was no chance for them to secure the elements of an education; but there was a fearful lack of interest on the part of many to take advantage of the means in reach.

The daily press at the beginning of this period was the *Savannah Georgian*, the *Savannah Republican*, the *Augusta Chronicle* and the *Augusta Constitutionalist*. There were, however, before the close of this era, the *Macon Telegraph*, the *Columbus Enquirer-Sun*, the *Atlanta Intelligencer*, the *Savannah News*, and some other short-lived dailies.

The weekly press had become greatly increased, and there were, in addition to the list we have given elsewhere, sundry other papers in each of the leading towns. There were at the beginning of the war a large number of weeklies which were largely supported by public advertising.

The *Southern Cultivator* was now a vigorous monthly edited by Daniel Lee and devoted to the development of southern agriculture. It was during this period that the Georgia Agricultural Society was formed, and it had its first fair at Stone Mountain in 1848, and afterward there was a fair held for several years in Atlanta, and one of the Atlanta streets is named Fair street in honor of the old fair ground.

In 1860 there was an exciting political campaign which resulted in the election of Abraham Lincoln and the triumph of the Republican party. Here my story ends. A new era begins, and a much larger volume than this would be necessary to tell the story of the four years from 1861 to 1865. I have tried to give the genesis of the Georgia people, to trace them back to their origin, and I think I have shown how absurdly they write who speak so flippantly of the Georgia people as descending from those who were in debtor's prisons and English almshouses, and how much more absurdly they write who declare that the middle Georgians were a lawless and ignorant horde of adventurers whom they call crackers. The facts are that some early Georgians were from England, Scotland, Germany and the north of Ireland, and some of them, not over 1,500 in all, received a small amount of help from the trustees; but they were of the best class of the plain people of the English yeomanry, the German farmers and the Scotch crofters; there came some Highland lairds and their clansmen with the Scotch, and some men of classical culture with the Germans, and some men of education and character with the English, and some enterprising and intelligent people with the Scotch-Irish, but by far the larger number of Georgians came from Virginia and North Carolina. There were a few Quakers and thrifty Jews among the early comers, and the cannie trader from Scotland, the daring adventurer from the north of Ireland, the mystical German, were all here before the Revolution; those broad-minded Englishmen, Noble Jones, John Wereat, James Habersham and Button Gwinnett, and Virginia gentlemen like Wm. Glascock and Geo. Walton, and Scotch chieftains like Lachlan McIntosh, and Puritans like Dr. Hall and Abraham Baldwin, all united in making the Georgia people. The native Celt—the pure Irishman from Cork or Tipperary—warm in his temper and Catholic in his faith, to whom Georgia was to be so greatly indebted in after time, was excluded by religious intolerance from coming at the first settlement, and it was only after the Revolution, and some time after it, that an Irishman like Wilde was found among her public men. The Irishmen who came to Galphin were Scotch-Irishmen and Protestants all, and it was not before 1840 that the south of Ireland people came in large numbers into Georgia. It may be best to give a summary of the different classes who have made up the Georgia people. They were: The English yeomanry, a few of the English gentry, the Scotch gentry, the Scotch peasantry, the Germans from the Tyrol who came from Hanover, the Germans from the Palatinate, the Scotch-Irish, the Virginians, Marylanders and Carolinians, a few New Englanders, a few Portuguese Jews, a few French Huguenots. These were the immigrants, and in after time there were no classes added to these save the German Jews who came as traders into the country. Those who came after the Revolution were of the same class as those who came before it, and do not find a separate place. The social features of the people took shape before the Revolution and underwent but little change in after time. There were then as in after time the gentry, the yeomanry, the crackers and the slaves.

I have up to this time attempted to give a description of each county and a short history of it as it came before me in order of time as organized, and as before the beginning of this period all the State had been divided into counties I have glanced at all parts of it. The counties as first made were very large but they were divided and subdivided, and for thirty years new counties were continually making their appearance. I do not think it necessary now to enter into the history of each, and I am compelled to omit a chapter giving an account of each of these newly formed counties.

CHAPTER XII.

RELIGION IN GEORGIA.

Georgia was settled by Christian men and from Christian motives. These Christians were of different denominations, and all forms of religious belief were tolerated except that held by the Roman Catholics. The founders of the colony were in the main Church of England people, and an English clergyman, as we have seen, came with the first immigrants. One of the first buildings erected was a board tabernacle, where Mr. Herbert, the rector, read prayers and preached. His health failed and he returned to England, and was succeeded by Mr. Quincy, one of the New England family of that name. Mr. Quincy remained only a short time and left the colony, and Messrs. John and Charles Wesley succeeded him. John remained in Savannah and Charles went with Mr. Oglethorpe to Frederica.

Of Mr. John Wesley's stay in Savannah we have told elsewhere, as that of Charles Wesley at Frederica. Both of these gifted brothers returned to England, and Mr. Geo. Whitefield came and took John Wesley's vacated place. He was compelled to leave his pastorate that he might raise funds for the support of his orphanage, and the church was somewhat irregularly supplied by the Church of England clergymen and by the officers of his orphanage. The church at Frederica ceased to have a pastor soon after the Spanish war, when the troops were disbanded and the town largely deserted by the people.

There was no other Episcopal church built in Georgia until 1757, when a church was built by the traders in Augusta, and Mr. Jonathan Copp was sent over by the Society for the Propagation of the Gospel to take charge of it and work as a missionary in the country about.

There was from the beginning and during the progress of the Revolution an entire abandonment of all the Episcopal churches except the one in Savannah, in which during the days of British occupancy there was occasional religious service. The only Episcopal clergymen who remained in Georgia and seem to have sympathized with the Americans were John Holmes and Mr. Abraham Piercey. The church in Savannah was supplied by Mr. Ellington after the Revolution. After the trustees of the Richmond academy had succeeded in building a church in 1789 Dr. Abraham Boyd, an Episcopal clergyman, was put in charge of it.

The church in Burke was abandoned to Methodists and Presbyterians and never reoccupied by Episcopalians. The church in Augusta was not regularly supplied until the Episcopal society in 1816 secured a gift of the lot on which St. Paul's church now stands, and succeeded in erecting the handsome structure which is now upon it. When the new cities of Macon and Columbus were laid out the Episcopalians built a church in each city as soon as it was settled, and Bishop Elliot was selected as the first Protestant Episcopal bishop of the diocese of Georgia in connection with the rectorship of Christ Church in Savannah.

LUTHERANS.

The Salzburghers, of whom we have already spoken as settling the Ebenezer colony, were the first Lutherans. They built a church at Ebenezer under the care of Pastors Bolzius and Gronau.

Another body of Germans made an abortive effort to establish a church at Frederica under the care of Mr. Driesler, and a church was built at Savannah probably before 1759, which was closed during the Revolution and not opened again till 1823. Before the Revolution the good Pastors Bolzius and Gronau died and Pastor Triebner took their places. He was a Loyalist and so were many of his flock, but many of them and leading ones among them were patriots.

After the war was over the old inhabitants returned to their homes near Ebenezer and renovated their churches. There was a body of German Lutherans, not Salzburghers, who were led to come to Georgia by Captain DeBrahm, who settled near Ebenezer and finally became identified with the Salzburghers. Some Lutherans from South Carolina, who were the descendants of the German emigrants to that colony, settled in upper Georgia after the opening of the new lands in 1825, and sundry congregations have been organized in the various counties of Georgia.

THE PRESBYTERIANS AND CONGREGATIONALISTS.

The Presbyterians were the third body of Christians who settled in Georgia and established churches. Pastor McLeod came with the Scotch colony from the Highlands and formed the first Presbyterian church in Georgia. He had service in a log hut at Darien. He, however, did not remain long in his parish, but went to South Carolina when this Scotch settlement was disintegrated, as it was soon after the Spanish war. There was no organized Presbyterian church after this until the coming, in 1751, of the Dorchester colony, who settled in St. John's parish and built a church at Midway; for while these people were not nominally Presbyterians, they were practically such, and Congregationalists and Presbyterians were regarded as the same body at that time and were in close alliance. The next church established in Georgia was in Savannah, where a number of Scotchmen had made their homes, and in 1759 a Presbyterian church, which was essentially a Congregational church, was organized and a learned Swiss clergyman, a Mr. Zubly, was secured as minister to it. The larger part of this congregation, with the pastor, took the side of the colonies, and Mr. Zubly was honored with an election to the Continental Congress. His course there we have seen, and the results of it. The church seems to have had no pastor during the war and was disorganized, and the house was in a dilapidated condition when the war ended. It was repaired and the congregation gathered again, and a pastor was secured. In 1760 there was quite a body of Scotch Presbyterians in St. George's parish, and they organized a church on Briar creek and one at Old Church and Walnut Branch, and had Rev. Josiah Lewis as pastor.

The rural Presbyterians were very strong in what was afterwards Jefferson county, where a body of Scotch-Irish people had settled. They do not seem to have had any church before the Revolutionary war, but were organized into kirks which met in private houses. Their pastor sympathized with the Loyalists and fled the country, and it was some time after the Revolution before a successor was secured. After the Revolution there came into upper Georgia, into Franklin and Jackson counties, a number of North Carolina and South Carolina Presbyterians, who formed several churches in Franklin county, then including a number of up-country counties.

There were several Presbyterian churches organized in Wilkes and Greene just after the Revolution, and several Presbyterian preachers were in charge of classical schools in the last days of the eighteenth and the first of the nineteenth century in different parts of Georgia. Many substantial citizens of Augusta were Scotchmen and were Presbyterians by inclination if not actually communicants. There was, however, no Presbyterian church organized until 1804, when one was regularly organized by Mr. McKnight, which held its services in the old St. Paul's church. In 1809 the congregation began to build a new church where the First Presbyterian church now stands on Telfair street, and a pastor was regularly employed after 1807.

BAPTISTS.

The early story of the Baptists has been already told in the current history.

Silas Mercer had come to Georgia just before the Revolution, and settled first in Burke and then removed to Wilkes. He, too, in common with Marshall and Bottsford, had been driven from Georgia during the war, but he returned and did most efficient work in Wilkes, and baptized his son Jesse, who became a great man among his people. While he was at work in Wilkes there were a number of Baptist preachers zealously preaching in Elbert, Lincoln and Oglethorpe, and they gathered a large harvest of souls. As the tide of settlement rolled westward the Baptist evangelist was always found with the foremost. As they were Congregationalists and demanded no educational qualification for license to preach, there was always a supply of earnest, enthusiastic preachers to push on the work.

Young James Screven, the son of General Screven, whose father was killed at Midway, while at school in Charleston had been converted and had joined the Baptist Church. When he grew to manhood and returned to Sunbury, where he fixed his home and near where he had an estate, he began to preach gratuitously to the people about him, and thus founded the Baptist Church in the low-country. During the year 1827 a very great religious awakening took place in all upper and middle Georgia, and the Baptists had a large part in the work and reaped a large return from their labors.

The Baptists by that time were among the wealthiest and most aggressive denominations in the State, and continued to press forward. Chas. D. Mallary, Sherwood, Dawson, King, Davis and Mercer were among the leading Baptist preachers. The *Christian Index*, of which we have spoken, is the organ of the Baptists, and has had a continued existence for eighty years.

METHODISTS.

In the current history an account of the coming of the first Methodists into Georgia has been given.

In 1788 the first conference was held in the fork of the Broad river, and that year the first church among the Methodists in Georgia was built. The second conference was held in that church in 1789. Hope Hull, a gifted young Marylander, came to Georgia at that time and had much to do with building up the church. There was at first rapid progress, and then after a few years a steady decline; and ten years after the first preacher came to the State there were fewer members in the churches than there were two years after they began.

In 1798 Stith Mead, a young Virginian belonging to one of the leading families in Georgia, came to Augusta and there established and organized the first Methodist Church in any city west of the Savannah river. He joined the South Carolina Conference and was made a presiding elder. He was a man of fine parts, and there was for some years a constant advance. The camp-meeting was introduced, and there were frequent revivals and rapid increase in members for ten years. The conference, which had been dependent on Virginia for her preachers, now, in the first year of the century, began to furnish them from her own body, and men like Lovick and Reddick Pierce and James Russell began to preach. There was a great revival in 1809 along the Broad and Little rivers under the preaching of Russell, in which many of the famous Broad river people were converted and joined the Methodist Church. Methodism had now extended her circuits until they reached every part of the State of Georgia.

In connection with the South Carolina Conference the Georgia Methodists established the *Southern Christian Advocate*, and afterward, surrendering their joint interest in the paper to South Carolina, they established the *Wesleyan Christian Advocate*, which is now published in Atlanta and has ten thousand subscribers.

From the beginning the Methodists paid much attention to the negroes, and have many adherents among them. The colored Methodists among the various bodies of negro Methodists are in close connection in the M. E. Church, South. The negro Methodists have handsome churches.

ROMAN CATHOLICS.

The Roman Catholics were excluded by law from Georgia at its first settlement and were not allowed a foothold until after the Revolution. The first church was established in 1796, in Wilkes county, at what is now Sharon or Locust Grove. The first church building was erected in Savannah in 1802.

A church was built in Augusta in 1811 on a beautiful lot given by the city. It is certain that, while a building was not erected until that time, there were services held for years before the house was built, and the same thing is doubtless true of Savannah.

In Macon and Columbus there were churches at an early day, and the Catholic church was one of the first erected in Atlanta. The Catholics have churches in nearly all the cities and larger towns of the State and a few in the rural districts. The first built in the country in Georgia was at Locust Grove, in Taliaferro county, and there is a mission church in Appling county. The Jesuits have an elegant establishment near Macon, a novitiate in which those of this order are prepared for the priesthood. There are elegant orphanages for boys in Washington and one for girls in Savannah. They have schools in all the cities. There has been a Catholic bishop in Georgia for over forty years, and the church is compactly and completely organized.

THE DISCIPLES,

or Christian Church, was brought into Georgia soon after it was established in the West. It has some strong congregations in the State. In Augusta and Atlanta it is a body of large influence and has an influential membership, and in Macon, Sandersville, Valdosta and in other places it has a following.

There are a number of other Christian bodies that are not found except in certain localities. There are a few Universalists, a congregation or two of Unitarians, and a small number of Congregationalists.

THE JEWS.

A small body of Portuguese Jews, about forty in number, came to the colony in 1733. The larger part of them removed to South Carolina, only a few families remaining in Savannah. These held firmly to their ancient faith and worshiped for many years in private houses. It was nearly a hundred years after the first Jews came before a synagogue was built. They then built a small synagogue and had regular services. They were Americans and people of position and wealth, and rigidly orthodox. The Germans, who were largely tinctured with the liberalism of the Reformed Jews, were not attracted to the little synagogue; and being people of means, they built a very handsome synagogue on a fashionable street. The Jews have other fine synagogues in other cities in the State, and regular services are held by the rabbis in each of them every Saturday.

TEMPERANCE REFORM.

In 1827 there sprang up almost simultaneously in different Atlantic States what were known as temperance societies, which aimed to diminish, if not entirely banish, the drinking habits of society. Adiel Sherwood established a temperance society in Putnam county in 1827, and in a short time the sentiment of temperance in the use of liquors became quite popular with serious people.

The movement passed through various forms and resulted in the formation of divers temperance orders. These first temperance societies had a large following among prominent men. Judge Lumpkin, Judge Charlton, Judge Longstreet, Judge Hillyer and many other prominent lawyers were leaders in the reform, but there was no attempt to suppress the sale by law. The antagonism to the sale of strong drink, however, reached so far that Josiah Flournoy, in 1839, canvassed the State to secure signatures to a petition forbidding the licensing of dram-shops. He was very sanguine of success, and when the Legislature, influenced by Judge Cone, summarily disposed of his favorite scheme, it was too much for him, and his health gave way under the shock. There were, however, granted by the Legislature charters for the towns of Oxford, Penfield and Culloden, in each of which the sale of spirituous liquor was forbidden, but no further effort to suppress the sale of liquor by law was made by the temperance men for some years. A license law was enacted and an effort was made to regulate the traffic. When the prohibition wave swept the North, and, following the example of Maine, State after State prohibited the sale of strong drink, some enthusiastic Georgians formed a prohibition party and nominated B. H. Overby, a prominent lawyer in Atlanta, as prohibition candidate for governor. He received only 6,200 votes, and the attempt to secure legal prohibition was given over for some years. It is hardly within the scope of this chapter to survey the field since the war, but the progress of the temperance cause has been constantly onward. The distillery has, except in some few parts of the mountain country, been put under the religious ban. County after county has secured special acts prohibiting the sale of strong drink in their boundaries, and by a general local option act in the whole State, with the exception of a few counties in which there are large cities or towns and a large negro vote, the whisky traffic has been positively prohibited and largely suppressed. Public sentiment is antagonistic to it, even in the cities, and while the retail trade is licensed, it is, in most of them, under careful regulation.

CHAPTER XIII.

EDUCATION IN GEORGIA.

First School at Ebenezer — Mr. DeLamotte in Savannah — Schools in Dorchester Settlements—School in Augusta—Constitutional Provision for Public Education—Academies Established and Endorsed—Old Field Schools—Appropriation for Poor Scholars — Appropriation for Academies — General Cobb's Measures for Public Schools—Private Academies and High Schools in Georgia—Mr. Whitefield's Effort to Establish a College—The Proposition for a State University—The Charter Granted and the University Established at Athens—First Graduates—A Glance at the History of the Institution—First Methodist School—School at Salem—Manual Labor School—Emory College Established—Glance at its History—First Baptist School at Enon—Manual Labor School at Penfield—Mercer University Established—Its History—Oglethorpe University—Sidney Lanier—First Female College in the World Established in Macon, Ga.—History of the Georgia afterward the Wesleyan Female College—Lagrange Female College — Georgia Female College—Monroe Female College—Andrew Female College—Young Harris College—North Georgia Agricultural and Military College—South Georgia College at McRae—Industrial College at Milledgeville — Technological College in Atlanta—Colleges for Negroes and Colored People—Cox Female College—Gainesville Female College—Shorter Female College — Dalton Female College—Lucy Cobb Institute—Gordon Institute—R. E. Lee Institute, Thomaston.

As this history has progressed the story of the efforts of the State to educate its people has been told. It is only necessary here to make a summary. There were before the Revolution public schools in Savannah and Ebenezer, and perhaps a few schools in the newly opened country. A provision was made in the first constitution for a general common school education. After this for years little attention was paid to general education; then the Cobb school law was made, and after the war a common school system was put into operation. Sundry private schools and academies, male and female, were established, to which attention has been called.

The first effort to found a college was made by Mr. Whitefield, who proposed to change his Orphanage into a college. Before his plans were perfected, but after he had secured a grant of land, begun work and the building was erected, Mr. Whitefield died. The property descended by bequest to Lady Huntington, but the buildings were burned, and soon after the war came on and the college, never fairly established, disappeared entirely.

THE STATE UNIVERSITY.

After the Revolution some gentlemen of the State procured a charter and an appropriation for the State University. The trustees selected were John Houston, James Habersham, Benjamin Taliaferro, Wm. Few, Joseph Clay, Abraham Baldwin, Wm. Houston, Nathan Brownson, John Habersham, Abel Holmes, Jenkins Davies, Hugh Lawson and Wm. Glascock. It was stipulated in the charter that all the officers selected for the institution should be of the Christian religion, and it was ordered that the board of trustees should be a *senatus academicus*, and should correlate all the academies with the University. While the Legislature granted the charter and 40,000 acres of land for endowment, it did not say where the University should be located, and made no provision for the erection of buildings.

The times were not favorable to the scheme. The country had not recovered from the desolations of the war, there was no money, and there were no pupils prepared for a college. The academies at Augusta, Sunbury and Mt. Carmel, in Wilkes, met all the needs of the times, and so the statute of 1785 lay dormant for nearly fifteen years. It was then decided to establish the University at Greensboro, but the people were not satisfied with the place, and in 1800 Mr. John Milledge proposed to give the State seven hundred acres of land in what was then Jackson, and is now Clarke county. The donation was accepted and he bought the land and gave it to the trustees, and the first college building was erected. A president was chosen, Josiah Miegs, and the first commencement was held on the 31st day of May, 1804. The graduates were nine: Henry Jackson, Gibson Clark, Jephtha Harris, Augustin Clayton, Thomas Irwin, Jared Irwin, Jr., Robert Rutherford and Wm. Williamson. The college had no endowment except in wild lands, and they brought a very small return. During the war of 1812 the college became almost moribund. In 1816 the lands were sold and the State took the notes from the purchasers and gave the college $100,000 in bonds for them. The college was slow in rallying, but was opened again under brighter auspices under Dr. Waddell.

He was succeeded by Dr. Alonzo Church, a Vermonter, who made a very efficient president for over thirty years, and after his resignation Dr. A. A. Lipscomb was made chancellor. He was a Marylander of national reputation as a man of fine culture, and he made a most efficient and popular officer. Dr. H. H. Tucker was then chancellor for four years. After his resignation Dr. P. H. Mell, who had been connected with the University for many years, was chosen. He was very popular and useful, and was succeeded by Dr. W. E. Boggs; and he by Hon. Walter B. Hill, the present chancellor.

The United States granted quite a generous quantity of the public domain to the various States for the establishment of colleges in which agriculture and the mechanical arts should be taught, and while Governor Smith was governor this donation was turned by him into the treasury of the University, which added an agricultural and technological department to its existing course and secured the benefit of the large endowment thus provided. The citizens of Athens gave to the University a handsome building for scientific work. There have been sundry bequests and

Seney Hall, Emory College.

large gifts to the University, notably those of Dr. Terrell, Governor Gilmer and Governor Brown. The University has attached to it a law school, located in Athens, and a medical school at Augusta. Some years since it adopted the plan of giving free tuition to all male citizens of Georgia who attended its literary, agricultural or mechanical departments, and it has so adapted its curriculum to the demands of all classes that it has put college advantages within the reach of all.

EMORY COLLEGE.

The Methodist Conference of 1789 projected a high school, to be located at some point in middle Georgia, and went so far as to raise a subscription for its establishment; and Bishop Asbury rode up the forks of the Ogeechee to select a place where the school should be located, but it was no time for establishing schools and the plan was not carried out.

If we do not recognize Hope Hull's academy as the first Methodist school, the first in Georgia was at Salem, in what is now Oconee county, which was adopted as a Methodist school by the South Carolina Conference in 1820.

Dr. Olin, who had married a Georgia lady and whose property interests were in Georgia, had been chosen president of Randolph-Macon College, Virginia, and was anxious to secure the support of all the Southern conferences, and asked the Methodists of Georgia to endow a chair in that college with $10,000 and to patronize the institution, giving them some special privileges in return. The conference consented to accept this offer and decided, in addition, to establish a high school in Georgia on the manual labor plan, so popular at that time. This manual labor school, as has been stated in the history of Newton county, was located near Covington. It was found to be impracticable to conduct a farm and a high school at the same time, and the conference, under the influence of Dr. I. A. Few, in 1836, decided to establish a college. A charter was secured and the spot was selected about two miles from the manual labor school. One thousand four hundred acres of land were bought, a village laid out, and in 1837 the corner-stone of Emory College was laid. Dr. Few was selected as president, the college was opened in 1839, and in 1841 the first class was graduated. Judge Longstreet succeeded Dr. Few as president. Bishop Pierce, then Dr. Pierce, followed him, and when he was elected bishop, Dr. Means, professor of Natural Science, was chosen as his successor. He resigned after a year and was succeeded by Dr. James R. Thomas, who was president when the war began. The college was necessarily suspended during the war and its buildings used as a Confederate hospital, and when the war was over they were fearfully dilapidated. The endowment was gone and the people impoverished, and there seemed little hope for its recovery from its prostrate condition; but Bishop Pierce made an earnest and successful effort to keep the college alive, and a faithful, self-sacrificing faculty stood bravely by him.

The Legislature now made a proposition to the three colleges which were opened. It would give them $100 in State bonds to pay the tuition fees of such wounded soldiers as desired an education, for each year they attended. The bonds were not salable, but Emory College consented to receive them, and filled up her vacant halls.

With the aid of Bishop Pierce's Endowment Society and with the devotion of the faculty, the college began a new career. New buildings were erected and new students began to pour in. Dr. Thomas had been elected to a college in California and Dr. Luther M. Smith made president. He was very successful in conducting the college, and when it had become firmly established he resigned, and Dr. O. L.

Smith was made president. He retired from the presidency and took a professorship, and Dr. A. G. Haygood succeeded him. While he was in office Mr. Geo. I Seney, a New York banker, was attracted by some broad views of the new president, and decided to give the college $150,000 for building and endowment. This gift of Mr. Seney and the buildings erected by Bishop Pierce gave the college a full equipment for its school work. Dr. Haygood succeeded in purchasing some large houses in which to provide helping halls where young men could board themselves at a low price; and as tuition prices were low and often remitted, many poor men had an opportunity to secure a first-class education. Bishop Haygood resigned, however, to take the important office of agent of the Slater fund, and Dr. Hopkins was chosen president; and when he was elected to the presidency of the Technological School, Dr. Candler was elected to the presidency of Emory. During his incumbency the college was much more largely endowed and more thoroughly equipped, a handsome library building was erected, and its patronage was largely increased. After Dr. Candler was elected bishop Dr. Dowman was elected president, and is still in charge.

MERCER UNIVERSITY.

The Baptists early in the century made an effort to establish a college on a healthy plateau near Augusta, to be called Mt. Enon College. Dr. Holcomb was the agent to collect funds and to secure the charter, but the Legislature refused to grant a charter for a college, and only a high school was established. The question of a college for Baptists then slumbered until 1829, when Mr. Josiah Penfield, of Savannah, bequeathed $2,500 to aid in educating poor young men for the ministry. With this sum increased by private gifts to twice the amount a manual labor school was established at a place in Greene county, which was called, in honor of the generous donor of the first large gift, Penfield. Dr. B. M. Sanders was made president. A manual labor school did not meet the demands of the Baptists, and a university was projected and was established in 1838. Dr. Jesse Mercer, who had been the liberal friend of the manual labor school, left the whole of a very considerable fortune to endow the university, and it had from the start a considerable fund for its support. In 1851 the endowment amounted to nearly $151,000.

It was a successful institution from the start. The first president was Rev. Otis Smith, who did not long remain at the head of the college. He was succeeded by Dr. J. L. Dagg, who was for a long time the able president. Dr. N. M. Crawford (the son of W. H. Crawford), Dr. Henry Holcombe Tucker, Dr. A. J. Battle, Dr. Nunnally and Dr. Pollock have all presided in turn over the college. The university, being in a secluded village, kept up its exercises during the war, and was the only college in Georgia which did so. After the war it suffered, as did all the other public institutions, and some of its friends urged a change of location. Macon was anxious to secure a male institution of high grade, and offered to furnish handsome grounds and a fine building to the university if it would change its location from Penfield to Macon. The trustees would not accept a donation, but agreed to give free tuition to twelve Macon youths *in perpetuo* in consideration of the buildings furnished, and the college was moved. The buildings are very handsome, and the patronage was considerable from its reopening. Colonel Gray, a wealthy man in Jones, left his whole estate to provide for the education of Jones county young men.

Mr. Rockefeller, the wealthy capitalist, gave the college a very handsome donation for a new chapel, and the Baptists of Georgia have made to the university many gifts. It has an excellent law school attached to it and a prosperous theological school, and was never more prosperous than it is at the present writing.

The Oglethorpe University, which was established by the Presbyterians on a beautiful hill near Milledgeville at the same time that Mercer and Emory began their careers, had a comparatively brief but highly honorable history. The college up to the war was under the care of Dr. S. K. Talmage. It is famous as the Alma Mater of Sidney Lanier. It never recovered from the effects of the war and was never reestablished after its close.

FEMALE COLLEGES.

The subject of female education engaged the attention of the Georgia people to a very limited extent in its early history, and when the Legislature gave a small bonus to academies for a number of years it refused to charter any exclusively female academies; but in 1827 it broke its record and chartered the first female academy under State patronage at Harmony Grove in Jackson county. There was not a female college which conferred degrees then in the world. A young lawyer named Chandler startled the public by declaring in a public speech at Athens that in his opinion women should have exactly the same advantages granted to men and should have the same degrees conferred on them. This view was heartily endorsed by many of the best people, and when the young city of Macon resolved to build a female academy of high grade, Rev. Elijah Sinclair suggested it should build a female college. The idea took readily, and the Ocmulgee Bank said if the Legislature would grant the bank a charter and charter the college it would subscribe $25,000. The conditions were met and the subscription was made and promptly paid. The people made large subscriptions also, and the Georgia Female College was enterprized. There was no intention to build a Methodist college but it was to be for all denominations. The buildings were planned on a large scale, and as soon as the main building was habitable Bishop Pierce, then plain Mr. Pierce, a young man, was made president and an able faculty selected to assist him. The college had large patronage from the beginning, but the great crash of 1837 came on just as the college began, and before the buildings were completed many of the largest subscribers were bankrupt. The builder closed his lien, the college was sold and bought by Bishop Pierce, and it seemed for some time that the first female college in the world was doomed to failure. Rev. Samuel Anthony was appointed agent by the conference, and through his influence Mr. Everett, a wealthy Houston planter, bought some scholarships under certain conditions, and one was that the college was to change its name and become a Methodist college. This was agreed to and it became the Wesleyan Female College. The trustees had provided a very imposing building and one very finely located, but there was no endowment and the college was dependent upon patronage for its support. Bishop Pierce resigned and was made agent, and Dr. W. H. Ellison leased the college and conducted it successfully. Dr. Edward H. Myers was then made president, and Dr. O. L. Smith, Dr. J. M. Bonnell and for over twenty-five years Dr. Bass were presidents. While Dr. Bass was president Mr. Seney decided to make a large donation to the female college equal to that he had made to Emory. He required, as a condition of his gift, that the house should be modernized and provided with all proper conveniences, and the old building was transformed and made more commodious and elegant.

The Lagrange Female College, also under patronage of the Methodists, is one of the old female colleges in the State. Beginning as a female school it developed into the Lagrange Female College conducted by the Montgomery brothers. It was afterwards sold to the Georgia Confer-

Southern Female College, College Park.

ence in 1855 and made a denominational college. It was unfortunately burned, but it sprang from its ashes and has never suspended, and is now better equipped and more largely patronized than it has ever been. It is now under charge of a veteran educator, President Rufus W. Smith, and is in vigorous life.

Not long after the Montgomerys established the Lagrange Female College Mr. Milton Bacon established the Southern Female College. It was under Baptist patronage and was largely attended. It too was burned, but it was rebuilt by the celebrated I. F. Cox, who for years conducted it in connection with his gifted family with distinguished success. After his death it was decided by the family, who owned the property and the charter, to remove to College Park and open the college there.

The people of Lagrange were so much opposed to the removal and the loss of the historic name that satisfactory arrangements were made by which the Southern Female College was still in existence. It is now a prosperous institution under the care of Dr. G. A. Nunnally.

The Southern Female College, at College Park, of which President C. C. Cox is the head, has a very elegant equipment and a very fine patronage.

The Agnes Scott Female College, in Decatur, which was the munificent gift of Colonel Scott, a celebrated manufacturer, is a fine institution.

The Andrew Female College, in Cuthbert, has a beautiful building and a good faculty. It is now under the care of Rev. Homer Bush.

There is besides these female colleges the Lucy Cobb Institute at Athens, which, while not claiming to be a college proper, does the finest work. It is conducted by Misses Rutherford and Mrs. Lipscomb and is in high favor.

The Gainesville College, which is a private undenominational college, conducted by Messrs. Pearce and Van Hoose, has elegant buildings and a very large patronage.

The Catholics have a number of high schools for young ladies, one in each important city in the State, generally conducted by the Sisters of Charity.

The great need for a college beyond the Blue Ridge, where tuition would be nominal and board low, and where opportunities could be afforded for those who wished to board themselves to do so, led to the founding of Young Harris College, in Towns county. It has had a very large patronage and is doing great good.

The Dahlonega Agricultural and Mechanical College, located in the old mint at Dahlonega and fostered by the State, is a very popular and largely patronized school, which has done much service for the State.

The needs of the wire-grass section led to the founding of the South Georgia College, which is located at McRae, and which aims to do for the young people of the low-country a work such as is done in the upper counties. It is a comparatively new institution but is doing good work.

The State having made ample provision for the education of its young men in agriculture, the arts and in literature, decided to do something as a State in the aid of its young women, and, as we have seen in the account of Baldwin, it established in Milledgeville the Industrial School for young ladies. It is under the care of President Chappell, and is a school of high grade with a very large number of students.

There are female colleges at Dalton and Thomasville.

TECHNOLOGICAL.

The Technological School, in Atlanta, supported by the State, is a very well-equipped institution, which aims to teach young men the mechanical arts and give them at the

Main Building North Georgia Agricultural College, Dahlonega.

same time literary training. It has a new textile school added to its other schools of handicraft.

In addition to other facilities a normal school, where the teachers of the State are taught, has been established by the State in the city of Athens.

There is no exclusively agricultural college in the State, but a professor of agriculture holds his place in the University, and there is some attention paid to this field of industry.

There have been established many schools for the negroes. The State has one near Savannah which is supported by it and which has an able faculty and is a useful school.

Atlanta University, an extensive institution for colored people, supported by the Congregationalists, has been long established, is well equipped and has an able faculty and a large patronage, and has been of great service to Georgia.

Clarke University is a very popular school, supported by Northern Methodists, and has a very large patronage. It is near Gammon Theological School, a well endowed Methodist college for training negro preachers.

The Baptists have an institution in Atlanta for training negro preachers, and the M. E. Church, South, has one in Augusta for the education of teachers and preachers, and there are beside these quite a number of high schools in the State.

Although it was not my original purpose to carry this history any further than 1850, I have found myself compelled, in order to give a glimpse of the present condition of education, to do so. There is now a well-organized common school system in the State. Schools are kept open for six months in the year, and in the cities and many of the towns for nine months, and all classes are now privileged to secure a liberal education at the expense of the State.

CHAPTER XIV.

THE CITIES.

SAVANNAH.

In the first chapter of this book much that concerns the early history of Savannah has been already written. To each settler was given a town lot, a garden lot and forty-five acres for a farm. These gardens were just beyond Liberty street and the farms where is now Gwinnett.

Mr. Moore, storekeeper for the trustees and a great friend of Mr. Oglethorpe's, came in 1735. He found Savannah a mile and a fourth in circumference. There was a sandy beach, long since covered by wharves, a mile along the river front, and an Indian town four miles above it. There were about one hundred and fifty houses. The house Mr. Oglethorpe occupied was such as the freeholders lived in—a frame of sawed timber 24x16, floored and ceiled with rough plank and shingled. There were a few better houses, some even two and three stories high. Generally they were surrounded with split boards for fencing, but some of the more pretentious had palisades made of turned wood palings. Some of the people had been thrifty and a few thriftless. Rum was cheap, and though forbidden, they managed to get it and drank too much, to their great injury. The common laborers had two shillings a day for their work and the carpenters from four to five shillings.

There was a garden of ten acres, in which not only the ordinary vegetables were grown, but in which the effort was made to raise all kinds of tropical fruits, with only very partial success, as the frost had cut down the orange trees. The efforts to make silk, after the first brilliant success in making enough to give a robe to the queen, were not encouraging. The Italians quarreled, broke the coppers, stole the eggs and ran away to South Carolina. Mr. Oglethorpe forbade any more silk to be loomed until eggs enough could be secured for another start.

So far Mr. Moore gives us an insight into the temporal affairs of the young colony, but for a correct account of the educational and religious we must have recourse to the journals of Mr. Whitefield and Mr. Wesley.

In a previous chapter we have spoken of Mr. Wesley's stay in Savannah.

After he went back to England Mr. Whitefield came. He saw the necessity for an orphanage, and with him when he saw a thing ought to be done was to decide to do it, and he at once made his plans to raise the money and establish one. The scheme was a very wild one. Mr. Whitefield was himself only twenty-four years old. The colony was just being settled. There were few children who needed the home, and there was no money at the back of his plans except what he might be able to raise by his public appeals. He was compelled to go to England to be ordained a priest. He went and was ordained, and began at once to raise the money for his asylum. He secured from the trustees a grant of five hundred acres, and his friend Mr. James Habersham, who had been teaching the parish school, selected the tract ten miles from the city where the present Bethesda school is located. Mr. Whitefield continued for quite a year in England, preaching continuously and raising money to build, and in the spring of 1740 he laid the first brick of the new home. He had, however, already put the Orphanage into operation, renting a house and taking the children he could find in the colony.

The first teacher of the parish school was Charles DeLamotte, one of the Holy Club at Oxford and a warm friend of Mr. Wesley's. He was a man of some means and taught a free school. He returned to England with Mr. Wesley, and Mr. James Habersham came with Mr. Whitefield and took up his work. Just before Mr. Wesley left the city a new secretary of the colony came to take the place of Charles Wesley. This was the excellent and painstaking William Stephens, Esq., son of an English baronet. He kept a journal and published it in 1742. It was somewhat notable that Mr. John Wesley and Mr. Whitefield and Mr. Stephens each kept and published journals of their lives in Savannah. Mr. Stephens's three volumes, now so rare, was the first book of any size ever written in Georgia or published by a citizen of the colony. Next to Pepys's famous Diary there are few more entertaining books. He records everything at full length. He was sent out by the trustees to look after things generally, and Mr. Causton's account particularly. Savannah had grown steadily, if slowly, up to his coming in 1737. There had come in some new English immigrants and quite a reinforcement of Scotchmen and Germans, and Mr. Stephens brought his son Thomas, who afterward gave him a world of trouble, and some indentured servants who were too lazy to work when they were well, and were generally sick, and with these he was trying to get his garden lot of five acres in cultivation and open his little farm. There was a public house where the justices Christie, Parker and Causton used to meet the secretary and take a glass with him. Mr. Causton was building a handsome house in the country where there is now Causton's Bluff.

There was a St. Andrew's society in Savannah, a lodge of Masons, and now and then a ball was given at the ordinary, attended by thirty people. Mr. Causton was no longer storekeeper and had gone to England to try to settle with the trustees, and Mr. Jones, the dissenter, was in charge of the storehouse. Mr. Williams bought some goats in South Carolina, and the old ram so annoyed Mr. Fitz Wal-

Synagogue Savannah.

ter by breaking into his garden that the irate Welshman incontinently slew him, and then Mr. Williams went out with his gun to kill Mr. Fitz Walter's harmless geese. Mr. Abram Minis had a store, and Mr. Pat Talifer, the doctor, sold rum and talked sedition in the Coffee House, and wrote scurrilous attacks on Mr. Oglethorpe until, despairing of causing a change of affairs, he and some of his Scotch companions left the colony for Charleston—no great loss, the secretary thought.

Mr. Oglethorpe went back to England and the secretary was made governor, but the village did not grow even though the trustees removed all restrictions on land holdings, but when, against the protest of the German and Scotch, at the instance of Mr. Whitefield and Mr. Habersham, negro slaves were allowed, planters began to move in from South Carolina. Then Governor Reynolds came and Governor Ellis and found things very dilapidated in the city and the colony in a very depressed condition, but matters were improving and wealth increasing. There was rice on the main and on the sea islands which were now occupied, indigo was planted and things might have prospered in the city but for the scheme of Governor Reynolds and Governor Ellis to move the capitol to Hardwick. This, however, was set at rest by Governor Wright, who came in 1762, and then Savannah began to build up with great rapidity. The traders now brought their goods to Savannah and sent them from thence to the nation and shipped their peltry from the port to England. Rice planting about Savannah became a large industry, the rice-fields coming to the very edge of the city, and there were soon thousands of slaves on the plantations. The upper parishes, St. George's and St. Paul's, were filling up with a thrifty population, who drove their cattle and brought hides and deerskins and furs to the Savannah market.

The sturdy Germans near by, in Ebenezer, had built a

Lutheran church in the city on the lot where it now stands, and Mr. Jonathan Bryan and Lachlan McGilveray and Edward Telfair secured subscriptions in 1769 and built a church for the Presbyterians, to which Mr. Zubly was to be minister. There was perfect harmony between the mother country and the thrifty young city. Then the stamp act passed and another chapter tells the results of this act of Parliament, but the storm soon blew over and Savannah continued to improve. The *Georgia Gazette* was established in 1763 and made its weekly appearance. The wooden houses on the bay gave way to ranges of brick and stone, and hundreds of ships of small tonnage came from the West Indies and the northern provinces and from across the Atlantic to unload goods and to take cargoes of rice.

Messrs. Cowper and Telfair brought cargoes of fine, healthy slaves from Sierra Leone to the wharves, and sold them at thirty pounds each to the planters. The ladies dressed in rich silk, handsomely trimmed. There were phaetons and horses and tables shining with plate in not a few of the homes. Decanters of brandy and rum and Geneva were on the sideboards of the gentlemen; Mahogany bedsteads and chairs were in their houses. The city had its quota of lawyers and doctors, and perhaps was not free from quacks, for Dr. Felix Pitt offered his services as a physician and proposed to wait on ladies and gentlemen and other persons, and closes his notice by saying: *Si curat morbum probatum est.* The country was full of new negroes and the workhouse was full of runaways. There was advertised, "A negro wench who cannot tell her name. Her upper teeth were filed; had on a wrapper of white cloth. Another with a slit in her ear and a scar on her cheek; a boy dressed in blue negro cloth with osnaburg trousers; and one with an iron on his leg," who were awaiting their owners.

There was shipped from the port live-oak timber, hides,

Pulaski Monument.

hogs of all sizes, and myrtle wax, in addition to tar, pitch and turpentine, rice and indigo.

Messrs. Bard & Thompson sold puncheons of rum and ladies' hats alike. Messrs. Pinkerd & Brown, Joe Goodwin, Richard Wright and Audley Maxwell were merchants. Mr. Lewis Johnson provost marshal.

Mr. Haddon Smith preached in "The Church," as Christ Church was called, and Mr. Zubly to his wealthy Scotchmen in the "Presbyterian meeting-house," which had been built on Bryan and St. Julian streets, near the present market. There was an ugly club, which had regular meetings. The old filature was used as an assembly room, and Tondee's long room, about where the custom house is now, was a famous place for gatherings. Governor Wright lived where Telfair Academy is now and Mr. Josiah Tattnell, as it was written then, on the opposite side of the square. Nearly all the gentlemen who lived in town had plantations in the country.

The English government attempted taxation without representation, and Savannah, which had been the petted child of the crown and never taxed at all, raised the standard of rebellion, and in Tondee's long room, where the king had been so often toasted in flowing glasses of Madeira, and where the young people danced on Mr. Oglethorpe's birthday, the meeting was held which resulted at last in the expulsion of Sir James Wright and in the terrors of a wasting war.

Savannah was occupied by a feeble garrison which was driven out by the British, who established their camp at the head of Broughton street, looking west. An effort at recapturing the city failed, but in 1782 Colonel Jackson's troopers rode into the evacuated city and General Wayne took possession. Three years of war and seven of stagnation in trade had wrought havoc, and when, in 1783, the court resumed its session after the "usurpation," as it was called, there was little that was cheerful in the outlook. But the stagnation was soon over and soon things brightened.

The grand jury complained that the court-house was in wretched condition, and the jail in worse, the churches without pastors and in great dilapidation, and there was no academy or school.

The State confiscated Governor Graham's magnificent place on the Savannah river and gave it to General Greene, and the home of Josiah Tattnall and gave it to Colonel Jackson, who himself bought Governor Wright's place near Savannah, on the Thunderbolt road, known as Cedar Hill, and took possession of it. Many other pieces of confiscated property were sold in the city, and the owners were exiled forever. The Legislature, after a few sessions in Savannah, ordered the capitol removed to Augusta, and, much to the annoyance of the people of Savannah, ordered the archives sent there also. Mr. Hunter opened a school where English branches were taught, and Mr. Bird attempted a classical school for young gentlemen, but, failing to get patronage, opened a mixed school where young ladies and young gentlemen were taught. There were up to 1789 no corporate powers granted to the city; then the city had a charter, and Mr. Houston was the first mayor. There were much disorder and confusion in the city even after that. Guns were fired, bells were rung and night made hideous with noise, but before that sometimes more serious things were done, for young Josiah Tattnall, not yet of age, and Mr. Claud Thompson and Mr. Goffe were at Wilson's on the night of the 4th of July, having "a night of extraordinary gladness," as the judge said, when they heard that the girls at Platt's tavern were playing on the hurdy-gurdy; they went up there and were refused admittance, and, attempting to make forcible entry, they were fired on by Mr. John Brice and Mr. Goffe was

WESLEY MONUMENTAL CHURCH, SAVANNAH.

killed. The Platt crowd were all tried for murder, and the man who fired the gun and Mary Platt, who loaded it, were both condemned to be hung. She was the first woman ever sentenced to be hung in Georgia, and she was pardoned by an act of the Legislature, as was also her companion in the crime.

Those were rollicking days. The hunting club was organized in 1783 to meet at the White Bluff Club House. Each man was to bring a beagle. There was to be a round of beef, some beefsteaks or a ham and some bread, and there was to be a supply of rum, brandy and Geneva.

General Washington visited the city on his southern tour and was generously entertained. There was a great fire in 1796, which destroyed the Episcopal, Presbyterian and Lutheran churches, leaving no churches in the city.

The town had an exchange located on the bay probably just opposite where the present one now stands, but in 1800 the present exchange was begun, and in 1807 it was finished. The Chatham Academy was incorporated in 1788, but not built until 1812.

The growth of the city was steady if not rapid. The first streets were all named after those who had befriended the young colony—Drayton, Bryan, St. Julian, Broughton, Bull, Whittaker. Then came South Broad, East Broad and West Broad streets. The hamlets of Yamacraw and of Ewensburg were where that portion of the city known as Yamacraw now is. King and Queen streets were changed into President and Congress, and State street was named when the State was established. After the Revolution there were Liberty street, Washington Square, Jefferson street, Lincoln, Gwinnett, Hall, Montgomery, McDonough and Perry, named after noted men.

The benevolent institutions of Savannah began with the establishment by Mr. Whitefield of the Orphan House in 1739. The Union Society, organized near that time, was formed by a Jew, a Scotchman and an Englishman. This society still exists, and has in its charge two orphanages, one for boys at Bethesda and one for girls in the city.

There was at an early date a city hospital, which still stands, an admirably managed, well-equipped institution.

There have been for years a Home for Aged Widows, an Episcopal Orphanage, a Hibernian Society and the St. Andrew's Society, formed one hundred and fifty years ago. There are German societies and sundry benevolent societies connected with the Catholic Church. An elegant Sailors' Home is under the care of the Port Society, where hundreds of sailors find lodging and refreshments and have religious services and amusements. The Masons were in Savannah from Oglethorpe's day. The Odd Fellows, Knights of Pythias and other fraternities came in due time.

The Episcopal Church was the first established in the young city, and Christ Church the first church building in it. For many years it answered the demands of the denomination, but as the city went westward it was thought advisable to build another church more modern in its appearance and more convenient to the residence part of the city, and St. John's Church was erected. As the city still grew other churches and chapels were necessary, and there is now in Savannah Christ Church, St. John's Church and several smaller churches.

The Independent Presbyterian Church is a Presbyterian Church in everything but its ecclesiastical government, and was the first of the name in the city. It has had a succession of very gifted men in charge of its pulpit, and is a very strong and influential body.

The Baptists first built a church, as we have seen, on Franklin square, and the first negro Baptist church now occupies this spot. There was a congregation and a church as early as 1796, but there was not a continuous pastorate, and I am not able to say who was the first pastor. It was under Dr. Henry Holcomb, a man highly gifted, of great intelligence and purity, that the church was organized about 1800. Dr. Holcomb exerted great influence in the city and wonderfully built up the church. In 1823 the present church on the corner of Lee and Agnew streets was built, and in the last few years the Duffy street church was also built. There are now two churches for whites and a number for colored people, some of which are very fine buildings with very large congregations and an immense membership.

The first Lutheran church in Savannah was built where it now stands as early as 1766. It was intended for the German-speaking people of the city. There was, however, a suspension of church services during and after the Revolution until 1824, when a new house was built on the old lot. This gave way to the building which still stands.

Although Mr. Wesley and Mr. Whitefield, who were both Methodists, had each preached in the city of Savannah, it was not until 1806 that Samuel Dunwody, who taught a small school, secured a room from Mr. Millen, a Presbyterian, and organized a Methodist society of three white people and four negroes. In 1812 James Russell came to Savannah and succeeded, with the aid of his up-country friends, in building a small church. This church served the little congregation for many years, and the pulpit was filled by men of great ability. In 1850 it was decided to build nearer the residence part of the city, and the handsome lot on St. James Square, where Trinity now stands, was secured and Trinity Church was built upon it. The elegant Sunday-school room attached to it was the gift of the benevolent W. R. McIntyre. A handsome church as monumental to John Wesley was projected by Rev. A. M. Wynn, and begun. Dr. J. O. A. Clarke did much to forward the work, and after years of effort the Wesley monumental church was completed. A neat and comfortable brick church was built on New Houston street and a good wooden building in a new part of the town, on Seventh street.

The Jews have three synagogues, and the one on Bull street is very handsome.

The Presbyterians have an organization connected with the presbytery known as the First Presbyterian Church, whose church is located on Bull street.

Before the Revolution there were no lawyers in any part of the colony except in Savannah, and the bar was noted for its ability. John Glen, John Stirk, Colonel Young, Colonel Farley, the Humes and Mr. Gibbons were among the leading counselors. After the city regained its prosperity there was quite a coterie of distinguished men. Nathaniel Pendleton, Matthew Hall McCallister, James Gibbons, Joseph Clay, James Jackson, Abram Jackson and Geo. Jones were famous men in that day, and from that day to this the Savannah bar has been noted for its great ability.

There has been in the history of Savannah a number of very decided changes in the nature of its society. For twenty years after it was settled it was an insignificant village, peopled largely by families in very humble circumstances. Mr. Whitefield said as late as 1770, in addressing the Legislature, that but for the employment given and the money paid for the Orphanage he established at Bethesda, many thought the colony would have been abandoned. There were a few Scotch shopkeepers, the officials, and in the city and neighborhood a few planters of moderate means, but the bulk of the people were very dependent. There was a broad line of distinction, however, even then between the classes. After Sir James Wright came, as we have seen, a tide of prosperity set in, and Savannah became a really elegant young city.

The classes were very distinct; they were the gentlemen

St. Paul's Episcopal Church, Augusta.

and the people. Although there was a break into these circles during the Revolution, it was only a few years afterward before the old English features of society were again apparent. For years Savannah society underwent little change. Near the bay and around the old squares there were the homes of the gentlemen. At the head of Bay street, what is now Yamacraw, was the home of James Habersham, when Sir. Patrick Houston's home was located on St. Julian square. General McIntosh lived on South Broad street, and General James Jackson near the present court-house. There was much refinement, much elegance and much dissipation.

The days of Savannah supremacy, when she controlled the markets of Georgia, were between 1812 and 1830. The ruling people in the social circles were the large planters and the great bankers and governors and the lawyers and doctors; but there came another day when the railroad came, and by slow degrees the old features of English life gave way, and Savannah presented few features not found in any other city of its size in the State.

Savannah has always been famous for the beauty of its old squares and the handsome monuments erected on some of them. The monuments to Generals Greene and Pulaski were the first erected, and were, for the time, considered very elegant shafts. There is a sad history connected with them. The body of neither hero is buried here. No one knows where either sleeps. Pulaski was buried no one knows where. General Greene's body was brought to Savannah and placed in a vault in 1785. When the vault was opened the body was gone, and though every inquiry was made it was never found. Mere conjecture has to be called to the aid of the inquirer, and there are decided differences of opinion as to where the old soldier was buried. It is at least certain that he was not buried on the square on which the monument stands. The monuments to Pulaski, to Gordon and to Sergeant Jasper are attractive works of art, and the one on the parade ground to the Confederate dead is very handsome.

The park in Savannah is a small but exquisite breathing place, with a beautiful growth of native trees and a fine fountain in the center of the grove.

Near the park is the Library of the Georgia Historical Society, which is not only the library of Savannah, but whose resources have been at the service of all the students of Georgia history. It has a very handsome building, which was largely the benefaction of Miss Margaret Telfair. In addition to its large collection of books bearing on Georgia history, it is rich in books bearing on the history of all the States

The history of Savannah has been carefully told, and nowhere so fully and accurately as in the History of Savannah by Colonel C. C. Jones.

AUGUSTA.

In the first chapter there is an account of the settlement of Augusta. For some years it was an important trading post. There was a fort and a considerable number of log houses occupied by the traders. The fort was located where the present St. Paul's Church is standing, and the houses built on the river bluff as far down the river as Elbert street. For twenty years after the settlement of the trading post the traders were dependent for supplies on South Carolina, where slavery was permitted.

Where the upper part of Augusta is now McCartan Campbell had a large river plantation, and on the south Wm. Glascock had his estate. The city was laid out and the lots granted in 1763. The streets were Reynolds, Market, Elias, and what are now Washington, Elbert and Center. The early settlers were largely Scotch traders, and when the Revolutionary troubles began some of them sympathized

First Presbyterian Church, Augusta.

with the mother country, but the larger part of the people were with the colonies, and Mr. Brown, a Scotch trader, was tarred and feathered—an indignity he amply avenged in a later day. After the troubles with the British a second fort was built near where was for years the upper market.

The history of Augusta during the war has been most carefully written by Colonel Jones, and it is not possible in the space appropriated to this account to do more than glance at it. The Legislature, when the British menaced Savannah in 1779, fled to Augusta, and when matters became still more serious, fled from Augusta to the frontier. Augusta fell into the hands of the British, and was attacked by Colonel Clarke, who was repelled, and was attacked again by Colonel Lee, Colonel Clarke and Major Jackson, and fell into the hands of the Americans. The Legislature now resumed its sessions in Augusta, and then, in 1783, the courts began their sessions. The judges were Wm. Glascock, Chas. Crawford, Wm. Few and Andrew Burns.

The old records show that the government of the city was vested in the board of trustees of the Richmond academy. This board let out the contract for building the academy to Colonel Wm. Candler. He took the contract for building the academy, but died before the completion of the work. The house was turned over to the county at a later date as a court-house and as a place for the legislative sessions. The school was, however, opened here in 1785, and Mr. Palmer was chosen as principal, and religious services were held at it until the church was built. The church was not made habitable until 1789, when it was so far completed by Colonel Wm. Mead, the contractor, that Parson Boyd was chosen by the vestry to hold services in it. Although Mr. Boyd was an Episcopalian and the vestry were of the same denomination, all other Christian bodies were permitted to hold services in the church. The salary was not large and pew rents were low. The list preserved shows that Mr. Edward Telfair paid as rent £6; Mr. Geo. Walton, £7 5s.; Colonel Seaborn Jones, £5 5s.; Colonel Abram Jones, £5; Major Forsyth, £5 12s.; Mr. Hunter, £5; Mr. Hills, £4; Mr. Longstreet, £4.

The tide of settlers came rapidly after the war ended, and Geo. Walton, the signer, removed from Savannah and settled near where the Augusta factory is now. The old building in which he resided is still standing—one of the few houses in the city that antedate the nineteenth century. There was a large influx of Virginians, and the immigration to the northern part of Richmond, now Columbia, and into the counties about was increasing the trade of the city largely, and its population grew rapidly.

Mrs. Fox had a tavern on the corner of Ellis and Center streets where the public sales were made, and the Tory Fox had a residence where the Virginia House is now. The court-house was on the corner of Elbert and Bay streets, and the jail opposite where the old market was.

There were two towns, the upper and lower; one which was largely fostered by the up-country tobacco-planter with his wagon trade, the other where the flatboats unloaded and where first the ferry and then the bridge crossed the Savannah river.

In 1798 Stith Mead, who had been educated in Augusta and whose father, Wm. Mead, lived in the city, had services in a private house on McIntosh street, the house of Ebenezer Doughty, and organized a Methodist society, and soon applied to the trustees for the grant of a church lot. They refused him, and he bought the two lots on which St. John's Church now stands, and succeeded, with the aid of the Methodists abroad as well as in the city, in building the Methodist church, which was occupied as early as 1802.

St. Paul's Church was too small for its congregation, and by private subscriptions and the aid of the trustees it was

Lower Greene Street, Augusta.

enlarged after 1800. New pews were added and rented, and Dr. Hull was put in charge of the church. The Presbyterians were organized into a congregation in the early part of the century and occupied this church, and the Episcopalians seem to have worshiped with them after the departure of Dr. Hull until they built their own church, which was begun in 1809. The lot on Telfair street was granted to them by the city.

The Catholics had services in Augusta as early as the beginning of the century, and a lot covering the square between Jackson, McIntosh, Walker and Telfair was given to them by the Legislature. Upon this lot, which was the same one the Methodists refused to purchase, a church was built in 1820.

In 1816 the lot on which St. Paul's Church now stands was granted to the trustees of the Episcopal society of the city of Augusta.

The board of trustees of Richmond academy was authorized to grant to the Baptists an acre of land for their building. Whether the lot the church is now on was the lot granted I am not able to say, but the church was built on this lot near this time, and Dr. W. T. Brantley was the first pastor.

The Christian Church, largely fostered by Mrs. Tubman, erected a good brick building on Reynolds street. As the city grew the demand for increased church accommodations was recognized.

The Episcopalians built the Church of the Atonement on the upper part of Greene street, and at a later period a handsome church on the hill.

The Presbyterians enlarged and beautified their handsome church on Telfair, and built a second church on Greene street.

The Methodists built a comfortable and commodious

church on lower Greene known as St. James's, and one near the cotton mill called Asbury, and one on upper Broad street; and when the factory was built in old Harrisburg they erected a handsome brick church called St. Luke's, and as the city extended westward one at Woodlawn.

The Baptists built the Kollock street and one on Broadway known as the Curtis Baptist and several other churches.

The Christian Church changed its location, and a very handsome church, with an attractive parsonage, was built by the bounty of Mrs. Tubman.

The Roman Catholics built an elegant church on their handsome lot, and recently have finished a very handsome church on upper Greene.

The Baptist negroes have several large churches. The various denominations of colored Methodists have each good churches, and there is no part of the city in which comfortable houses of worship are not to be found.

The account of establishing the first bank in Augusta has been given elsewhere. It was the Bank of Augusta. The Bank of the State of Georgia was at a little later date. The trade of Augusta reached as far as the extreme west of Georgia and took in much of South Carolina and western North Carolina, and the wagon trade was very large. The flatboats came down the river loaded with cotton and tobacco, and returned laden with rum, molasses, sugar, hardware and other merchandise. Petersburg, Vienna and Goshen, in the early days of the century, were flourishing towns tributary to Augusta. After the tobacco trade began to decline and cotton was largely cultivated, Augusta became a very important market for all middle and upper Georgia, South Carolina and North Carolina. After the building of the railways the trade of the city largely increased. There was steamboat connection with Savannah

St. John's M. E. Church, Augusta.

and railway connection with Charleston. The banks were strong and furnished the money to move the crops, and the city from 1812 to 1840 had a constant and steady growth.

In the early part of the century the old wooden stores gave place to brick blocks on the lower part of Broad street, and the old log houses with wooden chimneys gave way and long lines of elegant wooden houses were on lower Broad and Greene streets before the first fourth of the century was gone.

The jail had been removed from the corner of Washington and Broad streets to its present location. The first cemetery, which was on lower Broad street near the jail, was removed to the beautiful spot on which it is now, and no one, after 1816, was allowed burial in St. Paul's churchyard. The new academy was built on Telfair street, and in 1829 the elegant lot on which the court-house now stands was purchased from George Walton, Jr., for $11,000, and a handsome building costing $100,000 was erected as a court-house and city hall.

The question of transportation became a vital one. The roads in winter, when they were needed most, were execrable, and the river above the falls could only be navigated by flatboats at certain seasons.

The interest excited by the question of railroad building was growing, and it was decided in 1833 to apply to the Legislature for a charter for a railroad and turnpike company from Augusta to some point in the interior, either Eatonton or Athens, and in 1836 the act was amended, a bank was chartered and the Georgia Railroad was begun.

Of the building of this road we have spoken elsewhere. The great financial disturbance which began in 1837 affected Augusta in common with all the southern cities. The banks all suspended, but resumed and paid their obligations. In 1841 the first directory of Augusta was issued, and in it there are 1,236 names.

The city before 1860 had reached its lower boundary on Boundary street, and did not go further southward, but continued to grow toward the east and north, and Kollock, Campbell and Marbury were opened, and Springfield was joined to the city. The fearful slough on Campbell street was filled up, the Beaver dam was made a sewer and Hawk's gully in the north was bridged. Freshets came now and then, and the upper part of the city was swept by angry waves.

The city grew as the railroads went west, and while the wagon trade was no longer a factor, the railroads more than compensated for it, extensive as it had been.

The need of pure water led to the establishment of a system of water-works. The waters of Turnkett's Spring were brought in pine logs and distributed over the city, and when it was no longer possible to supply the demand from this source the river was utilized.

In 1839 Augusta was visited by a most serious yellow fever epidemic, and a second time in 1854; since that time there has been no return of the pestilence. The great wealth and solid character of the capitalists of Augusta led to the inauguration of a daring enterprise for those times. It was decided to begin a canal at the rocks on the river seven miles above the city and conduct the water of the river through the city, returning it to the river through Hawk's gully, so as to provide water-power sufficient for cotton and other mills. Who conceived this scheme I have not been able to discover, but a number of leading men in the city were its active promoters. The work was very expensive, much more so than was expected; some of the first ventures were unsuccessful, but it was soon evident no mistake had been made, and the canal was enlarged and new enterprises projected.

As we have seen, much of the land of the city of Augusta was granted by the first State government to trustees of the

Augusta academy; and although the trustees parted with a great deal of this land for a small price and used the proceeds of the sale for current expenses, they still held to enough of the corpus accruing from the sale of lands to give them a good income. The city has always had, since the academy was opened, a good classical teacher, and often more than one. Mr. George Walton, Mr. Edward Telfair, Mr. Wm. Glascock and many of the early citizens took great interest in education and in the Augusta academy. Many of the most distinguished men of the State received their early education here, and many of the most distinguished men in the land were teachers in this the leading academy in the State. When George Washington was making his tour through Georgia, he came by Augusta and stopped, as was his rule, at an inn. He was, of course, shown every attention by the citizens, and had the usual dinner and ball given to him; and while he was here the Augusta academy had an exhibition and prizes were given out by him. General Washington was kind enough to write the names of the prize-winners and his own in the books. There were a number given out, one of which was given to Judge Clayton and one to Dr. Tilman Dixon of Louisville, and to sundry others.

John Forsyth, the gifted statesman, was a youth when he came to Augusta, where his father, Robert Forsyth, was first a merchant and then marshal of the United States, succeeding Wm. Glascock, and, as we have seen, was killed by Beverly Allen. Mr. Forsyth graduated at Princeton. Judge Augustus Baldwin Longstreet, named for one of the first rectors of the academy, was born in Augusta and was one of the early students in the academy. There was quite a literary circle in the then small city, and a coterie of young men of real culture was to be found. Among these was Richard Henry Wilde, of whom we have spoken elsewhere, who afterwards became so famous as a man of elegant taste and extensive scholarship.

The sons of the people of means were sent to Princeton as a general thing to receive their degrees, until the State University was founded. The Augusta library was established on the corner of Ellis and McIntosh streets, and was the famous assembling place of the gentlemen of the old school who used to meet there and read the *National Intelligencer*, the *Richmond Whig* and Mr. Richie's States' rights paper. There was much stateliness and elegance in the society of those days between 1800 and 1850. Augusta was never in that first half of the century off its dignity. The old Virginians of the first decade—Glascock, Walton, Forsyth, the Watkinses, the old Scotchmen, Telfair, Cummings, Murray, Innes, Campbell and men like them, who wore their queues and drank their Madeira; who had their pews in St. Paul's and their summer homes on the hills about—were great sticklers for the proprieties of life; and while their sons were a little more democratic in theory, they were not less regardful of the old traditions and were as careful of decorum. The men of those early days were strict observers of old English manners. His black butler served the dinner on the return of the master from the counting-room, or the bank, or the law office, and uncorked the bottle of old Madeira or port, and the Episcopal vestryman or Presbyterian elder took his several glasses with great dignity and thankfulness. The press of the city of Augusta was the power in the State, and in those stirring days of Troup and the treaty of Crawford and Clarke, and especially of nullification, there were lively issues of the semi-weekly press, and when the fierce fight between the nullifiers and Jackson men was on, and the witty and satirical Longstreet edited the *Sentinal*, it was a lively journal, and there was more than one duel resulting from politics.

The sentiment against dueling had grown, but still it was regarded as a proper way to settle difficulties, and its true barbarity was as yet unrecognized.

For years, with the exception of the Richmond academy, all the paid schools were private enterprises except the Augusta free school, which was the result of a private bequest.

Mr. Houghton, a wealthy old merchant, established a free school in the lower part of the city and endowed it. When the city determined on adopting the common school system, these free schools were absorbed by the system, and one of the most complete systems in the State was established. The school buildings are of the best construction and the teaching force the most competent.

Mr. Tuttle, a childless old man, left a handsome sum to endow an orphans' home, and the endowment was largely increased by a bequest from Dr. Geo. M. Newton. A well-built and well-equipped hospital has been provided.

In 1830 a medical college, the first in Georgia, was established in Augusta and located on Telfair street. For many years it was the most famous medical school in the South. The fame of the school was largely due to the distinguished ability of its faculty.

It was in Augusta that the first book of Georgia laws was published. The Life of James Jackson, the first Georgia biography, was published from an Augusta press. Judge Longstreet wrote his "Georgia Scenes" in Augusta, and there Judge Starnes wrote a strong book in reply to "Uncle Tom's Cabin." The newspaper press in the city has been famous for its ability, and in the days of the *Constitutionalist* and *Chronicle* there was much vigor in the columns of the papers.

MACON.

In 1830, when the treaty was made by which the lands east of the Ocmulgee were surrendered to the whites, a fine section of land along that river, known then as the Ocmulgee old fields, and now included in and proximate to East Macon, was reserved by the general government, and in 1806 a trading post and a fort were built. This was called Fort Hawkins and was named in honor of Colonel Hawkins, the famous Indian agent. This reserve had long been occupied by the Indians and by the Mound-Builders who were before them, and was a favorite home of the migratory Creeks. There soon sprang up around the fort quite a village, in which there were two taverns, several stores and a printing-press set up by Simri Rose, before Macon was laid out. This little village was on the western boundary of the white settlements.

In 1820, after the treaty was concluded by which all the land between the Ocmulgee and the Flint was ceded by the Indians, Monroe county was laid out on the western side of the Ocmulgee and included Fort Hawkins on the east, but before the county was organized it was decided to subdivide it and make another county, which was called Bibb. The county was laid out in 1822, and immediately opposite the flourishing village of Fort Hawkins, on the west side of the river, a beautiful tract of land on a bluff was selected for the county site and as a place to found a city. The land was all owned by the State and four acres were granted for public buildings, and in 1823 forty lots were put on the market.

There had been for some years a ferry over the river near where the city bridge now stands, and before the town was laid off there were some log houses erected near the river on the western side. The town was laid out in 1823 by Oliver H. Prince, David S. Booth, Samuel Wood, Chas. J. McDonald and Seth Ward. The streets running north and south were numbered from one to eleven, and the cross streets were called by the names of the forest trees, with the exception of Ocmulgee or, as it was then called, Wharf

street. The little town, which began to be as soon as the first lots were sold, was encircled by high pine hills, which at that time were regarded as too remote for resident lots and too sterile for cultivation. It was evident to all that a great future awaited the new city, and the lots were eagerly bought and houses, mainly of logs, were built along Seventh, Sixth, Fifth and Fourth streets. At the log house of Mr. John Keener, on what is now Orange street, near the Mount DeSales Academy, in February, 1823, the county was organized by John Davis, Tarpley Holt, David Lawson and L. K. Carle. Mr. Butler says the first frame house was near the river about where the Southern railway station now is.*

There was quite a flourishing trade at Fort Hawkins, and Roger McCall and Harrison Smith had fixed their homes on Swift creek near by as early as 1818, where Mr. McCall had a sawmill.

A company built three flatboats and loaded them with cotton for Darien. There was no way of crossing the river except by canoes, and this led Messrs. Flanders & Willett to establish a ferry. A tavern on the west side of the river was a necessity, and the old Wayside Inn, at the foot of Mulberry street near the present jail, was built.

Near where is now the Lanier a temporary court-house of logs was built. The academy was opened by Oliver Danforth and a Masonic Lodge was chartered and began its work in 1823.

The settlers came in hordes into Houston, Crawford and Monroe, and Macon was the natural market of all who lived on the west side of the Ocmulgee. Cotton was brought in wagons and boated down the river to Darien, and in a short time after the town was laid out there were

*These facts are found in the History of Macon, by Mr. Jno. C. Butler, as are many others, for each of which I am not able to give him due credit but for which I am indebted to him.

seven hundred people in it. Mr. Sherwood says in 1826 there were forty stores and two hundred houses. A bank was a necessity, and a branch of the Bank of Darien was established. The business houses were located near the river bank.

The necessity for more speedy transportation for cotton led to the establishment of a line of steamers, and in 1826 there were seventeen thousand bales of cotton sent to Macon for shipment down the river.*

In 1825 the first bank in Macon was incorporated. It was known as the Bank of Macon. Harrison Smith, Timothy Mathews, Oliver H. Prince, Rice Durett, John T. Lamar, John Davis, M. T. Roseland, Luke Ross and James Flewellen were the corporators. The city now grew rapidly, and had become a place of almost two thousand inhabitants by 1827. There was at that time no church in the city. The Methodists had monthly meetings in the court-house, and had formed a small society. The first Methodist society was organized in 1826, and in 1827 the first protracted meeting ever held in Macon was held in a warehouse on Walnut street where Christ Church now stands. This meeting resulted in the building of the Methodist church, now known as Mulberry Street Church, on a lot granted by the Legislature that year. During the same year lots were also granted by the Legislature to the Episcopal, the Baptist and the Presbyterian churches. The Methodist church was the first church building erected in the city. The Presbyterian was built in 1829. It was on Fourth street near the Brown House, and was afterwards bought by the Catholics. The Baptists built a small wooden church on Sixth street near the old cemetery in 1829, which was soon abandoned and a new one built on Second street. The Episcopal church was built on the site Christ Church now occupies on Walnut

* Butler's History.

street some time near 1829, and was, according to White, a small but neat brick building.

The court-house was a very respectable brick building in a large square of four acres at the foot of Mulberry street. It was completed in 1830, and cost over $12,000. The tide of settlement rolled rapidly from the plain toward the hill. Macon filled up very rapidly with the best class of people, and became the cotton market of all central and western Georgia. From Putnam on the east and from Sumter on the south, and northward to Morgan and Newton, and westward to Talbot and Coweta, wagons came to the Macon market to bring cotton and carry back groceries. Real estate values were continually advancing. Men of great enterprise and nerve came to take charge of the heavy business. The bank of Macon did a heavy discount business, but there was wild trading, and the Macon bank failed in 1833. Its charter was forfeited and it went into the hands of a receiver. New banks were established, money was easy, and all along the hill were erected those stately ante-bellum dwellings, with their large rooms, broad verandas and handsome columns—houses that stand to-day unrivaled in beauty and elegance. A railroad was chartered to Milledgeville but never built, and one was chartered to Savannah and one to Forsyth, and both were afterwards completed. The municipal government of Macon was first by commissioners and an intendant. The first intendant was Ed. D. Tracy, in 1826, and the first mayor was Robert Augustus Beall, in 1835.

There was a school in 1824, but trustees for the academy in the city were not appointed by legislative act until 1832. The city was growing westward and the plateau of pine hills, two miles away, began to attract the people. Judge Strong fixed his residence in the midst of the pine forest on what is now Forsyth street, Vineville, and built his cottage. He planted a vineyard, and because the vines flourished so well he called his new home Vineville. New settlers came in and fixed their homes near him, and a village sprang up; an academy became a necessity, and one was built and a famous school was conducted by M. M. Mason. The growth of the village led to the building of a neat litte church in it and the establishment of the Vineville station of the Methodists.

The college was projected and begun, and the future was promising when the depression of 1837 began. After seven fearful years, with not a single solvent bank remaining and but few houses of good standing, the stricken city came out of the storm. Then came an era of prosperity, and Macon began to steadily advance. The manufacture of engines, mills and gins and then cotton was begun. The bankrupt college was put on its feet again, and soon there was a rage for improvement. The old wooden church of the Methodists gave way to a very handsome one of brick. The Presbyterians sold their large brick church on Fourth street, which, strangely enough, fell into the hands of the Catholics, and removed to the place where they now are. The Baptists built a handsome church on Second street. The Episcopalians built the present Christ Church. The colored Methodists and Baptists each built plain wooden churches before the war and had services of their own.

The State granted to the commissioners two lots for cemeteries, and the old cemetery was located in the valley beyond Seventh street; but through the influence of Simri Rose a most picturesque part of the reserve was selected for a new cemetery, and it was laid out by his direction; and in recognition of his able services, gratuitously given, it was called Rose Hill. A part of it was set off for a negro burial ground, and about 1884 a large body of land adjoining was purchased and laid out as the Riverside cemetery.

The *Messenger* was removed to Macon from Fort Hawkins in 1825 and published by Robinson and Rose. It was a

Christ Church, Macon.

stanch Troup journal, was bitterly opposed to Jackson and had a warm side for the nullifiers; was opposed to Van Buren, and finally fell into the ranks of the Whig party and was for many years a leading Whig journal. Mr. Bartlett published an opposition paper, the *Telegraph*. Dr. Andrews published a Universalist paper and then an independent weekly journal. The *Telegraph* and *Messenger* were published as dailies from 1860. Young Philip C. Pendleton enterprized and established the *Southern Ladies' Book* in 1838, the first venture of the kind made south of Richmond, and Bishop Pierce, then a young man, was his assistant editor. There was a considerable spirit of southern independence, and Mr. Griffin, a job printer, decided to publish a series of school readers, which were edited by his accomplished wife in connection with Dr. Mason, and printed and published by himself in Macon. These were the first school-books ever published in Georgia.

When the Monroe railroad, of which we have given an account, was begun, the station and depot for freight were near each other at the head of Cotton avenue, and the old passenger depot, now transformed into a dwelling, is still standing. The old depot for freight stood on the lot on which St. Paul's Church now stands, but after 1849 the belt around the city was built.

The population of Macon in 1825 was 700; in 1829, 2,635; in 1837, 4,000; in 1850, 5,720.

The first people of Macon were largely middle Georgians who came from the near-by counties, although from the beginning there was a considerable number of enterprising northern men who did much for the development of the young city. Judge Tracey, Governor McDonald, Robert Augustus Beall and Christopher B. Strong were among the members of the first bar, and Thomas Hardeman, Everard Hamilton, Thomas Napier, Robert Fort, Charles Campbell and Nathan C. Monroe were among the first business men.

The opening of the rich lands of Houston and Pulaski, and later of Baker, Dougherty, Lee and Sumter, brought into Macon a group of planters who, having large estates in the low-country, were not willing to expose their families to the isolation of a large plantation and risk their health in so malarious a climate. They bought handsome sites and erected elegant homes. Their plantations were supervised by overseers, and they gave them personal attention by making frequent visits. They were men of fine manners and broad views. They lived in affluence, entertained generously, educated their daughters at Wesleyan and sent their sons to either Athens, Oxford, Midway or Penfield for an education. They were of the best type of southern gentlemen and the society of the city had the highest social and moral tone.

With the coming of the railways there came a class of working men who were employed on the railroads, on the steamboats and in the workshops, and, as is the case in all cities, the two classes of people drifted apart. There were for the first fifty years of Macon history but few foreigners and very few Jews, and the large number of Hebrews and of people of European birth who are now in Macon have come in since the war between the States.

In 1850 the railroad to southwestern Georgia opened up a rich territory to Macon which had hitherto found its market on the Chattahoochee and the Flint, and large shipments of cotton were made to Macon that had hitherto gone down the Flint to Apalachicola or Fort Gaines, and Macon bankers furnished the funds which were needed by the planters of southwestern Georgia. There was some dissatisfaction at what Macon said was the unfriendliness of the Central railway to the city, and the Macon and Brunswick was projected and built. It opened up an almost entirely new country and made it tributary to Macon. A railroad to Augusta was projected in 1860 and completed after the war. It is not possible, in the limits we have been compelled to give to this account, to say much of the history of Macon since the war.

The citizens of Macon who have occupied official positions of honor and responsibility have been so many that we can only refer to a few of those who antedated the war. The Hon. Oliver H. Prince, who did such admirable work in making a digest of Georgia laws, a man of great wit and genius, had his residence here and repeatedly represented the county in the Legislature. He was lost in the wreck of the ill-fated Home on the North Carolina coast. Judge Eugenius A. Nisbett, one of the first judges of the Supreme Court and long one of the most prominent men in the State, noted for the purity of his character and the clearness of his intellect, lived in Macon. Judge Strong, one of the first of Macon's citizens and one of the most noted of Georgia's judges; Judge Tracey, famous for his genial spirit and legal learning; Colonel L. N. Whittle, noted for his public spirit and his philanthropy; Judge Barna Hill, long a leading lawyer and twice judge, were among the public men who occupied prominent places in the city before 1860; but Macon has perhaps a wider fame from having been the birthplace of that sweet singer Sidney Lanier, whose fame is as wide as the continent. Here he was born and here he married his gifted wife and began his career as an attorney.

It has not been the object of this book to give an exhaustive history of any part of the State or of any city. This work must be left largely to local historians. Macon has been fortunate in having Mr. Butler,* to whom I am much indebted, to preserve the story of the early years of the city of his birth.

---

* History of Macon, by J. C. Butler, 1879.

COLUMBUS.

The Creek Indians were originally known as Muscogees, and Coweta town, two miles below the present city of Columbus, was one of their chief Georgia towns. Here Mr. Oglethorpe came in 1735, when he desired to make a treaty with the Indians. After the withdrawal of the Indians from Georgia and the laying off of the western territory into counties, a very large county was laid out known as Muscogee, and Columbus was made its county site. It was to be on a plain two miles from Coweta town, at the head of navigation on the Chattahoochee river. It was laid off in 1827 and incorporated in 1828. The projected city was handsomely laid out into blocks of four acres each and extended one mile and a fourth along the river. In order that the young city might build a bridge over the river the State loaned it $16,000 and gave it half the public square for county buildings.

The unrivaled advantages of the young city at once drew to it a number of enterprising people, and, as was said of Macon, Columbus never had an infancy. The Muscogee academy was incorporated as early as 1828, and lots were granted to the Methodist, Baptist, Catholic, Presbyterian and Episcopal churches. Steamboats were put upon the river. The Bank of Columbus was chartered in 1828, and this was followed by other charters and bold projects on every hand. The rich lands on the Chattahoochee, below Columbus, had been the first land in the western part of the State to be settled, and large cotton plantations had been opened along the river above and below Columbus. The city had a large trade from its first settlement. The Indians were just across the river, and some of them were men of wealth who had large plantations, and Columbus was their market.

The times from 1826 to 1836 were flush times and Columbus was the financial center of all the country near it, and so business was brisk and large risks were taken in trade. Then came the Creek war and the next year the great crash. Every bank in Columbus suspended specie payments and then went into hopeless bankruptcy. There was, however, no possibility of crushing a city with the advantageous position which Columbus had, and it rallied and held its commercial superiority until the railroads diverted the cotton trade from Apalachicola to Savannah.

Columbus was surrounded with a tier of lofty hills. They were high, dry and healthy, and were naturally fitted for suburban homes. The rich lands on the western side of the river stretching toward Montgomery had been taken from the Indians and sold to settlers, and planters from eastern Georgia had bought plantations in Alabama, and many of them fixed their homes on the hills near Columbus; and besides these many planters who had plantations in the near-by counties in Georgia had homes also in the same vicinity.

These homes were very attractive and elegant, and as the planters had large incomes their style of living was luxurious. They were enterprising and prosperous and made a fine class of citizens, and the society of the city and villages about was noted for its wealth and culture. There had been granted to each of the churches—Baptist, Presbyterian, Methodist and Episcopal—an acre lot, on each of which was built a neat wooden church before 1830. The first church built in the city was the Methodist. Many Methodists from Greene and other eastern counties had made their homes in Columbus, and the Methodist preacher came with the first settlers. The first Methodist society was organized by James Stockdale in 1826. The other churches were organized soon after, and in 1833, when there were 1,600 people in the young city, there were three churches.

As it grew in wealth and in population new churches took the place of the old wooden buildings, and Columbus was provided with handsome and commodious brick churches for each of the leading denominations. Before 1860 St. Paul's, on Broad street, was built by the Methodists, and the Baptists also had a second church.

Columbus for the first twenty years after its founding was almost entirely dependent for prosperity on its commerce. Cotton, which constituted its main staple, was sent down the river to Apalachicola and shipped thence to New York and Europe. There was a fleet of steamboats constantly carrying cotton down and bringing goods back. There was no communication with the east other than by a stage line. Railroads had been projected but were not constructed; but at length, in 1851, the railroad from Macon reached the city and brought Columbus into connection with the Atlantic seaboard at Savannah, and not long after a road from the city reached Opelika, Ala., there was close connection with Montgomery and New Orleans. Before this time the great natural advantages of the city as a place for manufacturing were seen, and an attempt was made to utilize the water-power of the Chattahoochee. It was no easy task to bring the angry waters of the river to subjection, but it was at last accomplished. A dam was thrown across the river and great factories were erected on its banks. These factories have grown to large proportions, and Columbus has become next to Augusta—the chief manufacturing city of the State. In 1851, when Mr. White published his Statistics, there were the Columbus, the Coweta Falls and the Howard factories. These have, each of them, long since been merged into larger plants. In 1851 the famous Eagle and Phœnix factory was established. This factory is one of the most famous in the South for the extent of its plant and the variety of its work. Manufacturing in the city become its chief interest, as the railroads reached out in every direction from it and diverted its trade. The wholesale business after the war largely compensated for the lost trade of the planters. The society of Columbus before the establishment of the factories was a very homogeneous one. The ruling spirits were Georgians and the tone of society was that of the middle Georgia people. There was morality, refinement, hospitality, and, as in all river towns, there was a fair share of wild rowdyism, of gaming and drinking. With the building of the mills the city became largely populated by the mill people, who present the same features, to a large degree, wherever they are found. They were drawn from the pine woods and had the characteristics of the humbler class of rural people we have so often seen, but steady work and good wages, and especially religious teaching, have had their influence in elevating them, and there is perhaps not a better or more contented people than these.

The first newspaper in Columbus was the *Enquirer*, which was established by Mirabeau B. Lamar, afterward president of the Texas Republic. It was established in 1824, and Sherwood says had a circulation of six hundred copies.

The prominent men of old Columbus were many, and it would be impossible in a short sketch like this to do anything like justice to those who deserve notice.

Rev. John Slade, a graduate of the University of North Carolina and a Baptist preacher, a teacher of great repute, and at one time a professor in the Georgia Female College, removed to Columbus at an early day and opened his famous female seminary in the city, in which a great many of the young women of western Georgia were educated.

The Rev. Jno. E. Dawson, one of the most gifted of Baptist preachers, was pastor of the Baptist Church at two different periods. He was recognized as the leading preacher of his denomination in the State. The Baptist

Church has had in Columbus many very distinguished ministers, and the church being one of the leading Baptist churches of the State has commanded its best talent, but it never had in it a more devoted, persistent and untiring laborer than Jno. H. Campbell, to whose researches we have been so much indebted in preparing these pages. In his old age he gave himself to patient, untiring work among the poor people of the city and was looked upon as the benefactor of all.

The Methodist Church had its share of gifted men, but they were hardly to be called citizens of Columbus, as they spent so brief a time in the city, and there was not a man of distinction in the Methodist pulpit who did not have a pastorate in Columbus. Dr. Lovick Pierce had his home here and was recognized by the Columbus people as their special property, and he held his place in their esteem as one of the leading preachers of the land. He is buried in the city and his monument is there.

The bar of Columbus has been especially able. Walter T. Colquitt lived here in his brightest days, when he was matchless as an advocate and a stump-speaker, and he was living here when he received his death-stroke. His gifted son, Peyton H. Colquitt, was also living here when he went into the army and came back no more.

Colonel James M. Chambers, long recognized as a man of soundest judgment, resided in Wynnton.

Judge A. H. Chappell, to whom we as Georgians are so much indebted for sketches of early history, lived and died in Columbus.

Colonel Nicolas Howard the elder, who came to Columbus in its infancy and had much to do with its early history, died in the city; and Colonel John Howard had much to do with making the city. He commanded the Georgia troops in the Indian troubles of 1836, and after the war was over was one of the most energetic developers of the

Sacred Heart Catholic Church, Ivy Street, Atlanta.

material interests of Columbus. He built the railway from Columbus to Macon and did much other valuable work.

Colonel Seaborn Jones, a congressman and a leading planter and lawyer, lived and died here.

Colonel Henry L. Benning, who was judge of the Supreme Court, member of Congress and a general in the Confederate army, spent his life in Columbus; and Colonel Martin J. Crawford, long a leading man in this section, had his home here.

ATLANTA.

When the railway to Ross Landing was projected a village named after Miss Martha Lumpkin, Marthasville, was located at the terminus, in an unbroken forest of oaks, hickories and chestnuts, in which there was quite a quantity of pine timber.

Few spots were more attractive than the hills upon which the city was to be built. There were in every direction gushing springs and limpid rivulets. The hills were covered with magnificent forests, with an undergrowth of wild azaleas and chinkapins.

The spot chosen for the new village was a tract of which the Kimball house is now about the true center. Near it were located the three freight depots and a car-shed for a union station. The workshops of the Georgia railroad were located near where is now the present passenger station. A tavern was a necessity, and Dr. Thompson, a physician of Decatur, built a brick hotel, the first in Atlanta, where the Kimball house now stands, and James Loyd built a second hotel where the Markham house stood. It was a large two-story wooden building with long piazzas and numerous chambers.

There was no time to wait for the steam- or water-mill, and so sawmills run by horse-power were set up in what is now the heart of the city to cut the timber as it was cleared from the lots. Jonathan Norcross began his career in Atlanta by establishing the first of these sawmills run by horse-power. The little village of Marthasville soon was merged into the town of Atlanta and was incorporated as a town with an intendant and marshal. A calaboose made of hewn logs was built on some made earth near where the Hotel Jackson now stands. The lots near the projected depot and upon which it was to be built were owned by Samuel Mitchell, an Irishman, who lived in Zebulon. He had the city laid out, and gave lots to all the churches, and for the location of workshops and depots. As the various lots were owned by different men there was no one plan for a city, but each lot was laid out as the owner thought best. The village was very rapidly built up. There was no time to wait the slow process of brickmaking and bricklaying. Great wooden barns were filled with goods, and long rows of wagons came from all parts of the north and west of the State to trade at the terminus. It soon become evident that the village would be a city, and Mr. Garnett and Mr. Peters decided a good name for it would be Atlanta. It was a manufactured name, agreed on by the engineers, and the town of Atlanta was incorporated. In 1847 a charter was procured by John Collier and an election held for mayor and council. There was much rowdyism, and one street, for the number of gambling-houses and drinking-shops, was known as Murrell Row. There was no church and only two small schoolhouses. There was a great deal of business done. The West Point road was not built, and the trade of the western counties of Georgia and of the eastern counties of Alabama came to the new city. The whole of northeast Georgia was without a railroad and its produce was brought to Atlanta. There were a few large stores and many small shops. Jonathan Norcross had a very extensive establishment on the north side of the railroad, and Scott, Carhart & Co. a

Interior View Sacred Heart Catholic Church, Atlanta

very large grocery on the west side. There were a justice of the peace and a few lawyers doing small practice. The streets were unpaved and almost impassable in winter. Narrow sidewalks of plank made it possible for pedestrians to make their way comfortably if they did not cross the street, but when this was necessary there was no alternative but to brave the mud.

Before a church was erected a kind of village camp-meeting was held in the first warehouse built in Atlanta, on Wheat street. The meeting was conducted by several of the professors from Emory College. Where the First Baptist Church now stands a church was begun in 1847, and the First Methodist Church was begun at the same time. The Baptists had some aid from abroad in completing their church, and were able to finish it before their less fortunate neighbors; but the Methodists occupied their house some time before it was finished, and it was the first church opened for public worship in Atlanta.

In the course of a few years the Episcopalians built a church on the lot where their cathedral now stands, and the Presbyterians on the present lot of the First Presbyterian. The Catholics had worship in the city from its settlement, and built a neat wooden church where their present handsome edifice stands. The Christian Church was early organized and had a building on Pryor street.

The first brick store in the city was on the corner of Whitehall and Alabama and was occupied by McDaniel, Mitchell & Hulsey. The first mayor was Moses W. Formwalt, and the first marshal was German Lester. The whole police force was one deputy. The streets were unpaved, and during the winter, when traffic was heavy, wagons would sometimes be stalled on Whitehall street. Before the railroad to West Point was built Whitehall street was so crowded with wagons that it was not possible to cross without great difficulty.

The first postmaster was George W. Collier, and the post-office was on the corner of Decatur and Peachtree streets. The railroad to West Point was projected and, much against the will of the Atlanta people, was completed, and there were grave predictions that the loss of this western trade would be the ruin of the young city; but the city continued to grow, and a succession of fires, which burned the wooden buildings on Whitehall street, led to their being replaced with better structures. Afterward the disreputable shanties on Decatur and Peachtree streets gave way to better buildings. The old calaboose was removed, and the workshops were taken from the center of the city and moved where they now stand.

There were established already at the beginning of 1847 two newspapers—the *Enterprise* and the *Luminary* ; and an enterprising genius—printer, Baptist preacher and steam doctor—published a medical journal. In 1847 Col. C. R. Hanleiter established the *Miscellany* and Russell Reneau and his brother Jesse the *Republican* and about 1849, W. B. Ruggles owned and edited the *Intelligencer*. The Reneaus attempted a daily, but it soon died, but the *Daily Intelligencer* had a longer life. The schools in Atlanta were all private enterprises until after the war, and there was not a great deal of attention paid to education.

The class of people who settled Atlanta, and who in its first few years were its inhabitants, composed all classes of people and from every section of the land. Some of its most enterprising people were northern men from New England. Many were Irish, a few were Germans, and many more were Jews, and some were up-country Georgians and Tennesseeans. There were few people of wealth. Those who are among the wealthiest of its people now were poor boys who began life as employees in the stores of Jewish clothing merchants, and who have grown up with the city. For a long time there was little of refinement or cultivation

Trinity M. E. Church, South, Atlanta.

in the growing city, but there was a constant push forward and a fixed idea that Atlanta was to be the greatest place in all the nation, and year by year the city grew. There was always a small body of cultivated people, but after 1850 men of wealth began to come to it and invest in its enterprises. Mr. Peters had always had great faith in the city, and established the first steam flouring-mill in the city. Joseph Winship came from Morgan and opened his car factory, and after that his machine works, Messrs. Leyden & Dunning had a foundry, Mr. Markham built a large rolling-mill, and merchants of capital took the place of the small shopkeepers.

The central position of Atlanta made a place for conventions and it attracted people from every section. Hundreds of new people came to it every year. New territory was taken in, and just before the war Atlanta had two daily papers, two Methodist, two Baptist, two Presbyterian, one Episcopal, one Catholic, one Christian, and one Methodist Protestant Church.

The story of Atlanta during the war and since it ended it would take a volume to tell. For years the eyes of the whole land were turned upon it, and of how it fell and its people were exiled and its buildings burned I leave to others to tell. Much was destroyed, more was left. When peace came it took on at once vigorous life.

In some respects the story of the Atlanta people differed very greatly from that of the other cities of Georgia. There was nothing homogeneous in Atlanta society. Men brushed by each other on the streets who were from all sections of the United States and all parts of Europe. There was no question as to whence they came, but the question: what could the man do and what did he have?

Up to 1853 the people of Atlanta went to Decatur to attend to their legal business. There was no civil court in Atlanta except that of the justice of the peace ; but in

1853 the county of Fulton was made, and a court-house in connection with a city hall was erected where the State capitol now stands. This lot was afterwards given to the State by the city, and the State capitol was erected where it stands at the present time.

Although there was much whisky sold and used in Atlanta, there was always a strong temperance sentiment, and the Sons of Temperance, the Knights of Jericho and the Rechabites were well-supported societies before the war. The Masons had a lodge in Atlanta if not as soon, yet nearly as early as it received its name, and the Odd Fellows followed close after.

There was a volunteer fire company of a large number of enthusiastic members as early as 1849. The water supply upon which it relied was found in cisterns in the streets.

In 1851 there was a great improvement made in the city by extensive works begun for the State under the direction of Mr. Wadley. The spot where the present Western and Atlantis railroad depot is located was a beautiful grove around a bold spring. The lot was graded, and where the grove was the depot and shops are now located. The road was poorly equipped when he took hold of it, but with a large appropriation at his back and with fine judgment, he soon put the road where it has been ever since, and made it a profitable piece of property.

Atlanta in the early fifties was a straggling ragged town. The houses were scattered over a great area and were most of them very plain and cheap; business was still confined to a few houses on Marietta street and on Whitehall. In 1850 the population was 2,572. It was evident that, despite the fact that Atlanta had a poor country agriculturally on all sides, it could not be held back, and while its growth from 1847 to 1850 was comparatively slow, reaching only to a little over 2,000 by that time, the next decade saw a very great advance.

First Presbyterian Church, Atlanta.

During those early days in Atlanta both of the political parties held their mass-meetings in Atlanta. A Mr. Whitney, in 1847, made a famous speech at a railroad convention urging the construction of a railway to the Pacific along the line afterward taken by the Northern Pacific.

The temperance people had a grand convention at Walton Springs when Judge Robert M. Charlton and Judge Jos. Henry Lumpkin were leaders in the movement, and Judge George Hillyer, of Atlanta now, then of Monroe, a ruddy-faced boy, made his first appearance in Atlanta as an orator of the Cadets of Temperance at the same place. The famous split in the Democratic party, which had resulted in the election of Howell Cobb and the formation of what was known as the Tugaloo Electoral ticket, was healed in Atlanta after a glowing speech for General Henry R. Jackson.

My space is now taken, and it is superfluous to tell of the present condition of Atlanta. It is the Queen City of the South, with everything favorable to its future growth and development. After the war it was made the capital, and during Governor McDaniel's incumbency a handsome capitol building was erected. It has a complete system of public schools, street railways which cover all its streets, great wholesale houses, elegant homes and all kinds of benevolent institutions, and perhaps deserves the tribute given to it by a carrier's address of fifty years ago as—

"The greatest place in all the nation,
The greatest place for legislation
Or any other occupation,
The very center of Creation."

[NOTE.—I have been compelled for want of space to omit much I had prepared concerning the cities. Each city has its History. Augusta and Savannah by Colonel Jones and others; Macon by Mr. Butler, and Atlanta by Colonel E. Y. Clarke.]

ST. PHILIP'S CATHEDRAL, ATLANTA.

APPENDIX.

HEADRIGHTS GRANTED BY THE COLONIAL AND STATE GOVERNMENTS FROM 1754 TO 1800.

1743.—Geo. Foute, S Beltz, Urban Buntz, J Niedlinger, L McGilveray, Jno Niedlinger, Jno Rewter, D Hanler, W Gibbons, D Humbert, Henry Riedelsperger, R Houston, B Farley, W Gibbons, Geo Winkler, Jno Ryland, Jno Young, D Douglas, Geo Noble, Andrew Van Beverhought, John Van Beverhought, Wm Johnson, John Hamm, C Martin, J Simner, Peter Grant, Jacob Illy, Jno Pye, L Mitchell, D Humbert, J Bantli, J Swan, W Niedlinger, Hugh Ross, W Small, A Wylly, R Johnson, R Noble, Jno Barnard, F Kieser M Rhienstetter, J Berner, G Tyfe.

1745.—Wm Spencer, H Hamilton, Jas Grant, C Campbell, F Helvenstine, J Billinghast, Rich Kent, Robert Fox, R Raltoon, T Sparnell, J Waters, R Brufey, J Burgess, C Dasher, J Ross, D Dourezaux.

1746.—Jno Dobel, Jno Lawrence, J Fraser, Geo Frayer, Jno McIntosh, Jno McBean, Peter Baillon, J Barksdale, Wm Bearful, L McBean, Inigo Jones, A Camuse, D Bradock, J Rogerson, Wm Wilson.

1747.—John Penrose, Peter Shepherd, Thos Goodall, Wm Shoode, Jos Summers, Richard Lee, Jno M Bolzias, Thos Ross, John Atherton, Jno Oaks, R Johnson, Stephen Williams, Jno Wood, Thos Hill, John Wilson, Wm Clarke, Jno Kenedy, A Collins, John Alther, Gasper Hosteter, Wm Cooke, Geo Cubbege, Wm Beckett, B Wilson, R Hazzard, Wm Ewen, Geo Cubbege, Chas Ratcliffe, Jno Baxter, B Goldwire, Chas Mathews, John Mathews, Jno Barker, John Hencork, Peter McHugh, Abram Frisbie, John Mullryne, Jno Maxwell, Morgan Sab, John Hutchinson, P Delegal, H George, I Sheppard, John McIntosh, Major Horton, Wm Hester, Mark Carr, N Stevens, Lt-Col Heron, Kenneth Baillie, Lt Robt Howorth, M Evans.

1748.—A Dean, James Wall, John Horn, Chas West, Wm Case, David Black, P Brown, I. Nevie, John Farmer, John Ross, James Eads, I Caulkens, Wm River, Sam Mackay, Geo Cadagan, John Milligan. Jno Edwards, Jno Kellson, M Callerton,

John Ballowe, P Clarke, P Sutherland, J Marriot, J McKay, John Gordon, G Williams, M Boreman, W Clement, P Slyeman, R Jones McIntosh, Thos Goldsmith, L McIntosh, Wm Shrubsole, Jas Mackay, Jr, John Stevens, Thos Collins, R Cooper.

1759.—L Ogden, A Rose, Jno L Myer, L McGilveray, D Martin, Rev Geo Whitfield, I Ellison, Z Barrett, H Borguine, B. Borguine, I. Shepherd, Geo Dunbar, R Palmer, John Davis, Jas Finlay, A Maxwell, Ann Clarke, Isaac Lines, Donald Clarke, G Williams, R McIntosh, I McLaren.

1740.—James Habersham, Hugh Clarke, Angus Clarke, W Russell, I Stewart, D Demster, John Milledge, Isaac LaBow, C Lienberger, B Bacher, P Kohlieson, John Mohe, Geo Renicker, Martin Letler, Geo Meyer, A Scrimpt, N Crumenberger, M Switzer, Acn S Smith, Jno David Fisher, Edmond Gray, T Mitchell, M Allen, A Bourguine, Henry Parker, H W Parker, Rev Bart Zouberhuller, C Hopkins, Geo Galphin, J C Walhour, W Davis, M. Locher, Geo Hocker, V Leitner, I Sheraws, M Lochner, Geo Glasser, John Rhylander, P Metzcher, L Erst, Z Still, Thos Ellis, B Ore, Scuman, Thos Davis, John Bourguine, John Wesely, J Paris, J Bobb.

1750.—J G Bierpholt, J Papot, J L Myer, C Riedelsperger.

1751.—H Lempke, J T Kiefer, W Spenser, M Ziter, J Woolford, Noble Wymberly Jones, I Mahr, Jos Phillips, I Devaux, John Berham, Wm Jones, John Gray, Owen Day, M Gray, R Meadows, M Bossell, J Williams, A Lindsay, John Young, Geo Farris, Wm Payne, Geo Mackay, J McDaniel, J Edwards, W Johnson,.

17c2.—Nathaniel Watson, Jos Barker, A Seckinger, Mathew Seckinger, Geo Lambright, Martha Burkhardt, Pat Graham, David Graham, Wm Carr, Mark Carr, Thos Harris, J Finley, D Martin, J Thebault, J C Walthour, John Summers, D Kraft, A Rose, P Morrill, N Hunling, T Wilson, T Foreman, W Hargrove, Nathan Taylor, John De Vaux, Henry Sargeant, M Fenton, John Wilson, H McKay, R Hazard, J Parker, W De Brahn, J Gibbons, Isaac Young, D Slade, Jno Winn, Ed Sumner, R Spencer, Sarah Osgood, Sam'l Burney, Jos Bacon, Jona Bacon, R Woodcraft, Jno Edwards, Jno Elliot, Jos Way, Wm Graves, R Glass, D Ross, R Baker, J Oswald, Joshua Clarke, John Davis, John Maxwell, James Maxwell, Wm Maxwell, Jno Stevens, B Baker, J Osgood, S Stevens, B Norman, S Bacon, A Way, W Baker, Rich Girardeau, Janet Way, Ed Way, John Norman, N Way, I Mitchell, Sarah Mitchell, J Norman, I Steward, Sam'l James, J Quarterman, W Lupton, I Stevens, Jr, J. Weston, For Glebe, Wm Russell, David Fox, W West, Daniel Dunom, Isaac Dunom, Jno Graves, P Goulding, Jos Massey, N Bradwell, J Christen, H Dowse, E Simmons, P Goulding, Elizabeth Baker, Wm Chapman, J Baker, Rebecca Quarterman, Jos Stevens, Thos Stevens,

Jos Baker, Thos Way, John Shave, John Churchwell, Moses Way, Daniel Cannon, Jos Winn, J Gordon, Geo Cuthbert, David Graham, Jos Campbell, Jno Williams, Roderick Graynor, (Griener), W Aldridge Geo Applebee, J Parker, Henry Hyrne, (Hearn), Jas Dourezaux, Godleb Stiley, Turner Dixser, P Brown, W Ham, F Bailey, Wm Butler, Jas Butler, Wm Elliot, Wm Butler, T Butler, John Toomer, John Parker, Saml West, Jno Perkins, P Clarke, J Maxwell, John Davis, H Myers, D Delegal, Richard Milledge, J Jeansac, T Raspberry, John G Knabe, Paul Meyer, Melchoir Oachle, (Exley), John Lange, G Lang, John Eigin, M P Gerber, G Eichard, John L Nies, John Paulas, M Knapp, A Rauve, Geo Fisher, Jno G Griener, J Helvenstine, R Cooper, A Maxwell, E Carlton, L Muttair, Jno Kieley J Waldburg, Alice Stewart, Lucy Mauve, Wm Matthews, J Herle, J J Henselier, J Unold, Saefer, L Sallfer, Geo Balzenhard, M Ziegler, Jacob Ziegler, A Frey, J Martin Nies, I Meyer, Julan Hagmyer, C Prigsing, M Fisher, M G Kalbell, Jacob Guan, (Juhan), John Miller, Sol Hall, Jno Geo Mauls, Jacob Griener, Jno Melton Grier, Martin Belyenhagm, Geo Siebold, M Striegal, M Bader, John Meyer, J P Striegal, T Krause, Jacob Dice, Casher Rahn, T Kiefer, M Dasher, W Dews, Oliver Shaw, Jno Henry Grave, S Mercer, Geo Drieler, A Snyder, B Wealing, H Bishop, M Bader, John P Fleeger, John Shiera, M Echart, Geo Ballinger, M Sheranhamen, J Eberhard, C Van Munch, The Minister, C Van Munch, Adam Rhienstetter, J Matthews, J De Vaux, J Helvenstine, Seth Place, P Tondee, W McDonald, Jno C Boreman, A Baillie, W W Norton, W Harris, John Roe, (St George), L Johnson, S Adye, A Tabie, Edmund Tannatt, M Benz, P Guiard, Walter Flemming, W Bechet, David Fox, T Ready, Valentine Bostick, John Davis, John Coffee, A Gabel, H Hamilton, E Watson, I Phillips, D Unseed, W Butler, Jno Snook, J Danner, Jas Ed Powell, Hugh Kennedy, Jos Stanley, J Ottobugh, D Kennedy, James Paris, R Bennison, J Galachee, R Luden, W Barkshell, (Barksdale), E Goodall, T Beckett J G Nies, John Bennett, Richard Jones, J Cubbedge, Jno Bennett, C Gordon, T Trippe, T Lee, N Millar, Jno Pye, T Parker, A Ordner, D Flerl, W Kennedy, Jno P Miller, Christian Fullbright, F Arthur, M Roche, Geo McIntosh.

1754.—Sam'l Leon, Wm Thompson, David Truan, P Destemple, J Mackey, Jno McBean, Alex McDonald, S Hudson, Jno Fitch, Jno Hudson, John Brady, Edw Garmany, James Baillon, O Shaw. H Carvel, C Rabenhorst, J Mullryne, James Williams, Jno M Hink, Thos Carter, James Miller, Daniel Mackay, Geo McDonald, Angus McIntosh, Peter Grant, Jno R Purry, Wm McIntosh, D McKay, E St Julian, Richard Coxe, Sam'l New, James New, Richard Coxe, Jr., David Montague, V Bostick, J Butler, S Butler, Jno Thompson, Jno Todd, Jno Sheriff, F L Parry, Jno Fox,

Alex Low, R Baillie, Jos Godbe, J Matthews, Jno Greene, T Rasberry.

SAVANNAH AND C. C.

1759 to 1772.—Hannah Ash, Step and Annie Adge, Elzabeth Anderson, Thomas Ambrose.

ST. JOHN, ST. PHILLIPS AND ST. DAVID.

1751 to 1768.—Jas Andrew, Benj Andrew, Jas Andrew, Mary Arthur, Preserved Alger, David Anderson, Mary Ash.

ST. GEORGE'S, BURKE AND JEFFERSON.

1764 to 1774.—Sam'l Alexander, Hugh Alexander, Aaron Arnold, Benj Alen, Isaac Alexander, Wm Adams, James Anderderson, Elizabeth Anderson, Philip Alston, Davis Austin, Wm Allen, Wm Alexander, Wm Allen.

1787 to 1791.—Daniel Allen, Robert Allen, Jos Allen, Wm Allen, John Allen.

ST. PAUL'S.

1757 to 1774.—Joshua Atkinson, Ezikiel Abbett, Henry Abbett, Wm Alexander, James Anderson, Isaac Atwood, Abram Ayres, John Anderson, Rich Austin, Thos Ayres, John Allen, F Ashmon, Ed Ashton, Micajah Andrew, Nicolas Andrew.

1785 to 1788.—John Appling, David Allen, Gideon Allen, Samuel Allen, Isaac Atwood.

1793.—James Archer.

WILKES COUNTY.

1783.—Samuel Atkinson, Jos Abbitt, Rich Aycock, Asa Atkins, Wm Anglin, Jas Abbitt, Alex Autrey, Jacob Autrey, David Anglin, Thos Ansley, James Anderson.

1784.—Reuben Allen, James Allen, James Alford, Geo Alexander, Edmond Alexander, Jas Armstrong, Henry Anglin, Thos Avant, Samuel Alexander, Ben Allen, John Adams, Wm Anderson, John Ashley, John Autry, Gideon Anderson, James Adams, Joseph Allen, Wm Arthur, Wm Anderson.

1785.—Isaac Alexander, Martha Arthur, Robert Armstrong, Nathaniel Allen, Wm Allen.

1786.—Wm Allison, Mathew Arthur, John Ashmore, Abner Adkins.

1787 to 1796.—B Applewhite, Samuel Avara, Wathan Alexander, Nathan Alexander, Alex Autre, John Austin, Lich Allen, Wm Acre, Jos Anthony, Sarah Alexander, Jos. Alexander, Wm Averett, Henry Arrington.

GREENE COUNTY.

Andrew Armor, Chas Abercrombie, Jane Alford, Henry Allison, John Anderson, Jonathan Anderson, Benjamin Alexander, Chas Washington Allen, John Adkins.

CAMDEN COUNTY.

1784 to 1788.—Nath'l Ashley, Wm Ashley, Thomas Almond, Geo Albritton, Ludovick Ashley.

FRANKLIN COUNTY.

Wm Anderson, Nathaniel Allen, Wm Adkins, Thos Adkinson, Micajah Anthony, Wm Arnold.

WASHINGTON COUNTY.

[When Washington was laid out a large part of it was reserved for the Revolutionary soldiers and warrants were issued to them. In accordance with my plan I give the list of grantees as it is found on the books of the Secretary of State. These patentees were in all the older parts of the State and many of them never settled in Washington, but many did.]

1784.—Alex Autrey, Henry Allison, Jacob Autrey, Thomas Allen, Elijah Anderson, John Averitt, Jos Avent, Alex Anderson, Barclay Anderson, James Allison, Thos Ayres, Wm Ayres, James Allen, John Abbott, Ezekiel Alexander, Asa Alexander, Aycock, Chas Abercrombee, Alex Auglin, Robert Allen, Robt Adams, R Alexander, Jonathan Asbury, John Acordi, Jno L Alexander, Jonathan Asbery, Jno Anderson, James Adams, Virgil Alexander, Vincent Allenthorpe, Nathan Adams, Wm Anderson, Alex Armstrong, Thos Averett, John Arline.

SAVANNAH C. CHURCH.

1760.—Michael Burkhalter, Mary Bryan, Jno Gosher Betz, Jno Michael Betz, Wm Bradley, G W Brickhole, Peter Berger.

SAVANNAH, CHATHAM AND C. CHURCH.

1756.—David Brown, D C Braddock, Henry Bourquin, Jona Bryan, David Bear.

1757.—Michal Bowman, James Burnside.

1758.—Benj Bourquim, Jno Peter Briton.

1759.—Thos Bruce, John Barnes, Adams Bosomworth, Sigismund Belt.

ST. JOHNS, GREAT OGECHEE, LIBERTY, ST. ANDREW, ST. PHILLIPS.

1756 to 1774.--Elisha Butler, Elizth Baker, Wm Baker, Samuel Bacon, Joseph Bacon, Thomas Bates, John Bailey, Richard Baker, Samuel Bailey, John Baker, James Butler, Ed Baker, Jos Baker, Jos Bacon, Wm Bacon, Jos Barrington, Miles Brewton, Thomas Blackman, J Barnard, J Bullean, Ed Ball, Andrew Bird, S Bailey, F Briest, Rich Brown, Peter Berger, Moody Burt, James Bratcher.

1774 to 1793.—Wm Bamister, Ann Bamister, Daniel Brinson, B Brinkley, Martha Barrett, Hannah Bradwell, Wm Belcher, John Bledsoe, Thos Bellamy, Geo Beard, Ed Baker, Mathew Bryan, Hugh Blunt.

ST. MATHEWS, EFFINGHAM, SCRIVEN, BRYAN.

1758.—Ambrose Burr.

1759.—M Bidenback.

1760.—Mary Bosomworth, Jno Brady, Robert Boston, Jno Geo Bechet, Jno Gasher Bechet.

1765.—Geo Baillee, C Bittenback, M Bittenback, Usban Buntz, Wm Bland, Ed Boykin, Sol Boykin, Philip Box.

1761.—Jno Boykin.

1773.—Moses Bennett, Robert Bennett.

1791.—Martha Bishop, Wm Bishop, Charles Bailey.

1792.—Isaac Brackenridge, Heirs of Sylvanus Bird, Jas Butler, Wm Baker.

ST. GEORGE, BURKE AND JEFFERSON.

1770.—John Bradley, R Bowling, Patrick Brady, Thos. Battey, Alex Baggs, John Brown, Jas Blair, Wm Bennett, Jno Bowman, Saml Bevill.

1771.—Wm Blackman.

1789.—John Bass, Jno Barker.

1774.—Jas Beatty, Matthew Bass.

1775.—James Brown.

1784.—Jno Bell, S Beck, Mathew Bozeman, Geo Bryan, Elisha Burgeron, Reuben Byrum, John Burnet.

1785.—Daniel Bnrnett, Mathew Burnett, Jos Bigham, Brock.

1786.—Thomas Battle.

1787.—Geo Braswell.

—Ben Brock.

ST. GEORGE, BURKE AND JEFFERSON.

1760 to 1769.—Jno Brinson Lewis Bryan, Brinson, R Beard, John Burnside, Sol Boykin, Wm Boykin, John Brantley, Thomas Brantley, James Brantley, Sam'l Beckham, James Beckham, Wm

Burney, James Bowie, John Brinson, Bracey Randall, Jessee Brasher, Agnes Bryan, John Burney, Andrew Berryhill, S Bowen.

1790.—P Belcher, Bap Drewry, Abram Belcher, Jessee Boykin, Jos Burley, Peter Benson.

1791.—Jas Brewer, Sr.

1793.—John Brinson, Moses Brinson, Rev D Bothwell.

1794.—W M Byne, Jno Blanton, Adam Brinson.

1796.—Thomas Beasley, Ed Byne, Abner Belcher, L Beavers, Jos Brashet, Wm Brooks, George Bagby.

1799.—Wm Byne, Isaac Brinson, Mathew Brinson, R Beasley.

1788.—Bass Boykin, Needham Bryan, Isaac Brinsom, Gideon Bemy, Nancy Bird, Dr Wm Baker, Aaron Barber.

1779.—John Bryan, Ann Brown, Hugh Bell, Millboro Bennett, Mose Brinson, Wm Babcock, Charles Bell, Nathan Beall, Jno Berryhill, Henry Bell, Wm Baker, Anthony Bonnell, Jas Burkett, Jas Boyd, Samuel Boyd, Jas Bigham, Geo Brewer.

ST. PAUL'S OR RICHMOND COUNTY.

1760 to 1774.—Jacob Beall, Thos Bassett, Henry Bell, Jno Barton, Jno Bostwick, Jno Burns, Geo Brittie, Chas Bostwick, S Bugg, John Bugg, J Bradley, B Beaver, Wm Burgamy, James Brewer, Wm Blake, Shem Butler, Geo Beck, David Baldwin, Nathen Barnett, Wm Barnett, Jno Bennett, Jno Brean, Jno Burkes, Jno Bogg, Jno Bryd, James Richard, David Boyd, Biggott, Chas Bentz.

1774 to 1775.—Abram Booth, Coleman Brown, H L Bourguoin, Geo Barnes, Sal Barfield, Ches Bostwick, Ab Bedell, Tim Barnard, R Blanchard, A Burnes, C Bolton, Ed Barnard, A Bullock, Moody Burt.

1784 to 1786.—Abrm Baldwin, Chas Burches, Geo Breshfield, Wm Bacon, Dave Burwell, N Burnsides, F Brown, Dan Blair, Thos Barnett, L Bostwick, Nathan Beall, Hezikiah Beall, Wm Bails, Chesley Bostwick, W Barton, Wm Bryant, B Bayley, L Berryhill.

1785 to 1788.—James Bond, Brown, Same Blair, Thos Barrett, Littleberry Bostwick, Wm Bails, W Barton, B Bagley, W Bryant, R Bean, Jas Bowie, Lemuel Blair, S Berryhill, R Bonner, Elisha Bowdry, John Bird, Joel Barnett, L Brown, Jas Bryant, Elija Bragg, Rebecca Baker, Ed Burch, C Connell, L Bush, Jno Bryant, Jos Beaseley, Noble Butler, R Barron, A. Bryan, R Bulloch, W Blackstone, P Brady, I Buckalew, Jno Broth.

WILKES.

1783 to 1785.—Archibald Burton, Thos Burton, John Brown, Wm Berry, James Borean, Abraham Bedell, Auker Benton, Col

Chas Burke, Ed Bean, Jos Benson, Thos Banks, Ch G Bowers, Alex Brown, Bradshaw, Wm Brown, John Black, Wm Bradford, Jacob Bankston, Absalom Baker, Jacob Brooks, Prudence Brooks, Rebecca Bonar, Philip Brantley, Charles Bonner, Margh Brady, Andrew Burns, John Brooks, Martha Bemen, Wm Bowles, Thomas Brantly, Mal Bedell, Wm Bostwick, Thos Brown, Chas Berringfeld, Richard Barton, Wm Bonner, James Berry, Andrew Bell, Thomas Brown, M Burkhalter, Jacob Babbert, David Burnett, Wm Berry, Wm Best, Alex Brown, Isaac Bush, Jos Bell, John Benson, Daniel Burnett, John Buford, Wm Bailey, Francis Batty, Bud Braswell, John Brownfield, Nathan Bell, Jno Broughton, Pat Butts, John Burney, Jno Ball, Thos Bankston, Jno Bently, Stephen Bishop, John Bohanon, David Blackshear, George Bagley, Reuben Barfield, Sol Barfield, John Bayless, Philip Brantley, Nathan Bostick, Nathan Barman, Duncan Bohannon, John Buck, Jona Beard, John Brown, John Bell, M Baldwin, Ruth Bonar, Wm Billups, John Barnett, Peter Bankston, Elija Bankston, Jos Bailey, Jacob Ball, Jas Buchannon, John Buchannon, Bartram Bently, Jno Brewer, John Baker, Wm Bentley, Reuben Ballard, Thomas Burton, Rich Bellamy, ——— Burnett, Isaac Bussom, Zach Butts, Ed Black, Samuel Braswell, Nat Bradford, Andrew Brown, Jordan Buxton, Robert Bryan, John Burton, Jos Bennefield, Jere Baggess, Ben Ballard, Henry Buckhalter, Lamech Beckwith, John Burke, Jesse Bond, John Boyd, Alex Brown, Thomas Bond, Charles Brewer, John Bailey, Ab Bearden, Wm Buckhalter, Hinton Burnett, Wm Brewer.

1788 to 1790.—Thomas Briggs, Jno Boyd, Geo Brewer, Jos Blackwell, Reuben Ballard, Littleberry Bostwick, John Bentley, Richard Beasley, H Bohles, H Bussey, Joshua Ball, Tho Barron, Joshua Burnett, Henry Brown, Rosser Brooks, Jos Butler, G Banks, John Bentley.

1787 to 1788.—Francis Baldwin, Wm Bradshaw, Archie Burden, Thos Brannon, Chris Blanton.

1788 to 1790.—Wm F Booker, Francis Baldwin, James Blackie, John Baker, Thomas Black, James Brooks, Nat Bridges, Zach Butler, Jacob Babbett, Bradford Bynod, Nat Bullock, Geo Banks.

1792 to 1800.—Daniel Buford, Brazel Brawner, Benj Brown.

1795-96-98.—M Brown, A Burroughs, Prudence Barnes, Henry Bonner.

WASHINGTON COUNTY.

John Brown, John Bacon, H Beall Jas Brown, Jere Brigg, Chas Birch, Ed Birch Benj Bateman, Thomas Brannon, Wm Barnett, John Barnett, Jas Bishop, Ruth Bonner, Samuel Bloodworth, Jacob Brandon, John Beckham, Stephen Bishop, Jesse Brooks, Edward Boyd, Nicolas Bragg, Moody Burt, Sam Brannon, Jos

Burnett, Thomas Brantley, Reson Bowles, Jno Baggs, David Bronson Geo Barnhart, Joel Bowen, Thomas Bussy, Sam'l Berryhill, Isaac Betsall, Richard Buston, Archie Beall, Joshua Barnett, Richard Barfield, John Burke, Wm Bishop, Ed Beard Wm Breaddy, Wm Brown, Littleberry Bostwick, Ephram Bowen, John Bell, Simon Beckham, Joshua Burkhalter, Nathan Bostick Wm Barron, John Barnett, Nathan Brownson, John Braswell, A Bradley, Jesse Boykin, Wm Brinson, G Booker, Hugh Bell, Eliazer Bracks, Wm Blanchard Reuben Barron, John Bivings, John Bryan, M Burkhalter, Thos Barnett, Reuben Banks, David Baldwin, John Brown, Geo Bagley, Wm Burkhalter, John Brewton, Jacob Blount, Wm Bready, Allen Brown, John Bennett, Jno Baldwin, Wm Basford, Leonard Basford, Claiborne Bennett, John Barclay, Samuel Braswell, Jno Bales, Chas Burke, Randal Burney, Joshua Ballard, M Baldwin, A Brown John Burnsides, Thomas Brown, A Bailer, Lewis Boyd, Geo Bassett, Chas Brawner, John Bugg, Thos Brown Samson Braswell, Francis Boykin, Wm Berner, Hugh Brewster, Willoughby Barton, Allen Brown, Samuel Beckham, Zack Butler, David Burke, John Bush, Duncan Bryant, John Bryant, Benj Braswell, Fred Braswell, Richard Beasley, Edmond Byne, Oliver Bowen, Cornelius Batchelor, Spencer Branham, Aaron Burnes, Wm Blount, Jno G Blunt, Jas Bankston, Wm Berry, Wm Black, Jno Braswell, Jno Brown, Jno Briggs, Geo Bonner, Sherwood Bonner, Thomas Bray, R Barksdale, Samuel Barnett, Abram Barnett, Jno Barclay, M Burke, Wm Berry, Sam Braswell, Benj Braswell Richard Burney, Geo Burnhart, Geo Braswell, Jno Bender, Wm Brewer, Jesse Brown, Samuel Beckham, Solomon Beckham, Jesse Barbee, Joshua Baker, Daniel Butler, Jos Boyman, John Benson, Jos Baggs, John Brown, Wm Black, Jno Brittain, Samuel Bennett, David Bryant, Richard Burney, Wm Brewton, Nicolas Baker, David Bunery, Jos Barron, Sherwood Beckham, Thos Boyd, John Bugg, Gerard Banks, James Blunt, James Baxter, John Buchannon, S Bragard, Wm Burford, John Booth, Wm Bishop, Stephen Bishop, Geo Bagley, J Bankston Thos Brantley, Wm Burkhalter, Nathan Burnett, Samuel Burnett, Samuel Bannon, Wm Barnard, Thos Bonner, Samuel Bellah, Thos Bibb, Jos Burket, Sol Burnap, Wm Bracken, Jos Beddingfield, Arthur Burnett, Micheal Bird, John Bryant, John Brewer, Isaac Bracken, Christopher Butler, Jos Brown, Wm Beaver, Willie Bullard, John Burge, Laurence Bankston, John Black, Luke Beryman, Robert Braswell, Henry Brown, Elisha Banks, Wm Barron, Ben Brock, D Blackshear, Randall Burney, Jos Boswell, Benj Borland, Thomas Booker, Aaron Baxter.

FRANKLIN.

1785.—Richard Bellamy, Abram Bradley, Joshua Bradley, Wm Burnett Ed Bemus, Richard Berry, Stephen Blunt Jere Brantley, E Bugg, Cap Barker, John Bender, Henry Bird, Wm Bishop, Gilbert Burden, Obadiah Bosworth.

1786.—Thomas Banks, Ralph Banks, Wm Bailey, Wm Banks, Reynolds Barton, R Barrow, Jonathan Beard, John Boyd, Nathan Bostic, Thos Banks.

1790.—Wm Brewer, McCaw Belcher, Nathan Beall, Jos Bailey, Benj Brown, Peter Benson.

1791.—John Bickerstaff, Isaac Beall, Samuel Bird, Jno Bennett, Isreal Bird, Thomas Bray, Christopher Bailey, Martin Bowen.

1792.—Isaac Briggs, A Burns, E Burns, A W Burns, Bob Lewis.

1793.—James Brewton, John Bryan, Samuel Bryan, Jos Barren, Jno Brooks, Fred Buckalew.

1794.—Jesse Bird, Jonathan Black.

1797.—John Baker, Benj Beckham, Archie Bryan, Thomas Bryan.

HANCOCK, OGLETHORPE, WARREN, COLUMBIA.

James Bailey, Fred Buckalew, Jesse Bird, Jones Bradshaw, S Bostick, John Barnett, James Bullock, A Burnett, James Bridges, Frank Boykin, Francis Blackwood, Robt Burton, Benj Bryan, John Bryan; Robt Bryan, John Brewer, Geo Bledock, Philip Brantley, M Battle, Jos Bryan.

ST. JOHN'S ST. ANDREWS, ST. PHILLIPS, LIBERTY COUNTY.

1762 to 1774.—Arthur Carney, John Cuthbert, Jane Carney, John Carter, Bartram Clark, Chas Churchhill, Chas Couper, Alex Caswell.

1785 to 1790.—John Cooper, Wm Clark, John Cooper, A Caruthers, Jacob Clark, John Crafts.

ST. MATHEWS, EBENEZER, EFFINGHAM.

1758 to 1774.—Jno Cramer, N Croneberger, M C Cranweller, Alex Cameron, Jacob Ebenezer Crismon, James Conneck, Lawrence Clark, Wm Conyers, Jos Gray, Jona Cole, John Cadey, Chas F Chevaler, J Cantry, A Cunningham.

1778 to 1796.—Mathew Colson, Mary Ann Conway, Jas Copeland, James Cooke, Henry Cooke, Abram Cone, Aaron Crosby.

ST. GEORGE, BURKE AND JEFFERSON.

1761.—Wm Colson, Wm Case, John Conyers.

1764 and 1765.—Thomas Casey. Jno Caldwell, James Carter, Henry Cavanaugh. Samuel Crane, Wm Colson.

1767.—John Catlett, Jno Chub, N Cheny.

1774 to 1785.—John Casey, Alex Chestnut, James Castillaw, Zebulon Cock, John Cochran, Alex Casey, A Cavanaugh, Henry Cowper, Jesse Crawford, Thomas Chisholm, D Cannon, John Cade.

ST. GEORGE, OR BURKE, AND JEFFERSON.

1784 to 1799.—Alex Caswell, Wm Christie, Bailey Carpenter, Col Cocke, R. Crutchfield, Jno Campbell, Jno Culbreath, Martha Colson, Alex Custer, Elizabeth Corker, Elizabeth Clements, Fannie Chamberlain, Ebenezer Cook, Wm Caldwell, A Connell, Wm Chirstie, Wm Crane, Wm Clarke, Henry Caldwell, John Clements.

BURKE AND JEFFERSON.

1794 to 1796.—Sam Collins, Jos Clark, John Cornelius, Henry Caldwell, Casey Carny, Jno Clements, F Coleman.

RICHMOND COUNTY.

1756 to 1770.—Wm Clements, Sam Chew, —— Closman, Wm Clem, Wm Clark, R Crook, Geo Cornell, L Claiborne, R. Crook & Co, W Combs, David Callahan, Jno Christian, Wm Chandler, R Castleberry, Paul Castleberry, James Cheeves, C Cooksey, Geo Crumley.

1773 to 1774.—Ed Cartledge, Wm Combs, Chas Crawford, David Casey, Daniel Coleman, Isaac Cooper, Jacob Castell, Alex Caldwell.

1774 and 1775.—James Coats, McCarten Campbell, J Castle, Geo Conner, James Cobb, Peter Culbreath, Henry Coats, Nathaniel Coates, Wm Candler, James Caldwell, Elizabeth Crittenden, Thos Chadwick, Jno Cobb, C F Chevalier, R Carlton.

1784 and 1785.—Thos Childers, L Cartledge, Peter Cachary (Zackary), Gilbert Clarke, Anderson Crawford, Elijah Coombs, Wm Cone, John Castle, H Collins, Francis Collins, Wm Caussey, Jonathan Cook, Jacob Castleberry, Elizabeth Cornell, Peter Crawford, Nathaniel Cade, Ed Crisswell, Wm Crittenden, Alex Crisswell, James Culbreth, John Coleman.

SAVANNAH, CHRIST CHURCH.

1757.—Jno Casey, Jacob Casinall.

1759.—Rich Cooper, Thomas Clancy, John Clayton, Lopez Cash, Richard Capers.

ST. JOHN'S, LIBERTY, ST. ANDREWS, GLYNN.

Jessee Corker, Mary Crawford, Jno Cole, Jas Clubb, Geo Clubb, Wm Clubb, Thos Cryler.

ST. JOHN'S, GREAT OGEECHEE, LITTLE OGEECHEE, ST. ANDREWS, GLYNN.

1756 to 1761.—George Cuthbert, Jno Chapman, Richard Cox, Ed Carlton, Thos Carter, Andrew Collins, Wm Clifton, Henry Clark, Mark Carr, Thomas Carr, John Cain, Nathaniel Clark, Geo Cubbege, Wm Carr, Henry Clark, Henry Custer, Thos Collins, Thos Christie, Thos Cox, Moses Cone.

WILKES COUNTY.

1783 to 1785.—John Cargile, Chas Cargile, Wm Cooksey, Gen'l Elijah Clarke, Josiah Carter, Daniel Coleman, John Cunningham, Richard Cureton, John Cain, Richard Call, Seymour Catchings, Jess Cloud, Jos Catchings, Ed Cartledge, Wm and Thos Childers, Spencer Crane, Nathan Coats, John Cloud, Daniel Clower, Thomas Coil, Wm Candler, James Cone, Robert Carnthey, Nancy Cox, Wm Crutchfield, John Cannon, Henry Carr, John Clark, Hannah Conrad, Nath'l Coats, Hon Jacob Colson, Anthony Cooper, Wm Cunningham, Roger Cannon, Wm Coats, Michael Cope, Thomas Carter, Ben Crawley, Hugh Campbell, Lewis Clark, John Castleberry, John Calloway, Hart Champion, Wm Chapman, Thomas Canon, Daniel Connell, Francis Cook, Joshua Cook, Mary Cook, Thomas Cook, Dudley Cook, Jesse Connell, Philip Combs, Henry Carr, James Clark.

1786, 1787, 1788.—Richard Coulter, Jno Chappel, Rachael Cook, Joseph Cook, Mark Cook, John Coleman, John Cody, John Cox, Ed Collier, Joel Chandler, John Cooper, Jane Cannon, Wm Clifton, Ezekiel Cobb, John Copeland, Ezekiel Cloud, heirs of Peter Collier, Wm Cassells, Jos Crockett, Benj Catchings, Parable Clay, R Crowder, Rachael Cobb.

1792.—Lettice Cleghorn, Henry Clements.

1793.—Rich Castleberry.

1784, 1785.—Cornelius Cohorn, Christopher Clark, Robert Chambers, P Clymer, Jos Collins, Stanley Crews, Ambrose Crawford, Leona Carr, James Cook, Jos Catchings, Jno Calloway, Saml Cohorn, Geo Calhoun, Wm Carr, Christopher Chambless, Jno Cole, Charles Carroll, Abia Clay, Henry Castleberry, Edward Callahan, Samuel Creswell, Pat Cunningham, Jos Canon, Adam and David Canon, Thomas Canon, Abel Cobb, Francis Calloway, Cornad Cornelson, Wm Cureton, Henry Cade, Robert Carden, Sydnor Cosby, James Carroll, John Chisholm, Lemuel Crafford, John Campbell, Henry Candler, Merideth Catchings, Thomas

Carter, Chis Clark, Anthony Crumble, John Combs, Alex Cumings, Peter Curtright, Robert Casey, John Crockett, Jno Clements, James Culbreath, Charles Colley, Charles Cullen, Jno Commonpeck, Wm Caldwell, Martha Castleberry, Wm Clendeming.

WASHINGTON COUNTY.

1780.—Seymore Catchings, Jeremiah Cloud, Harris Coleman, John Clower, John Coleman, Dave Canon, Henry Camp, Anthony Crumley, Jno Candler, John Crutchfield, Gilbert Cribbs, John Cook, Jno Carlisle, Jos Cobb, Strother Crawford, David Clay, Wm Crockett, Henry Cooper, Elijah Clarke, David Creswell, Moses Collins, Wm Cauthon, Wm Camp, Wm Coulson, John Coates, David Creswell, Wm Campbell, Isreal Cauthorne, Jos Camp, James Calk, Henry Candler, Anderson Crawford, Moses Clark, Wm Camp, Jno Curb Jeremiah Cheves, Jos Coleman, Wm Cunningham, Daniel Conner, Mich'l Castellow, Nath'l Coates, Lewis Crane, John Collins, Robert Christmas, James Coleman, John Cook, John Campbell, John Chisholm, Geo Cook, Wm Childers, Ezekiel Cobb, Wm Chapman, Peter Castleberry.

1782.—Saml Cartledge, Ben Catchings, Jos Catchings, Thos Childers, Dave Childers, Henry Castleberry, Jacob Castleberry, James Culbreath, Peter Culbreath, Wm Culbreath, Thos Cribb, Wm Cone, Wm Collier, David Carr, Patrick Carr, Wm Candler, H Coleman, Wm Carroll, John Clowers, John Coleman, Wm Clarke, Rich Call, Ousley Carney, John Coleman.

RICHMOND.

1787 to 1789.—Alex Cameron, Mary Chambless, John Cobbs, Abia Clay, Thomas Carr, Martin Cox, Thomas Cain, Rich Call, Asa Cobb, Henry Candler, Chas Crawford, John Chambers, Heirs of Wm Candler, Stephen Collins. Paul Caldwell, Jno Cause.

1781.—Giles Carter, Wm Cowls.

1792.—Wm Conner, Wm Carroll.

1788 to 1794.—Thomas Crossley, Henry Champion Wm Culpepper, Jona Crooks, Henry Candler, Elizth Cobbs, Hoggate Collins, Frances Collins, Wm Clayton, Henry Candler, Philo Chance, Wm Conner.

WASHINGTON.

Vincent Chance, Pat Crookshanks, Samuel Colson, Thos Coates, Jona Coleman, Curtis Coleman, Jos Cooper, David Clay, James Cone, John Cotter, Geo Clamp, Gilbert Campbell, Jno Chappell, Jno Cobb, Wm Crosby, Wm Carter, Wm Cooksey, Jas Cooper, Thos Cobbs, John Childers, Thos Carr, James Crespus, John Cessna, Pat Connally, Samuel Cresswell, James Cresspell, Jno

Curtis, Moses Coleman, Samuel Camp, Robt Cresswell, Alex Curry, Wm Cochran, Robert Curry, Wm Curry, B Carter, Wm Cain, Reuben Cook, Ed Cocker, Samuel Camp, Jay Connelly, John Cessna, Drewry Cade, C F Chevalier, Wm Cureton, John Chambers, Jno Clarke, Jas Cooper, Peter Clymer, John Comer, David Cook, Thomas Crespus, John Cook, Emanuel Chaney, John Curry, John Crittenden, Thos Carr, John Clayton, John Culpepber, Thos Criddle, David Comins, Isham Carr. James Cobb, Lasley Coats, John Cook, Jas Cockersham, Jno Cox, Geo Crosby, Sampson Chance, Henry Cox, Jesse Conwell, Wm Cain, John Abnego Chandler, John Coleman.

FRANKLIN.

1784.—Ezekiel Cloud, John Cloud, Minion Cloud, Christopher Clark, Wm Causey, Jno Carter, Larkin Cleveland, Jona Cook, Jno Collier, Henry Compton, James Carter.

1784.—James Currier, Jno Craddock, Thos Connell, Ben Cleveland, Moses Clark, Peter Curry, Charles Clarke, Wm Clarke, Zach Cox, Richard Curry, Wm Crawford, John Cunningham.

1787.—John Cobbs, Sydnor Crosby, Jno Coulter, John Clarke, James Cockland, Thomas Cruse, Peter Carroll, John Carter, Schem Cook, Wm Cleveland, Jonathan Carter, Nathan Christmas, John Cumming, Samuel Creswell, Jos Carson, Elith Cunningham.

1788.—Suncock Cannon, Francis Coddington, Zach Cowart, M Cleveland, Aaron Campbell, Jonah Cole.

1786.—Jas Cowens, John Cole, Boling Clark, Samuel Camp, Wm Coran.

1789.—Richard Cain.

1798.—Orphans of Isaac Cook.

1792 to 1793.—David Culberson, Duncan Campbell, Alex Caldwell, Rich Colton, Isaac Carter, M Culpepper, Eden Coleman.

GREENE.

Josiah Carter, Peter Coffee, Daniel Conner, Colston Copeland, John Cane, Jos Cooper, Sterling Cato. John Curtright, Peter Curtright, Duncan Cameron, Geo Cowan, Chas Carroll.

BULLOCH AND SCREVEN.

Wm Crawford, Mary Crawford, Jos Cone, Milburne Coward, Jos Cooper, Jos Cone, Aaron Cone, James Comer.

CHRIST CHURCH.

1772.—Philip Delegal, Christopher Dawson, Jas Devany.

ST. JOHN'S, LIBERTY, ST. DAVID.

1764.—James Duck, Wm Dunnan.

1767 to 1769.—John Davis, Daniel Donnan, Samuel Devaux, David Dix, Andrew Darling, Wm Devaux.

1774.—Wm Dawson, Daniel Dunham, Samuel Deverau, Peter Deverau, Micheal Deverau, Jane Reed Deverau, Jos Dunlap, Jno C DeButts, P Demere, Wm Dunham, James Douglas, Andrew Douglas, James Dunwoody, Davis Duncan, John Dallas, John Deas, David Deas, John Drayton, Wm Duke, Lewis Davis, David Dix, Andrew Darling, Wm Devaux.

ST. MATHEWS, EFFINGHAM, ST. PHILLIPS.

1766 and 1767.—Martin Dasher, James Devaux, John Dunbar, Joseph Dickinson, Neal David, Geo Ducker, Mary Ann Delegal, H Douglas, Jno M Dasher, Jos Dickson, Wm Dunham, Henry Dixon, Jas Douglas, John Duncan, Phillip Delegal, Allen Dickson, Benj Daly, Thomas Darnell.

ST. GEORGE, BURKE, JEFFERSON.

1765 to 1772.—Daniel Douglas. Myrick Davis, Neal David, Jno Dickson, Wm Downey, Thomas Davis, John Davis, Jno Duhart, Samuel Davis, Jos D'Arcy.

1774.—Phillip Dell, Jno Dazby, R Danville, Robert Douglas, Wm Dukes.

1787 to 1789.—Joel Darcy, Jas Davis, Sarah Davis, Isaac DuBosce, Fred Douglas, James Douglas, Elias Daniel, Nancy Douglas, B Darcy, Ambrose Downs, Gehazi Davis, Ed Douglas, Chas Daniel, John Dryden, Wm Denny.

1784 to 1786.—Thomas Davis, Jos Davis, Jno Davis, Isaac DuBose, Mary Dyer, Sol Davis, Jno Davis, Wm Dunham, Thos Dilland, Benj Darcy, John Davenport Ben Davis.

ST. PAUL'S AND RICHMOND.

1750 to 1774.—Sephen Day, Dennis Duff, R Dickson, Isaiah Dary, Martin Dasher, Samuel Davis, Daniel Derazaux, Henry Downs, John Donnally, John Dobbins, John Dodds, Benjamin Dunn, John Dunn, Jno Duckworth, Abram Dennis, Jacob Dennis, Patrick Dennis, John Davis, Theophilus Davis.

1784 to 1789.—Meredith Davis, Cornelus Dyart, John Deam, Geo Divine, Magt Davis, David Douglas, Sarah Dunn, Jno Davis, R Dickson, James Donnelly, Clementine Davis.

1790 to 1796.—John Doss, Walton Drane, David Dremin. W Dunn, John Dougherty, Wm Drane.

WILKES COUNTY.

1783 and 1784.—Robert Day, Nathan Day, John Dennis, Eli Davis, Joseph Davis, Wm Davis, Susannah Davis, David Davis, Heir of Augustin Davis, Wm Davis, Absalom Davis, David Davis, Samuel Davis, John Davis, Absolom Davis Jr, Heir of John Dooley, Geo Darden, B. Darcy, Ceo Donley, Wm Darnell, Thomas Darnell, Thomas Dauthet Caleb Dorsey, John Dotten, M Doster, Henry Downs, Wm Downs, Ambrose Downs, Geo Douglas, Wm Douglas, Joel Doss, Nehemiah Dunn, Jeremiah Duckworth, Miles Duncan, Samuel Duncan, Henry Duncan, Jere Dukes, Taylor Dukes, Joel Dukes, Buckner Dukes, Wm Dukes, Chas Dukes, Wm Dudley, John Dudley, Reuben DeJarnett, Jacob Danshy, Martin Deadwyler, Jno Dale, Wm Davenport, John Dougherty.

WASHINGTON COUNTY.

Brock Davis, Ed Daniel, Robert Dick, John Dick, Wm Digbey, Geo Douglas, Wm Douglas, Alex Douglas, Jos Duncan, Luke Darden, John Dunn, Alex Douglas, Sol Davis, Wm Davis, John Dennis, Jacob Duckworth, Ed Daniel, Jos Duncan, Peter Devaux, Daniel Dampier, John Dean, John Davis, Jno Darby, Benj Davis, Lewis Davis, Samuel Davis, Christian Davis, Blandford Davis, Benj Darcy, James Donnelly, Rucker Duke, Thomas Darwell, Mathew Duncan, Mathew Declenden, John Dennis, Daniel Dennison, —— Davenport, Piler De La Playne, Benj D'Arcy, Edward Dickinson, Robert Day, Richard Darby, Geo Darden, Wm Daniel, Moses Davis, Abraham, Davis, Jno Darden, Robert Dickson, Henry Day, John Douglas, Miles Duncan, Wm Davis John Darby, Gilbert Dinkins, Jos Davidson.

FRANKLIN COUNTY.

1787.—Chas Daugherty, Benj Dawson, Joel Doss, Franklin Driver, John Darden, Jean Donaldson, Robert Donaldson, John Doolen, Stephen Denmark, Seth Dean, Jona Davidson, Rich Dawson.

MONTGOMERY AND FRANKLIN.

1794.—Nathe Denkee, Richmond Dawson.

ST. JOHNS, LIBERTY, G. O., L. O., ST. DAVID.

1754 to 1760.—Jones Elliot, Gov Henry Ellis, Wm Ewen, Gray Elliot.

1772.—Geo Eldridge.

1787 to 1797.—Jno Elliot, Alex Elliot, Stephen Ewbank, Wm Earnest.

ST. MATHEWS, EBENEZER, EFFINGHAM.

Geo Eagle, R Eshberger, Ludwig Ernest, Conrad Etcher, John Eppinger, John Everett, M Everage, Jas Emmett, John Everett.

ST. GEORGE, BURKE, JEFFERSON.

1760 to 1774.—David Emanuel, Asa Emanuel, Geo Eason, Philip Elephinstone, Jno Earle.

1787.—Wm Evans.

1786 to 1789.—David Emanuel, Hugh Evans, Daniel Evans, John Easley, Ben Edwards.

1790 to 1793.—Wm Elliot, Elijah Eastwood, Daniel Eubank, Elisha Eustis, Elisha Easter, John Even, Wm Edwards.

ST. PAULS.

1757 to 1770.—John Emanuel, Piles Elliot, Wm Ellen, James Emmett, Ed Echles, Mary Eaton, Gabriel Eberhardt, Jacob Elly, Michael Elly.

WILKES.

1783 to 1786.—Mary Edes, John Edes, David Evans, Abram Evans, Rich Ewbank, Abram Eiland, B Elliot, Jacob Early, Wm Edwards, Ambrose Edwards, Thomas Edwards, Edward Echols, Jos Elsbury, Michael Elsbury, Jere Elsbury, John and Hannah Elrod, David Eberhardt

1790 to 1797.—David Erwin, James East, John Edmond, James Echols.

GREENE.

Walter Ellace, Richard Easley, Ben Evans.

WASHINGTON.

John Evans, Gibson Evans, Daniel Evans, Stephen Evans, James Evans, Sam'l Elbert, Nath'l Eves, Stephen Ellis, Robert Ellis, Solomon Ellis, Jno Eads, Jacob Earnest.

FRANKLIN.

1786 to 1796.—Jeffry Early, Hugh Ector, John Erwin, Daniel Elam, Daniel Easley, Robert Elise, Henry Evans.

SAVANNAH C. CHURCH.

1758 to 1764.—Wm Frances. B Farley, D Fox, Jonatha Fox, Ab Frye, Rich C Fox, Fred K Fain, Walter Fleming, David Fisher.

1764 to 1772.—Nicolas Fisher, Alex Findley.

ST. JOHNS, ST. ANDREWS, ST. DAVIDS, L. O., G. O.

1755 to 1764.—David Fox, John Fox, John Farley, John Feaster, Sam'l Fulton, Simon Fraser, Barth Farrar, Thomas Fulker, Geo Finch, Elizabeth Fyfe.

1769 to 1774.—Sam'l Frink, James Forrester, David Fisher, Daniel Forbes, Geo Fox, John Fitzgerald, James Fordyce, Thomas Fleming, John Forbes, Wm Forsyth, Donal Forbes, Jno Forsyth, S Fulton.

1793.—Drury Fort, Abram Franklin, David Ferrand, James Fulcher, Seth Fountain.

ST. MATHEWS, EFFINGHAM, EBENEZER, SCRIVEN.

Philippa Finney, Geo Fowle, Jno Fitzer, H Fulzer, H Flyer, Wm Frances, Jos Ford, Thomas Fulker, Jonatha Felzer, Dyer Frazer.

ST. GEORGE, BURKE, JEFFERSON.

1763 to 1774.—Benny Fox, Zach Fenn, Ben Fox, James Fletcher, Donal Frantz, Thos Freel, Pare Fulton, M Frederick, J Fitzgerald, Thomas Fusel, Fletcher, Thomas Fussell, Jas Fox, Jas Finley, Thomas Frederick, Donal Forbes, John Fleming.

1789 to 1796.—John Farmer, Sarah Figgett, John Fulgham, Henry Forth, Robert Forsyth, John Freeman, Sr, John Freeman, Jr, James Finley, John Fayall, Eddy Floyd, Wm Fanney, Wm Freeman, Jesse Flarron Elija Floyd, Robert French, John Fulton, Thomas Fain, Thomas Fannell, Jas Fitzgerald, Jas Fenwick, Henry Forth, Robert Fain, Peter Fryermoeth, Rich Fleeting, Ab France, Samuel Ford, Laurence Folsom, Fielding Fryer, Lewis Fryer, Thomas Ford, Jonathan Fontain, John Fayle, C Fitzgerald, Mark Floyd, Jos Floyd, John Farmer.

ST. PAUL'S AND RICHMOND.

1764 to 1774.—John Fyfe, Wm Few, Ignatius Few, M J Fleming, Thomas Ford, John Farrell, Wm Farmer, Eli Ford.

1784 to 1792.—Ignatius Few, James Fleming, John Fendall, Robert Flournoy, Geo Fold, John Freel, Andrew Frazer, James Fox, Wm Farmer, Abraham Fears, Geo Franklin, Isaac Fuller, Jno Foster, Jos Ferguson, James Fulcher, Jno Fury, Eli Fort, John Fuller, Forrester, Sr, James Farley, James Fox, Joshua Fuller, George Franklin.

WILKES.

1783 to 1786.—James Freeman, Martin Freeman, Holman Freeman, John Freeman, George Freeman, Jno Fullelove, Samuel Foster, Wm Foster, Ignatius Few, Benjamin Few, Wm Few, Thos

Few, Wm Fitzjarrell, Jno H Foster, Samuel Finley, John Favour, Arthur Fort, Wm Fort, Lucend Folkes, Perryman Floyd, Andrew Frazer, Jno Fling, Phillip Franklin, Jos Fuller, Chas Finch, Meals and Forsyth, Tarpley Flint.

1786 to 1794.—Nathan Folsom, Joshua Farrell, Samuel Findley, Jno Flannagan, Jacob Finch, Nathan Foster, John Fergus, Robert Flournoy, Wm Fletcher, Perin Farrow, Jos Fitzpatrick, Chrs Felps, David Farrow, Dempsey Foster, Meals and Forsyth, J Fulgham, Abner Flewellen, Alex Flewellen (Warren), Chas Fain, (Elbert).

WASHINGTON.

Malech Frayer, Jacob Fair, James Fernell, Owen Fluker, John Fluker, Wm Fluker, Nathan Fowler.

FRANKLIN.

1785.—Geo Franklin, Jno Fuller, Jonas Fouche, John Flynn, Jno L Flint.

SAVANNAH.

1757 and 1770.—Wm Grover, Simeon Griener, John Gable, Aurith Gautier, Chas Gampher, Michael German, Wm Glen, David Gunter, Peter Gautier, Abner Graham, Jos Gibbons, Wm Grant.

ST. JOHNS, ST PHILLIPS, ST. THOMAS, ST. ANDREW, GLYNN.

1757 to 1759.—Francis Graham, Jere Gunn, Wm Gamble, Gray Gray, Jno Grienner, John Graham, Maj Granadge, Jno Gallache, Palmer Goulding, Sarah Goulding, Jno Graw, John Gordon, Jno Grayson, Wm Graves, Button Gwinnett, James Giginilliat, Jesse Gunn, Philip Grunder, Samuel Gurney, Jno Garrett, Henry Gimdrat, R Gough, Samuel Gary, John Goode, John Greene, John Gordon, Thomas Goldsmith, John Graves, John Grahame, J Girardian, Jasper Garbert John Graham, John Gieger, John Graves, Robert Gill, Wm Graves.

ST MATHEWS, EFFINGHAM, SCREVEN.

1763 to 1770.—John Grovenstien, John Goldwire, Geo Grain, Wm Gilbert, John Gruber, Anthony Gable, Peter Griener, Thomas Goldsmith, Aaron Griener, Wm Gilbert, John Gruber, John Goldwire, Jacob Greene, B. and Jos Goldwire, Sol Gros, Jno Grill, John Gugle, H Griener, James Gallach, Jesse Gunn, David Goodman, Wm Glascock.

ST GEORGE, BURKE AND JEFFERSON.

1757 to 1774—Jas Garvey, John Grady, Jas Gilespie, David Grier, Geo Galphin, Thos Galphin, Allen Grover, Catherine Griener, Andrew Griener, Jno Griener, Arthur Gibbons, Christian Gieger.

1773 to 1798.—Geo Galphin, Robt Gray, John Graham, John Gordon, Samuel Gandy, Thomas Gray, Jacob Gould, John Grant, Thos Golightly, P Goodall, Samuel Gandy, Basil Gray, Sam'l Gibson, Mungo Graham, Mary Goodall, Zack Gray, Wm Gibbons, Geo Griggs, Wm Goodbe, James Gilmon, John Gamble, Robert Gordon, Mathew Gray, Jno Gilmore, Samuel Gates, Samuel Gordon, James Gray, Judith Gannaway, Moses Green, John Green, Samuel Gates, B Gaven, Samuel Gurton, Mathew Gray.

RICHMOND, ST. PAULS.

1756 to 1774.—Geo Galphin, Robert Germany, Barbara Galphin, John Germany, James Groves, Robert Groves, John Green, James Grierson, John Green, Thos Garrett, Sir John Graham.

1789 to 1798.—Isaac Grubs, John Grienway, Ambrose Gordon, Penny Gray, Days Gill, John Gibson, Robert Graves, Jessee Grice, M Griffin, Moses Green, Robert Graves, Jessee Grice.

1774 to 1786.—Wm Garden, Sam'l Griffin, Michael Griffin, Jno Glover, Isaac Green, Isaac Gray, James Graham, —— Galphin, —— Grierson, —— Gudgean, Elyda Gun, Isaac Greathouse, Jas Gray, Nath Goff, John Garrett, Lewis Gardner.

WILKES.

1783 to 1788.—John Glover, Joshua Grenage, Jos Gunnells, Robert Gunnels, John Glover, Wm Glover, Geo Gray, Wm Grey, John Grigsby, John Garrett, Stephen Gafford, Rich Graves, Mathew Gaston, Abe Gonder, Littleberry Grisson, Duke Glenn, Jos Griffin, Hon Reuben Gilder, John Graves, Josiah Gales, Thos Goree, James Grigsby, Daniel Games, Daniel Gunnells, John Grantham, John Griffith, Robert Griffith, Humphey Graves, Jno George, John Gibson, Robert Guthrie, Thos and Chas Gillum, James Gorley, Major Green, Thomas Graves, Thomas Grimes, Wm Groves, Jno Golson, George Gresham, Stith and Glascock, Uriah Gilmore, James Gilmore, Rachel Graves, Ben Green, Wm Green, Sr, John Grantham, Jno Graves, Philip Gibbs, Isham Gardner, Thos Gamble, John Garrett, Jno Granade, Benj Gross, John Grimes, Amos Green, Joel Glass, Frances Gartrell, James Greenotreet, Wm Gordon, Aaron Grier, Moses Green, Sam'l Gilbert, Susannah Gardner, Nathan Gunnells, Hugh Gilliland, John Glass, Daniel Grant, Humphery Gilmer, John Glaspy, Wm Glascock Sam'l Griffith, John Gamble.

WASHINGTON.

Allen Fort, Ignatius Few, John Fuller, James Finley, Isaac Fuller, Zach Fenn, Thos Frederick, Holman Freeman, John Freeman, Thos Fuqua, Francis Fenn, Benj Few, Wm Few, Geo Folds, Wm Foster, Jos Ford, Arthur Ford, John Freel, David Felps, John Fuller, Jacob Fortine, Wm Fleming, Wm Franklin, Mack Fulgham, Jonathan Goldsburg, Thos Glascock, Aaron Grier, Robert Grier, Jno Grinsby, Alex Gaston, John Glass, John Garrett, Thos Gray, Jos Gray, Wm Glenn, Thos Grimes, Wm Gardner, E Gillett, Wm Germany, Richard Graves, Thos Gillilland, Wm Gillilland, Wm Godby, Jas Gilman, Josiah Goldsby.

FRANKLIN.

1786 to 1795.—Moses Guest, Thomas Gilbert, Samuel Gardner, Thos Gammage, Thorn Gilbert, Thomas Gilbert, Thos Gibbons, Dennis Glisson, Kemeth Gordon, Henry Garrett, Janes Goldsby, Mose Granbury, Sol Gross, I T Gardner, Frances Gideon, Thomas Gresham, F Grizell, Elijah Grimsley, Thomas Grover, Pleasant Goodall, John Gordon.

CHRIST CHURCH, SAVANNAH, VEMONSBURG.

1757 to 1759.—Harback, Ed Harold, Geo Hiesler, Pat Houston, Nicolas Homer, John Homer, Francis Harris, Thos Hamilton, Sam'l Hammer, Thos Hooper, Eliz'th Hendrick, Henry Hammond, Philip Howell, Wm Howell, Fred Helvenstein, Wm Handby, Fred Halsendorf, Fred Herb, John Hanleiter, Geo Hogue, Dame Priscilla Houston, Jas Hamilton, Jos and Annie Hunter, Francis Harris, Debora Houston, Robert Homer, Ed Hopton, Jacob Holbrook, James Hume, Gotlieb Harbert.

ST. JOHNS, ST. DAVIDS, ST. PHILLIPS, ST. JAMES, G. O., L. O.

1762 to 1765.—Robert Houston, David Hugenin, Gasner Hack, James Harly, Chas Hawkins, Charles Herring, Wm Harbard, Jas Heart, Jacob Helvenstine, Thomas Harris.

1791.—Sam'l Harris.

1757 to 1768.—Sir P Houston, James Houston, Jas Habersham, Geo Houston, Conrad Hower, Henry Hamilton, James Hurley, Wm Hopton, Isaac Hayne, Jas Hearn, Jas Habersham, Jos Habersham, Pat Houston, Geo Houston, James Houston, Nath'l Hall, Geo Hall, Daniel Hall, Thomas Hall, Geo A Hall, Michael Hames, Wm Handley.

1786 to 1792.—Robert How, John Houston, May Harrison, Jas Helvenstien, Jacob Helvenstien, Maria Hext, Eliza Hext.

CAMDEN.

1792 to 1796.—Joel Hobbs, James Hannah, Thomas Hannah, Wm Hedding, John Hardy, Leonora Harper, John Harrison.

ST. MATHEWS, ST. PHILLIPS.

1759 to 1762.—Wm Hearne, John Hearn, Geo Hartstien, Chas Hickson, Jacob Heisler, Joachin Harsten, John Hienley, Jno Hopkins, Fred Helvenstein, Michael Haverer, Geo Heckall, Elizabeth Hamack, Geo Henry, Samuel Hastings, John Humphries, Robert Humphries, Thomas Humphries, Wm Huntley, Geo Hyde, John Heinly.

1765 to 1774.—John Hall, Robert Hudson, Harmon Hinson, Thos. Hearn.

1770 to 1774.—John Harvey, Nicolas Horton, John Helvenstine, Fred Helvenstine, John Hagan, Emanuel Harvey.

1786 to 1796.—Wm Heyton, Bradley Hall, Miles Hunter, Abel Hite, Janes Hanley.

ST. GEORGE, HALIFAX.

1758 to 1765—James Huston, Samuel Hudson, Isaac Hawkins, Paul Haralson, John Hopkins, Samuel Hudson, Robert Hairston, Samuel Haynes, Nathan Hooker, John Howard, Jno Harwell, Geo Harmaugh, Anne Hopkins, Robert Hudson, James Huston, Davis Harwell, Wm Hobbs, David Holmes, John Howells, Jos Humphrey, Isaac Heaton, Pat Hannagan.

1770 to 1785—Mary Hilkey, V. Hollingsworth, Wm Harding, James Hart, James Haden, Wm Henkle, Berry House, Jos Haysworth, John Hampton, Henry Hayman, Alex Hendrick, Thos Hamilton, Wm Harding, James Hogg, Thos Harrison, Edna Hall, Robert Hamilton, John Hamilton, Charles Hedspeth.

1785 to 1790.—Jesse Horn, Step Hawthorne, R. Henley.

BURKE, JEFFERSON.

1786 to 1788.—Blasingame Harvey, Wm. Holly, Henry Hayman, Stanton Hayman, Ben Hart, Jacob Holland, John Hudson, Gilbert Harrison, Wm Hunt, Wm Hobbs, Jona Holley, Sarah Hord, H. Hargrove, Jas Harvey, Lewis Harrell, Martha Hooker, Mary Hughes. Sarah Hines, Dan'l Hagan, Sarah Haragan, Moses Horn, Luther Hallowell, Samuel Holton, Wm Hinson, B Hadley.

BURKE, JEFFERSON, ST. GEORGE.

1786 to 1788.—Martha Hooker, Jona Holly, Nathaniel Hicks, Mary Hogg, Wm Holmes, R Herrington, Jos Hampton.

1788 to 1790.—Michael Henderson, Geo Heydrick, Jesse Heydrick, Geo Harwell, H. Hillhouse, Mary Hogg, Z. Haslip, Thos Hannah, S Hayman, Wm Hines, Stark Hill, Jos Holiday, John Henry, C Harwell, John High.

1790 to 1798.—Thomas Hodges, Wm Herring, Wm Hudley, Richard Heath, Henry Horn, Jesse Handley, Moses Horne, Jos Harvill, Mary Hill, Thos Hilton, Wm Hart, Ed Hill, Blassingame Harvey, R. Herrington, Jordan Heath, Wm Hanmett, Milner Holiday, Samuel Hemphill, Ed Hill, Jacob Hoffman, Aaron Holiday, James Hudson, Wm Huston, Mary Hamage, Garland Hardwick, Jas Ham, Wm Holloway, Benjamin Haney, Silas Hilliard, Richard Hunt, Francis Holiday, John Humphreys, Mc Hawkins, Wm Holloway.

ST. PAULS.

1762 to 1774.—Abram Hood, Ezekiel Haviland, Thos Hickinbottom, John Heard, John Holloway, Leroy Hammond, James Heron, Steven Heard, Barna Heard, Thos Hogan, James Hart, John Howard, Wm Hixon, Sir Pat Houston, Peter Hart, James Hill, John Hume, James Hume, Jno Heard, Thos Henshaw, John Houston, Nathan Harris, Nathan Hampton, James Harris, Alex Horsack, Jno Howard, Jacob Henn.

RICHMOND.

1774 to 1790.—Ambrose Holliday, R Higginbottom, Samuel Hanson, Ben Harrison, Wm Hogg, Thos Hunt, Jno Hutchings, Jesse Hunter, Jas. Howell, Thos Hamilton, Richard Hills, Henry Hurd, Fitz M Hunt, Wm Hardy, Jos Hutchinson, Thos Hanson, Chas Hargrove, Ed Hicks, Arnold Hays, Thos Hays.

ST. PAULS AND RICHMOND.

1770 to 1798—Jas Hamilton, Wm. Hughes, Samuel Hammond, Joel Hill, Jos Harrell, Berry Hood, Thomas Hill, John Hickson, A Hawkins, James Hancock, O. Hatcher, Samuel Henson.

WILKES COUNTY.

1783 to 1785—Thomas Howell, Matthew Hubbard, John Hewett, Benj Howard, John Holmes, Jos Henderson, Michel Henderson, Micajah Hinton, Dempsey Hinton, James Hinton, John Hinton, Thos Hill, John Hill, James Hill, Isaac Hill, Joshua Hill, Isaac Hill, Abraham Hill, Theophilus Hill, Christian Hill, Geo Harriman, Samuel Hoff, Jacob Harding, Rhesa Howard, Julius Howard, Stephen Hay, Nathaniel Harvill, Wm Hammett, Susannah Hammett, James Hammett, Cuthbert Hudson, Asa Hooks, Mary Hudson, Thomas Holliday, Thomas Hubbard, Ben

Hubbard, John Hardeman, Uriah Hardeman, Charles Hardeman, Wm Hardeman, May Hollingsworth, Samuel Hunter, George Hamilton, Geo. Harper, Samuel Henderson, Jno Harley, Henry Hunt, Richardson Hunt, B Hammock, Fitz Maurice Hunt, Thomas Hailey, James Hurt, Wm Hughes, Chap Hughes, James Howell, Wm Hutchinson, David Harris, Elizabeth Huff, Thomas Hawkins, Jno Howsey, Thos. Hemphill, Geo. Hendon, Roberta Hendon, Rich Hamlin.

1783 to 1785.—Walton Harris, Robert Harper, Samuel Harper Andrew Hamilton, John Henderson, Mack Holloman, James Hart, Samuel Hart, Benj Hart, Thos Heard, Jesse Heard, Stephen Heard, John Heard, Charles Heard, Richard Heard, James Harvey, Richard Harvey, John Harvey, Thomas Harvey, Richard Hall.

1785 to 1792.—Jos Hays, Jno Hall, Wm Hall, Abram Heath, Lum Harris, David Harris, Jas Hog.

1787 to 1793.—James Himes, Wm Hardeman, Albert Hay, A Haladay, Geo Hall.

1787 to 1793.—Dalzel Hunter, Jos Higgenbottom, John Hightower, John Hendley, Shap Huse, James Hart, Moses Harris, Jno Herrington, Wm Hathorne Francis Higginbottom J Padury, Peter Stubbs, James Hatfield, Mary Hudson, Sylvester Hammond, John Hammond, Abraham (Abner) Hammond, Denis Headen, Robert Hambrick, Henry Haines, Richard Holmes, Richard Holland, C Hooper, David Harris, Thomas Hampton, D Holloman, Hillary Hendrix, David Howell, David Hillhouse, Thos Horton, G Hartfield, M Harback, John Harley, Peter Hoday, Wm Hathorne, Richard Hood, Jesse Hooper, Walter Hamilton, McHawkins, Jno Hollenshed, Jos Henderson, Wm. Holliday, Isaac Hardy, Wm Hatcher, Thos Harbens, Moses Hill, Wm Hathorne, James Hines, Geo Hamilton, Jas Hilton, W Harbas, James Haws, Wm Hog, Jno Hall, Wm Hay.

WASHINGTON.

Laurence Hause, Wm Huston, John Hicks, Tyne Harris, Jno Hill, Nicolas Hughes, Wm Hadden, James Hanna, Asa Haloday, Thomas Hawkins, John Hatcher, Miles Hunter, Thos Herrington, Christopher Hillery, Robt Howe, Robt Hodge, Ed Hall, James Hogg, Jas Hatcher, Hudson Hatcher, James H Harvey, David Howell, James Hilliard, Geo Hall, Benj Hobson, Andrew Hays, John Houston, Thos Hamilton, Thos Hartley, Wm Hogg, Wm Harper, David Haines, Michael Harback, Jas Hill, Joel Harvey, Samuel Hoff, James Hogan, Jesse Horne, Wm Hewitt, George Handlay, Rhesa Howard, Nat Harwell, Joshua Hampton, Setha Hammell, Andrew Hays, Michael Harback, Thos Harvey, Edward Hill, James Hamdon, Jno Hendley; Jno Hammock, Robt

Hines, Achilles Harris, Zack Harroll, Wm Hamilton, Wm Hill, Barnard Heard, Samuel Harvie, Thomas Howard, Nathan Harris, Edward Harris, Wm Harris, Daniel Harris, John Hill, James Howard, Samuel Hawkins, John Holmes, Jas Hammett, Michael Harvey, Jas Hogg, Thos Hathorne, Wm Herritt, Jas Harper, Wm Hunt, David Holloman, Mack Holloman, A Hone, Richard Hubbard, Rhesa Howard, John and B Howard, James Houston, Robert Hatcher, Benj Hammock, J Hinton, Wm Hill, Nicolas Hughes, Charles Harvey, Richard Harvey, John Harvey, Walton Harris, Buckner Harris, Samuel Holloman, Zack Henderson, A Hatcher, Francis Holton, Nathel Hicks, B Higginbottom.

FRANKLIN.

1786 to 1796.—Francis Holton, Jos Hudson, B Haines, Joshua Hill, Julius Howard, James Hogg, Cuthbert Hudson, Wm Hay, Jacob Horne, Thomas Holden, Jos Humphreys, Samuel Hunter, Sarah Hunter, A Haney, Geo Howard, Jos Humphries, Geo Herring, F Herrington, John Hall, R C Harris, John Heatley, Jas Harville, Zack Harrell, Jona Hilton.

GREENE COUNTY.

Thos Harris, James Houston, Joshua Houghton, Wm Heard, Wm Hogg, Thos Harvey, Newday Houseley (Ousley), Sarah Hagerty, Davis Harrison, James Hogg, James Harvey, Robert Hill.

COLUMBIA, ELBERT, LINCOLN, OGLETHORPE, WARREN.

1790 to 1799.—John Harris, Wm C Hunt, John Harrison, Major Hurst, Augusta Hamb, Thomas Haynes, Jesse Hardy, Luke Hamilton, Richard Hunt, Jos Hill, Jno S Hodges, Chas Hardeman, Ann Hay, Isaac Horn, Jos Harp, Israel Harris, Stephen Hartley, Jos Henry.

SAVANNAH, CHRIST CHURCH.

Wm Johnston, Lewis Johnston, Wm Johnston, Noble Jones, Noble W Jones, Mary Jones, Jean Jansack, Mary Inbert, Jacob Ihly.

ST. JOHN, ST. PHILLIP, ST. DAVIS, ST. ANDREW, CAMDEN, LIBERTY.

1756 to 1768.—Davis Jersey, Ben Irwin, J Jarvis, Andrew Johnson, Wm Johnson, Wm Jones, Joseph Johnson, Wm Jones, Samuel Jones, Joshua Jones, John Jameson, Alex Inglis, Peter Johnson, Alex Inglis, S Joiner, John Jones, Wm Jordan, Thomas

Jameson, Alethea Jones, Geo Ingils, Adam Irick, Abram Jones, Geo Johnson, James Jones, John Jones, Abe Jackson, John Jameson.

ST. MATTHEW'S.

1768 to 1787.—J Nesbitt Johnson, Anderson Johnson, Jacob Jeakly, Matthew Jones, Alex Inglis, Geo Inman, Henry Joice.

ST. GEORGE, BURKE, JEFFERSON.

1788 to 1789.—John Jeffers, Wm Jones, Richard Ingram, Elizabeth Jones, Ruth Jenkins, Sterling Jordan, Robert Irwin, Micajah Johnson, Jacob Joins, Charity Jordan, John Jones, S Johnson David Ingram, John Jordan, Elizabeth Irwin, Susannah Iverson, Wm Jones, Jesse Johnson, Francis Jenkins, J Jackson, Malachi Jones, Russell Jones, Reuben Jones, Irene Joiner, Wm Johnson, Thomas Johnson.

ST. GEORGE, BURKE, JEFFERSON.

1774 to 1785.—James Jones, Isabel Irvine, David Irvine, Wm Jenkins, Henry Jones, Ann Jarnigan.

1785 to 1800.—Henry Jones, James Jones, Joshua Inman, Jos Irwin, John Jones, Mary Inman, Batt Jones, Alex Irwin, Samuel Jordan, John Jones, John Irwin, R Ingram, John Jordan, Jacob Jordan, John Jeffers, Wm Jones, Richard Ingram, Elizabeth Jones, Ruth Jenkins.

ST. PAULS.

1757 to 1774.—Lewis Johnson, Wm. Johnson, John Jameson, Sam Jack, Isaac Justice, Henry Jones, H. Jernigan, Alex Johnson, Wm. Johnson, Wm. Jones, Thos Jones, John Jones, Francis Jones, Berry Jones, James Jarvirs, James Jackson, Isaac Jackson, Thomas Jackson, Berry Jackson, Absolom Jackson, Wm. Jackson, Walter Jackson, Andrew Jones, Henry Jones, Jacob Jones, Patrick Jones.

WILKES.

1784 to 1790.—Henry Josey, Wm. Jackson, Daniel Jackson, John Jack, Wm. Burnett Jack, James Johnson, Willis Johnson, John Johnson, Caleb Johnson, Wm. Johnson, Thos. Johnson, John Johnson, Reuben Johnson, Jonathan Jones, Hugh Jones, Philip Jones, Marshall Jones, Lucy Jackson, James Jack, Reuben Jackson, Amasa Jackson, Absolom Jackson, Peter Jackson, Ben Jackson, Nathaniel Jackson, Isreal Jordan, James Irvine, Nathan Jones, Zach Jones, Charles Jones, Braxton Jones, Jacob Jones, Sol Jones, Thomas Jones, Isaac Jones, Russell Jones.

WASHINGTON.

Alex Irwin, Jared Irwin, Hugh Irwin, Lawson Irwin, Pat Jarvis, Robert Jewett, Richard Jenkins, Benj Jenkins, Reuben Jackson, Peter Jackson, Randal Jackson, James Jackson, John Jackson, Job Jackson, Philip Jackson, Wm Jackson, Jonathan Jackson, Jesse Jackson, Frederick Jackson, Elias Jackson, Wm. Jackson, Samuel Jack, Joshua Inman, David Jones, Robert Jones, Simeon Jones, Seaborn Jones, Benj Jones, Jones Jones, Nathan Jones, Thos Johnson, Stephen Johnson, Daniel Johnson, Dempsey Justice, Berry Joiner.

FRANKLIN.

1784 to 1786.—Nicolas H Jarvis, Wm Johnston, Thomas Jones, James Jones, David Jones, Jas B Jones, Malachi Jones, John Johnson.

WARREN, HANCOCK, COLUMBIA.

1790 to 1800.—Malcom Johnson, Thomas Johnson, Joshua Jones, Hugh Ingram, Martin Johnson, John Justice, Harrison Jones, Heirs of Dev Garratt (Jarratt.)

SAVANNAH, VERNONBURG, SKEDAWAY, CHRIST CHURCH.

1756 to 1763.—Alexander Kellar, Kiefer, John Kelsale, Theobald Keifer, Jacob Keifer, Rich Kent.

ST. JOHN, ST. PHILLIPS, ST. ANDREW.

1756 to 1776.—Donald Kennedy, Peter Knight, Walter Kelly, Roger Kelsal, Thomas Kiser, Wilrich Roger, Thomas King, Jno King, Rufus King.

ST. MATTHEW'S, EBENEZER, EFFINGHAM, SCRIVEN.

1756 to 1799.—Peter Kohlinson, Leonard Rrause, Hugh Kennedy, Matthew Kough, Wm Knox, John Koln, John Kingall, Henry Kennan, Bryan Kelly, Wm Kennedy, Hugh Kennedy, Robert Kirkwood, Richard Kirkland, Henry King, Sam'l Krouse, John Knight, Wm Kirby, Wm King, John Koogler, Sam'l Krause, Arthur Kirby, Hannah Kirby, Richard Kain, Sol Kemp, Geo Koonce.

ST. GEORGE'S, BURKE AND JEFFERSON.

1756 to 1799.—Sol Kemp, John Knoblock, Jno Klien, James Kemp, Jno Kiebler, David Kelley, Jno Kemp, May Kennedy,

James Kislam, Chas Kimball, Dan'l Kemp, L Killebrew, Thos Kilpatrick, John Kent, Tandy C Key, Richard Kirsey, Jos Kimball, Wm Kennedy.

WILKES COUNTY.

1784 to 1786.—Jno Kirkes, John Kerns, Jno Kilgore, Jno King, Jacob Kinnebrew, John Kelly, Jno Kimborough, J Kendall.

WASHINGTON COUNTY.

1785 to 1790.—Wm Kimbro, John Kimbro, Wm Kelly, Ed Kelly, Jacob Kelly, Thos Kelly, John King, Jno Kemp, James Kemp, Thos Kilpatrick, Jos Kirkham, Jos Kennedy, Henry Kendrick.

WARREN COUNTY.

Samuel Knox, Kaden Ketton.

WASHINGTON COUNTY.

Wm Kimbro, John Kimbro, Wm Kelly, Ed Kelly, Jacob Kelly, Thos Kelly, John King, Thos Kemp, James Kemp, Thos Kirkpatrick, Jos Kirkham, John Kennedy, Henry Kendrick.

WILKES COUNTY.

1784 to 1786.—Mary Kinnan, Webb Kidd, Jacob King, Wm Kemp, Allen Kellog, Henry Karr, Richard King, Wm King, Andrew King, Ed Kelling, Thos Kemp, Jno Kellog, Absolom Knox, Benj Knox.

WASHINGTON COUNTY.

Jere Kendall, Edward Kendall, Ralph Kilgore, John Kilgore, Wm Kilgore, James Kelly, Jno Kell, Henry Kline.

GREENE COUNTY.

Henry Kerr, Alex King, John Kennedy, Peter Kender (Peter Render), Spencer Keely.

FRANKLIN COUNTY.

1786 to 1790.—R Kilgore, Pat Kneal (Neal), Henry Kair (Carr) Jno Kimbro, John Kield, John Kelly, Thomas Kilpatrick, Jere Kendall, Reuben Kennedy, Jno King, Robert King, James King, Ed Keating.

SAVANNAH, C. C., SKIDAWAY, ETC.

1756 to 1760.—James Love, Thomas Loyd, Andrew Loyer, Sam Lyon, Francis Lee, Anthony LeBon, —— LaRoche, Nicolas Lawrence, James Love, Alex LeMar.

ST. JOHNS, LIBERTY, ST. ANDREWS, ST. DAVIDS.

1756 to 1767.—John Lupton, Isaac Lines, Geo Love, Nicolas Lawrence, Jno Littmore, Wm Law, Wm Little, Jacob Lockeman, Isaac Limes, John Lawson, Benj Lewis, Wm Little, John Lynn, H Lownes, Henry Lownes, Jacob Lockeman, John Logstontine, Wm Leconte, John Lestinger, Isaac Lewis, Jos Lewis, Wm Lyford, R Lewis and others, Elijah Lewis.

ST. MATHEWS, BULLOCH, SCREVEN, EFFINGHAM.

1756 to 1774.—C Limberger, Viel Leckner, Viel Landfeller, Thomas Lee, Geo Lockner, Geo Lockner, Jr, Jno Lester, Jos Lutner, Andrew Lambert, James Leman, Benj Lanier, Samuel Lanier, Benj Lewis, Abraham Lewis, James Lucina, Thomas Lynn, Israel Lockner, Egerton Leigh, A Lewis, Eas Lyman, Samuel Langston, John Lauderdale, Joshua Louper, Bryan Lane, John Lane, Jordan Lewis, John Lee, Thomas Lane, Alex Lane.

ST. GEORGE, BURKE, JEFFERSON.

1786 to 1800.—Roger Lawson (1763), Abram Lindsay, Isaac Lindsay, Francis Lewis, Henry Lewis, Thomas Lewis, Samuel Lewis, Wm Lewis, Evan Lewis, Isaac Lewis, David Lewis, Jacob Lewis, Benj Lewis, Joseph Lewis, John Lot, Daniel Lot, Mary Larcy, Sol Lott, Moses Lindsay, Thos Lamb, Daniel Lott, Wm Lord, Philip Lightfoot, Rev Timothy Lawton, James Lowe, Samuel Lockhart, Thos Little, Thos Lindsay, Elijah Lawton, Thos Lamb, Jacob Long, Samuel Lowe, Thomas Lowe, John Lasseter, Isaac Lafevre, Jos Lancaster, Mathew Lively, Samuel Lasseter, Savannah Lester, John Lester, Henry Lowe, Sherrod Lewis, Thomas Lovett, Mason Lee, Fred Little, Wm Lance, L Lasseter, John Lasseter, Abraham Lester, Arthur Little, Jere B Longino, Acquillo Lowe, Eleazer Lewis, Francis Lodge. Nancy Lewis, Wm Lord, John Lawson, Ethelred Lane, Eliza Lindsay, Thomas Little, Hopkins Liptrat, Solomon Lowry, Isaac Lockhart, Wm Little, Sarah Lamar, Samuel Lett.

ST. PAULS, RICHMOND.

1759 to 1774.—John Lamar, James Laremore, Chas Lembacker, Geo Lembacker, David Lewis, Isaac Laremar, Isaac Lowe, R Lockridge, Wm LeConte, Jno Lee, Wm Lin, Thos Lin.

1784 to 1787.—John Leath, Wm Lee, Isaac Low, Thos Lawton, John Lamar, Jno Leonard, Jere Lumpkin, Moses Lindsay, Jacob Long, Wm Lockling, D Longstreet, Sarah Lamar.

1785 to 1800.—John Laremore (Lamar), Richard Lane, Archie Lane, Basil Lamar, Wm Lamar, Jno Lamar, Zech Lamar, T Luckins, Levi Lancaster, Fred Lipham, John Lindsay, Abram Lindsay, James Luckey, Wm Luckey, Geo Lumpkin, John Luckett, Henry Lyle, Wm Lawson, Thos Leverett, Saul Lakens, Nicolas Long, James Little, Basil Lamar, Wm Leatherton, Elizth Lofton, James Langston, M Liverman.

WILKES COUNTY.

M Linsacum, John Lowman, Wm Leverett, David Loyd, Sam'l Loyd, Samuel Lomas (Lomax), Mathew Ledbetter, Arthur Ledbetter, John Ledbetter, Wm Landrum, John Landrum, John Lee, Joshua Lee, Daniel Lardues, Elanor Lester, Richard Lovett, Philip Logan, Gabriel Lee, George Lea, John Lankford, John Linton, Henry Lyle, David Longstreet, John Locke, Wm Lynn, Rich Lockhart, Elisha Lyman, Wm Lea, Jno Lauderdale, James Lowry, Elijah Leonard, Elijah Lindsay.

WASHINGTON COUNTY.

Abner Legget, Henry Leverett, John Lamar, Thos Lamar, Sam'l Lamar, Wm Lamar, Robert Long, Jno Leslie, Sam'l Langston, John Larremor, Abram Lamb, Reuben Lott, Robt Lithgow, Jno Landers, Moses Lapham, Abram Lapham, Jno Ledbetter, Dennis Lindsay, Daniel Lowe, Thos Lester, Andrew Lawson, Thomas Lawson, Roger Lawson, Jos Lankford, Moses Lankford, John Linn, Jno Leverett, Jno Lange, Elijah Leonard, David Love, John Latever, Joel Lockhard, Wm Lott, Isaac Lenoir, Joel Lewis, Thomas Lane, Joel Lane, John Lane, Thomas Lane, Joshua Lee, Fred Ledbetter, Daniel Longstreet, Thos Lockey.

FRANKLIN.

1796 to 1800.—David Leeth, Jessee Lane, James Lander, Thomas Linn, Zach Lamar, Wm Langston, Henry Long, Wm Luckey, Freeman Lewis, Alex Luckey, David Luckey, R Lochart, John Lann, Rich Lewis, Thomas Lewis, Sr, Heirs of Thos Lewis.

WARREN, HANCOCK, COLUMBIA, OGLETHORPE.

1790 to 1900.—Thomas Leak, Wm Lyons, D Long, Jessee Lee.

SAVANNAH, CHRIST CHURCH, SEA ISLANDS.

1757 to 1759.—Peter Manly, Meeting House (Independent Presbyterian), John More, Pat Mackey, Thomas Mellichampe, Andrew

McIntosh, James Monroe, Jacob Monroe and wife, John Mullzyne, David Montaigut, Rich Milledge, Levi Marks, Thomas Mills, James Minter, Thomas Morgan, Geo Motte, Samuel Munday, C McCarty, James Miller, Chas McKenzie, Geo McKenzie, Wm Moon.

ST. JOHNS, ST. ANDREWS, ST. PHILLIPS, LIBERTY, CAMDEN, GLYNN.

1757 to 1769.—Angus McKay, Lewis Mettier, M McLeod, David Mackey, Abagail Morris, Alexander McDonald, Jno Maxwell, Wm Maxwell, Alex McKenzie, Jno McBean, Geo McDonald, Magt Miller, James Miller, Clement Martin, Lachlan McGilveray, Audley Maxwell, Sarah Mitchell, John McIntosh, Wm McIntosh, Jno More McIntosh, Lodi McIntosh, George McIntosh, Hugh Mackay, Jno McLellan, Ludwig Meyer, —— McIntosh, Wm Mills, Jno McLeod, Ed McGarr, Norman McDonald, Hugh Morrison, Jno Monroe, Donald Monroe, John Mathews, John Mullryne, Catherine Mullryne, John Mitchell, Henry Myers, M McLeod, May McLellan, James McLellan, Donald McIntosh, Jno McCulloch, Geo Moon, John Martin, John Middleton, widow Nath'l McCullock, Elizth McHuff, Jos Massey, Jno McLelland.

EFFINGHAM.

1774 to 1788.—David Mizell, Luke Mizell, Stephen Mills, Wm Mizell.

1788 to 1800.—David McCall, John Mathews, Jessee McCall, Wm Mikell, Wm McCall, Wm Means, John Marcus, Robert Marlow, John Myrick, Jessee McCall, Peter Martin, P McKenny, Jno C Miller, Henry McCarty.

ST. MATHEWS, EFFINGHAM, SCREVEN.

1756 to 1759.—Thomas Mack, Stephen Miller, John Meara, Jno L Meyer, Jacob Mohr, Magt Miller, John Miller, Jacob Meyer, Jacob Metzer, Mathew Mayer, Jona Michler, Geo Miller, Stephen Miller, Jacob Metzer.

1785 to 1800.—B Mack, Clement Martin, John Moore, James McHenry, Clement Martin, Jr, Jos Mack, Wm McCall, John Marcus, Jno Mikell, Mark May.

ST. JOHN, ST. ANDREWS, LIBERTY, CAMDEN.

1774 to 1785.—Elizth Mackay, Patrick Mackay, Lazarus Mallard.

1785 to 1800.—Gus McRea, Jno McRea, Ed McGray, James Montfort, Albert Mitchell, Palmer Minton, Arch Morrison, James Mann, Robert Montford, Daniel Miller, Isaac Munden, Wm Mills, Wm Moubray, Abner Mitchell.

ST JOHNS.

1756 to 1769.—Florence McCarty, Tattnell and Maxwell, Wm McCormack, Robert Miller, Henry Monroe, Alex McDonald, John Martin, Geo Mackey, John McKenzie, Thomas Moodie, Lewis Mather, Wm Miles, Thos Maxwell, M McLeod, Samuel Miller, Geo McKenney, John Monroe, Jno McCulloch, N Miller, May Milton, John McLean, John Mitchell, R Mackay' Jas Maxwell.

1769 to 1764.—John McDonald, Donald McLeod, Lewis Mathew, A McAlkey, McCulloah, May McDallard, Samuel McBride, McDaniel McDaniel.

1770 to 1775.—John McDonald John McDean, Thomas Morman, Chas Murray, John Mitchel, Henry Middletown, M Maddock

1774 to 84.—John Donald, L Monroe, Alex McDonald.

ST GEORGE, JEFFERSON, SCREVEN, HALIFAX.

1756 to 1764.—John McCollum, Aaron Morris, James McHenry, Carrie McAndrew, Mathew Miller, Wm Maner, McHenry, James Moore, John Mulkey, Thomas Morgan, Andrew McCurry, Wm McKenzie, Thomas Morgan, John Morris.

1767 to 1772.—B Montgomery, S McComic, Lewis Monroe, Wm Murphy, John Mulkey, Simon Monroe, Wm McDonald, John Murphey, Thomas Mobley, Jno Mercer, Geo Miller.

1764 to 1774—Richard Mark, James Martin, John Martin, Adam Morrison, Wm McConkey, Jas McCalvey, Daniel McNail, Mathew Marshall, David Mann, David McGowan, Daniel McMurphey, Nicolas Miller, Adam McLeroy, R McCormick, John Morrison, David Murray, James Martin, Isaac Murrey, Pat McGue, Wm McGiffech.

1774 to 1800.—John Morel, Jona Mulkey, James McKennon, John McGee.

BURKE, SCREVEN.

1784 to 1788.—Wm Murphy Samuel McNiel, Wm More, Jos McCollum, Isabel Martin, Jno Means, Mary McRead, Sarah Maxley, Mathew Marshall, Geo McMahan, May Martin, Jno McCulloch, John Morgan, E Mills, Wm McNorrell, Wm McNorrell, Michael Murphy, W L Mobley, J Music, James Mackay.

1788 to 1791.—Samuel More, Martin Martin, G McCroom, Clay McWatt.

1791 to 1800.—Jno Megomery, Meglarnery, Thos Mosley, Jas Mathews, Wm Martin, Thos McBride, J McCoy, Andrew Mack, F McKinney, Michael Murphey, Wm Murphey, Fred McMinn, Samuel McNeely, Moses McMahone, Thomas Mitchell, Brant

Moseley, Stephens Mills, B McCullen, Jno McAnaley, Nancy Mountain.

1785 to 1800.—Jno Means, L McCullough, B More, Jas McKay, John Magruder, Wm Manson, James Mackey, Mack McClary, Jas McConkey J McCuller, M Marshall, Willis More, May Mercer, Chas McDade, Wm Monroe, Morgan Morgan, N Mann, June Mathews, Mathew More, Jno Morrison, Wm Miller, W McCullough, Roger Moore, Jesse Morgan, Jno Martin, Pat McDaniel, Jere Milton, Robert Middletown, Daniel Murphy, Jno Megomery, Thomas Mountain, Maj McKinley, Jno Millen.

RICHMOND.

1756 to 1775.—Lachlan McGilveray, Daniel McGee, Macartan Campbell, Francis Macartan, Alex McIntosh, Henry Middleton, Matthew Marshall, W McMurren, Andrew McLean, John McDonald, Joseph Maddox, Ed Murphey, Robert McLean, Edw Murphey, Joseph Mooney, John Moril, Holland McTyiere, Jas. McFarlan, M Moore, Jos Maddox, Daniel McCarty, Wm Miles, Wm McIntosh, Rich Moore, Wm McFarlan, Thos McDonald, Thos Morris, John Mitchell, Thos Morris, John Mathews, Thos Morgan, John Marshall. Samuel Morton, John Miller, Thos Miller, Robert Middleton, James Mackay, Clement Martin, David Miller, Thomas Moodie, Daniel Miles, James Mossman, Andrew McLean, Wm Maxwell, Tattnall and Mulryne, Chas W. McKinnon.

1785 to 1787.—James McNeel, Rich Morris, Owen McGur, Rhoda Mercer, Jas McDonald, Thos Middleton, John Milledge, Wm Maddox, Ed Murphey, John Maddox, Thos Moore, R. Middleton, E Maxwell, Hugh Millegan, H. Middleron, Martin Moore, N O McGregor, John Marshall, Jas Mathews, Jesse McMill, Jas McDonald, Zep Math, B Moseley, J Morel, J Marcus, Hugh Magil, L Marbury, Hail McDaniel, Wm Martin, John McCartey, Gilbert McNair, M Mott, Mitch Mathews, Jesse Mathews, John McDonald, D McCarson, Wm McGee, John Moultrie, Daniel McMurphey, Jos McKinley, D McNeel, Jos May, Samuel McCullough, S Mitchell. David Maxwell, Martin Moore, Henry Martin, Offet McGruder, John Morris, John McDuffie, John McDonald, Joseph Mark, Alex Moss, Judge McCullough, Samuel McCullough, Andrew Mack, Chas McDade, John Milton, Wm McDaniel, Math McLemon, Jas McMannis, Jno H Montgomery, Wm Mead.

WILKES.

1783 to 1785.—Joel McLendon, Isaac McLendon, Jacob McClendall, Drury Manning, Lamentation Moss, Wm McKeen, Philip Mathew, Widower Morgan, David and Jas Mims, N

Marshall Martin, James McCannon, James McFarland, Ganaway Martin, John McDonald, Hugh McDonald, James McCaw, Jno Milligan, Austin Martin, Jos Moore, Geo Mathews, Ralph Mathews, Moses Mathews, James Mathews, Jeremiah Mathews, Philip Mathews, Micajah McGhee, Wm McGhee, John Milliner (Milner), Thos Morgan, Jas Morgan, Jas McLean, Ren McElmurray, Milly Mann, Mary Alsey and Darling McDaniel, Ed McGary, Solomon McAlpin, Josiah Moncrief, Thomas Mitchell, Wm Mitchell, Daniel McCarty, Ed Murphy, Benj Mosely, Jacob Mercer, Silas Mercer, Thomas Mercer, Robert Morris, Henry McCullers, Dave and Daniel McCullers, R McGary, Samson Monger, Thos McDowell, David Meriwether, Francis Meriwether, Thomas Meriwether, H McLeroy, James McLeroy, Jno Micklejohn, Wm Moon, Andrew McBride, Henry Mauldin, Wm Moss, John McVay, Geo Murray, R McCreary.

1786 to 1793.—Samuel Moffett, Sophia Moore, Wm Morgan, Benj Merritt, Aleghaney McGann, Wm May, John McLaughchin, John Myrick, John Mims, Pat McDonald, John McLeroy, David McCluskey, Mack McLendon, McCameron, Gideon Mason, James Meadows, Jos Magby, Jas Mays, Wm McCaw Jonathan Miller, Wm Miller, Jas Maroney, James Medlock, Brit McCuller, McCormack, Alex Jere Morris, Sam'l Mackie, John McEver, Ann Milligan, Hugh Myers, Silas Munk, Jas McCutcheon, Walter Mathis, Henry Monger, Jas McConnell, Jas McGown, R Madden, Thos Mosely, Sam'l McConathan, James McCowan, Wm McRee, Robert McNabb, Mary McNabb, Jos McMath, Alex McDougal, Ed McGary, Thos McCall, Jos Mott, Shadrick Mims, Drury Mims, Ezekiel Miller, Wm Moss, Horatio Marbury, Robert McDowell, Robert Middleton, Jas McCannon, James Morris, James Murphy, Alice Mills, Ruth McKamey, Israel Miller, Wm Mohorn, Wm McKinley, Jno McCornell.

1784 to 1786.—Isaac Milligan, John Mann, Wm Maddox, Stephen Michell, Jno McCarty, Daniel McCoy, Wm Mickle, Dav McClusky, Nathan Moss, Isham Morgan, Wm McRee, Mathew McLendon, Jas McCormack, J McCowan, Averton McLeroy, Heirs of John Meigs, Robert Middleton, Micheal Moore, Wm McLellan, John Moore, Berry Moore, John Mills, Clement Miller, R McCree, Wm Maxwell, Thos Moody, Alex McDowell Joshua Miller.

GREENE.

Wm Maddox, Robert Middleton, John McRay Andrew McComb, H Middleton, Wm McClelland, John Miller, Jere Moore, James McLendon, Robert Moreland, Wm Milton, Wm McGaughey, N McMullen, David Mitchell, Mapp, McCormick.

WASHINGTON.

Holland Middleton, Wm Morris, John Milton, John May, John Moore, Robert Mosely, Thomas Mosely, Berry Mosely, Neal Morgan, Asa Mercer, Israel Maxwell, Adam Manning, Alex McAlpin, Robert McGary, Thos McCormack, James Moore, Philip Morgan, James Martin, John Morris, Jacob McLendon, Thomas Marbury, Jonathan Miller, Ezekiel Miller, Thos Messer, John May, Van McGruder, Wm May, Jas McCoy, M Malone. Rev. Abram Marshall, Asa Morganson, Sol Marshall, Matthew Marshall, Sam'l Moats, Arch Michell, Wm Mathews, Moses Mathews, James Mathews, Meshach Mathews, Wm Morgan, Robert Middleton, Wm Mitchell, Sam'l McCulloch, Henry McKenney, Alex McDougal, John Mann, Arthur Mitcalf, Nathe Melton, Dave Madden, Louis McCulloch, Alex Moon, Zip Motle, Alex McGregor, Shadrack, Mimms, Sam'l Moon, John McIntosh, Wm McIntosh, Wm Minter, Peter Messer, Jere Mablely, Jesse McNiel, John Maddox, Drury Mims, Thos Mitchell, James McFarland, John McFarland, Joshua Miller, Wm May, Wm Motte, John McMunn, Jas Morse, Jesse Morgan, Leonard Moss, John Martin, D McNulty, Thos McGhee, Wm McGhee, James Martin, Owen McGurr, Thomas Mosely, Daniel McGilton, Ed Murphey, Wm Mims, Frances Moore, Wm Moore, Lachland McIntosh.

WARREN, COLUMBIA.

1790 to 1880.—James Miller, Wm Mims, Jos Mims, John Mims, Thomas Murray, Ab McDaniel, Henry McCarty, D D Moss, Wm McCune, Thomas McCord, Martin Macy, Jno Mackie, David McCoy, Tarquin McNiel, Jno Milner, Daniel MeNiel, Jas McGregor, Levit Marshall.

FRANKLIN AND JACKSON.

1786 to 1800.—Ed McGary, Thos McCall, Wm Mathews, Samuel Middleton, D McCowen, Jno May, R McCrary, Rosannah Mackie, Wm Mackie, John Millen, Thos Makee, Mills Murphey, Thomas Moore, Phelon Martin, H McCall, David Meriwether, Elijah Morgan, Wm Moss, Francis Mitchell, Daniel McBurnett, Thos Merriwether, Chas McDonald, Mary McNiely, Geo Mathews, John Morris, H McDonald, R McGowan, John McKee.

ST. JOHNS, LIBERTY, G. O., L. O., ST. PHILLIPS.

1756 to 1774.—P Nephew, James New, Sam'l New, And Nowland, Wm Norton, Geo Noble, Robert Nichols, Moses Nunez.

1787 to 1709.—Jno Niedlinger, James Nichols, Thos Nichols, John Nutt, Jno Neely, Wm Newman, Susannah Neel.

ST. MATHEWS, EFFINGHAM.

1756 to 1784.—Ulrich Niedlinger, John Neese, Thomas Noble, James Nix, George Nowlan, S Nobles.

ST. GEORGE, BURKE, JEFFERSON.

1756 to 1774.—Charles Neal, Jas Nesmith, John Nelson, Nicolas Nelson, John Neville, James Nichols, John Napper, John Neely.

1784 to 1800.—Charles Nelson, Rice Neely, Elisha Neal, Thomas Nelson, Mary Neely, James Neely, Thomas Neely, Samuel Neal.

ST. PAUL'S.

1756 to 1784.—Wm Newberry, Jas Nelson, Jonathan Neal, Jas Neal, Samuel Newton, Isaac Newton, Berry Nicholson.

WILKES COUNTY.

1784 to 1793.—John Neal, Royall Nelms, Jno Newton, Andrew Nay, Heirs of B Napper, Acquilla Nall, Edward Nugent, Samuel Nall, Nathan Nall, Sol Newsome, Claiborne Newsome, Austin Noland, Samuel Nelson, David Neal, Thomas Neal, John Nelson, Ed Nugent, Jno F Nunally, W W Nunally, Josiah Norris, Ben Nicholson, Jos Newton, John Nowlen, Wm Nicolas, Jesse Newby, Joshua Nall, Wm Norris, Thos Neasbett, Caleb Napper, James Napper, Wm Nicols.

FRANKLIN.

1784 to 1800.—Henry Nall, Rob Nall, Elizabeth Nunnally, Wm Nicols, Thomas Nesbett, W C Niblack' Geo Naylor.

ST. MATHEWS, EBENEZER.

Ch Oechley, S Ott, Adam Ordener, Charles Odenshall, David O'Bryan, Henry O'Bryan, Jas Oliver, David O'Bryan, Henry Obrey.

ST. GEORGE, BURKE, JEFFERSON.

Jas Oswell, Fred Odum, Peter Ogilvie, Isaac Odum, Jacob Odum, Jos Odum, Thos Oustin, Dame Occam, James Ogilbey, H O'Bryan, Fred O'Bryan, David O'Bryan, John Oates

1788 to 1800.—Sol Oaden, Robert Osborne, Wm Ogden, Wm Orr, Robert Osborne, John Oliver, James Oliver, Thomas Oliver, Elizabeth Odums.

RICHMOND.

1784 to 1785.—Alex Oliver, John Oliver, Samuel Oliver, James Orreck, Jepee Offutt, Ezekiel Offutt, Nathl Offutt, Eph Owens, Geo Ogg.

WILKES.

1784 to 1790.—Wm Oneal, Thos Owens, Dyonysious Oliver, Newday Owsley, Wm Owsley, John Oneal, David Ogletree, John Ogletree, Thos Ogletree, John Oliver, Jere Oates, Christopher Orr, Peter Oliver, James Oakes, While Outerbridge.

SAVANNAH, C. C.

1755 to 1765.—James Ed Powell, Thos Parker, Andrew Paget, Frances Parry, Agnes Parker, Thomas Palmer, John Parker, Geo Pickholt, Nathl Palmer, Samuel Pore, Samuel Parker.

ST. JOHNS, OGEECHEE, NEWPORT, DARIEN, ST. PHILIPS.

1755 to 1775.—Thos Peacock, Wm Peacock, Jno Perkins, Jno Philips, Ed Pearce, Jno Perkins, John Poulson.

1765 to 1775.—Ann Parker, Jean Ponsheer, James Papot, John Price, Jos Packaton, Isaac Powell, John Price, Martin Palmer.

1788 to 1794.—Job Pray, Henry Pittman, Wm Prince, John Pearce, John Piles, Piggot, Geo Parris, John Pilcher, James Payne.

ST. JOHNS, LIBERTY, ALTAMAHA, ST. ANDREWS.

1756 to 1774.—John Osgood, Joseph Osgood, J & J Stephens Osgood, W Outerbridge, J Oswell, David Ohphant, Thomas Osten, Owen Owen, Wm Oltver.

SAVANNAH.

1756 to 1785.—John Mary Oswald, Jos Ottalenghee.

ST. MATTHEWS, GOSHEN.

Jacob Posts, Jno Powling, Geo Posts, Saml Pelton, Jos Parker, Jno Patton, Wm Powell, Charles Pryce, Wm Panton.

EFFINGHAM.

1788 to 1793.—Jno Parrieos, Mark Pridgeon, Jno Posell, Jacob Prewatt, John Parton, Mark Pridgeon, Jno Powers, Thomas

Paramore, Nathan Paramore, Jno Powers, Arch Patterson, Saml Peacock, James Porter, Royal Philips, Gabriel Parker, Wm Pore, Samuel Patton, Mark Pridgeon, Wm Pitchford, Jos Plumer.

ST. GEORGE, HALIFAX.

1755 to 1765.—Jno Prothero, Micheal Power, Jos Perry, Wm Porter, Isaac Perry, James Pugh, Jas Perkins, Jno Phillips.

1765 to 1776.—Wm Powell, Wm Porter, Micajah Plummer, Aaron Pinson, Wm Penrose, Francis Pugh, John Perkenson, Thos Peacock, Sol Prather, Jos Pearcely, Robt Pier, Ed Pennington, Wm Pelcher, Sumter Porter, Wm Philpot, Lewis Powell, Catheron Poral, Henry Preston, James Pace

1765 to 1775.—Catherne Pell.

BURKE.

1784 to 1790.—Jno Patterson, Robert Patterson, Wm Patterson, Sarah Petttgrew, Geo C Perry, Wm Pickson, Thos Pennington, Philip Poole, Wm Price, Geo Palmer, Wm Price, Darcus Pickerson, Wm Parker, Stephen Powell, Wm Phillips, Frances Paris, B Perkins, F Pugh, Jno Paulet, James Porter, Wm Pool, Wm Proctor, Jas Power, R Parke, Mark Phillips.

ST. GEORGE, BURKE, SCRIVEN.

1788 to 1793.—Benj Powell, Job Price, Robert Prior, Anthony Powell, Jacob Parker, James Pinnion, James Pace, Jonahn Parker, Wm Paramore, Jessee Paulet, Mark Philips, Stephen Pierce.

ST. PAULS.

1756 to 1774.—James Paine, Jno Pettigrew, Jno Payne, Rich Pace, James Parris, Nath Pursley, Thos Pace, Knowles Pace, Peter Parris, Jno Phillips, Saml Payne, John Perkins, John Perkins, Peter Perkins, Z Pooler, B Pace, Ralls Perry, Wm Phillips, Charles Parks, Micagh Pauek, Thomas Pinson, John Parker, Silas Pace, James Phillips, James Puckett, Johnson Parrott.

RICHMOND.

1784 to 1793.—Thomas Pace, John Plak, Ed Prather, Beersheba Parker, Wm Pinson, Reece Price, E Primrose, Charles Porter, David Peterson, John Peak.

WILKES.

1783 to 1785.—Joel Phillips, Wm Pinkston, John Powers, Zach Phillips, Genl Pickens, Amos Ponder, Wm Parker, Saml Payne, John Paush, Sol Palmer, Geo Pettigraw Thos Pattoh, Wm

Painter, John Palmer, Jacob Perkerson, Wm Patrick, Henry Peebles, James Parks, Jesse Pye, John Pope, Wm Potts, James Potts, Joshua Perry, Jos Pulliam, Joshua Perkins.

1781 to 1786.—Benj Perkins, Fred Peters, Sarah Pendall, Jno Prestage, Thos Patton, M Patton, Elizabeth Partee, Denny Pace, Saml Phillips, Avnella Perkins, S Pennington, Ben Partie, Pettipool, James Perdue, Rich Parker, Philip Pitman, Jno Pitman, James Pollard, Paul Patrick, Jesse Partridge, Jose Presh, Stephen and W Potts, Ruth Peteet, John Pate, John Price, Henry Pace, Willie Pope, Elizabeth Patrick, Moses Powell, John Philips, Agnes Pruitt, Dan'l Park, Frances Powers, James Pye, Jane Patton, John Paine, John Patterson, Thoms Payne, Jno Perkins, Wm Poynter, Henry Pope, Moses Perkins, Jno Peters, Jno Pittman, Wm Parton, Jacob Pettijohn, Wm Patterson, G Pickens, Anna Parker, Philip Pool, Isaac Perry, Geo Pettigrew, Jesse Pye, Jacob Pinkston, Ed Prior, Ed Pharr, Mark Phillips, Ceader Powell.

WILKES.

1788 to 1789.—Carter Price, Sephen Potts, Jos Poyner, Wm Philpot.

WASHINGTON COUNTY.

1784 to 1793.—Benj Porter, Isaac Pinson, Samuel Phillips, Jos Phillips, Robert Pollard, Josiah Powell, Geo Powell, Dave Parker, Wm Perkins, Sol Pendleton, Wm Pollard, John Pattillo, Jesse Pugh, Edward Prather, Robert Parrott, Gideon Patterson, John Peak, Benj Posey, Thos Pennington, Cader Powell, Joel Phillips, Samuel Penn, Sol Palmer, Wm Penn.

GREENE COUNTY.

Jos Phillips, B Patrick, Jno H Pritchard, Oliver Porter, Wm Phillips, Jos Phillips, Jas Palmour, Robert Pullen, Dave Parker, James Pinkard.

FRANKLIN COUNTY.

1786 to 1800.—Thomas Patton, Nathaniel Pearre, Thos Payson, Barna Pace, Henry Parks, Isaac Perry, Richard Powell, Richard Purkins, Cullen Price, Wm Pullam, Robert Pullen, John Palmer, Jane Phillips, Baxter Pool, Arch Pettegrew, Johu Parton, Thos Perqua, Moses Potts, Callahan Price, Jno Parsons, Wylie Pope, Barnabas Pope, Wylie Pope, Sam'l Phillips, Benj Porter, Thomas Porter, Leroy Pope, Jos Phillips, Ezra Potts, Wm Patrick.

COLUMBIA COUNTY.

1794.—Jno Pierce, Thomas Payne, Moses Payne, Wm Pace, Rachel Powell, Thos Phelan, David Perryman.

LINCOLN COUNTY.

1792 to 1796.—John Piggot, Lewis Perkins.

WARREN COUNTY.

Blake Pierce, Jos Peavy, David Phelps.

MONTGOMERY COUNTY.

John Peterson, Thos Peterson.

ELBERT COUNTY.

Thos Pen, Richard Perryman, Martin Palmer, Nathiel Pearce, Thorn Phelan, Wm Patrick.

ST. JOHN'S, ST. ANDREW, ST. DAVID.

1756 to 1771.—Jno Quarterman, Jno M Quarterman, Rebecca Quarterman, Wm Quarterman, Thos Quarterman, Robert Quarterman, Wm Queen, Roger Quarles.

SAVANNAH C. C.

1756 to 1774.—Wm Russell, Governor Reynolds, David Randtuhler, John Roe, John Redick, Jno Revera, Wm Russell, B Romans, Fred Rosberry, John Ream, Samuel Read, Micheal Ruter, James Russell, David Reese.

ST. JOHN'S, ST. PHILIP'S, ST. ANDREW, ST. DAVID.

1756 to 1800.—T Robinson, Christian Rumph, Fred Resta, Jas. Read, —— Robinson, Isreal Raser, Chas Robertson, W R Reddick, Wm Ray, John Roberts, Wm Ready, John Richey.

ST. JOHN'S, LIBERTY, ST. PHILIPS, ST. DAVID.

1756 to 1774.—John Read, D Revera, Thos Rivers, John Rogers, John Rivers, Thos Ready, Henry Rogers, Henry Rosebery, Abram Ravot, Sylvester Robinson, C Roland, Geo Rolliman, Thomas Rasberry, Hugh Ross, Micheal Rector, Chushaw Rusk, Wm Rand, F Ruth, John Roane, Thomas Ross, Colin Reddick, Ann Rogers.

ST. MATTHEW'S, EBENEZER.

1756 to 1800.— —— Rattenberger, Christie Rabenhorst, Laner Ruter, Jno Ruter, Conrad Rahm, Chas Rattenberger, John Ruter, Pickering Robinson, Thos Roberson, B Ruter, F Rawlinson, Jno Roche, Thos Robinson, Geo Rollinson, Conrad Rahn, Daniel

Remshart, Simon Ruter, Bethazer Rienzer, Richard Raden, Jno Remshart, Elizabeth Ratliff, Fred Ruter, Jno Rollinson, Jos Ryan, Jos Rogers, John Rupert, Arthur Ryall, Samuel Ryall, Fred Rester, Greylock Roberts, Thos Redding, Daniel Remshart, James Russell, Wm Robertson, Wm Rushing, John Rushing, Palmer Rawles, John Rawles.

ST. PAUL'S.

1756 to 1775 —Jasper Rahn, Thos Red, John Roe, —— Roseborough, Charles Ring, James Ross, John Ramsay, Daniel Reese, Geo Routon, D Richardson, Wm Robinson, Jesse Reeves, Prissly Renn, David Robinson, Wm Ramey, Isaac Ramey, Wm Redman, James Ross, John Red, Randall Ramsay, Isaac Ramsay, David Robinson, Jordan Richardson, Timothy Ross, R Reynolds.

RICHMOND COUNTY.

1787 to 1798.—Ed Rowell, S Reeves, M Robertson, James Ryan, Thos Roberts, John Rhand, Isaac Randolph, James Robinson, Hugh Russell.

ST. GEORGES, HALIFAX.

1758 to 1762.—Sam'l Rouvier, Thomas Red, Paul Red, Hugh Ross, Jos Reynolds, Peter Randan, Mack Roche, Jno Royal, Samuel Royal, Sam'l Rhodes, Wm Rhodes, Hannah Roberts, James Red, Jethro Rountree, Jos Roberts.

1768 to 1774.—Josiah Roberts, Ann Roe, Wm Rountree, Frances Robe, Jas Roberts, Jas Read, John Robinson, James Robinson, Robert Rogers, Wm Read, James Reid, John Roberts, Wm Roberts, Wm Redding, Thos Rivers, John Ragin.

1783 to 1788.—John Rutledge, Henry Robinson, Magh Reeves, Wm Royal, Wm Rountree, Wm Rheney, Berlander Royal, Jessee Reeves, Sarah Reese, Walter Robertson, Mary Rogers, Elizabeth Roberts.

1788 to 1795.—Wm Robinson, Stephen Ryals, Jno Raiford, Mary Roberts, Anne Red, John Rankin, Wm Roland, John Roberts, Nicolas Reddick, Wm Ryalls.

BURKE AND SCREVEN.

Wm Rushing, John Rushing, John Rodgers, Jno Raiford, Richard Rowell, Jno Roberts.

WILKES COUNTY.

1783 to 1787.—Wm Richardson, Rich Runnalls, Wm Ramsay, Joha Ragan, Jno Robinson, John Rich, Geo Runnalls, Ben Ragland, Evan Ragland, R Ramsay, Drury Rogers, Herman Runnalls, Wm Rheny, Geo Reynolds, Jas Roquemore, J Riley, John Rutherford, Benj Rhodes, Jere Reeves, Simon Roberts, John Robertson, B Rhodes, Tunstuell Roan, Jane Runnalls, S Runnalls, Thos Runnalls, Preston Runnalls, Jona Robertson, Wm Robertson, James Ralston, Hugh Reese, Jos Riley, Jno Robert, Jno Rogers, Thos Rutledge, Presly Rucker, Jas Raley, Geo Reed, Robert Ross, Hugh Reese, R Radford, Reuben Ross, Jno Ross, Peleg Ross, John Rosser, Isham Richardson, Jos Richardson, Agnes Richardson, James Rendy, Thos Rose, Richard Ryan, Alex Rives, Roger Reese, heirs of John Ray, Robert Ratliff, Rich Rowland, Wm Reddick, D Robison, Amasa Royal.

1787 to 1788.—Jno B Renton, Jno Robinet, Jos Ryan, D Remshart, Jos Ross, Jno Rice.

GREENE.

1788 to 1798.—Andrew Reed, Samuel Reed, Abram Reddick, Mathew Robin, Adamson Ross, Jno Ratchford, Thos Roberts, Jno Ragan, Joel Reese, Ezekiel Robinet.

WASHINGTON.

Sam'l Ramsay, Isaac Ramsay, Thomas Ramsay, John Ramsay, Wm Ramsay, Randal Ramsay, John Richardson, Richard Ryan, James Ryan, Mathew Rushing, Elliot Rowell, John Rice, Michael Rafferty, Jos Robertson, Jona Robertson, David Robertson, Jonas Roberts, J S Reden, Geo Roseboro, B Rogers J Rickettson, Jas Reed, Thomas Reeves, Geo Redding, Peter Roquemore, Fred K Reynolds, Thos Roberts, John Reed, Jos Riley, Abram Reddick, Jno Roberts,Thos Reed, Joel Reese, Thos Read, Jno Reece, Jos Ray.

FRANKLIN.

M Rickeson, Leonard Rice, J M Rose, Jos Riley, Rich Rumalls, John Rench, Jacob Russell, Jose Russell, Ed Rice, Thos. Randall, James Russell, John Roberts, Michael Rogers, John Robertson. M Raiford, Rachel Rigg, John Rosseau, John Ryan, Ed Rice.

COLUMBIA.

Rich Randolph.

ELBERT.

Leonard Rice.

HANCOCK.

Geo Roan, Littleton Reese, Samuel Reed.

BULLOCK.

John Richardson, Sylvanus Robason, Jonathan Robason.

SAVANNAH, CHRIST CHURCH, SEA ISLANDS.

1758 to 1760.—Wm Steadman, Wm Smith, Lydia Somen, John Shick, Ann Stewart, John Simpson, Jno Snook, Mordacai Sheftall, Michael Switzer, —— Sackewille, Ben Stirk, Ed Summerville, Jas Simmer, M Salfner, Charles Story, Mordacai Sheftall, Gottlieb Staley, Jno Simpson, Paula Simara, Wm Stedman, Anthony Stokes, David Smock, Philip Snider.

1756 to 1758.—John Smith, Sam'l Stanhope, Wm Scales, B Sheftall, Michael Switzer, Wm Spencer, Mary Smith.

ST. JOHNS, ST. DAVIDS, ST. ANDREW, ST. PHILIPS, ST. MARYS.

1758 to 1768.—Robert Smallwood, Geo Senior, Mary Shortner, Jno Shave, M Smallwood, Jno Sartain, Jno Stewart, Ben Sheftall, Leah Sheftall, Gasper Stauker, Richard Spencer, John Shule, Alex Shephard, Robert Small, Marten Smallwood, James Stewart, Michael Stutz, Morgan Sab, Richard Savage, John Simpson, Jno Smith.

1768 to 1775.—Hamilton Scott, Jno Smith, Wm Sanders, John Stafford, Samuel Stiles, Joshua Stafford, Robert Smallwood, John Stewart, James Screven, James Spalding, Thomas Sullivan, Ellis Suguin, John Spencer, Anne Stuart, James Seagrave.

1775 to 1800.—Sam'l Smith, Wm Scott, John Stephens, Antonia Suavis, Thomas Spalding, Roger Sanders, Sam'l Smith.

ST. JOHNS, ST. DAVIDS, DARIEN, OGEECHEE, BRYAN.

1756 to 1758.—John Stewart, Jno Stewart, Robert Stewart, Jno Stephens, David Stephens, John Stephens, Rich Spencer, Jno Savage, Solomon Shad, Ed Sykes, James Scott, Angus Sylvester.

ST. MATTHEW.

1756 to 1758.—John Staley, Gabriel St ley, John Stewart, Fred Staley, Geo Shenan, M Snieder, M Schivehofer, John Smith, A Snider, David Stiner.

1760 68 --John Sheraws, John Starley, Michael Switzr, Aaron John Sheeling, John G Snieder, David Snieder, John Staley, Richard Scruggs, Geo Switzer.

1756 to 1758.---C Stiener, M Snieder, John G Snyder, Daniel Shubbrine, Geo Switzer, John Slaylerg, John W Slaylerg.

1775 to 1799. - May Shannon, Jane Snieder, G Scuggs, John Stewart, Andrew Snider, G Sitrow, Charles Smith.

ST GEORGE, BURKE, JEFFERSON.

1787 to 1788.---Geo Swaycord, Shad Scaword, John Smith, Moses Smith, Dill Sap, Simon Sherwood, John Stanland, Wm Sapp, Martin, Shirley, Francis Shivers, Geo Sloan, Geo Segar, John Sebert Phileman Sapp, John Sapp, Benj Sapp, Wm Sheffield, James Smith, Philip Scott, Jacob Shell, Wm Scell, Wm Skinner, Sarah Sapp, Sarah Smith, Wm Stinson, May Sykes.

1788 to 1790.---John Spurdock, Wm Slater, James Sharp, Wm Scott, James Sapp, John Sevair, Monroe Stradley, Samuel Smith, Moses Spencer, Jos Smith, Martin Shibey, John Shener, B Senem, Wm Smith, Moses Scarboro, John Stallings, L Scabbord, Aaron Scabboro, James Shivers, Calew Skell, John Sheffield Darbug Sapp, James Sapp, John Sterling.

BURKE.

1793 to 1800.—Ben Stephens, Samuel Samples, Nathan Samples, Mendal Stringer, Thomas Steptoe, Samuel Scutchen, James Stubbs, Wash Skinner, Jos Sykes, Wm Sykes, J Smith, Nathan Stephenson, Wm Skinner, J Stephens, Howell Saper, Michael Sharp, John Sharp, Michael Shelman, Joshua Stafford, James Smith, Jesse Slatter, James Shorter.

ST. GEORGE.

1767 to 1768.---Francis Spinger, Ed Sigmon, Eligah Sapp, Abram Sapp, John Stratton, Wm Sapp, Henry Sapp, John Sapp, Lydia Sharp, John Street, John Seely, Peter Stedler, John Smith, Wm Simpson, E Simpson, Stephen Smith.

1768 to 1774.----John Sapp, Wm Simpson, James Sherbert, John Star, Wm Shelly, R Smith, Wm Sanders, R Sullins, Geo Spain, John Strickland, Seth Slocumb, John Stanaland, Pat Stuart, Francis Strafer, Peter Stewart, Pat Stewart, Thomas Sherman, Sythe Studler, Wm Sheffield.

1784 to 1786.---Geo Sloan, John Sheffield Geo Sharon, Wm Spies, Joshua Smith, Jos Salesberry, Francis Scott, Samuel Smith, Daniel Sikes, Nicolas Skinner, Philip Scott, James Sandey, Jos Simpson, Sarah Strongman, Moses Spieght, John Sharp.

ST. PAUL'S.

1759 to 1774.—Loveless Savage, Jno Stewart, James Smith, Mordacai Sheftall, Chas Smith, Wm Stanley, Ivy Smith, Levi Sheftall, Richard Southerland.

RICHMOND COUNTY.

1787 to 1798.—Samuel Samson, Jno Stewart, Wm Stubbs, Henry Spalding, Charles Simmons, Joe Shoemaker, John Sorrells, Wm Sullivan, Robert Stanford.

ST. PAUL'S OR RICHMOND COUNTY.

1752 to 1774.—Thos Schruder, James Simpson, James Scriven, John Stubbs, John Slater, Jonathan Sell, John Sidwell, Richard Smith, Jno Stewart, Henry Sell, Samuel Sanson, Ann Stubbs, Debora Stubbs, Joshua Sanders, Robert Story, Arch Sturcey, Samuel Scott, John Scott, Thomas Stitsell, Nathaniel Shefford, Job Smith, Sarah Suter, John Smith, Aug Scott, Wm Shield, Wm Sims, Nathaniel Stubbs, James Shields, John Shick, Wm Stanley.

WILKES COUNTY.

Robert Sims, David Shaw, John Shannon, James Simpson, Martha Stuart, G Stuart, Abram Sanders, John Simmons, Wm Stark, Eliza Slayton, Moses Stephens, Francis Strippling, Thomas Seal, David Sidwell, John Sandage, Wm Stewart, Adam Stanley, Jno Sorrell, John Shelman, Francis Short, Benj Stick, Elijah Stinson, John Snead, John Slaton, Jos Scott, Weymouth Shaw, Wm Stokes, R Singleton, James Sterling, Alex Scott, Reuben Saffold, Enoch Seals, John Stephens, Thos Stephens, Jonah Spike, Acquilla Swann, Jos Spradling, Elizabeth Slaughter, Wm Stokes, Job Springer, Dudley Sneed, Francis Satterwhite, John Simpson, Jos Slaten, Isaac Stewart, Jesse Sanford, T Sheffield, Jos Scurlock, Peter Stubblefield, Jarvis Seal, Anthony Seal, Nancy Stephens, Samuel Slaughter, Reuben Slaughter James Swords, Hugh Sexton, Henry Shelton.

1786 to 1762.—Magt Steel, James Sims, Henry Starr, Fredrick Sims, Henry Sorrow, Henry Stokes, John Seal, Amos Shaw, Isaac Simpson, John Sawyer, Wm Stone, John Stokes, Newton Spikes, Basil Story, Joshua Stephens, H Scroggins, Leonard Switzer, Culbreath Shoal.

1783 to 1785.—James Scott, Benj Scott, James Scarlett, John Smith, Jug Smith, David Smith, Peter Smith, Jasper Smith, Sam'l Smith, Wm Smith, Heirs of Wm Smith, Hannah Smith, James Smith, Henry Smith, Thomas Smith, Nathan Smith, Ben Smith, Guy Smith, Frances Smith, Heirs of Jacob Smith, Richard Smith, Benagah Smith, Chas Smith, Green Smith, Barnard Smith, Abraham Smith, Nicholas Subtrine, John Steadman, Anna Sharp, Geo Sherman, Sarah Stroud, Geo Sewell, Joshua Sewell, Sam'l Sewell, Elisha Smallwood, Jarrett Strawnan, Wm Steel, Wm Satterwhite, David Sherrod, Thos Shannon, John Steward, Wm Sealmire, Samuel Stinson, Wm Stephens, Wm Sein, Peter Strozier, Esther Seabury, David Sloan, Enoch Stringfellow, Robert Sims.

WASHINGTON COUNTY.

Simon Salters, P. Stamper, Jno Sapp, Elizabeth Sapp, Wm Sapp, Dill Sapp, Martin Sanders, John Sanders, Jesse Sanders,

Thomas Shaw, David Shaw, Wm Saterwhite, James Stallings, Thos Shadrack, Jos Slaten, Thos Snelson, Chas Stewart, Clement Stewart, Wm Sheffield, Mark Sheffield, Jno Sheffield, Maure Sims, Nathaniel Smith, Thos Smith, Wm Smith, Jno Sitton, Wm Sikes, Wm Stiff, Andrew Shields, Aaron Sinquefield, John Stephens, Wm Sigmund, Dudley Sneed, M Sheftall, Henry Shelton, Jos Smith, Joshua Smith, Charley Smith, Geo Smith, Isaac Smith, Robert Smith, Jas Smith, John Smith, Wm Smith, John Strength, Steven Simmons, John Simmons, Isaac Simmons, Jos Simmons, Philip Steed, Robert Stewart, Jas Stewart, John Stewart, Samuel Simons, John Sheppard, Thos Sheppard, John Sharp, Michel Smally, Robert Savage, Jesse Stallings, Michel Sharp, Simon Salters, John Sharp, Johua Sharp, Jno Shackelford, Jos Samson, Leonard Switzer, Abraham Scott, Mich'l Scury, Wm Sullivan, Petter Scott, Phillip Sutton, R Spurlock, Charles Stone.

FRANKLIN.

John Shannon, Geo Shannon, Cornelius Scott, Thomas Snelson, Owen Shannon, John Simes, John Smith, Jos Swan, Geo Sticker, Wm Summerlin, Aaron Shelton, Thos Shaw, Alex Scott, Thomas Scott, W Strother, John Stubbs, John Sandage, Wm Sloan, David Sloan, Elias Stinson, Peter Strozer, Lewis Shelton, John Stonecypher, Wm Stinson, James Sawright, Andrew Sturgis, Wm Stith, Dudley Stead, James Steward, Wm Speed, John Smith, James Sewall, James Stewart, Moses Spencer, Ahimas Spencer, Geo Stewart, Francis Stripling, Wm Spencer, Joshua Sled, Wm Sparks, Davis Saxon, Benajah Smith, Henry Simonton, Jno Stewart, Robert Singleton, Jos Smalley, Thos Smyth, Geo Spain, Wm Stone, Simon Sherod, John Smith, Thos Smyth, Thos Shields, R Shipley, John Smith, Wm Spruce.

ELBERT, COLUMBIA.

John Stapler, T Saxon, Wm Stubblefield, James Sutton.

1790 to 1799.—James Sims, Owen Sullivan, John Shores, Jno Stone, Ann Stewart, John Smyth, James Smith, Henry Spalding, Jas Smith, Francis Smith, Jos Stubb, Wm Sims, Samuel Stubbs, Jacob Smith, Philip Steed, Jno Sibley.

MONTGOMERY.

1794.—James Shorter, James Sartin, Jno Spike, Samuel Shears, Valentine Smith, John Smith, John Shackleford.

LINCOLN.

T Slade, Jos Stafford, Anthony Seal, Lewis Smith.

WARREN.

1770 to 1800.—John Salles, John Smith.

GREENE.

Henry Seward, James Steward, Daniel Spellers, John Swepson, Daniel Spellers, James Scarlett, John Smith, Arch Smith, John Springer, Mathew Stone, John Swinney, Isaac Stocks, Thomas Steward, Geo Stokes, Samuel Slaughter, Ezekiel Slaughter.

SAVANNAH, CHRIST CHURCH.

1755 to 1774.—John Teasdale, Josiah Tattnall, Veneries Turner, Geo Thompson, John Tebean, Thomas Turner, Jos Tilley.

ST. JOHNS, LIBERTY, ST. DAVID, ST. PHILIP.

1765 to 1774.—Wm Trevin, Geo Tivener, James Taylor, Geo Teter, David Tebean, Jno Tanahall, John Tanner,.

1784 to 1800.---Lucy Thomas, David Tobear, Altho Thomas, Geo Theadcraft, Thomas Tomlinson.

ST. MATTHEWS.

1755 to 1774.—Josiah Tatnall, Wm Townsend, Lewis Tanner.

1784 to 1800.—Wm Thorn, David Thorn, Christian Tieutlen, Thos Thomson, James Tison, Asa Tanner, Wm Thompson, Elizabeth Tyner, Jas Taylor, Ben Thrasher, Wm Travis, Amos Travis, Adam Tanner, Fred Traddling, Charles Thelo, Lewis Turner, Peter Tondee, Thos Tumlin.

ST. GEORGE.

1765 to 1774.—Nicolas Thompson, James Thompson, Daniel Thomas, John Taylor, Samuel Tomlinson, Jno Turner, G Thomas, Jacob Taylor, Esther Tweedy, Jno Todd, Geo Thompson, Geo Thomas, John Thomas.

BURKE.

1784 to 1787.—Eleanor Tremble, Laban Thompson, Rachel Todd, Henry Todd, John Taylor, John Thompson, Wm Travis, Jno Tray, Josiah Taylor, Jno Taylor, Samuel Thomas, Jno Turner, Sarah Tucker, P Toquent.

BURKE, JEFFERSON, SCREVEN.

1786 to 1800.—Caleb Taylor, Ward Taylor, Ann Taylor, Chas Taylor, Aaron Taylor, Francis Tilman, Elisha Thompson, Thomas Tipton, Sarah Tucker, Wm Taylor, Ann Tomlinson, John Tallas,

Wm Tilman, John Turner, Elizabeth Tuckett, Eliza Todd, Daniel Thomas, Alex Thompson, Wm Tilman, Tarpley Tullis, John Treadwell, Agnes Tinley, R. Thompson, Ab Thomas, Samuel Thornton, Samuel Thomas, Thos Taggard, Jos Tannery, B Thompson, Wm Thomas, Mary Tannery, Jesse Taylor, P Tippens, Gideon Travis, John Taylor, John Tomlin, Celia Tomlin, Jno Tapley, New Tapley Wm Tillman.

ST. PAULS, RICHMOND.

Wm Tinley, David Tubear, Jno Tinckler, Ed Telfair, John Turpin, Wm Turpin, John Thompson, Nicodemus Thompson, Wm Tindall, Jas Tinley Henry Taylor, Jos Thomas, Wm Thompson, John Twiggs, John Tindall, Wm Thomason, Thos Taylor, Peter Thomas Jos Temple, David Tinsley, Jno Towns, B B Tindall, Heirs of Mack Tapley, John Toomer, Joel Tapley, Cunningham Tilley, James Tinsley, John Tudor.

WILKES COUNTY.

Francis Trawick, Jno Tankersville, Ben Thomson, Wm Tyler, Robt Thompson, Ben Thompson, Wm Thornton, Dozier Thornton, Samuel Thornton, Ethelred Thornton, Thos Thornton, Sol Thornton, Wm Terrell, John Terrell, John Tarver, Cam Thomas, Philip Thomas, John Torrence, Samuel Thomas, Benj Thomas, Michael Thomas, Theodocius Turk, John Townsend, Sarah Taylor, Wm Toombs, Gabriel Toombs, Jno Todd, R Tiner, Armistead Taylor, Benj Taylor, Francis Tennille, Wm Talbott, Peter Tatum, James Tate, Henry Tate, Henry Taylor, Henry Townsley, Jno Tanner, Jno Thomas, James Thomas, Thomas Tucker, David Tomlinson, Wm Triplet, Nathan Thurman, Martin Thurman, James Turner, Jno Tillery, Jno Troy, Henry Tompkins, James Thorn, James Thompson, Jno F Thompson, Jesse Thompson, Geo Thompson, Wm Thompson, Jos Thompson, Jud Thompson, Thomas Travis, Samuel Tuttle, Wm Teasley, Isaac Terry, Tallett, (Talley) Caleb Toole, Abner Talmage, Jno Tullis, Moses Tullis.

WASHINGTON.

John Taylor, Thos Tucker, Henry Trice, Jno Trail, Joshua Taylor, Geo Taylor, Henry Townsend, Laban Thompson, Wm Thompson, Benj Thompson, Jesse Thompson, Sol Thornton, Samuel Thornton, Henry Taylor, Francis Tennille, Gideon Thomas.

FRANKLIN.

Moses Trimble, R Taylor, J Turman, Wm Thompson, Ed Telfair, Daniel Terondet, Jno Twedie, B Trice, Hi Taylor, Ed

Taylor, H Tyler, Chas Taylor, Joel Terrell, R Taylor, Champion Taylor, David Thurman, Jas Terrell, David Terrell, John Trimble, Moses Trimble, John Templeton, Ely Thornton, Ab Tate, Massa Thomas, Abram Thompson, John Tarvins, Wm Thelford, Wiley Thriewit, Geo Theadgill, Jos Trapp, Hi Taylor, Ed Taylor, H Tyler, Chas Taylor, Elihu Thompson, Jesse Tennison, James Tate, J Taylor, R Thompson, Wm Tinson, Geo Thurman, Jona Towns, Joel Terrell.

WARREN.

Moses Thompson, John Trant, Cathran Thomas, John Tindall.

COLUMBIA.

Wm Tripp.

HANCOCK.

B Thompson.

GREENE COUNTY.

Jesse Thomson, Jos G Taylor, Robert Thompson, Sam'l Townsend, James Thweatt, John Tankersby, Wm Thompson, Ben Thompson, Zach Thompson, Roger Thornton.

SAVANNAH, CHRIST CHURCH.

David Unwild, Hannah Unwild, Geo Upton, Ches Van Munch, Thos Van Munch, Charles Van Munch, Thos Upton.

ST. JOHNS, ST. DAVIDS, ST. PHILIPS, ST. ANDREWS.

1756 to 1774.—Jere Vallalton, David Vallalton, James Vincent.

ST. GEORGE, BURKE, SCREVEN.

1756 to 1774.—David Vance, Geo Varner, Wharton Vaugton, Daniel Underwood, Wm Underwood, Agnes Underwood, Wm Underwood, David Usery, B Usery, Geo Varner.

ST. MATTHEWS.

Jos Underwood, Hannah Vincent, Thomas Vick, Isaac Van Zant, Benj Vermillion, Rich Vinson, Anthony Verdel, Dorcas Van Zant, James Vickers, Michael Vassar.

COLUMBIA.

Alex Vaughn.

MONTGOMERY.

Micajah Vasser.

ST. MATTHEWS.

Zach Upton.

RICHMOND.

Alex Vaught, Jesse Vaught, Jephtha Vivians, David Vincent.

WILKES.

1783 to 1788.—Wm Upshaw, John Upshaw, Wm Veazy, John Vann, Martha Vann, Wm Vardeman, John VanWinkle, Ezemah Verden, Ishmeal Vineyard, H Vanduzer.

WASHINGTON.

Sam'l Underwood, Abram Vickers, James Vann.

FRANKLIN.

Patrick Vance.

HANCOCK.

Thomas Vining.

SAVANNAH, C. C.

1756 to 1762.—Charles Watson, And Walker, Jno Weaver, Jos Wright, Sophia Williamson, Thos Wilson, James Wright, Geo Whitfield, Rich Warren, Charles Wilson, John Wilson, Michael Wickhauf, John Welcher, B Weddell, Alex Wyly.

ST. JOHNS, LIBERTY, OGEECHEE, L. OGEECHEE, ST. ANDREW, ST. PHILIPS ST. DAVIDS.

1756 to 1773.—Thos Way, Ed Way, Andrew Way, Thos White, Wm Watson, James Whitfield, Jacob Walthour, Jos Winn, Stephen Williams, James Wesley, Nath'l Way, Moses Way, Sam'l Way, Andrew Way, Moses Way, Abram Williamson, John Wereat, Andrew Watson, John Wetherington, Geo Whitfield, Alex Wright, Sam'l Wallace, Jos Wood, D Witherspoon, J Wertch, Stephen Williams, Jacob Wetter, Jno F Williams, D Witherspoon, Charles West, John Winn.

1773 to 1800.—Alex Wyly, Andrew E Wells, Geo Welch, Jas Ward, Jos Woodruff, Robert Watts, Jacob Weed, John Whitehead, Thos Worthington, John Wanden, Anthony Wayne, Abner Williams, Jacob Weed, Zach Wimberly, John Whitehead, John Williams, David Wood, Jno Webb, James Wilson, Mary Wright, Sarah Williams, Lazarus Walton, John Warren, Mathew Wood, Wm Weal, James Wood, Ed Welch.

ST. JOHNS, LIBERTY, BRYAN, McINTOSH, CAMDEN.

1796 to 1800.—Jas Warren, Mathew Wood, Jos Williams, Wm West, John Warren, Wilson Williams, Thomas Waters, Samuel Wright, Ann Webster, Sam'l Wade, Unity Williams, Fain Williams, Charles West.

ST MATTHEWS, EFFINGHAM, EBENEZER.

1756 to 1774.—Ludwig Wideman, Michael Weaver, John Wertch, James Wright, Jas Weston, Chaplain Williams, Abraham Wells, John Witherspoon, Andrew Willoughby, Stephen Wilmoth, Thomas Waters.

1790 to 1800.—Fred Wiggins, John Wisenbaker, John Wright, James Wilson, Daniel Wiltman. Zack White.

ST. GEORGE.

1761 to 1774.---Alex Wood. John Walters, B Williamson, Thos Whitehead, Peter Winn, John Wells, Jesse Wiggins, Francis Wynn, John Womack, Geo Walker, James Weston, Isaac Wimberly, Reason Whitehead, Geo Wyche, Jno Warnell, Arthur Wall, Jno Waters, Isaac Wood, Thomas Wimberly Richard Womack, Joel Walker, Chas Watron, Geo Williams, Jos Walker, Geo Wyche, James Waters, Benj Warren, Richard Womack, Geo Wells, Alex Walsington, Chas Williams, Thos Wigham, Wm Wall, Isaac Wood, Wm Wylly, Asa Williams, S Wilson, Jas Williams, Benj Warner, N Wade.

1784 to 1790.---Thomas Walker, David Wood, Ed Weather, Jas Warren, John Walker, Samuel White, Francis Wynne, Archie Wood, S Wiley, Wm Waddle, Mary Wall, C Whitehead, Willis Watson, Thomas Walker.

BURKE.

1886 to 1890.---John Williams, Robt Wine, E Williams, David Whitfield, May Williams, Jos Wade, James Ward, C Warren, Jas Wilson, Jas Woodhouse, Wm Whiler, Geo Wigginton, Samuel White, Sol Wiley, Platt Whittaker, E Whittaker, Hinch Warren, Stephen Weaver, Thos Whitehead, Nicolas Welch, Dempsey Welch, E Wynn, John Wicker. David Wood, Lewis Whitfield, Willis Watrow, Robt Walton, George Walton, James Welch, D Williams, Jos Wallace, Jos Waller, S Winket, Carlos Warren, Mary Womack, Richard Warren, Wm Wood, A Williamson, Alex Wigham. David Womack, A Walls, H G Walker, Abram Waters, Jno Whitehead.

ST. PAUL.

1758 to 1767.—Ben Williamson, Jos Wood, Francis Wyley, Sarah Wesley, Nehemiah Wade, Chas Weatherford, Isaac Wood,

Bryan Ward, Samuel Wright, Thomas Waters, John West, Daniel Westcoat. Peter Welche, Elias Walraven, Joel Walker, Thomas Weekly.

1770 to 1774.—Benj Wells, John Whitsett. Thomas Watson, John Welch, Jacob Watson, John Watson. Robert Walden, Sam'l Winslet. Martin Weatherford, Wm Wheat, Wm Wallace, Jacob Weldon, N Wood, John Walton, Samuel Waller, Isaac Weldon, Dyonysius Wright, Samuel Wells, Isaac Wood, W Williams, Sanders Walker, Wiggins, Sam'l Whislett, Humphrey Wells, Marshall Wright, Arthur Wall.

1784 to 1785.—.Shad Wright, Abednego Wright, Henry Walding, James Waters, Benj Wells. John Willingham, Ed Walker, Wm Wright, Wm Wilkins, Geo Walton, John Walton, Samuel Wright, Sion Wright, Sion Wilson, Geo Waggoner, Robert Walton, John Ward.

WILKES COUNTY.

1783 to 1784.—Wm Webb, Jno Webb, Jere Wooten, Geo Walton, Sanders Walker, Wm Wright, Susannah Williams, Wm Walker, Michael Whately, Phlineas Whately, Moses White, Jesse Walton, Wm Waggoner, James Waggoner, John White, Reuben White, Daniel White, Jere Walker, Micajah Williamson, Nehemiah Wade, Martha Ann Waters, John Winckfield, John Woodall, Clement Wilkins, Samuel Walker, Wm (2) Walker, Moses Walker, Robert Ware, Nicolas Ware, Henry Ware, Mary Whately, Lucy Whately, Thomas Walton, George Walton, Robert Watkins, Douglas Watson, John Webster, Alma Warnock, Henry Widerman, Sherrod Wise, Joseph Wise, Jos Williams, Isaac Williams, Bryant Ward, Samuel Walker, Wm Wiggins, Emphray Wheeler, Samuel Wallis, E Wambersee, Benj Wilson, Michael Hues Wall, Arthur Wright, Francis Wright, Abednego Wright, Thomas Wadsworth, James Woodall, Thos Weymouth, Andrew Wert, Ed Welborn, Wm Warthen, Richard Warthen, Henry Wall, Geo Waggoner, John Westbrook, Thomas Winkfield, Geo Whitsett, Garland Wingfield, Frederick Williams, Richard Ward, Heirs of Thos Webb, Thos Wooten, Amos Wright, Wm Wornack.

1785 to 1789.—Richard Worsham.

1781 to 1788.—Geo Wornack, Absolom Wornack, Jno Watson, Jno Watkins, James (2) Warren, Charles Waters, Elizabeth Wilder, John Walton, Wm Walton, Newell Walton, John Webster, Peter Williamson, Jos Wood, Jno Wall, Rachel Wells, Henry Woods.

1790 to 1800.—Clement Wilkins, John Winn, Wm Whitman.

GREENE.

Jno P Wagnon, Wm Willoughby, Curtis Wellburn, Thomas Wellburn, Isaac Williamson, Wm Wright, Thos Watts, Ethelrid

Wood, Matthew Wood, Aristarchus Wood, Silas Williams, James Ward, Willis Whately, Isaac Williams, Wm Washington, Jonathan Williams, John Wilson, James Wood, Dan'l Whately, John Wilkenson, Thos Wade, Wm Wilson.

WASHINGTON.

Geo Walton, Jesse Walton, Thomas Walton, Robert Walton, Newell Walton, William Walton, Charles Williams, Micajah Williamson, Charles Williamson, Jacob Winfree, Jesse Winfree, Wm Wilkins, J Welcher, Zach Wheeler, John Wiggins, Wm Wiggins, Nathan Wooten, Sam'l Whately, W Whately, John Whately, Mitchell Whately, Wm Willis, Richard Willis, Britton Willis, Jere Welcher, Joshua Wood, John Whitesides, Zach Wheeler, Charles Wilds, Geo Walton, John White, Sam'l White, Micajah Williamson, Nathan Woods, Jesse Winfrey, Joshua Welch, Sam'l Wilson, Peyton Wyatt, Thomas Wooten, David Walker, Gabriel Wilkins, Wm Wright, Arthur Whitten, Levin Watson, Joshua Watson, Thomas Watson, Daniel Wallace, Geo Wainright, Joshua Welch, Benj Wells, Charles Williams, Joseph Williams, Wm Where, Jonathan Wood, Henry Wood, Charles Waters, Joseph Woodruff, Wm Webster, Sanders Walker, Wm Wilder, Nehemiah Wade, Isaiah Willis, Abednego Wright, Israel Wright, Habakkuk Wright, Geo Williams, Sam'l Winslett, John Watts, Jno Wright, Nicolas Ware, Ed Williams, John Williams, Geo Wagner, Jas Wagner, Abner Webster, Geo Wyche, Jos Warnock, Jesse Warnock, Robert Walton, Richard Warthen.

FRANKLIN.

John Williams, Wm Walker, Willis Watson, Jesse Walton, Wm Walton, Thomas Walton, John Wingfield, Wm Wagner, Joshua Wynn, Saml West, John Wood, Thomas Walton, Jno P Wagnon, Malachi Wilder, Wm Walker, Ford Welcher, Benj Ward, E Wombersee, Rich'd Wood, Jos Waller, Wm Waggoner, John Waters, Penny Wilson, Peter Wiley, Rich White, David Wright, Ambrose Wheeler, E Weathers, Nathl Williams, Agnes Wilson, Mary Wilson, Absolom Wallis, Amos Whitehead, Mary Warnock. Valentine Warlick, Wm Wilkerson, Peter Williamson, Robert Williamson, Wm Williamson, James Williamson, Micajah Williamson, Jas Williams, Simon Walton, Walker Walton, W Welborn, Saml Woods, Micajah Wallis, Jno Wallis, J R Whitney.

ELBERT.

Wm Wise, Samuel White.

WARREN.

Geo Weatherby.

HANCOCK.

Sallie Williamson, Simeon Whitehurst, Geo Wyche.

OGLETHORPE.

1790 to 1800.—Patton Wise.

COLUMBIA.

John Williams.

Wm Yancey, Daniel York, Joe Youngblood.

1755 to 1757.—Frances Young, Henry Young, Mary Young, John Young, Isaac Young, Thomas Young, Jno Young, Thos Young, Thos Young.

1787 to 1800.—James Young, Jacob Young, John Young, Pleasant Young, James Young, Alex Young, John Young, Wm Young, Wm Young, Jr, James Young, David Young, Wm Young, Sr, Wm Young, Jr, Geo Young, Perigrine Young, Monah Yarborso, Thomas Yarborso, James Yarborso.

ZOUBEHUBLER, ZUNNERBRENNER.

P Zetterer, Jno Ziegler, J J Zubly, Jno Ziegler, Lucas Ziegler, Mathew Zettler, Solomon Zant, Henry Zang, John Zutheny, Philip Zimmerman.

LIST SOLDIERS OF THE LINE

Adam Alexander, secretary mate; Henry Allison, lieutenant; Danl A Cuthbert, captain; Edwd Carvan, lieutenant; Cornelius Collins, lieutenant; Raines Cook, captain; E P DeLaplaign, captain; John Ducains, captain; John Dollar, lieutenant artillery; Jos Day, captain; Thomas Davenport, lieutenant; Thomas Glascock, lieutenant; James Houston, surgeon; Christopher Hillary, lieutenant; Arthur Hays, lieutenant, Robert Howe, lieutenant; Wm Jordan, lieutenant; Wm Johnston, lieutenant; Philip Lowe, major; John McIntosh, colonel; John Meanly, lieutenant; Lachlan McIntosh, lieutenant; John Morrison, lieutenant; Wm McIntosh, captain; John Mitchell, lieutenant; Josiah Maxwell, lieutenant; Elisha Miller, captain; Robert Mosby, lieutenant; Clement Nash, captain; Nathl Peavre, lieutenant; Thos Payne, lieutenant; Jos Pannell, lieutenant colonel; David Rees, judge advocate; Fred Ridgely, surgeon mate; Frank Shick, lieutenant; Jas B Sharp, surgeon; Francis Tennille, lieutenant; Jno Peter Wagnon, lieutenant; Shadrack Wright, captain; Jno White, colonel; Wm Howard, Henry Gouze, lieutenant; Wm Lineby, lieutenant David Franklin, lieutenant; Peyton Smith, Saml Summerlin, Dimsey Summerlin, Thos Stockwell, Elijah Dauthan, Richard Turner, John Bird, Richard B Barnes, Wm Barnes. James Reeves, Robert Huggens, Hardy Davis, Jacob Wells, James Brown, Benj Bird, Saml Giles, Jerry Ellis, Jos Thompson, Thos Franklin, lieutenant, Hugh Robertson, lieutenant; James Wood, David Franklin, lieutenant; Henry Dulins, Danl Ollens. Thos Linby, Thomas Ferrell, Thomas John, Jas Gillons, Danl Ketley, Rich Baglewood, John Stots, John Howard, Thos Marney, John Johnston, Thos Worth, Thos Smith, Joshua Powell, Peter Stots, Jno Summerlin, Wm Hamilton, David Robeson, John Cheshire, R Summerlin, Jesse Lowe, Jesse Jones, Nicholas Tunis, Jas Summerlin, Wm Sinkfield, Stephen Hawkins, Nathan Spikes, Thos Duncan, Jas Lamar, Wm Simmons, John Farr, Benj Farr, Wm Compton, Jno Williams, Wm Lowe, Geo Surlock, Henry Fowler, Peter Fowler, Wm Pritchett, John Pritchett, Moses Brannon, Peter Clower, John Loyd, James Loyd, Wm Stewart, John Tankerson, Henry Persons, Saml Persons, Sol Butts, James Carter, John Swan, Edw Pratt, Wm Butler, Edmond Butler.

Geo Andrew, Wm Anglin, Asa Alexander, John Akins, Rich Austin, James Aldridge, Elijah Anderson, Benj Ashworth, Thos Ayres, John Anderson, John Adams, David Anglin, Alex Anderson, Wm Ammons, Richard Aycock, Danl Appling, Benj Andrews, James Allison, Alex Awtry, captain; John Awtry, captain; James Alexander, Robt Adams, John Appling, John Anderson, Wm Ayres, captain; Henry Allison, lieutenant; James Aldridge, Wm Anderson, Robt Alexander, Arthur Ashworth, Bartlett Aderson, Isaac Avera, Adam Ashworth, Robt Ammons, James Anderson, Hugh Adams, Alex Autrey, Danl Ayres, Hugh Alexander, Chas Adamson, Abram Ayres, Henry Anderson, John Abbott, Henry Allison, Jacob Awtry, Thomas Allen, John Averitt, Jos Avent, James Allen, Thomas Ansley, Ezekiel Alexander, James Ayres, Ayra (Ira) Alexander, James Adcock, John Allen, Robert Allen, John Ashmon, Henry Alexander, John Andrews, Jonathan Asbury, John Acord, Benj Andrews, James Adams, Andrew Armour, Alex Angelly, Chas Abercrombie, John Avery, Wm Ashley, lieutenant; Jno Anderson, Saml Andrew, Alex Armstrong, Thomas Averitt, Wm Aycock, Abram Ayres, Wm Allen, Chas Allen, Israel Averitt, Wm Adams, Wm Aaron, captain.

Willoughby Barton, Artemas Baker, Wm Brewer, Ed Boyd, John Bender, Allen Brown, Johnson Blair, John Brunson, Robert Beville, Joshua Barnette, Whitmarsh Baker, Wm Bready, Mial Barnett, W Baker, Wm Brunson, Wm Black, Jno Baker, colonel; Ben Bohanon, Thomas Blackshear, Nathan Bostick, Henry Black, Andrew Brown, Rich Barksdale, Jere Bugg, Danl Barnett, Geo Brevard, John Basnet, Saml Brassel, Robert Bell, Thos Burton, R Bowling, John Burnsides, Roger Brooks, Wm Blazer, Artemas Baker, Wm Burnard, Ed Burch, Ep Bowen, Chas Burch, Sherwood Bugg, Rich Bradley, Ford Butler, Thos Brown John Barnard, Sampson Ball, Wm Baker, lieutenant; John Burwell, Burton Barnett, Richard Burton, James Bevil, John Black, Nathl Brownson, Ed Bugg, Frances Brown, Saml Bugg, Rich Bradley, Nathan Barnet, John Berryhill, Jno Burton, John Brumley, John Benson, Jno Baxter, David Brunson, Wm Ball, Ebenezer Bronson, George Barber, Danl Burgsteiner, Geo Bagby, And Brown, Michael Bradley, Abner Beckham, Littleberry Bostick, Hugh Bells, Moody Burt, Wm Brady, Bryan Barker, Alex Brassard, Oliver Bowen, Joel Barnett, Jno Braddock, Zach Burley, Reuben Banks, Jacob Blount, surgeon's mate; John Brown, John Bennison, Bruns Boykin, Nathaneal Baker, Thos Baker. Robert Baillie, Paul Bevill, Arch Beall, Danl Bankston, John Brandon, John Black, Saml Bugg, Jos Buckhalter, Jos Brasswell, Danl Butler, Peter Beason, Joshua Bishop, Joshua Bradley, Jona Buggs, Jno Baggs, Joel Bowens, Geo Barnhart, Andrew Burns, John Bankston, Jno Bentley, Allen Beckham, Benj Brock, Wm Barker, Chas Beddingfield, Bolin Banks, Wm Braydon, John Buckhalter, James Brooks, John Bates, Hezekiah Bell, Lawrence Bankston, Theophilus Burke, Benj Borneman, Jona Busson,

Simon Beck, Wm Baldwin, sergeant; Sol Barfield, — Barksdale, Thos Bussey, Hezeker Bussey, Seny Bond, Jacob Babbetts, Chesly Bostick, Thomas Barrett, Abm Booth, Wm Barron, lieutenant; Thomas Brannon, Willoby Barton, Jos Burges, Jesse Brooks, Jno Bitsell, Nathan Beddingfield, Wm Buck, Rich Bonner, John Bender, Nicolas Bugg, Benj Blakely, Saml Beckham, John Barnett, Rich Bradley, Jeffey Barksdale, Erasmus Brewer, Gilbert Bardine, Wm Barron, Wm Brownlow, Simpson Braswell, John Burks, captain; Jeremiah Beal, captain; Jno Baggs, David Brown, Edward Beard, Robt Butler, James Brown, Saml Beatty, Danl Butler, John Butler, Reuben Bear, Robert Bain, James Brantley, Wm Bonner, Robt Bennefield, Garrett Beall, John Bell, Wm Bentley, Josiah Bradford, Ed Burks, Allen Braswell, Jno Burney, Philip Barnett, Danl Bankston, John Braddock, Robt Benton, Robert Boyd, John Briants, lieutenant; John Bearden, sergeant; Wilieby Barton, sergeant; Peter Burdey, Wm Bradey, lieutenant; Reuben Barron, Roger Brooks, Wm Braker, Jno Barber, David Baldwin, Mordacai Baldwin, lieutenant; David Baldwin, Zephaniah Beall, John Boid, Jos Burkes, Chas Booth, Geo Bodenner, David Burkes, Saml Branham, Henry Beal, Henry Brittian, Peter Bradshaw, Frances Butler, F Braswell, Ferdenan Braswell, Benj Blakely, sergeant; Wm Brady, James Braswell, George Braswell, Wm Barnes, Wm Beatty, R Barnard, Thos Bacon, Jonathan Bacon, John Bacon, Frances Barker, John Brooks, James Bryant, Saml Briggs, Wm Bryant, Wm Brady, Wm Blanchard, John Boyd, Geo Braswell, Jacob Bugg, Abner Beckham, Moses Brewer, Wm Barkaloe, Ford Butler, Benj Bryant, Saml Beatty, Wm Boderly, Wm James Baker, Thos Blacksell, Artemas Baker, Jacob Blunt, surgeon mate; John Butler, Roger Brooks, Rich Berry, Jacob Bowman, Jos Beasley, Thos Brantley, Sh Bakin, Simon Beckham, Ed Bugg, John Bentley, Chas Barker, John Bryant, Ed Boyd, Geo Brewer, John Burns, Jacob Bankston, John Berry, Henry Black, Randal Burney, Wm Bailey, Saml Branham, George Barker, Jesse Barnard, Stephen Blunt, Nathan Burnett, Paul Bevill, James Bevill, Hugh Bell, Thos Brown, James Bowen, Wm Brown, Jesse Boykin, Ed Burch, Danl Barnett, Wm Barry, Nathan Beal, Thos Burton, George Bagley, Moody Burt, James Beesley, Wm Beesley, Richard Jno Brazell, Jacob Brooks, Jose Burks, Byers Boykins, Nicodemas Boyd, Michl Buckhalter, Abrm Bradley, Reuben Blanchard, David Brunson, Wm Brady, sergeant; Micheal Bird, Chester Barber, George Bassett, Lewis Baughbank, Chas Brownen, David Braddock, James Burkes, Rich Barton, Rich Bradley, Fred Brown, Oliver Bowen, Jno Burney, Jr. Rich Bellamy, Saml Berryhill, Rich Barfield, James Boloth, Rich Burton, Jere Bugg, John Burnsides, Joseph Bags, Lott Boyce, Hardy Bass, Thomas Bass, Brantley Bass.

Thomas Carson, Littleton Chambless, Wm Carroll, Wm Clements, James Cone, John Connor, Thos Cribbs, Wm Corsea, Sol Collins, Jno Crutchfield, James W Calk, Wm Conyers, John Carson, Jos Carson, Sam'l Carson, Henry Curl, John Curl, Jno Chapman, sergeant; Cary Currey, Caleb Cock, John Clem, Henry Carr, John Clarke, Drewry Campbell, Henry Cullars, Thos Carson, John Clark, captain; Sam'l Camp, quartermaster; David Childers, Thomas Childers, John Conyers, John Conyers, Jr., Sam'l Creswell, surgeon; Wm Calson, Jas Cunningham, Jos Catchings, Gibson Clarke, Seymor Catchings, Pat Carr, major; Jere Chavons, Jas Cone, F Coleman, D Canon, Anthony Cooper, Adam Carson, Jacob Curry, Jacob Conley, Jas Coleman, Jacob Cauley, Wm Cowan, Jere Cloud, G Chaney, James Carter, Henry Carter, Pat Carlton, lieutenant; John Collins, Michael Cup, Rich Cauley, Lewis Clarke, John Caldwell, James Cartledge, Nicolas Curry, M Chandler, Lewis Crain, Ezekiel Cobb, Anthony Crumley, Wm Corbin, Steven Collins, John Collins, Wm Croker, M Carney, Isham Cook, Pat Cumming, Moses Collins, Jos Cobb, Pat Connally, Sam'l Clements, John Camant, Aaron Coats, Jos Conteratt, Wm Crudden, Wm Campbell, Alexander Campbell, Pat Carter, Ed Castello, Abednego Chandler, Wm Cureton, Wm Crook, Ousley Carney, Jno Chipen, Jas Cartledge, Sam'l Crawford, Benj Cox, Thomas Cannon, Wm J Cureton, Cornelius Carden, John Carson, Henry Cup, sergeant; John Collins, Emanuel Chaney, Jas Culbreath, Jas Cawthorne, Ezekiel Cloud, Drewry Cade, Thomas Chisholm, Benjamin Chisholm, Christopher Chambless, Wm Cone, Wm Camp, Isaac Clemmonds, Neaugh Cloud, Chestop Camberger, John Conyers, captain; John Crawford, Henry Carr, Wm Calhoun, Wm Cathern, Cornelius Carden, Thos Carson, Henry Castleberry, Abia Clay, Wm Cureton, Jas Cobb, Stephen Cantrell, Wm Cowns, David Creswell, Wm Clark, Jno Castleberry, David Caster, Chas Collins, John Coan, Jno Casey, Geo Cook, Rams Cook, John Cook, Caleb Cook, James Cole, Wm Casey, Jacob Castleberry, Roger Cannon, Geo Clondas, Sam'l Cartledge, John Coats, Leslie Coats, Jno Cudington, Daniel Coleman, Cornelius Cohron, Wm Cowns, Boling Cureton, Thos Cornell, David Corsea (Coursey), Alex Carswell, Wm Chapman, John Curtis, Henry Coats, Jos Culpepper, James Caldwell, Wm Colson, Thomas Chidney, James Cartledge, Peter Curry, Jno Cason, James Calk, Wm Cureton, lieutenant; Benj Chisholm, Jno Clark, Sr., Wm Crokes, Sam'l Cason, Sam'l Crabb, Jere Cloud, John Cole, Sr., Peter Clowers, John Carlyle, Thomas Cruze, John Chambers, John Camant, Nath'l Coats, Wm Cato, Peter Castleberry, Anderson Crawford, Drury Cade Wm Campbell, Daniel Conner, John Cunningham, major; Johnston Clark, John Cain, John Crutchfield, Jesse Connell, John Chisholm, sergeant; John Clements, lieutenant; Jos Camps, Jno Cole, John Cassells, Jos Culpepper, Jos Cullens, Jno Chambless, John Connell, John Chiles, Wm Candler, colonel; Jno Combs, John Cody, Jno Culbreath, Hepworth Carter, Spencer Crane, Wm Cassell,.Zach Canty, Nathan Crawford, Jas Carter, John Cargyle, Henry Candler, James Crispus, Chas F Chevalier, Benj Catchins, Rich Cureton, Jos Cauthon, Sol Camp, John Cloud, Dave Connor, Major Carr, Wm Clifton, Chas Clifton.

Rich Dowday, Sam'l Davis, Jeremiah Duckworth, Wm Downs, James Darsey, John Dunaway, David Davis, Abram Dennis, George Downs, Wm Davis, Geo Dorty, captain; Joseph Davis, Christian Dasher, James Dunwoody, Wm Dean, sergeant; John Dallas, lieutenant; Hull Dovly, lieutenant; Meredeth Davis, Chas Davis, sergeant; Dr. Davenport, surgeon; John Devaux, aid de camp; Jos Day, Wm Dawson, Martin Dawson, Elijah Dennison, Daniel Dannello, Joel Doss, lieutenant; Thos Dorton, Brittain Dawson, Benj Darney, Mathews Dalton, Rich Dowdy, Jenkins Davis, colonel; Moses Davis, Rich Darbe, John Duhart, Jona Downs, Absolom Davis, James Donnelly, Benj Davis, Jno Martin Dasher, Thos Dugan, captain; Asten Dabney, John Darby, Dan'l Dampier, Robert Day, Mathews Duncan, Gideon Davis, John Davies, James Darney, Ware Daus, John Darby, Clementine Davis, Luke Derbin, Dave Delaney, Jno Taylor Duke, John Donnelly, Solomon Davis, John Dethan, David Delk, Nathan Dickson, Wm Dukes, lieutenant; Henry Dukes, captain; John Taylor Dukes, Jr., Wm Dukes, Elizabeth Deaton, Mathew Declanchenes, Wm Dickson, Hugh Dixon, James Duncan, lieutenant; Mathew Duncan, Cornelius Donelly, Henry Driver, James Duffey, Sebua Dinkins, David Dickson, captain; Nathaniel Dickson, James Dunmon, Alex Douglas, Henry Dyer, Hardy Davis, Ware Daus, Wm Dunkin, Anson Dollar, John Donely, Stephen Day, Wm Davis, Wiley Davis, Robert Day, Anson Dollar, Joel Darcy, James Donnally, Myrick Davis, George Darden, Sr., George Darden, Jr., David Dick, Edw Davis, Ambrose Downs, Harry Day, Valthal Davis, Randolph Davis, Andrew Decks, James Duncan, Benj Dally, Wm Daniel, Nehemiah Davis, Austin Dabney, John Duchart, Chesley Davis, James Dukes, James Delaney, James Davis, Chas Deveraux, Josiah Dunn, John Dennis, Charles Denton, Wm David, Jacob Davis, David Dawson, Jos Davison, Jacob Dunn, Richmond Dennis, Isaac Dennis, Austin Dabney, John Dean, Lewis Davis, Jno Douglas, Wm Donoway, Wm Dean, Benj Dolly, Buckner Dukes, Taylor Dukes, Wm Dooly, John Dennis, Darby Dennison, Dave Dennison, Wm Darcy, Jacob Duckworth, Benj Daniel, John Dillard, Geo Douglas, Benj Daley, Chas Denman, Blandford Davis.

Wm Entechins (Enterkin), David Evans, Asa Emanuel, colonel; George Eimbeck, Danl Evans, Daniel Elliot, Daniel Earley, James Emmett, Saml Elbert, James Easton, John Eastwood, Stephen Evans, Jesse Embry, Wm Elliott Ephm Echols, Stephen

Ellis, Jacob Earnest, Steph Evans, David Emanuel, captain; Wm Earnest, John Elliot, Wm Evans, Wm Elliot, John Eady, Wm Entriccan, James Ellison, Absolom Etors, Wm Espey, David Emanuel, Enos Emanuel, M Embeck, Wm Elleas, Henry Elliot, James Eady, Jno Eagle, Jno Eustace, Robert Ellis, Danl Evans, Benj Evans, Abraham Edwards, Daniel Evans, Nathan Evans, colonel; Benj Evans, Wm Earnest, Wm Emtricken, Eph Eckles, Jno Evans, Peter Edwards, James Easter, Nathaneal Eves, John Eades.

Francis Foster, Ezra Fussell, John Ford, Mathew Fettler, Nathl Fettler, Wm Fame, Thomas Fukeway, John Freman, James Freman, Wm Freman, Wm Ferrul, John Fulton, Saml Fulton, Jos French, Travis Fane, Fredk Francis, James Flynn, John Fling, Jacob Farington, John Favens, James French, Joshua Ford, John Farvin, Joshua French, Steph Fuller, Conrad Fredman, David Felps, Jacob Fare, Jos Finshell, John Fain, Wm Foster, John Frier, Thomas Fussell, Benj Folsom, Zach Feras, Wm Farrell, John Frazier, Wm Flowers, Geo Folds, John Fann, Lawrence Fulsome, Saml Flemming, Geo Franklin, Thomas Ford, Arthur Fort, John Folsome, Joshua Fuller, Wm Fanner, Nathan Fowler, Thos Ford, Wm Fields, Jeremiah Fly. Conrad Fugonier, Isaac Fuller, Holman Freeman, Abram France, John Freeman, Asael Fanner, Wm Ford, Chas Fergason, Owen Fort, Thos Fluker, John Fluker, Wm Franklin, Jr, James Finley, Lewis Friels, Alex Frazier, John Fenn, Owen Fluker, Prater Fuqua, Wm Few, Jr, Wm Fean, Wm Few, Sr, Ignatius Few, John Ferkerson, James Flenneken, Owen Ford, Holman Freeman, Humphrey Freyar, Robert Flemming, John Frazier, Wm Franklin, Sr, Jacob Fortee, Malachi Frazier, Thos Frederick, James Ferrell, Chas Fitzgerald, Wm Fleming, Robt Flounray, Wm Fluker.

John Glampkin, Thomas Gilliland, Wm Grant, James Gilbert, Rob Gray, John Gamble, Wm Gilbert, Sam'l Garmany, Jos Gunnells, Jas Gray, Cary Godbe, James Green, Wm Green, Henry Green, Adam Grimsley, Joshua Gay, Rich Grinsey, Jno Glaspy (Gilespie), Philip Griner, Sam'l Griffith, Elam Greasell, George Garbet, Wm Gamest, John Goultney, Wm Godby, Jno Grimesley, Jas Graves, John Gray, Thomas Gray, Frances Gedings, Jno Giles, Thomas Galphin, John Golding, Henry Graybill, Jno German, Sr., Rich Graves, Jno German, Jr., Jno Ganson, Jno Gorham, Joshua Glass, Gilbert Grier, Wm Glascock, Thomas Grier, Matthew Griffin, John Graves, Wm Gent, Math Gray, Thomas Greene, Frederick Greene, Saliva Greene, Benj Greene, Lt Thos Glascock, Wm Gordon, Wm Giles, Arthur Giles, Absalom Gaines, Bagley Gaines, Sgt David Gaston, Rich Gibbs, Jesse Gordon, Sam'l Griffin, Thomas Greene, Lt Alex Gaston, Ely Garnett, Wm Golden, Wm Greer, Wm Gedions, Jacob Greathouse, John Grier,

Lewis Gardner, James Gorley, M Andrew Green, Robert Graves, John Girardeau, Wm Girardeau, Wm Graham, J Goldwire, Thos Greggs, Peter Grant, Hugh Gilliland, Jonathan Gift, Wm Gideons, Robert Grier, Pleas't Goodall, John Graves, Philip Griener, Thomas Goves, Nicolas Gunnells, Jno Grizzle, Sam'l Giles, Robert Graves, Jr., William Gay, Charles Gent, Aaron Grier, Capt Daniel Gunnells, Michael Griffin, Thomas Gragz, John Grierson, R M Gray, Sergt Elijah Grimsley, John Garrett, Rob't Grierson, Jos Grimsley, Wm Gilliland, Thos Gilliland, Step Gloveyer, Sullivan Green, McKeen Green, Jos Glase, Frances Grub, Thomas Grant, Jacob Gossett, Hardy Glover, William Germany, Josiah Goolsby, Jonathan Goolsby, Capt Grant, Benj Grubbs, Wm Grier, John Green, Curry Godbe, John Gamble, Benjamin Greene, Randal Griffin, Jacob Gray, Robert Giles, Andrew Giles, Andrew Grant, Joel Glass, Randolph Griffin, Peter Grant, Wm Greene, Ayres Gorley, Jesse Gordon, John Glass, Wm Graham, Wm Gardner, Clain Greazell.

James Harvey, Henry Heatley, Nicolas Hawkins, Beverly Holt, Wm Howard, Wm Hill, John House, Thos Hannah, Joshua Hill, Rich Heard, Stephen Heard, Wm Holiday, Rich Hubbard, Fitzmaurice Hunt, Jno Hubbard, Luther Holwell, Caleb Howell, Joel Harvey, Littleberry Harvey, James Hill, James Harvey, Jere Hatcher, George Heard, Ed Hagan, Dennis Hamby, Barnard Heard, Absolam Haliman, Joseph Harrill, Chas Hammond, John Hardy, Wm Hill, David Harris, Wm Howsley, George Haile, Thos Holiday, David Harris, Capt David Harris, Blasingame Harvey, Buckner Harris, Christopher Hillary, John Hicks, David Harrell, Private Wm Huntsman, Jno Hodge, Willoughby Hodge, Stanton Haymon, George Hammond, Sam'l Henson, Nath Hudson, Sam'l Hudson, Sergt John Haggett, Robert Hudson, Wm Hudson, Thos Handsard, Lt Nathaniel Hughes, John Hatcher, Robert Hatcher, Josiah Hatcher, Stephen Hawthorn, Jno Harris, Capt Archb'd Hatchett, Henry Heymond, Capt Isaac Hicks, Capt John Hardy, Surgeon James Hutson, Stephen Heyman, Joseph Heard, Rob Hodge, Abner Hammond, Wm Hatcher, Roger Hodge, Henry Hatcher, Sam'l Harris, Wm Hunt, Thos Hamilton, John Hart, Robert B Hamach, Wm Halymdorf, Phil Hornsby, Henry Houghton, James Hogg, Walton Harris, Travis Holton, B Hickinbotham, Joseph Hickinbotham, John Holmes, Benedick Hammock, Job Hinton, Edward Hagan, Jas Hammett, Michael Harvey, Thos Houghton, Edward Hall, James Hogg, David Holliman, Wm Hearthem, Robt Heatley, Jesse Horn, Miles Hunter, Robert Howe, Richard Hill, John Houston, Henry Hartle, Wm Harper, Michael Harback, James Hawthorn, Samuel Hoff, Wm Hewett, Rhesa Howard, Letha Hammett, Andrew Hays, Nicolas Harbuck, Thomas Harvey, Julius Howard, John Howard, James

Hilliard, Jno Horn, Robert Hines, Benjamin Harrison, Cuthbert Hudson, Evan Harvey, James Hawkins.

Jno Islands, Alex Irvine, Capt Joshua Inman, John Igle, Rich Ingram, Capt Shadrack Inman, Jno Lawson Irwin, John Irwin, Jared Irwin, William Irwin, Alex Irwin, Levater Irelow, Hugh Irwin.

Stephen Johnson, Edward Jones, David Jones, Jacob Jordan, Patrick Jarvis, Wm Johnston, Daniel Jackson, John H Johnson, Lt-Col James Jackson, Matthew Jones, Lt Thomas Johnson, Jesse Jones, Isaac Jackson, Benj Joiner, Francis Jenkins, Capt Richard Johnson, Michael Jones, Capt Wm Johnson, James Jeffries, John Hackner Johnson, Absolam Jackson, Jinsy Jordan, Job Jackson, Arthur Jenkins, Densey Justice, Robert Jones, Wm Jones, Wm Jackson, Benj Jackson, Robert Jarrett, James Jones, Thos Jones, Abraham Jones, John Jones, Drury Jackson, Daniel Josling, Seaborn Jones, Wm Jones, Michal Jenkins, Richard Jenkins, Isaac Justice, Elias Jones, S Jordan, Jos Jeter, Col Isaac Jackson, Sam'l Jordan, Robert Jenkins, Michael Jackson, Peter Jackson, Starling Jenkins, Benjamin Jenkins, Lewis Jardine, Reuben Jackson, Capt John Johnson, Capt Jonathan Jones, Thos Joiner, Baxton Jourdan, Jacob Johnson, Hugh Jones, Randolph Jackson, Chas Jourdan, James Johnston, Mark Jones, Henry Jones, Henry Jackson, Jos Jackson, Ben Jones, James Johnson, Frederick Jones, Simeon Jones, John Johnson, Thomas Jackson, Nathan Jones, Daniel Johnson, Lewis Jordan, Dev Jarrett.

Sephen Kersey, John Kennady, Stephen Kazey, Jacob Kelley, John King, Hugh Kelsey, Lieut John Kimborough, Private John Keliy, Robert Killgore, Thos Kilpatrick, Jacob Kinebrew, Jeremiah Kendall, Hezekiel Kendrick, Thomas Kelley, Jno Kielock, Ebenezer Kielock, John Kitchens, John Kelly, Sam'l Keith, Jr., Thomas Kemp, John Kitts, Thos Kendrick, Ralph Killgore, Jno Killgore, Henry Kain, Stephen Keesey, Archibald Kell, James Kemp.

Samuel Lamar, Lt Frederick Leapham, Andrew Lawson, Jacob Lewis, Obadiah Lowe, Hugh Lawson, Roger Lawson, David Lewis, Jr., John Leverett, John Leggett, Henry Leverett, James Little, Zech Lamar, Timothy Lee, Jno Lambrich (Lamback), Capt Clement Lanier, Richard Leven, Philip Logan, James Lane, Thos Lane, Geo Lowe, Thomas Lane, Rembern Lett, Isaac Lockhart, Benj Lanier, Dennis Live, Gheza Lewis, John Linn, Thos Linn, Nicodemus Lazarus, Wm Lambeth, Thomas Lunday, Theophilus Lunday, Jos Leslie, Sam'l Lankston, Jno Lawler, Jno Lauderdale, Ed Langworthy, Chaplain Josiah Lewis, Joel Lewis, Surgeon Evan Lewis, Thomas Lewis, John Landrum, David Long, Daniel Lowe, James Lucas, John Laramor (Lamar), Samuel Langston, Curtis Linn, Cornelius Lofton, John Lang, Abner Leggett, Archibald Little, Luke Lamar, Moses Lankford, Josiah Lankford, Dennis

Lindsay, Isaac Lowe, Sr., Isaac Lowe, Jr., Aaron Leverett, Wm Lane, John Lindow, John Lench, Samuel Lanier, Wm Lancaster, Charles Linn, Robt Leverett, Andrew Lee, Timothy Lee, Obadiah Lowe, Major Jos Lane, Major Jos Lowe, James Lewis, Wm Livingston, Thomas Lawson, Thos Lamar, Maj John Lindsay, Wm Lucas, Wm Lackey, Thomas Lanton, John Ledbetter, John Leath, John Lawson, Thompson Lawson, John Lawson, Sr., Levi Lancaster, Bev Lowe, Benj Lewis, Reuben Lett, Wm Lambeth, David Little, Thomas Locky, Roger Lawson, Sr., Abram Lamb, Robt Lithgood, Benj Lockhart, Bethial Lamb, Thomas Lamb, Andrew Lithgood, John F Lowe, Philip Logan, Joel Lockhart, Joshua Lee, Daniel Longstreet, Wm Lewis, Jas Lamar.

John Morton, James Martin, Merrian O McGruder, John Marshall, Jno W Martin, Wm Mills, Terry McHaney, Elisha Miller, Vance McGilton, James McGilton, Lachlan McIntosh, James McDowell, Thos Myers, Robert Moseley, Mannen (Manning), Daniel Moat, Daniel McNeily, John Milner, John McElhenry, Fred Minnus, William Mosely, Simon Moats, Luke Mann, John Mobley, Thos McGee, Martin Malone, Elijah Marsh, Capt John Morrison, Robert McMullen, Jno McCling, Bailey May, Benedick Middleton, Lewis McLean, Thomas Moore, Wm May, Frederick McMurry, James Morphett (Moffatt), John Mann, Wm Martin, John McCain, Leonard Moss, Isham Mathews, Daniel McNeil, Mordecai More, Christopher Morgan, Holland Middleton, Holland Middleton, Jr., Nicolas Miller, James Martin, Horatio Marbury, Jno McMunn, Michael McNeil, Archb'd McNeil, Benj Mosely, Wm Musteen, Philip Morgan, Jno Morgan, Thos McGhee, Capt Wm Mathews, Capt Thomas Maxwell, Lt Jno Mitchell, Brig-Gen George Mathews, William Mitchell, Joseph Maise, John Milledge.

Zadock McGruder, John McFarland, Alex McCalpin, Nath'l Milton, Reese Morris, R Mitchell, Asa Morgin, Wm Moates, Sol Marsh, Sam Moncrief, Sam'l McCullough, Jno Mattox, Levi Moates, Rob't Middleton, John Manning, Smith Miller, Jese, Mosley, James Mercer, Jacob McClendon, Isaac McClendon, Nathan Marsh, Jno Marsh, Hugh Milligan, R McNabb, Capt James Merriwether, Ed Martin, John Manen, George Moon, Ganaway Martin, Ed Murphy, Nathan Marshall, Jacob Mercer, Wm McKeen, Wm McMurray, Jos Mims. Drury Mims, Wm Miles, (Jas Moon,) John Mosely, Wm Moran, John Martin, Sr Wm Mines, Thos Meser, Daniel Marcus, Jos Money, Jno Marcus, Jacob Martin, Pat Mosee Dan'l McCoy, Capt Jas McKay, Josiah Moncrief, Alex Millen, James Manning, Elis Marcus, Rob't McGarry, Jere Morgan, Robert Morgan, Jno Mobley, David Miller, Wm Moore, Pat Money, Jos McCormick, Wm Moore, Pat McCullough, John Maddox, Wm Maddox, Arch Mahon, Thomas Mosely, Drury Manen, Edward McBride, Alex McDougal, Anthony Metcalf, Uriah Mott, John McClain, Abram

Chaplan Manhall, Thos Maxwell, Dan'l Mathews, Mathew McMurry, Col McNiel, Lt Col Martin, Luke Morgan, Dan'l McOwen, Thomas Mitchell, Henry McKenney, Alex Miller, John Manen, Jr, Ed Maxwell, John McCormick, Dan'l McCarty, Zach Mott, Miles Murphy, Jos McNatt, Robt McGenty, John Minus, Jos Monmouth, David McMurray, Jos May, Daniel McBurnett, Jacob Messer, Step Morgan, Francis Moss, Martin Moore, Thos Morphett, Travis McKinney, Benj McCormick, Sam'l Mahon, Lt Thomas McDowell, Wm Madkins, Jos Mott, James Morphett, Malicai Morgan, Jno McKenny, Thos McCain, Ed McGary, Martha Muban, Thos McCormick, Jesse Miller, Capt Henry Manadee, Michael Mathews, Hugh McNeely, Serg't Sam'l McCullough, Jno McCalvey Capt Robert Middleton, Nathan McKenny, Capt Hatton Middleton, Major Thos Maxwell, Rich Moon, Dunza Metcalf, Wm Mayborn, Hugh McDonald, Mathew Mayben, Jno McGill, Tekiah McDonald, Benj Mattox, Thomas McCall, James McRoy, Thos Marbury, Wm Mannon, Nathan Martin, Marshall Martin, Capt Jno Melvin, Capt Hugh McGee, Dan'l Miller, Daniel McMurphy, Thos Meyers, Wm Miller, Lt David Madin, John McDuffy, James Montgomery, James Maxwell, John Marshall, Ezekiel Miller, Lt Barclay Martin, Wm McCalvey, Jos Miller, Bat Moorines, Dan'l Mathews, Pat McMullen, Cornelus McCardell, Arch Mahon, Sol McNatt, Thos Mash, Rev Silas Mercer, Chaplain, James Morris, Jos McClendon, Jno McCarthy, Robert McGeary, Willis Murphy, Nathaniel Miller, Jno McCullock, Lazarus Matton, Lewis McGee, Thos McDowell, Thos Maffett, Simon Martin, Silas Moates, Wm Middleton, Owen Majar, Wm Mafield, John Mathews,(Jno Moon,) Wm Metcalf, John Mattox, Charles Millen, Geo Miller, Leonard Marbury, Jesse Morgan, Ed McGary, Henry McKenney, Wm Mathews, Thos McGee, Wm Mott, Asa Morganson, Jesse McNail, John McFarland, Jr, John McNunn, Meshack Mathews, Jos Marshall, Daniel Marshall, Zach Marshall, Reps Mabry, Alex McDougal, Zeph Mott, Francis Moore, Samuel Moore, Wm Moak, (Monk) Thos Mosely, Adrain Maning, Mill Murphy, Jonas Mann, Wm Marlow, Wm Marberry, Smallwood Middleton, Isaac McClendon, Sr, Francis Mitchell, Levi Marshall Jos McMath, Jos Mooney, Jonathan Miller, Jas McCutchen, Martin Mims.

John Newman, Thomas Newell, Michael Nuga, Elisha Nettles, Sol Newsom, Reuben Nail Henry Nail, John Nelson, Adam Nelson, James Nephew, John Gottlieb Needlinger, Capt Joseph Nail, Wm Nelson, Benj Nail, Capt Clement Nash, James Nelson, Wm Newman, Benj Nicolson, Geo Niele, Philip Nowland, Wm Newberry, Benj Nichols, Julian Nail, John North, Thos Neel.

Dixon O'Neal, Daniel Ormsby, (Fifer) James O'Bryan, Wm Oakland, John Offutt, Thos Owens, Ephriam Owens, Nathan O'Neal, Dyonnysius Oliver, Richard Oates Ezekiel Offutt, Peter

Oliver, John Oliver, Jane Oates, Ezekiel Offutt, Jesse Offutt, Nathaniel Offutt, James Oliver, Wm Odair, Uriah Odam, Duncan O'Bryant, Ladswick Outlaw, Chas Odingshels, Josiah Obear, James Oricks.

Lt Col Jos Pannell, Thos Pennington, Joel Philips, Capt Zach Philips, Wm Philips, Mark Philips, Reuben Philips, Lt David Philips, Richard Perkins, Wm Paterson, Col Francis Pugh, John Pittman, Thos Patton, Jno Paterson, Jr, Robert Paterson, Wm Payne, Abram Perkins, Jno Paterson, Sr, John Palmer, John Pendall, Elijah Perkins, James Parker, Isaac Pinson, Benj Porter, David Prestly, Wm Petty, David Prestley, Wm Petty, Thomas Pace, Sol Palmer, Wm Paret, Samuel Philips, S R Pennington, Peter Peavy, Jno Peal, Dial Peavy, John Paulk, Cader Parvill, Josiah Peters, Jos Parker, David Phelps Sol Paremoore, Timothy Pitman, Charles Parker, Christopher Putnal, Josh Parnell, Benj Parnell, Benj Plater, Sergeant David Phelps, Lt Nathaniel Pearre, Jas Pugh, Josiah Powell, Jos Plummer, Sam'l Payne, Sam'l Payne, Jos Penny, Capt James Powell, Robert Powell, Elijah Peters, Thos Pugh, Peter Parris, Jno Pattillo, Abner Pannell, Jno Pruitt, Sam'l Pounds, Gideon Patterson, Geo Powell, John Peavy, John Perkins, Ben Peteete, Rich Parham, John Peters, John Porter, Moses Powell, Barnard Pace, Lewis Powell, Jos Pulliam, Robert Parratt, Abram Peavy, John Pryor, Rob Peteete, Ed Prather, Samuel Prather, Simon Porteus, Philip Pittman, Elijah Pew, Peter Perkins, Jno Potts, Samuel Phelps, Lackland Pheny, Jos Phillips, Josiah Phillips, Isham Phillips, Hillary Phillips, Dempsey Phillips, Rob Penett, Jno Powell, Benj Perkins, Isaac Perry, Lt John Parker, Micajah Paulk, John Patterson, Sr, Lt Thomas Porter, George Parker, Wilder Phillips, Geo Palmer, Jones Persons, Robert Parrish, Job Price, Allen Parker, Burrel Phillips, John Partin, Jos Pullome, John Peak, Wm Pulliam Wm Piuson, John Pearce, Jesse Pearce, Lt Wm Paxton, Lt Col Joseph Pannell, Lt Jno Price, Jos Plummer, Wm Pearce, Reuben Pounds, Jesse Pugh, John Pugh, John Penell, Lt Payne, Henry Parks, Jona Palmer, Slep Powell, Daniel Parker, Wm Perkins.

John Querns, (Kerns) Wm Queen, Rogers Quarles.

James Roe, John Rowby, David Rogers, Jose Rose, Brittain Rodgers, Samuel Rutherford, John Robertson, Wm Riley, Jos Richardson, Fred Runnells, Isaac Ramsay, Sr, Isaac Ramsay, Jr, Drury Roberts, John Rawlings, Henry Rose, Alex Roberson, Dr Wm Read, Jonathan Ragan, Felix Ragan, Mathew Rushing, Malachi Rushing, Jos Ryley, Wm Ramsay, Randall Ramsay, Abram Ravoh, Thomas Rose, Reuben Rogers, James Ratliff, Caleb Rozer, John Rozer, John Roberts, Felix Ragan, John Roberts, George Roseborn, Samuel Ramsey, John Ramsey, Timothy Rickerson, Richard Ryan, Samuel Reed, Wm Robertson, Spencer Reeves, Peter Roquemore, Absolom Redick, Wm Rayne,

Thomas Reeves, Rea, Thos Robard, Wm Roseboro, Samuel Roberson, Benj Riden, Coleman Runnels, Edward Rowzer, Enos Richardson, Howell Rowell, Ed Rowell, John Ray, Geo Runnells, Hamilton Runnells, Geo Ray, Zach Ray, Darby Riggans, Wm Repatoe, John Rhodes, Francis Runn, Isaac Rasor, Davie Roberson, Sylvanus Roberson, Marmaduke Richerson, John Ryan, John Ragan, Tunstall Roan, Isaac Rayfield, James Rock, John Rench, John Ramsey, Jr, Samuel Rowland, John W Rawling, David Rawling, David Roberson, Lt John Richie, Thos Ramling, Sergeant Wm Rogers, Walter Roe, John Rice, Wm Riddle, Nathan Rice, Jamet Raior, Ainos Rayer, Wm Russell, Jacob Richards, Walton Row, David Rice, Barnard Ryler, Z Robertson, James Reeves, Edward Rogers, Francis Roberts James Ryan, Jos Robertson, Wm Ray, Jesse Roundtree, Oliver Roundtree, Lt Evan Ragling, Richard Ryan, Geo Robinson, Berry Ray, James Roberts, James Roan, Andrew Rae, Peleg Rogers, Daniel Reeves, Absalom Reynolds, John Read, John Rose, Benj Ragland, Jonas Roberts, Miche Rafferty, Caleb Rozer, George Redding, Isaac Razer, Ambrose Ray, Jos S Riden, Randal Ramsay, John Ragan, Burwell Rogers, James Red, Sam'l Red, Walker Richardson, Jonathan Richardson, Nathaniel Rumhey, Amon Roberts.

Samuel Smith, Ebenezer Smith, Cornelius Smith, Simeon Smith, Nathan Smith, David Smith, Saml Smith, Nathl Smith, Thomas Smith, James Smith, Arthur Smith, Frances Smith, Moses Smith, John Smith, Simon Smith, Burrell Smith, John Smith, John Smith, Sr, St Sandal Smith, George Smith, Israel Smith, Redick Smith, Wm Sessoms, David Shaw, Adam Shaw, Wm Simmons, James Sneads, Thos Shaddock, Isaac Stewart, James Summerlin, Simon Salters, Micheal Sharp, David Shaffer, James Simpson, John Sheffield, Henry Shelton, Mann Sims, Mordeca Shefball, Robert Spurlock, Chas Sumons, Dave Sikes, Robert Sims, James Snelson, Seth Stockham, James Sneads, Wm Sheffie (Sheffield), St James Stedman, Isaac Skinner, Wm Spencer, Peter Strozier, Elth Slocomb, Wm Sullivan, John Stuart, Wm Shields, John Stallings, Andrew Shields, Saml Sinquefield, R Sallett, John Strong, Thos Shadereck, John Shields, John Stanford, Andrew Smithers, Dempsey Standley, David Shadden, Capt Daniel Settler, John Summers, Jno Stedom, Jr, George Stickes, Stephen Shepherd. John Stranger, Wm Scott, James Simmons, Thos Sutherlin, John Sedmon, Jr, David Stout, Jno Studstill, James Stram, John Suves, Saml Stirk, John Stevens, Dudley Snead, Isaac Sanders, Richard Simmons, Dempsey Summers, Samuel Summers, Jacob Sanders, Peter Stratt, John Stratt, Corneliuls Stratt, Peter Stratt, Charles Stone, Clement Stewart, Samuel Stewart, Jacob Summerford, Sr, Jacob Summerford, Jr, Philip Steed, Edward Steed, Joshua Stone, Thomas Shaw, Thomas Snelson, Sr,

Simon Smith, Thomas Stephens, John Shelby, Benj Stephens, James Stewart, David Sherrell, Fred Shick, lieutenant; Wm Sims, Bender Stocks, Jos Straten, Frances Stripling, Alex Chaplain Scott, Rudolph Strohaker, Thomas Simmons, Robert Smart, Ezekiel Stallings, Jno Shacklelord, Loveless Savage, Jas Stalling, James Stalling, lieutenant; Emanuel Sapp, Jno String, John Sharp, Wm Sheffel, Wm Shares, Samuel Stiles, Mash Sheffel, Jno Sigman, James Simmons, Wm Stewart, Wm Simmons, Jr, Jessee Stallings, Malbourn Simmons, Wm Stanfard, Jacob Smith, Stevens Simmons, Wm Sykes, Samuel Stafford, Philip Scott, Abraham Sanders, Samuel Stokes, Chas Stewart, Wm Stiff, Nathan Spikes, James Swan, James Simmons, Daniel Safford, Sol Strickland, Wm Sessums, Thos Salsberry, Ralph Sutton, Captain Wm Scott, Andrew Shields, Wm Stuart, Thos Shamson, Jr, Thos Shamson, Sr, Elias Spikes, Dill Smart, Saml Standford, Eph Strange, Col John Stuart, Philip Suton, Robt Stuart, John Sawyer, Jos Scott, Jos Shackleford, Benj Shepherd, Thos Stone, Mark Sanders, John Sills, Wm Satterwhite, Wm Summerlin, Saml Simpson, John Sheffield, John Sitton, David Snell, Daniel Shaw, Abrm Scott, Fred Stanley, Owen Sullivan, Benj Scott, Reuben Samford, John Sapp, Leonard Switzer, Michl Smalley, Dudley Sneed, John Shaw, Owen Shannon, Edward Story, James Swain, Jno Strength, Jno Simmons, Jas Stubbs, John Sedmon, Joshua Sharp, John Stringer, Henry Shelton, Nicolas Scurry, Jacob Stewart, John Sallis.

Wm Todd, Wm Tomson, Sr, Robert Tucker, Joel Tanner, Moses Tremble, Gilshot Thomas, Jno Tankerfield, Garrott Turman Thos Tucker, Sr, Reuben Thompson, George Tureman, Peter Thomas, Laban Thompson, Allen Thomas, Samuel Turner, Thos Tucker, Jr, George Tucker, Saml Thomas, Peter Thomas John Taylor, Q Traywick, Peter Turner, Dennis Turner, Thomas Townsend, David Thorn, Henry Taylor, John Trapp, Benj Thompson, Jno Thurman, Robert Thompson, Isham Thompson, Richard Tyner, Peter Thompson, Benj Thompson, Jr, David Thompson, James Thompson, Geo Tuhantz, George Threadgirl, Capt Andrew Templeton, Wm Thorn, Samuel Thornton, Henry Townsend, Jno Tindall, Geo Turner, Wm Thornton, Sampson Turner, John Turner, Randolph Taylor, Capt James Taylor, Thomas Taylor, Josiah Taylor, Henry Turner, Nicolas Turvisa, John Tanneyhill, Jesse Thompson, Alex Thompson, John Thompson, Zachariah Thompson, Denny Thompson, Capt John Thompson, David Tomlinson, Josiah Taylor, Robert Taylor, Jr, Edward Taylor, Dennis Trammell, Solomon Thornton, Wm Tindall, Henry Truhantry, Jos Tommice, James Treeman, John Tweddle, David Turner, Denny Tolar, James Tommeross, Wm Turley, Henry Tune, Absalom Thurman, Geo Tarvin, Gideon Thomas, Rich Tate, John Trueman, John Thayott, Benj Tanner,

Meredith Tanner, Benj Talbott, Thos Thornbey, Wm Trammell, Andrew Tate, Josh Tindell, Wm Treadwell, Jno A Thorpe, Geo Thompson, B Thomas, Pascall Tucker, Chas Turner, Brigadier-General Jno Twiggs, Jno A Treutlen, John Trul, Jonah Taylor, Wm Tanner, Henry Turknett, Robert Terrell, Benedick Truce, John Talbott.

Samuel Underwood, Ed Upton, Philip Upton, David Usher.

Cader Vann, Jas Vann, Sol Vickers, John Vickers, Thos Vickers, Patrick Vance, Wm Vaughn.

James Wood, Richard Wood, Geo Weritte, Jos Wise, Andrew Wilson, Robert Winn, Stephen Wright, Dred Wilder, Jno Wyche, Daniel Walicon, John Wilcoxson, John Wade, Henry Wade, John Webb, John White, Jas Williams, Thomas Williams, Benj Waller, Wm Waller, Benj Wells, Dr. Humphrey Wells, An Walthour, Jno Winningham, Jno Palmer Wasome, Isaac Wright, John Whitecel, Edward Walsh, Captain George Walton, Robert Walton, Richard Wood, Joshua Wood, Robt Williamson, Lt-Col Micajah Williamson, David Welborne, Carroll Williams, Habakkuk Wright, Wm Walker, Isaac Walker, Jr., Isaac Walker, Sr., Thos Wooten, Robt Wooten, Robt Wilson (Clarke), Robt Wilson (Lee), Peter Winn, Jonathan Webster, James Webster, Walton Whateley, Samuel Whateley, John Way, John Way, Jr., Ed Way, William Wilkins, Absalom Wallis, Charles Wallis, Robert Willis, Jonathan Whitemore, Tom Wilder, Charles Wilder, Jeremiah Wells, Maj Joseph Woodruff, Mesheck Willis, Joseph Willis, Robert Willis, Samuel Whately, Zackariah Wheeler, Thos Wagnon, Chas Ward, Thomas White, Nicolas White, Benj Winn, John Winn, James Wise, John Wilkerson, Wm Wilkerson, Samuel Wilson (Clarke), Samuel Wilson (Lee), Capt John Wilson, Henry Ware, Chas Williams, John Williams, Joshua Williams, John Wilsher, Wm Wildair, Edward Walker, Nicolas Welch, Samuel Walker, Samuel Whitaker, Jesse Warnock, Thomas Woodworth, Ed Weathers, Austin Whitton, Henry Wood, Nehemiah Wade, Wm Webb, Geo Williams, Sam'l Williams, Henry Wagoner, William Way, Joseph Way, Lt John Wilson, Jas Wilson, Capt Wm Walker, Capt James White, Jesse Webb, Richard Willey, John Ware, Jos Winn, Daniel Wallicon, Arthur Ware, Wm White, Wm Wise, Hezekiah Wheat, Mesheck Wright, Robert Wells, Joshua Wynn, Newell Walton, Littleton Williamson, Samuel West, Jose Way, Stephen Westbrook, Wm Walker, Robt Walden, Wm Webster, Jno Welseley, Wm Whare, James Wright, John West, Demsey White, Tom Wise, Cornelius Whittingham, Jene Walten, Jere Welsher, Chas Williamson, Lieut Thomas Wooten, Jas Waters, John Wiggans, Jas Wallis, Gabriel Wilkins, Edwin Whately, John Whitesides, Thomas Wilburn, Burton Williams, Brittain Willis, Geo Wagoner, Geo Walton, Caleb Welch, Micajah Wilder, Joseph White, Ed Wilburn, James Ware, Frederick Williams, Leven Watson, Wm Willoughby, Benj Webster, Abner Webster, Thos Webster, Wm Wallace, Joseph Wood, James Wood, Capt Edward Wood, Major Ed Welch, Patrick Walsh, Micajah Williamson, Geo Watson, Jacob Watson, John Watson, Benj Watson, Thos Watson, Willis Watson, Jacob Wells, Joseph Wells, Capt Hezekiah Wade, Jno Wilkins, David Wilkins, John Williams, Butler Williams, Edward Williams, Nath'l Williams, John Wall, Francis Wall, David Wall, Nicolas Ware, Sylvanus Walker, Wm Wiggins, Jas Wood, Christopher Wood, Abraham Wood, John Wheat, Jos Waller, Robt Whitton, Jos Welch, Rawley Waters, Robert Wilson, Joseph Williams, John Williams, Christopher Wood, Abraham Wood, Samuel Ward, Wm Wallace, John Wikeman, John Wauden, Wm Wagoner, Wm Wallace, Sylvanus Walker, Jas West, Jas Weatherford, John Webster, Jesse Winfrey, Ed Wourd, Benj Wourd, Richard Williamson, James Wood, Amen Watley, Wooten Watley, Willis Watley, Sherwood Watley, Abednego (Benego) Wright, Jesse Welsher, Jordan Wells, John Wells, Jos Walker, John Wisenor, Philip Whitton, David Wilson, Hugh Wilson, Col Geo Walton, Lt Geo Walton, William Walton, Brittain Wallis, Jno Wereat, Charles Waters, Geo Wyche, Sam'l Wyche, Joseph Willis, Curtis Welborn, Curtis Welborn, Jr., Jacob Wareman, Philip Wilfred, Rich Whitt, Josh Woods, Joshua Woods, Jr., Hugh Ward, John Ward, Geo Watts, Jacob Watts, James Wagner, James Wooten, Isham Wheelis, William Wright, Malica Wilder, Jesse Womack, Rich Woods, James Wallis, Joseph Willis, Lewis Whilons, Adam Williamson, John Windfield, John Willingham, John Wright, Rich Walden, Zach Williams, Willis Walden, Benjamin Welch, William Wheeler, John Whately, Lieut J P Wagon.

Lieut Dave Young, Jon Young, Edward Young, Isham Young, John Young, Jr., John Young, Sr., Wren Young, James York, John York, Peter Youngblood, John Youngblood, Sr., James Youngblood, John Youngblood, Wm Younger, Littleton Yarborough, Thomas Yarborough, John Yankerfield, Peter Yates.

Jacob Zinn, Nath'l Zettler.

SOLDIERS PAID IN MONEY.

John Bird, Richard Barnes, Wm Barnes, Benj Bird, Rich Bazlewood, Moses Brannon, Samuel Butts, William Butler, Edmond Butler.

Peter Clowers, James Carter.

Wm Duncan, Elijah Douthan, Hardy Davis, Henry Dulins, Thomas Duncan.

Lt David Franklin, Lt Thos Franklin, Thos Ferrell, Jno Farr, Benj Farr, Henry Fowler, Peter Fowler.

Lt Henry Gauze, Sam'l Giles, Jas Gillons.

Robert Huggins, John Howard, Wm Howard, Stephen Hawkins, Wm Hamilton.

John Johnson, Jesse Jones.

Daniel Kitley.

Thomas Linley, John Loyd, James Loyd, James Lamar, Wm Lowe.

Thomas Masney.

Joshua Powell, Wm Pritchett, John Pritchett, Henry Persons, Sam'l Persons, Edward Pratt.

John Swan, Peyton Smith, Samuel Simmerlin, Dunsey Simmerlin, Thos Stockwell, Thomas Smith, Jno Summerlin, Peter Stots, Nathan Spikes, Wm Sinkfield, Wm Simmons, R Summerlin, Geo Spurlock, John Swan.

James Wood, Jacob Wells, Thos Worth, John Williams.

BOUNTY WARRANTS.

Robert Allen, Alex Armstrong, Edward Arnet, Bozeman Adair, Solomon Arnold, Matthew Anderson, John Angling, Capt Robt Anderson, Richard Aycock, Sol Arnold, Abraham Arnold, Levy Akridge, Jno Adams, Davis Akridge.

Lt and Ad Benj Bragg, Daniel Bruce, Ed Burke, Jere Barron, Charles Burke, Merander Berryhill, James Brooks, Capt Reuben Bennett, Prov Bridges, Lemuel Black, Capt Thomas Bornan, Thornberry Bowling, Peachy Bledsoe, Wm Bryant, Elijah Brockman, Ward Bruce, Henry Boles, John Bulloch, H Thomas Brown, Wm Brooks, Jonathan Burgess, Geo Bailey, Peter Bailey, Bledsoe Brockman, Rich Beasley, John Browning, John Bradley, Zechariah Bell, John Ball, Charles Burges, Harris Beasley, Jos Burgess, John Baker, Lemuel Brown, Casewell Brand.

Wm Clack, Wm Cochran, Thos Carter, Philip Cooper, James Clack, Wm Cronch, Jas Cox, Elisha Colbert, Wm Cowles, Joseph Colley, Ed Colwell, Sampson Culpepper, James Collins, Wm Cottingham, Caleb Cob, John Crouch.

James Davis, Jos Dobbs, James Dounnan, John Diamond, John DeGraffenried, Lewis Davis, Ishmael Dunn, Lt Jas Davison, Lt Isaac Daniel, Wm Daggett, Nimrod Dickens, John Danube.

Isaiah Eiland, Thos Elliot, Jno Easton, Willis Edwards, Thos Elkins, Henry English, Wm Ellis, Wm Edmondson, Roderick Early, Lt Jesse Evans, Wm Epps, John Eton, David Elder, Obadiah Echols, Wilder Early, Mitler Echols.

Thomas Franklin; Wm Franklin, James Fox, John Finch, John Furlow, Jas Ferguson, Roswell Freeman, Jas Griffith, Jas Glass, Wm Gresham, Laban Freeman.

Luke Gibson, Giles Ginnings, Wm Glenn, Geo Griggs, Lt-Col

Glascock, Major Ambrose Gordon, Wm Green, Wm Green, Sr., Sam'l Garner, Micajah Gnu, Jno Glen.

Hugh Hatherby, Capt Isham Hendon, Robert Haines, Ward Hudson, Frances Holland, Johnson Hendon, Frances Howard, Andrew Hartsfield, Michael Harris, Jos Hammock, Allen Harrison, Jere Harrison, Martin Hince, Jacob Hilby, Wm Hinton, Jno Hannah, Edward Harris, Wm Halliday, Capt Wm Harley, Theophilus Hill, Lt Sampson Harris, Michael Huntsman, Archibald Hudson, John Huff, Wm Hanson, Ansel Harper, Sam'l Hopkins, Jno Holeman, Duc Huggins.

John Ilas.

Jesse Johnson, Wm Johnson, Wm James, Jno Jeardean (Gerdine), Lt Edward Jones, Jas Johnson, Wm Johnson, Wallis Johnson, Abram Johnson, Jos Jones, Rich Jones.

David Kennan.

Jos Legit, Wm Lay, Wm Lumpkin, Wm Landrum, Capt James Landrum, Josiah Landrum, Henry Ledbetter, Wm Longstreet, Ansella Leigh, Moses Loyd, Jas Langford, Lt Geo Law, Charles Lane, Thos Lockette.

John Moon, Sharod McCartie, Jas Moore, Andrew Mays, Saml May, B Mathews, Bailes McDoreman, Richard Maxwell, Rich Mathews, Needham McElroy, Thos McEwin, Rowell McCirce, Gable Moffett, Alexander Moore, Jas Minis, Jno Middleton, Wm Mitchell, Martin Moore, Thos Mathews, Minor Mead, Saml Montcrief, Alex McMullen, Jno Mathews, Matthew Martin, Abednego Moore, Charles McKenney, Jonas Meador, Joel Meador, Garrett Morris, Burwell Mathews, Bailess McDoreman, Rich Mathews, Needham McElroy.

Jonathan Norton, Jas Norton, Jos Nixon, Jno Nixon, Mathias Newlin, Lt Wm Norton, Lt Richard Nalls.

Jonathan Oakes, John Olive, Christopher Orr, John Orr, Thos Owens.

John Pounds, Wm Parker, Hail Pain, Jno Powell, Josiah Patrick, Nicolas Poss, Frederick Pattison, Wm Porsten, Overton Phillips, Major Pullens, ——— Patrick, Capt Thos Patton, Capt Jno Pope, Lt Moses Potts.

Jeremiah Richards, Allen Richardson, Green Runnells, Daniel Rainey, Jos Rosberry, Jno Rainey, John Ross, Major Ryan, Jacob Reed, James Reddy, Samuel Robertson, Richard Rafferty, George Russell.

Joseph Samuels, Sherod Stroud, Robert Strong, Jesse Stirley, John St. John, Wm Smith, Owen Stroud, Reuben Stewart, Wm Stephens, John Simpson, Thos Sanson, Jas Simmons, Balson Strawn, Thompson Stone, Jabe Smith, Jas Stallings, Wm Smith, Jno Sandell, Wm Searce, Joshua Sykes, Wm Smith, Jno Stunbanks, Davis Sneid, Jno Stroman, Philip Stroud.

Richard Thompson, David Thrasher, Spencer Traywick, Alexander Terry, John Truball, Thomas Truall, Woodward Tucker, Thomas Terrell, Robt Toombs.

Thos Varner, Matthew Varner.

Wm Williamson, Moses Wilkes, Jas Winters, John Ward, Levi Webb, Peter Williamson, Boling Whittle, W G Wright, James Wallis, Thos Wade, Jno Wood, John Watson, John Wiatt, Ethelbert Wood, Jas Wood, Robt Whelton, Thos Wilcox, Jas Williford, Lt Thomas Watkins, Jesse Willingham, John Winn, Lt Richard Wooten, Emanuel Wambersie, Jno Walton, Charles Ward, Robt Watkins, Captain Charles Williamson, John Williams, Capt James Wood.

Henry Young, Leonard Young, Sanford Young.

Joshua Zoobers (Subers).

In this list are those whose grants are soldiers' grants, but other than this there is no positive proof that they were in the army:

James Alford, Baker Ayers.

John Beckham, Isaac Betsall, Jno Barclay, Joseph Ballard, Wm Burford, Jno Bush, Wm Brigg, Geo Bonner, Rich Burner, Heirs of John Bennett, Gideon Bussey, James Bowie, Robert Braswell, Andrew Borland.

Larkin Cleveland, James Collier, Edward Collier, Christopher Clark, Thomas P Carnes, Zach Cox, Bolling Clark, Samuel Camp, Robt Creswell, Robt Curry, Richard Call, B Curton, Jesse Conwell, Abednego Chandler, John W Connelly, Vincent Chance, Peter Carnes, Wm Crosby, Wm Cruddy.

Jeremiah Duck, Thos Dalton, Ambrose Dary, Michael Dickson, William Diamond, Robert Dixon, Peter DeBosk, David Dickson, David Dicks, Elijah Dounaphan.

Jonas Fouche, Peter Fair, George Fluker, Thomas Fail, Isham Fuller.

Charles Gilbert, Theod Goodwynn, Gilbert Grier, Joshua Gray, Daniel Green, Archd Gresham, Wm Guy, Thos Greers, George Galphin, Henry Gotcher, Edward Goode, Richd Gascoign.

Briggs Hobson, James Hodges, Jos Haughton, Wm Hay, Thos Holden, Samuel Haurst, Caleb Howell, George Harper, Nathan Harris, Jno Harrington, Ambrose Holliday, Nathl Hicks, Abimlech Hawkins, Chas Headspeth, Wm Hunt, Isham Huckably, Wm Hammett, Ed Hicks, Jos Humphreys, Fitzmaurice Hunt, Richard Hamlin, Hardy Hinton, Sampson Harris, Benj Hubbard, William Hightower, Henry Houston, Newell Housley, Absolam Hooper, Jonathan Holly, Jno Harrington, Benj Harvey, Jas Harnett, Hall Hudson, John Heatly, James Hutchinson.

Nathan Johnson, Wm Jameson, Chas Jones, John Jack, Abram Jackson, James Jackson, Sam'l Jordan.

John King, Ed Kenny, Lem Kieth, John Kieth, James Kenrick.

Rich Lockhart, James Lindsay, Joshua Lee, Daniel Longstreet, Wyatt Langford, John Loud, Wm Lewis, Wm Longstreet, Wm Lord, John Leonard.

Wm McCracken, John Morrison, James Madison, John McDonald, Jacob Martin, James McCutchin, Mordacai Moore, Jno Meanly, Shadrack McGee, John McConnell, John Mays

Geo Nailor, Thomas Nelson, Wm Niblack, Geo Newman, Thomas Neal.

Josiah Osgood.

Moses Payne, John Pack, John Phillips, Henry Pittman, Wm Pollard, Daniel Spinkston, Robert Purtin, John Pierson, Wylie Pope, Job Price, Daniel Parker, John Pickerton.

Benj Reese, David Russell, Geo Reeves, Amon Roberts, John Robinson, Jacob Reddick.

Robert Savage, Lewis Solomon, Andrew Sturgis, Charles Shepherd, Burney Simmeron, Micheal Shelman, Ezekiel Stallings, John E Smith, Geo Segar, Wm Shields, John Sebech, Wm Strong, John Shelman, Robert Singleton, Wm Sartain, Jos Sherrard, Wm Shaw, Moses Scarborough, John Shuffle.

Jesse Talbatt, Mark Tarpley, Moses Trimble, David Thurman, Asa Turner, Robert Tate.

Thomas Vining.

Picton Wyatt, Wm Wheeler, John Watts, John Warren, John Waldon, Chanet Wallis, Benj Ward, Sion Webb, Sherard Wise, Josiah Wood, Wm Wilborme, Micajah Wallis, Cammell Wallis, Benj Wilson, Thos Wadsworth.

Bartholomew Zackery, Geo Zeigler.

NOTE.—There are doubtless errors in the above list. The names as they have been copied from time to time have no doubt been often misspelled and sometimes the names changed. The name Housley is Ousley. The name Shuffle is Sheffield. I have, however, tried to give them as they appear in the Secretary of State's office.

NAMES OMITTED FROM WASHINGTON COUNTY.

Clement Nash, Thomas Neal, 1785; Benj Nichols, 1785: Geo Nede, 1785; Thomas Napier, 1786; Rene Napier, 1786; David Neal, 1787; Thomas Neal, 1788; John Neeley, 1789; Thos Neeley, 1789; Nehemiah Night, 1790; Elisha Neal, 1790; John Nutt, 1791; Benj Nicolson, 1791; John Newnham, 1793; Nall Martin, 1797; Wm Nelson.

WILKES COUNTY.

There are five manuscript folios in the Clerk's office in Washington containing plats of the various grants of land made in that county before the century began From those books I copied the list found in the body of the book. On comparing that list with the one in the Secretary of State's office I found some discrepancies. I have therefore decided to add to the appendix a copy of the list in the Secretary's office. The old clerks spelt proper names phonetically and those who examine the lists must draw their own conclusions.

1784 to 1800.—Alex Autry, Sam'l Alexander, John Anderson, Wm Anderson, Rich Aycock, James Adams, Jas Aycock, Joseph Allen, Thos Avent, Hannah Anderson, Arthur Atkins, Wm Anglin, Isaac Avera, Thos Ayres, Reuben Allen, Gideon Anderson, Thomas Ansley, Jacob Autry, Abr'm Ayres, George Alexander, James Allen, Jno Ashley, Richard Austin, Jas Alford, Jno Appling, Jno Austin, Martha Appling, Andrew Armor, David Anglin, Jno Autry, Arnold Atkins, James Awick, Ann Arnott, Lemuel Atkinson, Nath'l Allen, John Armstrong, Jno Adams.

1786.—Isaac Alexander, Martha Arthur, Wm Arthur, Abner Adkins, Wm Ayres, Benj Allen.

1787.—David Adams, Benj Ashworth, Wm Aycock, Henry Anglin, Thomas Ansley, Micajah Anthony, Jno Ashmore, Wm Allison, John Aylor, Wm Ayres, Asa Atkins, Wm Arnell, Abel Alexander, Robert Armstrong, Thos Ashley, Wm Aaron, Mathew Arthur, Richard Anderson, Benson Allenthorpe, Sam'l Avaid, Jas Abbott, Joseph Abbott, Sam'l Akin, Edmund Alexander, Ezekiel Alexander, Wm Averett.

1798 to 1800.—Reuben Allen, Wm Adair, Jos Anthony, Joshua Agee.

Absalom Biddle, Chas Burks, Thomas Brown, And Burns, Margt Brady, Step Bishop, Wm. Byers, Heirs of John Buckhalter, Wm Brantley, Jno Black, Rich Bellamy, Geo Barber, Jas Bishop, Wm Boner, Charity Bowers, Ed Black, Nath Bulloch, Christopher Blanton, Henry Bussey, Jno Banks, And Bell, Jno Borin, Thos Bethany, Jos Busson, Jere Bentley, R Bennett, Jona Beard, Josh Bradley, Jno Ball, Balam Brantley, Abraham Booth, Jeffry Barksdale, Jno Bates, Jno Barnard, Jack Barnard, Wm Barnard, Ruth

Bonner, Rebecca Bonner, Joel Brooks, Jno Beal, Job Brooks, Providence Brooks, Jos Brown, Chas Bonner, John Bently, Isham Barnett, Saml Barnett, Nathan Barnett, Benj Bridges, Isham Bayless, Nathan Bostwick, Henry Beall, Jacob Beall, Duncan Bohannon, Charity Bowen, Jesse Bond, Arthur Butler, Mordicai Baldwin, John Buchannon, Absolom Baker, John Bankston, Wm Baldwin, John Barksdale, Robert Bonner, Eleanor Brown, Richard Barefield, Jno Burney, Arnold Bruce, Thomas Burton, Jno Banks, John Boyd, Thomas Brantley, Isaac Busson, George Brewer, Wm Berry, George Bagby, James Bentley, John Brownfield, George Brewer, Nathan Barnett, Wm Buckhalter, Bird Braswell, Sol Barsfield, Jesse Barnett, Saml Braswell, Alex Brown, Philip Brantley, Wm Bishop, Absolom Beardin, John Barnett, James Boren (Boring), Obadiah Bosworth, Jeremiah Boggass, John Bracken, Daniel Burnett, Robert Bryan, John Barton, Wm Bawls, John Bush, Wm Buchanon, Wm Bradford, Joel Butler, Chas Burke, Isaac Briggs, Christopher Baker, Spencer Branham, Jacob Bankston, Daniel Bankston, John Benson, Archer Burton, Medel Buckhalter, Edmond Beard, Martha Benson, John Barnard, Francis Beard, John Bradshaw, Wm Barnett, Nathan Barnett, Jno Broughton, Richard Burton, Edward Butler, Bland Blackley, Isaac Bush, Azariah Baily, Charles Bedingfield, Wm Best, Francis Baty, Absolom Bedell (see Biddle), Jos Boon Isaac Briggs, Robert Barton, Thos Rice Brown, Lamentation Brazelle, Wm Bostick. Wm Braden, James Bailey, John Bailey, John Bohannon, John Barnett, Wm T Booker, Louis Bobo, Isaac Ball, Thos Brannon, Charles Bonner, John Burke, John Brownfield, Paty Burlison (heirs of), Mial Barnett, Frances Baldwin, John Bracken, Isaac Briggs, Wm Ball, Robert Boyd, John Brazell, James Bush, George Brewer, Nath'l Bradford, Thomas Burton, Zach Butler, Robert Bartlett, Sessmus Black, James Bradshaw, Richard Beasley, Benj Blake, Mial J Barnett, Nath'l Bridges, John Burnett, Wm Blake, Jas Butler, Reuben Blanchard, Bedford Brown, Zach Butler, Chas Burke, John Brown, Jos Blackwell, Robert Barnett, Frank Beasley, Littleberry Bostwick, Thos Brannon, Balam Bentley, Benj. Brown, Hezekiah Bailey, Jeremiah Baggess, Alex Brown, Reuben Ballard, Peter Bankston, Prudence Banen, Sam'l Braswell, Robert Burke, Mordacai Baldwin, Nath'l Bulloch, Thos Burke, David Bryan, Philemon Bird, James Brooks, Andrew Bell, Bird Braswell. James Bibb, Thomas Burke, Jos Beasley, James Brooks, Wm Best, Thomas Burke, Peachey Bletcher, Wm Brewer, James Bridges, Archold Borden, David Besey, Jacob Bobbett, Acquilla Barrons, Wiseman Broges, John Bush, Mary Burgamy, Jerse Bentley, Andrew Brown, James Heins Bentley.

Benj Catching, Meredith Catching, Seymour Catching, Joseph Catching, Daniel Coleman, John Cunningham, Elijah Clark, Hart Champion, Ed Cartledge, Samuel Crockett, Nathl Coates,

Anthony Cooper, Nash Cloud, Jeremiah Cloud, Rachel Cook, Lester Coats, Lewis Clarke, Jno Castleberry, Rich'd Carlton, Josiah Carter, Philip Combs, John Clements, Cornelius Cochran, Wm. Candler, Richard Call, Job Calloway, Michel Coats, Elias Cozart, John Conner, Samuel Creswell, Dan'l Conner, Bright Collins, John Clowers, Joshua Cook, Thomas Cook, Mary Cook, Dudley Cook, Francis Cook, Sarah Cook, Christopher Clark, Jno Cole, Drury Cade, Wm Coats, Wm. Campbell, Michael Culp, Henry Carr, Lewis Clarke, Thos Carson, Jos Carson, Adam Carson, David Carson, Hugh Campbell, James Cone, Spencer Crane, Benj Croley, Thos Carter, Daniel Connell, Zach Cocks, Jno Calloway, Henry Candler, Anthony Crumley, John Carson, Francis Calloway, George Cathorn, Wm. Cunningham, Drury Cook, John Cranch, David Clark, Edward Cowan, Ambrose Crawford, James Clark, Abia Clay, Edward Callahan, Jacob Colson, Robert Christmas, Jno Cargile, Charles Cargile, Susannah Calvert, Roger Casey, Wm Chapman, Stanley Crews, John Combs, Ambrose Cordin, John Chandler, Robt Cowden, Robt Cannon, Peter Clymer, Robert Chambers, John Crane, Jesse Clay, Timothy Covington, Moses Collins, Wm Caldwell, Daniel Clowers, George Carr, James Cockersham, George Cooper, Thomas Carter, Peter Curtright, Francis Coulter, John Crunnenpeck, Wm Carden, Lemuel Crawford, Alex Cumming, Jos Camp, Charles Carroll, Bolling Clark, John Cain, Thomas Curry, Franklin Cunningham, John Crutchfield, George Clancy, John Crawley, Mark Cook, John Coleman, Jos Crockett, Conrad Cornilison, Wm Cunningham, James Caldwell, Lewis Clark, Ed Collier, John Cox, Sydner Cosby, John Chappel, John Colley, John Cooke, Philip Connoway, Philip Combs, Thomas Coyle, James Ceath, Thomas Connell, Rachel Cobb, Abial Cobb, John Clements, Brantley Cox, Wm Clendennin, Wm Carr, Robert Carr, Sam'l Camp, John Carr, Heirs of Edmond Catching, Ezekiel Cloud, Robert Caruthers, Henry Castleberry, Matthew Clendennin, Barland Cureton, Drury Cade, John Copeland, Wm Cocks, Thomas Coleman, Wm Clack, James Coiley, Wm. Cassells, Martha Cartledge, George Cockburn, John Course, Edward Collier, Lettice Cleghorr, Peter Castleberry, Henry Clements, Wm Campbell, James Cottonhead, Jesse Chappell, Jos Crockett, Thomas Carven, Wm Crew.

Absalom Davis, Augustine Davis, Henry Downs, Jonathan Downs, William Downs, Robert Day, Wm Daniel, Geo Darden, Joel Doss, Margt Davidson, Jere Duck, Wm Dean, James Davis, Wiley Davis, Wm Davis, Geo Dooly, Margt Dawster, Jacob Dansby, Isaac Dennis, John Dennis, Benj Davis, James Denley, (Dannely) Richard Davenport, Thomas Daniel, Wm Davenport, Thos Duke, Samuel Davis, John Davis, Joseph Davis, Lewis Coxen Davis, Wm Davenport, Nehemiah Dunn, Jno L Dickson, John Donaway, George Dawson, Henry Duncan, Wm Dudley Susan-

nah Davis, Martin Deadwyler, James Dowdell, Geo Douglas, Jno Douglas, Reuben Dejarnett, John Dameron, Samuel Duncan, Isaac Dennis, Wm Davidson, David Davis, John Doolin, Stephen Doss, John Darden, Jno Doss, John Dickson, John Decker, Jere Duckworth, Wm Delany, Wm Douglas, Charles Duke, John Dobbs, Wm Daniel, David Duncan, Thos Dalton, Robert Dick, George Douglas, Buckner Dukes, John Dickens, Joe Doughty, Jesse Dodd, John Dysert, Wm Dunn, Stephen Doss, Charles Dean, Wm Dismukes, Martin Dawson, Charles Dean, John Dayner, Jno Davidson, John Dooly, Silas Dixon, Henry Dukes, Nathaniel Day, Brook Davis, Gilbert DeBarbearange.

Wm Evans, David Evans, James Easter, James C Edwards, Peter Edwards, Wm Ellis, Jacob Early, James Elliot, Wm Elliot, Francis Edmonds, Mary Eades, Ed Eckles, Jacob Elsberry, Hugh Exton (Ector), Benj Elliott, Jos Eason, Hugh Egur (Ector), Neemiah Edge, David Eberhardt, Abram Eades, Wm Embry, Lewis Elliott, John Embry, Wm Edwards, Arden Evans, Andrew Evans, John Embry, Absalom Eiland, Richard Eubanks, Reuben Edwards, David Ervin (Irwin), John Eads, Jesse Eads, James Elrod, John Edmondson, Jeffry Early, John Edwards, Jos East, George Elliott.

Ignatius Few, Benj Few, Wm Few, James Freeman, Holman Freeman, James Finley, John Freeman, Nathan Fowler, Samuel Fugate, Owen Fluker, John Farmer, Wm Fitzgerald, Andrew Frazer, Arthur Fort, John Friel, Samuel Foster, M H Foster, Jas Foster, John Farmer, Phillis Flanagan, P Favior, Alex Foster, Jno Fielding, John Fling, Paremon Floyd, Jas Fuller, Robert Flournoy, John Fullilove, Ephraim Farr, Bartholomew Farrow, John Fielder, John Fuller, Thos Forrister, Robert Forsyth, Thomas Florence, Wm Fletcher, John Farrall, Jacob Fresh, John H Foster, Wm Fort, Thomas Findley, Wm Finley, John Folsom, David Fulton. John Flemming, John Firgus, David Felps, Mathew Fulgham, John Fuller, Wm Finch, Ephraim Fair.

Henry Graybill, Jos Griffin, Thos Glascock, John Gamble, Jno Giles, James Graves, Jos Gray, Samuel Gilmore, Thomas Grigg, Elizth Griffin, Stephen Gilmore, John Gilmore, Wm Greene, Thos Greer, John Gibson, Lewis Graves, Richard Gray, Josiah Gates, Jos Gibbons, James Gillaspie, Robert Guttory, Stephen Garner, John Griffith, Daniel Gunnells, Wm Glass, Isaac Gorley, John Graves, Daniel Grant, Thos Gregg, Chan Grazeal, Charles Gilham, Robert Graves, Randall Gibson, Henry B Gibson, John George, Aaron Grier, James Green, Wm Glenn, Duke Glenn, George Gray, Henry B Gibson, Steven Gafford, Wm Graves, Jonathan Goodsby, Joshua Glass, Geo Gresham, Richard Graves, Thomas Glascock, Thomas Grimes, Robert Guttery, Daniel Gaines, Isaiah Goolsby, Samuel Gardner, Burges Goldsby, James Goldsby, Abe Gonder, George Gray, John Golson, Thomas

Grantham, Humphrey Gilmore, George Griffith, Jno Gunnells, John Garrett, Wm Gilbreath, Wm Golden, Wm Glover, Jas Glover, Benj Green, Peter Goldsby, John Gresham, William Gary, Thomas Gorden, Jas Gray, Thomas Gilbert, Philip Guise, Francis Grubbs, John Granade, John Grantham, Nicolas Guise, John Guise, Miles Gathright, Wm Graves, Humphrey Gilmore, John Griffey, Jas Gray, Benj Goss, Wm Graves, Henry Greene, Thomas Giles, James Greene, Francis Gartrell, Alex Gordon, Richard Goldsby, James Gilmore, Richard Golding, Francis Gideon, Samuel Gilbert, William Gamack, Amos Green, Robert Griffith, Wm Gearlin, Humphrey Graves, Henry Gaines, John Greene, Rogers Green, Susannah Green, Abel Gowers.

James Harvey, Thomas Harvey, John Harvey, Michael Harvey, James Hogg, Steven Heard, John Heard, John Holliday, Margt Holliday, Robert Harper, Nathaniel Howell, Charles Heard, James Hardwick, Thomas Harper, Evan Harvey. Walton Harris, Rich Heard, Sam'l Hawkins, Jno Hammett, Wm Hammett, Andrew Hambleton, Sam'l Hunter, Benjamin Howard, Sam'l Hix, Churchwell Hooker, John Hubbard, John Holmes, Sam'l Hook, Wm Heard, Jacob Hambleton, Mark Halliman, Cuthbert Hudson, Mathew Hubbard, Asa Hooks, Julius Howard, Jos Henderson, Jas Hill, Wm Hughes, Barnard Heard, Jas Howell, Thos Hawkins, Stephen Hogge, Jacob Hinley. Wm Holiday, Jno Harris, Sam'l Harper, Mary Hollingsworth, Richardson Hunt, Sam'l Houstoun, John Hurley, Nath'l Harvill, Thos Hill, Wm Hightower, Wm Housley (Ousley), James Hines, Buckner Harris, David Harris, Ambrose Holliday, Andrew Hamilton, Jno Hausey, Jas Hart, Luck Hamilton, Rich'd Hamblin, Godfrey Hartsfield, Charles Hudson, Henry Hunt, Fitzmaurice Hunt, Eliz'th Huff, George Hamilton, Edward Hagan, Robt Hammock, Wm Hawthorn, Thos Habvard, John Hutchings, Abram Hill, Benj Hubbard, Jno T Harper, Thos Holliday, Ed Harper, John Hammock, George Hammock, John Hightower, John Harris, Benedick Hammock, Wm Hutchinson, Magt Holland, Charles Holland, Abraham Holliman, Isaac Hill, Sam'l Hart, Thos Herndon, George Heard, Tharp Huse, Sam'l Hoff, Sylvester Hammond, Benj Hart, Edward Harrison, Henry Haines, Charles Hardman, Uriah Hardman, Jno Henley, John Harrison, Jno Hill, Dalzell Hunter, Archibald Hodge, Isaac Hodge, Benj Higginbottom, Jos Higginbottom, Mary Hudson, Sam'l Hunter, Susan Hammett, Drury Hearn, Churchill Hooper, John Harrington, Wm Higginbottom, David Hillhouse, Thos Hintch, Francis Hawkins, Dan'l Hollifield, Robinson Hendon, Job Hinton, Rich'd Holmes, Jessee Hooper, Abram Heath, John Hodges, David Howell, Francis Higginbottom, Henry Hill, Rich'd Hilliard, Hillery Hendricks, Wm Hodge, Wm Hansard, George Herndon, Dennis Henby, Job Hannah, Thos Hall, Thos Hampton, Nath'l

Hunt, Baird Hinman, Moses Hay, Moses Hill, Wm Herritt, Jas Hannah, Michel Hinsman, Moses Herring, John Harrington, Nicolas Hawkins, Alex Hughman.

1789—Isham Huscabee, Micajah Hinton, Adam Hardin.

1790—Isaac Hardy, Peter Hodo, John Howell, Geo Hall, Lambeth Hopkins, Ezekiel Harling, Wm Hardman, Thos Harben, Thos Horton, Benj Hambricks, George Hamilton, Joshua Hale, Jessee Hale, Wm Hay, Abram Hilton, John Hollingshead, Thos Hawthorn.

1790-1800—James House, Theophilus Hill, Asaul Harber.

1790—David Holliman, George Harris, Rich Hartsfield, Thos Hughsmith, Jessee Heard, Rhesa Howard, Wm Hatcher, Steven Hansberger, Wm Hatchcock, Michel Harbuck, Timothy Holtzclaw, James Hughes, Wm Hughes, David Henan.

John Jones, Edward Jones, Wm Jackson, Richard Jones, Sarah James, Daniel Jackson, Priscella Jones, Sterling Jenkins, Peter Jackson, Joseph Jackson, Charles Jackson, Hugh Jones, Jona Jones, Jno H Johnson, Wm Johnston, Daniel Johnston, Wm Jarvis, Philip Jones, John Johnston, Robert Jenkins, Moses Jones, Reuben Jackson, George Johnson, Abr'm Islands, Wm Johnson, Nathan Johnson, Wm Jones, Nathan Jones, Needham Jerninghan, Lucy Jackson, Absolom Jackson, Russell Jones, Marshall Jones, James Irwin, Thomas Johnson, Alex Johnson, Miles Jennings, Davarix Janatt (Deveraux), Amasa Jackson, Zach Jordan, Joshua Jordan, Charles Jordan, Solomon Jordan, Nathan Jordan, Baxter Jordan, Jacob Irish, David Irwin, Joshua Jones, Robert Jamison, Willis Johnson, Isaac Jones, Jacob Johnston, Jno H Johnston, Henry Josey, John Jennings, Jacob C John, Absolom Jackson, James Jack, John Johnson, George Johnson, Enoch James, Warren Judeath, Caleb Johnson, Benj Jackson, Reuben Johnston, Thomas Jones, Wilson Johnson, Henry Jones, Caleb Jennings, James Jennings.

Randorp Key, Jonathan Key, John King, Joel King, Andrew King, Jacob Kimbrough, Wm Kimbrough, Thos Kemp, Jno Kelly, Edward Keating, John Keating, James Kidd, Webb Kidd, Andrew Kidd, Wm Kelly, Joab Kinnebrew, Caleb Kirk, Robert Kilgore, John Kilgore, Jesse Kendall, Hugh Kelly, James Kerr, Jno Kirk, Jno King, Henry Karr, Allen Killough, John Keis (Key), George Karr, Barnard Kelly, Stephen Kersey, Candler Knox, John Kilgore, Peter Kilgore, Isaac Killough, David Killough, James Kinman, Massey Keen, Richard Kain, Gilbert Keen.

Fred'k Leapham, Hez Linsecum, Marion Linsecum, Zachariah Linsecum, Thos Leverett, Wm Leverett, Robert Leverett, John Lamar, Basil Lamar, Thomas Lamar, Wm Lamar, Wm Lawson, John Lindsay, Abner Leggett, David Luckie, Alexander Luckie, James Luckie, Wm Luckie, James Lambert, John Long, George Lambsen, John Ledbetter, Fred'k Ledbetter, Nicolas Long,

David Love, Thos Little, James Little, Jonathan Loper, Elizabeth Landrum, John Landrum, Wm Landrum, John Lawrence, Levi Lancaster, Abr'm Landers, George Lumpkin, Sterling Lane, John Larremol (Lamar), George Lee, Wm Linn, Benj Lewis, Jno Loyd, Jas Loyd, Elenore Leslore (Lesuer), Philip Logan, Wm Layson (Lawson), Daniel Ladner, Jno Lamb, Richard Lockhart, George Lea, Joshua Lea, Aaron Livingston, Sam'l Lomas, Henry Lyle, Daniel Longstreet, John Linton, Mathew Ledbetter, Richard Lovett, Abraham Livingston, Jas McLayson, Thos Lockey, Jno Lovell, Jno Lock, Wm Lackey, Isaac Levins, Jas Lane, Wm T Linton, Jno Lauderdale, Wm Linn, Wm Littleton, Jno Lespridge, Wm Lee, John Lankford, Elihu Lyman, Wm Love, Zach Lawrence, Giles Lee, Henry Lowry, John Lindsay, Elizth Lindsay, Thos Lindsay, Rhoda Lyle, Charles Lane, John Lawrence, Elijah Lindsay, Elijah Leonard.

Nath'l Martin, Ganaway Martin, Austin Martin, James McNeil, Catherine McNeil, James McFarlane, John Milner, Abraham Marshall, Sol Marshall, Edward McGary, Robt McGary, Maxcy Moncrief, Mary Moncrief, Silas Mercer, Thos Mercer, George Muncy, Aaron McNabb, Alex McAlpin, Wm Moss, Lamentation Moss, Jno Middleton, Robert Middleton, George Mathews, Donny McCrullen, David McCrullen, James McConnell, Newell McConnell, Francis McKenney, John McKenney, Ann Millegan, Baptist Millegan, Isaac Millegan, Thos Mitchell, Stephen Mitchell, Jas May, Wm May, Jacob Martin, Jno McDonald, Jacob McLendon, Jacob McLendon Jr, Isaac McLendon, Joel McLendon, Levi Marshall, Mathew Marshall, Edward Murphy, Daniel Murphy, Daniel McCarty, Sampson Monger, Henry Monger, Ally McDaniel, Mary McDaniel, Darling McDaniel, Mary Morgan, Thomas Morgan, Jas Morgan, Benjamin Mosely, Thos Mosely, David Mims, Jos Mims, Shadrick Mims, James McCannon, John McVay, Hugh McDonald, Jno McDonald, Wm McKey, Geo Martin, Sam'l Martin, Alex McAlpin, Sol McAlpin, Micajah McGhee, Robert McGough, Richard Madden, Thos Moffatt, James Moffatt, Jos Moore, Wm Moore, Michael Moore, Sophia Moore, Robert Moses, Moses Mathews, Thos McCall, Wm McRee, Alex McDougal, John McGowan, James McLerry, Josiah Moncrief, John McCormick, Thos McCormick, James McLean, John McLean, John McLanahan, Jos McMathis, John McDowell, Wm Muse, Wm Miles, Robert McGinty, Wm McLeroy, Hannah Mendengal, Marmaduke Mendengal, Jos Mott, Wm Mims, John Mims, George Murray, Hugh Marrs, Wm McClellan, Horatio Marbury, Israel Miller, Francis Mitchell, Dixon Marshall, Joseph Moler, John May, Druny Manning, John Mann, Wm Maxwell, Thos Mason, Thomas Meriwether, Francis Meriwether, Charles McDonald, Nathan Morgan, John Morgan, Wm Morgan, Robt McRory, Benj

Moore, Thos Moody, John Maynor, Geo Martin, John Mills, David Martin, Benj Merritt, Philip Mathews, Robert Mosely, Wm Mosely, Henry Mosely, Noble McCowan, Amie McCuller, Jas McLemurray, John Mobley, John McCarty, John Mason, Gideon Mason, John McLaughlin, Milly Mann, David Murray, Patrick McDonald, Richard Melear, Jos Miller, John McConnell, John Manor, Hugh Maiers, Robt McRay, Magt Machon, David McClarkey, James McClarkey, Jeremiah Mathews, Oliver Mathews, Allen McDonald, Cornelius McCardell, Hugh McCall, David Moore, Sallie Moore. Jno McFall, Richard McRee, Adrian McKinzie, Jno Myrick, Jas McKey, Jas Magba, Joseph May, Jonathan Miller, James Mathews, Daniel McBurnett, James Meroney, Isaac Mulligan, Baalam May, Thos Morris, Henry McKay, George McCall, James Marks, Alex Mills, Alice Mills, Silas Monk, James McCowan, Robert Martin, Reuben McLeroy, Wm McLin, Wm Miller, Robert Moses, Travis McClendon, Abednego Moon, David McCallmen, John Menell, Jas McCarmon, John Myrick, Walter Mathews, Daniel Morris, Pitman Milner, Ewing Morrow.

Sol Newsom, Claiborne Newsom, Ed Nugent, Wm Norris, Joseph Nail, Julius Nail, Samuel Niele, Robert Neile, Stephen Nobles, Wm. Nobles, Samuel Nelson, John Nelson, Nathan Nall, John Nall, Martin Nall, Thomas Neal, David Neal, John Nelson, David Nelson, Thomas Norton, Levi Newton, Wm. Nazary, George Newman, Wm. Noland, Acquilla Nail, Benjamin Nicolson, Jacob Nealy, Wm. Norris, Julian Nail, Benjamin Nipper, Jas Nipper (Napper), Jas Newmuller, John Nelms, Noyal Nelms, Thomas Nasbet (Nesbitt), Wm. Nichols, Samuel Newman, W. W. Nunnalee, Josiah Norris, John Neel, Caleb Napper.

Thomas Owens, Dyonesius Oliver, Axom John O'Neal, Wm. O'Neal, James Orrick, John Ogletree, Wm Ogletree, John Oliver, Peter Oliver, John Owens, Glen Owen, Jere Oates, Wm. Odair, Daniel Oar, Anthony Olive, Wm. Overstreet.

Moses Powell, Jr., Cader Powell, John Pinkston, Zach Phillips, Wm. Phillips, Joel Phillips, Joseph Phillips, Joshua Perry, Sol Palmer, George Palmer, Charles Parks, Andrew Pickens, Ed. Pharr, Jacob Pruit, Elijah Partee, John Peters, Jesse Pugh, Samuel Payne, John Pittman, George Pettigrew, James Patrick, Lewis Powell, John Pope, Sarah Pendal, John Paris, Stephen Pennington, Eph Pettipool, John Pierce, Wm Powell, Philip Pitman, James Pitman, Pattie Pittman, Jesse Pittman, Wm. Pollard, Wm Pulliam, Joseph Pulliam, B Pettie, Benjamin Perkins, Joshua Perkins, Averilla Perkins, L Berry Perkins, Thomas Patton, Wm Peters, John Peters, Rich Petiet, Richard Parker, Wm Parker, Barna Pace, Dyal Peavy, Saybret Perkins, John Payne, Thomas Patton, Matthew Patton, John Paterson, Isaac Perry, James Potts, Wm Potts, Meredith Price, John Price, Jesse Partridge, John Pate, Francis Powers, Wm Painter, John Prestage, Daniel Parker, Benj Partee, Samuel Pickern, Burrell Pope, Ruth Powell, Henry Pace, James Patton, Samuel Patton, Joseph Paze, Jehu Pugh, John Phillips, Agnes Parrett (Parrott), Henry Pope, Wm Patrick, Paul Patrick, Lewis Pierce, Robert Parks, Richard Powell, Wm Pilison, Philip Pool, Jas Pope, Moses Perkins, Peter Perkins, John Page, Ed Pharr, Alex Patrick, John Palmer, Mildred Palmer, Jesse Perkins, Aventon Perkins, Jos Priest, Gab Pickens, Amos Ponder, Wm Pascall, Thos Payne, Jr, Willis Pope, George Pettigrew, Jas Patterson, John Patterson, Samuel Poole, John Perkins, Benjamin Perkins, Wm Parten, John Parten, Levi Phillips, Henry Peebles, Sam'l Pharr, Jacob Pharr, Abel Pennington, Thomas Pew, Jones Person, Edward Palmer, Levi Pruitt, Harris Pettigrew, Henry Pass, Wm Paradise, Jesse Pew, Jacob Parkerson, Wylie Pope.

John Querns, Wm Queer.

Randolph Ramsay, John Ramsey, Benj Riden, Evan Ragland, John Rutherford, Jonathan Ragan, John Robert, Wm Ramsay, Jane Runnells, Rich Runnells, Harmon Runnells, Geo Runnells, Turnstall Roan, Jonathan Ragan, Benj Rhodes, Jno Robinet, Jno Robinson, Jen Reeves, John Rufus, Reuben Rufus, George Reed, Adonijah Read, Wm Rheney, Saml Riley, Hugh Rees, Saml Roe, Henry Roe, Jas Rockmore, Walker Richardson, Reuben Ratchford, Drury Rogers, John Robinson, James Roan, Thos Rutledge, Spencer Runnells, John Russell, Andrew Ray, Abr'm Reddix, Wm Rasberry, Thos Robertson, Jona Robertson, Charles Ray, John Rice, John Ross, Geo Ray, Preston Runnolds, James Raley, Wm Reddox, Robert Ross, Agnes Richardson, Richard Ryan, Joseph Ryan, Wm Richardson, Thos Rose, Alex Rees, Roger Rees, Wm Rhany, Peleg Rogers, Wm Rogers, Robert Ratliff, Benj Ratliff, Daniel Ramshart, Wm Ratliff, James Ready, Jno B Ruston, James Ralston, John Robinet, Thos Russell, Jas Rockman John Rice, James Ross, Wm Railey, Jas Ryley, John Roberts, Susannah Ruff, Reuben Radford, Mack Ragan, Wm Richards, Ignatius Rains, Jeptha Rush.

Saml Scott, Jas Scott, Benj Scott, Saml Sewell, Starns Simmons, Robert Simmons, Joshua Sanders, Isham Shap, Seth Stubblefield, Peter Strozier, Wm Smith, Peter Smith, Wm Smith, Saml Smith, Enoch Stringfellow, John Simmons, John Sallis, Nicholas Subtrine, Joseph Subtrine, Wm Stark, David Sidwell, Thos Shannon, Gravenor Stewart, Henry Stewart, Martha Stewart, Wm Sanson, Loveless Savage, Geo Sorrill, John Sorrill, Robt Sorrill, Jas Scarlet, Israel Smith, Jasper Smith, Henry Smith, Jesse Spurling, Frances Short, Moses Stephens, Francis Stripling, Alex Scott, Robt Singleton, Thos Smith, David Smith, John Stedham, Heirs of James Stapler, Heirs of Lewis Salenon, Sarah Stroud, John Shamon, Henry Sewell, Esther Seahmy, John Sellers, John Shelman, Joshua Sewell, Wm Stewart, Job Springer, Dudley Sneed, Charles Seal, Enoch Seal, Eliza Stinson, Peter Stubblefield, Robt Shinman, John Stephens, Wm Smith, James Shepherd, Jesse Stallings, Henry Sizemore, Wm Stith, White Salter, Wm Salter, Ezekiel Salter, Thos Seal, Zach Sheffield, Eder Stanley, Jos Scott, Benj Scott, Thos Scott, Jas Scott, Josiah Spikes, John Smead, Saml Simpson, Andrew Sterges, Thomas Stephens, Jno Shackelford, Reuben Saffold, Jas Sims, Henry Steele, Claiborn Sandege Berry Stringfellow, John Smith, Robert Smith, Benjamin Smith, Arthur Smith, Drew Smith, Needham Smith, Francis Smith, Henry Stokes, Elizth Sailor, Burna Simmerman, John Ga Snider, James Spratlin, Wm Shropshire, Jno Sawyers, Benj Stirk, Wm Strong, Ebenezer Sternes, Reuben Slaughter, Saml Slaughter, James M Stewart, Frederick Sims, Wm Smith, Benegah Smith, Richard Smith, Isaac Stewart, Jas Sutton, Isaac Simonton, Wm Stokes, Asa Simmons, Adam Simmons, David Smith, Gabriel Smith, Jacob Smith, Jesse Sanford, Nancy Stephens, Henry Sorrow, Jas Sewell, John Stokes, Fred Sims, Jno Seals, Jarvis Seals, Anthony Seals, Guy Smith, Jos Slaton, Joshua Scurlock, Chas Smith, Jasper Smith, Hugh Saxon, Amos Shaw, Joseph Stubbs, John Shields, Abram Silvey, John Sawyer, Henry Simmons, Henry Starr, Christopher Saylors, James Sanson, Gibson Santherton, Bail Story, Ed Story, James Stewart, Henry Shelton, Acquilla Swann, Isaac Stewart, Isaac Stocks, Seth Stubblefield, Joel Simms, Jno Statham, Archer Skinner, Wm Scudder, Frances Sutterwhite, Frances Stripling, Simeon Shaves, Robert Sanders, Joshua Sledd, Sol Strickland, Abram Smith, Robert Sturges, Robert Sellfbridge, Pattillo Sponser, Wm Scott, Isbell Strader Nathan Smith, Burrell Smith, John Sorrell, Robert Sims, Micajah Stone, Henry Summerlin, Nicolas Slade, Wm Stubblefield, Nathan Spikes, Geo Sorrell, Jas Smith, Thos Screvener, Jas Stuart, Jennie Sims, Jas Stringer, Culbreath Steal, Leonard Switzer, Robt Stamper, Archbald Simpson, James Smart, James Shields, Wm Sewell, Henry Snow.

Benj Thompson, Wm Thompson, John Thompson, Geo Turman, Garnett Turman, John Turman, Francis Trawick, Sam'l Tyner, Rich Tyner, Mark Thornton, Mary F. Townsend, Sam'l Taylor, Benj Thomas, Thomas Tucker, Jno Teasley, John Thurman, Jos Turnbull, Wm Tyler, Robert Thompson, David Terrell, William Terrell, Tabetta Thompson, Elzth Thompson, Jas Todd, Robt Tate, James Tate, Jos G Taylor, Wm Triplett, Moses Trimble, Isham Thompson, George Thompson, Wm Thompson, Th Thornton, Sam'l Thornton, Wm Thornton, Herad Thornton, John Talbott, Wm Toombs, Dozier Thornton, Dread Thornton, James Thomas, Michael Thomas, John Torrence, John Troy, Sarah Taylor, John Thurman, Alex Thompson, Henry Thompson, Daniel Terondett, Robert Thompson, John F Thompson, Jesse Thompson. John Tallett (Talley), Jas Turner, Humphrey Tompkins, Ann Transon, Abner Tatam, John Trimble, Nancy Townsend, John Townsend, Mary Thomas, Amistead Taylor, M Taylor, Francis Tenille, John Turner, Wm Triplett, Francis Traywick, Henry Tate, James Tate, Wm Tate, John Todd, Philip Thomas, Moses Tullis, David Thurman, Wm Thurman, Jas Thomas, Mathew Talbot, John Tanner, Jos Thompson, Wm Thompson, Elihu Thompson, Berry Taylor, Gabriel Toombs, David Tomlinson, John Tweedle, Wm Teasley, John Teasley, John Tindall, Alex Thompson, Moses Trimble, Demp sey Towler, Thomas Travis, Jesse Talbott, Henry Thompson, Dempsey Toler, Caleb Tode, John Townsend, John Tiller, Noel Thornton, Wm Taylor, Chan Thomas, Henry Townley, John Tillery, John Templeton, Nicolas Tuttle, James Tuttle, Wm Tyler, Martin Tunman, John Tindall, Ethelred Thomas, Thos H Thornton, Wm Thornton, John Tarver, Thomas Talbott, Samuel Thomas, Wm Traylor, Silas Teasley, John Thunmond, David Thunmond, Wm Tinch, John Tabor, John Tatum, Geo Tucker, John Tanner, John Todd, Jacob Teaver, Henry Trent, Ed Taylor, Abel Tatum, Benj Thomas, Benj Talliferro, Noel Thornton, Thos Taylor, Benj Taylor, John Towns, Robert Toombs, Daniel Thetcher.

Jesse Veazy, James Veazy, Patrick Vance, Davis Vance, Anthony Verdell, Geo Vinon, James Vineyard, Wm Vickery.

Sanders Walker, Wm Walker, Jere Walker, Geo Walker, John Wingfield, Garland Wingfield, Thos Wingfield, Nehemiah Wade, Micajah Williamson, Mary Whately, Willis Whately, Wyley Whately, Jos Williams, John Williams, Susannah Williams, Jos Sherrod Wise, Henry Ware, Nicolas Ware, Robert Ware, Wm Waggoner, Jas Waggoner, George Waggoner, Thos Wadsworth, Jas Wadsworth, Henry Weideman, John White, Nicolas White, Joseph White, Rhoda White, Ed Wilburn, Thos Wilburn, Joshua Wilburn, Tisdall Whately, Rich Whately, Shirley Whately, Mich'l Whately, Jno Webb, Wm Webb, Osten Webb, Jesse Walton, Thos Walton, Robert Walton, Newell Walton, John Walton, Sam'l Waller, Ed Watts, Susannah Wall, Mary Wall, Andrew West, Christian West, Wm West, Wm Wiggins, John Whitesides, Benj Wilson, Andrew Wilson, Wm Wilson, Samuel Wilson, David Wells, Humphrey Wells, Robert Wells, Rachel Wells, Dread Wilder, Wm Wilder, Elizth Wilder, Wm Wilmouth, Thos Wilmouth, Martha Waters, Elijah Williams, Isaac Williams, Wm Williams, Ezekiel Williams, John Woodall, Thomas Wooten, Richd Woods, Middleton Woods, James Woods, Douglas Watson, John Watson, Sam'l Whately, Rebecca Whately, Ornan Whately, Jas Whately, John Whately, Amon Whately, Walton Whately, Lucy Whately, Daniel Whately, Wm Wortham, Richard Wortham, Caleb Welch, John Westbrook, Arthur

Wright, Francis Wright, Wm Wright, Amos Wright, Moses White, Thomas White, John White, Reuben White, Daniel White, Demsey White, Wm White, Zach Wheeler, Wm Wheeler, Euphony Wheeler, Geo Whitesell, John Winn, Obadiah Winn, Margt Wallace, Oliver Wallace, John Wallace, Wm Wallace, James Wallace, Corsey Welborn, Emanuel Wambersee, Bryan Ward, Thos Ward, Abner Webster, Ann Webster, John Webster, Jonathan Webster, Archer Webster, Benj Whitehead, Wm Wagner, Abm Wamack, Wm Wamack, George Walton, Isaiah Walton, Wm Walton, John Wilson, James Wilson, Joseph Wilson, Ann Willis, Thos Watts, George Watts, Fred Williams, Roland Williams, Charles Williams, Bazil Williams, Nehemiah Williams, Daniel Williams, Peter Williams, Christopher Williams, James Wooten, Jeremiah Wooten, John Wilkins, Clement Wilkins, Rich Worsham, Septumus Wetherby, John Willis, James Wood, John Wood, Robert Wadkins, Ben Welch, Elzth Wyley, Jesse Wright, Elisha Wright, Richard Wright, Jane Warren, John Weaver, Charles Waters, John Watkins, Benjamin Watkins, Jno Wheat, Benj Wilcher, Cornelius Whittington, Isham Whallis (Wheelis), Jos Wheelright, Henry Walker, Moses Walker, John Walker, Joseph Woodall, George Willis, Pleasant Walker, Ed Williams.

Wm Yancey, Jas Young, Wm Yarboro, James Yarboro, Wm Yonge, Wm Young, John Young, John York, James York, Peregrine Young.

Wm Zachary, Philip Zimmerman.

I have not attempted to give the dates at which these grants were made. They were recorded all along from 1783 to 1800. A search in the Secretary of State's office will show the date and location of the grant.

SOLDIERS OF THE LINE—ADDITIONAL.

Thomas Atkinson, Thos Adcock, Wm Adkins, Henry Aughn, James Amos, Matthew Arthur, Strong Ashmore, Moses Allen.

Major Wm Baker, John Black, John Brown, Fred Bradewell, Andrew Berryhill, Sam'l Barron, Benj Burleson, Gibson Berry, Britton Brantley, Daniel Burlock, Jacob Bausworth, Dempsey

NOTE.—There was no roster of revolutionary soldiers preserved. The above list includes, as does the list on a previous page, the names of those certified to by some officer of the army as having rendered military service. These names have been discovered in various ways by Captain Johnson, to whom reference is made in the preface, and many of them appeared in my first edition. The list has been carefully gone over, and these additional names, omitted there, are placed here.

Baker, Charles Barber, Stark Brown, David Batson, John Brown, John Bromfield, Stancel Barber, Amos Brantley, Jas P Buchannon, Wm Bazer.

David Canon, Jere Cloud, Jr, Wm Crosby, Gilbert Campbell, Michael Castellaw, Stephen Corsey, Jr, Wm Cone, Moses Clark, James Clarke, Ralph Cobb, Rich Childress, Geo Cooper, Wm Copeland, Gresham Cofield, Elisha Cook, Reuben Cook, John Cone, Jos Cooper, Tuner Christian, Jas Camp, Ed Cartledge, Jno Cooper, Lt Col.

Peter Devaux, Frances Danieley, Elijah Dumaplir, Robert Darington, Wm Dunford, Isaac Davis, John Darby, John Daniel, John Dantignal, Jesse Doles, Thomas Dalton, John Dyche, Nicolas Darby, John Dudley, Chas Damson, John Duck, Jere Duck, Michael Dickson.

Thos Espey, Capt; Levi Emanuel, Enos Emanuel, Thos Ellett, Walter Ellet, Robert Eimenson.

W Few, Lt Col; James Fleming, Major; Benj Frazier, Benj Few, Col; Travis Fenn, Samuel Fulsom, Pinnon Floyd, Wm Furlow, Geo Foals, John Ford, John Fuller, Sr, John Freeman, Abram Frauly, James Fincher, Jas Felps, David Flemington, Samuel Flemington, Fielding Fryer, Pat Fitzpatrick, Lt, John Frazier, Lt.

Isaac Green, Allen Gay, George Grenswell, Jehu Gwalthney, Wm Graves, Rabun Grier, Lt; John Gray, Robt Ginkins, John Gibson, Thos Geddings, Wm. Garland, Herod Gibbs, Isaac Gilder, Thos Glassaway, Jas Gordon, Thos Gibbons, John Garnett (Lt), John Garnett, Thos Greer, Joshua Gress, Thos Gress.

James Harvey, Nicolas Hawkins, Sam'l Hanson, John Harvey, Ambrose Holiday, James Hawkins, Wm Hadden, John Hampton, Jos. Hudson, Samuel Harper, Capt, Robert Harper, Lieut, Jas Hudson, Tyre Glenn Harris, Rich Halliman, Lewis Holloway, Wm Holt, James Hammack, Richard Horn, Wm Harben, Monoah Hubbard, Christian Hiedt, Jos Hodges, Thos Hinsley, Isaac Hollingsworth, Stephen Howell, John Hawthorn, John Hinnard, Benj Hampton, Benj Harris, Jno Hogg, Zach Henderson, Lieut, Wm Hopkins, Wm Harris, Samuel Haugh, Ben Hart, Samuel Hicks, Matthew Hobson, Geo Hawley.

Stephen Johnson, Philip Jones, Jno Jackson, Ben Jones, Jr., Absalom Island, David Jackson, Frederick Jones.

Ed Kelly, Jos Kemp, Wm Kimbrough, Wm Kelly, William Killgore, Jos Kircum, David Kieth, Patrick Kneal, Thomas Kirk, Jno Kilgore, Henry Kair.

Basil Lamar, Wm Larkey, Rich Livins, Jno Linn, Zach Landrum, John Linton, Elijah Leonard, Jno Leggett, Jno Lowe, Wm Lamar, James Lett, Fred Ledbetter, Jos Langford, Isaac Lockhart, Elegno Lewis, Jonathan Langford, Wm Little, Robert Long, Jno Lawson, Jr.

Geo Melvin, Jas McCoy, Samuel Miller (commissary), Wm McKenny, Josiah Maxwell, Lieut, Austin Martin, Wm Morgan, Wm Moats, Lettice McFarling, Jos Mancen, Simeon McClendon, John McCarty, Joshua Miller, Moses Miller, Jas McLain, Jas Matthews, Daniel McNiely, Matthew McKenny, Alex Moore, Nicolas Mehan, Reuben Matthews, Cornelius Martin, Henry Morecock, Jacob McClendon, Joshua Moss, Thos McClendon, Wm Morris, John McCall, Wm McCulloch, John Morris, John McManus, Samuel Maddox, Jno Miller, John Maeur, Andrew McLean, Jos Moore, Jessee Mercer, James McCaller, Malone Mullins, Siles Mercer, Moses Marshall, John Middleton, John Meanly, Jno McIntosh, Lieut, Wm McIntosh, Capt, Littleberry Mosley, Elisha Miller, Capt, Clem Mash, Capt, John Morel, Capt, David Mahan.

Geo Nix, Jno Niely, Rich Norwood, Arch Nixon, Wm Nichols, Wm Nealy, Jere Nelson, John Newigate, John Newman.

Robert Owens, Wm Oharn, Ed Outlaw, Sol Ogden.

John Palmore, John Phelps, Ben Powers, Robert Pollard, Robert Peteete, Francis Parker, Moses Potts, Warren Philpot, Adam Perkins, Joel Perkenson, Rich Pollett, Ed Penny, Sam'l Pate, Wm Peters, Capt Job Pray, Wm Passmore.

Peter Quarles.

James Roe, Jno Read, Jere Rogers, Jas Read, Robert Raines, Mathew Rabun, Henry Ryalls, Jona Royal, Isaac A Ray, Thomas Robertson, Josh Rivers, Jno Rivers, James Ridge, Rehem Redding, Chas Raley.

Reddick Smith, Wm Sessums, Michael Sharp, Wm Sizemore, Simon Sanders, Jno Scott, Sr, Jno Scott, Jr, Cornelius Scott, Charles Stewart, John Stuart, Elijah Sapp, Jno Stapler, Joshua Sanders, John Swint, Geo Spann, John Stevens, Josiah Spikes, George Smith, Wm Sapp, Thos J Smith, Wm Sapp, Jr, Benj Simmons, Aaron Springfield, Henry Sapp, Vawn Scott, Wm Shirley, Robert Sanna, Houston Sheddell, John Screven, Thos Sutton (Lt), Jas Sherrar, Gen'l Jas Screven, Adam Showers, Philip Simmons, Wm Satterwhite, Wm Summerlin, Wm Satterwhite, Wm Summerlin, Sam'l Simpson, John Sheffield, John Sitton, Israel Smith, David Snell, Daniel Shaw, Abraham Scott, Frederick Stanley, Owen Sullivan, Benj Scott, Reuben Samford, John Sapp, Leonard Switzer, Michael Smalley, Dudley Sneed, John Shaw, Owen Shannon, Edward Story, James Swain, John Strength, John Simmons, James Stubbs, John Sedmon, Joshua Sharp, John Stringer, Henry Shelton, Nicolas Scurry, Jacob Stewart, John Salles, Timothy Simpson, David Shay, Wm Smith, John Simpson, Nicolas Stegal, Richard Stephens, George Sway, John Stiles.

Joshua Thomson, Thos Tucker, Jr, Geo Tucker, Sam'l Thomas, John Taylor, Geo Tucker, John Torrence, James Thomson, Benj Thompson, Jr, Dan'l Thompson, Sam Tomlinson, Jas Thompson,

Jno Tharp, Nehemiah Turnnett, John Towns, Jno Troy, Jas Trapp, Ben Thomas, Robert Taylor, Jr, Denny Thompson, Jno Thomson, Ed Taylor.

Isaac Van Zant, James Vawn.

Thos Williams, Jesse Womack, Abednego Wright, Stephen Westbrooks, Thos Walker, John Webster, Jona Whitemore, Jno Walker, Andrew Wilder, Jno Wallace, Robt Williamson, Sanders Walker chaplain, Robert Walton, John Williams, Wm Wilder, Geo Williamson, Jere Warren, Adam Wideman, Robert Wilson, Isaac Williams, Chas Ward, Sam'l Webster, Jno Winn, Wm Willey, John Whiteset, Sam'l Williams, Elisha Walker, Sampson Wylder, Thos Whitely, Isham Wells, Jos Wells, Ed Wood Capt, Geo Watson, Thos Webster, Andrew Wells, Jona Whittmore, Wm Wood, Robt Wilson, Sam'l Ward, Jos Walker, Sylvan Walker, Jno Wells, Brittan Walls, Jno Wereat, Chas Waters, Chas Williams, Jos Willett, Jno Webster, Jesse Winfrey, Ed Woods, Richard Williamson, Owen Watley, Worton Whatley, Willis Whatley, Sherrod Whatley, Banigo Wright, Jesse Welcher, Richard Willey.

Adam Youngblood, James Youngblood, Wm Yarborough, John York.

Bounty warrants for military services, but certificates as Revolutionary soldiers wanting. (Probably, but not certain.)

Charles Williams, Wm Gresham, Hiram Howard, James Jenkins, Williamson James, Thomas Mitchell, James Moore, Andrew May (or Way), Samuel May (or Way).

GOVERNORS.

James Edward Oglethorpe, July 15, 1732 to 1751.
Wm Stephens, acting Governor, 1743 to 1751.
Henry Parker, 1751 to 1754.
John Reynolds, 1754 to 1757.
Henry Ellis, 1757 to 1760.
James Wright, 1760 to 1771.
James Habersham, acting, 1771 to 1773.
James Wright, 1773 to 1775. Deposed.
Wm Ewen, 1775 to 1776.
Arch Bullock, 1776 to 1777.
Button Gwinnett, February 22, 1777, to May 8, 1777.
John Adam Trentlea, May 8, 1777, to January 8, 17,8.
John Houston, January 8 to December 29, 1778.
John Wereat, 1778 to 1779.
Geo Walton, November 4, 1779, to January 7, 1780.
Richard Howley, January 7, 1780, to 1781.
Stephen Heard, Prt Ex council, 1781 to August, 1781.
Nathan Brownson, August, 1781, to January, 1782.

John Martin, 1782 to 1783.
Lyman Hall, 1783 to 1784.
John Houston, 1784 to 1785.
Samuel Elbert, 1785 to 1786.
Edward Telfair, 1786 to 1787.
George Mathews, 1787 to 1788.
George Handley, 1788 to 1789.
George Walton, 1789 to 1790.
Edward Telfair, 1790 to 1793.
George Mathews, 1793 to 1796.
Jared Irwin, 1796 to 1798.
James Jackson, 1798 to 1801.
David Emanuel, President of Senate, acting Governor, March, 1801, to November, 1801.
Josiah Tattnall, 1801 to 1802.
John Milledge, 1802 to 1806.
Jared Irwin, President of Senate, acting Governor, September, 1806, to November 7, 1806.
Jared Irwin, November, 1806, to November, 1809.
David B Mitchell, November, 1809, to 1813.
Peter Early, November, 1813, to 1815.
David B Mitchell, 1815 to 1817. (Resigned.)
Wm Rabun, President Senate, Governor *ad interim*, November, 1817.
Wm Rabun, November, 1817, to October, 1819. (Died.)
Mathew Talbot, President Senate *ad interium* to November, 1819.
John Clarke, 1819 to 1823.
Geo M Troup, November, 1823, to 1827.
John Forsyth, 1827 to 1829.
Geo R Gilmer, 1829 to 1831.
Wilson Lumpkin, 1831 to 1835.
Wm Schley, 1835 to 1837.
Geo R Gilmer, 1837 to 1839.
Charles J McDonald, November, 1839, to 1843.
Geo W Crawford, 1843 to 1847.
Geo W Towns, 1847 to 1851.
Howell Cobb, 1851 to 1853.
Herschel V Johnson, 1853 to 1857.
Joseph E Brown, 1857 to 1865.
James Johnson, Pro Governor, July, 1865, to December, 1865.
Charles J Jenkins, 1865 to 1868.
Brigadier-General T H Ruger, acting Governor, January, 1868, to July, 1869.
Rufus B Bulloch, July, 1869, to October, 1871.
Benj Conley, President Senate, October, 1871, to 1872.
James M Smith, January, 1872, to January, 1877.

Alfred H Colquitt, 1877 to November, 1882.
Alex H Stephens, November, 1882, to March, 1883. (Died.)
Jas S Boynton, President Senate, March, 1883, to July, 1883.
Henry D McDaniel, July, 1883, to November, 1886.
John B Gordon, November, 1886, to November, 1890.
Wm J Northen, November, 1890, to 1894.
W Y Atkinson, November, 1894, to 1898.
Allen D Candler, 1898 to 1902.

LIST OF COUNTIES,

Showing names, for whom named, when laid out, county seats, and population, from census of 1890.

NAMES.	FOR WHOM NAMED.	COUNTY SEATS.	LAID OUT.	POPULATION. Whites.	Colored.	Totals.
Appling	Colonel Daniel Appling	Baxley	1818	6,214	2,462	8,676
Baker	Colonel John Baker	Newton	1825	1,595	4,549	6,144
Baldwin	Abraham Baldwin	Milledgeville	1803	5,262	9,346	14,608
Banks	Dr. Richard Banks	Homer	1858	6,999	1,563	8,562
Bartow	General Francis Bartow	Cartersville	1861	14,574	6,042	20,616
Berrien	John M. Berrien	Nashville	1856	8,277	2,417	10,694
Bibb	Dr. W. W. Bibb	Macon	1822	19,029	23,341	42,370
Brooks	Preston L. Brooks	Quitman	1858	6,342	7,637	13,979
Bryan	Jonathan Bryan	Clyde	1793	2,833	2,687	5,520
Bulloch	Arch. Bulloch	Statesborough	1796	9,023	4,689	13,712
Burke	Edmund Burke	Waynesboro	1777	5,817	22,684	28,501
Butts	Captain Sam. Butts	Jackson	1825	5,167	5,398	10,565
Calhoun	John C. Calhoun	Morgan	1854	2,239	6,199	8,438
Camden	Earl of Camden	St. Mary's	1777	2,041	4,137	6,178
Campbell	Duncan C. Campbell	Fairburn	1828	5,621	3,494	9,115
Carroll	Charles Carroll	Carrollton	1826	18,450	3,851	22,301
Catoosa	Catoosa	Ringgold	1853	4,795	636	5,431
Charlton	R. M. Charlton	Trader's Hill	1854	2,465	870	3,335
Chatham	Earl of Chatham	Savannah	1777	22,965	34,775	57,740
Chattahoochee	Chattahoochee River	Cusseta	1854	1,837	3,065	4,902
Chattooga	Chattooga River	Summerville	1838	9,204	1,998	11,202
Cherokee	Cherokee Indians	Canton	1832	13,904	1,508	15,412
Clarke	General Elijah Clarke	Athens	1801	7,072	8,114	15,186
Clay	Henry Clay	Fort Gaines	1854	3,002	4,815	7,817

Clayton	A. S. Clayton	Jonesboro	1858	5,220	3,075	8,295
Clinch	General D. S. Clinch	Homerville	1850	4,292	2,360	6,652
Cobb	Thomas W. Cobb	Marietta	1832	15,510	6,776	22,286
Coffee	General John Coffee	Douglas	1854	6,621	3,862	10,483
Colquitt	Walter T. Colquitt	Moultrie	1856	4,317	477	4,794
Columbia	Christopher Columbus	Appling	1790	3,243	8,038	11,281
Coweta	Chief town of Coweta Indians	Newnan	1826	9,740	12,614	22,354
Crawford	Wm. H. Crawford	Knoxville	1822	4,159	5,156	9,315
Dade	Major Francis Dade	Trenton	1837	4,614	1,093	5,707
Dawson	Wm C. Dawson	Dawsonville	1857	5,353	259	5,612
Decatur	Stephen Decatur	Bainbridge	1823	9,116	10,833	19,949
DeKalb	Baron DeKalb	Decatur	1822	11,214	5,975	17,189
Dodge	Wm. E. Dodge	Eastman	1870	6,143	5,309	11,452
Dooly	Colonel John Dooly	Vienna	1821	9,232	8,914	18,146
Dougherty	Charles Dougherty	Albany	1853	1,975	10,231	12,206
Douglas	Stephen A. Douglas	Douglasville	1870	5,993	1,801	7,794
Early	Governor Peter Early	Blakely	1818	3,670	6,122	9,792
Echols	Robert M. Echols	Statenville	1858	2,059	1,020	3,079
Effingham	Lord Effingham	Springfield	1777	3,388	2,211	5,599
Elbert	Governor Sam. Elbert	Elberton	1790	7,492	7,884	15,376
Emanuel	Governor David Emanuel	Swainsboro	1812	9,396	5,307	14,703
Fannin	Colonel J. W. Fannin	Morganton	1854	8,612	112	8,724
Fayette	General LaFayette	Fayetteville	1821	5,654	3,074	8,728
Floyd	General Floyd	Rome	1832	17,970	10,421	28,391
Forsyth	Governor John Forsyth	Cumming	1832	9,866	1,289	11,155
Franklin	Benjamin Franklin	Carnesville	1786	11,372	3,298	14,670
Fulton	Robert Fulton	Atlanta	1853	49,238	35,417	84,655
Gilmer	Governor George R. Gilmer	Ellijay	1832	9,005	69	9,074
Glascock	General Thomas Glascock	Gibson	1857	2,552	1,168	3,720
Glynn	John Glynn	Brunswick	1777	5,669	7,751	13,420
Gordon	W. W. Gordon	Calhoun	1850	11,030	1,728	12,758
Greene	General Nathaniel Greene	Greensboro	1786	5,332	11,719	17,051

LIST OF COUNTIES—Continued.

Names.	For Whom Named.	County Seats.	Laid Out.	Population.		
				Whites.	Colored.	Totals.
Gwinnett	Governor Button Gwinnett	Lawrenceville	1818	16,903	2,996	19,899
Habersham	Joseph Habersham	Clarkesville	1818	9,984	1,589	11,573
Hall	Governor Lyman Hall	Gainesville	1818	15,280	2,767	18,047
Hancock	John Hancock	Sparta	1793	4,739	12,410	17,149
Haralson	Hugh A. Haralson	Buchanan	1856	10,199	1,117	11,316
Harris	Charles Harris	Hamilton	1829	5,999	10,798	16,797
Hart	Nancy Hart	Hartwell	1853	7,930	2,957	10,887
Heard	Stephen Heard	Franklin	1830	6,215	3,342	9,557
Henry	Patrick Henry	McDonough	1821	8,629	7,591	16,220
Houston	Governor John Houston	Perry	1821	5,272	16,341	21,613
Irwin	Governor Jared Irwin	Irwinville	1818	4,241	2,075	6,316
Jackson	Governor James Jackson	Jefferson	1796	13,780	5,396	19,176
Jasper	Sergeant Jasper	Monticello	1812	5,392	8,487	13,879
Jefferson	Thomas Jefferson	Louisville	1796	6,450	10,763	17,213
Johnson	Governor H. V. Johnson	Wrightsville	1858	4,673	1,456	6,129
Jones	Hon James Jones	Clinton	1807	3,931	8,778	12,709
Laurens	Col. John Laurens	Dublin	1807	7,654	6,093	13,747
Lee	Richard H. Lee	Leesburg	1826	1,432	7,642	9,074
Liberty	Liberty	Hinesville	1777	4,207	8,680	12,887
Lincoln	General Ben. Lincoln	Lincolnton	1796	2,473	3,673	6,146
Lowndes	Wm. J. Lowndes	Valdosta	1825	7,128	7,974	15,102
Lumpkin	Governor Wilson Lumpkin	Dahlonega	1838	6,453	414	6,867
McDuffie	George McDuffie	Thompson	1871	3,267	5,522	8,789
McIntosh	McIntosh Family	Darien	1793	1,258	5,212	6,470
Macon	Nathaniel Macon	Oglethorpe	1837	4,001	9,182	13,183
Madison	James Madison	Danielsville	1811	7,361	3,663	11,024

Marion	General Francis Marion	Buena Vista	1827	3,467	4,261	7,728
Meriwether	General David Meriwether	Greenville	1827	9,201	11,539	20,740
Miller	Andrew J. Miller	Colquitt	1856	2,701	1,574	4,275
Milton	Homer V. Milton	Alpharetta	1857	5,536	672	6,208
Mitchell	Colonel Thomas Mitchell	Camilla	1857	4,800	6,106	10,906
Monroe	James Monroe	Forsyth	1821	6,621	12,516	19,137
Montgomery	General Richard Montgomery	Mt. Vernon	1793	5,590	3,658	9,248
Morgan	General Dan. Morgan	Madison	1807	5,043	10,998	16,041
Murray	Thomas W. Murray	Spring Place	1832	7,977	484	8,461
Muscogee	Muscogee Indians	Columbus	1826	12,395	15,366	27,761
Newton	Sergeant John Newton	Covington	1821	7,146	7,164	14,310
Oconee	Oconee River	Watkinsville	1875	3,881	3,832	7,713
Oglethorpe	General James E. Oglethorpe	Lexington	1793	5,686	11,265	16,951
Paulding	John Paulding	Dallas	1832	10,443	1,505	11,948
Pickens	General Andrew Pickens	Jasper	1853	7,832	350	8,182
Pierce	Franklin Pierce	Blackshear	1857	4,396	1,983	6,379
Pike	Zebulon M. Pike	Zebulon	1822	8,223	8,077	16,300
Polk	James K. Polk	Cedartown	1851	10,289	4,656	14,945
Pulaski	Count Pulaski	Hawkinsville	1808	6,558	10,001	16,559
Putnam	Israel Putnam	Eatonton	1807	3,939	10,903	14,842
Quitman	General John A. Quitman	Georgetown	1858	1,421	3,050	4,471
Rabun	Governor Wm. Rabun	Clayton	1819	5,440	166	5,606
Randolph	John Randolph	Cuthbert	1828	5,794	9,473	15,267
Richmond	Duke of Richmond	Augusta	1777	22,346	22,848	45,194
Rockdale	Rockdale Church	Conyers	1870	4,127	2,686	6,813
Schley	Governor Wm. Schley	Ellaville	1857	2,238	3,205	5,443
Screven	General James Screven	Sylvania	1793	6,916	7,508	14,424
Spalding	Hon. Thos. Spalding	Griffin	1851	5,835	7,282	13,117
Stewart	General Daniel Stewart	Lumpkin	1830	4,198	11,484	15,682
Sumter	General Thos. Sumter	Americus	1831	7,008	15,099	22,107
Talbot	Governor Matthew Talbot	Talbotton	1827	4,019	9,239	13,258
Taliaferro	Col. Ben. Taliaferro	Crawfordville	1825	2,464	4,827	7,291

LIST OF COUNTIES—Continued.

Names.	For Whom Named.	County Seats.	Laid Out.	Population.		
				Whites.	Colored.	Totals.
Tattnall	Josiah Tattnall	Reidsville	1801	7,138	3,115	10,253
Taylor	Zachary Taylor	Butler	1852	4,598	4,068	8,666
Telfair	Governor Edward Telfair	McRae	1807	3,142	2,335	5,477
Terrell	Dr. Wm. Terrell	Dawson	1856	5,334	9,169	14,503
Thomas	General Jett Thomas	Thomasville	1825	11,122	15,032	26,154
Towns	Governor George Towns	Hiawassee	1856	3,990	74	4,064
Troup	Governor George M. Troup	LaGrange	1826	7,062	13,661	20,723
Twiggs	General John Twiggs	Jeffersonville	1809	2,748	5,447	8,195
Union	Union	Blairsville	1832	7,584	165	7,749
Upson	Stephen Upson	Thomaston	1824	6,065	6,123	12,188
Walker	Major Freeman Walker	LaFayette	1833	11,350	1,932	13,282
Walton	Governor George Walton	Monroe	1818	10,312	7,155	17.467
Ware	Nicholas Ware	Waycross	1824	5,178	3,633	8,811
Warren	General Joseph Warren	Warrenton	1793	4,201	6,756	10,957
Washington	George Washington	Sandersville	1784	10,312	14,925	25,237
Wayne	General Anthony Wayne	Jesup	1805	5,290	2,195	7,485
Webster	Daniel Webster	Preston	1856	2,423	3,272	5,695
White	Colonel John White	Cleveland	1857	5,489	662	6,151
Whitfield	Rev. George Whitefield	Dalton	1851	10,984	1,932	12,916
Wilcox	Captain John Wilcox	Abbeville	1857	4,825	3,155	7,980
Wilkes	John Wilkes	Washington	1777	5,616	12,465	18,081
Wilkinson	General James Wilkinson	Irwinton	1803	5,567	5,214	10 781
Worth	General Wm. J. Worth	Isabella	1853	5,872	4,176	10,048
137 Counties.				978,357	858,996	1,837,353

INDEX.

A

B

C

D

E

F

G

H

I

J

K

L

M

N

O

P

Q

R

S

T

U

W

Y

Z